# TOWARDS HUNGER FREE INDIA
## Agenda and Imperatives

# TOWARDS HUNGER FREE INDIA
## Agenda and Imperatives

*Proceedings of*
National Consultation on
'Towards Hunger Free India'
New Delhi, 24–6 April 2001

*Sponsored by*

United Nations
World Food Programme

Planning Commission
Government of India

M.S. Swaminathan
Research Foundation

*Published by*

MANOHAR
2004

First published 2001
Reprinted 2004



ISBN 81-7304-437-6

*Published by*
Ajay Kumar Jain for
Manohar Publishers & Distributors
4753/23 Ansari Road, Daryaganj
New Delhi 110 002

*Typeset at*
Digigrafics
D-69, Gulmohar Park
New Delhi 110 049

*Printed at*
Lordson Publishers Pvt. Ltd.
C5/19 Rana Pratap Bagh
Delhi 110 007

# Contents

SECTION III: NUTRITION, FOOD ABSORPTION AND UTILIZATION



SECTION IV: GLOBALIZATION AND FOOD INSECURITY



SECTION V: POLICY RESPONSE TO FOOD SECURITY

# Contributors

WASIM AKHTAR: Collector and DM, Jhabua, Madhya Pradesh

G.S. BHALLA: Professor Emeritus, Centre for Study of Regional Development, Jawaharlal Nehru University and Former Member, Planning Commission, New Delhi

PRADEEP BHARGAVA: Senior Fellow, Institute of Development Studies, Jaipur

P.S. BIRTHAL: Senior Fellow, National Centre for Agricultural Economics and Policy Research, New Delhi

MEERA CHATTERJEE: Senior Social Development Specialist, The World Bank, New Delhi

BIPLAB DASGUPTA: Professor of Economics and Member, Rajya Sabha, New Delhi

A. DUSTAGHEER: Project Officer (Nutrition), UNICEF, New Delhi

PATRICE L. ENGLE: Chief, Nutrition/Child Development, UNICEF, New Delhi

C. GOPALAN: President, Nutrition Foundation of India, New Delhi

WOLFGANG HERBINGER: Regional Programme Adviser, UN World Food Programme, New Delhi

INDIRA HIRWAY: Professor of Economics and Director, Centre for Development Alternatives, Ahmedabad

A.K. SHIVA KUMAR: Adviser, UNICEF, New Delhi

ANJANI KUMAR: Senior Fellow, National Centre for Agricultural Economics and Policy Research, New Delhi

AMITABH KUNDU: Professor, Centre for Study of Regional Development, Jawaharlal Nehru University, New Delhi

M. MAHAMALLIK: Senior Research Fellow, Department of Economics, Sambalpur University, Burla, Orissa

S.S. MEENAKSHISUNDARAM: Additional Secretary, Department of Space, Government of India, Bangalore

V.K. MEHTA: Ex-Director, Planning Commission/Management Consultant, New Delhi

UTE MEIR: Programme Officer, UNESCO/WFP Co-operative Programme, UNESCO, Paris

JOS MOOIJ: Visiting Fellow, Centre for Economic and Social Studies, Hyderabad

SARASWATI RAJU: Professor, Centre for Study of Regional Development, Jawaharlal Nehru University, New Delhi

NIRA RAMACHANDRAN: Senior Visiting Fellow, Institute for Human Development, New Delhi

V.M. RAO: Visiting Professor, Institute for Social and Economic Change, Bangalore

D. NARASIMHA REDDY: Professor and Coordinator, Department of Economics, University of Hyderabad, Hyderabad

V. RATNA REDDY: Senior Fellow, Centre for Economic and Social Studies, Hyderabad

KAILAS SARAP: Professor, Department of Economics, Sambalpur University, Burla, Orissa

AMITA SHAH: Professor, Gujarat Institute of Development Research, Ahmedabad

VINOD K. SHARMA: Professor, National Centre for Disaster Management, Indian Institute of Public Administration, New Delhi

RAVI S. SRIVASTAVA: Professor, Centre for Study of Regional Development, Jawaharlal Nehru University, New Delhi

R. THAMARAJAKSHI: Ex-Secretary, Department of Statistics, Ministry of Planning and Programme Implementation, Government of India

# Foreword

On 15 August 1997 which marked the fiftieth anniversary of India's independence, the President of India, Shri K.R. Narayanan pointed out that commitment to a democratic system of governance and achievement of self-sufficiency in food are the twin major accomplishments of the first 50 years of freedom from colonial rule. Recently, the Prime Minister of India, Shri Atal Behari Vajpayee has reminded us that in accordance with Mahatma Gandhi's vision of independent India, we should strive to move from overall food self-sufficiency to nutrition security at the level of every child, woman and man by the sixtieth anniversary of independence, i.e. 15 August 2007. This publication is therefore timely, since it contains authoritative analyses of the various steps involved in the food production-distribution-consumption chain.

*The Food Insecurity Atlas of Rural India* produced by MSSRF and WFP provides guidelines for a plan of action designed to achieve a sustainable end to both Protein Energy Malnutrition (PEM) and hidden hunger caused by micronutrient deficiencies. In this context, I would like to deal briefly with the uncommon opportunities India has today to leapfrog in the area of achieving freedom from hunger through a Community Centred and Controlled Food Bank Network. I would like to briefly refer the major components and ground rules of such a decentralized and location and culture specific system.

## 1. ADOPT A WHOLE LIFE CYCLE APPROACH TO NUTRITION SECURITY

### A. PREGNANT MOTHERS

Overcoming maternal and foetal under- and malnutrition is an urgent task, since nearly 30 per cent of the children born in countries in South Asia are characterized by Low Birth Weight (LBW), with the consequent risk of impaired brain development. Half of the world's malnourished children are in India, Pakistan and Bangladesh. LBW is a proxy indicator of the low status of women in the society, particularly of their health and nutrition status during their entire life cycle.

B. NURSING MOTHERS

Appropriate schemes will be necessary to provide support to enable mothers to breast feed their babies for at least 6 months, as recommended by WHO. Policies at work places should be conducive to achieving this goal.

C. INFANTS (0 TO 2 YEARS)

Special efforts will have to be made to reach this age group through their mothers, since they are the most unreachable at present. Before the age of two 80 per cent of brain development is completed. The first four months in a child's life is particularly critical, since the child is totally dependant on its mother for food and survival.

D. PRESCHOOL CHILDREN (2 TO 6 YEARS)

A revitalized and community controlled Integrated Child Development Service (ICDS) will help cater to the nutritional and health care needs of this age group.

E. YOUTH (6 TO 18 YEARS)

A nutrition based Noon Meal programme in all schools (public and private and rural and urban) will help improve the nutritional status of this group. However, a significant percentage of children belonging to this age group are not able to go to school due to economic reasons. Such school 'push-outs' or child labourers need special attention.

F. ADULTS (18 TO 60 YEARS)

The Nutrition Safety Net to cater to this category should consist of both an Entitlements programme like Food Stamps and Public Distribution System (PDS), as well as a Food for Eco-development programme (also called Food for Work Programme). The Food for Eco-development Programme will promote the use of food grains as wages for the purpose of establishing water harvesting structures

(Water Banks) and for the rehabilitation of degraded lands and ecosystems. Thus, many downstream benefits and livelihood opportunities will be created. In designing a nutrition compact for this age group, persons working in the organized and unorganized sectors will have to be dealt with separately.

### G. OLD AND INFIRM PERSONS

This group will have to be provided with appropriate nutritional support, as part of the ethical obligation of society towards the handicapped.

The above whole-life cycle approach to Nutrition Security will help ensure that the nutritional needs of everyone in the community and at every stage in an individual's life, are satisfied.

## 2. ADOPT A 10-POINT ACTION PLAN TO ACHIEVE SUSTAINABLE NUTRITION SECURITY AT THE LEVEL OF EACH INDIVIDUAL*

The ten points are:

- *Identification*: Identify those who are nutritionally insecure through the local community. Trained Community Volunteers will be useful for this purpose.
- *Education and Information Empowerment*: Empower those who are not aware of their entitlements about the nutritional safety nets available to them and also undertake nutrition education. An entitlements database can be developed for each area and household entitlement cards can be issued, indicating how to access nutritional, health care and educational programmes.
- *Overcome Protein-Calorie Under Nutrition*: The various steps indicated under the whole-life cycle approach will have to be adopted. The problems of child labour and of persons working in the unorganized sector will need specific attention.
- *Eliminate Hidden Hunger caused by the Deficiency of Micronutrients in the Diet*: Introduce an integrated approach including the consumption of vegetable and fruits, millets and grain legumes and the provision of fortified foods like iron and iodine fortified salt and oral dose of Vitamin A.

* Refer to Appendix for the full text.

The basic approach should be a food based one, with emphasis on home and community nutrition gardens, wherever this is socially and economically feasible.

- *Drinking Water, Hygiene and Primary Health Care*: Attend to the provision of safe drinking water and to the improvement of environmental hygiene. Also, improve the primary health care system.
- *Sustainable Livelihoods*: Improve economic access to food through market-linked micro-enterprises supported by micro-credit. Also, create an economic stake in the conservation of natural and common property resources. Ensure that agreements under the World Trade Organization (WTO) provide a level playing field for products coming from decentralized small scale production (production by masses or farmer's farming) as compared to those emerging from mass production technologies or factor farming.
- *Pay Special Attention to Pregnant and Nursing Mothers and Pre-school Children*: Measure progress through monitoring MMR, IMR, incidence of LBW children and male-female sex ratio. Iron-folate supplements during prenatal care should be accompanied by steps to overcome protein-energy deprivation.
- *Strengthening Food Based Safety Nets:* Create lasting individual, household or community assets through Food for Work activities. Focus on the most vulnerable with respect to gender, age, social status and geographic location.
- *Linking Disaster Mitigation with Development*: Establish grain and water banks in order to strenthen households' and communities' ability to cope with disasters. Food assistance should be targeted to people in the most disaster prone areas in order to increase their food security.
- *Greater Market Access to Farm Products:* Avoid trade restrictions. Open the global and national markets for Indian agricultural products.

## 3. COMMUNITY FOOD BANK AS AN INSTRUMENT OF SUSTAINABLE FOOD AND NUTRITION SECURITY

Community Food Bank (CFB) can be started at the village level, with initial food supplies coming as a grant from governments and donor agencies. Later, such CFBs can be sustained through local purchases and from continued government and international support for Food for Eco-development and Food for Nutrition programmes. The CFB can be the entry point to not only bridging the nutritional divide, but also for fostering social and gender equity, ecology and employment. They can also be equipped to cater to emergencies like cyclones, floods, drought and earthquakes.

The CFBs can be organized with the following four major streams of responsibilities.

- *Entitlements*: The benefits of all government and bilateral and multilateral projects intended for overcoming under- and malnutrition can be delivered in a coordinated and interactive manner (as for example those intended for overcoming the deficiencies of macro- and micro-nutrients).
- *Ecology* : Food for Eco-development with particular reference to the establishment of water banks, land care, control of desertification and afforestation.
- *Ethics*: This group of activities will relate to nutritional support to old and infirm persons, pregnant and nursing mothers and infants and pre-school children.
- *Emergencies*: This activity will relate to the immediate relief operations following major natural catastrophies, like drought, floods, cyclone and earthquake as well as to meet the challenge of seasonal slides in livelihood opportunities.

Each of the above four streams of activities can be managed by four separate self-help groups of local women and men. This will help generate a self-help revolution in combating hunger. The overall guidance and oversight may be provided by a multi-stakeholder Community Food Bank Council.

## 4. RESOURCES CENTRES FOR CFBs

For the CFB movement to succeed there is need for training managers of such Food Banks and for building the capacity of the Community Oversight Council to plan and monitor the different programmes. Training modules will have to be prepared for this purpose. Accounting and monitoring software will have to be developed and members of the Self-Help Groups will have to be trained in the use of the software and in managing the computer-aided knowledge centres, linked to CFBs. Four different training modules, each relating entitlements, eco-development, ethics and emergencies will have to be developed, so that each SHG is headed by a professionally trained woman or man. A network of institutions which will provide the necessary managerial, technical and training support to managers of self-help groups and CFBs will have to be organized in different parts of the country.

I wish to record our sincere gratitude to Shri M.D. Asthana, Principal Advisor, Planning Commission and his associates for their tireless and visionary efforts which went into the preparation of this book. Our heart-felt thanks also go to Mr. Pedro Medrano and his associates in the World Food Programme for their technical and financial support.

M.S. SWAMINATHAN

# Preface

In April 2001, on the occasion of the release of the *Food Insecurity Atlas of Rural India*, the Indian Government in collaboration with M.S. Swaminathan Research Foundation and the United Nations World Food Programme held a consultation on 'Towards Hunger Free India'. The consultation was attended by leading food security experts from the academic world, Government Departments, Non-Governmental Organizations, UN and donor agencies. This book comprises papers submitted by eminent participants that analyse and highlight the various dimensions of food insecurity in India and present recommendations on how food assistance can improve the livelihoods of the poor.

The issue of food security was discussed comprehensively taking into account all dimensions of the problem. The focus was not only on agricultural production and trade, but also on vulnerability to natural disaster, economic access to food as well as on food utilization, including intra-household distribution of food resources, childcare and physical absorption. Equal importance was given to the public response to food insecurity and India's food based safety nets. As an outcome of this consultation, a Ten Point Agenda was formulated that will be considered in India's Tenth Five-Year Development Plan.

India has the biggest food assistance programmes in the developing world. The three largest schemes together cover almost one-third of India's entire population. At the same time more than one-fifth of the population, or some 208 million people, are malnourished. This paradox of ample availability of food versus high malnutrition and incidence of hunger, could be resolved by adopting a policy approach that addresses the different dimensions of food insecurity.

The various aspects of food insecurity are linked in complex ways to diverse social, economic and cultural phenomena, e.g. gender hierarchies, labour market fluctuations, environmental factors, etc. If these crucial linkages are pinpointed and systematically incorporated into development policies, food-based interventions will have a more comprehensive and lasting impact on the lives of people. By shedding light on these issues, the book creates the rationale for food assistance programmes to adopt new perspectives and to expand accordingly. Such programmes could be strengthened, for example, through better targeting of the most vulnerable—especially women and children—more decentralized and participatory management and improved disaster responsiveness.

The various papers in the consultation point to a general conclusion: strengthening opportunities and diversifying options are the key to poverty alleviation and hunger eradication. The persisting question of how to achieve sustainable and equitable food security, is thus addressed; while the phenomenon of hunger is inextricably connected to poverty, illiteracy, etc., the initial answer lies in the basic, grass roots approach to intervene with food. This is the crux of the matter and this is also where the United Nations organizations such as WFP can contribute significantly.

WFP seeks to combat hunger and malnutrition, especially among women and children, with food as the primary and essential tool. Our singular focus is on the role of food as an instrument of sustainable development, by enabling and involving people who are otherwise marginalized. In India, we are very pleased to be closely associated with the government in its endeavor to increase the developmental impact of food assistance. WFP plays an important catalytic role through piloting new approaches of food assistance that can be scaled up and that serve as a basis for leveraging policies and resources for the hungry poor. The conviction that food, particularly when managed by women and consumed by children, makes a critical and positive difference both in the immediate well-being of a person as well as in his/her long-term development, is our driving force, the thrust of our presence here.

The consultation indicates a commonality of approach and of purpose among all involved. The challenge before us right now is to achieve this common purpose in the most efficient and integrated manner. Effective targeting, as highlighted in the *Food Insecurity Atlas*, and continued innovative research, would be of utmost importance. The priority, however, is to achieve a strategic synergy among different interventions, an effective marriage of various ideas, in order to chart out an action-oriented pathway to our collective goal, i.e. the goal of achieving substantial freedom from hunger by 2007, the dream of Food for All by 2015. The government's initiative and leadership, coupled with the contributions of civil society organizations such as M.S. Swaminathan Research Foundation and the international community, will set the right pace for this challenging journey. If we, as partners in development, solemnly commit our respective strengths and resources toward meeting this challenge, then in due time we can prove that this consultation represents more than a mere romantic vision, but that it lays the groundwork for food policies and interventions to make a positive dent in the food security of India.

PEDRO MEDRANO

# Acknowledgements

This book is a record of the main proceedings of the national consultation on 'Towards Hunger Free India' and is the result of the combined efforts of the Planning Commission, the World Food Programme (WFP) and the M.S. Swaminathan Research Foundation (MSSRF). We are most grateful to the Hon'ble Shri Atal Behari Vajpayee, Prime Minister of India, for giving the inaugural address to the Consultation. We also take this opportunity to express our grateful thanks to the Hon'ble Deputy Chairman, Planning Commission who fully supported the joint initiative of Dr. M.S. Swaminathan and the WFP for organizing the consultation at the national level.

The Consultation also owes its success to Ms. Catherine Bertini, Executive Director, WFP for her unstinted support. While she keenly looked forward to visit New Delhi and be present during the event, she had to cancel her visit due to unavoidable reasons. We take this opportunity to express our grateful thanks to Mr. Namanga Ngongi, Deputy Executive Director, who represented Ms. Catherine Bertini and the WFP, United Nations, at the inaugural session. Grateful thanks are also due to Hon'ble Mr. Som Pal, Member, Planning Commission for the Special Address.

The Consultation could not have been such a success without the support of Dr. N.C. Saxena, Secretary, Planning Commission. Mention may also be made of Ms. Feroza Mehrotra, Adviser, Dr. Sharat Kumar, Director, Mr. B.B. Mukhopadhyay and Mr. V. Srinivasan, Protocol Officers, Planning Commission, for their unequivocal support in organizing the Consultation.

The moving spirit behind the whole initiative was indeed Dr. M.S. Swaminathan. It was his stature as the architect of the 'Green Revolution' in India that brought everyone together. Needless to say, the Consultation finally owed greatly to the numerous contributors, participants, chairpersons and rapporteurs from Delhi and different parts of India as well as from abroad. Thanks are also due to Dr. A.N. Sharma, Director, Institute of Human Development, New Delhi and his team of co-workers for their contribution towards the success of the technical sessions.

The WFP India regional office worked round the clock with a missionary zeal for the event. Special mention ought to be made in this regard of Mr. Wolfgang Herbinger, Regional Programme Adviser, Dr. Minnie Mathew, Ms. Eela Choudhuri and Ms. Kavita Verma. The credit for the subsequent editing goes to all the members of the Editorial Board. We also wish to acknowledge here the contributions of Manohar Publishers who could bring out the book at such a short notice.

M.D. Asthana
Pedro Medrano

# Abbreviations

AAY : Antyodaya Anna Yojana
AED : Academy for Educational Development (USAID Funded)
AFS : APEC Food System
AMS : Aggregate Measure of Support
AMU : Amrit Mahila Udyog
ANCOVA : Analysis of Co-variance
ANM : Auxiliary Nurse Midwife
ANOVA : Analysis of Variance
AOA : Agreement on Agriculture
APL : Above Poverty Line
AVHR : Advanced Very High Resolution
AWW : *Anganwadi* Worker
BCG : Bacillus of Calmette and Guerin
BIMARU : Bihar, Madhya Pradesh, Rajasthan, Uttar Pradesh
BMI : Body Mass Index
BPL : Below Poverty Line
CACP : Commission for Agricultural Costs and Prices
CAP : Common Agricultural Policy
CARE : Cooperative for Assistance and Relief Everywhere
CBO : Community Based Organization
CDPO : Child Development Project Officer
CIP : Central Issue Price
CMIE : Centre for Monitoring Indian Economy
CODEX : Alimentarious Commission for Harmonization of Food Standards
CPI (ML) : Communist Party of India (Marxist-Leninist)
CPL : Common Property Land
CPR : Common Property Resources
DDP : Desert Development Programme
DES : Dietary Energy Supply
DGE & T : Director General of Employment and Training
DPAP : Drought Prone Area Programme
DPT : Diphtheria, Pertussis, Tetanus

DRDA : District Rural Development Agency
DSB : Dispute Settlement Body
DTDP : Dispersed Tribal Development Programme
DWCRA : Development of Women and Children in Rural Areas
EARRS : Earthquake Affected Relief and Rehabilitation Services
EAS : Employment Assurance Scheme
EC : European Commission
ECCSGD : Early Childhood Care for Survival Growth and Development
ECLAC : Economic Commission for Latin America and the Caribbean
EDTA : Ethylene Diaminete Traacetic Acid
EEC : European Economic Community
EGS : Employment Guarantee Scheme
EPW : Economic and Political Weekly
ERC : Expenditure Reforms Commission
EU : European Union
FAO : Food and Agriculture Organization of the United Nations
FAOSTAT : FAO Statistical Data Bases
FCI : Food Corporation of India
FFW : Food for Work
FPS : Fair Price Shops
FRESH : Focusing Resources on Effective School Health
GATT : General Agreement on Tariffs and Trade
GCC : Gross Calorie Content
GDP : Gross Domestic Product
GIPIB : Government of India, Press Information Bureau
GLASOD : Global Assessment of Soil Degradation
GMF : Genetically Modified Food
GMO : Genetically Modified Organisms
GOI : Government of India
HAZ : Z-score of height-for-age
HCR : Head-Count Ratio
HS : Harmonized System
IAY : Indira Awas Yojana
ICAR : Indian Council of Agricultural Research
ICDS : Integrated Child Development Services
ICMR : Indian Council of Medical Research

| | | |
|---|---|---|
| ICRISAT | : | International Crop Research Institute for Semi-Arid Tropics |
| IDD | : | Iodine Deficiency Disorders |
| IDEA | : | Iron Deficiency Elimination Action |
| IDPAD | : | Indo-Dutch Programme for Alternatives in Development |
| IFPRI | : | International Food Policy Research Institute |
| IHD | : | Institute of Human Development |
| IIP | : | Intensive Intervention Project |
| IJRY | : | Intensified Jawahar Rozgar Yojana |
| ILO | : | International Labour Organization |
| ILSI | : | International Life Science Institute |
| IMD | : | Indian Meteorology Department |
| IMF | : | International Monetary Fund |
| IMPACT | : | International Model for Policy Analysis of Agricultural Commodities and Trade |
| IMR | : | Infant Mortality Rate |
| INCAP | : | Instituto de nutricion de Centro America y Panama |
| INP | : | Integrated Nutrition Programme |
| IPCL | : | Improved Pace and Contents of Learning |
| IRDP | : | Integrated Rural Development Programme |
| IRRI | : | International Rice Research Institute |
| ISO | : | International Standards Organization |
| ITDA | : | Integrated Tribal Development Agency |
| ITDP | : | Integrated Tribal Development Programme |
| IWDP | : | Integrated Watershed Development Programme |
| JCI | : | Janpath Citizens' Initiative |
| JFM | : | Joint Forest Management |
| JRY | : | Jawahar Rozgar Yojana |
| KBK | : | Kalahandi, Bolangir and Koraput |
| KRIBP | : | Kribhco Indo-British Project |
| LBW | : | Low Birth Weight |
| LDC | : | Less Developed Countries |
| LES | : | Linear Expenditure System |
| MADA | : | Modified Area Development Approach |
| MDM | : | Mid-Day Meal |
| MFN | : | Most Favoured Nations |
| MICS | : | UNICEF Surveys |
| MLA | : | Member of Legislative Assembly |
| MMR | : | Maternal Mortality Rate |
| MNC | : | Multi-National Corporation |

MPCE : Monthly Per Capita Expenditure
MPW : Multi-Purpose Worker
MSP : Minimum Support Price
MSSRF : M.S. Swaminathan Research Foundation of India
NABARD : National Bank for Agriculture and Rural Development
NADAMS : National Agricultural Drought Assessment and Management System
NAS : National Accounts Statistics
NCAER : National Council of Applied Economic Research
NFHS : National Family Health Survey
NFI : Nutrition Foundation of India
NFIDC : Net Food Importing Developing Countries
NGO : Non-Government Organization
NHS : National Health Survey
NIN : National Institute of Nutrition
NIPCCD : National Institute of Public Corporation and Child Development
NIRD : National Institute of Rural Development
NNG : National Nutrition Goals
NNP : National Nutrition Policy
NOAA : National Oceanic and Atmospheric Administration
NPNSPE : National Programme for Nutritional Support to Primary Education
NREP : National Rural Employment Programme
NSDP : Net State Domestic Product
NSS : National Sample Survey
NSSO : National Sample Survey Organization
NTB : Non-Tariff Barriers
NTM : Non-Trade Measures
OBC : Other Backward Caste
OC : Other Caste
OECD : Organization for Economic Cooperation and Development
ORMAS : Orissa Rural Marketing Apex Society
ORS : Oral Recipe Solvent
ORSTOM : Organisation pour la Recherche Scientifique dans les Territoires Outre-mer (Government of France)
PCY : Per Capita Income
PDS : Public Distribution System
PHC : Primary Health Centre

PIA : Project Implementing Agencies
PLW : Pregnant or Lactating Women
PMGY : Pradhan Mantri Gramodaya Yojana
PP I : Population Projection I
PP II : Population Projection II
PR : Panchayati Raj
PRA : Participatory Research Approach
PRI : Panchayati Raj Institution
PROBE : Public Report on Basic Education in India
QR : Quantitative Restriction
RD : Rural Development
RIDF : Rural Infrastructure Development Fund
RLEGP : Rural Landless Employment Guarantee Programme
RPDS : Revamped Public Distribution System
S&D : Special and Differential
SAARC : South Asia Association for Regional Corporation
SAP : Structural Adjustment Programme
SAT : Satellite Phones
SC/ST : Schedule Caste/Schedule Tribe
SCM : Subsidies and Countervailing Measures
SD : Standard Deviation
SDP : State Domestic Product
SEWA : Self-Employed Women's Association
SFC : State Food & Civil Supplies Corporation
SGA : Small for Gestational Age
SGSY : Swaranjayanti Gram Swarozgar Yojana
SHG : Self Help Group
SLC : Survey of Living Condition
SPS : Sanitary and Phytosanitary Standards
ST : Scheduled Tribe
TBT : Technical Barriers to Trade
TDCC : Tribal Development Cooperative Corporation
TE : Triennium Ending
TFP : Total Factor Productivity
TPDS : Targeted Public Distribution System
TRIPS : Trade-Related Aspects of Intellectual Property Rights
TRQ : Tariff-Rate Quotas
TRYSEM : Training of Rural Youth for Self Employment
TSP : Tribal Sub-Plan
UC Davis : University of California, Davis
UK : United Kingdom

UNCTAD : United Nations Conference on Trade and Development
UNDP : United Nations Development Programme
UNICEF : United Nations International Children's Educational Fund
UNRISD : United Nations Research Institute for Social Development
UP : Uttar Pradesh
UPOV : International Union for the Protection of New Varieties of Plants
USA : United States of America
UT : Union Territory
VAM : Vulnerability Analysis and Mapping
VER : Voluntary Export Restraint
VGD : Vulnerable Group Development
WAZ : Z-Score of weight-for-age
WDC : Watershed Development Committee
WDP : Watershed Development Project
WEF : World Education Forum
WFP : World Food Programme
WHO : World Health Organization
WHZ : Z-Score of weight-for-height
WPI : Wholesale Price Index
WPR : Workforce Participation Rate
WTO : World Trade Organization

# Inaugural Address

*Hon'ble Shri Atal Behari Vajpayee*
*Prime Minister of India*

> . . . the responsibility of mitigating the hunger of the poorest of our brethren cannot be that of the Government alone. Concerned citizens and non-governmental organizations can contribute immensely to the success of our 'Food for All' mission . . .

It gives me great pleasure to be here with you at this inaugural session of the consultation on 'Towards a Hunger Free India'. I compliment the Planning Commission, the World Food Programme, and the M.S. Swaminathan Research Foundation for this commendable initiative. This is a unique instance of the coming together of the Government, an international agency, and a non-governmental organization to deliberate on a critical challenge before our nation—namely, how to ensure Food for All.

Democracy and hunger cannot go together. A hungry stomach questions and censures the system's failure to meet what is a basic biological need of every human being. There can be no place for hunger and poverty in a modern world in which science and technology have created conditions for abundance and equitable development.

India has progressed on many fronts since Independence. We have achieved self-sufficiency in food, even though our population has more than trebled to cross the one billion mark in five decades. I compliment our hard working *kisans* and our agricultural scientists for increasing the growth rate in food production from 0.3 per cent a year in the half century before Independence, to 3 per cent in the half century since.

We have sufficient stocks of foodgrains. No one needs go hungry in this country. Nevertheless, it is true that many millions of our countrymen still go hungry to bed every night. Malnourishment, especially among women and children, is widespread. We are determined to change this situation. In this, we are guided by the commandment of the Upanishads:

अन्नं बहु कुर्वीत
*Annam Bahu Kurvita*

It means: 'Multiply food production many-fold. Ensure an abundance of food all around.'

While we need to substantially increase our food production, we are faced with the paradoxical problem of surplus food stocks. There is also the related problem of substantial quantities of food being wasted. This has happened because of inadequate attention in the past to its storage, preservation, processing, and proper distribution.

I am reminded here of the proverbial *Akshay Patra*—or the inexhaustible plate—in the *Mahabharat*. The plate was blessed with the powers of producing unlimited food, provided no part of it was wasted. What this metaphor teaches us is that, India can produce enough food to feed all her citizens and much more, but no part of it should be wasted.

The Government has drawn up policies and schemes to address all the critical issues in efficient food chain management. We are providing many incentives and facilities to farmers, their co-operatives, and to private entrepreneurs to set up godowns, silos, cold storages, and food processing units.

Few people outside the Government are aware that India has the world's largest officially supported food and nutrition security programme. This initiative encompasses not just the public distribution system with its elaborate system of production incentives, marketing support, buffer stocking, and distribution, but also includes nutrition supplements to young children and mothers, mid-day meal schemes, food grants to the destitute, and food for work programmes for the working population.

We have doubled the allocation of food to all poor families under the PDS. The *Antyodaya Anna Yojana*, which is a new scheme for the poorest 10 million families, gives a sharper focus to our commitment to reduce hunger.

To a great extent, these interventions have addressed the problem of access to food, both physical and economic, and have provided a basic safety net to our people. However, there is still a long way to go before we can assume that all our people are food secure at all times.

Regional and seasonal variations, fluctuations in the purchasing power of the poorest households, natural calamities, etc., all combine to create conditions for continuing food insecurity to large sections of our people. The challenge before the Government is to devise its strategies in such a manner so as to be able to anticipate and provide for these conditions of insecurity and ensure year-round food security at the household level.

In this regard, the comprehensive document on food insecurity in rural India being released today, is most timely. It complements the Government's own efforts over the past few years to target subsidized food more accurately at the most needy regions and groups.

The high cost of managing our food stocks is a major problem in the way of reaching cheaper food to a greater number of needy families. There is an urgent need to ensure that the Central Government's annual food subsidy, which has gone up five times in a decade to reach Rs. 13,000 crore this year, is better targeted.

One way to reduce costs is to decentralize the buying and distribution of food. Instead of one agency, the Food Corporation of India, buying food at one price, and then moving it to States, this year's budget has proposed to give individual States the freedom to buy food from anywhere and to distribute it themselves. The Centre will provide financial assistance for this purpose.

I hope that this measure will encourage our State Governments to take creative steps to buy the cheapest food that they can get from the nearest sources and distribute it in the most efficient way possible. This will ensure that the Central subsidy can benefit more poor people than is the case today.

I must, however, point out that the implementation of the PDS is not living up to the people's expectations. Our Targeted Public Distribution Scheme does not seem to be working well many places—specially in the poorer north and north-eastern States. The limited off-take in the States where the majority of our poor live, points to serious deficiencies in the administrative capability of the system. I urge the concerned State Governments to effectively remedy this situation at the earliest.

Even the implementation of free food provided to school children under the mid-day meal scheme leaves much to be desired. This is a matter of serious concern. We owe it to the nation to run and operate all our beneficiary programmes in a cost-effective manner.

I believe that the shortcomings at the implementation level can be overcome by ensuring greater people's participation and monitoring. Our Panchayati Raj Institutions and other citizens' organizations have to play an active role in making these laudable schemes successful.

We shall examine whether the surplus food stocks can be used in innovative ways. For example, to promote female literacy programmes and attendance in schools. India would be happy to learn from the experience of such exercises undertaken elsewhere under the auspices of the World Food Programme.

Friends, the responsibility of mitigating the hunger of the poorest of our brethren cannot be that of the Government alone. Concerned citizens and non-govermnental organizations can contribute immensely to the success of our 'Food for All' mission. As a matter of fact, they are already engaged in many admirable initiatives. I especially applaud the countless mass-feeding activities by religious institutions, belonging to all communities.

We in India have a long tradition of *Anna Dan*—giving and sharing food. The full potential of this noble tradition has not been realized in modern times. Therefore, a specific idea I would like to place before your consultation is how we can activate mass-feeding programmes by religious and social institutions on a far wider scale. They are especially needed in times of natural calamities. I assure you that the Government would facilitate and support such activities in all ways it can.

I shall conclude by stressing my belief that the sacred mission of a 'Hunger Free India' needs the cooperative efforts of the Central and State Governments, local self-government bodies, non-governmental organizations, international agencies, and—above all, our citizens. We can indeed banish hunger from our country in a short time. Let us resolve today to make this mission substantially successful by 2007, which will mark the sixtieth anniversary of our Independence.

Thank you.

# Keynote Address

*Hon'ble Shri K.C. Pant*
*Deputy Chairman, Planning Commission*

> . . . agricultural Growth must be viewed not merely as a means towards food security, but as a strategy to subserve the broader goal of poverty eradication . . . the effort must be to broad-base our agricultural growth pattern so that every part of the country participates to the extent possible in increasing our agricultural output . . .

During the first two decades after independence, India had to import large quantities of food grains to meet shortfalls in domestic production. The extent of vulnerability came into sharp focus during the severe drought of 1965 and 1966. The cessation of food aid because of the Indo-Pakistan war of 1965 led to unacceptably high famine deaths in the country. It is a lesson we should never forget. Geo-political conditions are still not such that food security can be dropped from its position as a central element of our economic strategy.

It is this strategy which powered the green revolution, and in a relatively short period of time the country started producing enough not only to meet its internal demand, but also to generate a small surplus. This in itself is not a mean achievement as the country's population has more than trebled since independence. However, this should not be a cause for complacency since per capita production and availability of food grains remain below the normative needs of our population. National Family Health Survey (NFHS) -2 of 1998-9 has shown that undernutrition, especially in children, is still widely prevalent. Almost half of the women in the age group of 15-49 years and an 3/4th of children have been found to be anaemic.

Increasing food grains production in the country should therefore continue to be a major element of our agricultural strategy. In the past, surplus food grains production was realized primarily in Punjab, Haryana and Western UP. However, there is a tendency among farmers in this region to diversify towards crops other than foodgrains. Alternatives must, therefore, be developed. The region in the country which has the maximum potential for increase in foodgrain production, particularly of rice, is the eastern region. The next stage of the Green Revolution in the country has to come about in this region.

But the rest of the country cannot be neglected either. Even today, the extent of poverty in the country is unacceptably high. There is considerable research which suggests that the sector which has the most beneficial effect on poverty reduction is agriculture. Therefore, agricultural growth must be viewed not merely as a means towards food security, but as a strategy to subserve the broader goal of poverty eradication. Looked at this way, the effort must be to broad-base our agricultural growth pattern so that every part of the country participates to the extent possible in increasing our agricultural output.

Although there is considerable potential for accelerating agricultural growth in the country, including allied activities such as horticulture, animal husbandry, dairy and fishery, the pace of progress has been slow and certain weaknesses are becoming increasingly evident. Among the factors of concern are environmental considerations such as land degradation and water depletion, inadequate market integration leading to localized shortages and gluts, tardy progress of technology diffusion, inadequacy .of appropriate infrastructure, and others. What is also worrying is that the pace of employment creation in agriculture has slowed significantly in recent years. This has ominous implication for the future.

India's efforts to attain better yields and productivity has also been less than adequate. In fact, we seem to be slipping down the productivity ladder in most agricultural products compared to the rest of the world. Some of these issues can be addressed by increased investment, but many cannot be. In particular, a gradual shift in the geographical pattern of agricultural production in order to bring it in line with the resource endowments appears essential.

The single most important issue in raising agricultural production is land and water management. Large parts of the country are already suffering from water stress and corrective action has to be taken immediately. Almost 62 per cent of net sown area is rainfed. Latest estimates of 1993 made by the Ministry of Agriculture show the extent of degraded land in the country was more than 173 million hectares. Public investment in irrigation, rainwater harvesting and watershed management, coupled with greater participation of the people in managing these common resources, must, therefore, be accorded immediate priority.

Malnutrition among a large section of the people has been identified to be on account of factors other than the availability of food grains and other forms of nutrition alone. For example, even if all the food with adequate complements of all nutrients were available, its absorption physiologically may be problematic because of lack of good quality of drinking water and a clean environment. The problem of hunger, nutrition and food security, is thus related to the whole development process. We have had a growth of almost 6 per cent in the recent past. It may not be disappointing, but it is not enough to account for the major development issues which relate to the quality of life of our people. The Honourable Prime Minister has, therefore, directed us to examine the feasibility of doubling per capita income in the country over the next ten years. We are in the process of undertaking this exercise keeping in view the availability of resources. To reach such a target, we must be prepared to jettison concepts and policies which are no longer relevant. Today, India is no longer an economy of shortages, but an economy where overall adequacies are maldistributed.

This is amply borne out by the huge surplus of food grains that have been accumulated in the FCI godowns. The government is concerned about the fact that in spite of surplus production of food grains, we have still not been able to eradicate hunger. It appears perhaps, that the food procurement policy is itself becoming a vehicle for supporting high prices of food grains. The government, therefore, has to strike a balance between what is necessary for the welfare of the farmers and for the welfare of the customer. The poor in the country will certainly benefit from low prices of foodgrains in the market, but if this comes through unremunerative prices to the farmers then the pace of future progress will necessarily be adversely affected. Therefore we will have to tread a narrow path.

I hope this consultation will suggest how best we can tackle the problem of ensuring Hunger Free India.

# Special Address

*Mr. Namanga Ngongi*
*Deputy Executive Director*
*World Food Programme*

> . . . what is impossible today—an India where everbody has access to enough food to lead a healthy and active life—can become reality tomorrow. . . .

'We are daily witnessing the phenomenon of the impossible of yesterday becoming the possible of today' (M.K. Gandhi).

We are meeting here today because we share a vision—and that vision is an India free from hunger. Yes. That is an ambitious goal, but it is one that can be achieved with the right kind of development strategies.

The two publications we are launching at this consultation, we hope, will help the people and the Government of India to shape those strategies. One is an *Atlas* that depicts and analyses food insecurity problems in India. The other, *Food Assistance in South Asia*, focuses on challenges often faced in food assistance programmes and presents recommendations on how such assistance can improve the livelihoods of poor people. This is the first time that food insecurity in India and in South Asia has been analysed in depth taking into account all dimensions of the problem. The book also provides, for the first time, a comprehensive overview on the evolution of food based interventions in the region.

For WFP, this evening is, however, more than just another inaugural session. This evening and the next two days mark the culmination of a very fruitful collaboration with the Government of India and M.S. Swaminathan Research Foundation. In the name of WFP, and especially on behalf of colleagues here in India, I would like to thank the Planning Commission and M.S. Swaminathan Research Foundation for the privilege of working together.

Today, all of us gathered here, I believe, share a common aim of linking food security analyses with the elaboration of policies that have a clear poverty focus. Such policies should also lead to the design and implementation of targeted programmes in order to truly reach people in need.

Our collaboration, among WFP, the Planning Commission and the M.S. Swaminathan Research Foundation has sought to apply lessons learnt and develop new models of food assistance to reach out to the hungry poor.

As an illustration, *The Food Insecurity Atlas* provides a sound basis to improve targeting of national food assistance programmes in India. And the book stresses the importance of linking food security policies with food assistance. It is a great achievement that the results of this collaborative effort will be considered in India's Tenth Five-Year Development Plan.

Let me now concentrate on an issue that is central to the consultation as well as to the two books: The focus on women and children.

We often talk about giving food aid programmes a stronger poverty focus. There are no better ways to do that than by targeting women and children in need. Yet, it is women and children who are least empowered and who have little or no voice in the world of politics. From a political perspective, they are the easiest to neglect; from a developmental perspective they are the least served.

Women and children are worst affected by hunger. Malnutrition among young children in India is among the highest in the world. More than half of all children under the age of five, or some 70 million, are underweight. That means that some 35 per cent of the world's malnourished children live in India.

On the other hand, there are more than 40 million metric tons of food grains in stocks. Obviously, in South Asia, India is not alone in this paradox of hungry people living next to overflowing warehouses.

What is particularly worrying is that hunger is handed over from one generation to the next. Poor nutritional status of girls and women can result in an inter-generation cycle of malnutrition. Sixty per cent of women in their childbearing years are stunted as a result of inadequate nutrition during their own childhood. During pregnancy their anaemic condition is further aggravated. A malnourished, anaemic woman is likely to deliver a baby with low birth weight. This baby is disadvantaged by the bequest of hunger even before birth, and will carry this handicap throughout its life.

Another reason to focus on women is that women are the main nutritional caretakers for the whole family. They prepare the food and feed the children. What they eat also influences the growth potential of the unborn baby in their womb. Their role in the gender division of labour is inextricably linked to food security and nutrition. And it is under their control that food resources are more likely to benefit children and increase household food security.

In the past, not enough progress was made in reducing malnutrition despite growing food production. To confront the intractable problem of widespread hunger, the Government of India has built the biggest food assistance programmes in the developing world. The three largest schemes together cover almost one third of India's entire population. Some 24 million children and mothers are covered by the Government's Integrated Child Development Services. About 98 million school children get a daily snack or meal in their schools and almost 200 million poor people benefit from subsidised food distribution.

Successive governments of India have clearly shown their commitment to eradicate malnutrition. And, Honourable Prime Minister, your presence here this evening reinforces the importance your government assigns to the issue of food security. But, we all agree that a lot more needs to be done. One of the key recommendations the book *The Food Assistance in South Asia* makes is to work more through women. Women are mostly marginalized and have only a very limited role in decision-making. Their needs are not adequately considered as their voices are often not heard.

'Make women the key players' is thus the first recommendation of the book. Involve women in all aspects and stages of food assistance programmes, because this is a prerequisite for success.

Half-a-century ago there lived an exemplary Indian scholar and statesman, Dr. Ambedkar, who said: 'I measure the progress of a community by the degree of progress which women have achieved.'

The big challenge that remains not only here in India, but also in most countries in the world is to create an environment in which women can be equal partners to men in the development process. It is Dr. Ambedkar's dream that we call today 'gender equality'.

Thirty-six years after Dr. Ambedkar's death, the Indian government took an important step by strengthening women's role in the Panchayat Raj system. The 73rd amendment of 1992, was a path breaking decision on the inclusion of women in governance. It tackled 'institutionalised inequalities' through 'institutionalised counter measures'.

I am sure, if Dr. Ambedkar would still be alive, he would also passionately applaud you - Honourable Prime Minister - for declaring the year 2001 as the 'Women's Empowerment Year'.

Food-based assistance has a comparative advantage over other kinds of interventions in contributing to women's empowerment. Food is one of the few resources that most women traditionally manage as part of their household responsibilities. Food is a good vehicle for initiating changes in the lives of women, for increasing their awareness and self-help capacities. With food, women can be reached who otherwise are often excluded from public events and programmes.

In India, WFP is piloting a programme approach that focuses on women as key agents of change. It is the women's educational level, nutritional status and control over food resources and assets that determine household food security. Consequently, the problem of food insecurity is addressed from various angles.

Three different food-based interventions - Supplementary feeding, food-for-work and incentive schemes for girls' school attendance - are promoted in the same area, in carefully identified and targeted communities.

Supplementary feeding ensures that small children receive nutritious food and alleviates mother's burden to scrounge around for food. Food for school attendance acts as an incentive to send girls to school. FFW offers employment to women as well as men within the community and helps to check migration to already overcrowded urban areas. Assets created through community work such as irrigation channels, wells or protected watersheds improve livelihoods of the entire family and community.

It is the combination of these interventions that can make a difference in the lives of the poor people, and particularly of women. Strengthening opportunities and options is the key to alleviating hunger and poverty. It is the key to a hunger free India.

Honourable Prime Minister, I firmly believe that what seems impossible today - an India where everybody has access to enough food to lead a healthy and active life - can become reality tomorrow.

Just think back: Only four decades ago India was desperately struggling to cover its food shortfalls. It could not produce enough food to feed its 440 million people. Thanks to the commitment of successive governments and the dedicated work of people like Professor Swaminathan, the father of the 'Green Revolution', today, India with a population of one billion has surplus food stock.

I am optimistic - Honourable Prime Minister - that with the strong commitment of your government working together with civil society organizations and the international community to target the most vulnerable and to invest in the country's human resources development, we can realize the vision of a hunger free India.

# Special Address

*Hon'ble Shri Som Pal*
*Member, Planning Commission*

Dr. Swaminathan and friends,

I deem it my privilege to be able to address this 'Consultation on Towards Hunger Free India'.

When we talk about food and hunger, we need to first understand the special characteristic of agriculture. Agriculture is different from other sectors of the economy since it is not possible to fully control production. Prices tend to be determined by supply and demand in agriculture, unlike industry where prices are 'administered'—being determined on the principle of cost plus the 'mark up' for profits. A good production in agriculture may cause a fall in prices reducing incomes of the farmers despite a higher volume of sale. The Minimum Support Price (MSP) for agricultural products is indeed a safety mechanism to protect the farmers from such an eventuality. The MSP, however, has come under criticism on account of many aberrations that have crept in its implementation over the years. There is no denying that it needs to be re-examined in the light of the emerging situation. It has, nonetheless, to be recognized that in view of the large number of farmers who take disjointed decision, there would always be a need for something like the MSP to guide them as to how much acreage to allot to different crops.

In this regard, I would like to refer to the Bhanu Pratap Committee Report which recommended that instead of procuring and buying agricultural commodities at the declared price, the Government should announce the average price based on the existing market prices and should intervene in those cases only where the market prices show a variation of more than 15 per cent on either side. In this way, it would be protecting the interests

*Special Address to the National Consultation on 26 April 2001.

of the producer (farmers) as well as the consumers. This would require continuation of the existing policy of buffer stocking of food grains in the range of 20 to 30 million tons, annually.

So far as subsidy to infrastructure in Indian agriculture is concerned, it is not so as it is made out to be. Much of the subsidy on electricity shown against agriculture includes 'distribution losses' on account of pilferage/theft. In a way, this amounts to 'fudging' in the absence of correct classification of data. The fertilizer subsidy is yet another case in point. There are two components of this subsidy; as high as 58 per cent of subsidy is pocketed by the industry and only 42 per cent reaches the farmers.

Equally worrying is the trend of increasing higher expenditure on direct inputs in agriculture since 1968. As is well known, this is the negative aspect of the 'Green Revolution'. There is a need to restructure the cropping pattern through introducing well designed alternative cropping and multiple cropping to reduce our dependence on the use of chemicals in agriculture. Use of chemicals could certainly be reduced by 50 per cent within the next 3 to 5 years. Agriculture products available in the open market contain high residues of pesticides. The 1,172 samples collected from 52 milk producing districts only proved this point, showing toxic residues of DDT alone to the tune of 4.2 per cent against the internationally CODEX of 0.05 that is 84 times higher than what is desirable! The high yielding varieties of wheat and rice being produced in Punjab and Haryana are found deficient in zinc causing diabetes in a big way; 25 per cent of the rural population is affected by diabetes in Punjab.

Public distribution system of India is indeed the largest of its kind in the world. It supplements the policy of buffer stocking under which the effect of rising prices on account of supply constraints is modulated by market intervention. Attempts are also on to supply about 40 per cent food grain requirements of very poor families at much below the market price and to indigent old people even free of cost. However, these do not seem to be succeeding on account of administrative failure. Diversion away from the targeted population has been assessed to the extent of 33 to 93 per cent of foodgrains supplied.

In my view, the problem of food access for the most vulnerable sections of population can be best ensured through improving their 'entitlement'. Under the weak finances of the States and the Central Government, it is not feasible to dole out the food stocks procured by the public agencies at hugely subsidized rates. This is not a sustainable proposition. Entitlement, in turn, can be best guaranteed by improving the purchasing power of the poor people. The Bhanu Pratap Committee Report (1990) to which I referred to earlier had brought to the notice that around 90 million hectares of land is lying unutilized in India. Since 1990, there has been some improvement in the situation; nonetheless, the latest figures available with the Planning Commission suggest that even now around 80 million hectares of land is lying unutilized. Its distribution to the poor by removing legal obstacles will empower the poor economically. The Union Government can certainly convene a meeting of the Chief Ministers (of states) and put across the idea of allotting such land on either lease basis or permanent ownership basis enabling the poor to put it to productive use. It will at the same time tremendously enhance their dignity and feeling of well being, contributing to public welfare massively. In order to impart urgency to the task, a feasible time frame could be thought off.

I would also like to draw your attention to corruption. Various Poverty Alleviation schemes, with huge plan outlays, are being implemented in the different States. Some of these are meant for lactating mothers and malnourished children. But if these schemes/ programmes are doled out for implementation to those who offer the highest graft, no welfare objective can be achieved. The general public perception about these programmes being a source of corruption has to be changed by better delivery mechanism. Moreover, it may perhaps be better to use these funds to buy land and allot it to the poor to permanently alleviate them.

There is, moreover, a need to increase plan allocation for agriculture. Sixty-seven per cent of India's agriculture is still thirsting for water. It is rain-fed areas where the poor of India mostly live. During my tenure as a Minister in the Ministry of Agriculture, I constituted a Committee to estimate the expenditure required for watershed development at the national level. The estimate given to me amounted to Rs. 75,800 crore. With this expenditure, we can certainly insulate 80 per cent of Indian agriculture from the vagaries of nature. It would be a measure towards mitigating the effects of drought in the different parts of the country. This public sector expenditure, however, is not forthcoming due to priorities shifting in other directions.

With these words, I express my heartfelt gratitude for being invited to speak on this occasion.

Thank you very much.

# Valedictory Address

*Hon'ble Shri Nitish Kumar*
*Union Minister for Agriculture and Railways*

> . . . the crucial issue today is long-term sustainability of our agriculture. While we must produce more, we should produce it through technologies rooted in the principles of ecology and equity. Increase in production in the future will come not from area expansion, but from enhanced productivity through improved and sustainable agricultural practices. . . .

I am very happy to be with you today to discuss the action plan for making India hunger free by the year 2007. With the guidance of persons of the calibre of Professor Swaminathan, I am confident that this goal is achievable. In the same manner that he took the lead in bringing about a Green Revolution in the country, we need his support and inspiration to make his vision of an 'Ever-Green Revolution' a reality.

*The Food Insecurity Atlas of India*, which was released by the Prime Minister on Tuesday, is an extremely useful document that will enable us to formulate appropriate interventions to making India hunger free. I congratulate the United Nations World Food Programme and the M.S. Swaminathan Research Foundation for this important contribution. The Atlas reveals that every State in the country has its strengths and weaknesses in relation to achieving the goal of sustainable food security. A food security balance sheet of strengths and weaknesses must be developed on similar lines for each State, and even at lower levels, in order to identify priorities for programmes, action, and investments. While India has made significant progress in agricultural development in the past 50 years, it has increasingly become evident that micro-

*Valedictory Address to the National Consultation on 26 April 2001. Due to preoccupation in Parliament, Shri Nitish Kumar's address was not delivered personally.

level planning and targeted programme implementation will be required to sustain and extend the gains, achieved so far.

While at the macro-level the objective of self-sufficiency of foodgrains seems to have been met, there are important concerns of household food security that need to be addressed urgently. Though the food stocks held by the Government are very large, yet almost one third of the Indian population is still below poverty line and has limited access to food. Sustainable food security, however, is not simply a product of purchasing power. It involves physical, economic, social and ecological access to balanced diets, and it is to be viewed not on the basis of each household but each individual. I agree that we cannot wait for per capita income growth to trickle down. We must confront the issue in a targeted and focused manner.

The studies conducted by the M.S. Swaminathan Research Foundation have thrown up several interesting findings that will assist in policy formulation. Moreover, the Action Plan to free India from hunger by the year 2007, is an extremely useful exercise towards ensuring that every individual will lead a productive and healthy life in perpetuity. Based on the slogan 'think, plan and act locally, and support nationally and globally', the Action Plan provides a blueprint for sustainable development, while addressing the needs of individual farming families.

The crucial issue today is long-term sustainability of our agriculture. While we must produce more, we should produce it through technologies rooted in the principles of ecology and equity. Increase in production in the future will come not from area expansion, but from enhanced productivity through improved and sustainable agricultural practices. Innovative packages are needed which harness our traditional skills and strengths to novel cropping systems, precision farming methods and advances in frontier sciences and technologies. While we attempt to derive maximum returns from farmland, an important fact that is increasingly coming to the fore is that nature must be nurtured. Existing systems of pricing and subsidy have, particularly in some parts of the country, resulted in alarming depletion and degradation of the soil through unsuitable cropping patterns and excessive or disproportionate use of water and nutrients. In order to build on the gains of the Green Revolution, it is imperative to review prevailing system and come up with sustainable solutions.

In attempting to bring about a productivity revolution in farming we are fortunate that there is a fairly significant gap between potential and actual yield in most crops. In order to bridge these gaps, special attention should be devoted to conservation and enhancement of land and water resources. Traditional 'Green Revolution' areas are in urgent need of integrated natural resource management so that future prospects are not eroded. Conjunctive use of water will ensure optimum use in an integrated manner of river, rain, ground and other water so that every drop yields maximum return. The ongoing National Watershed Development Programme in Rainfed Areas, implemented by my Ministry, aims at an integrated strategy for optimum utilization of water resources for crop oriented strategies in poorly endowed areas. The programme is based on community participation and 'ownership'. In view of the fact that extensive areas of the country are becoming prone to soil degradation, community based programmes for conservation and enhancement of land and water resources combined with sustainable system of use, need to be developed through micro-studies and micro-planning.

We have many success stories to emulate, but each region and each area must evolve their respective solutions. Recognizing the importance of regionally differentiated strategies, we have formulated a programme, which will be launched shortly for harnessing the ample groundwater resources of the eastern region. This scheme will assist in harnessing the enormous untapped potential of this region, which is expected to result in additional food grains production of about 40 lakh tons per year. You may be aware that similar scheme for boring of shallow tube wells has made Assam surplus in foodgrains last year. The recently introduced Macro Management Scheme too is designed to assist States in identifying and implementing targeted area-specific strategies. In the budget for the current year, we have provided Rs. 850 crore for this programme. Each State has prepared a detailed workplan identifying its strengths and weaknesses and indicating region-specific interventions. Several innovative schemes have been taken up in the Work Plan made to meet local needs and requirements. The concept Eco-Regional Technology Missions can be dove-tailed with the Macro Management Scheme. A Technology Mission for Integrated Development of Horticulture in the North-Eastern region will also be launched soon. This envisages support for all activities relating to Horticulture Development in the region, extending from the development of seed and planting materials, through cropping methods and systems, to post-harvest interventions, processing and marketing.

The realities of the agriculture scenario today underscore the importance of diversification. Horticulture has proved to be an ideal alternative to agriculture. Not only does it improve the productivity of land in terms of biomass production and returns per unit area, but it also provides increased employment opportunities. Similarly, the livestock and fisheries sectors provide excellent livelihood opportunities. Apart from these, new avenues for gainful employment are the production of eco-foods, bio-fertilizers, bio-pesticides, bio-processing, health foods, herbal medicines, etc.

Diversification of agriculture, supported by efficient and low-cost, environment friendly technologies especially for on-farm storage, post-harvest processing and value addition is a pressing need. Diversification to horticultural crops has, in addition, proved to be a good alternative in land use planning. The horticulture sector improves the productivity of land as well as returns per unit area. It also provides higher opportunities for employment and value addition. Of course, this would require concomitant investments in infrastructural components such as cold storage, modern processing, etc., to realize the full potential of diversification. Price policy also needs to be used as a tool for encouraging diversification in agriculture, with emphasis on sustainable growth.

The livestock and fisheries sectors provide another set of avenues for supplementing farmers' incomes and generating gainful employment in the rural sector particularly among landless, small and marginal farmers, and women. India has already become the world's largest milk producing country and is likely to reach the production level of 81 million tons during the current year. India is now the sixth largest producer of fish in the world and second largest producer of freshwater fish after China. The present availability of animal protein in Indian diet needs to be increased at least two-fold from the present level of 10 grams with special emphasis on maintaining the nutritional levels of growing children and nursing mothers. Animal husbandry and fisheries is an area, which is likely to assume increasing importance in the future. Already this sector accounts for 25 per cent of agricultural GDP and its growth far outstrips that of agriculture. The returns from this sector too are extremely rewarding, particularly to small and marginal households. It is expected that a major in-road can be made on rural poverty through strengthening this sector.

It is disturbing that about 10 per cent of food grains, 30-40 per cent of the horticultural produce, and around 10-12 per cent of livestock and fisheries produce of the country get spoiled or damaged for want of adequate post-harvest and processing facilities. We can ill-afford to incur such huge losses. The processing levels of agricultural produce in the country are extremely low, even in comparison with other developing countries. Increasing the processing levels from the present 2 per cent to 10 per cent, and value addition from 7 per cent to 35 per cent in the next ten years is likely to involve an investment of around Rs. 1,40,000 crore. Obviously, the lion's share of this investment will have to come from the private sector. Government, on its part, will provide a facilitative climate. In the current year, it is proposed to extend excise exemption to this sector, besides a package of other incentives.

Agriculture today, is capital-starved. The share of agriculture in Gross Domestic Capital Formation has been steadily declining. As regards its share of GDP too, agriculture accounts for only 25 per cent now, against 35 per cent in 1980-1. Considering the fact that about two-thirds of our population depends on agriculture for their livelihood, it cannot be disputed that investment in agriculture needs to be stepped up on a massive scale. The areas of investment, which have immediate impact on agriculture production and development, are irrigation, technology, infrastructure and education. While the Government is trying to increase its share of investment, the private sector must come forward to invest in agriculture, particularly in infrastructure, technology and education. The profitability of farming and consequently, the viability of the farm sector as a whole, can be substantially increased, if improved technologies can be made available to farmers in respect of farm machinery and equipment, water conservation methods, improved varieties of seeds, post harvest management practices and value addition to primary products through agro-processing and agri-business.

India has considerable strength in agricultural research and education. Our scientific community is one of the strongest in the world. The challenge is to take the fruits of research to the farmer's field. With rapidly changing technologies available in the field of agriculture, transmission of knowledge and skills from lab to land is a particular challenge. Innovative solutions are called for.

Recently, it occurred to me that the services of thousands of agriculture graduates that our universities produce each year could be meaningfully tapped to strengthen our extension system. Accordingly, we are formulating a scheme to assist these persons to set up 'agri-clinics' and 'agri-business' centres, which would provide a package of services to the farmers. The scheme envisages provision of credit to individuals or groups of agriculture graduates, along with a small subsidy component, for setting up units to provide extension and consultancy services to farmers, as well as for setting up soil testing laboratories, seed and fertilizer testing facilities, etc. The scheme will not only make available much needed extension services, but also create gainful employment for agriculture graduates who can operate the single window 'bio-centres' mentioned in your Action Plan.

Marketing is increasingly becoming the critical factor in agricultural development and food management. The fact that the Indian farmer receives, as a proportion of what is paid by consumers, much less than his counterpart in other countries, highlights the inadequacies and inequities of our marketing system. Producers have evolved remarkable innovations in some States in order to promote direct marketing. This is an area that requires increased focus. Moreover, empowerment of producers through provision of market intelligence with the use of information technology should also be an area of high priority. In the new millennium, marketing will assume increasing importance and it is likely to be crucial in improving the lot of the farmer.

Many apprehensions have been voiced about our ability to cope with the WTO regime. The recent removal of all remaining QRs has led people to predict large-scale imports of agricultural products detrimental to our farm sector. However, I wish to assure you that the Government will be vigilant in protecting the Indian farmer and in preventing dumping of surplus agricultural products by developed countries. We have many instruments at our disposal, such as import duties, anti-dumping and countervailing duties, safeguard measures, and sanitary and phyto-sanitary standards, which can be used to protect the interest of domestic producers. During the past year alone, import duties have been revised four times to prevent surge of imports. As announced recently, an effective system will be established to monitor the entry of agricultural and other goods and to orchestrate a Quick Response to any threat to domestic agriculture or industry. While, on the one hand, we will ensure that imports do not affect the interest of Indian farmers, on the other hand we need to capitalize on the opportunities afforded by the WTO for increasing exports from India.

Liberalization of world trade in agriculture has opened up new vistas of growth. India has a competitive advantage in agricultural exports because of near self-sufficiency of inputs, relatively low labour costs and diverse agro-climatic conditions. Export can be the engine for bringing about a major shift in agricultural growth and overall economic development. The recently announced EXIM Policy seeks to give a fillip to agricultural exports with the creation of agri-export zones. India must exploit its comparative advantage in areas such as eco-foods, organic products, herbal and medicinal plants, etc. A major challenge in exploiting our export potential relates to raising the quality of agricultural produce to global standards. Quality consciousness among farmers and agro processors needs to be created and grading and standardization of agricultural produce promoted. Given the competitiveness of world trade, unless we are able to upgrade and maintain consistent quality standards, sanitary and phyto-sanitary measures, ISO and *Codex Alimentarius* standards, our export potential will be severely restricted. Harnessing information technology, E-commerce and quality management will not only yield returns in terms of export earnings, but also provide stimulating and rewarding employment, which will attract and retain youth in farm-related occupations.

I wish to commend the M.S. Swaminathan Research Foundation and the World Food Programme on the comprehensive Action Plan they have developed aimed at making India hunger free. There are several valuable suggestions in the Action Plan, which I will use while formulating programmes in my Ministry, particularly for the Tenth Plan. I look forward to the continued guidance of Professor Swaminathan and others like him in developing public strategies and programmes for attaining our common goals. Once again, I thank you for giving me this opportunity to interact with you and assure you that your Action Plan will receive my most profound consideration. JAI HIND.

# Introduction

*M.D. Asthana*

Hunger is the worst form of deprivation as it comes in the way of fulfilment of the most basic need of every human being. Everyone has a fundamental right to be free from hunger and have access to sufficient, safe and nutritious food and its effective utilization for an active and healthy life. There can be no place for hunger and poverty in a modern world in which science and technology have created conditions for abundance and equitable development. Accordingly, at the 1996 World Food Summit, a commitment was made to achieve food security for all, eradicate hunger in all countries and halve the number of people suffering from hunger and malnutrition by the year 2015. The progress towards the achievement of this goal has been less than adequate and it is realized that the urgency for eradicating hunger and malnutrition would necessitate determined policies and sustained and effective actions. The policy interventions would have to target in particular: (a) the chronically undernourished people (whose calorie intake is below specified minimum energy requirements); (b) underweight children below 5 years (with weights two standard deviation below normal); (c) those who suffer from hidden hunger (unbalanced diets leading to vitamin A, iodine and iron deficiencies); and (d) transitory insecure due to exposure to recurrent disasters. As pointed out by Drèze and Sen (1989), hunger should not be seen in terms of food deprivation alone; non-food factors such as medical attention, health services, basic education, sanitary arrangements, provision of clean water, eradication of infections and epidemics are also equally important.

Over the last fifty years, India has made significant strides in its food grain production with staple food production recording a peak of almost 209 million tons by 2000 and self-sufficiency in food has been achieved to meet the demand of the population which has burgeoned to one billion mark. In the 55th Round of the National Sample Survey (NSS), 92 per cent of rural population and 97 per cent of urban population reported subjectively that they get two square meals a day. It is reported that due to increase in cereal production, per capita calorie intake has risen from 2,200 in the late 1980s to 2,500 at the end of 1990s (Rao and Radhakrishna 1997; Haller 1999). While at the macro-level, the objective of self-sufficiency in food grains has been met, there are important concerns of household food security and intra-household distribution problems. The problem of malnutrition is a cause of concern—over 207 million people were undernourished in 1996–8 with lack of inadequate access to enough food to meet their basic nutritional needs. National Family Health Survey (NFHS-2) of 1998–9 has shown that malnutrition, especially in children is still widely prevalent. India has 20 per cent of the world's children but 40 per cent of its malnourished children (Measham and Chatterjee 1999); 30 per cent children have birth weight less than 2.5 kg and 53 per cent children below 5 years are underweight. About half of the women in the age group of 15–49 years and three-fourth of the children have been found to be anaemic. The economic cost of this problem is estimated at 1.27 per cent of the Gross Domestic Product (GDP) (Ross and Horton 1998). It may be relevant to note that the prevalence of malnutrition is not only on account of lack of access to food but has also to do with the deficiency of safe drinking water, sanitation, environmental hygiene, primary health care and awareness. The problem of hunger, nutrition and food security is thus related to the whole process of development.

The question of hunger needs to be viewed in a framework of food insecurity which covers the following dimensions: (1) availability of food—to meet demands of growing population and changing dietary needs; (2) access to food, which is a function of purchasing power, sustainable livelihoods and employment opportunities and also entitlement to subsidized schemes; (3) absorption and utilization of food, which is a function of access to clean drinking water, environmental hygiene and primary health care and nutrition practices; (4) vulnerability, which covers external factors affecting food security, viz., natural and man made disasters; and (5) sustainability which involves attention to the conservation and enhancement of natural resources like land, water, forests and biodiversity. These dimensions of hunger were discussed by leading food security experts at a consultation on 'Towards Hunger Free

India' convened jointly by the Planning Commission, the World Food Programme, and the M.S. Swaminathan Research Foundation of India (MSSRF) and held at Vigyan Bhavan, New Delhi, on 24–6 April 2001. Besides the papers presented at the consultation, two publications—*The Food Insecurity Atlas of Rural India*, a joint initiative of the MSRRF and WFP and a book titled *Enabling Development: Food Assistance in South Asia* prepared by WFP—formed the backdrop of the discussions.

## FOOD AVAILABILITY

Agriculture plays a pivotal role not only in ensuring the food and ecological security of the country, but also in providing opportunities for jobs and income and subserve the broader goal of poverty eradication. With the advent of Green Revolution, there has been a sizable growth in cereal production, mainly on account of rice and wheat. The per capita availability of cereals has gone up to 173.7 kg per year for the triennium ending 1999 as against 143.9 kg for the triennium ending 1963. Over the same period, the per capita availability has registered a decline in case of coarse cereals (from 42.5 kg to 25.5 kg) and pulses (from 23.2 kg to 13.3 kg) (Thamarajakshi, Paper 1). A disturbing trend in the recent period has been the significant deceleration in the growth rate of agriculture both in terms of gross product and in terms of output. The yield growth rate for all crops taken together has registered a decline from 2.65 per cent per annum during the 1980s to 1.38 per cent during the 1990s—the decline has been steep in the case of rice, wheat and cotton.

Alternative estimates of perspective demand for food grains have been made by several experts and organizations based on different assumptions about base level consumption, expenditure elasticities, and expected growth of income and population, as also the demand for milk and milk products and the derived demand for cereals for feed. In this context, it is relevant to note that the NSS data on consumption expenditure for various rounds reveals that the per capita consumption of cereals per annum has gone down from 173 kg to 154 kg in rural areas and from 134 kg to 124 kg in urban sector. On the other hand there has been an increase in consumption of non-food grain items, viz., vegetables, milk and milk products and meat and eggs and fish. It seems that the food consumption basket is getting diversified in favour of items in as much as expenditure elasticities for cereals are very marginal and even negative. In this context, it is relevant to note that the average per capita net apparent consumption of cereals during 1998–2000 stood at 429 grams per day which is 4 per cent lower than the average for the period 1990–7 (GOI 2001). It is generally observed that cereal consumption has gone down with the increase in incomes and diversification of diets. But a sharp increase in cereal prices in real terms (30 per cent higher relative to all commodity Wholesale Price Index (WPI) in 1999–2000 over the 1990–1 level) appears to have played a major role in restraining cereal demand. The food consumption of the bottom deciles of population, as shown by different surveys, is just 30–40 per cent of the top deciles of the population. It seems that affordability of the poorest segments has been seriously affected by the observed increase in real prices of cereals. There is a wide range of variation in several projections on the total demand for food grains for the year 2020 (from a low of 250 to as high as 375 million tons). The range in these estimates reflects different assumptions about per capita income growth and on how the Indian diet evolves in future (Haller 1999). A broad substitution of cereals with 'superior food' such as animal protein, would lead to a steep increase in the demand for cereals to feed livestock (see Paper 1, Thamarajakshi, and Paper 2, Bhalla). The likelihood of a rapidly growing demand for livestock products and food grains presents an important opportunity to increase incomes and employment and to reduce poverty in rural areas through additional investment in agriculture development. Livestock products are an important source of food particularly of high quality protein, minerals and vitamins and micronutrients and their higher intake in human diet could play an important role in reducing the undernourishment particularly in vulnerable groups. Even though there has been some increase in the consumption of livestock products, the per capita consumption levels in India are much lower than world standards and even those recommended by Indian Council of Medical Research (ICMR). The feed and fodder scarcity has one of the most limiting factors in improving livestock productivity in India. Lack of adoption of improved livestock technologies and prevalence of diseases add to the problem. Removal of these constraints would help in improving the income levels of livestock owners (mainly small farmers) and contribute positively to their food and nutrition security (Paper 5, Kumar and Birthal).

Most of the increase in projected food requirements would have to come from the increase in domestic food production because dependence on large quantities of imports would make India not only vulnerable to year-to-year fluctuations in world prices, but could itself lead to price increases. Besides, large-scale dependence on imports may result in foreign exchange difficulties and also security implications given the current geo-political conditions.

Although there is considerable potential for accelerating agricultural growth, the pace of progress has been slow and serious weaknesses are becoming increasingly evident. The challenge that lies ahead for India includes both raising food output, and ensuring that growth is sustainable, stable and widely shared. There is a fairly significant gap between potential and actual yield in most crops. Regionally differentiated strategies need to be adopted to remove the technological, infrastructural, social and policy constraints responsible for the prevailing yield gaps. In many irrigated areas, productivity can be raised significantly and environmental stress reduced considerably by bridging the large technical efficiency gap through adoption of improved management practices. Scientific land and water management is crucial to raising agricultural production. With a view to increasing and preserving the quality and availability of water, the following may be undertaken: (a) develop appropriate policies and plans for water and watersheds and water management techniques; (b) promote economically, socially and environmentally sound irrigation improvements (small scale irrigation). The World Bank estimates that even a 10 per cent increase in efficiency of existing irrigation facilities could add 7–8 million hectares of irrigated land in India without utilizing additional water resources. Public investment in irrigation, rainwater harvesting and watershed management coupled with greater participation and involvement of people in managing these common resources should be accorded high priority. Panchayats/local bodies which have been given constitutional responsibility for management of land, water and Common Property Resources (CPR) must be enabled to discharge the assigned functions effectively and in an environmentally and socially sustainable manner. Water rights should be delinked from land rights through appropriate legislations and institutional arrangements so that small and marginal farmers could benefit from public investment in watershed development and get equitable share in common resource and are able to achieve sustainable food security (Paper 4, Reddy). Technologies for elevating and stabilizing yields are available for semi-arid and dry farming areas, as a result of the work done by the Indian Council of Agricultural Research (ICAR) and International Crop Research Institute for Semi Arid Tropics (ICRISAT), etc. There is a close linkage between livestock and livelihoods in these areas and they are ideal for cultivation of low water requiring but high value pulses and oilseeds. Also, agricultural intensification in dry areas can reduce pressure on degraded lands and forests and contribute to improved soil fertility. Developing and adopting technologies to meet complex, location specific environments in unfavourable areas will require greater participation of intended users. The resource base for agriculture is under stress and is threatened by problems such as desertification, deforestation, losses of biodiversity as well as inefficient use of water, climate change and depletion of ozone layer. Latest estimates of 1993 made by the Ministry of Agriculture show that extent of degraded land in the country was more than 173 million hectares. To prevent the debilitating effect of degradation on food output growth, precise nature of soil degradation should be identified and scientific restoration measures must be developed. An urgent action is needed to combat pests, drought and natural resource degradation and erosion of biodiversity. Diversification of agriculture, supported by efficient, low-cost, environment friendly technologies especially for on-farm, post-harvest processing and value addition will provide more jobs and income in rural areas. Without enhanced efficiency in the production and post-harvest phases of agriculture, Indian farmers will not be able to face the challenge of globalization in terms of cost-effectiveness, quality of produce and consistency of supply. Small and marginal farmers would need access to best practice in precision farming, affordable credit, crop insurance, farm inputs and modern farm equipment in order to increase productivity. Support facilities like demand projections for crop planting, soil testing and weather forecasting to guide them in their planting, inputs and harvesting would also be necessary. Mid Term Review of the Ninth Five Year Plan states that 'the extension system has not only become outmoded but totally ineffective'. It 'should be replaced with a more modern and vibrant system' to create a credible structure for dissemination of all relevant knowledge and system. Biotechnology holds promise for significantly increasing productivity in long term but short term gains will most likely caused by reducing susceptibility to pest and disease losses. Care should be taken to see that new technologies like biotechnology do not by-pass poor regions and farmers. As in the past, public investment in the rural infrastructure, agricultural research and extension and education and health of rural people will have to play a key role in the agricultural growth. The marginal returns to several infrastructure investments are higher in many rainfed areas. There is also scope for reducing the cost of providing public grants in rural areas by involving (a) the local bodies and panchayats to take better advantage of alternative and lower cost sources of supply of public goods, and (b) improving the efficiency of public supply institutions through improved management, more transparent procurement and operational procedures and greater accountability to end users.

## DISASTER MITIGATION

Food shocks could be caused by unusual seasonal shortages, natural disasters or economic disruptions. Natural disasters are a major factor affecting food security. In disaster affected areas, food insecurity is often present in all dimensions: food stocks or harvests are destroyed, households lose their assets and employment opportunities, nutrition and health problems are rampant. It is estimated that over 39 million people in India are affected every year by recurrent natural disasters such as floods, cyclones and droughts. The severity of natural disasters and their devastating effects are steadily increasing, interdependent with environmental degradation. Natural resource management is thus an important component of disaster mitigation programmes that must be coordinated across national borders. There is a need to establish a vulnerability information and mapping system analysing the major causes of vulnerability and identifying disaster prone areas and groups of people that are at greatest risk of becoming food insecure in the event of a disaster. This would help in devising appropriate policies to prevent the most serious effects of recurrent natural disasters and undertake swift humanitarian response and recovery operations once the disaster has struck. The active involvement of communities, local authorities and institutions and grass root relief initiatives and structures should be solicited in implementing emergency operations and better identification of population and areas in greatest risk. Targeting must focus on those who cannot cope with recurrent disasters, not just those who live in disaster prone areas. As women's roles as caregivers expands dramatically during and after a disaster, they should be fully involved in assessment of needs and in management and evaluation of relief operations. Response must be timely and effective to meet transitory and emergency food requirements in ways that encourage recovery, rehabilitation, development and a capacity to satisfy future needs. Special care is needed for those who cannot produce or procure enough food for an adequate diet especially when affected by natural disaster or climate related ecological change. Well articulated contingency plans coupled with early warning systems based on application of climate forecast information for surveillance and earth warming, drought, flood, other natural disasters, pest and disease alertness, help protect the affected to the extent possible while preventive measures involve the construction or restoration of rural infrastructure that directly protects against natural disasters, soil and water conservation measures, and erosion or desertification control. Food for work programmes should support preventive measures such as water harvesting in drought prone areas and strengthening river embankments in flood prone areas. From the perspective of enabling development, short term hand outs for several weeks following a disaster do little to address the underlying cause of vulnerability. It should be ensured that relief and recovery operations do not undermine a household or communities' existing coping strategies to ease these short term shocks. Local capacities and existing coping mechanisms have to be strengthened by involving communities in defining priorities and directing initiatives.

Food for work programmes have a significant potential to mitigate disasters. Ongoing food assistance programmes should be designed in such a way that they can be easily expanded and used as a channel for reaching disaster victims. Pre-designed 'off the shelf' projects need to be available for implementation at the first signs of trouble. Trained staff have to be close at hand in order to respond quickly. Village level storage facilities and local grain banks in vulnerable areas help families during period of shortfall and reduce logistics problems associated with disaster relief. At the onset of a disaster, the scaling up of ongoing food for work programmes as a kind of safety net to protect against shortfalls has proven to be an effective means of intervening before destitution sets in (WFP 2001). Moreover, supplementary feeding and school feeding programmes can help stabilize food consumption among the most vulnerable population groups through a temporary increase in the ration size or outreach.

Linking food relief to the creation of appropriate infrastructure to limit future damage and consequent development in disaster prone areas, provision of food safety nets, improving the warning system for drought and improving delivery systems through Public Distribution System (PDS), etc., to backward areas and vulnerable population groups could be effective disaster mitigation strategies. There is a need to provide policy support to replicate the water harvesting mechanism on the line of Maharashtra Pani Panchayats which has helped improve coping mechanism among vulnerable population groups through equitable sharing of rain water harvested by community participation (Paper 6, Sharma). Regeneration and efficient use of natural resources like land, water and forests is crucial to improving the sustained availability of water and fodder which is very crucial for drought affected people, especially resource poor households. There is a need for re-orienting the project planning and implementation of watershed development programmes and also integrate them with overall macro level policies to ensure ecological balance. Careful planning would ensure natural resource development including common property resources, their sharing among households and creating a requisite buffer at the community level. There is a need to explore wider options (sometimes outside the micro-settings of watershed projects) such as linkage of micro/village level efforts with water resources at various levels, devising pricing and subsidy structure to promote more efficient water use, improvement by enhancing access/availability of fodder through comprehensive land use planning which facilitate both physical access to pastures and other CPRs and at the same time ensure resources for investment in various activities essential for development; developing markets for inputs and outputs through road and transport network, promotion of agro-processing and strengthening of social infrastructure for health and education; and creating a buffer stock of food grains and fodder by involving the development agencies and institutions to meet the drought disasters (Paper 7, Shah). Since disasters are frequent and devastating, they should not be treated as random events and policies and systems should be evolved to tackle them in a systematic way so as to ensure food and nutrition security to affected people. A sound management of environment through a long-term strategy and undertaking a variety of steps like constructing cyclone resistant or earthquake resistant buildings could reduce devastation. The experience of recent earthquake and drought in Gujarat shows clearly that decentralized structures involving communities and local people have been more successful than centralized interventions in mitigating the disasters (Paper 8, Hirway).

## SUSTAINABLE LIVELIHOODS

A sustainable livelihood can be defined as the one that can cope with and recover from stresses and shocks and maintain or enhance its capabilities and assets both now and in the future, while not undermining the natural resource base (Chambers and Conway 1992). Subsistence farm families depend on natural resources (often in the commons around them—forests, grazing lands, road sides, rivers and ponds) for their very survival as this is one of the few productive assets they have access to. The tragedy of the commons is that these resources tend to be over exploited and it is the poorest families that can least afford to worry about long term sustainability at the expense of a meal today. The depletion and/or excessive deterioration of natural resource base leads to change in livelihood patterns including cultivation on fragile lands accompanied by impoverishment and increasing inequities. A sustained effort would be required to rejuvenate/regenerate common property resources in an environmentally and socially sustainable manner for which panchayats should take a lead. As the regeneration of CPRs capable of meeting sustainable livelihood needs is likely to be a time consuming process, the households which depend on degraded natural resources for their food security would need to be enabled to make a shift to more sustainable livelihoods. Environmental rehabilitation and social forestry has special relevance to rural women who face severe difficulties in accessing fuelwood in degraded CPRs.

Support under the existing food assistance programmes can be provided to offset any short term losses to enable people to take the risk to improve their farming systems and increase sustainable yields from their natural resource base. While designing food interventions, the following principles may be kept in view: (a) programmes should build on the traditional knowledge, particularly of indigenous communities about natural resources; (b) food assistance should support more efficient and sustainable livestock production systems through improving grazing techniques, fodder crops and the use of multiple sources of animal feed; (c) community forest management can be the key to sustainable production and use of forest products such as food, fodder and fuel; and (d) food intervention should be accompanied by appropriate knowledge/technology transfer that is especially targeted at women, such as training in new farming methods or food processing technologies, natural resource management, etc. (WFP 2001).

Sustainable livelihood approach based on community's strength and assets, human capital (as also accretions), social, physical and financial capital (micro credit) and above all the institutions which bring together one or all the above is critical to reducing the target groups' vulnerability to food insecurity in both rural and urban areas and in combating poverty. The policies promoting a variety of livelihood options within the broad parameters of limited resource base would be more effective in meeting food security needs of such people/groups (Paper 10, Ramachandran). Over time there has been an increasing trend of casualization among female workers. This has implications for the relationship between female work, its sustainability and intra-household food distribution through women's income and any policy measure for hunger free India (Paper 11, Raju).

Kundu (Paper 9) argues that food security and nutrition must be viewed within the frame work of a development strategy to generate employment and income. The analysis of nutrient intake across states reveals that much more than affordability, the intake of nutrients are determined by food habits and cropping patterns in the region. The development process in post reform period has not brought forth many jobs either of regular or of self-employment variety. Casualization of work force and unemployment seem to result in low nutritional intake which may reflect low affordability of households. The penetration of market forces as a result of economic reforms has rendered many of the household activities non-viable, particularly those engaging female workers. The State has to play a positive role by helping small and marginal farmers as also those setting up small-scale units in their survival strategy through a support system. The infrastructural investment in public sector needs stepping up to sustain agricultural growth and alleviate poverty on a sustainable basis in rural areas.

Jhabua district in Madhya Pradesh is pioneer in undertaking several innovative schemes to improve opportunities to sustainable development and livelihoods. The watershed development mission in the district has been successful in effective, efficient and site-specific soil and water conservation and regeneration of degraded forests. There is an active involvement of the people's representatives and community organization in preparation of action plans. The community assisted water harvesting tanks have been constructed and several food for work programmes have been undertaken with assistance from Government of India and WFP to combat drought conditions. These programmes have further been linked with state-run *Pani Roko Abhiyan* under which water harvesting works are taken up to combat existing drought conditions and also to increase water holding capacity of the district to minimize similar natural crises in the future. Peoples' participation in the scheme is in the form of labour and micro tanks, stop dam, desiltation of tanks, dug wells and tube wells deepening/recharge, field bunding. WFP assisted intensive intervention project intends to ameliorate conditions of vulnerable groups by taking up several activities (Akhtar, Paper 25).

## ACCESS TO FOOD

As already stated, access to food is a function of purchasing power, sustainable livelihoods and employment opportunities and also entitlement to subsidized schemes. Lack of cash to purchase food often coincides with limited food availability in the market at certain times of the year, causing great hardship to families and undernourishment. The 1997 NSS data show that 42 per cent of our rural population and 49 per cent of urban population receive less than the accepted daily calorie intake norm—and these proportions have virtually remained the same in the last decade. Cereals contribute over 80 per cent of the calories of people in the lowest income segment, decreasing to about 50 per cent as we move up the income curve. Of late, food consumption basket is getting diversified in favour of non-food grain items, viz., vegetables, milk and milk products and meat, egg and fish. The consumption of these items is however very small compared to ICMR norms and income increases could make people consume more of these items resulting in improved overall nutrition. Sustainable progress in poverty eradication is critical to improve access to food. There is a need to adopt policies to create conditions encouraging stable employment especially in rural areas including off-farm jobs so as to provide sufficient earnings and improved access to food. The augmentation of production in poorer and backward areas, such as eastern and central India would help poor in these regions either to produce themselves or have enough purchasing power to buy subsidized food grains. Revitalization of rural areas is possible on the twin planks of productivity improvement in agriculture and the creation of thriving food processing, livestock and fisheries sectors. This would not only help arrest rural-urban migration but also achieve food security for all. The funds available under the Rural Infrastructure Development Fund (RIDF) should be effectively used for the purpose. Apart from these, new avenues for gainful employment are the production of eco-foods, bio-fertilizers, bio-pesticides, bio-processing, health foods, herbal medicines, etc.

With a network of around 4,51,000 Fair Price Shops (FPS) distributing commodities worth over Rs. 150 billion to around 180 million households, the Public Distribution System (PDS) in India is perhaps the largest distribution network of its type in the world and represents an important policy response to the problem of food access arising on account of poverty. However, the system has not been able to translate macro level self-sufficiency into a micro level availability of food grains for the poor households due to several implementation problems such as excessively high cost of delivery; inability to reach the poor effectively; marginal income transfer to poor households; urban bias; negligible coverage in the states with the highest concentration of rural poor; and lack of flexible, transparent and accountable arrangements for delivery. An attempt has been made to reorient the PDS into a Targeted Public Distribution System (TPDS) so as to improve the cost effectiveness in reaching the poor and better targeting the mounting food subsidy to the really needy.

Under the new TPDS in operation since June 1997, differential pricing is being followed for the Above Poverty Line (APL) and Below Poverty Line (BPL) populations. During the initial period of the scheme, the prices paid by the BPL population were either reduced or kept unchanged limiting the increases only to APL category. The adoption of economic cost linked prices with effect from April 2000 (APL supplies at economic cost of the Food Corporation of India and BPL supplies at half the economic cost) resulted in sharp price increases for both APL and BPL populations. However, in overall terms, as compared to the situation immediately preceding the introduction of TPDS, the Central Issue Prices (CIPs) in real terms (relative to all-commodity WPI) in December 2000 were 11 to 13 per cent lower for BPL population while they were higher to the extent of 73.6 per cent for wheat and 44.2 per cent for rice in respect of APL population. The steep increase in issue prices consequent to introduction of TPDS has led to a sharp reduction in APL offtake from PDS between 1998–9 and 2000–1, from 7.4 million tons to 1.8 million tons in case of rice and from 5.3 million tons to only 0.3 million tons in case of wheat. More significantly, the offtake by BPL population has also fallen short of allocation mainly due to inadequacies in the operation of TPDS. It is estimated that the total consumer subsidy for the BPL population in 2000–1 is much less than budgeted and unlikely to exceed Rs. 5,000 crore. Despite this, the total food subsidy for the year is projected to go up to Rs. 13,000 crore against the budgeted Rs. 8,210 crore mainly on account of the higher outgo on carrying cost of excessively large Central Pool stocks and fiscal burden arising out of attempts to dispose off accumulated excess stocks at below cost prices through open market sales and exports.

The large accretions to the Central Pool stocks is the result of combined effect of high levels of Minimum Support Prices (MSP)—relative to all-commodity WPI in 2000–1, the MSP was higher by 24.9 per cent and 9.5 per cent for wheat and paddy respectively from 1996–7 level—and CIP leading to sharp increase in procurement and reduced offtake from PDS. This has also resulted in much higher increase in market prices due to withdrawal of large quantities of grains from market affecting adversely the food security of the poor who still have to buy most of their grain requirements from the market. The present levels of the MSP are too high and need to be rationalized not only to send proper signals to farmers on cropping pattern and prevent inefficient use of scarce resources like water leading to soil degradation but also to enable public procurement agencies to defend the MSP successfully, given shortage of storage space and the likely absence of private trade. Due care has to be taken to ensure that prices received by farmers do not become unremunerative and MSP operations are effective, particularly in states such as Assam, Bihar, Orissa and Uttar Pradesh, where farmers have reported to have been receiving prices below MSP. The problem is particularly acute for small and marginal farmers who have low marketable surplus and inadequate infrastructure and are forced to sell their produce to traders at much lower prices (Reddy, Paper 4).

The government has announced measures on 12 July 2001 to revive the offtake from PDS and reduce excess stocks in the Central Pool. These include: increase in BPL quota from 20 kg to 25 kg per month per household and supplies at 48 per cent of economic cost against 50 per cent earlier and supplies to APL population at discounted rate of 70 per cent of economic cost rather than at economic cost. These measures are not expected to have any negative fiscal impact since the current cost of holding stocks exceeds the proposed increase in consumer subsidy. The reintroduction of subsidy to APL category (to the extent of 30 per cent of economic cost) is also being justified as necessary cost to revive the viability of FPS and avoid negative impact on BPL food distribution. Diversion of PDS allocations in unauthorized channels is one malaise which defies solution. According to a study by Tata Economic Consultancy Services, it was found that at the national level, there was a diversion of 36 per cent of wheat supplies, 31 per cent of rice and 23 per cent sugar. The diversion is more in northern, eastern and north-eastern regions; it is comparatively less in southern and western regions (Planning Commission 2000). Based on her study of PDS in Bihar, Jos Mooij (2000) concludes that a large group of beneficiaries including PDS dealers, officials involved in inspection and monitoring, local politicians who can appoint people in vigilance committees and others participate or benefit from the diversion of the food grains and the whole 'malfunctioning system' functions actually very well when one looks at it from the perspective of these vested interests. There is no doubt the need to take measures to improve the economic viability of FPS, for instance by linking commission to the quantity of wheat and rice distributed rather than on basis of price (so that dealer is not disadvantaged on account of lower prices for BPL population), encouraging FPS owners to have their own business in addition to the distribution of commodities under PDS, organizing weekly distribution of PDS to reduce tied up capital, etc. But the real improvement in TPDS could only come through adoption of following measures on a priority basis: (i) effective involvement of Panchayati Raj Institutions (PRIs) in identification of beneficiaries and in implementation through formation of vigilance committees at PDS level; (ii) making available essential information relating to entitlement of BPL families, fair average quality of food grains, procedure of issue of ration cards, inspection and checking, etc., to enable satisfactory access to benefits; (iii) improvement in the infrastructure to handle food grains including construction of sufficient number of good quality godowns/depots at nearby places and the financial position of State Food and Civil Supplies Corporations; (iv) distributing coarse cereals which have high nutrition value; (v) integrate PDS with ongoing poverty alleviation programmes relating to self employment, wage employment or area development; and (vi) organizing and educating beneficiaries and other stakeholders to ensure that supplies reach FPS in proper quantity and quality and are sold to genuine buyers. Citizen's charter incorporating consumer friendly suggestions and adequate checks and balances regarding every aspect of functioning of PDS needs to be strictly ensured. Vested interests have seen to it that the charter is only partially implemented or not implemented at all.

Several useful insights have been provided in the papers included in this publication on improving the efficacy of PDS to make it an effective safety net for the poor. The diverse experience among states as regards the coverage and functioning of PDS can be explained in the context of structures of state and society resulting in different levels of political support and commitment to the system. The policy solution to improve the performance has to take into account these local conditions (Mooij, Paper 22). Only 33 per cent of the rural households in India reported the use of PDS on a regular basis (Shariff 1999) but with the introduction of highly subsidized prices for the poor, the focus has shifted to rural population. In his study on rural Uttar Pradesh, Srivastava (Paper 23) finds that poorer groups depend more on market purchases to meet their cereal requirements and there is a seasonal pattern in such purchases (the proportion of poorest households purchasing rice and wheat in lean season goes up to 61 per cent and 68 per cent respectively as against only 16 per cent and 9 per cent in post-harvest period). This calls for a new orientation in distribution which should take into account the enhanced requirements of poor in rural areas during the lean season instead of the existing pattern of monthly rationing suitable for the cities. In the case of chronically drought prone districts in Rajasthan, the ability of household to meet their food grain consumption requirements goes down sharply in a drought year and during these periods PDS and Food for Work Programmes can play a crucial role in ensuring food security (Bhargava, Paper 24). Rao (Paper 3) suggests that the criteria for identifying the poor should be such that only genuine poor are included. To check leakages under TPDS, the system should be based on local grains normally consumed by poorer sections and those figuring low in preference scale of non poor. PDS system based on local grains would also serve to provide incentives for their production. Broad based agricultural growth would generate local supplies of food grains on which the PDS could draw. In view of the possible difficulties in complete switch-over to coarse grains (coarse grains are grown by small farmers for subsistence and hence difficult to collect in sufficient quantities; production is totally from rain fed areas and may collapse in a drought year; prices of coarse grains may be higher than wheat and rice; and short shelf life of coarse cereals would not permit centralized procurement, stocking and distribution), it may be necessary to organize grain banks at the village itself preferably through the PRIs, making use of local facilities for stocking and distribution (Meenakshisundaram, Paper 21). Without adequate purchasing power and timely credit, the poor are not in a position to acquire food grains even when they have access to PDS. It is therefore imperative that PDS is integrated with other anti poverty programmes particularly those offering employment and micro credit.

The reintroduction of APL subsidy to improve the PDS offtake may have been necessitated due to peculiar situation of excessive stocks but goes against the basic rationale of TPDS to effect savings by removing non-poor from PDS and target the food subsidy entirely to BPL population. It would be a much better idea to utilize the existing excess food stocks to step up employment schemes, both as relief measures in drought affected regions and to step up rural infrastructure in less developed regions which would improve incomes on a sustainable basis over medium and long term. It is heartening to note that the Government of India has decided to provide flexibility for undertaking Food for Work (FFW) programme by (a) including Food for Work Component in all labour-intensive schemes with first priority to drought-proofing including water conservation/harvesting measures; (b) implementing flexible norms for wages and material component and allowing APL families eligible for employment under the FFW; and (c) undertaking FFW in the event of other natural disasters besides drought.

## FOOD NUTRITION, ABSORPTION AND UTILIZATION

There are three principal components of food utilization—nutrition practices, physiological absorption and intra household distribution. Availability of micronutrients and incidence of poverty also influence the nutritional status of the people. Nutritional practices cover dietary pattern, childcare and nutrition knowledge and are strongly influenced by culture and tradition. There are strong links between education, childcare practices and nutrition. Literary skills are required to access information about improved food preparations or child practices. High level of literacy especially among women is a major factor explaining the success of nutrition improvement experiments (UNICEF 1999).

Today it is accepted that if special nutritional needs of women and children are not met, then physical and psychological disabilities of individuals become a drag on the development potential of the entire household for multiple generations (Sub-Committee on Nutrition 2000). It is therefore a matter of concern that in India, there are gender differentials in access to food (especially micronutrients) nutrition, health care and primary education. Maternal Mortality Rate (MMR)—an indicator of gender bias, is very high at 420 per 1,00,000 live births in India and one-fifth (2,00,000) of maternal deaths in world occur in India alone.

Achievement of nutrition security (with a focus on pregnant and lactating women, infants below 6 months age, children under 5 years of age and school children) is one of the important objectives of India's five year plan and is even enshrined in the Indian Constitution. Reduction of malnutrition among infants and young children and the reduction of micronutrient deficiencies (iron, iodine, etc.) among poor sections of the society is achieved by supplementary food at the village level *anganwadi* centres, by enhancing micronutrient fortification of stable food items, by expanding coverage of health and nutrition education and by promoting kitchen gardening to help improve availability of green leafy vegetables.

The issues in regard to nutrition, utilization and absorption necessitate focussed action to: (a) promote access to clean water and sanitation for all people especially in poor communities and rural areas; (b) school feeding programmes with particular attention to children in rural areas and to girls; (c) nutrition, sanitation and health education for public and promote technologies and training programmes on nutrition, home economics, environment protection, food supply and health; (d) community based food security and nutrition programmes that encourage self reliance, utilizing participatory planning and implementation processes; and (e) prevention and control of specific micro nutrient deficiencies (vitamin A, iron, iodine); (f ) to enable young children and expectant and nursing mothers to meet their special nutritional and nutrition related health needs.

Low birth weight not only perpetuates inter generational malnutrition, it also establishes the conditions for chronic disease in later adulthood such as diabetes and heart disease at the same time. Micro nutrient deficiencies are another result of poor food utilization and are mostly attributable to an inadequate intake and absorption of essential vitamins and minerals that are required for normal growth and development. Legislative ban on non-iodized salt which was recently rescinded in India, was widely criticized by eminent nutritionists in the country.

Food acts as an incentive that brings women to health centres. But going to the health centres by itself will not improve the nutritional status of women and their families. Nutritional education is also needed, along with supplementary feeding for those at critical points in their lifecycle such as pregnant or nursing mothers or infants and young children. Lessons learnt from best practices in supplementary feeding programmes include the following: (a) interventions targeted to expectant and nursing mothers and to children, should utilize food that is fortified with micro nutrients; (b) greater use of blended foods in supplementary feeding programmes can improve the targeting outcome: while these foods are ideal for the intended beneficiaries, they are unfamiliar to, and less appreciated by others; (c) local capacity to produce blended food should be strengthened wherever this is feasible, and possibilities of social marketing must be explored; (d) community based centres (such as *anganwadi* centres) can be an effective alternative channel to health clinics for the provision of mother and child health and nutrition care; (e) home visits by field workers can strengthen outreach and effectiveness of supplementary feeding programmes; and (f) supplementary feeding targeted to pregnant women and mothers should always be combined with nutrition and health education.

School feeding programmes represent an effective tool for increasing enrolment of children from food insecure families in schools, as well as for ensuring that short term hunger does not inhibit the capacity to learn. The following principles have proven to help strengthen the effectiveness of food assistance in support of training and education: (a) school feeding programmes work best in geographic areas with food insecurity and low overall rates of elementary school enrolment; (b) girls' access to schooling will be strengthened if the feeding component is complemented by the creations of supportive conditions such as availability of girls' hostels and appropriate latrines; (c) food as an incentive for school attendance may not be needed year round as fluctuations in attendance are often related to agricultural seasons; (d) opportunities should be sought to integrate de-worming treatment in school feeding programmes; and (e) the provisions of take home food incentive rations tied to enrolment and regular attendance of girls can dramatically improve the gender balance in schools.

Food assisted training programmes should be designed in light of the various demands on women's time, so that women can participate without being overburdened. Right timing is also important in supplementary feeding programmes, since there are particular periods when pregnant women and small children need special nutritional attention.

Gopalan (Paper 13) discusses different aspects of nutrition situation as it prevails in the country and covers topics such as changing nutrition scene in the country, major health problems afflicting children, adolescent girls and women, need for nutritional orientation of food production programmes and supplementation with synthetic nutrients and harnessing emerging biotechnology. Besides, the paper also goes into issues like intra familial distribution and mobilizing the community. It is suggested that production should be diversified in terms of fruits, vegetables, etc., for ensuring a balanced diet.

Shiva Kumar (Paper 14) argues that it is not the food availability but the adequate knowledge about proper feeding practices and quality of care and attention when being fed that are critical to preventing malnutrition during early infancy and improving food security. As there is a close linkage between child malnutrition and maternal malnutrition and both are strongly dependent upon the level of schooling attained by women, the universalization of education should be achieved on top priority basis. The schemes like Mid-Day Meal (MDM) if properly managed and administrated could ensure high retention and reduce malnutrition and to a large extent contribute to the food and economic security of poor households.

Chatterjee (Paper 15) provides an excellent review of working of Integrated Child Development Services (ICDS) in India. ICDS attempts to provide expectant and lactating mothers and young children health care, nutrition support, health and nutrition education and early childhood education in an integrated manner. The paper notes that despite soundness, scope and high expenditure level the scheme has had insufficient impact on the problem of child malnutrition in the country. The main problems affecting ICDS that have bearing on its effectiveness in reducing malnutrition are: (a) lack of attention to very young child (0–2 years old) particularly in their proper feeding at home; (b) inadequacy of services to pregnant/lactating women; (c) insufficiency of food supplementation; (d) poor training of *anganwadi* and health workers particularly in nutrition; and (e) inadequate community involvement. To improve the impact, the author argues that instead of expanding the scheme to uncovered areas, it is better to improve the quality of services and implement these schemes in a more decentralized manner with community participation. There is also a need to enhance the access of the poor to the ICDS.

Meir (Paper 16) reviews the school feeding programmes in India—both the feeding of children at school and distribution of dry food rations to school children. The objectives of the MDM scheme are: (i) to enhance the nutritional status of children (alleviate short term hunger in malnourished or otherwise well nourished and overcome lack of specific micronutrients in school children); and (ii) to promote universal elementary education by encouraging poorer parents to admit and retain their children in school. The implementation of scheme is faced with several problems. The author suggests improvement in scheme along following lines: (a) adjust the design of school feeding to fulfil nutritional objectives; (b) target the scheme to families that lack resources to adequately provide for their school age children; (c) involve communities/parents in operation of the scheme; (d) improve food logistics and management and monitoring and evaluation. In addition school feeding should be combined with other school health interventions notably treatment for intestinal parasites (de-worming), improvement of sanitary conditions at school or health and nutrition education. The successful experiments in states like Tamil Nadu, Kerala, Gujarat and WFP experiences all over developing world could be studied to derive lessons for the improvement of the scheme.

Proper care practices are critical to the optimal growth and development of children and their ability to profit from schooling and also their nutritional status. The most feasible intervention is to support positive existing practices related to care, or to change them to be appropriate and relevant. Attention must also be given to improving the resources for care, such as setting up community childcare facility, improving community response to needs for child referral or strengthening women's capacity to make decisions affecting community decisions. A successful approach to improving care for development requires cooperation among different sectors, strong community involvement and participation and investment in resources for care (Paper 17, Engle and Dustagheer).

## GLOBALIZATION AND FOOD INSECURITY

As a result of multinational production networks, mobility of capital, freer trade and new technologies, labour has become more susceptible to global economic forces than ever. Competition for foreign investment and the greater ability of employers to shift production to other locations has weakened labours' bargaining ability. It has also resulted in rising internal inequality due to unequal distribution of the skills and infrastructure needed to participate in the economy, the high demand for skilled labour, and substantial profit income. Many of the new job opportunities have been low paying and characterized by poor social protection.

Considerations of flexibility and competitions have also resulted in greater resort to subcontracting, outsourcing and informalization of work. But it also shifts many of the costs of the market volatility to workers, making them more vulnerable to recessions and threatening their job and income security. Suitable policy measures including safety nets will be necessary to help these vulnerable groups to cope with insecurity. Our economic and trade policies should focus on securing livelihood of millions engaged in small-scale production. At the same time, every effort should be made to confer the power of efficiency and scale on small producers through sustainable institutional structures.

India has a competitive advantage in agricultural exports because of near self-sufficiency of inputs, relatively low labour costs and diverse agro-climatic conditions. This potential can be exploited by establishing well functioning internal marketing and transportation systems to facilitate better links within and between, domestic, regional and world markets and diversifying trade. The Uruguay Round Agreement on Agriculture (AOA) was expected to improve market opportunities for efficient agricultural producers and food processors in developing countries. But these gains have not materialized. Excessively high tariff peaks continue to apply to products that constitute exports or offer a potential for export diversification in developing countries. In addition to tariff and non-tariff barriers that hinder access to markets of developed countries, agricultural subsidies by developed countries, whether in the form of direct export subsidies, processing subsidies or direct payments to farmers, also deter entry into markets. The reform process envisaged in Article 20 of AOA should ensure that developing countries are well-informed and equal partners in the process of evolving effective solutions to improve their access to markets. It should also be ensured that environmental (and labour standards) measures do not unfairly affect market access for developing countries' food and agricultural exports.

There are genuine concerns on quality and safety of food supplies in international markets. Given the competitiveness of world trade, unless we are able to upgrade and maintain consistent quality standards, sanitary and phyto-sanitary measures, International Standards Organization (ISO) and *Codex Alimentarius* standards, our export potential will be severely restricted. This calls for strengthening of normative and controlled activities in areas of human, animal and plant health and safety (important for exports as well as imports) and effective enforcement of food legislation which is currently hampered by a number of constraints such as lack of capacity for monitoring, assessing and controlling food quality, lack of accurate data, the incidence of food borne diseases, inadequate facilities to identify chemicals and pesticides in food and insufficient involvement and coordination of concerned ministries and public institutions handling food safety issues. It is necessary to put in place measures for effective prevention and progressive control of plant and animal pest and diseases, including especially those which are of transboundary nature, such as rinderpest, foot and mouth disease and desert locust, where outbreaks can cause major food shortages and trigger trade measure.

From April 2001, the quantitative restrictions on imports have been removed. The government has taken recourse to WTO-compliant measures such as import duties, anti-dumping and countervailing duties, safeguard measures, and sanitary and phyto-sanitary standards to prevent surge of imports that may threaten domestic agriculture.

Dasgupta (Paper 18) argues convincingly that food security by way of trade is not a feasible alternative and that such a shift is unwarranted and motivated. The global trade is not so integrated that one can take as much of what one needs from the world market; very few countries of the world having a surplus in food production and such a supply is not available without costs. The competitiveness of agricultural exports by developed countries is not on account of their competitive advantage but due to colossal subsidies given by them to their agricultural producers. Such a situation is likely to continue in future also because developed countries have been able to get provisions in World Trade Organization (WTO) favourable to them.

Narasimha Reddy (Paper 19) discusses the implications of WTO provisions and their implementation on food security in the context of small farmer economies like India. Given that the agriculture is not a commercial venture for small-marginal farmer, agriculture in developing countries cannot bear the onslaught of free imports from developed countries and needs protection to avoid destitution. Due to very limited capability of developing countries to invent, the intellectual property rights regime would make such countries dependent on Multi-National Corporations (MNC) who have proprietary rights over seeds derived from biotechnology.

This may undermine the competitiveness and the very survival of small farmer economy. The author suggests a strategy for review of AOA to incorporate the concerns of developing countries by giving a special dispensation to these countries to undertake policy and support measures in consonance with their food security concerns.

There are concerns that several existing WTO agreements put limits on the range of policy options available to pursue the domestic policy goals including food security concerns. As a part of the built-in-agenda on agriculture and discussions in several WTO committees, the issues relevant to food security are being deliberated upon. The paper by Mehta (Paper 20) provides an assessment of the effects of these developments and offers suggestions on the strategies that may be pursued by India to get a favourable outcome in future negotiations so that appropriate WTO-compliant policies could be put in place to eradicate hunger and malnutrition and achieve food security for all as early as possible.

## HUNGER FREE INDIA: AGENDA AND IMPERATIVES

The national agenda for governance of the present government promises to ensure food security for all and create a hunger free India. This vision can be achieved at the earliest with the right kind of development strategies that offer opportunities and options to all to develop their potential to the maximum. For this to happen, the government has to play a facilitating role by creating an enabling environment for private and group initiative (with the cooperation and participation of all members of society) to devote their skills, efforts and resources and in particular investments towards the common goal of food for all through effective participation of all people in decisions and actions that affect their food security. It is imperative that rapid growth in food grain production is accompanied by comprehensive plans and programmes to address the key concerns of poverty eradication and improvement in household income, particularly of the poor households which are more prone to hunger and malnutrition. It has also to be ensured that increased production comes from pathways that are environmentally sustainable and are rooted in the principles of ecology, social and gender equity and livelihood and employment generation. The role of the government is critical in mobilizing public and private resources to strengthen social and physical infrastructure, support community food security and improve the entitlement of vulnerable groups and pursue the eradication of hunger and sustainable food security at the national and household level. Difficult decisions have to be made about how to allocate and possibly redistribute limited resources and improve the efficiency in resource use to make deeper and faster cuts in the number of food insecure people. A national food insecurity and vulnerability information and mapping system indicating areas and populations including at local level, affected by or at risk of hunger and malnutrition and elements contributing to food insecurity is crucial to focussed efforts in eradicating hunger and attaining sustainable food security at the national and household level. In this context, *The Food Insecurity Atlas of Rural India* brought out jointly by the UN World Food Programme and the M.S. Swaminathan Research Foundation is the first attempt to systematically identify areas and populations affected by or at risk of food insecurity by tracking the nineteen selected indicators relating to food availability (5 indicators), food access (8) and food availability (6). Within food availability, the analysis considers deficit and fluctuations in production, transitory food insecurity due to natural disasters and long term sustainability affected by forest area cover, ground water availability and soil degradation. In food access, besides the problems relating to overall physical access to food, issues relating to gender and social discrimination in food access, livelihood vulnerability (poverty and casual employment) and rural infrastructure (electricity, water, road, etc.) have also been considered. The food absorption is affected by chronic energy deficiency, severely stunted and wasted children under five, infant mortality rate, lack of safe drinking water and health care facilities. The Atlas reveals that every state in the country has strengths and weaknesses in relation to achieving the goal of sustainable food security. Such detailed information (which should be collected also at sub-state levels) would facilitate formulation of appropriate interventions by identifying region specific priorities for programmes, actions and investments in making India hunger free. Information should be collected on a regular basis on nutritional status especially of poor, women, children and vulnerable and disadvantaged groups to monitor and improve their household food security. Goals and programmes aimed at food security and poverty eradication should be safe-guarded in difficulties of economic transitions, budget austerity and structural adjustments. The gram panchayats should be effectively involved in identifying the really poor and a mechanism should be evolved to provide precise information to eligible persons to their entitlements under various government schemes, methods of accessing benefits, functionaries responsible for delivery and redressal channels in case of grievances. Poverty alleviation programmes need to (a) focus more on aspects like vulnerability, seasonality, coping mechanisms and intra household distribution of resources; and (b) broaden their focus to include other vulnerable households who are at risk of becoming chronically poor and food insecure. Priority should be accorded to people-oriented investments in education, health and nutrition in order to promote broad based economic growth and sustainable food security. The strengthening of rural health infrastructure would be crucial in reducing infant and child mortality, improving life expectancies and nutrition status.

India has the world's largest official supported food and nutrition programmes providing targeted-in kind-food to vulnerable groups. Almost 200 million people benefit from subsidized food distribution under targeted public distribution system, 98 million school children get a daily snack or meal in their school under Mid-Day Meal scheme and 25 million children and mothers are covered by the Integrated Child Development Service. Besides these food grants are given to destitutes and food for work programmes is undertaken for working population. The *Antyodya Anna Yojana* (AAY), a new scheme for the poorest 12 million families, gives a sharper focus to the India's commitment to reduce hunger. The impact of these interventions would be greater if effective targeting and cost effectiveness is ensured and the focus is more on creating lasting assets (physical and human). Distribution of low-cost and high-calorie/protein/micronutrient cereals like *jowar, bajra, ragi* and millets through PDS, knowledge of childcare and health care practices as well as supplementary nutrition including distribution of fortified food for vulnerable groups through ICDS could help eliminate protein calorie malnutrition and energy deprivation and hidden hunger. Besides improvement in design of programmes, implementation based on consensual, participatory and transparent processes are necessary. Shift from conventional welfare thinking towards focusing on enhancing human capital and removing bottlenecks pays rich dividends as demonstrated in the case of Samurdhi concept in Sri Lanka which seeks to mainstream the poor and link them with investment, training and credit, while seeking to remove development obstacles or roadblocks with the help of food assistance.

For accelerating the shift from food for work to work for assets, the following design principles will be of importance: (a) issues of sustainability, operation and maintenance as well as environmental implications need explicit attention, as these considerations have a direct impact on the benefits to be derived; (b) participatory approaches should be used in the selection and design of activities. Community participation is crucial to establish ownership as a precondition for sustainability and for devising more appropriate interventions (Herbinger, Crawshaw and Shaw 1999). Special efforts have to be made to ensure food security and education of impoverished sections of people who had not been reached by the government through their planned efforts. Decentralized management, synthesizing of the various programmes, better targeting, giving women pivotal role, quicker responsiveness for disasters would catalyse the existing programmes; the combined effort of all these is to facilitate the deprived sections of the population to enter the development stream (Herbinger, Paper 26).

Women's roles in the gender division of labour are inextricably related to household food security and nutrition, and food resources under women's control are more likely to benefit children and increase food security than when controlled by men. It has to be ensured that they have equal opportunity to participate in activities, that they also benefit from assets created, and that they have some measure of control over the food resources provided and the assets produced. Evidence suggests that countries which under-invest in their women, and which fail to lower existing gender inequalities, eventually pay the price in terms of slower growth and lower incomes (UN 1999). Education of girls has a direct impact on child malnutrition. A recent study by the International Food Policy Research Institute (IFPRI) concluded that 44 per cent of the reduction in child malnutrition between 1990 and 1995 is attributable to increases in women's education. When women's education is combined with an improvement in their social status, these factors account for over 50 per cent of reduction in child's malnutrition (IFPRI 1998).

Safe drinking water is an important factor in influencing the biological absorption of food in body. Despite heavy investment in the scheme to provide safe drinking water to every village in the country in a time-bound manner, independent reports show that at present only 50 per cent of the villages may be having safe drinking water. Under the new policy initiated in April 1999, states have been asked to set up village water and sanitation committees, and enforce 10 per cent of capital sharing and 100 per cent sharing of O&M cost by users as precondition for disbursal of funds so as to improve capacity of local people to manage water resources and ensure long-term viability. Strong political and administrative commitment would be required to implement these necessary reforms to tackle the serious problem of availability of adequate quantities of safe drinking water.

In line with the goal of achievement of food security consistent with the World Food Summit commitments in a time bound framework, the Approach Paper to the Tenth Plan has suggested time bound targets for several social indicators crucial to achieving the goal of 'Hunger Free India'. These targets would be central to the attainment of the objectives of the Plan and include *inter alia:* (a) universal access to primary education by 2007; (b) reduction of gender gaps in literacy and wage rates by at least 50 per cent by 2007; (c) increase in literacy rates to 72 per cent by 2007 and 80 per cent by 2012; (d) reduction of Infant Mortality Rate (IMR) to 45 per 1,000 live births by 2007 and to 28 by 2012; (e) reduction of Maternal Mortality Rate (MMR) to 20 per 1,000 live births by 2007 and to 10 per cent by 2012; (f) increase in forest and tree covers to 25 per cent by 2007 and 33 per cent by 2012; and (g) all villages to have access to potable drinking water by 2012. In addition to substantial allocation of resources to the social sector, major improvements in governance would be undertaken to make effective use of allocated resources. The successful achievement of these targets would go a long way in making the mission of 'Hunger Free India' substantially successful by 2007. While national efforts must continue to remain the main element of any strategy to eradicate hunger, it is equally important to forge a global coalition for global action to promote food security.

# Opening Remarks to the Technical Sessions

*Dr. N.C. Saxena*
*Secretary, Planning Commission*

Friends! It gives me great pleasure to be here welcoming you all to the Technical Sessions on 'National Consultation on Towards Hunger Free India'. As you all know, the Consultation is designed to identify first the problem around the key issues relating to food security, namely, food availability, food access and food absorption and finally to discuss the policy response to the identified problems. You already had the Prime Minister and the Deputy Chairman, Planning Commission speak on these issues yesterday and now we look forward to your input through the technical sessions.

As also observed by Dr. Swaminathan in his Welcome Address, the issue of food availability has been somehow solved. However, 'food access' and 'food absorption' are the two issues on which we still have to do a lot of work. The former is closely related to the question of poverty. According to one estimate, poverty has come down from 36 per cent to 26 per cent between 1993–4 and 1999–2000. However, if one looks at the net state domestic product (NSDP) of a state like Bihar, it is observed that its slow growth does not match with the rapid fall in poverty figures during the last seven to eight years.

It is equally important to realize that although food production has gone up, per capita food availability has declined on account of rising population. According to some observers, food consumption pattern of people is changing in favour of vegetables, fruits, milk and meat. As such, since there is lower per capita demand for food grains, the aggregate demand for food grains is also coming down. But then, why is it that the food consumption

*Opening Remarks to the Technical Session on 25 April 2001.

of the bottom 10 per cent of the population, as shown by the different surveys, is 30 to 40 per cent of the food consumption of the top 10 per cent?

Poverty is concentrated in the poorer states of Bihar, Orissa, Madhya Pradesh and Uttar Pradesh. Everyone agrees that if one wants to reduce hunger, we need to concentrate on agriculture. In my view, technology holds the key especially in relation to irrigation. While food grains production increased significantly in the 1980s, it stagnated in the 1990s. I am familiar with the scene of Uttar Pradesh where a large number of farmers have had to shift from power driven pump sets for irrigation to diesel driven pump sets because of irregular and erratic power supply. Lessons may, nonetheless, be learnt from Bangladesh where diesel pumps have been substituted with manual labour and yet the production has gone up.

The various Poverty Alleviation Schemes in India, namely, the Jawahar Rozgar Yojana (JRY), the Integrated Rural Development Programme (IRDP), the Employment Assurance Scheme (EAS), the Integrated Child Development Scheme (ICDS) and Indira Awas Yojana (IAY), all together involve a staggering plan expenditure of Rs. 18,000 to Rs. 19,000 crore a year. However, as mentioned in the Mid-term Appraisal of the Ninth Five Year Plan, by and large, the gains have been modest. Apart from leakages, there are conceptual weaknesses in the scheme, which need to be tackled. Opportunities of self-employment would be higher when the growth in the economy is high (and there is market expansion) and not simply through providing subsidy on credit. I am not saying that credit is not important; credit is important but credit should be available at a reasonable rate of interest to anyone willing to set up an enterprise. Today, the subsidy, provided for loans, for example under IRDP/SGSY scheme, has become a source of corruption—involving the bank officials, village/district officials and the beneficiary.

Similarly, the Employment Assurance Scheme was originally intended to address incidence of hunger in specific pockets. Universalization of this scheme to all regions, in my opinion, was not a good idea. The original objective was lost when the scheme was introduced even in states of Punjab and Kerala where wage rates have been much above the subsistence level. We need to have, instead, asset building programmes in the form of watershed development, tank rejuvenation, waste land development, afforestation and creation of rural roads. The side benefit would naturally be creation of employment. In my opinion, instead of monitoring employment, we should monitor how many community assets have been created and adequate provision should be made for their maintenance.

There is another factor we need to examine today. The Government of India may have increased allocation for Poverty Alleviation Schemes, but it presupposes counterpart funds from the states. Can financially weak states of Orissa and Assam draw the entire amount made available to them in the absence of their share of counterpart funds? This is all the more worrying since the state finances, in general, have deteriorated over the years. Until the Sixth Plan, the (federal) states were contributing 28 per cent to their plan outlay; Centre's (Government of India) contribution being equal to 45 per cent. The picture has totally changed now with state's own contribution being (–)52 per cent. With Centre's contribution remaining the same at 45 per cent, borrowings by states having increased from 27 per cent earlier to 107 per cent. States today have fallen into a debt trap and are borrowing to pay the salaries to their employees. In the eyes of the general public, this only means the government is of the government and for the government.

While the State Governments and the Ministry of Rural Development (Government of India) claim that 95 per cent of villages have been covered with supply of drinking water, Planning Commission's own independent review shows that only 50 per cent of villages may be having safe drinking water. There is either a seasonal problem or other problems of 'quality' in data enumeration for this difference; but the fact remains that the situation is far from satisfactory despite having spent Rs. 45,000 crore on this scheme over the years. I am afraid drinking water may emerge as a serious problem during the Tenth Plan and call for remedial measures in advance. These are some of the issues having a bearing on 'food access'; 'food utilization' and public health, which have been bothering me. I am sure the consultation, during its deliberations, would be addressing these issues. The timing of this event is very opportune as we are in the process of finalizing the 'Approach Paper to the Tenth Plan'. I am sure the output of the deliberations would be of high order and I look forward to your recommendations.

Thank you!

SECTION I

# Food Availability and Vulnerability to Natural Disasters

# 1. Demand and Supply of Food Grains in 2020

*R. Thamarajakshi*

Alternative estimates of perspective demand for food grains have been prepared from time to time. The National Commission on Agriculture in the 1970s had done pioneering work on supply-demand projections for the year 2000. Besides the Planning Commission, which has been carrying out such exercises for the five-year plans, individual professionals have put out estimates based on different assumptions about base-level consumption, expenditure elasticities and expected growth of income and population, as also the demand for milk and milk products and the derived demand for cereals for feed. Demand projections have to be validated in the light of production and apparent consumption trends, stocks with public agencies, and inventories with private trade, as these reflect what the market has been absorbing.

## PRODUCTION TRENDS

During the past four decades, there has been a sizeable growth in cereal production; average production in the triennium ending (TE) 1999–2000 was 2.7 times that in TE 1962–3. Between TE 1982–3 and TE 1999–2000, production rose by 57 per cent, the corresponding increases being 29 and 33 per cent in the decades, TE 1973–83 and TE 1963–83 respectively. The increase has been mainly on account of wheat and rice. Production of coarse cereals, which increased during TE 1963–83, remained almost unchanged thereafter. Production of pulses has fluctuated; it declined in TE 1963–73, rose by 1.73 million tons during TE 1983–93, again rose during TE 1993–2000 (Table 1). In the post-1990s, there has been a deceleration in the growth rate of rice: it fell from 3.7 per cent during 1980–1 to 1991–2 to 2.1 per cent during 1992–3 to 1999–

TABLE 1: PRODUCTION OF FOOD GRAINS (TRIENNIUM AVERAGES) 1960–1 TO 1999–2000

(million tons)

| Period/Crop | TE 1962–3 | TE 1972–3 | TE 1982–3 | TE 1992–3 | TE 1999–2000 |
|---|---|---|---|---|---|
| Rice | 34.5 | 41.5 | 51.3 | 73.94 | 86.0 |
| Wheat | 11.3 | 25.0 | 38.9 | 56.01 | 71.1 |
| Coarse cereals | 23.9 | 26.1 | 29.3 | 31.96 | 30.7 |
| Total cereals | 69.7 | 92.6 | 119.5 | 161.91 | 187.8 |
| Pulses | 12.0 | 10.9 | 11.3 | 13.03 | 13.8 |
| Total food grains | 81.7 | 103.5 | 130.8 | 174.94 | 201.6 |

*Source*: Government of India, Ministry of Agriculture.

2000; corresponding decline in the case of pulses was from 1.4 per cent to 0.8 per cent, while coarse cereals recorded a negative growth rate of 1.6 per cent in the latter period. Consequently, despite continuous good monsoons and general improvement in food grains' terms of trade, the growth rate of food grain production declined from 2.9 per cent during the decade TE 1982–3 to TE 1992–3 to 2.0 per cent during the period TE 1992–3 to TE 1999–2000. Notwithstanding this decline, absolute levels of food grains production are now high, the per capita availability of which did not show much of a rise till the early 1980s, increasing to 173.7 kg in TE 1999–2000. On the other hand, per capita availability of pulses successively declined from 23.2 kg in TE 1963 to 17.0, 14.1, 13.5 and 13.3 kg in TE 1973, 1983, 1993 and 1999, respectively. Per capita availability of food grains, which declined somewhat from 167.1 kg in TE 1963 to 165.2 and 163.8 respectively in TE 1973 and 1983, increased remarkably to 175.1 kg in TE 1992–3 (Table 2).

TABLE 2: PER CAPITA NET AVAILABILITY OF FOOD GRAINS

(kg per year)

| Period/Crop | TE 1962–3 | TE 1972–3 | TE 1982–3 | TE 1992–3 | TE 1999–2000 |
|---|---|---|---|---|---|
| Rice | 71.9 | 68.5 | 68.2 | 77.8 | 75.4 |
| Wheat | 29.5 | 42.3 | 48.9 | 56.4 | 59.5 |
| Coarse cereals | 42.5 | 37.4 | 32.6 | 27.4 | 25.5 |
| Total cereals | 143.9 | 148.2 | 149.7 | 161.6 | 160.4 |
| Pulses | 23.2 | 17.0 | 14.1 | 13.5 | 13.3 |
| Total food grains | 167.1 | 165.2 | 163.8 | 175.1 | 173.7 |

*Source*: Government of India, Ministry of Agriculture.

A distinguishing feature of the food grain economy in recent years has been the misalignment of market prices and administered prices, consequently, it is unclear if production trends reflect operation of market forces. The annual average increase in MSP of rice and wheat during 1992–3 to 1999–2000 at 10 per cent and 10.8 per cent is much higher than the respective increases of 7.5 per cent and 6.2 per cent during 1980–1 to 1991–2. Procurement/support prices have been raised at a faster rate than the index of wholesale prices. Due to the practice of setting procurement prices at levels higher than what the market can offer and the commitment of the State to purchase all quantities offered at MSP, the State has, over the years, become a dominant buyer, while private trade is perhaps not finding it worthwhile to carry inventories; out of the crop of 1999–2000, more than 40 per cent of rice and wheat have been bought by public agencies (Table 3). However, there appears to be slackness in the demand for grain allocated for sale through PDS outlets; offtake has been persistently lower than allocation (Table 4). This is despite the TPDS under which families below the poverty line receive rice and wheat at lower and highly subsidized prices. As a result, cereal stocks with the government have risen from 23 million tons in January 1985 to an estimated level of 45.7 million tons in January 2001, compared to a minimum buffer stock norm of 16.8 million tons with associated problem of storage, handling losses and rising food subsidy.

TABLE 3: MARKETED SUPPLY AND PROCUREMENT

| Year | Rice | | | Wheat | | |
|---|---|---|---|---|---|---|
| | Procurement (million tons) | Procurement as % of production | Procurement as % of market supply | Procurement (million tons) | Procurement as % of production | Procurement as % of market supply |
| 1993–4 | 14.26 | 17.8 | 41.6 | 11.87 | 19.8 | 37.8 |
| 1994–5 | 13.40 | 16.4 | 38.4 | 12.33 | 18.7 | 35.7 |
| 1995–6 | 9.95 | 12.9 | 30.2 | 8.16 | 13.1 | 25.0 |
| 1996–7 | 12.22 | 15.0 | 35.0 | 9.30 | 13.4 | 25.5 |
| 1997–8 | 14.33 | 17.4 | 40.7 | 12.65 | 19.1 | 36.4 |
| 1998–9 | 11.84 | 13.8 | 32.3 | 14.14 | 19.8 | 37.8 |
| 1999–2000 | 17.27 | 19.3 | 45.2 | 16.35 | 21.6 | 41.3 |

*Note*: Marketed supply estimated by using the average rates of 42.71 per cent for paddy/rice production and 52.44 per cent for wheat production vide GOI, Department of Statistics, National Accounts Statistics (NAS), Sources and Methods, 1989.

TABLE 4: FOOD GRAIN ALLOCATION AND OFFTAKE UNDER PDS

(million tons)

| Year | Wheat | | Rice | |
|---|---|---|---|---|
| | Allocation | Offtake | Allocation | Offtake |
| 1991–2 | 10.30 | 8.83 | 11.36 | 10.17 |
| 1992–3 | 9.25 | 7.85 | 11.48 | 6.96 |
| 1993–4 | 9.56 | 5.91 | 12.41 | 8.87 |
| 1994–5 | 10.80 | 4.83 | 13.32 | 8.03 |
| 1995–6 | 11.31 | 5.81 | 14.62 | 9.75 |
| 1996–7 | 10.72 | 8.52 | 15.10 | 11.14 |
| 1997–8 | 10.11 | 7.08 | 12.83 | 9.90 |
| 1998–9 | 10.11 | 7.95 | 12.93 | 10.74 |
| 1999–2000 | 10.37 | 5.00 | 13.84 | 10.95 |
| 2000–1 | 7.51 | 2.72 (Apr.–Dec. 2000) | 10.96 | 5.75 (Apr.–Dec. 2000) |

*Source*: Government of India, *Economic Survey, 1999-2000.*

## TRENDS IN CONSUMPTION

As against this scenario of production and demand for PDS cereals, a decline is observed in actual levels of consumption of cereals based on NSS results. Per capita consumption of cereals per annum in the rural sector declined from 173 kg to 154 kg and from 134 kg to 124 kg in the urban sector during 1987–97. The triennium average for 1994–5 to 1996–7 was 156 kg in the rural sector and 126 kg in the urban sector, the weighted average for the country as a whole being 148 kg (Thamarajakshi 1999). Similar decline is observed in the consumption of pulses. Besides, the level of consumption is also very low: 9.1 kg in the rural sector and 10.3 kg in the urban sector. Compared to decline in cereal and pulses consumption, NSS data reveal increasing trends in non-food grain items, viz., vegetables, milk and milk products and meat, egg and fish. It seems the food consumption basket is getting diversified in favour of non-food grain items, inasmuch as expenditure elasticities for cereals are very marginal and even negative.

There is a viewpoint that the burgeoning stocks of cereals do not necessarily imply that domestic production has reached a level which is much more than what the market or PDS can absorb. It is argued that these surpluses are a transitory phenomenon due to inter-year variation in production, and do not represent a real surplus after meeting the genuine needs of food security but are surplus realized due to structural constraints on effective demand (World Bank/Suryanarayana March 2001). This, however, could not be a sustainable position: the surpluses which are much more than minimum buffer stock norms and the highly subsidized prices for BPL families act as a depressant on ruling market prices, which enable at least the better-off among the BPL families to turn to the open market, contributing to low offtake. Further, when PDS prices for BPL families are at a highly subsidized rates, it is not clear why food security objective should elude achievement.

We have to distinguish between food supply and access to available food. India is currently food surplus at the national level, but this does not preclude intra-household distributional problems. This cannot quite be interpreted as prevalence of hunger. In one of its recent rounds, the NSS found that on an average, 92 per cent of the rural and 97 per cent of the urban population gets two square meals a day. It is reported that due to increase in cereal production, per capita calorie availability has risen from 2,200 in the late 1980s to 2,500 at the end of the 1990s (Rao and Radhakrishna 1997; Haller 1999). There is, of course, utmost need to attend to the problem of malnutrition and to empower the vulnerable sections of the population to have a balanced diet in terms of requisite nutrients, and this calls for a diversified food consumption basket. But malnutrition is not only on account of lack of access to food, but has also to do with that of safe drinking water, sanitation, environmental hygiene, primary health care and awareness. Here, it is gratifying to note that 37 developing countries accounted for a decline of 100 million undernourished persons, with India and China contributing two-thirds of this number (FAO 1999).

## FOOD GRAIN DEMAND PROJECTIONS

Alternative projections of cereal demand are available for 2020 covering direct consumption needs and cereals required for livestock feed. For estimating direct consumption, the conventional approach is to superimpose income and population growth factors and expenditure elasticities on a base-level per capita consumption. Past trends of per capita consumption show a saturation tendency in regard to cereal intake and diversification in favour of non-food grain items of the food basket. In the light of the above, there may not be much scope for increase in per capita consumption on account of the income factor. At the same time, it would not be realistic to assume the past declining trend to continue in future. Recently, the NSS have observed in their 55th round that a 7-day reference period in the survey showed a higher level of consumption than that on the basis of a 30-day reference period. However, the 55th round had sought to elicit responses on the basis of both 7-day and 30-day reference periods from the same sample population, thereby giving room to the possibility of bias in both the results, apart from non-comparability with results from earlier rounds. The results of the 55th round are not, therefore, used here. It is decided to assume that the observed level of per capita consumption of cereals as in the triennium 1994–5 to 1996–7 would hold good for the coming years too.

As for population projections for 2020, we have taken as base the provisional population totals of 1,027 million persons as on 1 March 2001 as per the *Census of India*. The decadal growth of population between 1991–2001 is 21.34 per cent. Assuming the same decadal growth for the next 20 years, population in 2020 would be 1,485 million; we may call this 'Population Projection I' (PP I). The current decadal growth of 21.34 per cent represents a decline of 10.6 per cent over the previous decadal growth of 23.86 per cent during 1981–91. Assuming the same rate of decline in 2001–11 and 2011–21, population in 2020 would be 1,411 million; we may call this 'Population Projection II' (PP II). Projections on future rate of urbanization range between 33.5 per cent and 40 per cent; the present study has taken the rate of urbanization at 35 per cent. On this basis, cereal requirements for human consumption in 2020 works out to 216 million tons on PP I, and 205 million tons on PP II.

Cereal requirements for livestock feed constitute derived demand and hence depend on the future demand for livestock products. A review of available estimates of requirements for livestock products and feed needs is considered necessary to arrive at a realistic estimate. The current level of feed use is reported as 3.7 million tons. The Planning Commission has estimated milk consumption at 180.8 million tons in 2011–12 compared to 66 million tons in 1996–7; they have not estimated cereals needed for feed. Dyson and Hanchate have extrapolated past trends and estimated the demand in 2020 for milk and meat respectively at 170.3 million tons and 16.1 million tons; they estimate feed needs of cereals as 30 million tons. Bhalla et al., have adopted high demand elasticities for livestock products to reflect structural shifts in tastes over time, and derived much higher demand projections at 289.6 million tons for milk and 19.9 million tons for meat and eggs, and derived demand of feed requirements at 50.1 million tons; the authors, however, admit that there is no precise way of forecasting 2020 elasticity values. Estimates by Rosegrant and Kumar of cereal needs for feed are respectively 13.7 million tons and 16.9 million tons; yet another estimate is that by Bansil at 30.6 million tons. The ICMR's recommended norms of consumption of livestock products compare with projected levels as per Rosegrant et al., and Kumar, hence it is assumed here that the ICMR norm would imply feed demand of an average of 15 million tons.

Our two estimates of demand for cereals for direct consumption for 2020 are 205 million tons and 216 million tons, and after providing for seed, feed and wastage at current rates, and allowing for accelerated demand for livestock products for inter-year fluctuations as also for exports, production target for cereals could be placed at 274 million tons and 287 million tons. Table 5 presents available projections. The lowest of these projections would mean an addition of 36 million tons over that achieved in the triennium ending 2000, while the highest projection would

TABLE 5: ALTERNATIVE PROJECTIONS OF CEREAL DEMAND, 2020

(million tons)

| | | Human consumption | Feed requirements | Total |
|---|---|---|---|---|
| Present study | (i) | 205.0 | 69.0* | 274.0* |
| | (ii) | 216.0 | 71.0* | 287.0* |
| Dyson & Hanchate@ | | 193.5 | 30.1 | 223.6 |
| Rosegrant et al.@@ | | 223.6 | 13.3 | 237.3 |
| Kumar@@ | | 237.6 | 16.9 | 254.5 |
| Bansil** | | 227.8 | 30.6 | 258.4 |
| Bhalla et al.@@ | | 246.1 | 50.1 | 296.2 |
| Nutritional requirement | | 212.0 | 15.0 | 227.0 |
| Planning Commission for 2011-12 | | 238.7 | | 307.5* |

*Notes*: * Includes seed and wastage and allows for inter-year fluctuations and export possibilities besides feed needs at accelerated demand for livestock products.

\# Production target.

@ Dyson, Tim and Amresh Hanchate.

@@ G.S. Bhalla, Peter Hazell and John Kerr.

** Cited in @.

mean an addition of 108 million tons. In this connection, it would be useful to note the feasibility of production increases; as against the plan target of production of cereals of 217.5 million tons at the end of the Ninth Plan (2001–2), estimated production in 2000-1 is only 184 million tons.

Regarding pulses, they are important sources of protein. Presently, consumption levels are very low, and are not rising. Action is needed to create awareness about their nutritional properties. If we carry forward to 2020 at the current levels, requirements would be around 13 million tons, even lower than current level of production of 14 million tons. The Planning Commission had expected demand of the order of 19.5 million tons in 2001–2, but fixed a lower target of 16.5 million tons; for 2011–12, it worked out consumption at about 25 million tons. Provisional estimate of production in 2000–1 is 12.3 million tons. Having regard to the progress of production, requirements are assumed to be 30 million tons by 2020 in the present study; the total requirements of food grains in 2020 would be 304/317 million tons as against an average production of 201.6 million tons in the TE 1999–2000.

## SUPPLY PROSPECTS

Increases in food grain production have to come mainly from step-up in yield levels as net sown area under food grains has reached a plateau. Within food grains, rice and wheat have gained at the cost of coarse cereals, while area under pulses has remained unchanged. Cropping intensity has not shown improvement in the 1990s and has remained at around 1.3. It is disconcerting to note that growth rate of yields in the 1990s in the case of rice, wheat and pulses were considerably lower than in the 1980s (Table 6). Further increases have to come from rainfed areas and the eastern region. Only 40 per cent of the area under food grains is irrigated. Steps should be taken to raise productivity in rained areas through ground water development and watershed management. The eastern region's untapped potential with its abundant surface and ground water was counted upon by the Planning Commission for 50 per cent of the planned incremental production in the Ninth Plan. This has to be pursued; the mid-term appraisal has pointed out that exploitation of ground water potential, especially in the eastern region, is sub-optimal and that procedural delays and

TABLE 6: GROWTH RATE OF FOOD GRAIN YIELDS (COMPOUND GROWTH RATE)

(per cent per annum)

| Crop | 1979–80 to 1989–90 | 1989–90 to 1998–9 |
|---|---|---|
| Rice | 3.82 | 1.21 |
| Wheat | 3.65 | 1.96 |
| Course cereals | 1.84 | 1.63 |
| Total cereals | 3.43 | 1.52 |
| Pulses | 2.63 | 0.65 |
| Total food grains | 3.33 | 1.42 |

*Source*: Government of India, Ministry of Agriculture.

heavy transaction costs have reportedly inhibited the pump schemes operated by the state governments that leave little real subsidy for the farmers. Decline in public investment in agriculture has substantially contributed to slackening of agricultural growth; only 6.5 per cent of Ninth Plan outlay has been allocated to irrigation. The slowdown in irrigation has affected cropping intensity and yields. It is also known that fertilizer use is not widespread across the states. The yawning gap between agriculturally prosperous states and backward states in fertilizer use, proportion of irrigated area and yields shows the scope for improvement towards widespread growth provided appropriate location specific strategy is adopted.

Policy makers and planners are fully aware of the components of strategy for raising productivity and have spelt out the same in many documents for quite some years now. However, there are slippages in critical areas like irrigation, efficiency of water use, fertilizer use and development of rainfed regions and the eastern region. For instance, the Ninth Plan had targeted growth of 4.5 per cent in the Plan period for agriculture and allied sectors for meeting both domestic and external demand. But actual performance during 1997–2001 has turned out to be a mere 1.5 per cent only.

# 2. Demand and Supply of Food and Feed Grains by 2020

*G.S. Bhalla*

India faced serious problems on its food front right from the day it achieved independence in 1947 and food deficits persisted right up to the mid-1970s. Consequently, the country had to resort to food imports to feed its rising population. India imported, on an average, 2.1 million tons of food grains during the 1950s and as high as 4.5 million tons of food grains during the 1960s, when the food situation became quite serious. Because of the persistent food scarcity, and the need for improving the productivity and income level of a large proportion of the workforce dependent on agriculture, Indian planners accorded high priority to accelerating agricultural growth in general, and growth of food grains in particular, from the very beginning of planning in 1951.

The strategy adopted was to implement land reforms and to undertake large investments in irrigation, rural electrification, agricultural research and extension, roads, markets, communications, credit and other rural infrastructure. The introduction of new seed and fertilizer technology during the mid-1960s marked a new stage of development in Indian agriculture and led to unprecedented increase in the output and yield of two major cereals, namely, wheat and rice. Large-scale planned investment in rural infrastructure, combined with concerted efforts undertaken to extend the Green Revolution to almost all the regions in India, resulted in substantial increase in the production of food grains in the country. As a result, India became almost self-sufficient in food grains production by the middle of the 1980s. Besides

*This paper is based on the study entitled 'Prospects for India's Cereal Supply and Demand to 2020', by G.S. Bhalla, Peter Hazell and John Kerr, IFPRI Discussion Paper 29, Washington, DC, November 1999.

increasing yields technological developments also resulted in reducing the cost of production and led to reduction in the real price of wheat and rice, conferring real gains to the poor. The institution of a comprehensive system of food management consisting of procurement of food grains, their stocking and distribution through a PDS network deepened and enhanced the food security of Indian people in general, and the Indian poor in particular.

Recently, there have been some indications of erosion in the system of food security. One clear indication is a very hefty rise in the administered price of rice and wheat, which is hurting the poor. The availability of large stocks to the tune of 40 million tons has imparted a sense of complacency to the policy makers in India. Although the Food Corporation of India (FCI) has not been disbanded, its operations have been curtailed leading to serious problems for the farmers. Some serious changes have also been made in the PDS. The recent trend of diversification in the food demand basket and decline in per capita consumption of food grains on the one hand, and increase in consumption of superior foods and animal husbandry products on the other, has further added to the sense of complacency of the policy makers. The liberalization of the economy and the signing of WTO have given added incentive to the drive for and relative neglect of accelerating food grains production in the country. It is being thought that India hardly needs any further emphasis on food grains production.

Economic liberalization has resulted in giving much larger importance to the operation of the market. It is argued that given a proper price climate and higher prices for agricultural commodities (prices that are no longer lower than border prices and do not discriminate against the farmers), large investments would be forthcoming from the private sector including the farmers themselves. The persistence of large deficits is a drastic cut down of real public outlay on rural (and urban) infrastructure and a sharp decline in public investment in agriculture. The result of continued neglect of public investment in agriculture is a significant deceleration in the growth rate of food grains.

The long-term policy implications of such a policy are likely to be quite serious. This is particularly because with expected rapid rise in per capita income, the direct and indirect demand for food grains is likely to rise at a much faster rate than being envisaged by the policy makers. On the other hand, because of continuing neglect of the supply potential, the prospects for future growth are becoming quite dim.

## DEMAND ESTIMATES

The main purpose of this paper is to concentrate on the supply potential of Indian economy. However, it is important to understand the dimension of food demand for undertaking any fruitful discussion about the supply scenario. In the following section, we only give a brief review of the existing estimates about food demand till 2020.

Recently, there has taken place a heated debate in India on food demand projections to the twenty-first century. By using both log linear and Linear Expenditure System (LES) equations, the Planning Commission has derived some estimates of food demand till 2010. The NSS data on consumer expenditure for various rounds has brought out that there is a distinct change in tastes and consumption habits, and, over time, consumers are spending larger proportion of their income on superior foods and in many rich states, their per capita consumption of food grains has gone down significantly. More important, even poor households with inadequate calorie intake did not use additional income to purchase additional calories in the form of food grains, the cheapest available source (GOI, NSSO 1991). Keeping in view these developments, some scholars have predicted that with an acceleration in per capita income (PCY) growth, there would be a further decline in the growth rate of demand for food grains.

On the other hand, we have predicted a rapid rise in total cereal demand primarily because of rising feed requirement of meeting rapidly rising demand for milk, meat and other animal husbandry products emanating from rapidly rising per capita income.

It is the requirements of the livestock sector that would become a very important determinant of future demand for cereals. Rapid economic growth, particularly if it is accompanied by significant reductions in poverty, will lead to escalating demand for cereals, milk, eggs and meats. These, in turn, will likely require changes in livestock production methods, with much greater use of cereals for livestock feed.

According to our estimates, if current livestock feeding practices continue, then total cereal demand in 2020 would amount to only 258 million tons, with a PCY growth of 2 per cent per annum (p.a.). With PCY growth of 3.7 per cent p.a., a growth rate that India achieved during the 1980s and the 1990s, the total food and feed demand would reach 296.2 million tons, including 50.1 million tons (or 17 per cent) for feed and 246.1 million tons (or 83 per cent) for direct human consumption. This means doubling of cereal demand over 1993, which is the kind of increase that India experienced over the last 30 years.

The total cereal demand would increase to 374.7 million tons if PCY grows at 6 per cent p.a. [Gross Domestic Product (GDP) growth at 7.5–7.7 per cent p.a.], including 107.5 million tons (or 28 per cent) for feed. This level of cereal demand seems quite reasonable when expressed in per capita terms (0.077 kg per capita per day), and would bring India more into line with the level demanded in China in 1993 (0.073 kg per capita per day). It is also only about one-third of the current level in the United States. If per capita income growth slows down to 2.00 per cent p.a. (GDP at 3.5 to 3.8 per cent p.a., the pre-1980 growth rate), then total cereal demand in 2020 is projected at 257.3 million tons, a modest 70 per cent increase over 1993 demand.

If economic growth is also accompanied by significant reductions in the proportion of poor people, then cereal demand could record further increases. This is because moving the poor above the poverty line would necessitate provision of higher quantities of food grains to the poor for direct and indirect consumption. Again, making the entire population attain adequate nutritional levels would imply higher consumption of milk, meat and other foods, thereby once again increasing the indirect demand for food grains.

The projections of food demand given above are higher than the projections given by other scholars. For example, for a PCY of 3–4 per cent p.a., the International Model for Policy Analysis of Agricultural Commodities and Trade (IMPACT) model projects the total demand at 237.3 by 2020 (Rosegrant et al. 1995) and Kumar a figure of 254.5 million tons (Kumar 1998) against our figure of 296 million tons. Notably, the differences are entirely because of different assumptions about the livestock sector. Unlike other scholars, we have assumed structural changes in the demand for livestock products that will lead to higher income elasticities. We have also assumed that rapid growth in livestock demand will have to be matched by a shift towards more cereal-intensive

TABLE 1: PROJECTED CEREAL REQUIREMENTS FOR INDIA AND COMPARISON WITH OTHER COUNTRIES FOR 2020

(million tons)

| Country/year/source | Food | Feed | Total | kg per capita per day |
|---|---|---|---|---|
| *India* | | | | |
| 1999 actual | 165.025 | 4.59 | 169.615 | 0.48 |
| 1993 actual | 147.121 | 3.712 | 150.833 | 0.47 |
| Authors' projections with per capita income growth of: | | | | |
| 2 % | 231.510 | 25.749 | 257.259 | 0.53 |
| 3.7 % | 246.080 | 50.111 | 296.191 | 0.61 |
| 6 % | 267.210 | 107.522 | 374.732 | 0.77 |
| 2020 IMPACT* | 223.6 | 13.3 | 237.3 | 0.51 |
| 2020 Kumar** | 237.6 | 16.9 | 254.5 | 0.55 |
| *China* | | | | |
| 1993 (actual) | 251.243 | 72.640 | 323.883 | 0.73 |
| 2020 (IMPACT)* | 293.441 | 177.989 | 471.430 | 0.90 |
| *Pakistan* | | | | |
| 1993 (actual) | 20.361 | 1.313 | 21.674 | 0.47 |
| 2020 (IMPACT)* | 42.426 | 2.826 | 45.232 | 0.49 |
| *United States* | | | | |
| 1993 (actual) | 34.822 | 158.200 | 193.022 | 2.03 |
| 2020 (IMPACT)* | 42.390 | 202.101 | 244.491 | 2.08 |

*Notes*: *IMPACT model baseline results (Rosegrant et al. 1995).
**Kumar's projections (Kumar 1998).

livestock feeding systems. These are controversial assumptions, but not implausible given the experience of many other countries, including neighbouring countries in Asia. Demand estimates to 2020 given by us and other scholars are summarized in Table 1.

## ESTIMATING CEREAL SUPPLY BY 2020

India's total cereal production which averaged 2.7 per cent p.a. during 1949–50 to 1990–1, has decelerated to 1.39 per cent p.a. during 1990–1 to 1998–9. Although, initially, India started as a highly food deficit country, India was able to become self-sufficient by the beginning of 1980s. At present, the country has foodstocks worth 40 million tons.[1] Although, initially, expansion of area and increased irrigation played an important role in growth of cereal production, after the introduction of new technology during the mid-1960s, it was the increasing use of improved seeds and inorganic fertilizers that played a crucial role in increasing production. For example, irrigated area increased from 38 million hectares in 1960–1 to 79.9 million hectares by 1995–6. And fertilizer consumption from 2.92 million tons in 1960–1 to 180.7 million tons by 1999–2000.

With production growing at 2.7 per cent p.a., to 2020, production would increase to 243 million tons or one and a half times the production level of 198 million tons achieved in 1998–9. But it would be unrealistic to make such an extrapolation for various reasons. First, further expansion of the irrigated area will be more costly, as agriculture must increasingly compete with other water users (e.g. industry and urban households) for limited water resources. Second, there is now limited scope for the further expansion of the Green Revolution technologies and production gains from the greater use of improved varieties of fertilizers. Finally, resource degradation is also impacting on productivity growth in irrigated and rainfed areas. If it is not corrected, it would become a significant constraint on future growth rates of cereal production.

A brief analysis of some of the options are given below.

## POSSIBILITIES FOR FUTURE GROWTH

For analysis of technology options, the various regions in India could be divided into irrigated and high-potential and low-potential rainfed areas. It may be underlined that in all the three types of areas, future growth would have to continue to depend on yield increases, since there is no scope for area increases. This is because the left out land in all types of areas is unproductive and cultivating it would be costly and could result in deforestation and soil erosion. Yield increases, in turn, will require the continued spread of yield-enhancing technologies, improved natural resource management, and greater technical efficiency. In some of the most productive areas, research is needed to boost potential yields in order to create a new source of yield growth. On the other hand, in many other areas there are still large yield gaps between farmers' yields and demonstration plots, suggesting those significant gains could be made just by spreading existing technology. Another imperative is to minimize natural resource degradation, which threatens to undermine the gains already made.

The scope for further expansion of irrigated area now being limited, production growth in irrigated areas will increasingly have to come from growth in the productivity of existing land and water resources. Unfortunately, there is increasing evidence to suggest that productivity growth is stagnating in many irrigated areas for two main reasons. First, the Green Revolution has already run its course in irrigated areas, and there is less scope than in the past for obtaining additional output from the greater use of improved varieties and fertilizers. Second, environmental stresses associated with intensive irrigated farming are reducing productivity growth in many high-yielding areas (Bhalla and Singh 1997). Salinity, alkalinity, and waterlogging of land are even leading to the degradation and loss of significant areas of irrigated land. More work is needed to understand the nature of these problems, how serious they are, and what is required to solve them (Hobbs and Morris 1996). Possibilities for increasing production in irrigated areas include the following.

*Genetic Improvement*

There is scope for continued development of new varieties. For rice, hybrids could result in a one-time yield increase of 15–20 per cent. International Rice Research Institute's (IRRI) 'super rice' that drastically modifies plant architecture may bring additional gains of up to 30 per cent (Pingali et al. 1997). Other crops continue to enjoy modest advances through the development of second-generation modern varieties. Biotechnology holds some promise for significantly increasing productivity in the long-term, but short-term gains will most likely arise by reducing susceptibility to pest and disease losses.

*Crop Management*

This area is generally neglected in India so far. There are significant opportunities to raise productivity by reducing the large technical efficiency gap in many irrigated areas. While there has been widespread adoption of modern varieties, fertilizers, and irrigation, much less adoption of improved management practices has taken place that could boost productivity and reduce environmental stress. Though often very knowledge-intensive, some incremental management changes—relating to site- and season-specific pest, water, and nutrient management—provide the potential for reducing this efficiency gap. As elsewhere, however, this type of 'precision farming' will require greatly improved knowledge-transfer systems and skilled and educated farmers to be successful in India. This suggests a need for major changes in the agricultural research system to promote work that is more on-farm, more interdisciplinary, more focused on crop management (in addition to plant genetics), and that promotes more feedback from farmers.

*Spreading Irrigation*

Increasing the irrigated area, either by investing in new sources or by using existing irrigation facilities more efficiently, could also be a source of future growth. Irrigation now covers about 38 per cent of gross cropped area, but the potential is as high as 50 per cent. However, expanding irrigation facilities to the maximum potential area by the year 2020 is probably not feasible. There are several constraints.

First, most of the 'easy' options for increasing irrigated area have already been exploited. The remaining possibilities for large-scale canal irrigation involve higher financial, environmental, and social costs than previous projects, so progress in expanding irrigation potential is likely to be increasingly slow.

Second, water demand is rising in non-agricultural sectors, and agriculture's share in total water use is certain to drop during the period up to 2020. The World Bank estimates that agriculture's share in 2025 will be 73 per cent, compared to 87 per cent in 1985. This means a significant share of any expansion of irrigation facilities will simply go to maintaining existing potential.

Third, ground water, which is currently India's fastest growing source of irrigation, also faces limits to growth. In many dry areas, ground water has been tapped so heavily that the water table has fallen precipitously over the years. In the dry areas, where irrigation can have its greatest impact, the prospects for additional well investment are the lowest. Even without creating new irrigation potential, however, better management of existing water resources could have a large impact on output. Currently, irrigation water is underpriced and poorly managed, causing widespread waste. In canal-irrigated areas, water tariffs are so low they do not even cover maintenance costs.

Farmers on the upper end of distribution channels use scarce water for water-intensive crops, leading to waterlogging and salt problems and reducing water availability for farmers at the tail end. In many areas irrigated by wells, free or nearly free electricity causes over-pumping, which leads to ever lower water tables and widespread well failure.

Careful management of available water resources could go much farther, raising overall irrigated area and irrigated crop yields. The World Bank estimates that even a 10 per cent increase in efficiency of existing irrigation facilities could add 7–8 million hectares of irrigated land in India without utilizing additional water resources (World Bank 1998).

Institutional reforms are needed to better coordinate irrigation management. Watershed management, ground water development, canal irrigation, lift irrigation and agriculture are all managed independently of each other, even though they are strongly linked and potentially complementary. Similarly, social and environmental externalities that cross the boundaries of narrowly organized government line departments receive inadequate attention in project planning (Repetto 1994). Irrigation development proceeds with inadequate attention to drainage or soil conservation, resulting in shortened project lifespans due to soil salinity or sedimentation of reservoirs. As a result, reorganizing the irrigation administration is needed not only to increase productivity of existing irrigation capacity, but also to prevent its decline.

*High-potential Rainfed Areas*: Agriculture in favourable rainfed areas has performed well in recent years. Production will probably never match that in the most productive irrigated areas due to inferior agro-climatic conditions, but some growth potential still exists. Projections of continued growth in these areas are based on two factors. First, for the past two decades these areas have consistently adopted improved varieties and other inputs, but with a lag compared to irrigated areas. This trend should continue. Second, additional growth is possible with improvements in crop management. In high-rainfall areas with deep, black, water-retentive soils, for example, improved drainage practices will enable more area to be brought under double-cropping even without irrigation.

Adoption of such management practices depends largely on increased farmer knowledge and higher output prices. In some areas of eastern India, unravelling complicated tenure arrangements should encourage land-improving investments, such as irrigation and flood control, which are critical to further intensification (Repetto 1994).

On the whole, high-potential rainfed areas (mostly in the eastern region) represent India's best option for expanded production. Historical trends suggest that improved varieties and inputs will continue to spread to these areas. In addition, they are among the poorest least-educated, and least-developed areas in the country. Continued improvements in infrastructure will raise the returns to agriculture in these areas, while increases in education may increase the scope for adoption of better management practices.

*Low-potential Rainfed Areas*: Other rainfed areas lag behind in agricultural production and yield growth. In particular, semi-arid rainfed areas have seen only limited adoption of modern inputs. They produce mainly coarse grains like sorghum and millet, and in some places yield growth has been negligible over the last three decades. In recent years, there has been a shift to oilseeds, which have performed well in response to high output prices. But on the whole, progress has been limited in semi-arid regions. This is largely a result of unfavourable growing conditions, natural resource degradation, and farmers' unwillingness to invest in costly inputs due to the high risk of crop failure.

Technical solutions are less clear than in more favourable environments, and output growth is likely to be limited. Farmers in unfavourable environments pursue complex, risk-minimizing strategies for producing food and earning their livelihoods. This complicates the introduction of new production technologies, which may not be adopted if they are incompatible with some component of existing livelihood systems, thus imposing unacceptable opportunity costs. Some technical recommendations, such as watershed management, require collective action among farmers that is difficult to attain. So far, the promise of dryland watershed development in raising agricultural productivity has been fulfilled only in a few isolated cases. Researchers and development practitioners are increasingly realizing that developing and adapting technologies to meet complex, location-specific requirements in unfavourable areas will require greater participation of intended users. Encouraging such hands-on, participatory approaches is difficult where research or development systems traditionally work in a top-down manner.

On the bright side, the experience with oilseeds in recent years shows that favourable incentives can encourage productivity increases even in relatively unfavourable areas. High output prices for oilseeds have induced increases in both area and yield. Another positive sign is that agricultural intensification in dry areas may be associated with environmental improvements, not degradation. Water harvesting and moisture concentration measures also bring soil conservation and application of organic matter and other nutrients. Where water becomes available, farmers often invest in improved livestock, which require stall-feeding rather than open grazing. Their manure can be saved for use both as fuel and as organic matter to be applied to croplands. As a result, intensification can reduce the pressure on widely degraded rangelands, and forests and contribute to improved soil fertility. Meanwhile, chemical inputs in low-potential rainfed areas will remain below polluting levels.

### *The Role of Fertilizers*

Fertilizers can play an important role in increasing cereal production, either through increased fertilizer applications or improved efficiency. After expanding at a rapid pace since the early 1960s, fertilizer consumption averaged about 120 kg per hectare in 1990–1 in the major states of India.

However, current use rates are still far below the amount that would maximize production, estimated at a national average of 334 kg per hectare of NPK fertilizer (Gandhi et al. 1998). Of course, this average figure reflects variations both within and across states. It represents the agronomic optimum, at which yields no longer increase with an additional unit of fertilizer applied. It is higher than the economic optimum, at which net returns (the value of output less the cost of fertilizer) no longer increase with an additional unit of fertilizer applied. As with irrigation expansion, raising fertilizer use to maximum levels is also unrealistic, for at least four reasons.

First, unless fertilizer prices plummet and food prices rise dramatically, the economically optimal quantity of fertilizer will not likely approach the agronomic optimum.

Second, many fertilizers are petroleum-intensive, and tripling their use may have unmanageable foreign exchange implications. Third, high fertilizer application rates would lead to chemical pollution and impose unacceptable off-site costs, especially through leaching into ground water.

And fourth, as mentioned earlier, in drier rainfed areas, fertilizer application will remain constrained by risk. To illustrate the difficulty of a threefold increase in average fertilizer use, it is helpful to consider that the current average in highly intensive Punjab is about 210 kg per hectare, and there is some evidence that marginal returns are low at this rate. It is difficult to imagine the all-India figure exceeding the current Punjab level by the year 2020.

On the other hand, there are reasonable prospects for increasing the efficiency of existing fertilizer inputs, specially on rainfed lands. Studies suggest that the profitable use of fertilizer in many unirrigated areas will generally require greater fertilizer efficiency through a balanced dose, timely planting, improved time of application, and improved placement. In marginal areas, it is likely that fertilizer will only be profitable in some years and locations (Dvorak 1992). This suggests a movement away from general recommendations to more specific recommendations conditional on factors such as crop rotation, moisture availability, and time of planting. It implies that substantial increases in yield could be achieved through better management; the yield increases would exceed the increase in fertilizer application. Relaxing various supply constraints like marketing and access to credit can also help increase fertilizer use, particularly in many rainfed areas.

## FUTURE SUPPLY PROJECTIONS

With increased demand for livestock, the agricultural sector will have to produce more feed grains. Ordinarily this should induce a shift away from rice and wheat, which currently account for around 80 per cent of total cereal production, towards maize, sorghum, and millet. Direct human consumption of these coarse grains is falling in India (Singh and Morris 1997; ICRISAT and FAO 1996), while yields are rising. But the tendency during the last decade was nearly 5–7 per cent area under coarse cereals shifting to wheat and rice and oilseeds. This trend needs to be reversed.

TABLE 2: ALTERNATIVE CEREAL SUPPLY PROJECTIONS FOR 2020

(million tons)

| Scenario/projection basis | Production | Seed and waste | Available supply |
|---|---|---|---|
| 1993 Actual | 168.6 | 12.6 | 156.0 |
| Supply projection, 2020 | | | |
| Scenario 1 | | | |
| 1962/65–93 trend extrapolated (2.7 % production growth per year) | 347.1 | 26.0 | 321.1 |
| Scenario 2 | | | |
| IMPACT model (baseline) | 256.2 | 19.2 | 237.0 |
| Scenario 3 | | | |
| 1993 fertilizer use is tripled to an all-India average of 334 kg/hectare (to reach the agronomic optimum level) | 287.5 | 21.6 | 265.9 |
| Scenario 4 | | | |
| 50 % of gross cultivated area is irrigated (100 % irrigation potential is achieved) | 236.3 | 17.7 | 218.6 |
| Scenario 5 | | | |
| Fertilizer use rises to 334 kg/hectare and 50 % of gross cultivated area is irrigated (most optimistic fertilizer and irrigation scenario) | 389.6 | 29.2 | 360.4 |
| Scenario 6 | | | |
| Fertilizer use doubles to 227 kg/hectare and 41.5 % cultivated area is irrigated (half of the increased irrigation and fertilizer compared to Scenario 5) | 279.4 | 21.0 | 258.4 |
| Scenario 7 | | | |
| Fertilizer use rises 50 % to 173 kg/hectare and 41.5 % cultivated area is irrigated (25 % of the fertilizer rise and 50 % of the irrigation rise compared to Scenario 5) | 251 | 18.8 | 232.2 |
| Scenario 8 | | | |
| Scenario 7, plus genetic and technical efficiency improvements | 281 | 21.1 | 259.9 |

*Note*: According to Sarma and Gandhi (1990), the Ministry of Agriculture (GOI) deducts 5 per cent for the seed and 2.5 per cent for waste when calculating available grain production. We have therefore deducted 7.5 per cent from total production to obtain the available supply for food and feed.

## TREND PROJECTION

As mentioned earlier, the simplest method for projecting future production of cereals is to extrapolate past growth trends, which produces an estimate of 347 million tons by 2020, or more than twice the 1993 production level (Table 2). If one were to project the growth rates during 1990–1 to 1998–9, the output in 2020 comes out to be 280.3 million tons and available supply to 259.2 million tons. However, for reasons discussed above, such a projection is probably too simplistic. The gap between total production (plus net imports) and total demand is about 10 per cent in the IMPACT model results.

## IMPACT MODEL

The IMPACT by IFPRI provides cereal supply projections to 2020 for India. This model endogenously determines area under cultivation, responding to price changes but constrained by available area. According to IMPACT estimates, annual increases in area under cereals would be only 0.7 per cent, consistent with figures over the last three decades, so production growth must come from yield growth.

Both exogenous and endogenous components determine yield growth. The exogenous component is based on various assumptions about future conditions in public and private research and extension, and the spread of markets, infrastructure, and irrigation. The endogenous yield growth component is based on price response, with prices set to clear markets. The growth contribution of modern inputs such as fertilizers is accounted for in price effects in the yield response function, and as a complementary input with irrigation and with the modern varieties generated by research (Evenson and Rosegrant 1995).

The projected annual yield growth rates to 2020 are 1.53 per cent for wheat, 1.43 per cent for rice, and 1.42 per cent for all cereals. The rates for all cereals are brought down by the low rates for coarse grains. The projected growth rates would be sufficient to raise yields from 2.4 tons per hectare for wheat in 1993 to 3.6 tons per hectare in 2020, and 1.9 tons per hectare to 2.7 tons per hectare for rice. Total cereal production would grow from 168.6 million tons in 1993 to 256.2 million tons in 2020 (Table 2).

## KUMAR'S PROJECTIONS

Kumar (1998) developed a detailed econometric model of the cereal production system in India that simulates planted area, input use, and yields by cereal type. The model includes assumptions about changes in output prices, the price of fertilizer, wage rates, and trends in Total Factor Productivity (TFP) growth. He provides two supply scenarios for 2020, one with constant growth in TFP, and one with a decelerating rate of growth in TFP. In the first case, total cereal production in 2020 is estimated at 309 million tons. If growth in TFP slows down, then total production in 2020 will only be 269.9 million tons. The latter is remarkably close to the IMPACT forecast.

### EXPANDING IRRIGATION AND FERTILIZER

Another way to examine future growth is to consider the prospects for increasing output simply by extending the use of inputs that have proven successful in raising output in the past. As mentioned above, sizeable yield gaps remain between national averages and those attained on experiment stations, suggesting that existing technology can go a long way towards meeting India's growing food requirements.

As previously discussed, the main sources of growth have been irrigation, modern varieties, and fertilizer. We examined possible increases in food grain production through further expansion in the use of these inputs. In the projections under the most optimistic scenario, all remaining irrigation potential is fully utilized, and fertilizer use is raised to agronomically optimal levels in the year 2020.

The exercise requires comparing current irrigation and fertilizer levels with the ultimate potential, comparing yields with and without irrigation, and with different levels of fertilizer, and then calculating additional production if these gaps were closed. These scenarios imply that irrigated land would spread from the current level of 33 per cent of gross cropped area to 50 per cent, and that fertilizer use would rise on average from 120 kg per hectare to 334 kg per hectare. The results of this exercise are shown in Table 2 (Scenarios 3–5). If fertilizer use is tripled, cereal production would increase from the 1993 level of 168.6 million tons to 287.5 million tons in 2020 (Scenario 3). If irrigation were expanded to 50 per cent of gross cropped area, the 2020 production figure would be 236.3 million tons (Scenario 4). And if both fertilizer and irrigation were expanded to these levels, cereal production in 2020 would be 389.6 million tons (Scenario 5), or 42.5 million tons above the trend projection (Scenario 1).

It is important to note that these optimistic figures simply show what is theoretically possible given existing technology. But for reasons explained above, they are not realistic due to the high costs of completely closing the gaps in both irrigated area and fertilizer use. Accordingly, Table 2 also shows what would happen under more realistic and less optimistic assumptions about expansion of irrigation and fertilizer use. If the irrigation and fertilizer gaps are closed by 50 per cent instead of 100 per cent (Scenario 6), irrigation would spread to about 41.5 per cent of cultivated area, and average fertilizer use would rise to an all-India figure of about 227 kg per hectare (representing a doubling of current rates). This scenario assumes that the 50 per cent shortfall below the most optimistic projection is spread evenly throughout the country. Under this scenario, cereal production would increase by 110.4 million tons to a total production level of 279 million tons in 2020.

This scenario is probably still questionable. The irrigation figures may be attainable through a modest increase in irrigated area, coupled with significant improvements in irrigation efficiency. But fertilizer quantity probably remains an overestimate for the reasons given above. Under a still less optimistic projection, irrigation is assumed to increase to 41.5 per cent as under the previous scenario, but fertilizer increases by 50 per cent instead of doubling. In this case, additional cereal production would be 82 million tons, for a total production level of 251 million tons (Scenario 7), which is similar to the IMPACT projections.

## OTHER SOURCES OF GROWTH

As discussed above, modern varieties still have a role to play in increasing yields. Introduction and diffusion of the hybrid and 'super' rices mentioned earlier, combined with similar advances in wheat and other crops, could eventually lead to additional annual rice production of 10–30 million tons. Additional spread of the current generation of modern varieties will also continue to stimulate gains. Improvements in technical efficiency, principally through site-specific measures to reduce pests and raise soil fertility, will add 10–20 million tons as well. If genetic improvement and technical efficiency raise production by an additional 30 million tons, combining this with the estimates based on the spread of irrigation and fertilizer could bring total production to 281 million tons by 2020 (Scenario 8).

## EFFECTS OF NATURAL RESOURCE DEGRADATION

Several studies have estimated degraded land area in India. Sehgal and Abrol (1994), using the guidelines of the Global Assessment of Soil Degradation or GLASOD (Oldeman 1988), estimated the national figures shown in Table 3. Sehgal and Abrol relied on several sources of information, including a generalized soil map of India, remote sensing data from selected areas, and published information on forestry and soil degradation problems. Unlike other studies, they also gave a rough estimate of the effects of land degradation on crop yields (Table 4).

The data presented in Tables 3 and 4 raise at least three interesting issues. First, the area under degradation is quite large, even after adjusting the figures to cover only agricultural land. If the numbers are correct, they may help explain the low yields found in many areas of the country. Second, continued spread of degradation could have a debilitating effect on food output growth. Third, if the current level of degradation were reduced through

TABLE 3: EXTENT OF SOIL DEGRADATION SEVERITY IN INDIA

(million ha)

| Type of degradation | Severity of degradation | | | | |
|---|---|---|---|---|---|
| | Low | Medium | High | Very high | Total area |
| Water erosion | 5.0 | 24.3 | 107.2 | 12.4 | 148.9 |
| Wind erosion | | | | | |
| Loss of top soil | — | — | 6.2 | — | 6.2 |
| Loss of top soil or terrain deformation | — | — | 4.6 | — | 4.6 |
| Loss of soil due to terrain deformation or due to over-blowing | — | — | — | 2.7 | 2.7 |
| Chemical deterioration | | | | | |
| Loss of nutrients | — | — | 3.7 | — | 3.7 |
| Salinization | 2.8 | 2.0 | 5.3 | — | 10.1 |
| Physical deterioration | | | | | |
| Water logging | 6.4 | 5.2 | — | — | 11.6 |
| Total area | 14.2 | 31.5 | 127.0 | 15.1 | 187.7 |

*Source*: Sehgal and Abrol, 1994.
*Note*: – Is a nil or negligible amount.

TABLE 4: YIELD IMPLICATIONS OF SOIL DEGRADATION*

| Severity | Yield implications |
|---|---|
| Low | Negligible loss (up to 15 %), easily manageable |
| Medium | Moderate loss (15–33 %), soils can be managed at farm level |
| High | Significant loss (33–67 %), affected area not economical to cultivate, could have other uses such as agro forestry |
| Very high | Unmanageable and uneconomical to use |

*Source*: Sehgal and Abrol, 1994.
*Note*: * The rough area figures were suggested by Abrol in a personal communication.

investments to improve soil conditions, then presumably yields could rise. Shortages of land and rising food prices often provide the needed incentive for farmers to invest in their land, reversing degradation and increasing productivity (Scherr and Hazell 1994). For example, by 1986–7, 42 per cent of salt-affected land in Punjab had been reclaimed using soil amendments and other management practices (Joshi 1997), and reclamation has proceeded further since then. On rainfed lands, there is abundant evidence that farmers conserve soil, plant trees, and undertake other measures to protect natural resources where the net returns warrant them (Pender and Kerr 1996).

To consider the effects of changes in the level of degradation, we take a very simple look at what would happen to current levels of national food production if degradation levels were to either improve or deteriorate beyond the levels estimated by Sehgal and Abrol. We assume that current food production levels reflect the yield-reducing effects of degradation cited by Sehgal and Abrol, and then simulate the change in production that would be associated with a 50 per cent reduction of degradation and a 50 per cent increase in degradation on agricultural lands. This exercise is only intended to give a rough idea of the implications of changing natural resource management conditions. It is important to note that Sehgal and Abrol's estimates of the yield effects of degradation are very broad, so precision is impossible. Also, the exercise should really be done at a disaggregated level, matching local degradation conditions to crop yields to capture differences in yield effects of degradation across different types of agriculture, and then summing to the national level. But such an undertaking is beyond the scope of the present study.

The exercise is conducted separately for irrigated and rainfed lands because they are subject to different kinds of degradation problems. For example, rainfed lands are more prone to soil erosion, while irrigated lands are susceptible to salinity. In the scenario of reduced degradation, it is assumed that for each type of degradation, 50 per cent of the area affected at different levels of severity shifts to a reduced level of severity. For example, 50 per cent of the slightly affected area becomes non-degraded, 50 per cent of the 'medium' area becomes 'low', and so on. For the increasing degradation scenario, the same area of land shifts in the opposite direction. The base land area used in the calculations is the area that is subject to changes in yield as a result of degradation or improvement on different types of land. Then the percentage of production change is calculated under the full range of yield changes in Table 4.

Under the scenario of an improved land degradation situation, and assuming a 50 per cent increase in fertilizer use and that 41.5 per cent of the cropped area is irrigated, projected 2020 food production would increase by 7.2 per cent—from 251.0 million tons to 269.1 million tons (Table 5, Scenarios 7 and 12). Varying the assumptions about the impact of degradation on food production to Sehgal and Abrol's high and low points, this percentage change ranges from 4.7 per cent to 10 per cent. If the degradation situation worsens by the same magnitude, the numbers are slightly smaller because there are some degraded areas that have prospects for raised production, but no prospects for dropping any further (such as wind-blown areas of Rajasthan and waterlogged river bank areas of eastern India). The average decline in production is 6.8 per cent (with a range of 4.5–9.5 per cent), leading to a decline in total cereal production from 251 to 233.9 million tons (Table 5, Scenario 11).

These figures are constant across all the 2020 food supply projections listed in the previous section, because it was assumed that the area under irrigated and rainfed conditions is roughly constant across projections. As a result, worsening degradation reduces the range of supply projections from 250–80 million tons by about 6.8 per cent to 233–61 million tons, and reducing degradation increases the range by about 7.2 per cent to 268–300 million tons. These results are generally consistent with simulations con-

TABLE 5: ALTERNATIVE CEREAL SUPPLY PROJECTIONS FOR 2020, WITH LAND DEGRADATION

| Scenario | Projection basis | Production | Seed and waste | Available supply |
|---|---|---|---|---|
| | 1993 actual | 168.6 | 12.6 | 156.0 |
| | 1998 actual | | | |
| | Supply projection, 2020 | | | |
| 2 | IMPACT model (baseline) | 256.2 | 19.2 | 237.0 |
| 9 | With additional land degradation | 235.0 | 817.7 | 218.1 |
| 10 | With reduced land degradation | 271.0 | 20.3 | 250.7 |
| | fertilizer use rises 50 % to | 173 | | |
| | kg/hectare and 41.5 % cultivated area is irrigated | | | |
| 7 | Base calculation (Scenario 7 in Table 2) | 251.0 | 18.8 | 232.2 |
| 11 | With additional land degradation | 233.9 | 17.5 | 216.4 |
| 12 | With reduced land degradation | 269.1 | 20.2 | 248.9 |
| | plus genetic and technical efficiency improvements | | | |
| 8 | Base calculation (Scenario 8 in Table 2) | 281.0 | 21.1 | 259.9 |
| 13 | With additional land degradation | 261.7 | 19.6 | 242.1 |
| 14 | With reduced land degradation | 301.2 | 22.6 | 278.6 |

*Note*: According to Sarma and Gandhi (1990), the Ministry of Agriculture (GOI) deducts 5 per cent for the seed and 2.5 per cent for waste when calculating available grain production. We have therefore deducted 7.5 per cent from total production to obtain the available supply for food and feed. The gap between total production (plus net imports) and total demand is about 10 per cent in the IMPACT model results.

ducted with the IMPACT model (Rosegrant et al. 1995; Table 5, Scenarios 9 and 10). In this case, additional land degradation is projected to reduce cereal production by 8 per cent, from 256.2 to 235.8 million tons. Reduced degradation leads to a 5.8 per cent increase in production to 271 million tons.

## CONCLUSION AND POLICY IMPLICATIONS

By combining the demand and supply projections from previous sections, we can now assess the likely cereal gaps for India in 2020. These gaps are reported in Table 6 for some of the more important demand and supply scenarios.

TABLE 6: MATRIX OF PROJECTED CEREAL GAPS IN 2020 UNDER ALTERNATIVE DEMAND AND SUPPLY SCENARIOS

(million tons)

| Supply scenario | Total supply (net of seed and waste) | Demand (food + feed) scenario Authors' projections with per capita income growth | | |
|---|---|---|---|---|
| | | 2 % | 3.7 % | 6 % |
| Total demand | | 257.3 | 296.2 | 374.7 |
| | | (supply minus demand) | | |
| 1962/65–93 trend extrapolated | 321.1 | 63.8 | 24.9 | –53.6 |
| Reasonable increse in fertilizer and irrigation use* | 232.2 | –25.1 | 64.0 | –142.5 |
| Plus genetic and technical efficiency improvements** | 259.9 | 2.6 | –36.3 | –114.8 |
| With additional land degradation*** | 242.1 | –15.2 | –54.1 | –132.6 |

*Notes*: * Scenario 7 in Table 2. Fertilizer use increases to 173 kg/hectare and half the remaining irrigation potential is exploited.

** Scenario 8 in Table 2.

*** Scenario 14 in Table 5.

Our results show that whether India will have a manageable cereal demand in 2020 depends critically on what happens to the livestock sector. Rapid economic growth, particularly if it is accompanied by significant shifts in consumption patterns and reductions in malnutrition, could lead to escalating demands for milk, eggs and meats. These, in turn, would require changes in livestock production methods, with increasing reliance on cereals for livestock feed. A distinguishing feature of our paper is that we look beyond the bounds of past patterns of consumption behaviour and livestock feeding systems in India, and consider the possibility of significant structural shifts in these variables as the Indian economy continues to grow rapidly and modernize and as more people become exposed to a wider range of food types, including more processed foods. The per capita consumption of livestock products is currently very low by international standards, and also falls well below the standards set by the ICMR. Any significant correction of these abnormalities would quickly lead to large cereal gaps than other forecasters have estimated. Given plausible assumptions about how expenditure elasticities and livestock-feed coefficients will change over time and per capita income growth of 3.7 per cent or more p.a., India may need nearly 300 million tons of cereals by 2020. But short of significant changes in the agricultural sector, the country's production capacity is not likely to exceed 260 million tons (net of seed and waste). This implies a cereal gap (excess demand over domestic production) of 36 million tons or more per year by 2020. The cereal gap would be even larger if India were to become a 'Tiger' economy. For example, with 6 per cent growth in per capita income each year, the gap could reach 115–42 million tons by 2020. Even if the Indian economy slows down to more historical rates of growth, the cereal gap could grow to as much as 25 million tons by 2020.

These findings contrast sharply with results from several other studies, which are much more sanguine about the prospects for continued national self-sufficiency in cereals. The IMPACT model projects a market-clearing situation in which domestic production and demand are almost in balance at 237 million tons in 2020. Kumar (1998) also projects small cereal gaps for 2020. In his case, projected demand is 265.8 million tons, and production is either 286.1 or 245.9 million tons (both adjusted for seed and waste), depending on whether TFP growth continues unabated or whether it slows down. In the first case, India would have a cereal surplus of 20.3 million tons, but in the second case there would be a cereal gap of 19.9 million tons. Yet our higher figures for India involve less cereals (including feed grains) per person in 2020 than some other Asian countries are already using today.

Of course, large cereal gaps could never materialize in a market economy. There would be an inevitable upward pressure on prices, which would serve to close the gap by dampening demand, inducing new sources of supply, and encouraging more imports. Price increases would be particularly hard on the poor, and, as in the past, it is likely that the government would give continuing priority to either keeping basic food prices at acceptable levels, or targeting assistance to the needy. Either approach would help maintain cereal demand. The gaps would, therefore, have to be filled through increased domestic production or imports. Imports could take the form of rice and wheat for human consumption, livestock feeds (such as maize), or livestock products themselves.

## POLICY IMPLICATIONS

The likelihood of a rapidly growing demand for livestock products and feed grains presents an important opportunity to increase incomes and employment, and to reduce poverty in rural areas through additional investments in agricultural development. There is considerable scope for additional agricultural growth that is economically efficient, that would better exploit the country's comparative advantage, and that would contribute to the generation of rural employment and poverty alleviation. This would require additional public infrastructure investment in rural areas, which has been woefully neglected for the last two decades.

The policy reforms begun in the early 1990s tried to bring about market reforms and eliminated many of the domestic controls on commodity movement and trade. Most important, the exchange rate reforms that resulted in substantial devaluation of Indian currency led to a surge in agricultural exports. The Indian policy makers also tried to raise domestic administered support-cum-procurement prices of many of the important agricultural commodities like rice and wheat to bring these in line with the world prices with the avowed objective of turning the terms of trade in favour of the farmers. Over the years, the prices were further raised under the pressure of the kulak lobby, with the result that currently the prices of many of these commodities are higher than international prices. Besides undue rise in domestic price, another reason for international non-competitiveness is the very sharp decline in international prices of cereals, primarily because of large subsidies being given to farmers in the developed countries.

The Indian farmer is now facing the threat of cheap imports. In addition, because of declining efficiency of inputs, the profit margin of the farmers is declining very sharply. Many farmers have been squeezed between the rising costs of key inputs (as subsidies have been removed) and unsure market for their produce, because of diminishing role by the FCI.

As in the past, public investment in rural infrastructure, agricultural research and extension, and the education and health of rural people will continue to play a key role in determining the rate of agricultural growth (Fan et al. 1998). It will also require that rainfed areas receive a larger share of any additions to public investment. There is clear evidence that infrastructure investments have been biased towards irrigated areas, and this has compounded the natural advantage enjoyed by irrigated over rainfed areas (Binswanger et al. 1993). Recent evidence suggests that while in the past these investments have yielded the highest returns in irrigated areas, this has been less true in the post-Green Revolution era (Fan and Hazell 1999). In fact, the marginal returns to several infrastructure investments are now higher in many rainfed areas, and they also have a potentially greater impact on reducing rural poverty. This suggests the possibility that investment in infrastructure in rainfed areas can offer India a 'win-win' strategy for addressing productivity and poverty problems.

The Indian government undertakes large expenditure on agriculture. Besides giving large subsidies on farm inputs, particularly fertilizers, credit, water, and electricity, it used to undertake large investments in rural infrastructure. Many state governments also supplemented the efforts of the central government in undertaking expenditure on rural infrastructure. Recent data show that the public investment in infrastructure by both the central and state governments has gone down perceptibly. Although input subsidies have also gone down, expenditure on subsidies continues to be quite high. There is no doubt a need for rationalizing the subsidy on agricultural inputs and diverting it for public investment in rural infrastructure. This would no doubt make available some resources. But merely reducing input subsidies would not yield enough resources for undertaking the requisite level of investment in rural infrastructure, which has been woefully neglected for nearly two decades. An important step would be to reduce expenditure on public administration and avoid extravagant increases in salaries undertaken in the Fifth Pay Commission. Keeping in view the declining efficiency in agriculture, the real need is for substantially increasing public-sector investment in agriculture. There is also scope for reducing the cost of providing public goods in rural areas by involving: (1) the local bodies and the Panchayats to take better advantage of alternative and lower cost sources of supply of public goods; and (2) improving the efficiency of public supply institutions through improved management, more transparent procurement and operational procedures, and greater accountability to end-users (Rao and Gulati 1994; World Bank 1999).

Several of our supply-side scenarios for 2020 implicitly assume that the government will continue to invest in new technology and rural infrastructure. But a combination of greater productive investments plus more efficient and scientific use of available technology could bring about an additional 20–30 million tons of cereals by 2020. With parallel increases in livestock productivity, the projected food gaps should be manageable.

The policy alternative would be to fill the cereal gap through increased imports. The import of 36–64 million tons of cereals (or its equivalent in livestock feeds or livestock products) would place a heavy burden on the country's trade balance, and divert funds from more economically productive investments. It would also do much less to alleviate the most crucial gap of all—the growing gap in incomes, wealth, and opportunity between India's rural and urban areas.

## CURRENT CRISIS IN INDIAN AGRICULTURE

The liberalization of the Indian economy initiated during the early 1990s was launched with a view to accelerating agricultural growth by ending discrimination against agriculture and turning the terms of trade in favour of agriculture through a large, real devaluation of the currency and increase in output prices of agriculture. This policy was expected to bestow immense benefits to this sector through accelerated growth and increased exports. By the beginning of the 1990s, the *Economic Survey* was in an upbeat mood and predicting a substantial gain to India, running into billions of dollars from increased agricultural exports.

A decade after the beginning of economic liberalization, instead of experiencing an unprecedented boom in growth, the agricultural sector in India is facing some serious crises. This is reflected in a

TABLE 7: GROWTH RATES OF GDP AND PER CAPITA INCOME 1950–1 TO 1998–9

(at 1980–1 prices)

| Years | GDP | GDP agri. | Secondary | Tertiary | Per capita income |
|---|---|---|---|---|---|
| 1950–1 to 1998–9 | 4.16 | 2.61 | 5.61 | 5.15 | 1.77 |
| 1950–1 to 1990–1 | 3.77 | 2.49 | 5.49 | 4.76 | 1.41 |
| 1967–8 to 1990–1 | 4.20 | 2.80 | 5.20 | 5.20 | 1.64 |
| 1950–1 to 1964–5 | 4.00 | 2.65 | 7.73 | 4.61 | 1.69 |
| 1967–8 to 1979–80 | 3.45 | 2.10 | 4.43 | 4.49 | 1.11 |
| 1980–1 to 1990–1 | 5.46 | 3.94 | 6.86 | 6.58 | 3.01 |
| 1990–1 to 1998–9 | 6.23 | 1.95 | 7.45 | 8.24 | 4.30 |

*Source*: *Economic Survey*, various issues.

significant deceleration in the growth rate of agriculture, both in terms of gross product and in terms of output.

Thus, the growth rate of gross product from agriculture including allied sectors declined sharply from 3.2 per cent p.a. during 1980–1 to 1990–1 to only 1.93 per cent during 1990–1 to 1998–9 (Table 7).

Again, taking the output of the crop sector alone, as compared with a growth rate of 3.5 per cent p.a. during the 1980s, the growth rate of agricultural output decelerated to only 2.37 per cent p.a. during the 1990s. This was the lowest growth achieved during any period (Table 8).

Second, a more serious development during the 1990s was that the yield growth for all crops taken together decelerated from 2.65 per cent p.a. during the 1980s to 1.38 per cent p.a. during the 1990s. There was a sharp decline in the yield growth rates of wheat, rice and cotton. The growth rate of yield in rice decelerated from 3.21 to 1.27 per cent and in wheat from 3.15 to 1.58 per cent p.a. In the case of cotton, yield growth rate has gone down from 4.15 per cent p.a. during the 1980s to only 0.18 per cent during the 1990s (Table 8).

TABLE 8: ALL-INDIA COMPOUND GROWTH RATES OF AREA PRODUCTION AND YIELD OF MAJOR CROPS

| Crop | 1949–50 to 1964–5 | | | 1967–8 to 1980–1 | | | 1980–1 to 1990–1 | | | 1990–1 to 1998–9 | | |
|---|---|---|---|---|---|---|---|---|---|---|---|---|
| | Area | Prod. | Yield | Area | Prod. | Yield | Area | Prod. | Yield | Area | Prod. | Yield |
| Rice | 1.21 | 3.5 | 2.25 | 0.77 | 2.22 | 1.46 | 0.53 | 3.76 | 3.21 | 0.53 | 1.81 | 1.27 |
| Wheat | 2.69 | 3.96 | 1.27 | 2.94 | 5.65 | 2.62 | 0.51 | 3.68 | 3.15 | 1.70 | 3.30 | 1.58 |
| Coarse Ce | 0.90 | 2.25 | 1.23 | | | | | | | -2.12 | 0.18 | 2.09 |
| T. Cereals | 1.25 | 3.21 | 1.77 | 0.37 | 2.61 | 1.7 | -0.21 | 3.02 | 3.25 | 0.05 | 2.00 | 1.51 |
| T. Pulses | 1.72 | 1.41 | -0.18 | 0.44 | -0.4 | -0.67 | 0.23 | 1.87 | 1.63 | -0.14 | 0.81 | 0.55 |
| Food grain | 1.35 | 2.82 | 1.36 | 0.38 | 2.15 | 1.33 | -0.13 | 3.04 | 2.82 | 0.05 | 1.86 | 1.39 |
| Sugar cane | 3.28 | 4.26 | 0.95 | 1.78 | 2.6 | 0.8 | 1.87 | 3.27 | 1.37 | 1.37 | 2.87 | 1.23 |
| Oilseeds | 2.67 | 3.2 | 0.3 | 0.26 | 0.98 | 0.68 | 2.85 | 5.99 | 3.06 | 1.51 | 2.83 | 1.60 |
| Cotton | 2.47 | 4.55 | 2.04 | 0.07 | 2.61 | 2.54 | -0.96 | 3.15 | 4.15 | 3.25 | 3.06 | 0.18 |
| Non-food grains | 2.44 | 3.74 | 0.89 | 0.94 | 2.26 | 1.19 | 1.46 | 4.16 | 2.42 | 1.51 | 3.11 | 1.34 |
| All Crops | 1.58 | 3.15 | 1.21 | 0.51 | 2.19 | 1.28 | 0.26 | 3.46 | 2.65 | 0.37 | 2.38 | 1.37 |

*Source*: Government of India, Ministry of Agriculture, *Agricultural Statistics at a Glance*, 1999.

TABLE 9: STATE-WISE GROWTH OF AGRICULTURAL OUTPUT, 1962–5, 1970–3, 1980–3, 1993 AND 1996–9

| State | 1970–3 over 1962–5 | 1980–3 over 1970–3 | 1990–3 over 1980–3 | 1996–9 over 1990–3 |
|---|---|---|---|---|
| Haryana | 4.65 | 3.02 | 5.04 | 1.98 |
| Himachal Pradesh | 3.33 | 0.96 | 2.74 | -0.11 |
| Jammu & Kashmir | 5.37 | 3.47 | 0.17 | 0.49 |
| Punjab | 6.63 | 4.74 | 4.22 | 0.73 |
| Uttar Pradesh | 2.54 | 2.77 | 3.06 | 2.47 |
| North-West Region | 3.60 | 3.21 | 3.55 | 1.91 |
| Assam | 1.85 | 2.80 | 2.42 | 1.31 |
| Bihar | 1.12 | -0.41 | 2.12 | 3.33 |
| Orissa | 0.99 | 2.65 | 2.92 | -5.14 |
| West Bengal | 2.37 | 0.68 | 5.97 | 2.99 |
| Eastern Region | 1.57 | 1.09 | 3.63 | 1.25 |
| Gujarat | 1.78 | 3.12 | 0.86 | 6.83 |
| Madhya Pradesh | 1.97 | 1.28 | 4.53 | 3.86 |
| Maharashtra | -3.64 | 6.57 | 2.12 | 3.29 |
| Rajasthan | 4.29 | 1.26 | 6.06 | 4.90 |
| Central Region | 0.73 | 3.13 | 3.33 | 4.50 |
| Andhra Pradesh | 0.93 | 3.61 | 3.42 | 1.52 |
| Karnataka | 2.64 | 2.32 | 3.68 | 3.62 |
| Kerala | 4.09 | -0.91 | 1.92 | 3.60 |
| Tamil Nadu | 2.76 | -0.57 | 4.00 | 3.25 |
| South Region | 2.40 | 1.38 | 3.43 | 2.19 |
| All States | 2.08 | 2.38 | 3.44 | 2.83 |

*Source*: Government of India, Ministry of Agriculture, *Area and Production of Principal Crops in India*, various issues.

Third, agricultural growth has decelerated in almost all the regions in India during the 1990s. Moreover, the hitherto under-developed states in eastern and central India that had for the first time recorded notable acceleration in their growth rates during the 1980s have also experienced significant deceleration in their agricultural growth during the 1990s. In the context of food security, another serious development is that the food surplus states of Punjab and Haryana recorded a sharp decline in their growth rates during the 1990s (Table 9). The refusal of FCI to procure paddy on time during the *kharif* harvesting season of 2000 has further added to the prevalent uncertainty on the agricultural front.

The result is that the prospects of maintaining food security and meeting emerging demand from domestic production has become even more difficult than the scenario presented above in the paper. This underlines the need for giving top priority to accelerating public sector investment in rural infrastructure.

## NOTE

1. The surplus during this period is mainly due to demand contraction brought about due to very high increases given to administered prices of wheat and rice during the last few years.

# 3. Agricultural Price Policy and Food Security: Need for a New Paradigm

*V.M. Rao*

India has by now over three decades of experience in operating an agricultural price policy along with a countrywide PDS. The critical food situation which the country faced as a result of two successive years of severe drought in the mid-1960s proved to be a blessing in disguise as it triggered a major transformation in India's strategy to overcome the food problem. As is well known, independence brought in its trail severe disruptions, intensifying India's vulnerability on the food front. 'Grow More Food' campaigns and relief activities during years of scarcity have been familiar features in India's development programmes right from the beginning of planning in the early 1950s. In comparison, the policy-makers' response to the droughts of the mid-1960s was of a very different kind in terms of the ambitiousness of the target, namely, achievement of self-sufficiency in food grains and the political will and the systemic commitment with which the target was pursued. The result was spectacular: in less than a decade, food imports were dispensed with; a stable arrangement for price support to rice and wheat was put in place; food grain surpluses with the government helped in building up a PDS and in spreading it in rural areas; most important, the rapid spread of the Green Revolution demonstrated the inherent capacity of Indian agriculture to be an engine of growth and development, unlike its earlier image as a backward and stagnating part of the economy.

This paper, however, is concerned with a less pleasant theme, namely, even successful strategies sour over time and turn sick if they fail to adjust to a fast-changing world. Currently, agricultural price policy and the PDS are in the news for the wrong reasons: disregard of economic criteria in price fixation, high cost and wastage in the operations of the FCI, erosion of international competitiveness of Indian agriculture, limited impact of the PDS on the poor and its virtual absence in the hard-core poverty areas. The disease underlying these symptoms is far from difficult to diagnose. The agricultural price policy has to take note of three major ongoing processes of change. First, the era of economic reforms which began in the early 1990s makes it necessary to test the agricultural price policy against the economic criteria underlying the reforms. Second, compared to the situation that prevailed in the late 1960s, Indian agriculture has now a much broader growth base in terms of regions and crops. The strategy has to focus now on effective utilization of surpluses of food grains rather than on management of shortages. Third, the emergence of Panchayati Raj institutions as the third tier of government carrying substantive responsibility for planning and implementation of development programmes for rural areas and people is an important milestone in promoting self-help and participatory initiatives among the rural people in areas such as provision of food security to the poor.

The purpose of this paper is to provide a few glimpses of these processes with a view to bringing out the need for a thorough-going reform of agricultural price policy and the PDS. The first section describes the present status of the price policy for wheat as perceived by the Commission for Agricultural Costs and Prices (CACP). The section is based on the reports of the CACP mentioned in the section. The second section presents a brief narration of the evolution of the PDS and its linkage with the price policy. The point to be noted is that the principal consideration that has shaped the PDS is not so much provision of food security to the poor as defending, however weakly, the price policy for rice and wheat and the related operations as the only effective way to tackle the problem of food security for the country as a whole. The third section indicates briefly how the recent trends in agriculture and in decentralized governance offer an opportunity to restructure the PDS to better serve the needs of the poor. It could be argued that such restructuring would be consistent with the paradigm of liberalization, the new agricultural policy, and, above all, with the perspective of empowerment and human development which is gaining weight in the polcy making for eradication of poverty.

## PRICE POLICY FOR WHEAT

It is indeed paradoxical that the price policy for wheat which was a spectacular success in the early years of India's agricultural price policy is now like a millstone around its neck. The following sequence of phases led to this outcome. By the late 1970s, the Green Revolution lobby had already arrived on the political scene. A farm member was added to the CACP around this time. The minutes of dissent by the farm member became almost a routine part of CACP reports after the 1970s. By the late 1980s, the Green Revolution lobby had become politically dominant enough to persuade the government to review the components forming the cost of production of a commodity so that the prices recommended by the CACP met the norm of 'remunerativeness'. In the early 1990s, the CACP was reconstituted to include three full-time farm members—and there followed a phase of unprecedented increases in Minimum Support Price (MSP). The practice of announcing procurement prices for paddy and wheat was stopped, which meant that the FCI had to purchase all the grains offered by the farmers irrespective of PDS and buffer stock requirements.

It may be recalled here that the MSP was effective only for paddy and wheat in the Green Revolution areas. The MSP for other commodities were fixed more for record than for effective enforcement in the field. Hence, Table 1 gives only the MSP fixed for paddy (common) and wheat. It can be seen from Table 1 that in 4 out of 9 years in the case of paddy and 5 out of 9 years in the case of wheat, the MSP fixed by the government was higher than

TABLE 1: MSP FOR PADDY (COMMON) AND WHEAT

| Marketing year | Paddy (common) (Rs.) | Wheat (Rs.) |
|---|---|---|
| 1991–2 | 230* | 225 |
| 1992–3 | 270* | 275* |
| 1993–4 | 310 | 330* |
| 1994–5 | 340 | 350 |
| 1995–6 | 360* | 360 |
| 1996–7 | 380* | 380 |
| 1997–8 | 415 | 475* |
| 1998–9 | 440 | 510* |
| 1999–2000 | 490* | 550* |

*Source*: *Kharif* and *Rabi*, 1999–2000.

*Note*: * The price fixed by the government was higher than that recommended by the commission.

that recommended by the commission. The commission's observations in the last three reports show clearly that the commission (including, interestingly, the farmer members) are unhappy and very apprehensive about the consequences.

Referring to the bonus of Rs. 55 for wheat (over MSP of Rs. 455 fixed earlier) given in the marketing season 1997–8, it observed,

Not only were market pries at the beginning of April, 1998 comparable to the MSP fixed earlier, wheat stocks with the government were also comfortably above minimum stipulated norms as a result of imports made earlier in the year. Procurement would have been 9 to 10 million tons without bonus. The bonus this year has put the Commission in a dilemma, since this may set a precedent . . . (Commission) does feel constrained to point out that the whole economic rationale of the present system of MSP fixation could be threatened if the bonus becomes a regular feature and, in particular, if the bonus-inclusive effective procurement price in any particular year is treated as the floor for the effective procurement price in the subsequent year . . . the ratchet effect will mean that the effective determinant of future procurement prices will no longer be the cost of production of the crop, nor any other consideration in the terms of reference of the Commission, but simply the highest market price previously reached [*Rabi* 1998–9], chasing the market prices for arriving at the level of MSP is neither in the interests of the farmers nor of the economy. (*Rabi* 1997–8)

Pointing out that the world wheat prices were low and likely to decline below even MSP without bonus, the commission warns that:

Not only has India already been priced out of world markets, but also Punjab-Haryana wheat would be priced out of many consumer markets within India if free trade was allowed. . . . It must be appreciated that unless pricing operates within a rational framework, it will be difficult not only to keep food affordable for poor consumers but also to protect Indian producers from the vicissitudes of a world market dominated by rich countries which give huge subsidies to their farmers. (*Rabi* 1998–9)

Looking ahead to the long-term effects on agriculture it further observed:

The real difficulty is, however, that although ecologically unsustainable in the long-run, the wheat-rice cycle is highly remunerative in comparison with the other options currently available. And the existing system of incentives, involving subsidised fertilisers, water and electricity along with assured and remunerative markets only for rice and wheat helps to perpetuate this situation. (*Rabi* 1998–9)

The MSP for wheat for the 1999–2000 marketing season was fixed at a level which exceeded the Commission's recommendation by an unprecedented margin of 12 % (from Rs 490 per quintal to Rs 550). . . . Not only will the current MSP cover cost $C_3$ in all the major wheat growing states, it will exceed by 20 % to 40 % the cost $C_2$ in states such as Punjab, Haryana and UP which contribute to most of the procurement. When the government fixes prices different from recommended, the reasons for this may be stated. . . . Roller Flour Mills Association has informed the Commission that its members in South India are finding it cheaper to source supplies from abroad rather than to buy North Indian wheat either from private trade or through the open market scheme being implemented by the government . . . the offtake of PDS wheat (above poverty line) has virtually ceased in the Northern and Central States. (*Rabi* 1999–2000)

It may seem that the commission is quite harsh in its strictures on the government. It is necessary to mention that this reflects more the commission's worry about the consequences of sharp increases in MSP rather than lack of appreciation of the enterprising role of the Green Revolution farmer in increasing the production of food grains. A decade earlier, when increases in MSP were relatively modest, the Commission had argued:

There is no case for upward revision in the prices on account of rise in cost of production, increase in the prices of inputs or trend in market prices, yet the Commission is of the view that an upward revision in the prices is called for because the repeated pronouncements made by the government at various levels since October, 1989 accompanied by substantial increases in the administered prices of *kharif* and *rabi* crops over and above those announced earlier have raised the farmers' expectations. If administered prices are not suitably adjusted upward, their enthusiasm in sustaining the tempo of growth in farm investments and agricultural output may get adversely affected. (*Kharif* 1990–1)

The hikes in the MSP of wheat in recent years, which seem highly irrational on economic criteria, could easily be explained if one takes into account the political context and processes influencing the fixation of administered prices for wheat. Ashok Mitra, who headed the CACP in its initial years and has been a critical observer of India's agricultural scenario, describes the emerging situation thus:

In this unequal society where 65 per cent of the total arable land is concentrated in the hands of only 10 per cent of the farmers, the new agricultural strategy became the exclusive monopoly of big farmers and rich peasants. The latter constituted a powerful political lobby given their clout in the countryside, they exercised influence over a large section of the electorate. In the areas where the experiment with the high yielding varieties of seeds yielded lush dividends, the dominance of the farm lobby was therefore altogether pronounced. Very soon, pressure began to be exerted on the government that, never mind the decisions of the agricultural prices commission, procurement prices must be pushed up almost to the level of market prices. But the lobby did not even stop there . . . with ample food grains available in the areas where the new agricultural strategy succeeded beyond measure, the market price for grains tended to fall, and, in some instances, even fell below the level of the procurement price. A sensible policy in this situation would have been to purchase grains at minimum support prices. Political forces were, however, at work; the Kulak lobby would not hear of any such practice. Over the years, they bullied the government into buying grains at procurement prices that were higher than the market price as well as the minimum support price. And such procurement prices were not fixed by the agricultural prices commission, but at the initiative of the government itself. (Ashok Mitra, Starvation Amidst Plenty', Rediff web site, 23 December 2000)

The interesting point to note is that the gains of the farm lobby came not at the cost of non-agricultural/urban sectors, but at the cost of the rural poor. It is indeed quite logical that if those with political clout gain, those without it should lose! A look at the emerging situation in the PDS, which follows, is of help in seeing the flip side.

## THE PUBLIC DISTRIBUTION SYSTEM: ORIGIN AND EVOLUTION

India has had a historical past marred by devastating famines. Conquest of famines has been among the notable achievements in independent India. The post-Independence period has witnessed a rising trend in agriculture. There has been a decisive break in this respect from the pre-Independence decades during which agriculture was marked by prolonged and persistent stagnancy. As Amartya Sen has pointed out, rising agricultural production is a necessary but not a sufficient condition for eradication of famines. Complementary policy measures to reach food grains to the population in distress are as important as growth in production. India has achieved a measure of success in combining these two anti-famine strategies.

Paradoxically, while India has been able to subdue famines, its success in building up a PDS for food grains to ensure food security to the needy during the normal years has been limited. In a country of continental size like India, there would be pockets of scarcity even in a normal year. Agricultural markets cannot always be relied upon in ensuring that adequate quantities of food grains reach such pockets in time to avert distress. Further, agricultural markets are notorious for speculative operators capable of creating artificial scarcity and generating inflationary spiral in prices. Even a modest fall in production can trigger hoarding and market turbulence, developing quickly into a crisis. On the other hand, rising production often causes fall in prices to levels low enough to frustrate the very sections among the farmers adopting new technologies and investing in modern inputs to improve yields.

It is important to understand the weaknesses in our food security system and the historical process which has given rise to them. The beginning of the present food security system could be traced to the severe food crisis of the mid-1960s, which compelled the country to seek supplies from abroad on humiliating terms. The policy makers learned the bitter lesson that a country which begs for food commands no respect, much less any influence, in the comity of nations. A quick breakthrough in the production of food grains was perceived as a priority goal to be achieved by mobilizing all the resources and talents available in the country. It is enough for our purpose to note that these efforts were rewarded handsomely in the form of a Green Revolution in rice and wheat which helped the country in just about a decade to eliminate dependence on imported food grains and achieve, probably for the first time in its history, a growth rate in food grains above the rate of increase in population. It is essential to realize that the Green Revolution was made possible by the hard work and enterprise of the farmers in the Green Revolution areas. Policy support was necessary, but the crucial role was played by the producers who translated the policy support into increased production on farms.

The Green Revolution in rice and wheat provided a powerful thrust to the development of a PDS. India's earlier experiences were confined to management of food economy during periods of extreme scarcity. Organizing famine relief has been an activity with a long history, and the country has by now enough expertise to handle situations of severe drought. Hunger and migration on a mass scale—typical of famines—are now memories of the past.

The Second World War created another typical situation of scarcity, namely, cessation of imports over a prolonged period, necessitating statutory rationing in selected large urban centres. The PDS now prevailing in India has been an outcome not of scarcity, but of bountiful harvests provided by the green revolution. It may seem strange, but it is true that the problems in the present PDS arise from India's lack of experience in using food surpluses to promote development! If the logistics of acquisition, storage, transport and distribution of food grains are difficult enough in situations of scarcity, the problems become much more difficult to tackle when food grain surpluses far exceed the quantities which the PDS needs or can handle. Situations of extreme scarcity in food grains call for centralized and hierarchical organizations and arrangements, along with strict restrictions on the normal market and trade channels handling food grains. Situations of plenty, on the other hand, would need a different approach, relying on decentralized operations targeted at the poor and allowing markets to operate freely unless an emergency was apprehended. An interesting hypothesis suggested by the present PDS is that it is based on the perspective and policy tools appropriate to situations of scarcity than of plenty!

To understand this paradox, one has to take into account the political processes which have shaped and continue to shape the PDS. Particular mention needs to be made of two sets of policies which have their origin in the political processes characterizing the Green Revolution period and the later decades. First, the explicit concern with the problem of poverty and the strategy of designing an array of special programmes for the poor can be traced back to the early 1970s, which also witnessed the beginning of the Green Revolution. If the Green Revolution took care of the supply side of the PDS, the anti-poverty programmes provided the thrust from the demand side. The PDS assumed soon the status of being the centre-piece in the anti-poverty programmes. The plentiful supplies of food grains generated by the Green Revolution were matched by the ambitious target of extending the PDS to cover the entire population—both rural and urban. Further, since poverty was measured by the 'calorie' norm, it was only natural to assume that poverty could be eradicated by the simple expedient of reaching enough food grains to the poor. In the changing supply situation, it would have been more logical for the policy maker to choose a system targeted at the poor rather than one universal in coverage. Our hunch is that this did not happen, because neither the policy maker nor the elite in society who influence policies were quite convinced that the days of food scarcity were finally over for India. Even today, with food grains production crossing the mark of 200 million tons, compared to a mere 50 million tons around 1950, experts are not lacking in sounding alarm bells about the food situation ahead.

Further, it is possible to suspect that the Green Revolution itself nurtured policies which hindered the development of a broad-based PDS which India, with its continental spread, required. The Green Revolution strategy was designed to obtain a quick breakthrough in production. It concentrated on limited areas and sections of farmers who were in a position to bring about substantial increases in production in a relatively short period. These selected areas and sections of farmers were helped with a wide range of incentives: research and extension support; heavily subsidized inputs like irrigation, fertilizers, electricity and credit; remunerative prices; a virtual guarantee of purchase of marketable surplus by government agencies, thus eliminating the price and market uncertainties. The production response was spectacular, but the Green Revolution left untouched large parts of Indian agriculture which benefited little from the development programmes implemented in the Green Revolution areas. India has a rich variety of local staples suited to the varying growing conditions in different regions, as well as to diverse tastes and preferences characterizing the people in these regions. Creating favourable growth conditions across regions would have stimulated the production of local staples, providing a broader and stable foundation for the PDS besides enabling the poor farmers to become self-sufficient in their staple food grains. By the time the Green Revolution strategy reached its culmination, a strong farmer lobby emerged in the Green Revolution areas making it difficult for the policy maker to shift the focus of agricultural strategy from the Green Revolution areas to areas which had remained neglected so far and needed priority attention. Thus, the PDS could not develop beyond the stage it reached as a result of increased food grains production brought about by the Green Revolution strategy.

Indian agriculture has now reached a phase where a further breakthrough in the PDS has become imminent as well as essential. How the breakthrough might be achieved is outlined in the next section. We conclude this section by enumerating the principal features of the PDS as it stands now with brief remarks about its inadequacies.

1. The PDS now handles about 20 million tons of rice and wheat procured almost wholly from Punjab, Haryana, and western Uttar Pradesh. Neither other grains nor other areas play any role in sustaining the PDS. States like Karnataka should take note of complete absence of coarse cereals in the PDS. It is quite common in the present system for a tribal consuming local millets to be offered superfine rice at a subsidized price he cannot afford!
2. Agricultural scientists warn that the rice-wheat rotation which now feeds the PDS is extremely injurious to the fertile soils of Green Revolution areas. If the rotation is continued indefinitely, the soils may eventually lose their productivity.
3. Procurement of huge quantities of food grains from a limited area, and their storage and distribution to remote corners in the country is an inherently costly operation. When implemented by a centralized, hierarchical and bureaucratic organization, the operation provides unlimited scope for corruption, wastage and leakage.
4. Owing to the politicization of support price fixation, the burden of subsidies on the government increases, while the offtake from the system declines leading to accumulating stocks and sharply rising storage costs.
5. Despite the gigantic scale of the PDS, the poor in the country derive little benefit from the system. Hard-core poverty states like UP and Bihar remain virtually left out. Taking the country as a whole, less than a half of the poor are estimated to have access to the PDS. Even those having access get only a fraction of their needs from the PDS. Judged by the criterion of providing food security to the poor, the present PDS has to be regarded as a dismal failure.

## CONCLUSIONS: RESTRUCTURING THE PUBLIC DISTRIBUTION SYSTEM

It is best to begin by taking note of the difficult tasks involved in providing food security to the poor. We focus our discussion on the rural poor, as the present PDS has been much less effective in the rural than in the urban areas:

1. The rural poor are dispersed widely across small communities. Even within the community, some of the poor live in separate hamlets with poor connectivity. This settlement pattern makes it difficult for the development personnel and institutions to reach the rural poor. The problems get particularly serious in top-down bureaucratic organizations where the local level personnel neither have rapport with the poor, nor are they accountable to them.
2. The criterion to identify the poor (based on annual household income) allows almost everyone in the village to be reckoned as poor. While the national sample survey estimates show around a third of the population as poor, the household surveys carried out by the state governments to enumerate the poor for selection of beneficiaries for the anti-poverty programmes cover almost 80 per cent or more of the households in the village! In the process, the hard-core poor get overlooked.
3. The long chain of functionaries from the state headquarters downwards merely increases the cost of administration, without improving supervision, monitoring and implementation. It is not an accident that it is common to assess the anti-poverty programmes by indicators like expenditure incurred or number of beneficiaries covered, having no relationship with the validity of the selection procedure used to choose the beneficiaries or the benefits actually received by the poor.
4. Rice and wheat are superior cereals consumed by the richer sections in the rural areas. The PDS based on rice and wheat would be severely handicapped in focusing the supplies on the poor. A targeted PDS confined to the poor would well-nigh be impossible to organize unless it is based on local grains normally consumed by the poorer sections in the population. Leakages towards the non-poor would be minimal in the case of such grains, as they figure low in the preference scale of the non-poor. Further, the PDS based on local grains would also serve to provide incentive for their production. Few seem to realize that cheap rice and wheat—as compared to the prices of local grains—made available by the PDS could be a factor in the decline in the areas under local grains observed in recent years.

5. Even a restructured PDS by itself would not provide adequate food security to the poor. For this purpose, the PDS would need to be integrated with other anti-poverty programmes, particularly those offering employment and micro-credit. Without adequate purchasing power and timely credit, the poor would not be in a position to acquire food grains even when they have access to the PDS.

Would it be possible to restructure the PDS to enable it to meet the requirements noted above? Two major changes occurring in the rural areas since the early 1980s provide some ground for hope in this respect. These are ongoing processes of change whose pace and thrust depend on policy support. First, Indian agriculture has witnessed a fair measure of diversification and broad-based growth since the early 1980s. This is particularly noticeable in the areas which were untouched by the Green Revolution and lack the advantages of fertile soil, abundant irrigation and subsidized inputs. These areas include some regarded as the most backward, where agriculture had remained stagnant over a long period. What is remarkable about this development is that it appears to have been an outcome of farmer enterprise responding to market signals. While the Green Revolution provided a glimpse of the capabilities of Indian agriculture, the growth observed in the last two decades carries a more substantial promise of the potential of Indian agriculture for sustained growth. Interestingly, even the coarse cereals—the crops which have benefited the least from government policies or market stimulus—show rising trends in yields since the early 1980s. In the light of agricultural trends in more recent years, continuation of a PDS based on rice and wheat surpluses procured in Green Revolution areas must indeed seem quite puzzling. As regards the future, it needs to be borne in mind that production and yields are plateauing in Green Revolution areas, and other areas would have to share larger responsibility for sustained growth and technological change in agriculture. The new agricultural policy recognizes the need for a major shift in the agricultural strategy in favour of the neglected parts of Indian agriculture. However, considering the political economy of lobbies and pressure groups, the shift in strategy may neither be quick nor smooth.

The second major change having a bearing on the restructuring of the PDS is the move towards decentralized governance through the Panchayati Raj institutions. The goal of decentralized governance is to entrust the processes of agricultural and rural development to the rural people, along with matching devolution of financial resources and decision-making powers. There is a built-in provision for adequate representation of lower strata and of Scheduled Castes and women in the Panchayati Raj institutions. The poor would have an opportunity to participate in the formulation and implementation of anti-poverty programmes. The technical and administrative personnel of the Panchayati Raj institutions would be accountable to the local people. Decentralized governance would help in placing the anti-poverty programmes on a strong foundation of local participatory institutions. These institutions, in turn, would be in a position to tackle effectively the critical tasks in eradicating poverty, namely, identification of felt needs and priorities of the poor; distinguishing between different categories of poor ranging from the near-destitute to near-non-poor; effective targeting of anti-poverty programmes using the information about subcategories of the poor; continuing help, guidance and supervision of beneficiaries.

A little reflection would show that the processes of change described above provide the conditions necessary for a restructured PDS to operate. Broad-based agricultural growth would generate local surpluses of food grains on which the PDS could draw. This would mean that it would be possible to shift over from the rice and wheat surpluses procured from the Green Revolution areas to a wide range of grains procured and distributed locally. In comparison with the present PDS, the new system would be simple, transparent and cost-effective. When the PDS is administered by the Panchayati Raj institutions, there would be enough room for the beneficiaries to play an active role in the operation of the system. As these institutions would also be involved in other anti-poverty programmes, the problems of providing adequate employment to those not having enough purchasing power and meeting the credit needs of those with irregular income flows would be relatively easy to tackle. More important, the decentralized PDS administered by the Panchayati Raj institutions would be in a better position than the present system to achieve tight targeting of the benefits of the PDS on the poor. Targeting would be facilitated by the choice of local grains for distribution, and by the ability of the village-level panchayat to identify the subgroup among the poor in need of food security.

There are indications that the subgroup would be much more modest in size than the large numbers now reckoned as poor. The panchayat should face no great hurdle in establishing regular contact with this subgroup. Thus, the emerging situation could be favourable for restructuring the PDS to make it a more effective instrument for providing food security to the poor.

However, it is only fair to note that the policy support needed for restructuring the PDS could remain weak and fitful. Broad-based agricultural growth has been a policy priority for a long time without matching action. Critical programmes for afforestation, watershed development and spread of new technologies for rainfed crops receive lots of funds, but show limited enduring impact. There is no assurance at the moment that the coming years will witness a steady trend towards broad-based agricultural growth. There are indications that market forces and farmer enterprise are working in this direction but there could be shocks and interruptions unless the process is backed up by strong policy support. The story of the Panchayati Raj institutions is even more dismal. It is now almost a decade since the enactment of the constitutional amendment to make the Panchayati Raj institutions a full-fledged third tier of the government operating at the level of district and below. However, the ground-level situation in most areas continues to be the same as it was before the constitutional amendment. It would be premature to expect any major re-structuring of the PDS to take place before a firm trend towards broad-based agricultural growth and activation of Panchayati Raj institutions gets established.

The oppressive costs of maintaining the present PDS and the pressure they exert on the policy maker could be a factor favouring restructuring of the system. A recent study by the National Council of Applied Economic Research (NCAER) reports (based on *Deccan Herald*, 19 February 2001):

1. The food stocks with the government are estimated to go up from 44 million tons in November 2000 to about 60 million tons by the end of June 2001.
2. The procurement of wheat during the current marketing year was over 16 million tons, nearly 16 per cent higher than the record procurement of 14 million tons during the last year. The northern states successfully pressurized the central

government into procuring even wheat below the prescribed quality norms.

3. Procurement of rice during 1999–2000 (October to September) marketing year went up by nearly 47 per cent over that in the preceding year as a result of political pressures from Andhra Pradesh and Bihar.
4. The combined offtake of both rice and wheat from the PDS during the first seven months of the current year (April to October 2000) was about 8 million tons, nearly 22 per cent lower than the offtake in the corresponding period last year. The open market sales of wheat have remained a non-starter, as issue prices were much higher than the market prices. The possibility of rice export too is low due to price depression in international market.
5. A news item in the Government of India web site (Press Information Bureau, 23 February 2001) informs viewers that a standing committee of Parliament has recommended dumping of food grains rendered unfit for consumption owing to remaining in godowns for long periods into the sea to make room for fresh procurement of food grains!

# 4. State Intervention in Grain Markets: Implications of Liberalization for Food Security[1]

*V. Ratna Reddy*

State intervention in grain markets in India dates back to the Second World War. In order to address food scarcity and maintain price stability, the government had acquired powers to regulate production, transport, storage and distribution of any item. This was followed by the establishment of the Food grain Policy Committee in 1943 in the wake of the Bengal famine. Under conditions of scarcity, free trade may not be satisfactory in terms of maintaining price stability and fair distribution (Tyagi 1990). The legacy of state intervention in food grain markets is continuing till date despite changes in the food security scenario of the country. While food self-sufficiency and surplus in the economy make State controls redundant, continuing price and output fluctuations indicate the need for intervention. The need of the day is to alter these interventions, which were primarily meant for scarcity conditions to address the spacio-temporal price fluctuations. These fluctuations occur mainly due to the fact that our agriculture continues to be rainfall-dependent to a large extent. Low price elasticity (short-run), and demand as well as supply of food grains often result in price swings due to fluctuations in demand and supply (Jones 1998).

Further, international grain markets are dominated by a small number of countries and are hence prone to price fluctuations due to supply instability in any of these large producing countries. Therefore, State intervention in grain markets continues to be critical as long as food self-sufficiency and security continue to be our policy objectives. This is true of developing as well as developed countries, as no one wants to sacrifice their food security irrespective of their free market ideology. This is more so in the developing countries, where 50 per cent of the expenditure goes towards food among poor households. As a result, the state's role in food grain markets becomes crucial from welfare as well from the political point of view, e.g. during 1999, unprecedented rise in onion prices in India resulted in the fall of governments. These features prompt widespread state intervention in food grain markets. These interventions are meant for (1) preventing supply crises, (2) self-sufficiency, (3) cheap and stable consumer prices, (4) supporting and stabilizing producer prices, and (5) to induce structural change in the rural economy (Jones 1998). Compared to the objectives during the 1940s, the objectives of self-sufficiency and price stability have become politically very important in the recent past. Besides, interventions are being used to protect the farming community by providing remunerative prices to various commodities. These prices, along with other incentives such as subsidies are used to promote certain crops, e.g. cotton, oilseeds, etc., in order to meet the demand internally.

But the crux of the problem is the extent of the state's role and the costs involved, as the state's involvement in food grain trade and storage is proving to be costly when compared to private traders (Jha and Srinivasan 2000). Moreover, their effectiveness in achieving the policy objectives of fair prices and distribution is rather ambiguous. The idea is to identify the areas in which state intervention is required to safeguard food self-sufficiency and security. Besides, the alternative options available in this regard need to be examined. This would help us in tuning our policies to the changing scenario. This paper is an attempt in this direction. The specific objective here is to review the food market liberalization policies and the implications for food security in the Indian context. For this purpose, we draw from the experiences of other developing countries where different policy (liberalized) options are in practice, and their applicability in India.

## LIBERALIZING FOOD GRAIN MARKETS: REVIEW OF APPROACHES

Food grain market reforms can be grouped under six broad categories.[2] These include (1) regulatory reform, (2) price reform, (3) reforming market agencies, (4) subsidy policies, (5) macro/trade policy, and (6) support systems. Here, we discuss these approaches in the Indian context.

REGULATORY REFORMS

Regulatory reforms include removing constraints on the performance of marketing functions, such as primary marketing, grain movements across administrative boundaries and storage for speculation purposes, and removal of price controls. While the regulatory policies are meant to tackle scarcity conditions, they turn redundant and inefficient in surplus conditions. India has moved from being a net importer to a net exporter in recent years (Annexure: Table I). Net per capita availability of food grains has increased substantially, though there are imbalances in the composition (Annexure: Table II). While per capita availability of cereals is increasing the availability of pulses has halved during the last 35 years. On the other hand, extent of public distribution of food grains amounts to one-third of the procured grains (mainly rice and wheat), leading to a huge pile-up of foodstocks. While the minimum buffer stock norms for food security reasons remained more or less stagnant, actual stocks ballooned from 22 million tons to 45.7 million tons between January 1994 and January 2001 (Table 1).[3] This is mainly attributed to the active involvement of state's marketing agencies in the primary markets in the name of price stability as also serveral other implicit objectives for growth of agriculture. The effectiveness of these interventions becomes clear from recent experience.

TABLE 1: CENTRAL FOOD GRAIN STOCKS AND MINIMUM BUFFER STOCK NORMS

(million tons)

| Beginning of the month | Wheat | | Rice | | Total (Wheat and Rice) | |
|---|---|---|---|---|---|---|
| | Min. norm | Actual stock | Min. norm | Actual stock | Min. norm | Actual stock |
| Jan. 1994 | 7.7 | 10.8 | 7.7 | 11.2 | 15.4 | 22.0 |
| Jan. 1995 | 7.7 | 12.9 | 7.7 | 17.4 | 15.4 | 30.3 |
| Jan. 1996 | 7.7 | 13.1 | 7.7 | 15.4 | 15.4 | 28.5 |
| Jan. 1997 | 7.7 | 7.1 | 7.7 | 12.9 | 15.4 | 20.0 |
| Jan. 1998* | 7.7 | 6.8 | 7.7 | 11.5 | 15.4 | 18.3 |
| Jan. 1999* | 8.4 | 12.7 | 8.4 | 11.7 | 16.8 | 24.4 |
| Jan. 2000* | 8.4 | 17.2 | 8.4 | 14.2 | 16.8 | 31.4 |
| Jan. 2001* | 8.4 | 25.0 | 8.4 | 20.7 | 16.8 | 45.7 |

*Source*: *Economic Survey, 2000-2001.*

*Note*: * Provisional.

The recent intervention measures of the state in the primary food grains markets are rather ill-advised. These market intervention send wrong signals to the farm sector and delays its integration with the market system. More importantly, it is benefiting the trading community and the large farmers rather than protecting the small and marginal farmers for whom it is actually meant. Due to the low marketable surpluses, lack of infrastructure, etc., small and marginal farmers are selling their produce to traders at a much lower price than traders receive from the FCI. The declining rural consumer price index (while the urban consumer index is rising) is a clear indicator that farmers are not getting the support price. The poor quality of rice this year further depressed the price farmers receive from the traders. On the contrary, the FCI is forced to buy the grain at a higher price (Rs. 540 per quintal irrespective of the quality), which is the maximum price in terms of cost of cultivation.[4] This higher price is an incentive for traders to make a quick buck. In situations like this the support price should be at the minimum level, i.e. cost $C_1$ (all paid-up costs + imputed value of family labour) or $C_2$ ($C_1$ + rental value of land), rather than at the maximum level i.e. cost $C_3$ ($C_2$ + additional value of human labour based on statutory wages + 10 per cent of the first two components to account for managerial input of the farmer). For instance, $C_1$ and $C_2$ costs for paddy in Andhra Pradesh were Rs. 277 and Rs. 405 for the year 1996–7 (the latest estimates available). Even after adding the expected increase in the costs (based on the previous years), the minimum support price will be in the range of Rs. 325 ($C_1$) and Rs. 450 ($C_2$) per quintal for the current year. In addition to this, the FCI's procurement, transport and storage costs (including losses), which are double those of private traders, will further push the FCI into the red. While making such comparison, due regard is to be made to the fact that the FCI cost includes more than 1,000 km of transportation and eight to nine months of storage and serves important national goals of agricultural price policy. At the going rate of Rs. 540 per quintal, the FCI is losing a minimum of Rs. 150 and a maximum of Rs. 600 per quintal, as the acquired stocks would ultimately go waste if there was no storage capacity with the FCI. In fact, the committee on FCI suggested that 5 million tons of grain should be dumped into the sea, as it was not suitable for consumption. In the long run, these stocks may neither serve speculation purposes nor be used for free distribution. On the contrary, the storage costs are

TABLE 2: BENEFIT-COST RATIOS (CONSUMER BENEFIT/ GOVT. COST + PRODUCER COST)

| Year | Rice | Wheat |
|---|---|---|
| 1990–1 | 0.40 | 0.08 |
| 1991–2 | 0.53 | 0.27 |
| 1992–3 | 0.54 | 0.21 |
| 1993–4 | 0.41 | 0.09 |
| 1994–5 | 0.48 | 0.16 |
| 1995–6 | 0.59 | 0.16 |
| 1996–7 | 0.63 | 0.33 |
| 1997–8 | 0.62 | 0.43 |

*Source*: Jha and Srinivasan, 2000.

increasing over time and these costs are directly related to the volume of stocks (Jha and Srinivasan 2000). More importantly, benefit-cost ratios (consumer benefit/government cost + producer cost) are much below 1 for both rice and wheat, though it appears to be on the rise during the recent past (Table 2).

While the policies of State intervention in primary grain markets and maintaining stocks above the norms is still being pursued actively, restrictions on grain movements have been lifted recently as these do not serve any useful purpose in the present context of aggregate surplus. On the contrary, they resulted in cross-border price variations, damped producer prices in the producing (surplus) states, and increased consumer prices in the non-producing (deficit) states, adding to the costs of the PDS in terms of transportation costs.

## PRICE REFORM

Prices are often used to protect producers from volatility in grain markets. Prices are also used to correct bias in terms of trade against agriculture during the initial years. In India procurement prices are used to maintain price stability in grain markets. These prices are arrived at on the basis of cost of cultivation and several other specified factors rather than on demand-supply basis. Cost-based pricing becomes necessary to provide incentive to produce more. But it becomes a burden on the state when there is a glut in the market. There are some indications that this approach over the years has led to lopsided allocation of resources like land and water resulting in production inefficiencies. In the light of increasing rice and wheat prices, farmers have increased their land allocation to these crops, often bringing even marginal lands into cultivation. This has further pushed the cost of cultivation and the procurement prices up, resulting in a vicious cycle. This is mainly due to the combination of unrealistic price fixation and active participation of state agencies in the primary markets of rice and wheat. In the case of pulses, supply response to prices is not evident despite price rise, because pulse crops are poorly placed as far as technological breakthroughs are concerned and hence continue to be low-yielding (low overall profit per unit of land).

Unless price distortions are corrected and linked to demand and supply, farmers tend to misallocate their resources. In fact, some scarce resources like water are used inefficiently leading to ecological problems in the long run, such as land degradation. These policies seem to be driving the farm sector to the brink, instead of making it vibrant. Farmers are not allowed to adjust to the integration of local markets with global ones. On one hand, they are deprived of higher prices for crops like cotton, on the other, they are not allowed to adjust the cropping pattern in accordance with the markets. As a result, the potential for private initiative is depressed. Past policies might have served the purpose of increasing national food security improvement in physical and economic access to food for the masses and shift in the cropping pattern in favour of more remunarative crops, but there is a need to relax some of these interventions in the present context of surpluses.

The main objective of intervention to protect the farmers from losses is thwarted by the trading community. Traders are gaining the most from FCI interventions, as they are dumping the poor quality rice (purchased from farmers at a much lower price) with the FCI. As a result, small and marginal farmers are not receiving the remunerative prices. Another perceived benefit is self-sufficiency and food security. It is apprehended that the glut in grain markets may shift the cropping pattern away from food grains, resulting in food shortages. This appears to be imaginary, as farmers do not change their cropping pattern due to price fall in one year. This is more so in the case of food grains like paddy due to socio-cultural and physiological constraints. Farmers are attached to food grain crops (especially paddy), as they are concerned with food security at the household level. In Andhra Pradesh, a shift away from paddy would be a long-term prospect, as it is physiologically difficult to convert paddy fields to other crops in the short run. Moreover, paddy is known as the lazy man's crop, hence farmers prefer it to other remunerative crops in the short run. Therefore, unless the glut continues in coming years, it is unlikely that farmers will shift away from paddy.

These distortions can be corrected without adversely affecting the farming community or jeopardizing the food security goal. Price fixation should reflect the demand-supply situation. The state should fix the floor and ceiling prices in order to protect the producers as well as consumers in the event of exigencies of excess supply or deficit supply, instead of actively participating in the primary markets. For maintaining food stocks, the State should buy grains from the open market. This would reduce the burden on the state in terms of procurement and storage costs. It will need to be decided how this support will be extended, and whether in this scenario the price paid by the public agency would be higher or lower than MSP. More investment should go in to increasing productivity of land, which would ensure food security in the long run as well as making our agriculture competitive in the international markets.

## ROLE OF FCI

The FCI was established during the years when the country was facing acute shortage of food grains. During this period private trading was completely restricted in expectation of undue price fluctuations. The FCI continues to play the same role despite the change in situation. It continues to manage all the three operations mechanically without minding the costs and benefits, as between 1990–1 and 2000–1, the economic costs of wheat and rice have more than doubled while FCI's sales realization has remained constant (for below poverty line population) (Table 3). It is interesting to note that the increases in MSP for wheat and rice were below the Wholesale Price Index (WPI) between 1980–1 and 1991–2 (pre-reform period), the increase was higher between 1992–3 and 1999–2000 (post-reform period). On the other hand, increase in issue prices was higher than the MSP during the pre-reform period while the reverse is true in the post-reform period. Despite increasing subsidy on per unit basis, food grain offtake is continuously declining. In fact, in absolute terms the offtake has come down from 8.83 million tons in 1991–2 to 5 million tons in 1999–2000 in case of wheat, which may further decline in 2000–1.

TABLE 3: ECONOMIC COST AND CONSUMER SUBSIDY

(million tons)

| Fiscal Year | Economic costs | | FCI's/average sale realization | | Consumer subsidy | |
|---|---|---|---|---|---|---|
| | Wheat | Rice | Wheat | Rice | Wheat | Rice |
| 1991–2 | 390.79 | 497.04 | 251.68 | 365.58 | 139.11 | 131.46 |
| 1992–3 | 504.10 | 585.27 | 279.36 | 442.40 | 224.74 | 142.87 |
| 1993–4 | 532.03 | 665.10 | 355.88 | 500.42 | 176.15 | 164.68 |
| 1994–5 | 551.17 | 694.71 | 407.89 | 600.75 | 143.28 | 93.96 |
| 1995–6 | 583.95 | 762.82 | 411.94 | 613.34 | 172.01 | 149.48 |
| 1996–7 | 640.16 | 847.69 | 433.20 | 610.57 | 206.96 | 237.12 |
| 1997–8 | | | | | | |
| BPL | 786.35 | 939.33 | 250.00 | 450.00 | 536.35 | 589.33 |
| APL | | | 450.00 | 673.58 | 336.35 | 265.65 |
| 1998–9 | | | | | | |
| BPL | 797.16 | 1,026.67 | 249.57 | 401.81 | 547.59 | 624.86 |
| APL | | | 449.57 | 751.81 | 347.59 | 274.86 |
| 1999–2000 | | | | | | |
| BPL | 824.74 | 1,095.03 | 261.29 | 366.77 | 563.45 | 728.26 |
| APL | | | 693.29 | 921.77 | 131.45 | 173.26 |
| 2000–1 | | | | | | |
| (BE) | 830.00 | 1,170.00 | 415.00 | 565.00 | BPL 450.00 | 590.00 |
| | | | | | APL 415.00 | 565.00 |

*Source*: *Economic Survey, 2000–2001.*

TABLE 4: FOOD GRAIN ALLOCATION AND OFFTAKE UNDER PUBLIC DISTRIBUTION SYSTEM

(million tons)

| Year | Wheat | | Rice | |
|---|---|---|---|---|
| | Allocation | Offtake | Allocation | Offtake |
| 1991–2 | 10.30 | 8.83 | 11.36 | 10.17 |
| 1992–3 | 9.25 | 7.85 | 11.48 | 9.69 |
| 1993–4 | 9.56 | 5.91 | 12.41 | 8.87 |
| 1994–5 | 10.80 | 4.83 | 13.32 | 8.03 |
| 1995–6 | 11.31 | 5.81 | 14.62 | 9.75 |
| 1996–7 | 10.72 | 8.52 | 15.10 | 11.14 |
| 1997–8 | 10.11 | 7.08 | 12.83 | 9.90 |
| 1998–9 | 10.11 | 7.95 | 12.93 | 10.74 |
| 1999–2000 | 10.37 | 5.00 | 13.84 | 10.95 |
| 2000–1 | 7.51 | 2.72* | 10.96 | 5.75* |

*Source*: *Economic Survey, 2000–2001.*

*Note*: * April–Dec.

The ratio of offtake to allocation has declined from 85 per cent to 48 per cent in the case of wheat, and from 90 per cent to 79 per cent in the case of rice during the same period (Table 4). Therefore, the demand for food grains from public distribution is on the decline, which may be attributed to declining price differential between public and private grain markets and quality of the grains.

The indications are clear that FCI is slowly losing its importance and relevance as an effective marketing agency of the State. This is mainly due to the fact that it failed to tune itself to the changing conditions of food grain markets. In the changed circumstances, it should only concentrate on maintaining the required (minimum norm) stock grains to meet any eventuality, and act as a monitoring agency while entering the market. In order to maintain the stocks, it should buy from the market rather than buying from the producers. It should concentrate on maintaining quality stock and managing the allocation and offtake balance so that stocks do not go waste. This calls for improving the storage facilities and efficiency of the institution.

## SUBSIDY POLICIES

Food subsidies are seen as income transfers to the poor. They have also served the important role of providing price support to the farmers, economic access and grains for the vulnerable sections, and food security at national level. Targeted subsidies (to the poor alone) are expected to be cost-effective, with minimum leakage to non-target groups. Alternatives to subsidies include cash transfers and food stamps/vouchers. While cash transfers may not ensure food security at the household level (due to spending on non-food items), food stamps programme is one of the widely adopted measures. India has been thinking of adopting this approach since the early 1990s, but so far no concrete policy has been formulated in this regard. This year, some states like Andhra Pradesh are talking in terms of introducing food stamps. Since the beginning of the plan era, food grains are being distributed through the PDS/FPS at subsidized rates. Food subsidy has been rising over the years, putting pressure on the exchequer. Food subsidy accounts for 2.29 per cent of the government expenditure and 0.66 per cent of the country's GDP (GOI 2001). The earlier programme of PDS was revamped in 1997–8 in order to reduce the leakage of benefits to non-poor and make it targeted. As a result, issue prices are different for below poverty line and above poverty line population. Subsidy is higher in the former case. However, the inefficiencies of FCI reflected in rising economic costs and declining offtake haunt the food subsidy programme. Some are arguing for abandoning the PDS altogether in the light of its inefficiencies. According to them employment guarantee schemes are more cost-effective compared to PDS.

Despite all its shortcomings, the food subsidy programme in the country is viewed positively in addressing food security and poverty alleviation (Tyagi 1990; Vyas 2000). However, in the light of the changing economic scenario the subsidy programme needs to be made cost-effective and target oriented sooner rather than later. The alternative of food stamps may be introduced on an experimental basis, as it has proved to be effective elsewhere (Suryanarayana 1995). It is necessary to draw lessons from these experiments. After reviewing the programme in four countries, Suryanarayana (1995) concludes that food stamps programme may be confined to urban locales in India due to the paucity of socio-economic data. This could be a starting point, and the process of creating socio-economic data in the rural areas may be initiated in order to make it acceptable in rural areas later. Further, issue of food stamps needs to be inflation neutral, i.e. the value of the stamps should be in terms of physical quantities rather than in cash terms.

### MACRO/TRADE POLICIES

Macro/trade policies are seen as critical for food security as they determine our dependence on external economies for food. India joining the WTO and the recent lifting of Quantitative Restrictions (QR) on a number of agricultural commodities is seen as a threat to our food security. Though QR are lifted, there is no immediate threat to our agricultural products due to the imposition of high tariffs. However, these tariffs are likely to be phased out in the course of four years. The main threat is from the developed countries, where agriculture is heavily protected when compared to our agriculture, which is negatively subsidized. This uneven competition puts us in a disadvantaged position. Therefore, protection levels in these countries should be phased out in line with the phasing out of our tariff structure. In the absence of such agreement our farmers are likely to suffer in the long run. In the short run, we should make full use of the flexibility provided in the WTO to protect our farm sector.

The real threat from free trade, however, comes from countries like China, Taiwan, etc., where per unit cost of production is very low due to high yield levels compared to us. The only way to meet this competition by fair means is to enhance our productivity levels. Presently, we are having a huge gap between potential and actual yields (as much as 50 per cent in some cases). This gap can be bridged only through proper land and water management. This calls for strengthening our extension network, which is in a poor state. Food security in the long run can be attained only through productivity enhancement. The present status of self-sufficiency may not continue, if recent agricultural performance is any indicator, and during the latest year, for the first time since the Green Revolution, our agricultural growth rates have fallen below the population growth rate. If this trend continues, even the aggregate food security could be a serious problem. Therefore, macro/trade policies should be in tune with the changing agricultural situation.

Declining public investment and a shift towards private investment in agriculture is an indication of such a policy shift. However, issues of self-sufficiency and food security could be of serious concern, as private investment is resulting in a shift away from food crops. Recent Central Statistical Organization (CSO) data indicate a clear shift in favour of horticultural and floricultural crops. In the context of globalization and swelling food grain stocks, it is a welcome sign, at least to those who believe in the benefits of globalization. This is well supported by the recent glut in the food grain markets. Perpetuation of this process is no less a sort of revolution, provided the two most important policy objectives of poverty and inequalities are taken care of by the process automatically. Unfortunately, the recent indications warn us about any complacency with regard to food security. In this context, we cannot neglect the importance of biotechnology.

## SUPPORT SYSTEMS

Support systems in terms of free information flows, dissemination of technology, freeing internal trade, quality control of external trade, etc., are vital in safeguarding our food security. These systems play an important role in bridging the gap between real and potential production levels. Free and integrated information system makes farmers' cropping decisions easy. Economic data on a variety of crops need to be provided on a regular basis through a wider network of information systems. Freeing internal trade in terms of allowing futures trade in food grains would help in filling these information gaps. The extension network should be strengthened in order to have wider adoption of new technologies and cultivation practices. Unfortunately, the trend seems to be in the reverse direction, as some states (like Andhra Pradesh) have initiated programmes for privatization of the extension network, which may not be effective in the context of fragmented Indian agriculture (dominated by small and marginal farmers).

The state machinery assumes an important role as a monitoring agency once QR are removed. The quality of imported produce needs to be checked and consumers need to be educated as regards the likely impacts of such products. This is very important in a country where literacy and awareness levels are low. Even the educated urban consumers may fall prey to the charm of imported goods. It is likely that developed countries might dump low quality products in the markets of developing countries at subsidized rates. For instance, meat products from Europe, rejected elsewhere, may find their way to these countries, where consumer awareness of 'mad cow' or 'foot and mouth' diseases is marginal. Similarly, milk and milk products are often hormone-induced, which may be harmful to health.[5] Proper information in this regard could work as a deterrent to the flooding of foreign goods.

## CONCLUDING REMARKS

If the recent trends are any indication, we should not be complacent about our food security even in the medium run, as our present situation is a result of 10 successive (unprecedented) good monsoons. The drought during the last year has pulled our agricultural growth rates below population growth rates for the first time after the Green Revolution. Production of food grains has fallen from 208 million tons to 196 million tons. But this is no reason to defend the mess we have created in the food economy. The distortions created in this sector need to be addressed immediately before it gets too late. A number of countries have adopted one or more of the policies/approaches described above.

The results are mixed, at the best, mainly due to the reason of late adoption and half-hearted attempts (Jones 1998). However, the situation in India is totally different from these countries (mostly African), as most of them were facing food scarcity at the time of adopting these policies. We have passed though that state and aquired the shock absorbing capacity for taking hard decisions in the direction of an improved and sustainable food security system. In order to achieve this, our food security system should not be a burden on our budget, adding to our fiscal deficit.

There are wastages and inefficiencies in the system, which need immediate attention. Without reforming the food security system, any cut in the budget will adversely affect the poor, as targeting is not proper in the present set-up. Further, the system is biased towards cereals, specially rice and wheat, whereas pulses are totally neglected. This creates problems for the nutritional balance, which is ultimate in food security (Vyas 2000). The approach should be towards reducing these imbalances and targeting it to the really needy. For this purpose, there is need for redefining the role of state institutions like the FCI in food grain marketing. It should not operate in the primary markets. It should purchase grains at the prevailing market prices for stocking purposes. Stocks should be maintained at required levels and should be managed as per the allotment/offtake ratios. There is an urgent need to look into the reasons for the dwindling of these ratios. In this regard, the declining poverty ratios across the states should be kept in mind.

The most contested option is the opening up of grain markets to global competition. Total integration would be advantageous to our farmers in some products and disadvantageous in others. Rice is one commodity where India is not price-competitive and hence global integration will push the prices down further. However, in the long run, left to market forces, prices would stabilize and area adjustments will take place in accordance with the price responsiveness of farmers. Our buffer stocks (45 million tons) with FCI will suffice to see us through the period of the adjustment process. As a result, farmers will benefit due to the shift in the cropping pattern towards more remunerative crops as well as higher prices for their produce (like cotton) subject to the technical problem of shifting crops due to land conditions. Further, there is a possibility that some precious water will be available if the cropping pattern shifts in favour of less water-intensive (when compared to paddy) crops like floriculture, cotton, etc. However, there is one hitch in this process. While FCI stocks can guarantee food security at the national level, how do we ensure viability of agriculture in poorer regions and of the poorer (small and marginal) sections of the farming community. Neglect of the interests of these sections would jeopardize the policy objectives of self-sufficiency and food security in the long run.

For instance, in the fragile resource regions, groundwater tables are shrinking faster in the absence of public investment to replenish them, resulting in the drying up of wells. More importantly, intra-regional disparities are on the rise, as most of the small and marginal farmers in these regions are not able to invest in groundwater exploitation and hence remain outside the purview of the liberalized markets. These farmers cannot afford to grow commercial crops due to their limited access to water. For instance, in most of the arid tracts, few marginal farmers grow *rabi* crops, as they do not have water. One of the reasons for the cotton farmer's suicides in Andhra Pradesh was the indebtedness consequent to well failure. Though public investment in watershed development programmes in these regions would reduce their fragility by increasing in situ soil moisture and groundwater tables, it is unlikely to address the equity issue. For watershed development per se will not guarantee access to water to all sections of the farmers due to the capital-intensive nature of groundwater exploitation. As a result, public investment in watershed development would improve the groundwater, a common resource, for the purpose of private exploitation. In the process of liberalization it would be beneficial to large, medium and corporate farmers to acquire land. At the same time, it is rational on the part of small and marginal farmers to sell their lands as they cannot grow commercial crops for the market.

In the absence of alternative employment avenues, these farmers will add to the unemployed labour force. In the light of shifting cropping patterns and corporatization of agriculture, it is unlikely that the agricultural sector will be able to support the increased labour force. The only way to make small and marginal farms viable and profitable is by strengthening their resource base. Access to groundwater to all sections of the rural population is a necessary condition. At the policy level, water rights need to be de-linked from land rights through appropriate legislation and institutional arrangements. South Africa has done this within two years of getting independence. This would bring in equity in the distribution of the most important common pool resource. The State policies should be directed towards achieving this objective, at least in the long run. This would ensure sustainable food security. At the same time, care should be taken to see that new technologies like biotechnology will not bypass poor regions and farmers.

## NOTES

1. Here, food security is taken at the macro-level, though household-level food security is equally, if not more, important.
2. Adopted with modification from Jones (1998).
3. It may be noted that the lower offtake from PDS and stocks excceding the norms has happened in the past also. Similarly, there were also situations when stocks deflected to the levels lower than the prescribed norms.
4. The linkage between cost and minimum support price, is not direct as there are other considerations involved in fixing MSP.
5. Consumers in Europe are shifting towards organic milk, as most of the milk is found to be hormone-induced.

## ANNEXURE

TABLE I: NET AVAILABILITY, PROCUREMENT AND PUBLIC DISTRIBUTION OF FOOD GRAINS

(million tons)

| Year | Net Produc-tion of Food-grains | Net Imports | Net availab-ility of food-grains | Procure-ment | Public distribu-tion | Coln. 3 as % of coln.4 | Coln. 5 as % of coln. 2 | Coln. 6 as % of coln. 4 |
|---|---|---|---|---|---|---|---|---|
| 1 | 2 | 3 | 4 | 5 | 6 | 7 | 8 | 9 |
| 1951 | 48.1 | 4.8 | 52.4 | 3.8 | 8.0 | 9.2 | 7.9 | 15.3 |
| 1952 | 48.7 | 3.9 | 52.0 | 3.5 | 6.8 | 7.5 | 7.2 | 13.1 |
| 1953 | 54.1 | 2.0 | 56.6 | 2.1 | 4.6 | 3.5 | 3.9 | 8.1 |
| 1954 | 63.3 | 0.8 | 63.9 | 1.4 | 2.2 | 1.3 | 2.2 | 3.4 |
| 1955 | 61.9 | 0.5 | 63.2 | 1.3 | 1.6 | 0.8 | 2.1 | 2.5 |
| 1956 | 60.7 | 1.4 | 62.6 | neg. | 2.1 | 2.2 | neg. | 3.4 |
| 1957 | 63.4 | 3.6 | 66.2 | 0.3 | 3.1 | 5.4 | 0.5 | 4.7 |
| 1958 | 58.3 | 3.2 | 61.8 | 0.5 | 4.0 | 5.2 | 0.9 | 6.5 |
| 1959 | 69.0 | 3.9 | 72.3 | 1.8 | 5.2 | 5.4 | 2.6 | 7.2 |
| 1960 | 67.5 | 5.1 | 71.2 | 1.3 | 4.9 | 7.2 | 1.9 | 6.9 |
| 1961 | 72.0 | 3.5 | 75.7 | 0.5 | 4.0 | 4.6 | 0.7 | 5.3 |
| 1962 | 72.1 | 3.6 | 76.1 | 0.5 | 4.4 | 4.8 | 0.7 | 5.7 |
| 1963 | 70.3 | 4.5 | 74.8 | 0.8 | 5.2 | 6.1 | 1.1 | 6.9 |
| 1964 | 70.6 | 6.2 | 78.1 | 1.4 | 8.7 | 8.0 | 2.0 | 11.1 |
| 1965 | 78.2 | 7.4 | 84.6 | 4.0 | 10.1 | 8.8 | 5.2 | 11.9 |
| 1966 | 63.3 | 10.3 | 73.5 | 4.0 | 14.1 | 14.0 | 6.3 | 19.2 |
| 1967 | 65.0 | 8.7 | 73.9 | 4.5 | 13.2 | 11.7 | 6.9 | 17.8 |
| 1968 | 83.2 | 5.7 | 86.8 | 6.8 | 10.2 | 6.5 | 8.2 | 11.8 |
| 1969 | 82.3 | 3.8 | 85.8 | 6.4 | 9.4 | 4.5 | 7.8 | 11.0 |
| 1970 | 87.1 | 3.6 | 89.5 | 6.7 | 8.8 | 4.0 | 7.7 | 9.9 |
| 1971 | 94.9 | 2.0 | 94.3 | 8.9 | 7.8 | 2.1 | 9.3 | 8.3 |
| 1972 | 92.0 | -0.5 | 96.2 | 7.7 | 10.5 | -0.5 | 8.3 | 10.9 |
| 1973 | 84.9 | 3.6 | 88.8 | 8.4 | 11.4 | 4.0 | 9.9 | 12.8 |
| 1974 | 91.6 | 5.2 | 97.1 | 5.6 | 10.8 | 5.3 | 6.2 | 11.1 |
| 1975 | 87.4 | 7.5 | 89.3 | 9.6 | 11.3 | 8.4 | 10.5 | 12.6 |
| 1976 | 105.9 | 0.7 | 95.8 | 12.8 | 9.2 | 0.7 | 12.1 | 9.6 |
| 1977 | 97.3 | 0.1 | 99.0 | 9.9 | 11.7 | 0.1 | 10.1 | 11.8 |
| 1978 | 110.6 | -0.6 | 110.2 | 11.1 | 10.2 | -0.5 | 10.0 | 9.2 |
| 1979 | 115.4 | -0.2 | 114. | 13.8 | 11.7 | -0.2 | 12.0 | 10.2 |
| 1980 | 96.0 | -0.3 | 101.4 | 11.2 | 15.0 | -0.3 | 11.6 | 14.8 |
| 1981 | 113.4 | 0.7 | 114.3 | 13.0 | 13.0 | 0.6 | 11.4 | 11.4 |
| 1982 | 116.6 | 1.6 | 116.9 | 15.4 | 14.8 | 1.4 | 13.2 | 12.6 |
| 1983 | 113.3 | 4.1 | 114.7 | 15.6 | 16.2 | 3.5 | 13.7 | 14.2 |
| 1984 | 133.3 | 2.4 | 128.6 | 18.7 | 13.3 | 1.8 | 14.0 | 10.4 |
| 1985 | 127.4 | -0.4 | 124.3 | 20.1 | 15.8 | -0.3 | 15.8 | 12.7 |
| 1986 | 131.6 | 0.5 | 133.8 | 19.7 | 17.3 | 0.4 | 15.0 | 12.9 |
| 1987 | 125.5 | -0.2 | 134.8 | 15.7 | 18.7 | -0.1 | 12.5 | 13.8 |

(contd.)

TABLE I (contd.)

| 1 | 2 | 3 | 4 | 5 | 6 | 7 | 8 | 9 |
|---|---|---|---|---|---|---|---|---|
| 1988 | 122.8 | 3.8 | 130.8 | 14.1 | 18.6 | 2.9 | 11.5 | 14.2 |
| 1989 | 148.7 | 1.2 | 147.2 | 18.9 | 16.4 | 0.8 | 12.7 | 11.1 |
| 1990 | 149.7 | 1.3 | 144.8 | 24.0 | 16.0 | 0.9 | 15.0 | 11.0 |
| 1991 | 154.3 | -0.1 | 158.6 | 19.6 | 20.8 | neg. | 12.7 | 13.1 |
| 1992 | 147.3 | -0.4 | 148.5 | 17.9 | 18.8 | -0.3 | 12.2 | 12.7 |
| 1993 | 157.5 | 3.1 | 149.8 | 28.1 | 16.4 | 2.1 | 17.9 | 10.9 |
| 1994 | 161.2 | 1.1 | 154.8 | 26.0 | 14.0 | 0.7 ] | 16.1 | 9.1 |
| 1995 | 167.6 | -2.6 | 166.7 | 22.6 | 15.3 | -1.5 | 13.5 | 9.0 |
| 1996 | 157.9 | -3.1 | 163.3 | 19.8 | 18.3 | -1.9 | 12.5 | 11.2 |
| 1997 | 174.5 | -0.5 | 176.2 | 23.6 | 17.8 | -0.3 | 13.5 | 10.1 |
| 1998 | 168.2 | -2.0 | 159.6 | 26.3 | 18.4 | neg. | 15.6 | 11.5 |
| 1999 | 177.7 | -1.3 | 169.4 | 30.8 | 17.0 | -0.8 | 17.3 | 10.0 |
| 2000 | 180.2 | -1.0 | 170.5 | 35.5 | 12.1 | -0.6 | 19.7 | 7.1 |

*Source*: *Economic Survey, 2000–2001*.

TABLE II: NET AVAILABILITY OF CEREALS AND PULSES

(million tons)

| Year | Population (millions) | Cereals | | | | Pulses | Per capita availability per day (grams) | | |
|---|---|---|---|---|---|---|---|---|---|
| | | Net production | Net imports | Changes in govt. stocks | Net availability (coln. 3+4-5) | Net availability | Cereals | Pulses | Total |
| 1 | 2 | 3 | 4 | 5 | 6 | 7 | 8 | 9 | 10 |
| 1951 | 363.2 | 40.1 | 4.1 | 0.6 | 44.3 | 8.0 | 334.2 | 60.7 | 394.9 |
| 1952 | 369.2 | 40.7 | 3.9 | 0.6 | 44.0 | 8.0 | 325.4 | 59.1 | 384.5 |
| 1953 | 375.6 | 45.5 | 2.0 | -0.5 | 48.0 | 8.6 | 349.9 | 62.7 | 412.6 |
| 1954 | 382.4 | 53.6 | 0.8 | 0.2 | 54.2 | 9.7 | 388.1 | 69.7 | 457.8 |
| 1955 | 389.7 | 51.7 | 0.6 | -0.8 | 53.1 | 10.1 | 372.9 | 71.1 | 444.0 |
| 1956 | 397.3 | 50.4 | 1.4 | -0.6 | 52.4 | 10.2 | 360.4 | 70.3 | 430.7 |
| 1957 | 405.5 | 52.8 | 3.6 | 0.9 | 55.5 | 10.6 | 375.6 | 71.8 | 447.1 |
| 1958 | 414.0 | 49.5 | 3.2 | -0.3 | 52.9 | 8.8 | 350.3 | 58.5 | 408.6 |
| 1959 | 423.1 | 57.4 | 3.9 | 0.5 | 60.8 | 11.6 | 393.4 | 74.9 | 468.3 |
| 1960 | 432.5 | 57.1 | 5.1 | 1.4 | 60.8 | 10.4 | 384.1 | 65.5 | 449.5 |
| 1961 | 442.4 | 60.9 | 3.5 | -0.2 | 64.6 | 11.1 | 399.7 | 69.0 | 468.7 |
| 1962 | 452.2 | 61.8 | 3.6 | -0.4 | 65.8 | 10.2 | 398.9 | 62.0 | 460.9 |
| 1963 | 462.0 | 60.2 | 4.6 | neg. | 64.8 | 10.1 | 384.0 | 59.9 | 443.9 |
| 1964 | 472.1 | 61.8 | 6.3 | -1.2 | 69.3 | 8.8 | 401.0 | 51.0 | 452.0 |
| 1965 | 482.5 | 67.3 | 7.4 | 1.1 | 73.7 | 10.8 | 418.5 | 61.6 | 480.1 |
| 1966 | 493.2 | 54.8 | 10.3 | 0.1 | 64.8 | 8.7 | 359.9 | 48.2 | 408.1 |
| 1967 | 504.2 | 57.6 | 8.7 | -0.3 | 66.6 | 7.3 | 361.8 | 39.6 | 401.4 |
| 1968 | 515.4 | 72.6 | 5.7 | 2.0 | 76.2 | 10.6 | 404.1 | 56.1 | 460.2 |

(contd.)

TABLE II (contd.)

| 1 | 2 | 3 | 4 | 5 | 6 | 7 | 8 | 9 | 10 |
|---|---|---|---|---|---|---|---|---|---|
| 1969 | 527.0 | 73.1 | 3.8 | 0.5 | 76.5 | 9.1 | 397.8 | 47.3 | 445.1 |
| 1970 | 538.9 | 76.8 | 3.6 | 1.1 | 79.3 | 10.2 | 403.1 | 51.9 | 455.0 |
| 1971 | 551.3 | 84.5 | 2.0 | 2.6 | 84.0 | 10.3 | 417.6 | 51.2 | 468.8 |
| 1972 | 563.9 | 82.3 | -0.5 | -4.7 | 86.5 | 9.7 | 419.1 | 47.0 | 466.1 |
| 1973 | 576.8 | 76.2 | 3.6 | -0.3 | 80.1 | 8.7 | 380.5 | 41.1 | 421.6 |
| 1974 | 590.0 | 82.8 | 5.2 | -0.4 | 88.4 | 8.8 | 410.4 | 40.9 | 451.2 |
| 1975 | 60.35 | 78.6 | 7.5 | 5.6 | 80.6 | 8.8 | 365.8 | 39.7 | 405.5 |
| 1976 | 617.2 | 94.5 | 0.7 | 10.7 | 84.4 | 11.4 | 373.0 | 50.5 | 424.3 |
| 1977 | 631.3 | 87.3 | 0.1 | -1.6 | 89.0 | 10.0 | 386.3 | 43.3 | 429.6 |
| 1978 | 645.7 | 100.1 | -0.8 | -0.3 | 99.6 | 10.7 | 422.5 | 45.5 | 468.0 |
| 1979 | 660.3 | 104.8 | -0.3 | 0.4 | 104.1 | 10.8 | 431.8 | 44.7 | 476.5 |
| 1980 | 675.2 | 88.5 | -0.5 | -5.8 | 93.8 | 7.6 | 379.5 | 30.9 | 410.4 |
| 1981 | 688.5 | 104.1 | 0.5 | -0.2 | 104.8 | 9.4 | 417.3 | 37.5 | 454.8 |
| 1982 | 703.8 | 106.6 | 1.6 | 1.3 | 106.8 | 10.1 | 415.6 | 39.2 | 454.8 |
| 1983 | 718.9 | 103.0 | 4.1 | 2.7 | 104.4 | 10.4 | 397.8 | 39.5 | 437.3 |
| 1984 | 734.5 | 122.0 | 2.4 | 7.1 | 117.2 | 11.3 | 437.8 | 41.9 | 479.7 |
| 1985 | 750.4 | 116.9 | -0.3 | 2.7 | 118.9 | 10.5 | 415.6 | 38.4 | 454.0 |
| 1986 | 766.5 | 119.9 | -0.1 | -1.6 | 121.5 | 12.3 | 434.2 | 43.9 | 478.1 |
| 1987 | 782.7 | 115.2 | -0.4 | -9.5 | 124.4 | 10.4 | 435.4 | 36.4 | 471.8 |
| 1988 | 799.2 | 113.2 | 2.3 | -4.6 | 120.1 | 10.7 | 411.5 | 36.7 | 448.5 |
| 1989 | 815.8 | 136.6 | 0.8 | 2.6 | 134.7 | 12.5 | 452.6 | 41.9 | 494.5 |
| 1990 | 832.6 | 138.4 | neg. | 6.2 | 132.2 | 12.5 | 435.3 | 41.1 | 476.4 |
| 1991 | 851.7 | 141.9 | -0.6 | -4.4 | 145.7 | 12.9 | 468.5 | 41.6 | 510.1 |
| 1992 | 867.8 | 136.8 | -0.7 | -1.6 | 137.7 | 10.9 | 434.5 | 34.3 | 468.8 |
| 1993 | 883.9 | 145.8 | 2.6 | 10.3 | 138.1 | 11.7 | 427.9 | 36.2 | 464.1 |
| 1994 | 899.9 | 149.6 | 0.5 | 7.5 | 142.6 | 12.2 | 434.0 | 37.2 | 471.2 |
| 1995 | 922.0 | 155.3 | -3.0 | -1.7 | 154.0 | 12.7 | 457.5 | 37.8 | 495.3 |
| 1996 | 939.5 | 147.1 | -3.6 | -8.5 | 152.1 | 11.3 | 443.6 | 32.6 | 476.2 |
| 1997 | 955.2 | 162.0 | -0.6 | -1.8 | 163.2 | 13.0 | 468.2 | 37.3 | 505.5 |
| 1998 | 970.9 | 156.9 | -2.8 | 6.1 | 147.9 | 11.7 | 417.3 | 33.1 | 450.4 |
| 1999 | 986.6 | 164.7 | -1.5 | 7.0 | 158.2 | 13.2 | 433.7 | 36.7 | 470.4 |
| 2000 | 1002.1 | 168.7 | -1.0 | 8.7 | 159.1 | 11.4 | 434.8 | 31.2 | 466.0 |

*Source*: *Economic Survey, 2000–2001.*

# 5. Growth of Livestock Sector in India: Implications for Food and Nutrition Security

*Anjani Kumar and P.S. Birthal*

The concept of food security is interpreted in many ways. However, physical and economic access to food at the household level, at all times, to ensure healthy and active life is the crux of food security (Vyas 2000). If this definition of food security holds true, livestock can make a major contribution. Unfortunately in theoretical and empirical literature, food security is usually defined with reference to food grains only. This is misleading for a country like India where livestock products account for around 15 per cent of the food budget. Moreover, foods other than cereals supply 40 per cent of total food energy in the country. Exclusion of livestock is not appropriate, as livestock may contribute to food security through increased output of livestock and non-livestock products, and by income and employment generation that assures

TABLE 1: PRODUCTION AND PRODUCTIVITY OF MAJOR LIVETSOCK PRODUCTS, 1997–8

| Product | Production (million tons) | Productivity (kg/animal/annum) |
|---|---|---|
| Milk | | |
| Cow Milk | 35.51 | 1,085 |
| Buffalo milk | 35.33 | 1,341 |
| Meat | | |
| Cattle meat | 1.38 | 103 |
| Buffalo meat | 1.40 | 137 |
| Goat meat | 0.46 | 10 |
| Sheep meat | 0.22 | 12 |
| Poultry meat | 0.53 | — |
| Pig meat | 0.55 | 35 |

*Source*: *FAO Production Year Book.*

access to food. In this background, this paper examines both direct and indirect contributions of livestock to food and nutrition security. The paper specifically focuses on the growth dynamics of the livestock sector, availability of livestock food, consumption pattern, supply and demand, and the prospects of livestock growth in India.

## TRENDS IN PRODUCTION AND YIELDS

Table 1 provides the estimates of production of important livestock products. In 1997–8, India produced 71 million tons of milk, 4.54 million tons of meat, and 28.5 billion eggs. India is now the largest milk producer in the world.

### MILK

Between 1972–3 and 1997–8, cow and buffalo milk production grew at the rate of 5.2 and 4.4 per cent a year (Table 2). The productivity of cow and buffalo increased at a rate of 3.2 and 1.9 per cent, respectively and thus contributed about 61 per cent and 44 per cent to their respective output growths. Over time, the growth in production as well as in productivity has accelerated. But productivity has increased faster than the production, indicating that milk production growth is gradually becoming productivity centred. In case of cattle, acceleration in productivity growth is partly because of increase in the population of high-milk-yielding crossbreds.

Average milk yield of a crossbred in-milk cow in 1993–4 was 5.8 kg/day, which was about 3.5 times more than that of an in-milk indigenous cow (Table 3). In-milk crossbred cows comprised 14.2 per cent of the total in-milk cows and contributed 36.3 per cent to total cow milk production. Buffalo accounted for 45 per cent of total in-milk bovines and contributed 57 per cent to total milk production.

### MEAT

Total meat production in the country between 1972–3 and 1997–8 grew at a rate of 4.2 per cent a year. The growth in contributions from different species, however, varied widely. Maximum growth occurred in beef and veal output (7.1 per cent), followed by pork

TABLE 2: ANNUAL GROWTH RATES IN PRODUCTION AND YIELD OF LIVESTOCK PRODUCTS, 1972–97

(in per cent)

| Commodity | 1972–88 | | 1989–97 | | 1972–97 | |
|---|---|---|---|---|---|---|
| | Production | Yield | Production | Yield | Production | Yield |
| Milk | | | | | | |
| Cow milk | 5.19 | 3.03 (58.4) | 4.88 | 4.04 (82.8) | 5.15 | 3.16 (61.4) |
| Buffalo milk | 4.36 | 1.66 (38.1) | 4.73 | 3.82 (80.8) | 4.41 | 1.94 (44.0) |
| Meat | | | | | | |
| Beef and veal | 7.50 | -0.13 (-1.7) | 4.21 | 2.07 (49.2) | 7.08 | 0.15 (2.1) |
| Buffalo meat | 4.04 | -0.07 (-1.7) | 4.57 | 0.39 (8.5) | 4.11 | -0.01 (-0.2) |
| Mutton and lamb | 1.98 | 0.33 (16.7) | 3.86 | 3.34 (86.5) | 2.22 | 0.07 (3.2) |
| Goat meat | 2.46 | 0.62 (25.2) | 1.68 | -0.02 (-1.2) | 2.36 | 0.52 (22.0) |
| Pig meat | 6.44 | 0.13 (2.0) | 5.07 | -0.01 (-0.2) | 6.26 | 0.12 (1.9) |
| Poultry meat | 5.11 | — | 9.31 | — | 5.65 | — |
| Total meat | 4.17 | — | 4.61 | — | 4.22 | — |
| Eggs | 6.15 | — | 3.92 | — | 5.58 | — |

*Source*: Computed from data in *FAO Production Year Book*, various issues.
*Note*: Figures in parentheses indicate percentage share of yield growth in output growth.

TABLE 3: CONTRIBUTION OF CROSSBRED COWS TO MILK PRODUCTION, 1993–4

| | Indigenous cow | Crossbred cow | Buffalo |
|---|---|---|---|
| Share in milch stock (%) | 47.40 | 7.90 | 44.70 |
| Share in milk production (%) | 27.70 | 15.80 | 56.50 |
| Milk yield (kg/animal/day) | 1.69 | 5.81 | 3.65 |

*Source*: Government of India, Ministry of Agriculture, Department of Animal Husbandry and Dairying, 1999.

(6.3 per cent), poultry meat (5.6 per cent), buffalo meat (4.1 per cent), goat meat (2.4 per cent) and mutton and lamb (2.2 per cent). Growth in total meat production has accelerated slightly in recent years mainly owing to the acceleration in growth of meat from buffalo, sheep and poultry.

Growth in meat production is largely due to growth in number of animals slaughtered, as yield growth is negligible in case of almost all the species. Recent trends, however, indicate improvements in meat yield of cattle, buffalo and sheep, and a decline in meat yield of goat and pig. A number of factors are responsible for poor meat productivity and growth therein. Large animals, that is cattle and buffalo, are raised mainly for milk and provide meat as an adjunct. Animals slaughtered are of poor quality. It is only surplus buffalo males and unproductive stock of both cattle and buffalo, often old, infertile and malnourished which find their way to slaughterhouses. Stagnation in yields of small ruminants is a matter of concern. The main reason being deterioration of common grazing lands (Jodha 1991; Pasha 1991) that affects the consumption requirements of small ruminants and that of supplementary feeding. Improved nutrition and veterinary care would generally help raise meat yields in the short run. However, in the long run, genetic improvement would be a key factor in sustaining the output growth of these animals.

### EGGS

During 1972–97, egg and poultry meat production increased at a rate of 5.6 per cent a year. However, in recent years poultry meat production increased at an increasing rate, while egg production growth witnessed substantial deceleration. Genetic improvement efforts contributed substantially to faster growth of the poultry sector. About two-thirds of the total egg production in the country in 1993–4 came from improved layers that comprised 48 per cent of the total egg laying population (Table 4). The average egg yield of an improved layer is 232 eggs/annum, which is more than double the yield of an indigenous layer. Clearly, there is considerable scope for increasing egg production through substitution of indigenous layers with the improved layers.

## SOURCES OF GROWTH IN THE LIVESTOCK SECTOR

Research and development efforts have contributed significantly to gross output growth of the livestock sector. Since 1970–1 the livestock sector has been growing at a rate of about 3.6 per cent a year. And technology has contributed substantially to this (Table 3). The TFP index, a measure of contribution of technology,

TABLE 4: SHARE OF IMPROVED POULTRY IN TOTAL EGG PRODUCTION, 1993–4

| | Unit | Fowls | Ducks |
|---|---|---|---|
| Population | Thousand | | |
| Improved layers | | 65,077<br>(48.1) | 539<br>(5.1) |
| Indigenous layers | | 70,225<br>(51.9) | 9,967<br>(94.9) |
| Total | | 1,35,302<br>(100.0) | 10,506<br>(100.0) |
| Egg production | Lakh nos. | | |
| Improved layers | | 1,50,953<br>(66.3) | 1,039<br>(8.4) |
| Indigenous layers | | 76,719<br>(33.7) | 11,395<br>(91.6) |
| Total | | 2,27,672<br>(100.0) | 12,434<br>(100.0) |
| Egg yield | No./annum | | |
| Improved layers | | 232 | 193 |
| Indigenous layers | | 109 | 114 |

*Note*: Figures in parentheses are percentages of total.

has been growing at an annual rate of 1.4 per cent since 1970, while in the pre-1970s, growth in the TFP index was marginally negative. This implies that gradually technology is becoming a driving force in the growth of the livestock sector. It, may however, be noted that it is only the dairy, poultry and pig sectors that have witnessed some adoption of livestock technologies, mainly breeding technologies.

## GROWTH IN LIVESTOCK SECTOR AND FOOD SECURITY

The spectacular growth of livestock products, especially milk, meat, eggs and poultry meat has played an important role in ensuring food security in India. This is evident from the contributions of livestock products in terms of Gross Calorie Content (GCC). The GCC of live-stock output has increased by more than 4 times from 1.9 thousand billion calories in 1950–1 to 8 thousand billion calories in 1997–8. The contribution of the livestock sector to the total production of calories has also improved, especially after the 1970s

TABLE 5: GROSS CALORIE CONTENT OF LIVESTOCK OUTPUT

| Year | Total in billion calories | Per capita in calories |
|---|---|---|
| 1950–1 | 18,899 | 143 |
| 1960–1 | 22,691 | 141 |
| 1970–1 | 23,402 | 119 |
| 1980–1 | 37,028 | 147 |
| 1990–1 | 63,244 | 203 |
| 1997–8 | 80,108 | 231 |

*Source*: Satyasai and Viswanathan, 1996, *IJAE,* vol. 51, no. 4.

(Satyasai and Viswanathan 1996). As the human population increased from 36 crore in 1950–1 to around 95 crore in 1997–8, it is relevant to examine the per capita per day GCC of livestock output. It is to be noted that there was tremendous improvement in the per capita GCC provided by the livestock sector from 143 calories in 1950–1 to 231 calories in 1997–8. Considering a daily requirement of 2,400 calories for a rural adult, and 2,100 calories for an urban adult, the GCC provided by the livestock sector increased from 6 per cent in 1950–1 to around 10 per cent in 1997–8 (Table 5).

## LIVESTOCK SECTOR AND NUTRITION SECURITY

Balanced and nutritious food is a primary indicator of quality of life, human welfare and development. Livestock products are important sources of food, particularly of high quality protein, minerals, vitamins and micronutrients. The value of dietary animal protein is in excess of its proportion in diets, because it contains essential amino acids that are deficient in cereals. The intake of even a small amount of animal products corrects amino acid deficiencies in cereal based human diets, permitting more of the total protein to be utilized because animal proteins are more digestible and metabolized more efficiently than plant proteins (FAO 2000). Proteins of high biological values are mainly derived from animal sources, and these are essential for growing children, expectant and nursing mothers, the old and the infirm, and heavy manual workers. The nutrition expert group of the ICMR has recommended 300 g of protein for pre-school children, 250 g for school children (up to 18 years of age), and 200 g for adult men and women, and an additional 125 g for expectant mothers. These recommendations are for vegetarian populations. For meat-eating populations the recommended requirements range from 200 g for children to 160 g for adults. The empirical evidence at the macro-level also emphasizes the role of livestock products in human diet.

### GROWTH OF LIVESTOCK SECTOR AND EQUITY

Land and livestock are the two most important assets in rural India, thus their relative distribution influences the pattern of equity (Birthal et al. 1999). Livestock is an important source of income and employment for the small and marginal farmers and landless households. Unlike land, the distribution of livestock is much more equitable (Table 6). For instance, during 1992–3 marginal farm households that comprised 48.3 per cent of the rural households had a commensurate ownership share in populations of different livestock species. Shares of small, medium and large farm households in livestock populations of different species was more than their proportionate share in household distribution. Thus, the gains of improved livestock output are likely to be distributed more equitably than those of crop output.

## DEMAND AND SUPPLY OF LIVESTOCK PRODUCTS

### CONSUMPTION OF LIVESTOCK PRODUCTS

Despite rapid growth in production, per capita consumption of livestock products in India is very low as compared to many developed and developing countries. For example, per capita consumption of milk is about half of the level in Australia and the

TABLE 6: DISTRIBUTION OF LAND AND LIVESTOCK, 1991–2

| Size & Class of landholding | % of households | % area owned | Distribution of livestock (%) | | | | |
|---|---|---|---|---|---|---|---|
| | | | Cattle | Buffalo | Sheep and Goats | Pigs | Poultry |
| Landless | 21.8 | 0.0 | 2.4 | 2.8 | 5.1 | 7.7 | 6.4 |
| < 1.0 ha | 48.3 | 15.5 | 47.1 | 36.1 | 46.2 | 49.5 | 54.8 |
| 1.0–2.0 ha | 14.2 | 18.6 | 24.0 | 26.7 | 19.3 | 20.4 | 19.0 |
| 2.0–4.0 ha | 9.7 | 24.2 | 16.6 | 20.2 | 15.0 | 13.9 | 14.4 |
| 4.0–10.0 ha | 4.9 | 26.4 | 8.3 | 14.4 | 9.7 | 7.1 | 4.2 |
| > 10.0 ha | 1.1 | 15.3 | 1.6 | 4.8 | 4.7 | 1.0 | 1.1 |

TABLE 7: PER CAPITA ANNUAL CONSUMPTION OF LIVESTOCK PRODUCTS

| Commodity | Rural | | Urban | | All | |
|---|---|---|---|---|---|---|
| | 1987 | 1993 | 1987 | 1993 | 1987 | 1993 |
| Milk (litres) | 38.40 | 47.28 | 51.12 | 58.68 | 41.52 | 50.28 |
| Mutton and goat meat (kg) | 0.72 | 0.72 | 1.56 | 1.32 | 0.96 | 0.84 |
| Beef and buffalo meat (kg) | 0.36 | 0.48 | 0.84 | 0.72 | 0.48 | 0.60 |
| Poultry meat | 0.24 | 0.24 | 0.24 | 0.36 | 0.24 | 0.28 |
| Egg (nos.) | 6.24 | 7.68 | 17.16 | 17.76 | 8.88 | 10.32 |
| Fish (kg) | 1.92 | 2.16 | 2.04 | 2.40 | 1.92 | 2.28 |

*Source*: NSSO 50th Round, 1997.

United States. Per capita meat consumption is extremely low. This is mainly because of socio-cultural factors. Table 7 presents the annual per capita consumption of livestock products in India.

Demand for livestock products is highly income-elastic. Expenditure elasticities for milk and milk products, meat and eggs have been found to be more than unity both for rural and urban consumers indicating that sustained rise in per capita incomes will further boost demand for livestock products. At present, dairy products comprise an important component of consumer budgets. Milk and milk products have a share of 13.7 per cent and 14.1 per cent of expenditure on food in rural and urban areas respectively (Table 8). Meat accounts for 3.7 per cent of the food budget of a rural consumer and 3.2 per cent of an urban consumer. The share of egg is estimated below 1 per cent for rural as well as for urban consumers. On an average, an Indian consumer spends about one-fifth of the total food expenditure on livestock products (excluding fish).

## BEHAVIOUR OF LIVESTOCK PRODUCT PRICES

Increased output influences the prices of commodities via supply. An increase in supply of commodity brings down its price, ceteris paribus, and the reduced price facilitates better access across categories. Fig. 1 shows trends in real wholesale prices of major livestock products and by-products, during the period 1970 to 1998.

During the 1970s, milk price was characterized by fluctuations. It showed some stability during the 1980s and thereafter it started

TABLE 8: PER CAPITA MONTHLY EXPENDITURE ON LIVESTOCK PRODUCTS, 1993–4

(in Rs.)

| Commodity | Rural | Urban | All |
|---|---|---|---|
| Milk and milk products | 26.52<br>(13.67) | 36.12<br>(14.08) | 31.32<br>(13.90) |
| Mutton and goat meat | 3.07<br>(1.58) | 5.99<br>(2.33) | 4.52<br>(2.01) |
| Beef and buffalo meat | 2.12<br>(1.09) | 2.20<br>(0.86) | 2.16<br>(0.96) |
| Poultry meat | 2.04<br>(1.05) | 2.52<br>(0.98) | 2.28<br>(1.01) |
| Eggs | 1.50<br>(0.77) | 2.39<br>(0.93) | 1.95<br>(0.87) |
| Fish | 10.2<br>(5.26) | 11.99<br>(4.67) | 11.10<br>(4.92) |
| Other food | 148.55<br>(76.57) | 195.41<br>(76.15) | 171.98<br>(76.33) |
| Total food | 194.0<br>(100.0) | 256.62<br>(100.0) | 225.31<br>(100.0) |

*Source*: NSSO 50th Round, 1997.
*Note*: Figures in parentheses are percentages.

declining. A simliar trend is observed in prices of milk products, especially those of butter and ghee, though their prices during the 1990s started showing an upward trend. This is probably due to diversion of milk towards processed products such as ice creams, the demand for which is income-elastic and increasing with sustained rise in per capita incomes and urban population. Ghee and butter are essential commodities, and diverisification of milk towards products away from *ghee* and butter would make their prices rise.

Mutton price has been on a rising trend, though with slight fluctuations. This is expected because of slow growth in mutton output. On the other hand, beef price showed a declining trend from 1974–5 to 1985–6, and started increasing thereafter. Price of pork declined till 1983–4, and thereafter the trend is marred with fluctuations. Whereas, the real price of eggs has been declining steadily, the real prices of dairy, poultry and pig products have either declined or remained stable.

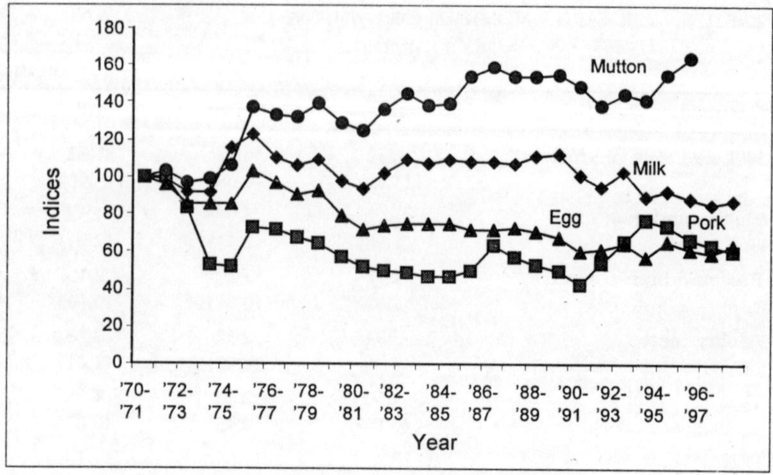


FIG. 1: TREND IN REAL WHOLESALE PRICES OF LIVESTOCK PRODUCTS, 1970–97.

DEMAND AND SUPPLY OF LIVESTOCK PRODUCTS

Two trends will shape the future demand for livestock products namely, (a) the shift from vegetarianism to diets containing meat and (b) income and price elasticity of demand for livestock products. Demand for livestock products is income-elastic and real prices too have been declining (Birthal 2000). Improvements in market efficiency, particularly in rural areas, will further facilitate this.

Sustained economic growth, rising per capita incomes and declining real prices of livestock products will boost their future demand. The demand for livestock products for 2020 as projected by Bhalla and Hazell (1998), Kumar (1998), World Bank (1996) and Dastagiri (2001) are given in Table 9.

Estimates of milk production by Bhalla and Hazell are extremely high. This is probably due to the assumptions made by them. Milk estimates by Kumar and World Bank seem to come closer to the reality, and indicate that milk demand in 2020 will be about three times more than the demand in 1993. Estimates for meat and eggs vary widely. Bhalla and Hazell estimate meat demand at about 10 million tons, while estimates of Kumar put demand for meat at 6.3 million tons. Whatsoever may be the reason for variation in estimates, demand for livestock products is expected to grow faster.

TABLE 9: DEMAND PROJECTIONS OF LIVESTOCK PRODUCTS TO 2020

| Commodity | Bhalla and Hazell (GDP growth of 5.5 %) | Kumar (GDP growth of 5 %) | World Bank (GDP growth of 5 %) | Dastagiri Actual |
|---|---|---|---|---|
| | 2020 | 2020 | 2020 | 1993 |
| Milk (million tons) | 496.28 | 142.7 | 147.21 | 46.18 |
| Mutton and goat meat (million tons) | 2.75 | | 12.72 | 0.83 |
| Beef and buffalo meat (million tons) | 3.95 | | 1.15 | 0.49 |
| Pork (million tons) | 1.79 | | — | — |
| Poultry meat (million tons) | 1.50 | | 0.81 | 0.25 |
| Eggs (million) | 7.68 | | 44.06 | 9.62 |
| Total meat | 9.99 | 6.3 | — | — |

*Note*: Bhalla and Hazell's estimates against row mutton and goat meat include sheep meat only. Dastagiri's estimates for egg are in terms of billion numbers.

Bhalla and Hazell have estimated the supply of different livestock products and argue that if current production trends (annual growth rates for milk, 5.6 per cent; eggs, 6.6 per cent; poultry meat, 6.5 per cent; and sheep and goat meat, 3.5 per cent) continue, demand for most of the products will be met from domestic production except milk. Assuming Bhalla and Hazell's growth rate in milk production and the demand estimates of Kumar and of Dastagiri, it appears that the milk demand too will be met from domestic supplies.

## PERFORMANCE OF LIVESTOCK SECTOR TRADE

The trade of livestock products has experienced significant change over the last two decades. A close perusal of the time series data revealed that we were net importers in livestock products till 1988. The scenario has changed drastically during the 1990s. This sector now holds good export potential, as its exports exceed imports significantly. A comparison of these figures in the total agricultural and the total merchandise trade brings out the fact that while the agricultural sector provided surplus foreign exchange, trade deficit

TABLE 10: PERCENTAGE SHARE (OF EXPORTS AND IMPORTS) OF TOTAL LIVESTOCK PRODUCTS IN THE EXPORTS AND IMPORTS OF TOTAL AGRICULTURAL, MERCHANDISE TRADE AND LIVESTOCK GDP

| Triennium | Exports | | | Imports | | |
|---|---|---|---|---|---|---|
| | Total agricultural exports | Total merchandise exports | Livestock GDP | Total agricultural imports | Total merchandise imports | Livestock GDP |
| 1981–2 | 3.50 | 1.02 | 0.60 | 14.27 | 1.41 | 1.44 |
| 1984–5 | 3.61 | 0.91 | 0.50 | 5.25 | 0.61 | 0.55 |
| 1987–8 | 3.42 | 0.66 | 0.37 | 5.48 | 0.51 | 0.42 |
| 1990–1 | 3.27 | 0.53 | 0.42 | 4.79 | 0.21 | 0.21 |
| 1993–4 | 3.93 | 0.54 | 0.57 | 2.98 | 0.17 | 0.20 |
| 1997–8 | 6.22 | 1.05 | 1.01 | 1.52 | 0.10 | 0.22 |

*Sources*: *FAO Trade Year Book* (relevant_issues) and *National Accounts Statistics.*

in the non-agricultural sector was the main cause for the problem of balance of payments. It is interesting to note that the share of exports from the livestock sector in the total agricultural exports increased continuously (Table 10). The ratio of livestock exports to livestock GDP has also improved from 0.6 per cent in TE 1982 to a little over 1 per cent in TE 1998. The reverse was observed in the case of livestock imports.

Export from the livestock sector has increased at an impressive growth rate of 8.43 per cent p.a. during 1980-98 (Table 11). Exports of eggs registered the highest annual growth rate (31.57 per cent)

TABLE 11: COMMODITY-WISE GROWTH RATES OF EXPORTS AND IMPORTS OF LIVESTOCK PRODUCTS

| Commodities | ACGR - Exports (%) | | ACGR - Imports (%) | |
|---|---|---|---|---|
| | 1980–90 | 1991–8 | 1980–90 | 1991–8 |
| Total merchandise exports | 8.28 | 10.22 | 5.11 | 12.37 |
| Total agricultural products | 1.03 | 13.11 | -1.99 | 24.72 |
| Total livestock products | -0.06 | 24.15 | -12.25 | 3.82 |
| Live animals | 0.86 | -16.97 | 31.16 | -20.82 |
| Meat and meat preparations | 0.10 | 25.22 | -14.09 | 25.46 |
| Dairy products | 13.07 | 7.37 | -12.78 | -1.92 |
| Eggs | -4.85 | 45.70 | 12.65 | -1.24 |
| Hides and skins | -13.85 | -12.13 | 51.73 | 13.01 |
| Animal fats | -3.57 | 49.55 | -48.04 | 5.82 |

followed by dairy product (18.44 per cent) and meat and meat preparations (9.18 per cent). The export of animal fats, which was facing negative growth during the 1980s, has witnessed the highest growth during 1990s. The import of hides and skins slowed down in the 1990s (13.01 per cent) from 51.73 per cent in the 1980s, which is attributed to the various measures taken to enhance the domestic availability of raw hides and skins to meet the growing demand of the leather industry.

## CONCLUSION AND OUTLOOK

Despite substantial growth in production, a huge untapped potential remains and the future growth in the livestock sector would be crucially dependent on generation and diffusion of technologies related to genetic enhancement, nutrition and health. In the dairy sector, there remains presently a large gap between obtainable and realized yield. During 1993–4, mean annual yield of an indigenous cattle was 618 kg, while the lactation yield on research farms for some of the important milch breeds varies from 1,137 kg to 1,931 kg. In case of crossbred cows and buffaloes the yield gap, however, is not as large as for indigenous cows. The average milk yield of a crossbred cow was 2,127 kg a year, as against the obtainable lactation yield range of 2,326 kg to 3,196 kg. Similarly in case of buffalo, the annual milk yield was 1,333 kg, while the obtainable yield varies from 1,111 kg to 1,855 kg per lactation depending on the breed. Regional gaps, however, merit more attention. In eastern and north-eastern states, yield is abysmally low. In Orissa, Nagaland, Mizoram, Meghalaya and Assam, the average milk yield of indigenous cattle ranges between one-fourth to one-half of the national average. Buffalo milk yield too is much less than the national average. These figures indicate both opportunities and severity of constraints in raising milk production in such areas.

As observed in previous paragraphs, productivity of small ruminants is abysmally low, and a major breakthrough is yet to take place. Adoption of livestock technologies has remained limited and sporadic. Only 7.5 per cent of the cattle population is of crossbreds. In case of other animal species too, the status of crossbreeding is not much different. Hardly about 5 per cent of the sheep and 15 per cent of pigs represent crossbreeds. The probable reasons could be non-acclimatization and high incidence of morbidity and mortality in crossbred animals. The success in the poultry sector, however, is notable. The share of improved poultry in total poultry population is about 34 per cent. Crossbreeding is also practised in other species—statistical information, however, is lacking.

Feed and fodder scarcity has been one of the most limiting factors in improving livestock productivity in India. Crop residues and by-products comprise the main feedstuff accounting for 40 per cent of the total feed and fodder consumption (World Bank 1996). Green fodder contributes 26 per cent, while concentrate feed contributes only 3 per cent to the total feed consumption. The rest comes from grazing. Stall-feeding is largely confined to buffalo, crossbred cattle and draught animals. Small ruminants largely feed on forage from village commons, roadsides and harvested fields, and supplementary feeding is lacking except in large commercial herds.

A large gap exists between the requirement and availability of feed and fodder at the national level. Recent estimates indicate that India is short in dry fodder by 31 per cent, green fodder by 23 per cent and concentrate feed by 47 per cent. Regional deficits, however, are more important than the national deficit. Out of 55 micro-agro-ecoregions, 43 are deficit in feed and fodder (Singh and Mazumdar 1992). Most of the deficit regions lie in the arid and semi-arid tracts. The feed and fodder deficiency is because of heavy population pressure, quantitative and qualitative deterioration in common grazing lands resulting in low biomass production for animal feed, and lack of adoption of fodder production technologies such as urea treatment of straw-urea molasses mineral blocks and bypass protein.

Disease is another constraining factor to increasing livestock production. Diseases such as rinderpest, foot-and-mouth, haemorrhagic septicaemia, mastatis, brucellosis, tuberculosis, black quarter, etc., still prevail and cause enormous economic loss. Though animal health infrastructure has witnessed uncontrolled growth during recent years, occurrence of diseases and in severe proportions is quite frequent (Birthal 2000).

The livestock sector has witnessed an impressive growth in the recent decades and has contributed positively to food and nutrition security. Increased livestock output in India has added to food security in several ways. It has enabled the livestock owners (the majority of them being marginal and small farmers) direct access to more food of livestock origin. Increased production has kept livestock product prices down or stable enabling even low-income groups access to such food. Increased domestic production has promoted exports and reduced imports.

# 6. Food Availability and Vulnerability to Natural Disasters

*Vinod K. Sharma*

Natural disasters directly impact economies, agriculture, food security, water, sanitation, the environment and health each year. Therefore, they are the greatest concerns for the affected nations. Different natural hazards cause varying levels of physical damage to infrastructure and agriculture with implications for their indirect and secondary impacts. Droughts cause heavy crop and livestock losses over wide areas of land, but typically leave infrastructure and productive capacity largely unaffected. Floods and cyclones cause extensive damage to both infrastructure and agriculture, depending on their timing relative to the agricultural cycle. However, earthquakes have little impact on standing crops (excluding localized losses) but can cause widespread devastation of infrastructure and other productive capacity over relatively large areas.

India is among the world's most disaster prone areas with high degree of vulnerability to natural hazards, resulting in unprecedented damage to sectors like agriculture and disruption of socio-economic activities. The massive damage to agricultural areas and consequent loss of production affects food security in the region, with the people belonging to lower-income groups being the hardest hit. Disruption of agricultural activities restricts employment opportunities in the rural areas. The wide gap in income potential between rural and urban areas, loss of employment opportunities and increasing poverty aggravates the food availability and its equal distribution.

## THE FOOD SITUATION IN INDIA

The *India Human Development Report* released by the NCAER in 1999 reveals some startling facts.

1. The average per capita consumption of food grains in India is 14 kg per month, which corresponds to 467 g per day. This estimate is less than the nutritional norms of intake for the rural population. Moreover, there is a wide variation across states with average per capita monthly consumption ranging from 9 kg in Kerala and 10 kg in Gujarat to 17 kg in Himachal Pradesh and Rajasthan.
2. The PDS, an income transfer programme aiming to provide food security to the masses, is found to be almost non-existent in states with high levels of poverty and under-nutrition.
3. Of children aged 0–4 years, 37 per cent have second-degree malnourishment or 'stunting'. About 29 per cent of children aged 5–12 are stunted. About 5 per cent of children aged 0–14 years suffer from wasting. Stunting and wasting are found to be insensitive to economic, occupational, landholding, and social group differences.
4. The nine districts of western Orissa, known collectively as 'KBK' (Kalahandi, Bolangir and Koraput) belt present an irony of sorts. Despite being among the biggest contributors to Food Corporation of India's Orissa pool, several poor people continue to die due to their inability to buy food.

## NATURAL DISASTERS IN INDIA

India is hit by one major natural disaster or the other almost every year wherein the loss of life is accompanied by losses of property, loss of development opportunities, etc., that cannot be clearly counted or scaled. Over a period of 10 years (1987–96), about 57 million people have been affected by natural disasters in India.

The costs of disaster are clearly inequitable, falling heaviest particularly on those belonging to the lower-income groups who have limited resources to cope and take a long time to pull out of such situations. Disasters result not only in loss of shelter but also create hardships, lack of food availability, temporary loss of livelihood and disrupt socio-economic activities. Some of the losses may be redeemable and compensated for through disaster relief and insurance. However, apart from the economic dimension, such disturbances have psychological and social dimensions as well, which need to be studied and documented. Some of the major disasters during last decade included the Latur earthquake of 1993 killing about 10,000 persons, the Andhra Pradesh cyclones of 1990 and 1996, killing about 1,000 persons each, the Gujarat cyclone of 1998 killing over 3,500 persons and the Orissa super-cyclone of 1999 killing about 10,000 persons. Besides these major events, there were smaller earthquakes in Uttarkashi, Chamoli and Jabalpur, and frequent floods in the north-east, Uttar Pradesh, Bihar and Kerala. Unfortunately, these disasters were not taken up as learning opportunities, and lessons were not drawn from them to the extent to be usable in combating future disasters. What happened in Gujarat recently and the way it was handled are grim reminders of the fact that we still need to learn and improve much.

## EARTHQUAKES

The recent earthquake that struck the state of Gujarat on 26 January 2001 created havoc for many and resulted in devastating losses. It caused heavy damage to life and property both in rural as well as the urban areas. Though the loss of life in rural areas has been less in comparison to urban areas, their economic losses are much more critical since their vulnerability is higher. This is due to their assetless and resourceless situation.

Gujarat has been reeling under severe drought conditions for more than two years now, and the rural areas especially have lost all means of earning livelihoods.

Of all the categories of affected people, the maximum severity of the situation is borne by women, children and the elderly population. It is for the woman to provide for the household needs of the family members (food, water, etc.) and with this onerous task on her shoulders she has to take on added responsibility of working in fields, looking after the cattle, etc.

Recurring drought conditions have made their lives miserable and the earthquake added on to their adversity, resulting in a critical and irreplaceable loss of assets. This loss has left the population further vulnerable to future shocks and stresses. Some of the male members have migrated to other towns and cities for want of work, with the result that the work burden on women has increased. Walking long distances in search of food and water, working in fields and also rebuilding their devastated homes, etc., has a telling effect on their health status.

### DROUGHTS

1. In India, about 68 per cent of total sown area is drought-prone.
2. Two-thirds of the country is arid, semi-arid and dry sub-humid, prone to recurrent droughts.
3. Sixteen per cent of the country's total area is drought-prone.
4. On an average, more than 50 million people are affected annually by drought conditions.
5. Drought is a perennial feature in some states of India.

Drought is a significant environmental problem as it is caused by less-than-average rainfall over a long period of time. Agricultural droughts result due to the imbalance between soil moisture and evapo-transpiration needs of a crop for a fairly long period, causing damage to the standing crop and reduction in crop yield. The imbalance may be caused by: (1) annual precipitation being less than normal; (2) late onset of monsoons; (3) early withdrawal of monsoons; and (4) long inter-dry spells in the monsoon period.

### OTHER NATURAL DISASTERS

In India, agriculture and food availability are also adversely affected by other natural hazards such as cyclones, floods and thunderstorms. The Indian Ocean is one of the six major cyclone-prone regions of the world. Every year cyclonic depressions are formed in the Arabian Sea and the Bay of Bengal. About a fourth of all cyclonic depressions formed in the Bay of Bengal become severe cyclone storms with wind speeds exceeding 47 knots. When such cyclones enter the mainland, they create havoc for agriculture, especially along the coasts where the accompanying tidal waves inundate vast tracts of agricultural land with saline water.

The north-eastern parts of India generally experience thunderstorms, severe local weather phenomena known as '*Kaal Baisakhi*'. These thunderstorms are characterized by very strong winds (reaching 200 km per hour) for a very short duration over a limited area.

### PEST ATTACKS

India has a desert area of more than two hundred thousand sq km covering the states of Rajasthan, Gujarat, Punjab and Haryana. Locust breeding occurs in one part or another of the vast desert area. Occasionally, it reaches endemic proportions and attacks vegetation and agricultural crops. Locusts caused substantial damage during the period 1926 to 1941, 1940 to 1946, 1949 to 1955 and 1959 to 1962. In recent years, India experienced a large-scale locust invasion in 1978. Again, during July 1993, the country experienced a substantially large locust invasion. The swarm persisted till October 1993; a total of 172 swarms entered the country.

### FLOODS

About 6 per cent of the country's land area (40 million ha) is prone to flooding. An average of 8.6 million hectares of land is flooded annually. Floods are caused mainly in the Ganga–Brahmaputra–Meghna basin, which carries 60 per cent of the nation's total river flow, affecting over 30 million people annually.

Floods are chiefly caused due to the peculiarities of rainfall in the country: 75 per cent of the total annual rainfall in the country is concentrated over a short monsoon season of three to four months. As a result, there is a very heavy discharge from rivers during this period, causing widespread floods.

The problem is further compounded by recurrence of different disasters in the same area. In India, most of the states experience more than one type of disaster (Table 1).

## DISASTER MITIGATION AND FOOD AVAILABILITY

Lack of food availability is among the biggest problems faced in disaster scenarios. One of the most important tasks, therefore, is to devise disaster mitigation strategies that directly address problems of food availability. Some of these strategies have been outlined here.

### LINKING FOOD RELIEF TO DEVELOPMENT IN DISASTER-PRONE AREAS

The World Food Summit declaration made in 1996 provides a common legal framework for countries to deal with natural and man-made disasters. Its commitment five states:

> We will endeavor to prevent and be prepared for natural disasters and man-made emergencies and to meet transitory and emergency food

requirements in ways that encourage recovery, rehabilitation, development and a capacity to satisfy future needs.

There is a clear recognition in the commitment of the fact that while national and international relief operations are often the only solution for hungry people facing immediate starvation, and should continue to be a priority, emergency food assistance cannot be a basis for sustainable food security. Stepped up rehabilitation and development promotion activities, which prevent recurrence of and reduce vulnerability to food emergencies, are essential elements of food security. Accordingly, steps need to be taken to ensure that emergency operations will foster the transition from relief, through recovery, to development.

The South Asia Association for Regional Cooperation (SAARC) in its first South Asian Region Report prepared following a workshop on natural disaster reduction in South Asia region in 1994 organized by the SAARC Secretariat too points out that the linkages between natural disasters and development are often

TABLE 1: NATURAL DISASTERS OCCURING IN VARIOUS STATES/UTs IN INDIA

| Name of State/UT | Drought | Flood | Cyclone | Earthquake | Total |
|---|---|---|---|---|---|
| Andhra Pradesh | * | * | * | | 3 |
| Bihar | * | * | | * | 3 |
| Gujarat | * | | * | * | 3 |
| Jammu & Kashmir | * | * | | * | 3 |
| Haryana | * | | | | 1 |
| Karnataka | * | | | | 1 |
| Madhya Pradesh | * | | | * | 2 |
| Maharashtra | * | | * | * | 3 |
| Rajasthan | * | | | | 1 |
| Orissa | * | * | * | | 3 |
| West Bengal | * | * | * | * | 4 |
| Arunachal Pradesh | | * | | * | 2 |
| Assam | | * | | * | 2 |
| Himachal Pradesh | | * | | * | 2 |
| Manipur | | * | | * | 2 |
| Nagaland | | * | | * | 2 |
| Sikkim | | * | | * | 2 |
| Meghalaya | | * | | * | 2 |
| Andaman & Nicobar | | * | * | | 2 |
| Tamil Nadu | * | | * | | 2 |
| Uttar Pradesh | * | * | | * | 3 |

*Source*: Government of India, National Centre for Disaster Management.

overlooked. Development programmes are at times designed, ignoring the impact of hazards. This has accentuated the vulnerability of the areas and the people to natural disasters. As the region is being exposed to repeated disasters, often in the same locality, there is an urgent need for dovetailing disaster reduction concerns in the national plans and for taking up specific projects focusing on disaster reduction.

Mitigation activities could include measures to prevent or moderate the potential threats from occurring, from escalating or from affecting productivity into the next season. Prevention may involve constructing or restoring rural infrastructure to limit the damage of flood water or slow the advance of desertification, for example. A physical structure such as a sea dike, gabion or small dam may prevent damage from a flood, or a shelter belt along a coastal beach could help to reduce loss from a hurricane. The use of food aid for such purposes will, of course, be appropriate only in areas where food consumption is a problem.

## FOOD SAFETY NETS AND COPING MECHANISMS

In many countries, shocks to food systems occur frequently. The main causes of these shocks are recurrent natural disasters, setbacks in the process of recovery of food price hikes as a result of economic adjustment. Food-based Safety Nets are defined as institutional arrangements that use targeted food assistance programmes to prevent poor people's access to food from temporarily falling below minimum acceptable standards.

The World Food Programme (WFP) has initiated one such intervention in Bangladesh: 'Development' Safety Net Programmes. The WFP contributes to safety net provisions in Bangladesh through two regular 'development' food aid programmes and through occasional relief food interventions in response to man-made and natural disasters. The regular programmes use food for work and for training to improve not only access to food, but at the same time promote Rural Development (RD) and Vulnerable Group Development (VGD).

RD activities such as construction, rehabilitation and maintenance of large-scale public works (including coastal embankments, drainage and irrigation canals, and rural link roads) are critical to the national disaster prevention strategy against floods and cyclones. VGD measures assist in diversifying the income base of vulnerable women and their families, thus reducing the impact of production and market risks.

Both RD and VGD have proven to be mechanisms that can be employed in response to disaster. Of these two, VGD procedures can be instituted more rapidly, as the process of selecting women beneficiaries is well understood at the lowest level of local government. The main constraint to rapid response is the quantity of grain in the government's local storage depots. In the case of RD, mechanisms for the assembly and payment of the workforce are as familiar to government and local government agencies as VGD beneficiary selection. The key constraints to RD as an immediate emergency response are climatic and soil conditions persisting after floods and cyclones, and the time required to identify useful earthworks.

### IMPROVING WARNING SYSTEMS FOR DROUGHT

The Indian Meteorology Department (IMD) has made efforts to provide a long-range forecast of monsoon rainfall. In 1988, a Parametric Power Regression Model was developed on the basis of global and regional meteorological and oceanic parameters (physically related with monsoon and rainfall) for estimating the monsoon rainfall of India. The model has been successful in estimating the correct nature of monsoons during the past few years. For instance, it has been observed that when the rainfall is less by 10 per cent of the long period average value, a large part of the country suffers from deficient rainfall. Such information can be utilized for advance drought mitigation planning.

Besides this, IMD carries out rainfall monitoring up to district level on a real time basis. All this helps in estimating the drought conditions over an area/region.

On the basis of long-range forecast of monsoon rainfall over the country, government and other agencies can take appropriate measures to minimize the effect of drought conditions.

The National Agricultural Drought Assessment and Management System (NADAMS) is being developed by the Department of Space for the Department of Agriculture and Cooperation, and is primarily based on monitoring of vegetation status through National Oceanic and Atmospheric Administration (NOAA) Advanced Very High Resolution (AVHR) data. The drought assessment is based on a comparative evaluation of satellite-observed green vegetation cover (both area and greenness) of a district in any specific time period, with that of any similar period in previous years. The comparative evaluation helps in fixing the current situation in the scale of historic agricultural situations. In 1989–91, drought assessment was intimated to drought-affected states and districts within 48–72 hours of every biweekly period by telex/telegram and printed bulletins despatched within 10 days. During 1992, the frequency of drought report was changed to monthly interval, but with more detailed assessment of seasonal conditions and integrating ground observations of rainfall and agricultural situation with satellite data. This nationwide early warning service has been found to be useful for providing first alert of drought systems.

### IMPROVING DELIVERY SYSTEMS

The most important food security policy in India today is the Public Distribution System (PDS). The PDS in India has a network of over 4.5 lakh FPS and serves about 180 million families, and is perhaps the largest such programme in the world. The system is intended to translate the macro-level self-sufficiency in food grains to micro-level by ensuring access to food and other essential items to poor families. However, the PDS has been widely criticized for its failure to reach the poor effectively, and is found to be almost non-existent in states with high levels of poverty and under-nutrition.

The challenge lies in improving the delivery system so that it is possible to target the most backward areas and vulnerable population groups. An initiative has been taken in this regard by revamping the PDS to cover in a more targeted fashion the population below the poverty line in all areas. The TPDS has now been implemented in quite a few States and Union Territories (UT). The results of this new strategy and its impact in reducing the vulnerability of the population in disaster-prone areas remains to be seen.

### DEVELOPING COPING MECHANISMS

Natural disasters are not by definition disasters. It is people's inability to cope in the face of a natural phenomenon which creates a disaster. The increase in occurrence of natural hazards due to environmental degradation has got combined with the increasing vulnerability of people (particularly the poor) settled in vulnerable locations for economic reasons, to result in sharp increase in natural disasters and damage incurred by them.

Thus, capacity building of the people themselves could prove to be critical in reducing vulnerability and improving food availability. Currently, healthy trends in rain water harvesting that are being experimented upon in many of the rainfed areas of India[1] provide hope for improving coping mechanisms among the vulnerable population groups. There is a need to replicate such mechanisms on a larger scale in disaster-prone areas.

## CONCLUSION

Food availability becomes a critical issue in almost any disaster situation. Regions suffering perennially from natural disasters such as droughts, floods and cyclones remain in need of adequate food supplies to feed the vulnerable population groups. While the importance of immediate relief in the form of emergency food assistance cannot be denied, the linkage of food relief to development in disaster-prone areas should be established to deal with the problem on a sustainable basis. Several coping strategies developed at local level could reduce dependence of the population on the vagaries of the weather and at least provide for enough to feed themselves. However, food availability and its link to overall development, particularly to livelihood, is yet to be given the boost it needs. Food safety nets provide a good example worth emulating and are a hope for removing food imbalances in the country and improving management of disasters on the whole.

## NOTE

1. Fifty km from Pune in Maharashtra is the village of Mahur, which receives on an average 500 mm of rain every year. Most of it used to run off in seasonal streams due to hilly terrain, leaving little water for irrigation. In 1971, the state government had built a minor irrigation dam in the village to store rain water, but people did not know how to make proper use of it. The villagers depended on rainfed agriculture and the village experienced recurrent droughts. The rate of out-migration used to be very high, with one member of every family living in Mumbai. But now, from an undeveloped, rocky, barren area, Mahur is showing signs of prosperity. The village is now dotted with

fields of lilies, tuberoses and other flowers, chickpeas, custard apple and maize. Cropping patterns have changed for the better; farmers now cultivate short-term seasonal crops which fetch better returns. The change in the face of Mahur village has come about through a successful experiment of water harvesting and its equitable sharing among villagers under the unique scheme of Pani Panchayat. Mr Vilas Salunkhe, the brain behind the scheme, a mechanical engineer by profession, has been instrumental in the success of this venture which was initially started by him in 1974 in Naigaon village in Purandar taluka and has been adopted in Ambegon, Meval and Phaltan talukas of Pune.

The scheme represents an excellent example of micro-watershed development, land and water management aimed at making people self-reliant. For water harvesting, a percolation tank was built and fields were lined with contour bunds. Innovative low-cost community irrigation schemes were designed and various water regeneration techniques were employed to improve production. Three 30 hp pumps were installed to draw water in the fields of members for irrigation purposes. In recognition of the fact that apart from micro-watershed development, the economic needs of the village had to be met, the scheme had a provision that each family could irrigate a maximum of 2.5 acres of land, considered sufficient for sustaining a family of five. One trained person ensured that no one was denied his share. Equal rights given to water use also resulted in more equitable land sharing. Emphasis was placed on cultivating low-water-requiring short-term cash crop. The involvement of the community in the scheme was ensured through setting up of a 'Gram Gaurav Pratisthan' which was expected to contribute 20 per cent of the cost of the project, with the balance coming from government subsidy. The scheme proved quite successful as evident by its adoption by surrounding villages. Social justice and water distribution helped villagers to cope up with the drought problem and improve agricultural production and employment.

The Pani Panchayat Model has attracted interest in other parts of the country, such as in Bihar's Palamau district and Karnataka. There is a need to incorporate principles of this scheme in the planning process so that replication is not a problem.

# 7. Drought-proofing: Exploring Wider Options

*Amita Shah*

There is a significant relationship between occurrences of droughts as well as fluctuations in agricultural production, and variations in level of poverty (Ahluwalia 1978). Unlike other natural disasters like cyclones and earthquakes, which though severe in their impact are nonetheless discrete events, droughts (dry or wet) have certain specific features such as higher frequency, larger coverage of space and people, and more crucially, a sustained adverse impact on the sources of food production, viz., land, water and vegetation. This tends to make people in drought-prone regions generally perceive droughts as an overarching reality, within which they have to shape up their coping strategy (Joshi 1999). To a large extent, the coping strategies among drought-affected people involve migration and/or severe decline in food consumption.

Over the past 50 years, droughts in India have occurred almost once in every three years, although, meteorologically, there has not been any change in the frequency of droughts over the past 100 years. Nevertheless, what is of concern is that the intensity of their impact has increased significantly over time (Mathur and Jayal 1993). This is primarily because of three reasons: (1) increased demand for water (vis-à-vis the more or less same level of precipitation); (2) low technical efficiency in water use; and (3) unequal distribution of water among households. Even though low level of precipitation is the basic cause of drought, human suffering has further been compounded due to unwise human actions leading to economic disaster.

It is well-recognized that unplanned overexploitation of natural resources and neglect of conservation measures are responsible for substantial imbalance in the ecology of drought-prone areas. There is a need to take concerted policy measures to facilitate the processes that enhance basic investment in natural resources in these regions, so that the frequency and/or intensity of droughts could be mitigated on a sustained basis.

## EXISTING PROGRAMMES FOR DROUGHT-PROOFING

The Drought Prone Area Programme (DPAP), launched by the Government of India in the early 1970s marked the beginning of a drought-proofing approach for mitigation of disaster in the event of droughts in different parts of the country. Over the years, the coverage of the programme was extended and its emphasis shifted from employment generation to asset building in the Fourth Five Year Plan, to restoration of ecological balance on a watershed basis in the Fifth Five Year Plan, and further to sustainable agricultural development, and finally to drought-proofing and control of desertification as specific objectives during the Seventh Plan. Despite the identified objective and strategies for drought-proofing in the later phases of the programme, it left ample scope for activities not directly related to drought mitigation, and the programme began to be implemented in a segmented manner without adhering to the watershed approach for area development (Ministry of Rural Development 1994). This eventually led to merging of the DPAP (and three other schemes, viz., JRY, IWDP and Desert Development Programme (DDP) with the Watershed Development Project which seeks to: (1) promote economic development of the village community; (2) encourage ecological balance; and (3) improve the conditions of resource-poor and the disadvantaged sections of the watershed community (Morae 1995). Together, these objectives should help in mitigating the adverse impact of droughts on people's livelihood. Though not stated explicitly, Watershed Development Projects (WDP) have become the major plank for drought-proofing in the large tracts of dryland regions in the country. It was recognized that significant changes in approach of project planning and implementation would be necessary for WDPs to achieve the stated objectives. Since certain environmental, structural and administrative constraints cannot be resolved within the project's framework, drought-proofing or sustainable improvement in people's economic status would need certain macro-level policies for ensuring overall ecological balance and adopting feasible options for drought-proofing, at least in the medium term.

The present paper provides a brief profile of poverty in the

TABLE 1: POVERTY—DPAP INTERFACE

| State | Total districts | Districts under DPAP | | | High and very high poverty districts | |
|---|---|---|---|---|---|---|
| | | Total | High poverty | Very high poverty | Total | DDP |
| Andhra Pradesh | 23 | 8 | — | — | — | — |
| Assam | 23 | — | — | — | 13 | — |
| Bihar | 42 | 8 | 5 | 2 | 42 | 7 |
| Gujarat | 19 | 12 | — | — | — | — |
| Haryana | 16 | 6 | — | — | — | — |
| Himachal Pradesh | 12 | — | — | — | — | — |
| Karnataka | 20 | 15 | — | — | — | — |
| Kerala | 14 | — | — | — | — | — |
| Madhya Pradesh | 45 | 11 | — | 4 | 23 | 3 |
| Maharashtra | 30 | 12 | 4 | — | 15 | 4 |
| Orissa | 13 | 4 | — | 2 | 13 | 3 |
| Punjab | 12 | — | — | — | — | — |
| Rajasthan | 27 | 17 | 3 | — | 3 | 3 |
| Tamil Nadu | 21 | 12 | 1 | — | 5 | 1 |
| Uttar Pradesh | 63 | 17 | 6 | 5 | 34 | 6 |
| West Bengal | 17 | 3 | — | — | 8 | — |
| Total | 397 | 125 | 19 | 13 | 156 | 27 |

*Source*: Centre for Monitoring Indian Economy (CMIE), *District Profiles (1993)*, Mumbai.

drought-prone regions and, discusses some policy issues pertaining to drought-proofing in these regions by drawing upon the experiences from various watershed projects in some of the dryland regions in India.

## POVERTY IN DROUGHT-PRONE REGIONS: A PROFILE

It is observed that drought-prone regions do not always coincide with high or very high incidence of poverty. For instance, only 32 out of the 125 DPAP districts have high or very high incidence of poverty. Of the 156 districts with high/very high incidence of poverty, only 27 are DDP districts (Table 1). It has been noted that for many of the poor households in these regions, poverty is acute and transient rather than chronic or perpetual (Sagar 1996).

TABLE 2: DROUGHT-PRONE DISTRICTS IN INDIA, 1993

| State/district | Relative growth of index of pop. | | Urban-ization | Liter-acy | As % of main workers | Average holding (ha) | Value of output of major crop, 5 yrs. ending (Rs./ha) | Per capita food grain prod. (kg) |
|---|---|---|---|---|---|---|---|---|
| | Index | % | | | | | | |
| Andhra Pradesh | 99.0 | 2.2 | 26.9 | 44.1 | 70.4 | 1.7 | 4,392.0 | 150.0 |
| DPAP Total | 80.9 | 4.6 | 22.5 | 42.1 | 74.1 | 2.4 | 3,376.6 | 106.3 |
| Bihar | 43.0 | 2.1 | 13.1 | 38.5 | 81.1 | 0.9 | 3,017.0 | 118.0 |
| DPAP Total | 38.1 | 2.1 | 9.3 | 40.5 | 84.3 | 1.1 | 2,948.8 | 152.4 |
| Gujarat | 114.0 | 1.9 | 34.5 | 61.3 | 59.3 | 3.3 | 2,446.0 | 77.0 |
| DPAP Total | 99.8 | 1.8 | 30.5 | 58.4 | 62.0 | 4.2 | 2,193.7 | 81.6 |
| Haryana | 136.0 | 2.4 | 24.6 | 55.8 | 58.7 | 2.8 | 4,564.0 | 474.0 |
| DPAP Total | 118.4 | 2.1 | 17.9 | 56.6 | 61.6 | 2.8 | 4,086.2 | 396.8 |
| Karnataka | 117.0 | 1.9 | 30.9 | 56.0 | 66.7 | 2.4 | 3,495.0 | 146.0 |
| DPAP Total | 91.5 | 1.8 | 22.7 | 50.4 | 75.7 | 2.5 | 3,798.2 | 162.9 |
| Madhya Pradesh | 73.0 | 2.4 | 23.2 | 44.2 | 76.6 | 2.9 | 2,170.0 | 208.0 |
| DPAP Total | 66.5 | 2.6 | 6.0 | 38.3 | 80.5 | 3.8 | 2,164.7 | 192.8 |
| Maharashtra | 164.0 | 2.3 | 38.7 | 64.9 | 61.1 | 2.6 | 2,202.0 | 115.01 |
| DPAP Total | 83.0 | 2.4 | 24.8 | 58.6 | 72.8 | 2.8 | 2,112.2 | 40.7 |
| Orissa | 63.0 | 1.8 | 13.4 | 49.1 | 74.9 | 1.5 | 2,425.0 | 162.0 |
| DPAP Total | 61.3 | 1.7 | 9.8 | 39.5 | 81.5 | 1.8 | 2,551.3 | 199.5 |
| Rajasthan | 69.0 | 2.5 | 22.9 | 38.6 | 70.6 | 4.3 | 1,559.0 | 163.0 |
| DPAP Total | 54.4 | 2.5 | 20.9 | 35.5 | 72.7 | 6.3 | 1,281.3 | 124.8 |
| Tamil Nadu | 135.0 | 1.4 | 34.2 | 62.7 | 61.5 | 1.0 | 6,622.0 | 124.0 |
| DPAP Total | 105.7 | 1.3 | 29.4 | 63.3 | 63.6 | 1.0 | 5,324.7 | 101.7 |
| Uttar Pradesh | 72.0 | 2.3 | 19.8 | 41.6 | 72.9 | 0.9 | 4,502.0 | 220.0 |
| DPAP Total | 58.0 | 2.0 | 14.5 | 43.8 | 76.9 | 1.2 | 3,048.5 | 214.2 |
| West Bengal | 97.0 | 2.2 | 27.5 | 57.7 | 55.7 | 0.9 | 5,139.0 | 152.0 |
| DPAP Total | 55.7 | 1.9 | 9.2 | 54.9 | 73.7 | 2.0 | 5,046.7 | 217.3 |

*Source*: CMIE, *District Profiles (1993)*, Mumbai.

Managing the natural resources for drinking water and fodder, rather than mainly for food, is very crucial for drought-affected people for whom lack of purchasing power is not as critical a problem as physical availability of water and fodder. How do these people in drought-prone regions fight against adverse agronomic conditions? The data relating to several socio-economic indicators for DPAP regions vis-à-vis the overall position in respective states presented in Table 2 reveal the following:

1. Despite the relatively lower land productivity, per capita production of food grains is higher or more or less the same among the DPAP districts vis-à-vis the state average. Since the difference in the average

size of landholdings is very small except in Gujarat, Madhya Pradesh and Rajasthan, higher or almost the same level of food grain production per capita in DPAP districts might be due to lower rate of growth of population among these districts.

2. Most of the DPAP districts have lower level of overall development index, literacy rate and urbanization vis-à-vis the state average (except for Bihar, UP and Tamil Nadu). These combined with lower rate of population growth (in 7 out of the 10 districts) indicate net outmigration of workers from these regions.
3. Migration can be an effective strategy only when it is combined with alternative economic avenues in the growing industrial and tertiary sectors. In industrially developed states like Gujarat, Maharashtra, Tamil Nadu and Karnataka, migration might result in upward mobility in economic conditions of people in DPAP regions due to market support for better investment opportunities and higher reservation price among these intra-state migrants. But for high-poverty states with lower level of industrialization, this involves long-distance migration, often to industrially/agriculturally developed regions like Gujarat, Maharashtra, Punjab and Haryana. This kind of migration may also have significant social costs, besides other hardships that they might have to undergo during the migration.
4. While migration as a coping up strategy among people in dryland regions is widely prevalent (NIRD 2000), not much is known about the outcomes of such migration, specially in terms of the social costs and economic upward mobility in the long run. What is, however, fairly well-recognized is that unless efforts are made to develop the home economy, outmigration from drought-prone regions may only shift poverty from rural to urban or from dryland to agro-climatically better-endowed regions. Higher level of industrial growth combined with market development, however, may help improving the outcome of such migration.

The interface between droughts and poverty emphasizes the need for promoting integrated farming systems in drought-prone regions. The next section deals with this aspect.

## FOOD, FODDER AND WATER: IMPERATIVES FOR DROUGHT-PROOFING

Essentially, a drought-proofing strategy involves sustained availability of food, fodder and water, specially among resource-poor households. In an ideal situation, a well-designed as well as implemented watershed project should be able to attain this goal at least in the long run. But experience from various watershed projects suggests that enhancing the availability of these three vital commodities, particularly fodder and water for drinking purposes, is difficult. As a result, these activities are found to be missing in a large number of otherwise well-performing watershed projects. Primarily, the difficulties arise because development of both fodder and drinking water resources involves working on Common Property Resources (CPR) like pastures, village tanks and drainage lines, etc. This becomes particularly important if the objective is to cater to the needs of the resource-poor who do not directly benefit from a significant increase in crop-production (and the resultant increase in crop residue) because of their limited land base, and at the same time do not have their own sources of water like wells, farm ponds or irrigation from check dams, etc.

Of course, the resource-poor can also derive benefits through percolation mechanisms, provided the overall farm economy in the village is substantially improved. For instance, a significant improvement in cropping intensity can enhance wage income among the resource-poor, who, in turn, can access food from open markets, fodder from crop fields and markets, and water from private sources from within and outside the village. In fact, this can even reduce their dependence on livestock (hence need for fodder) for generating supplementary income. But the percolation mechanism to work effectively requires that: (1) the aggregate increase in cropping intensity be fairly significant; (2) institutional arrangements for sharing of resources like crop residue and water are well in place; and (3) market operations are appropriately regulated so as to insulate the resource poor households from fluctuations in prices as well as supply of food, fodder, and water.

Ensuring increased access to food, fodder and water specially among resource-poor households should, therefore, necessitate careful planning for resource development, including CPRs, sharing mechanisms among households and creating a requisite buffer at the community level. As watershed projects cannot address these issues entirely within the micro-setting, there is a need for macro-level policy interventions by exploring wider options in terms of geo-hydrology, farm technology, market support, legal-administrative restructuring, and resource allocation. These are discussed as under.

## GEOGRAPHICAL OPTIONS

Ensuring water, specially, for drinking and domestic use, is the top priority under a drought condition. The usual approach for achieving this is in situ conservation and harvesting of rain water through various measures like gully plugs, check dams, village and farm ponds, field bounding and trenching, and recharging of wells, etc. In practice, water harvesting structures are generally the most preferred activities, as observed in a large number of micro watersheds in dryland/drought-prone regions (Shah 2001). While this is a fairly valid approach in a situation where water is the most critical operative constraint for crop productivity, such measures however, often overlook the need for ensuring drinking water during scarcity periods. There is also a problem of water availability beyond February in a large number of water harvesting structures such as checkdams, recharging tube-wells or village ponds.

Given the wide variation in groundwater availability and water retention capacity within a micro-region, measures for developing water resources have to account for such factors at the planning stage. The priority of harvested water for drinking purposes has to be spelt out explicitly. There is need for storage and distribution of water in the event of scarcity by exploring innovative measures like rooftop water harvesting systems, lining of ponds, and other devices for improving water retention in wells, etc., both for micro-watersheds and through linkage with development of water resources at various levels, viz., regions, basins, catchments, sub-catchments and watersheds (Shah et al. 1998). The integration of micro-level efforts with water resources development planning at the macro-level would also help in improving the effectiveness of water harvesting structures for drought-proofing

## YIELD AUGMENTING TECHNOLOGIES AND WATER USE EFFICIENCY

Promoting improved technologies for various segments of the farming system is equally important as conservation of natural resources. This is particularly true in the case of water, where the effective availability depends both on how much is harvested and how efficiently it is used. At present, the pricing as well as subsidy structure does not provide much incentive for more efficient use of water. As a result, the additional water harvested through various measures often gets used for growing a more water-intensive crop. Shifting to cotton, spices and other high-valued, high-irrigation-intensive crops is a common experience in many of the watershed projects being implemented in drought-prone regions.

This kind of response to conservation efforts limits water availability not only during a drought year, but also across households within a watershed community. This happens because planning for water harvesting measures is often silent about its use pattern as well as sharing mechanisms. For instance, if a check dam constructed under the project recharges groundwater, its beneficiaries are automatically defined by virtue of owning land in the catchment area of the structure. And the rest of the village community has very limited share, say, in the pattern of water use by a few landowning households.

In this context the Technical Committee on DPAP, headed by Prof. Hanumantha Rao (1994), had suggested a cautious approach for water use allowing tapping only of the rechargeable water, without exploiting the static water. It also asserted that drinking water be accorded priority during drought years. These aspects need a fresh emphasis in the watershed projects. Also, it is essential that water use efficiency becomes the concern of the entire community, rather than only those who directly access it. Apart from an active negotiation process at the community level, a useful mechanism for promoting water use efficiency is to shift a part of the subsidy from construction of water harvesting structures to adoption of water saving devices like drip irrigation systems, land levelling, trenching, etc. A similar approach could be adopted for promoting other agronomic practices like manuring, mulching, vegetative barriers, etc.

## IMPROVING ACCESS TO FODDER

Unlike development of water resources, intensifying investment on pastures and CPRs for increasing fodder supply is difficult proposition since a bulk of the Common Property Land (CPL) is already encroached upon and faces severe neglect. The problem is further accentuated due to emphasis on natural regeneration rather than on cultivation of fodder, which takes a longer time. To bring fodder development to the centre stage of drought-proofing would require a three-pronged approach of enhancing the availability of fodder, improving the quality of livestock, and managing its distribution both during normal as well as drought years. A prerequisite for developing the fodder sector is comprehensive land use planning which facilitates both physical access to pasture and other CPLs, and at the same time ensures resources for investment in various activities essential for development.

### DEVELOPING MARKETS FOR INPUTS AND SERVICES

In a drought-prone region, the central focus of the area development approach is on ecological regeneration, economic gains and drought-proofing. Due to resource limitations, it is suggested that area development programmes like watershed development in DPAP region should focus on certain clearly identified sectors/ activities. In addition, alternative mechanisms for strengthening the following infrastructure-related activities should be explored: (1) developing markets for inputs, outputs and various services related to agricultural operations; (2) providing road and transport networks; (3) promoting agro-processing; and (4) strengthening the social infrastructure for health and education.

Watershed projects do recognize these as important activities to be undertaken at a later stage, presumably by the village watershed committees. The scope for promoting private initiatives for a large number of such services should be explored promoted. A number of activities such as establishing seed, grain and fodder banks directly relate to drought-proofing and have already been successfully implemented by several Non-Government Organizations (NGO). In the past, such activities have been effectively undertaken by some of the project implementation agencies, e.g. Kribhco Indo-British Project (KRIBP). While this agency already had significant experience in various aspects of promotional marketing and cooperative functioning, more such agencies can be encouraged to promote agriculture-related services and input markets in drought-prone regions. Such activities, in turn, can be supported through self-help groups promoted under watershed projects and/or by seeking credit support from institutions like National Bank for Agriculture and Rural Development (NABARD).

## MIGRATION AND DIVERSIFIED FARMING SYSTEMS IN TRIBAL REGIONS

Tribal areas often constitute a substantial part of drought-prone or desert regions. These regions, apart from having poor physical infrastructure, also suffer from the problems of limited asset base in terms of land and/or livestock. In fact, a large number of households, specially in the tribal regions, are semi-landless. These households are invariably compelled to earn their livelihood by migrating out. While most of these migrants continue to till the land, farming activity becomes more or less marginal for their livelihood base. Those who stay back are generally women, children and old people, with limited capacity to look after their land and livestock. In the process, whatever asset base they have, also starts degrading in terms of quality. Droughts tend to intensify the process of migration and land degradation, making it further difficult to sustain the livestock. Eventually, a large number of these households bring roadside labourers, leaving their land to sub-optimal use.

Strengthening the land base among these tribal households operating marginal holdings would, therefore, need a different kind of policy intervention whereby group cultivation can be promoted especially for growing food as well as fodder crops. Such an approach might also help adoption of various soil moisture conservation measures, which otherwise remain neglected for want of family labour to work on the fields.

Thus, the imperative for an effective drought-proofing strategy is to adopt a location-specific approach, which can cater to varying conditions in terms of soil type, topography, hydrology, landholding size, livestock base, and, above all, cultural practices. The next stage of a watershed project should try to address these issues by adapting to the local needs and at the same time looking beyond the resources—technical, financial, and organizational—provided within the project's frame.

## LINKING DROUGHT RELIEF WITH DROUGHT-PROOFING

While the above discussion suggests the wider options to be explored for an effective drought-proofing strategy, it nevertheless cannot entirely prevent droughts from occurring. The general prescription, therefore, is to link up the programmes for the development of drought-prone regions. In this context, the following aspects need special attention.

1. At present, drought relief work tends to concentrate on some of the traditional measures like deepening of wells, desilting village ponds, construction of bunds, etc. Since these measures are repeatedly undertaken under relief work, it has led to a mindset that these assets belong to the state, hence people do not have any responsibility towards maintaining them. To reverse this process, the menu of relief work can be widened to include more physical infrastructure like roads, school buildings, public places, repairing of houses, water storage facilities, etc., for which funds are already being allocated under separate schemes. Soil-water conservation measures should generally be undertaken in a well-planned manner where people contribute a substantial part of the costs. This is essential for creating people's stakes in the long run.
2. Distribution of water and fodder should be linked with the local institutions/enterprises that could be created under the developmental programmes. This will not only help in stabilizing their economic operations, but will also reduce the administrative burden of the relief machinery, and perhaps reduce potential leakages. Ideally, each village or cluster of villages should keep a buffer of grain and fodder, which is managed by the local institutions/enterprises. A part of the funding to be provided under drought relief may be channelized to these agencies for maintaining the stocks at the cluster level.
3. Given the acute shortage of water in most parts of drought-prone areas, large-scale measures like inter-basin transfer of water, and water storage systems, etc., should be considered as part of the drought-proofing system, to be planned systematically rather than as a crisis fighting mechanism. Such a systematic approach would also arrest serious damage to the groundwater systems.
4. Financial norms for subsidies should be made flexible according to the economic status of the households. A uniform norm, for instance, for providing fodder may be counterproductive to the long-term goal of rationalizing the livestock population.

5. Finally, a cess for using irrigation water in different parts of the state can be tried out to generate a separate budget for drinking water. Developmental agencies and people's organizations could be involved in managing the funds both during the drought as well as non-drought years. In fact, a state-level committee consisting of the various stakeholders could be constituted to look after the developmental activities as well as the relief operations for supplying drinking water in the drought-prone regions.

## CONCLUSION

The foregoing discussion on the policies and practices of drought-proofing has brought out some important lessons for the next stage of watershed development projects, specially in the dryland regions in India. While there is a close association between droughts and poverty as well as food security, in a large number of situations, occurrence of a drought is only a trigger event—its disastrous consequences are often caused by the inappropriate use of natural resources like land, water and forests. Given the increasing demand for such resources, regeneration as well as efficient use of these resources are the essential features of an effective drought-proofing strategy in the long run. The recent shift towards watershed development programmes is a manifestation of this realization.

But watershed development is essentially an approach rather than a developmental scheme or a project with limited objectives. An effective drought-proofing strategy will have to go beyond the project mode and explore wider options in terms of geo-hydrological resources; technology for water use efficiency; land use policy with a central focus on fodder development; strengthening of the input/output markets and services for supporting various segments of farming systems; and creating a buffer stock of food grains and fodder by involving developmental agencies and institutions to meet drought disasters in these regions.

# 8. Food Security in Disaster Management

*Indira Hirway*

It has been observed that 95 per cent disaster-related deaths in the world occur in developing countries. Asia is considered to be the most disaster-prone area, with India and Bangladesh being two of the most disaster-prone nations in this region. According to official information, 24 states in India have been declared as disaster-prone states, the major disasters being cyclones, floods, droughts, landslides, hailstorms as well as earthquakes. On an average, about 50 million people in the country are affected by one or the other disaster every year, besides loss of property worth several million (Table 1). Good management of disasters and ensuring food security to disaster-affected people is, therefore, an important task for the central and state governments in India.

Ensuring food supply to disaster-affected people, which is one of the basic components of disaster management, tends to be one of the toughest tasks in a country like India where the incidence of nutrition-based poverty is significant. The present

TABLE 1: ANNUAL DAMAGES DUE TO NATURAL DISASTERS IN INDIA

| Year | People killed or missing | People affected (in million) | Houses damaged (fully/partially) | Property losses (Rs. in million) |
|---|---|---|---|---|
| 1990 | 1,855 | 3.17 | 10.20 | 1,708.92 |
| 1991 | 1,860 | 34.27 | 11.90 | 1,899.33 |
| 1992 | 1,367 | 190.90 | 05.71 | 2,047.61 |
| 1993 | 9,936 | 26.24 | 15.30 | 5,795.55 |
| 1994 | 2,344 | 23.53 | 10.51 | 1,830.47 |
| 1995 | 2,508 | 54.35 | 28.88 | 4,732.18 |
| 1996 | 2,789 | 54.99 | 23.77 | 5,431.22 |
| 1997 | 1,881 | 44.38 | 11.04 | NA |

*Source*: Government of India, National Centre for Disaster Management, *Natural Disasters in India: Some Recent Case Studies.*

paper discusses some of the challenges involved in this task. The paper is divided into three sections: The first section discusses the nature and types of disasters as well as challenges of ensuring food security; the second discusses the recent experience of ensuring relief and food security to earthquake-affected and drought-affected Gujarat, while the third section draws inferences and lessons from the discussions in the first two sections.

## FOOD SECURITY AND DISASTERS

Disaster can be defined as a 'disruption of human ecology which cannot be absorbed by the adjustment capacity of the affected community within its own resources. It is an event concentrated in time and space, which contributes a social, economic, cultural and political devastation, and affects people and community' (United Nations 1986). This 'disruption' in human ecology leading to 'devastation' can be divided into two categories based on their genesis: natural disasters, originating from natural factors, and man-made disasters or man-made devastation. It is important to note, however, that the frequency and intensity of natural disasters often depend on man-made factors, and in that sense natural disasters also are man-made disasters to a considerable extent. For example, the intensity of floods or droughts is affected by management of natural resources, the destruction of an earthquake is affected by the implementation of building codes, or adverse effect of any disaster depends considerably on the preparedness of the community. Disaster management is an important instrument of helping people in natural or man-made disasters. A good management of disasters frequently reduces the frequency of their occurrence as also their intensity and adverse impact. It ensures food security, which includes availability as well as access to food supply of affected communities.

Major natural disasters are floods, cyclones, droughts, landslides, earthquakes, etc., while major man-made disasters are chemical disasters like massive gas leakage, accidental fire, bursting of dams, explosions of power plants, etc. Both types of disasters have some common features that need to be noted while managing disasters:

1. Disasters occur suddenly, almost without any warning.
2. Their onset is fast, leaving very little time for emergency actions.

3. Their scale is huge which covers overwhelmingly large areas and large size of population making its impact severe.
4. Losses of disasters are also huge, as survival of life and property are in danger during a disaster.
5. Disasters totally disrupt the usual systems/mechanisms of life, creating tremendous problems in maintaining life and livelihood.
6. Disasters tend to hurt the vulnerable groups like Dalits, poor, women and children the most, as they are the least equipped groups to face a disaster, and are easily bypassed in relief and rehabilitation assistance.
7. Disasters have long-term after-effects which need long-term support and action. A country takes a long time to come to normalcy after a disaster.

All the above features make the task of disaster management urgent as well as difficult. The challenge of disaster management lies in taking care of these features of disasters by suitable strategies and actions to ensure support, including food security to affected people.

When a disaster occurs, affected people and regions need the following types of support, in the order mentioned below.

## TYPES OF SUPPORT

### *Rescue*

The first task is of rescuing human life and then animal life, as far as possible to minimize the loss of life of people, and whenever possible, of animals. Rescue operations involve reaching affected human beings and removing them to a safe place, and to medical help when needed.

### *Relief*

Rescue needs to be followed by relief, which implies assuring food, water, shelter, clothing and medical help to the affected. Since these minimum needs in the disaster area are usually destroyed, it is important to acquire these at the earliest. Both rescue and relief need to take care of socio-psychological support to people to help them come out of the trauma that they have faced.

*Resettlement*

Relief should also help people to get resettled gradually, though not necessarily on a permanent basis. Providing temporary shelter, cooking facilities and rations, access to water supply and its storage, sanitation, etc., to affected families to enable them to stand on their own (though temporarily) are the major components of this phase. Restoring infrastructure like water supply, electricity, transportation, communication, health facilities, schools, etc., helps people to settle down gradually in their new life.

*Rehabilitation and Reconstruction*

The next stage is of moving towards medium-term and long-term rehabilitation and reconstruction. The major tasks to be undertaken during this phase involve revival of livelihood, revival of the economy, restarting of educational systems, and constructing *pukka* shelter and structures to enable people to move to a normal life. This phase helps people to earn and buy their own food.

*Resuming Economic Development*

The last task is to put the economy back on the track of development. That is, to go back to the status of normalcy.

Ensuring food security is a part of all the tasks discussed above. That is, ensuring availability, accessibility and utilization of food to affected people, particularly to the vulnerable sections like women, children, Dalits, poor, etc., is an important aspect of all the above tasks to be undertaken after a disaster.

During rescue and relief, the task is to provide food packets or cooked food on an emergency basis. Since disaster-affected people are in no position to cook any food, the first requirement is to provide cooked food to all through community kitchens in relief camps, or through distribution of food packets to the survivors of disasters. This task essentially needs (1) accessing/cooking food, (2) packaging it in a healthy way, and (3) arranging for the distribution in a way that all the sections of the affected population, even in remote areas, receive it without any loss of human dignity.

Community kitchens cannot and should not run for long, as they hurt human dignity, and as each family would like to be on its own as soon as possible. During the relief and resettlement phase, therefore, it is necessary to provide food rations (monthly supply for the family) which would include rice, wheat flour, or *bajra* flour, *dal*, oil, tea, sugar, *gud*, salt, spices, etc. Such food kits can be prepared and distributed along with a kit of utensils, a cooking stove, kerosene and other basic needs like quilts, buckets, soap, etc., and a temporary shelter for the family to live on its own. This phase is important for physical and psychological settlement of families on the one hand and for moving to the next stage of rehabilitation on the other hand.

The first two phases of community kitchens (and food packets), and of distribution of ration are meant for all affected people without any exception, as all affected, rich and poor, need this support. These two phases are of welfare and charity. The task of the government is to organize it efficiently and effectively without hurting the dignity of people. During both these phases, it is important to take special care of vulnerable sections like women, children, disabled, Dalits and the poor, as also people living in remote areas, as these are likely to be bypassed by the administration.

Charity should not go on forever, and, therefore, the next phase is to revive the livelihood of people to enable them to buy food rather than receive it as charity. Revival of livelihood requires that (1) economic activities are revived, (2) physical and economic infrastructure is restored, (3) economic institutions like banks, shops, trade, transport, small and large factories, cottage industries or rural artisan work, agriculture, etc., are revived. This calls for planned action on the part of the government. Grants, loans and other support will be essential here. Revival also includes revival of agricultural activities like crop cultivation, animal husbandry, etc. Loss of standing crops, death of animals and loss of equipment and machinery usually puts farmers in a very vulnerable situation. It is important that they be immediately supported through appropriate actions. Repair of irrigation systems, cleaning of farms, revival of water tanks, wells, etc., digging wells for immediate irrigation, distribution of input kits to farmers to enable them to cultivate the next crop, providing animals/bullocks or equipments on loan or grant, are some of the very critical steps here. Revival of agriculture goes a long way in raising food production and ensuring food security.

An important aspect of revival of the livelihood and the economy is to use the process of reconstruction as a major means of employment generation and revival. That is, the massive employment generated in reconstruction of temporary and then permanent shelters, reconstruction and repairs of infrastructural facilities like roads, bridges, school buildings, hospitals, banks, etc., can contribute to regenerating the economy by functioning as the engine of revival. Such activities can have accelerating effect on the economy, as they will promote several other economic activities like brick kilns, building materials, masonry and carpentry, and massive construction activities. Systematic planning of these activities by choosing the right technology, local building material, local skill training and local labour could help considerably in reviving the economy and promoting the livelihood of local people.

Other efforts of economic revival will include provision of grants and easy loans to producers, giving financial incentives and subsidies to enterprises, drawing up special schemes for promoting economic activities like handicrafts, rural artisan work, etc., and giving special facilities and concessions to small producers belonging to vulnerable sections of the society.

It needs to be noted that efforts for economic revival as well as rehabilitation and reconstruction give an opportunity to correct and improve the earlier infrastructure and the past development path. This opportunity must not be missed.

## CRITICAL AREAS IN REHABILITATION AND RECONSTRUCTION

Some of the critical inputs needed for successful rehabilitation and reconstruction are good administration, availability of funds and involvement of people.

### *Administration*

A major input in disaster management in general and food security in particular is administrative efficiency. The success of the 'Five Rs' namely, rescue, relief, resettlement, rehabilitation and reconstruction depends critically on the efficiency and effectiveness of the administration. The administration is expected to focus particularly at the following aspects:

1. *Coordination*: Since a large variety of organizations such as grass roots organizations, a variety of NGOs, donor agencies,

global organizations, central government, state government, panchayat bodies, etc., are likely to be involved in these operations, it is important that the efforts are well-coordinated through a formal agency of the state (government).

2. *Efficient Delivery*: In time of crisis (of a disaster), reaching remote areas, Dalits, poor and women, without leakages or delays is extremely important. Even the administration that does not perform very well during normal times must rise to the occasion to reach the affected regions and people without delay.
3. *Monitoring*: As the situation in a disaster changes from day to day, constant monitoring is critical to delivering the required services in response to changing needs.
4. *Accountability and Transparency*: And lastly, accountability and transparency in financial accounts as well as in performance is another major administrative challenge. Disasters attract huge funds, from within the country as well as from outside the country. There is, therefore, always a temptation of misappropriating the funds. It is important that the accounts are made public for everybody to see. This helps in maintaining the morale of all the concerned agencies.

*Funds*

Rescue, relief, resettlement, rehabilitation and reconstruction need huge funds, the extent of funds needed depending on the nature and extent of the damage. Such funds are usually not available with any government, and particularly a state government in a country like ours.

Special tax or a levy, public contribution, and funds from global and foreign agencies are the major sources that need to be tapped. It is important to underscore that domestic funds—tax or levy and public contributions—need to be tapped fully, followed by donations from outside and then soft loans from global organizations. Repayment of such soft loans is a burden on the state, and, therefore, it is necessary that its use is minimized.

*People's Involvement and Decentralization*

Rehabilitation and reconstruction in general and food production and food distribution in particular under disaster management need to be organized in a decentralized manner, where people and people's organizations are involved closely. It should be kept in mind that the objective of rehabilitation and reconstruction is not merely to construct structures, but to rebuild people's lives. This has to be done as per their own needs and priorities.

## DISASTER PREVENTION, MITIGATION AND PREPAREDNESS

Disaster management has attracted a lot of attention of scholars and policy makers in the recent years, which has led to a better understanding of disasters and a better approach to disaster management. Increase of disasters on the one hand and the emerging new understanding of disasters on the other hand prompted national and global agencies to declare the decade of the 1990s as the decade for disaster management. With the new understanding, the major focus on disaster management has shifted from post-disaster relief actions to preparedness, mitigation, and, if possible, prevention of disasters. In addition, the new thinking on disaster management also focuses on (1) generating public awareness and education, (2) community participation and bottom-up approach to planning disaster management, (3) enhancement of organizational strengths and training of specialists, and (4) social audit of disaster management by people and people's organizations.

### PREPAREDNESS

Preparedness involves establishing authorities and responsibilities for emergency actions and garnering the resources to support them; a jurisdiction must assign or recruit staff for emergency management duties and designate or procure facilities, equipment and other resources for carrying out assigned duties. Preparedness measures should not be improvised or handled on an ad hoc basis, but should be systematized very well in administration. This requires formulation and maintenance of valid and up-to-date counter-disaster plans which can be brought into effect whenever required, public education and training, drilling of concerned machinery so that it can spring into action when required.

Preparedness is required to undertake the following:

1. Emergency communications for warning about disasters and evacuation of people to safe places.

2. Emergency communication for assistance and immediate delivery of resources, organizing search and arranging relief to crisis-affected people on a war footing.
3. Quick survey and assessment of the situation and organizing emergency assistance of food, shelter and medical support.
4. Accessing the help required and requesting help from outside if needed, and coordinating help from different agencies to avoid overlaps.
5. Bringing in necessary lifeline systems, such as power, communication, water, sanitation, and transportation to an acceptable level.
6. Maintain law and order and retain the confidence of people in the system.

## DISASTER MITIGATION AND PREVENTION

Mitigation of disaster implies lasting, often permanent, reduction of exposure to disaster-led hazards. This can be done in different ways for different types of disasters. For example, improved codes of buildings that ensure drought-resistant or earthquake-resistant construction can break the cycle of having to rebuild again and again after every event of flood, earthquake or cyclone; better management of land and water resources, and cultivation of drought-resistant varieties of crops can reduce the intensity of droughts considerably, or planting thick mangroves on sea coasts can reduce the intensity of cyclones considerably. Though natural disasters cannot be eliminated completely, reduction in their frequency and intensity can surely be achieved by adopting appropriate strategies.

Mitigation or prevention of disasters calls for (1) a careful analysis of the causes and effects of disasters, (2) formulation of a long-term strategy to reduce their frequency and intensity, and (3) designing of a systematic action plan for the purpose. It will be necessary for a disaster-prone state to set up a special department on disaster management to plan and implement disaster mitigation activities. Disaster mitigation also requires careful monitoring of the situation. In fact, it will be desirable that a disaster-prone state establishes a monitoring system for natural disasters.

The first step in disaster mitigation is to set up a scientifically efficient and efficiently functioning observation network for

(1) hydrological data collection, (2) seismological observations, (3) wind velocity, (4) cyclone growth, etc., through scientific instruments like radar, satellite imagery, etc. This step should help in identification of hazard zones and hazard assessment vulnerability and risk assessment for different sections of the population settlements and regions. All this should ultimately help in preparing a sound strategy and action plan for disaster mitigation, which can be formulated by scientists, economists, planners, administrators and social scientists working together.

Disaster mitigation also requires that the general public is made aware of how to act during disasters and support disaster management and mitigation.

In short, disasters should not be treated as disturbances that occur randomly in a society, to be faced by ad hoc actions of the administration. Disasters need to be understood, analyzed and integrated in the strategy of development planning so that their frequency and intensity are minimized and the devastation as well as the sufferings of people are reduced to the extent possible.

## DISASTER MANAGEMENT IN INDIA

The national approach to disaster management in India has evolved over a period of time. At present, the primary responsibility of managing natural disasters is with state governments. The centre's role is limited to one of providing resources to the states and acting in a supportive manner. The dimensions of the response by the central government are determined by the (1) gravity of the calamity, (2) scale of relief operations, and (3) need to augment financial resources available with state governments.

The disaster management plan for the country is supposed to have four essential components, namely, application of scientific inputs for forecasting; designing relief programmes by applying scientific inputs and timeliness in relief delivery; people's participation in relief; and rehabilitation as well as in monitoring and contribution to resilience of societies and areas for improvement in quality of life. The major focus of the policy, however, has been on relief and restoration, neglecting the preparedness and mitigation dimensions of disasters. According to the official policy, a committee at the national level (under the chairmanship of Cabinet Secretary) may be set up by the central government in the event of a disaster. This committee is meant to provide directions in the matter of relief and restoration. Nodal ministries in the event of disasters are Agriculture (national disasters), Environment and Forests (chemical disasters), Department of Atomic Energy (nuclear disasters), Health (biological disasters) and Home (civil strife).

At the state level, the Relief Commissioner/Revenue Secretary is the nodal agency for relief efforts. A state level committee chaired by the Chief Minister acts as a policy formulating forum and monitoring body. At the district level, the District Collector is the focal point for all relief efforts. While some states have formed a Special Committee for Disaster Management, others have not. Most state governments worry about disaster only when one occurs in their respective states. Disaster management includes three major tasks, risk analysis and vulnerability assessment, response plan and mitigation strategy, which are usually performed by the state revenue department in consultation with other concerned departments. The armed forces are expected to play a critical role in rescue and relief operations after a disaster takes place. Supportive efforts are made by state governments and NGOs. In short, the disaster management system that has been set up in India is temporary and has a focus mainly on relief and restoration. It does not include, in any effective way, preparedness, mitigation or prevention of disasters.

Recently, after the devastating earthquake in Gujarat, some efforts have been made at the all-India level to improve the management of disasters in the country. An all-party meeting on 3 February 2001 decided to set up a National Committee on Disaster Management. This committee is headed by the Prime Minister and has 37 members from different political parties. The committee is mandated to (1) suggest short-term, medium-term and long-term steps for relief, rehabilitation and reconstruction in earthquake affected areas; (2) deliberate on the necessary institutional and legislative measures needed for an effective long-term strategy to deal with national calamities in the future; and (3) suggest parameters defining a national calamity.

The mandate of the committee itself suggests that India is still in the initial stages of scientific disaster management. However, one hopes that progress is quick enough to reach a sound level of disaster management very soon.

## FOOD SECURITY UNDER TWO DISASTERS IN GUJARAT: RECENT EXPERIENCES

Gujarat experienced a devastating earthquake on 26 January 2001 at 8.46 a.m. measuring 7.9 on the Richter scale. Since its epicentre was in Kachchh, it suffered maximum devastation. The quake also created damage and destruction in many other districts of Saurashtra ( Jamnagar, Rajkot, Surendranagar, Bhavnagar, Amreli) north Gujarat (Banaskantha, Patan, Ahmedabad, Mehsana) and south Gujarat (Bharuch, Surat and Valsad). It has been estimated that about 20,000 persons lost their life and 1.67 lakh persons got injured (Table 2). In all, about 159 lakh of the population of the state was affected by the quake. Nearly 12.19 lakh houses/huts were affected, of which 3.54 lakh were completely destroyed. Over 20,000 cattle were killed in the quake.

Over 85 per cent of the losses occurred in Kachchh. The other districts which suffered substantial losses are Rajkot, Jamnagar, Surendranagar, Ahmedabad and Banaskantha. The total loss to the state is estimated at Rs. 21,262 crore. About 52 per cent of the loss is in household properties, estimated at Rs. 11,195 crore. Damage to property of industrial and commercial establishments has been estimated at Rs. 8,000 crore accounting for 38 per cent of the total losses. Public infrastructure and utilities have estimated the loss to their property at Rs. 1,680 crore (Table 3).

The Army, local people and NGOs played a critical role in the first few days of the earthquake. In spite of constraints like not

TABLE 2: DEATHS AND INJURED POPULATION IN THE EARTHQUAKE

| District | Dead | Injured | District | Dead | Injured |
|---|---|---|---|---|---|
| Kachchh | 18,212 | 1,36,048 | Porbandar | 9 | 90 |
| Ahmedabad | 751 | 4,040 | Junagadh | 8 | 89 |
| Rajkot | 433 | 11,951 | Gandhinagar | 8 | 241 |
| Jamnagar | 119 | 4,930 | Bhavnagar | 4 | 45 |
| Surendranagar | 113 | 2,909 | Anand | 1 | 20 |
| Surat | 46 | 190 | Vadodara | 1 | 270 |
| Patan | 38 | 1,695 | Kheda | 0 | 28 |
| Banaskantha | 32 | 2,770 | Mehsana | 0 | 1,339 |
| Navsari | 17 | 52 | Sabarkantha | 0 | 56 |
| Bharuch | 9 | 44 | Amreli | 0 | 5 |
| | | | Total | 19,801 | 1,66,812 |

*Source*: CMIE, *Monthly Review of the Gujarat Economy.*

TABLE 3: ESTIMATED LOSS OF PROPERTY

| Type of property | Rs. in crore | % share |
|---|---|---|
| Household property | 11,195 | 52.6 |
| Industrial est. | 5,000 | 23.5 |
| Commercial est. | 3,000 | 14.1 |
| Public infrastructure amenities | 1,080 | 5.1 |
| Public utilities | 600 | 2.8 |
| Personal property | 387 | 1.9 |
| Total estimated loss | 21,262 | 100.0 |

*Source*: CMIE, *Monthly Review of the Gujarat Economy*.

many troops being available in the affected areas and the heavy casualities, the Army moved switfly to the area for providing rescue and relief. It set up control rooms for rescue, medical help, and started rescuing trapped persons, removing dead bodies and debris, shifting injured to makeshift hospitals or to distant hospitals in Ahmedabad, Mumbai, Pune, Delhi, etc., providing drinking water, running free kitchens and patrolling. About 25,000 troops were deployed in Kachchh (20,000), Ahmedabad (4,000), Jamnagar (600) and Dhangadhra (400). About 500 persons were rescued alive, 2,500 bodies were recovered, 11,000 surgeries performed, and 20,000 persons were treated in Army hospitals. It set up 48 relief camps, 39 tented colonies and ran 39 free kitchens for people.

Voluntary organizations along with the general public were quick to respond, and they also played a critical role in providing food to people. An NGO, for example, provided lunch to 15,000 people in Kachchh on 26 January itself! It provided free lunch till 10 March. NGOs set up 24-hour control rooms, relief camps and mobilized resources to reach affected people. Innumerable households in neighbouring towns and villages cooked food at home, prepared packets and sent them to affected areas as soon as they heard about the crisis. The road to Bhuj was full of trucks with food, blankets, quilts, clothing, etc. Several local organizations supplied food in Ahmedabad, Bharuch, Jamnagar, Rajkot, Banaskantha, Surendranagar districts. As one would expect, there was some wastage, and some remote villages were left out of the help. But the spontaneity of the public and NGOs was overwhelming.

The Government of Gujarat was late in responding to the crisis because of the holidays, and because of the breakdown in communication with affected areas. The emergency communication systems, the Sattelite (SAT) phones could not work due to technical faults. Government also got defunct as many of the staff died or was affected and did not report on duty and many of the office buildings in Kachchh collapsed. It took some time before it could get into action. There was no emergency machinery to jump into action to take up fixed duties in the crisis. It lacked what is called 'preparedness' in disaster management.

Massive NGO networks started operating almost immediately and started, as far as possible, channelizing efforts of people. The Janpath Citizens' Initiative[1] (a network of about 200 NGOs of Janpath, 75 NGOs of Pravah, 22 NGOs of *Abhiyan* in Kachchh and some academics and professional organizations) came into existence on 27 January. A team of some leading NGOs had already left for Kachchh on 26 January before the Janpath Citizens' Initiative (JCI) came into being. The JCI was supported by innumerable members of civil society, such as doctors, nurses, businessmen, teachers, engineers, architects, traders, manufacturers, students, etc. The Earthquake Affected Relief and Rehabilitation Services (EARRS), another major NGO network, Self Employed Women's Association (SEWA), the Kachchi Samaj, Swaminarayan Organizations, Rashtriya Seva Sangh, etc., all got involved in providing food and relief to affected people, and did a good job. However, one is not sure that all the affected people, particularly in remote areas were reached. There were many complaints from these areas.

After running community kitchens for a few days, the focus shifted to providing food grain kits to people (consisting of monthly supply of rice, wheat flour, *dal*, tea, sugar, oil, salt, spices and *gud*) along with a kit of utensils and another kit of miscellaneous items like a stove, blankets, buckets, storage for drinking water, soap, towels, candles as well as a shelter (tent or tarpaulin if possible). About 30,000 food kits were distributed by the JCI, and a few thousands by other NGOs.

The Government of Gujarat restored electricity and communication within three to four days of the earthquake and supplied drinking water to all the affected areas. It also announced free distribution of food grains to affected people till 31 March 2001, and issued 2 lakh temporary ration cards to affected families. All this aimed to ensure food security to people in the immediate period of the disaster. The government also announced cash doles of Rs. 1 lakh for loss of a life, doles for loss of household items, as well as doles for food and livelihood.

No systematic assessment has been made so far about the effectiveness of the measures taken by NGOs and the government for ensuring food supply to people during the rescue and relief period, till about the end of March. One can, however, make the following observations:

1. The immediate food security was provided by local organizations, NGOs, the general public and the Army. The government could not act immediately due to its constraints and could not manage to reach remote areas.
2. The next stage of providing food grains was attempted both by NGOs and the government. However, it took some time for the government to distribute cash doles as well as free food grains. The government, however, was successful in restoring power and water supply in most places.
3. Coordination of the efforts of different NGO networks, donor agencies, public and government departments could not be managed which resulted in wasteful duplication on the one hand, and deprivation of some regions on the other hand.
4. The government also could not manage the distribution of huge supplies which came from outside Gujarat and outside India on a large scale. Governance failed in the region to undertake these tasks successfully. Lack of temporary shelter was a major failure as enough tents, shelters could not be procured.

## RESTORATION OF LIVELIHOOD AND AGRICULTURE FOR FOOD SECURITY

At present, Gujarat is experiencing two natural disasters simultaneously, namely, the earthquake, and the drought. Both these disasters need to be addressed simultaneously, as both are overlapping considerably in terms of their geographical coverage and problems. Both have created serious problems for food security as both have disrupted the livelihood of people in the affected areas.

The earthquake has upset the life and livelihood of people almost totally. Earning members have died in many families, many have been injured and a large number of households have been rendered without home, shelter and without their worldly possessions. They need considerable support to pick up the threads of their lives and to start living afresh. The main occupations of people in the earthquake-affected areas are agriculture, animal husbandry, handicrafts, salt manufacturing and other small and medium industries. The earthquake has destroyed their assets as well as the basic infrastructural facilities and destroyed their livelihoods.

It has damaged infrastructural facilities like water supply, electricity, roads and bridges, dams and reservoirs, banks and godowns, markets, post offices and public buildings very badly in several areas, upsetting the economy badly.

It has also damaged, partly or fully, health and educational facilities like hospitals, community health centres, primary health centres/subcentres, dispensaries, school rooms, *anganwadis*, higher secondary schools, technical institutes and colleges.

It has also destroyed dams and irrigation structures in the affected areas: 21 earthern dams are severely affected, 164 dams need major repairs, 58 irrigation schemes have moderate or minor damages, and many small water harvesting structures have been damaged/destroyed.

Losses in agriculture and livestock to private producers have been estimated at Rs. 509.60 crore, as standing crops have been damaged/destroyed, equipment and machinery are damaged, bullocks and milch animals have died and agricultural lands are damaged. The agricultural losses in the public sector include damage to public buildings, damage to bore wells, pump houses, pumps, tanks, godowns, etc., totalling a loss of Rs. 35.30 crore. It has been estimated that the total damages would cost about Rs. 11,000 crore in terms of repairs and reconstruction (Table 4).

The damage to industrial buildings, machinery, inventory, godowns, as well as destruction of handicrafts, raw materials, equipment, machinery, etc., have been widespread. About 3,000 small-scale industries, 20 medium to large units and thousands of cottage units are affected. In addition, damage to markets, shops, trading centres, storages have been immense (CMIE 2001).

Food security to the affected people can be ensured mainly by undertaking massive repairs and reconstruction works of buildings and infrastructural facilities and by extending financial and other support to the various economic activities.

TABLE 4: PRELIMINARY ESTIMATE OF ASSET LOSSES AND RECONSTRUCTION COSTS, AS OF 23 FEBRUARY 2001

| Sector | Asset losses (Rs. in crore) | Reconstruction loss[a] (Rs. in crore) |
|---|---|---|
| Housing | 5,166[b] | 5,148 |
| Health | 219 | 279 |
| Education | 670 | 837 |
| Subtotal: social sectors | 6,054 | 6,264 |
| Irrigation | 186 | 419 |
| Rural water supply | 233 | 451 |
| Municipal infrastructure | 140 | 209 |
| Public buildings and monuments | 339 | 442 |
| Power | 186 | 456 |
| Transport[c] | 321 | 358 |
| Ports | 98 | 121 |
| Telecommunications | 51 | 121 |
| Subtotal: infrastructure | 1,553 | 2,576 |
| Agriculture and livestock* | 544 | 344 |
| Industry* | 339 | 205 |
| Services* | 1,163 | 930 |
| Subtotal: productive sectors | 2,046 | 1,479 |
| Subtotal: environment[d] | 256 | 256 |
| Grand total | 9,909 | 10,575 |
| Public assets[e] | 2,497 | 3,864 |
| Private assets[f] | 7,412 | 6,710 |

*Source*: Government of Gujarat and Assessment Mission Estimates.

*Notes*: [a] Replacement of immovable assets, with improved earthquake/cyclone resistance.

[b] Includes value of household contents such as consumer durables; reconstruction excludes replacement of these assets.

[c] Includes roads and bridges, railways, and airports.

[d] Includes costs of rubble removal in urban and rural areas.

[e] Public assets above include: health, 70 per cent of education assets, irrigation, rural water supply, municipal infrastructure, public buildings and monuments, power, transport, ports, and telecommunications, plus the environment.

[f] Private assets above include housing, 30 per cent of education assets, and production assets in agriculture and livestock, industry and services.

* Asset losses and reconstruction costs to agriculture, industry, and services, exclusive of sectors listed above.

The Government of Gujarat has set up a Disaster Management Authority under the chairmanship of the Chief Minister to coordinate the comprehensive earthquake recovery programme. A Task Force has also been constituted under the chairmanship of the

Chief Secretary, and a high-power Central Implementation Committee has been set up for implementing, monitoring and quality control. These committees and the Task Force consist of the concerned ministers, government officers and prominent MLAs.

The state government has also set up a state level advisory committee for public/private partnership under the chairmanship of Prof. Y.K. Alagh, which consists of representatives from NGOs and civil society. In addition, advisory committees have been set up at the district and village levels in the affected districts/villages. The district-level advisory committees are headed by the collector with the additional collector as its member secretary and Zila Panchayat president and concerned officers as its members. (Note that the Zila Panchayat president is just an ordinary member and there are no other members from panchayats or civil society on the committee.) Similarly, the village ievel committee is headed by the deputy collector or *mamlatdar*, with the *talati* as its member secretary. There is no proper or adequate representation to panchayats (non-existing in most cases) or NGOs/CBOs.

District, taluka and village-level executive committees have been for implementing the different disaster related packages in severely affected regions. These committees consist only of government officers from the concerned departments. The district level three-member executive committee consists of the district collector, the district development officer and the executive engineer, and the taluka-level executive committee consists of the additional collector in charge of the taluka, the additional district development officer in charge of the taluka and the executive engineer. These committees do not have any members either from local panchayat bodies, NGOs or Community Based Organisations (CBO).

The Government of Gujarat has declared several schemes and packages for the revival of economic activities. The major schemes include the following.

1. Housing rehabilitation by (a) temporary shelter arrangement to all by the beginning of the monsoon, (b) rubble removal, (c) raw material banks to ensure availability of building materials, (d) building centres for demonstration, training and capacity building, and (e) cash doles/assistance and loans to people. The government envisages private/public partnership and a definite role of village committees and NGOs in this sector.

2. For health and education sectors, the government has decided to rebuild and reconstruct totally devastated facilities, repair damaged facilities and construct extra facilities to provide the required facilities and support. In the health sector, for example, it has been proposed to construct splint workshops, orthotic/prosthetic workshops, mobile workshops and physiotherapy/occupational therapy centres, while for education it has proposed to construct temporary buildings, leading to permanent structures later on.
3. The government has also designed programmes and schemes for reconstruction of economic infrastructural facilities of different kinds. Repair and reconstruction of dams, irrigation facilities, water harvesting structures, wells, tanks, etc.; construction of storage facilities, pipelines and repair of existing storage for drinking water supply; repair of roads and bridges, repairs and reconstruction of public buildings, etc., are the major activities to be undertaken under these programmes.
4. Village Adoption Scheme: Villages with more than 70 per cent houses destroyed will be fully reconstructed and, if demanded by local people, shifted to other sites. About 229 villages (172 in Kachchh, 25 in Rajkot, 19 in Jamnagar and 13 in Surendranagar) are such villages. It has been estimated that, on an average, each of these villages will need about Rs. 3 crore (Rs. 30 lakh for land, Rs. 70 lakh for infrastructural facilities, Rs. 180 lakh for housing and Rs. 20 lakh for meeting urgent expenses). Under the village adoption scheme, an NGO (including corporate houses, also) has to contribute 50 per cent of the expenses to adopt a village, with the other 50 per cent coming from the state government. Several corporate houses have adopted such villages. There are several unresolved problems, however, with respect to the relocation and adoption, participation of all sections of the local community, involvement of NGOs which cannot shell out 50 per cent of the funds and so on.
5. Industrial units damaged or destroyed in the earthquake will receive cash assistance, soft loans as well as several concessions and subsidies. Special schemes have been prepared for artisans, salt manufacturers, handicrafts, handloom/weaving and for self-employment ventures.
6. All these revival efforts are expected to be implemented in a

decentralized fashion, with the participation of people, village committees, district committees, NGOs, etc. It is expected that these efforts will revive the economy, generate employment and livelihood of people leading to ensuring food security for people within a span of a short time.

## THE SECOND CONSECUTIVE DROUGHT AND FOOD SECURITY

The second disaster, the second consecutive drought, however, is much more serious than the earthquake in terms of spread and its frequency in the state. As it is, 52 talukas of the total of 184 talukas of Gujarat have been declared as drought-prone and are covered under the Drought Prone Area Programme (DPAP), and 47 talukas have been declared as desert areas and covered under the Desert Development Programme (DDP). That is, 99 talukas, covering more than 60 per cent of the area of the state are generally subjected to frequent droughts. In addition, some other talukas are also covered under droughts when the droughts are major (like the present one).

It has been observed that the frequency, coverage and intensity of droughts have increased in the state over the years. Some of the new characteristics of droughts observed to be prevalent in the state in the recent decades can be listed as follows:

1. Deaths due to famines have almost been eradicated, as food grains are made available to affected areas.
2. However, droughts are now accompanied by severe shortage of drinking water as Gujarat has experienced a serious depletion of its water resources in recent decades. Such shortages were not experienced in the 1960s and even in the 1970s when digging of wells to access drinking water was not a difficult proposition.
3. Since the frequency and intensity of droughts have increased in the state, massive scarcity works are being undertaken where people work as unskilled labour under the hot sun of the summer to earn a meagre living.

The main approach of the state government for helping drought-affected people consists of the steps laid down in the age-old Scarcity Manual:

1. A major approach is to start scarcity works on a large-scale to provide unskilled employment to affected people so that they earn wages to buy food grains from local ration shops, where food grains are sold at subsidized rates.
2. Since the size of the population that demands such works is very large, beyond the affordability of the state exchequer, the government has put certain restrictions on scarcity works. First, not all adult members of a household are allowed to work on such works. If the size of a family is 4 to 5, only two members can work, if the size is 6 to 8, only three members can work and so on. Second, the workers are not entitled to receive the legal minimum wages declared by the government under the Minimum Wages Act. This Act is temporarily withdrawn for scarcity works, with the result that the workers receive wages according to SOR, which comes to much less than the minimum wages.
3. People do not have a right to demand scarcity works as it is left to the sweet will of the administration to start such works. Scarcity works thus do not necessarily cover all the villages or all the affected people.
4. A scarcity work lasts till the funds sanctioned for the work last. Though it is necessary to stop a work only after it is taken to 'a safe stage', the work usually stops when the funds are over, even though the safe stage is not reached.
5. Selection of scarcity works is not done in a planned way, keeping the long-term priorities of the area in mind. It has been suggested, however, that works of drought proofing, such as deepening of tanks, as well as road construction, etc., may be taken up under scarcity works.
6. The government is expected to provide a shade, drinking water and footwear to people who come on scarcity works.
7. The government also is expected to provide fodder and water for animals, and water to people, even by tankers to affected villages.

In short, the strategy of the government for drought management is to line up affected people, after every few years, begging for scarcity works from the administration. There is no guarantee of work or of minimum employment, no assurance of minimum wages, and no assurance of long-term drought-proofing so that one day they or their children need not stand in the sun with a begging bowl!

The present drought is the second consecutive drought which is a major one, and much worse than the first drought. It may be the biggest of the decade, or of the century. About 13,133 villages of the total of 18,114 villages (more than 73 per cent) are severely affected by this drought. The drought has spread to 23 districts of the 25 districts, covering 2.9 crore of the 5 crore population!

All the districts affected by the earthquake are also suffering from the drought which makes the situation extremely difficult for the people living in these districts.

The Chief Minister has drawn up a Special Action Plan for facing the present drought.

1. Large-scale scarcity works have been started at 2,734 locations, where about 15.5 lakh persons are working. The state government is spending Rs. 6 crore per day on the works.
2. These workers get Rs. 40 as wages and receive 20 kg of subsidized grains, wheat at Rs. 2 a kg, and rice at Rs. 5 a kg (though this has not been observed to be correct by the present author in her ongoing survey in the state).
3. About 1.18 lakh destitutes, pregnant women, etc., are getting cash doles, which comes to Rs. 10 lakh per day.
4. The state has created a buffer stock of 2,00,000 tons of fodder, and 0.3 million animals have been taken in *panjrapol* which are run with the help of NGOs. The government has also acquired 3,000 tons of cattlefeed.
5. As far as the drinking water is concerned, the main approach has been to dig tube wells/bores or to get tankers from outside. This year, two major steps have been: (a) getting Narmada waters through pipelines (a big pump at Maliya Miyana has been constructed to cater to the needs of Kachchh, Surendranagar, Jamnagar and Rajkot) and (b) arranging water tankers (about 1,648 tankers are in operation on a continuous basis to provide water to 2146 villages) and running water trains (two trains to Rajula have already been sent and many more are planned).

Both the crises together will cost more than Rs. 11,700 crore to the state exchequer, about Rs. 11,000 crore for the earthquake and Rs. 700 crore for the drought. It is indeed a massive challenge faced by the state government in managing both crises simultaneously.

## ISSUES IN REVIVAL OF LIVELIHOOD AND FOOD SECURITY

The state government plans to revive the economy for livelihood of disaster-affected people using the packages discussed above. It is expected that this revival will contribute significantly towards ensuring food security of the affected population. There are, however, several issues that need to be tackled in this context.

### *Raising Finances for the Revival*

The two disasters have affected the state exchequer in two different ways. On the one hand they have reduced, and are likely to reduce in the coming years, the revenue considerably, while on the other hand, they have pushed up the expenditure drastically. This calls for a very careful planning of public finances in the state.

The negative impact of disasters on the fiscal balance will depend on the (1) terms at which the government obtains finances for meeting the expenditure; (2) extent to which it rationalizes expenditure by improving its efficiency and improves its own revenue collection in non-earthquake affected areas; (3) standards used for reconstruction of housing and other assets; (4) extent to which beneficiaries and the private sector share the costs of reconstruction and rehabilitation; and (5) extent to which the state is able to control leakages and corruption.

It is important, therefore, that the areas, sectors as well as sections of the population to be covered under rehabilitation and reconstruction are prioritized and targeted properly. This calls for decentralization of the efforts, participation by people including the poor, and accountability and transparency. Close collaboration between the government, the private sector, NGOs and the general public is very important in this context.

The total cost of reconstruction of assets damaged by the earthquake has been estimated at Rs. 11,000 crore approximately. The expenditure on public goods and services like power, water supply, health, roads, bridges, irrigation, etc., will come to around Rs. 8,496 crore. In addition, more than Rs. 700 crore will be needed for managing the drought, and Rs. 100 crore will be needed for Narmada-based water supply pipelines. This expenditure will have to come from the public exchequer. Unless the public finances are managed well, the state is likely to face a huge burden of debt servicing without satisfactory achievements of the goals. What is worse is that this will force the state to reduce welfare and social sector expenditure in the coming years.

*Management of Droughts*

Management of droughts in the state seems to be suffering from several limitations.

1. Selection of works to be undertaken is done without a long-term focus on drought proofing. Though some watershed development programmes have given positive results in the state, scarcity works do not include such works.
2. Selection of works also is not based on any systematic plan for the region. In most cases, these are selected on an ad hoc basis or with some short-term considerations. This work thus neither contributes to drought-proofing, nor to any systematic development of the region.
3. Duration of a scarcity work does not depend on the time required to complete the work, but on the amount sanctioned for the region. As a result, resources are frequently wasted year after year on the same work.
4. Drought-affected people have no right to demand scarcity works as the decision about starting a work is an administrative one taken by the district collectorate. Also, not all those who want work are allowed to work on these sites as there are strict rules restricting participation. People usually wait with a begging bowl for the sweet will of decision makers.
5. The wages paid on scarcity works are much less than the minimum wages declared by the state, as the Minimum Wages Act is not applicable for such work. Studies have shown that the actual wages are frequently around Rs. 20 to Rs. 30 per day! (the officially accepted rate is Rs. 40 per day).
6. Each work site is expected to provide shade and drinking water. This is not always observed to be existing.
7. Studies have shown that the quality of assets created is poor, and there are also large-scale leakages and corruption.
8. There is no provision of providing works under scarcity relief that could be undertaken at homes (such as handicrafts). There is a need to take a fresh look at such restrictions.

In short, scarcity works neither provide short-term relief nor any long-term relief to people. Such works provide part support for survival, but this is far from adequate. As a result, a study by United Nations International Children's and Educational Fund (UNICEF) has shown, the frequent droughts have had a highly adverse impact on the nutrition and health of the poor who live in drought-prone areas in the state (*Times of India*, April 2001). The study shows that:

1. Very hard work on the one hand and poor food intake on the other hand seem to have affected the nutrition level of the poor living in drought/desert-prone areas in Panch-mahals, Dahod, Kachchh and Jamnagar.
2. Lack of adequate supply of water does not allow scarcity workers to consume green vegetables, which results in malnourishment and anemia.
3. Children are observed to be affected by night blindness or blindness due to low consumption of vitamins.
4. Women and children in these regions have become easy victims of diarrhoea, dehydration, hepatitis, typhoid, etc. The incidence of such diseases is also observed to be high in men in these regions.
5. There is a general deterioration of health and nutrition of men, women and children living in drought-prone and desert areas in the state.

### *Rehabilitation and Reconstruction for Earthquake-Affected People*

As regards rehabilitation and reconstruction of earthquake-affected people, there are several issues that need careful attention of all those concerned.

The first important issue is regarding the database of the damage, particularly of housing of people in non-Kachchh areas. As the major focus has been on Kachchh, which has suffered 85 per cent of the losses, non-Kachchh areas are relatively neglected. There is an urgent need to conduct a fresh survey of damage of properties owned by individuals, and particularly the poor (Hirway 2001; Utthan 2001).

Our long experience with disasters has shown that satisfactory rehabilitation does not take place if (1) it is not decentralized,

(2) if people are not involved in decision making, and (3) if livelihood is not ensured to people. The government administration, however, has poor capacity to undertake all the three tasks. It requires special efforts to do so. In the case of Gujarat this is particularly difficult as there is no village panchayat at the village level (the elections were postponed because of the drought last year).

Discrimination against Dalits, minorities and the poor has been a common complaint coming from many areas of the state even during the rescue and relief phase. It is important, therefore, for the government to see that (1) discrimination is minimized, (2) grievances in this field are immediately attended to, and (3) special focus is kept on these vulnerable sections who are usually easy victims of deprivation and exploitation.

Several affected areas, particularly outside Kachchh have not yet set up a proper system of public distribution of food grains. Shops have not been repaired, supplies are not regular and ration cards have not been distributed in some areas. It is important to take up these tasks on a war footing.

Many women, particularly widows, have been left with no source of income. These women and their dependent families need immediate support in terms of assistance or in economic activities. Special attention needs to be paid to such women and households.

Corruption is a widespread characteristic of our society, and the government administration is no exception to this. The huge amounts of money involved in disaster management are likely to attract unscrupulous elements to this work, which will affect the interests of the poor the most. There is a need to organize a system of transparency and accountability. Some NGO networks have suggested setting up of a high-level committee for this purpose.

The speed was another major challenge to the state and it is important to provide the following before onset of monsoons: (1) temporary shelter to all affected; (2) temporary buildings for schools, hospitals, dispensaries, etc.; (3) repair of agricultural infrastructure, distribution of inputs and equipments to farmers in time; (4) economic revival so as to enable people to work in their own occupations by then; and (5) repair or construction of some water harvesting structures to collect rain water in these drought-prone areas.

The government has announced several packages for rehabilitation and reconstruction in the field of housing, infras- tructure, social services, agriculture, industries, trades, and services along with concessions, subsidies and easy credit. Right now there is an element of uncertainty and vagueness about these. There is a need to concretize and operationalize these packages, if necessary, in partnership with professional organizations. The government has many professionals—the best doctors, nurses, architects, engineers, planners, businessmen, educationists, managers, chartered accountants, scientists, technocrats and NGOs. The government so far has not provided enough space to involve these people in the tasks of rehabilitation and reconstruction. It is high time the government took the help of these professionals who are more than willing to help. The results will depend on how successful the government is in involving these experts.

## LESSONS TO BE LEARNT

Major observations emerging from the first two sections can be listed as follows:

1. Ensuring food security to disaster affected people in the short, medium and long term is an important task that needs careful attention of policy makers and planners. In a country where disasters are frequent and devastating, it is important to evolve polices and systems that provide food security to masses of people that suffer from disasters every year.
2. Unfortunately, we are not yet well prepared for this task as disasters are mostly seen as random events and addressed more or less in an ad hoc fashion. Consequently, there is neither preparedness nor systematic efforts for mitigation or prevention (in some cases) of disasters. Though some beginning has been made in this direction in the recent years, we have a long way to go.
3. Each type of disaster has its own origin and impact. Also, not all disasters can be predicted well (for example, occurrence of earthquakes cannot be predicted). It is important to understand the causes and impact of each type of disaster so as to face it satisfactorily. It seems that mismanagement of natural resources is, to a large extent, responsible for the frequency and intensity of the several disasters like floods,

cyclones, landslides, droughts, etc. Sound management of the environment through a long-term strategy will, therefore, go a long way in reducing devastation of disasters.

4. All disasters, to a small or large extent, are man-made. Destruction caused by disasters can be reduced considerably by undertaking a variety of steps like constructing cyclone-resistant or earthquake-resistant buildings in such disaster-prone areas.
5. A top-down approach never works in disaster management as the local situation changes from place to place and the situation also changes from day to day in disaster-affected areas. Somehow our governments have not learnt to work in a decentralized structure by putting faith in the abilities of local people. As a result, most rehabilitation and reconstruction activities have given poor results. It is high time that our governments understand this truth and put faith in decentralized democratic structures, and kept space for CBOs, NGOs and various experts to participate in rehabilitation and reconstruction activities.
6. Disasters are painful to people, and particularly to the poor. Frequent disasters have a highly adverse impact on nutrition levels of the poor. Disasters are also very expensive as the government as well as the general economy and society have to pay a big price for these. They halt economic progress, put a brake to the process of poverty reduction, tend to reduce social sector expenditure and slow down the general development of the society. It is, therefore, important to learn how to manage disasters well.

## NOTE

1. The author is a member of the 7 members JCI Coordination Committee.

SECTION II

# Sustainable Livelihood and Economic Access to Food

# 9. Nutritional Deficiency, Poverty and Unemployment: Trends and Interrelations and their Implications for Food Security

*Amitabh Kundu*

The 1990s heralded the beginning of a new era as far as the strategy for ensuring food security in India is concerned. The total production of food grains, including feed and seed, touched the two hundred million metric ton mark in 1998–9 and exceeded that by about 10 million tons the following year. This has been pronounced as a landmark for the agricultural sector. Importantly, the country experienced high demographic growth during the first four decades of planned development, hovering between 2.1 and 2.3 per cent per annum. This resulted in an increase in population by about 130 per cent. Despite this high population growth, India could achieve self-sufficiency in food grains as cereal production more than trebled during this period. The fact that the country has built the capacity to meet any challenge on account of natural calamities like droughts or floods through its buffer stock without recourse to food aid or imports is no mean achievement.

The fact that that this self-sufficiency has been obtained primarily due to slow growth in demand for cereals should, however, be a matter of serious concern.[1] The major explanation for the slower growth in cereal demand would be reduction in per capita cereal consumption both in rural and urban areas. It is argued that there has been diversification of dietary habits due to steady income growth over the past decades, demonstration effect, exposure to fast globalizing media, etc. The decline in the consumption of food grains in per capita terms for rural areas is substantial, the figure declining from 185 kg per year in 1980 to 165 kg in the mid-1990s. In urban areas, the figure has stabilized at around 130 kg. The demand for cereal as livestock feed has also not grown much, almost getting stabilized at 5 million tons per year. The components in the consumption basket to register a significant increase are milk, meat, eggs, etc., their growth rates being about 6 per cent per annum.

Given this production and consumption scenario, it has been argued that food insecurity and malnutrition are no longer only problems of production. The average production in any year, if distributed evenly across regions and households, should eliminate hunger and starvation. The fact that there are still nutritional deficiencies, leading to problems of wasting and stunting in several regions points to major deficiencies in distribution of food. Understandably, there are households that do not have the purchasing power to buy adequate cereals from the market. Many among these are not covered under the PDS or do not get adequate quantities. Also, a few may not be able to afford the grains even at the subsidized rates due to their low and fluctuating income levels. Food security and nutrition must, therefore, be viewed within the framework of a development strategy to generate employment and income.

Keeping this perspective in view, the present paper analyses the aspects of nutritional deficiency in the context of the changing pattern of poverty, unemployment, and income generation at the national as also state levels. The second section of the paper, which follows the present introductory section, analyses the macro-scenario of nutritional deficiency and looks at it in the context of the changing employment structure, poverty scenario, sectoral composition of income and employment, etc. Sectoral growth performance, shifts in workforce structure and their implications for poverty and nutrition have been discussed in the third section. In the fourth section, an attempt has been made to analyse the regional scenario through indicators pertaining to the selected dimensions, separately for rural and urban areas, taking the states as the basic observational units. This has been done largely by using the data from the quinquennial rounds of National Sample Survey (NSS) since the early 1970s. Indicators of state (net) domestic product, female literacy, and infant mortality rates have also been incorporated in the inter-state analysis from other sources. The fifth section analyses the nature of interdependency between nutritional levels and the selected socio-economic indicators. The changing pattern of interdependencies during the 1970s, 1980s and 1990s has been examined for understanding the factors behind food insecurity and nutritional deficiency. The impact of nutritional deficiency on health indicators has been assessed in the sixth section using indicators for the 1990s. The last section summarizes the findings and examines their policy implications.

## NUTRITION, POVERTY[2] AND EMPLOYMENT TRENDS AT MACRO LEVEL

It has been argued that despite relatively high income growth together with an increased availability of food grains during the past three decades, food consumption has declined substantially in per capita terms. What is, however, more disturbing is that the intake of some of the major nutrients show a decline in calories in varying degrees. Calorie consumption per capita in rural areas has gone down from 2,266 in 1972–3 to 2,221 in 1983, and then to 2,153 in 1993–4. Even in urban areas, the figure has gone down, but at a slower rate. Per capita calorie intake has declined marginally by less than 1 per cent during the two decades from 1972–3 to 1993–4. Unfortunately, there is no evidence of a compensatory increase in protein consumption in per capita terms, as its level has stabilized at 60 grams in rural and about 56 grams in urban areas. The same thing can be said about consumption of fats as well.

Notwithstanding the problems in the computation of poverty, it is impossible to deny the need for having poverty estimates during the intervening period for guiding policy decisions. Poverty and unemployment are issues too critical for Indian polity to wait for five long years for receiving attention of policy makers in a dispassionate manner.

Available evidence shows that poverty has declined steadily at the national level as also in rural and urban areas during 1970s, 1980s and early 1990s as seen from the following tables: The percentage of people below the poverty line as per research studies based on NSSO data (Table 1), percentage of persons employed as per usual and weekly status to total population (Table 2), percentage of workers in the 15–59 age groups, in different NSS Rounds by usual, weekly and daily status (Table 3), percentage of unemployed person-days to labour force/labour days in Rural areas (Table 4) and urban areas (Table 5) and percentage of usually employed persons to type of employment (Table 6).

Based on the above data, one would infer that the growth rate of employment seems to have had a boost until the early 1990s due to the growth of short-term jobs, possibly in the informal

TABLE 1: PERCENTAGE OF PEOPLE BELOW POVERTY LINE IN RURAL AND URBAN AREAS OF INDIA EMERGING FROM DIFFERENT STUDIES

| Years | Rural | | | Urban | | |
|---|---|---|---|---|---|---|
| | Mod EG | Gupta | T & S | Mod EG | Gupta | T & S |
| 1972–3 | 56.4 | NA | 57.2 | 49.0 | NA | 47.0 |
| 1977–8 | 53.1 | NA | 54.5 | 45.2 | NA | 42.9 |
| 1983 | 45.6 | 45.6 | 49.0 | 40.8 | 40.8 | 38.3 |
| 1987–8 | 39.1 | 39.1 | 44.9 | 38.2 | 38.2 | 36.5 |
| 1993–4 | 37.3 | 37.3 | 39.7 | 32.4 | 32.4 | 30.9 |
| 1994–5 | NA | 38.0 | 43.6 | NA | 34.2 | 34.1 |
| 1995–6 | NA | 38.3 | 40.1 | NA | 30.9 | 28.7 |
| 1997 | NA | 38.5 | 38.3 | NA | 33.9 | 31.0 |
| 1998 | NA | 45.3 | 44.9 | NA | 34.6 | 31.6 |
| 1999–2000 | | NA | NA | | NA | NA |

*Note*: The poverty estimates are based on the quinquennial and annual rounds of NSS pertaining to consumption expenditure.

TABLE 2: PERCENTAGE OF PERSONS EMPLOYED AS PER USUAL (PRINCIPAL AND SUBSIDIARY) AND WEEKLY STATUS TO TOTAL POPULATION

| | Usual status | | | | Weekly status | | | |
|---|---|---|---|---|---|---|---|---|
| | Rural | | Urban | | Rural | | Urban | |
| | Male | Female | Male | Female | Male | Female | Male | Female |
| 1972–3 | 54.5 | 31.8 | 50.1 | 13.4 | 53.0 | 27.7 | 49.1 | 12.3 |
| 1977–8 | 55.2 | 33.1 | 50.8 | 15.6 | 51.9 | 23.2 | 49.0 | 12.5 |
| 1983 | 54.7 | 34.0 | 51.2 | 15.1 | 51.1 | 22.7 | 49.2 | 11.8 |
| 1987–8 | 53.9 | 32.3 | 50.6 | 15.2 | 50.4 | 22.0 | 49.2 | 11.9 |
| 1993–4 | 55.3 | 32.8 | 52.1 | 15.5 | 53.1 | 26.7 | 51.1 | 13.9 |
| 1994–5 | 56.0 | 31.7 | 51.9 | 11.2 | 54.1 | 24.1 | 51.1 | 11.7 |
| 1995–6 | 55.1 | 29.5 | 52.5 | 10.7 | 53.8 | 23.3 | 52.0 | 10.9 |
| 1997 Jan.–June | 55.0 | 29.1 | 52.1 | 11.1 | 53.5 | 22.2 | 51.3 | 11.4 |
| 1998 | 53.9 | 26.3 | 50.9 | 9.9 | 52.4 | 20.2 | 50.4 | 9.9 |
| 1999–2000 | 53.1 | 29.9 | 51.8 | 13.9 | 51.0 | 25.3 | 50.9 | 12.8 |

sector. This process, however, had a setback since the mid-1990s, reflected in a decrease in the Workforce Participation Rate (WPR) in the annual as also five-yearly rounds. Importantly, significant increase in employment by current (weekly and daily) status and a corresponding decrease in unemployment during 1983–93 were welcomed by policy planners in the country. This was seen as a growth of part-time subcontracted jobs that had a healthy impact on the conditions of workers at lower levels, leading to decline in poverty. Unfortunately, the increase in such low productive jobs

TABLE 3: PERCENTAGE OF WORKERS IN 15–59 AGE GROUP IN DIFFERENT NSS ROUNDS BY USUAL, WEEKLY AND DAILY STATUS

| Year/Round | Rural male | | Rural female | | Urban male | | Urban female | |
|---|---|---|---|---|---|---|---|---|
| | Principal | Principal + subsidiary | Principal | Principal + subsidiary | Principal | Principal + subsidiary | Principal | Principal + subsidiary |
| 1977–8 (32nd) | 90.2 | 92.0 | 40.7 | 54.2 | 79.6 | 81.0 | 19.3 | 24.6 |
| 1983 (38th) | 88.4 | 90.4 | 40.1 | 54.5 | 79.5 | 81.0 | 18.7 | 23.4 |
| 1987–8 (43rd) | 86.2 | 88.7 | 39.8 | 51.6 | 77.9 | 79.3 | 18.3 | 23.5 |
| 1993–4 (50th) | 86.5 | 88.4 | 36.7 | 51.6 | 78.8 | 79.7 | 18.4 | 23.4 |
| 1999–2000 (55th) | | | | | | 78.5 | | 20.9 |
| | Weekly status | Daily status | Weekly status | Daily status | Weekly status | Daily status | Weekly status | Daily status |
| 1977–8 | 87.1 | 81.5 | 37.7 | 31.4 | 78.6 | 75.7 | 19.6 | 17.1 |
| 1983 | 85.4 | 80.2 | 36.4 | 31.6 | 78.3 | 75.2 | 18.4 | 16.5 |
| 1987–8 | 84.0 | 83.5 | 35.3 | 33.2 | 77.3 | 75.1 | 18.5 | 17.0 |
| 1993–4 | 85.1 | 80.9 | 42.0 | 34.3 | 78.2 | 76.0 | 20.9 | 18.1 |
| 1999–2000 | | | | | 77.1 | 74.4 | 19.1 | 16.7 |

*Source*: NSSO (1988, 1990 and 1996).

TABLE 4: PERCENTAGE OF UNEMPLOYED PERSONS/PERSON-DAYS TO LABOUR FORCE/LABOUR-DAYS IN RURAL AREAS

| Year/Round | Male | | | Female | | |
|---|---|---|---|---|---|---|
| | Usual pri + subs status | Weekly status | Daily status | Usual pri + subs status | Weekly status | Daily status |
| 1977–8 (32nd Round) | 1.3 | 3.6 | 7.1 | 2.0 | 4.1 | 9.2 |
| Jan.–Dec. 83 (38th Round) | 1.4 | 3.7 | 7.5 | 0.7 | 4.3 | 9.0 |
| 1987–8 (43rd Round) | 1.8 | 4.2 | 4.6 | 2.4 | 4.4 | 9.0 |
| 1989–90 (45th Round) | 1.3 | 2.6 | — | 0.6 | 2.1 | — |
| 1990–1 (46th Round) | 1.1 | 2.2 | — | 0.3 | 2.1 | — |
| July–Dec. 91 (47th Round) | 1.6 | 2.2 | — | 0.7 | 1.2 | — |
| Jan.–Dec. 92 (48th Round) | 1.2 | 2.2 | — | 0.6 | 1.2 | — |
| 1993–4 (50th Round) | 1.4 | 3.1 | 5.6 | 0.9 | 2.9 | 5.6 |
| 1994–5 (51st Round) | 1.0 | 1.8 | NA | 0.4 | 1.2 | NA |
| 1995–6 (52nd Round) | 1.3 | 1.8 | NA | 0.7 | 0.9 | NA |
| 1997 (53rd Round) | 1.2 | 2.0 | NA | 0.7 | 1.8 | NA |
| 1998 (54th Round) | 2.1 | 2.9 | NA | 1.5 | 2.7 | NA |
| 1999–2000 (55th Round) | 1.7 | 3.9 | 7.2 | 1.0 | 3.7 | 7.0 |

TABLE 5: PERCENTAGE OF UNEMPLOYED PERSONS/PERSON-DAYS TO LABOUR FORCE/LABOUR-DAYS IN URBAN AREAS

| Year/Round | Male | | | Female | | |
|---|---|---|---|---|---|---|
| | Usual pri + subs status | Weekly status | Daily status | Usual pri + subs status | Weekly status | Daily status |
| 1977–8 (32nd Round) | 5.4 | 7.1 | 9.4 | 12.4 | 10.9 | 14.5 |
| Jan.–Dec. 1983 (38th Round) | 5.1 | 6.7 | 9.2 | 4.9 | 7.5 | 11.0 |
| 1987–8 (43rd Round) | 5.2 | 6.6 | 8.8 | 6.2 | 9.2 | 12.0 |
| 1989–90 (45th Round) | 3.9 | 4.5 | — | 2.7 | 4.0 | — |
| 1990–1 (46th Round) | 4.5 | 5.1 | — | 4.7 | 5.3 | — |
| July–Dec. 1991 (47th Round) | 4.1 | 4.8 | — | 4.3 | 5.6 | — |
| Jan.–Dec. 92 (48th Round) | 4.3 | 4.6 | — | 5.8 | 6.2 | — |
| 1993–4 (50th Round) | 4.1 | 5.2 | 6.7 | 6.2 | 8.4 | 10.4 |
| 1994–5 (51st Round) | 3.4 | 3.9 | NA | 3.4 | 4.0 | NA |
| 1995–6 (52nd Round) | 3.8 | 4.1 | NA | 3.1 | 3.5 | NA |
| 1997 (53rd Round) | 3.9 | 4.3 | NA | 4.0 | 45.8 | NA |
| 1998 (54th Round) | 5.1 | 5.4 | NA | 6.8 | 7.8 | NA |
| 1999–2000 (55th Round) | 4.5 | 5.6 | 7.3 | 5.7 | 7.3 | 9.4 |

*Source*: NSSO (1998, 1996 and 1994).

has also been stalled in recent years. Interestingly, the volume of employment available, measured through number of daily-status workers per thousand usually-employed persons, had gone down during 1987–2000 among rural males from 926 to 897, while this remained stable at 940 for urban males. These suggest an increase in the rate of underemployment. In case of females, however, the corresponding figure has gone up significantly from 638 to 676 in rural areas. In urban areas, too, the increase is substantial, from 716 to 791.

Casualization of the workforce in rural and urban areas is yet another disturbing trend. This has come about along with a substantial decline in the share of regular male workers. For rural women, it is the percentage of self-employed workers which has gone down. For urban females, however, there has been growth of low productive jobs available on regular basis. The impact of all these on the welfare of different groups of workers would have to be examined by considering their earnings and poverty status and intake of nutrition.

TABLE 6: PERCENTAGE OF USUALLY EMPLOYED PERSONS (PRINCIPAL AND SUBSIDIARY) BY TYPE OF EMPLOYMENT

| Year | Rural male | | | Rural female | | |
|---|---|---|---|---|---|---|
| | Self-employed | Regular employees | Casual labour | Self-employed | Regular employees | Casual labour |
| 1977–8 | 62.8 | 10.6 | 26.6 | 62.1 | 2.8 | 35.1 |
| 1983 | 60.5 | 10.3 | 29.2 | 61.9 | 2.8 | 35.3 |
| 1987–8 | 58.6 | 10.0 | 31.4 | 60.8 | 3.7 | 35.5 |
| 1993–4 | 57.9 | 8.3 | 33.8 | 58.5 | 2.8 | 38.7 |
| 1994–5 | 60.4 | 6.8 | 32.8 | 57.0 | 2.2 | 40.8 |
| 1995–6 | 59.0 | 7.7 | 33.3 | 56.4 | 2.4 | 41.2 |
| 1997 | 59.4 | 7.3 | 33.3 | 57.0 | 2.1 | 40.9 |
| 1998 | 55.3 | 7.0 | 37.7 | 53.4 | 2.5 | 44.2 |
| 1999–2000 | 55.0 | 8.8 | 36.2 | 57.3 | 3.1 | 39.6 |
| 1977–8 | 40.4 | 46.4 | 13.2 | 49.5 | 24.9 | 25.6 |
| 1983 | 40.9 | 43.7 | 15.4 | 45.8 | 25.8 | 28.4 |
| 1987–8 | 41.7 | 43.7 | 14.6 | 47.1 | 27.5 | 25.4 |
| 1993–4 | 41.7 | 42.1 | 16.2 | 45.4 | 28.6 | 26.0 |
| 1994–5 | 40.4 | 43.1 | 16.5 | 42.6 | 30.1 | 27.3 |
| 1995–6 | 41.0 | 42.5 | 16.5 | 40.0 | 33.2 | 26.8 |
| 1997 | 40.0 | 41.5 | 18.5 | 39.7 | 31.3 | 29.0 |
| 1998 | 42.5 | 39.5 | 18.1 | 38.4 | 32.7 | 28.8 |
| 1999–2000 | 41.5 | 41.7 | 16.8 | 45.3 | 33.3 | 21.4 |

*Source*: NSSO (1988 and 1996).

## SECTORAL GROWTH PERFORMANCE, SHIFTS IN WORKFORCE STRUCTURE AND THEIR IMPLICATIONS FOR POVERTY AND NUTRITION

A major apprehension while launching the Structrural Adjustment Programme (SAP) in 1991 was that it would slow down the tempo of economic growth and decelerate growth in employment resulting in food insecurity and nutritional deficiency. Available evidence, however, reveals that the first few years of the period of reform were characterized by reduction in unemployment and increase in the volume of employment, although most of the jobs were for short duration and part-time in nature. The second half of the 1990s certainly gives warning signals as the employment situation seems to have worsened significantly. The is further confirmed by the data from the Economic Census suggesting that the growth rates of non-agricultural enterprises and employment therein in the 1990s were half of that of the 1980s. The performance of the economy measured in terms of growth in national income, on the other hand, has been rather satisfying in the 1990s. The growth of GDP in real terms has never been negative, even after the formal launching of the programmes of structural adjustment.

Critics have pointed out that the high growth of the Indian economy in the post-liberalization phase cannot be taken to reflect the success of SAP. They hold that the performance of the economy is due, in no small measure, to growth in agriculture, which has been very high, thanks to the excellent monsoons, year after year. In any case, agriculture so far is a sector least affected by SAP in the country; its good performance cannot, therefore, be attributed to liberalization.

Despite the Indian economy registering high growth rate in the 1990s, sectoral composition of income has fluctuated significantly, but the overall growth rate has been maintained at above 5 per cent in real terms, which is much above that registered in any decade until the 1980s. Critics of SAP, therefore, do not have much ground for complaint on the growth front.

The same, however, cannot be said with regard to poverty level in the country, computed from the thin sample data. It went up significantly in 1992, 1995 and 1998, and in all the three years, one observes that agricultural production had either remained stationary or declined. Interestingly, a growth rate of 5 per cent in the 1980s, which ultimately led to economic crisis in the early 1990s, had made a dent on poverty, bringing it down by 4 percentage points. In contrast, a very high annual growth of over 7 per cent during 1994–8 made no impact on poverty in rural or urban areas. Similarly, a growth of 5 per cent in 1997–8 pushed up the level by 2 percentage points. The emphasis of policy makers focusing on poverty alleviation must, therefore, shift from the magnitude of growth to its composition, as the latter holds the key to poverty.

The fall in the growth in agriculture in a particular year brings down the supply, but that can be taken care of through storage and the PDS. But the low growth of agriculture also depresses affordability among the vulnerable sections and their capacity to access food even from the government system, because of the recent changes affecting prices and coverage. Similarly, the fluctuations in the highly labour-intensive sectors like mining and quarrying and construction are also responsible for increase in poverty and decline in nutritional intake.

Manufacturing is a sector wherein the growth of income during the 1990s has been high—over 7 per cent, as was the case in the 1980s. Unfortunately, this has not been accompanied by growth in employment. The percentage of workers in manufacturing, as obtained from the Population Census and NSS data, has gone down significantly during the past three decades (Tables 7 and 8). The decline is sharper after 1987–8, specially in urban areas. This, besides a downward trend in labour intensity in the organized sector, can be explained in terms of jobs being subcontracted out by large and medium manufacturing units to smaller units, often carried out at household level. Many of these subcontracted workers identify themselves as providers of services and, thus, get classified under the tertiary sector. The number of workers in organized manufacturing covered under the Director General of Employment and Training (DGE&T), Ministry of Labour has been stable or gone up marginally during the 1990s. The figure has gone down in absolute terms since then, which confirms the apprehensions noted above.

The share of construction workers has fluctuated over the years under consideration. It increased during 1983–7 particularly in rural areas. During 1987–93, however, there was a decline in rural areas, as there was an expansion in government-sponsored construction activities in the wake of the severe drought in 1987–8. The share of construction workers increased during 1983–7, and the trend has been sustained during 1987–2000 as well. However, there has been a decline in the absolute number of workers in the public sector since 1994–5. One would infer that much of the growth of employment in construction activities has taken place outside the formal sector at a low level of productivity and wage rate. This is confirmed by the analysis of the growth in real wages during the 1980s and early 1990s in urban areas (Table 9). The growth in real wages for regular male workers during 1983–7 was 5.6 per cent per annum, which has come down to 0.7 per cent only during 1987–93. Correspondingly, for women, it has declined from 4.8 per cent to –3.7 per cent. Equally dismal is the scenario for the casual workers. For males, the growth rate has declined from 3.7 per cent in the first period to 1.2 per cent in the second period. The corresponding percentage figures for female casual workers are 5.0 and 3.2 respectively (Table 10).

The incidence of poverty among casual and self-employed workers in urban areas has been noted to be extremely high—much higher than among regular workers. Similarly, agriculture,

TABLE 7: SECTORAL DISTRIBUTION OF URBAN MAIN WORKERS AS PER POPULATION CENSUS

(percentage)

| Sector | Male | | | Female | | |
|---|---|---|---|---|---|---|
| | 1971 | 1981 | 1991 | 1971 | 1981 | 1991 |
| Cultivators | 5.2 | 5.2 | 4.9 | 4.1 | 4.6 | 5.1 |
| Agri. Labourers | 4.7 | 4.7 | 5.4 | 17.7 | 16.7 | 15.6 |
| Forestry, fishing, etc. | 1.6 | 1.8 | 1.7 | 2.0 | 1.8 | 1.5 |
| Mining and quarrying | 1.0 | 1.1 | 1.2 | 1.0 | 0.7 | 0.7 |
| Manufacturing HH | 4.4 | 4.2 | 2.5 | 10.0 | 10.4 | 7.5 |
| Manufacturing NH | 24.3 | 26.0 | 23.2 | 13.0 | 14.6 | 14.1 |
| Construction | 3.5 | 4.3 | 5.3 | 2.9 | 3.1 | 3.3 |
| Trade and commerce | 21.4 | 21.3 | 23.7 | 8.2 | 8.9 | 10.0 |
| Transport | 10.7 | 10.0 | 9.2 | 3.2 | 2.2 | 1.9 |
| Other services | 23.3 | 21.4 | 22.8 | 37.9 | 37.0 | 40.1 |

*Source*: *Census of India* (1971, 1981 and 1993).

TABLE 8: PERCENTAGE DISTRIBUTION OF USUALLY EMPLOYED PERSONS (PRINCIPAL AND SUBSIDIARY STATUS) IN RURAL AREAS

| Sector | Male | | | | |
|---|---|---|---|---|---|
| | 1977–8 | 1983 | 1987–8 | 1993–4 | 1999–2000 |
| Agriculture (0) | 80.5 | 77.8 | 74.6 | 74.0 | 71.4 |
| Mining and quarrying (1) | 0.5 | 0.6 | 0.7 | 0.7 | 0.6 |
| Manufacturing (2 & 3) | 6.5 | 7.0 | 7.4 | 7.0 | 7.3 |
| Electricity (4) | 0.2 | 0.2 | 0.3 | 0.3 | 0.2 |
| Construction (5) | 1.7 | 2.2 | 3.7 | 3.2 | 4.5 |
| Wholesale/ret. td. (6) | 4.0 | 4.4 | 5.1 | 5.5 | 6.8 |
| Transport, sto., etc. (7) | 1.2 | 1.7 | 2.0 | 2.2 | 3.2 |
| Financial, ins. serv. (8) | 0.2 | 0.3 | 0.4 | 0.4 | 0.5 |
| Community, etc., serv. (9) | 5.2 | 5.8 | 5.8 | 6.6 | 5.6 |
| **Sector** | **Female** | | | | |
| | 1977–8 | 1983 | 1987–8 | 1993–4 | 1999–2000 |
| Agriculture (0) | 86.8 | 87.8 | 84.8 | 86.1 | 85.4 |
| Mining and quarrying (1) | 0.3 | 0.3 | 0.4 | 0.4 | 0.3 |
| Manufacturing (2 & 3) | 6.1 | 6.4 | 6.9 | 7.1 | 7.6 |
| Electricity (4) | 0.0 | 0.0 | 0.0 | 0.1 | 0.0 |
| Construction (5) | 0.7 | 0.7 | 2.7 | 0.9 | 1.1 |
| Wholesale/ret. td. (6) | 2.3 | 1.9 | 2.1 | 2.1 | 2.0 |
| Transport, sto., etc. (7) | 0.1 | 0.1 | 0.1 | 0.1 | 0.1 |
| Financial, ins. serv. (8) | 0.0 | 0.0 | 0.0 | 0.1 | 0.1 |
| Community, etc., serv. (9) | 3.7 | 2.8 | 3.0 | 3.3 | 3.6 |

*Source*: NSSO (1986, 1990, 1997 and 2000a).

TABLE 9: PERCENTAGE DISTRIBUTION OF USUALLY EMPLOYED PERSONS (PRINCIPAL AND SUBSIDIARY STATUS) IN URBAN AREAS

| Sector | Male | | | | |
|---|---|---|---|---|---|
| | 1977–8 | 1983 | 1987–8 | 1993–4 | 1999–2000 |
| Agriculture (0) | 10.2 | 10.3 | 9.1 | 9.0 | 6.6 |
| Mining and quarrying (1) | 0.9 | 1.3 | 1.3 | 1.3 | 0.9 |
| Manufacturing (2 & 3) | 27.7 | 27.0 | 25.7 | 23.5 | 22.4 |
| Electricity (4) | 1.1 | 1.1 | 1.2 | 1.2 | 0.8 |
| Construction (5) | 4.2 | 5.2 | 5.8 | 6.9 | 8.7 |
| Wholesale/ret. td. (6) | 21.6 | 20.2 | 22.0 | 21.9 | 29.4 |
| Transport, sto., etc. (7) | 9.9 | 9.9 | 9.7 | 9.7 | 10.4 |
| Financial, ins. serv. (8) | 3.0 | 3.5 | 3.5 | 3.8 | 4.5 |
| Community, etc., serv. (9) | 21.5 | 21.4 | 21.7 | 22.6 | 16.5 |
| **Sector** | **Female** | | | | |
| | 1977–8 | 1983 | 1987–8 | 1993–4 | 1999–2000 |
| Agriculture (0) | 25.1 | 32.0 | 29.4 | 24.7 | 17.7 |
| Mining and quarrying (1) | 0.6 | 0.8 | 0.8 | 0.6 | 0.4 |
| Manufacturing (2 & 3) | 29.4 | 27.1 | 27.0 | 24.1 | 24.0 |
| Electricity (4) | 0.1 | 0.0 | 0.2 | 0.3 | 0.2 |
| Construction (5) | 2.6 | 3.3 | 3.7 | 4.1 | 4.8 |
| Wholesale/ret. td. (6) | 9.8 | 9.0 | 10.0 | 10.0 | 16.9 |
| Transport, sto., etc. (7) | 1.2 | 1.6 | 0.9 | 1.3 | 1.8 |
| Financial, ins. serv. (8) | 0.7 | 0.4 | 1.2 | 1.9 | 2.5 |
| Community, etc., serv. (9) | 30.4 | 25.8 | 26.6 | 33.1 | 31.7 |

*Source*: NSSO (1986, 1990, 1997 and 2000a).

construction and trade are the three sectors that reported much higher levels of poverty than the national average (Kundu 1994). Significantly, these are the categories and production sectors that have gained in terms of the share in total employment. The incremental workforce, getting absorbed largely as casual and self-employed workers in low productive sectors certainly cannot be taken as a healthy development from the viewpoint of workers' welfare or future urban development.

## CHANGING LEVELS OF POVERTY, EMPLOYMENT AND NUTRITION: AN INTER-STATE ANALYSIS

The inter-state variations in poverty, employment/unemployment and nutritional levels have been analysed only for those years for which quinquennial data are available from the NSS, as the thin

TABLE 10: ANNUAL COMPOUND GROWTH RATES OF REAL WAGES FOR ADULT (15–59 AGE GROUP): REGULAR/SALARIED AND CASUAL WORKERS IN DIFFERENT SECTORS

| Sector | Regular/salaried workers | | Casual workers | |
|---|---|---|---|---|
| | 1983–7 | 1987–93 | 1983–7 | 1987–93 |
| *Males* | | | | |
| Agriculture | 11.4 | 1.2 | 3.1 | 2.0 |
| Mining, quarrying and manufacturing | 7.6 | 2.8 | -0.2 | -0.4 |
| Div. 2 | | | | |
| Div. 3 | 2.8 | 1.6 | 4.7 | 1.4 |
| Electricity, etc. | 5.3 | 0.5 | -1.5 | 1.5 |
| Construction | 5.8 | 2.5 | 3.2 | 5.0 |
| Trade | 5.6 | 0.7 | 3.3 | 1.8 |
| Transport | 3.1 | 1.8 | 3.7 | 1.2 |
| Other services | 5.8 | 0.6 | 3.4 | 2.1 |
| Div. 8 | 4.7 | 2.6 | 3.8 | -0.9 |
| Div. 9 | 7.6 | 1.4 | 7.8 | -0.9 |
| All | 6.3 | 1.3 | 3.3 | 1.6 |
| *Females* | | | | |
| Agriculture | 8.5 | 6.0 | 2.8 | 3.9 |
| Mining, quarrying and manufacturing | 9.9 | 2.6 | 10.7 | 1.9 |
| Div. 2 | 4.4 | 4.9 | 5.3 | 1.9 |
| Div. 3 | 0.4 | 0.3 | 9.5 | 0.9 |
| Electricity, etc. | 2.6 | 2.8 | | 4.0 |
| Construction | 4.8 | -3.7 | 5.0 | 3.2 |
| Trade | -1.3 | 5.2 | 1.0 | 6.2 |
| Transport | 10.2 | -1.0 | 6.7 | -4.4 |
| Other services | | | | |
| Div. 8 | 6.0 | 2.1 | 22.2 | -0.4 |
| Div. 9 | 9.8 | 0.1 | 5.9 | 2.9 |
| All | 9.2 | 0.6 | 5.3 | 2.9 |

sample data do not provide reliable estimates at the state level, as noted above. The poverty levels for the states obtained by different scholars basically using the methodology recommended by the Expert Group on Measurement of the Number and Proportion of the Poor are given in Table 11. It has been pointed out that the percentage of the poor in rural areas has always been above that in urban areas, although the differences have been changing over time. Surprisingly, however, for a large majority of the states, this is not the pattern. Only a few like Assam, Bihar and Orissa among the backward states and Maharashtra and West Bengal among the developed ones exhibit rural poverty higher than that in urban areas. Most of the less developed states like Andhra Pradesh, Kerala, Madhya Pradesh, Uttar Pradesh and Rajasthan report higher levels of urban poverty in many of the years under consideration. This is also the pattern in Punjab, Haryana, Karnataka and Gujarat—the developed states in the country. What explains the opposite result at the national level is that the states that conform to the national pattern, report rural poverty to be higher than urban poverty by a huge margin.

The spatial variation in rural poverty shows a clear pattern and strong negative relationship with economic development during the 1970s, 1980s and early 1990s. A study analysing the pattern of interdependencies among infrastructural and economic development indicators in the 1970s and 1980s confirms that rural poverty declines smoothly with development. This is not the case with urban poverty (Kundu 2001). The dynamics of development in urban areas in different states during the past two decades

TABLE 11: PERCENTAGE OF PEOPLE BELOW POVERTY LINE BY STATES: 1973–93

| | 1973–4 | | | 1977–8 | | | 1983 | | | 1987–8 | | | 1993–4 | | |
|---|---|---|---|---|---|---|---|---|---|---|---|---|---|---|---|
| | R | U | C | R | U | C | R | U | C | R | U | C | R | U | C |
| AP | 48.4 | 50.6 | 48.9 | 38.1 | 43.6 | 39.3 | 26.5 | 36.3 | 28.9 | 20.9 | 40.1 | 25.9 | 15.9 | 38.3 | 22.2 |
| AS | 56.7 | 36.9 | 51.2 | 59.8 | 32.7 | 57.2 | 42.6 | 21.7 | 40.5 | 39.4 | 9.9 | 36.2 | 45.0 | 7.7 | 40.9 |
| BH | 63.0 | 53.0 | 61.9 | 63.3 | 48.8 | 61.6 | 64.4 | 47.3 | 62.2 | 52.6 | 48.7 | 52.1 | 58.2 | 34.5 | 55.0 |
| GJ | 46.4 | 52.6 | 48.1 | 41.8 | 40.0 | 41.2 | 29.8 | 39.1 | 32.8 | 28.7 | 37.3 | 31.5 | 22.2 | 27.9 | 24.2 |
| HR | 34.2 | 40.2 | 35.4 | 27.7 | 36.6 | 29.6 | 20.6 | 24.2 | 21.4 | 16.2 | 18.0 | 16.6 | 28.0 | 16.4 | 25.1 |
| KN | 55.1 | 52.5 | 54.5 | 48.1 | 50.4 | 48.8 | 36.3 | 42.8 | 38.2 | 32.8 | 48.4 | 37.5 | 29.9 | 40.1 | 33.1 |
| KL | 59.2 | 62.7 | 59.8 | 51.5 | 55.6 | 52.2 | 39.0 | 45.7 | 40.4 | 29.1 | 40.3 | 31.8 | 25.8 | 24.6 | 25.4 |
| MP | 62.7 | 57.6 | 61.8 | 62.5 | 58.7 | 61.8 | 48.9 | 53.0 | 49.8 | 41.9 | 47.1 | 43.1 | 40.6 | 48.4 | 42.5 |
| MH | 57.7 | 43.9 | 53.2 | 64.0 | 40.1 | 55.9 | 45.2 | 40.2 | 43.4 | 40.8 | 39.8 | 40.4 | 37.9 | 35.2 | 36.9 |
| OR | 67.3 | 55.6 | 66.2 | 72.4 | 50.9 | 70.1 | 67.5 | 49.1 | 65.3 | 57.6 | 41.6 | 55.6 | 49.7 | 41.6 | 48.6 |
| PB | 28.2 | 28.0 | 28.1 | 16.4 | 27.3 | 19.3 | 13.2 | 23.8 | 16.2 | 12.6 | 14.7 | 13.2 | 12.0 | 11.4 | 11.8 |
| RJ | 44.8 | 52.1 | 46.1 | 35.9 | 43.5 | 37.4 | 33.5 | 37.9 | 34.5 | 33.2 | 41.9 | 35.2 | 26.5 | 30.5 | 27.4 |
| TN | 57.4 | 49.4 | 54.9 | 57.7 | 48.7 | 54.8 | 54.0 | 47.0 | 51.7 | 45.8 | 38.6 | 43.4 | 32.5 | 39.8 | 35.0 |
| UP | 56.5 | 60.1 | 57.1 | 47.6 | 52.2 | 49.1 | 46.5 | 49.9 | 47.1 | 41.1 | 43.0 | 41.5 | 42.3 | 35.4 | 40.9 |
| WB | 73.2 | 34.7 | 63.4 | 68.3 | 38.2 | 60.5 | 63.1 | 32.3 | 54.8 | 48.3 | 35.1 | 44.7 | 40.8 | 22.4 | 35.7 |
| AI | 56.4 | 49.0 | 54.9 | 53.1 | 45.2 | 51.3 | 45.6 | 40.8 | 44.5 | 39.1 | 38.2 | 38.9 | 37.3 | 32.4 | 36.0 |

*Source*: Government of India, Press Information Bureau (GIPIB), 'Estimates of Poverty', New Delhi, 11 March 1997.

*Note*: R = Rural, U = Urban, C = Combined, AI = All India.

unfortunately has not led to a corresponding decline in poverty. It would appear that there has been a delinking of the rural and urban labour markets as also of the processes generating growth and poverty.

The intake of nutrients, viz., calorie, protein and fats in per capita terms reveals an interesting pattern across the states (Table 12). The intakes were consistently higher in states like Punjab, Haryana, Himachal Pradesh, Jammu & Kashmir and Rajasthan for all the three nutrients in rural areas. This can be explained in terms of high affordability and rich food in case of Punjab and Haryana, while for the other three states it is due to the nature of cereals consumed and other specificities affecting food habits. It is indeed very surprising that the states like Bihar, Uttar Pradesh, Madhya Pradesh and Rajasthan have higher nutrition intakes than Gujarat, Karnataka, Tamil Nadu, West Bengal and Maharashtra.

The pattern in the case of urban areas is similar. States like Himachal Pradesh, Jammu & Kashmir and Rajasthan have high intake of calorie and protein. The developed states in general have lower intake, which includes even Punjab and Haryana. In case of protein and fats, however, developed states like Punjab, Haryana and Gujarat do somewhat better. Still, Rajasthan and Bihar

TABLE 12: PER CAPITA CALORIE INTAKE (kcal) PER DAY

| State | Rural | | | Urban | | |
|---|---|---|---|---|---|---|
| | 1972–3 | 1983 | 1993–4 | 1972–3 | 1983 | 1993–4 |
| Andhra Pradesh | 2,103 | 2,204 | 2,052 | 2,143 | 2,009 | 1,992 |
| Assam | 2,074 | 2,056 | 1,983 | 2,135 | 2,043 | 2,108 |
| Bihar | 2,225 | 2,189 | 2,115 | 2,167 | 2,131 | 2,188 |
| Gujarat | 2,142 | 2,113 | 1,994 | 2,172 | 2,000 | 2,027 |
| Haryana | 3,215 | 2,554 | 2,491 | 2,404 | 2,242 | 2,140 |
| H.P. | 2,954 | 2,636 | 2,324 | 2,961 | 2,429 | 2,416 |
| J&K | 3,151 | 2,569 | 2,507 | 2,467 | 2,234 | 2,392 |
| Karnataka | 2,202 | 2,260 | 2,073 | 1,925 | 2,124 | 2,026 |
| Kerala | 1,559 | 1,884 | 1,965 | 1,723 | 2,049 | 1,966 |
| M.P. | 2,423 | 2,323 | 2,164 | 2,229 | 2,137 | 2,082 |
| Maharashtra | 1,895 | 2,144 | 1,939 | 1,971 | 2,028 | 1,989 |
| Orissa | 1,995 | 2,103 | 2,199 | 2,276 | 2,219 | 2,261 |
| Punjab | 3,493 | 2,677 | 2,418 | 2,783 | 2,100 | 2,089 |
| Rajasthan | 2,730 | 2,433 | 2,470 | 2,357 | 2,255 | 2,184 |
| Tamil Nadu | 1,955 | 1,861 | 1,884 | 1,841 | 2,140 | 1,922 |
| U.P. | 2,575 | 2,399 | 2,307 | 2,161 | 2,043 | 2,114 |
| West Bengal | 1,921 | 2,027 | 2,211 | 2,080 | 2,048 | 2,131 |

showing high protein intake, Jammu & Kashmir, Himachal Pradesh and Rajasthan showing high fat intake similar to that of Punjab and Haryana is striking. One would argue that much more than affordability, the intake of nutrients is determined by food habits and cropping patterns in the region.

## GROWTH, EMPLOYMENT GENERATION AND POVERTY: AN ANALYSIS OF THE FACTORS AFFECTING NUTRITIONAL ADEQUACY

In an attempt to analyse the spatial pattern of economic growth, poverty, unemployment and their impact on nutritional levels, a set of 10 indicators have been built taking 15 large states as the units of observation. First, we have constructed indicators taking data from the quinquennial surveys of NSS for the years 1972–3, 1983 and 1993–4. These give: (1) average consumption levels of calories, protein and fats along with poverty estimates for rural and urban areas separately; (2) per capita income at current prices; and (3) the percentages of the female literate, male workers, casual workers, manufacturing workers and unemployed persons in the early 1990s. Except female literacy data that are from the Population Census of 1991, the others pertain to the year 1993–4 and are taken from the 50th Round of NSS. Separate indicators have been constructed for rural and urban areas, although for correlation analysis, the two data sets have been combined to look at cross-category interrelations. The list of the indicators is given below:

1. Average calorie intake (kcal) per day in rural and urban areas for each of the years 1972–3, 1983 and 1993–4.
2. Average protein intake (grams) per day in rural and urban areas for each of the years 1972–3, 1983 and 1993–4.
3. Average intake of fats (grams) per day in rural and urban areas for each of the years 1972–3, 1983 and 1993–4.
4. Percentage of people below poverty line in rural and urban areas for each of the years 1972–3, 1983 and 1993–4.
5. Per capita net state domestic product at current prices for each of the years 1972–3, 1983 and 1993–4.
6. Female literacy for 7+ years population in rural and urban areas, 1991.
7. Percentage of rural and urban male workers (usual status 15+ years), 1993–4.

8. Percentage of casual to total male workers in rural and urban areas 1993–4.
9. Percentage of workers in manufacturing (M + F) in rural and urban areas 1993–4.
10. Unemployment rate by usual status (adjusted) in rural and urban areas, 1993–4.

The analysis begins with an overview of interdependencies between indicators of per capita income and poverty levels in rural and urban areas. An attempt is made here first to assess the impact of sectoral patterns of economic development on the levels of poverty across the states and focus on the differences in development dynamics between rural and urban areas. The impact of the economic factors on nutritional intake has then been analysed in the later part of this section in some detail.

A significant point emerging from the inter-state analysis is that the inequality in poverty levels over the years has gone up, both in rural as well as urban areas (Table 13). The coefficient of variation in the percentage of poor in rural areas has gone up from 22.2 per cent in 1973–4 to 37.6 per cent in 1993–4. The corresponding increase in case of urban poverty is slightly higher—from 20.4 to 38.8. This implies that poverty reduction has been uneven across the states, especially in urban areas; an important point about the inter-state variation is that poverty in rural areas is very high in economically backward states. One observes a strong negative correlation between per capita State Domestic Product (SDP) and percentage of people below the poverty line, as expected, in the 1970s.[3]

The correlation between rural poverty and SDP is strongly negative, viz., –0.71 in the year 1973–4. The figure is significant at 1 per cent level. The correlation coefficients are about the same for all the years for which NSS quinquennial data are available, as may be seen in Table 13. The coefficients are highly stable and vary marginally between –0.6 and –0.7 during the period from the early 1970s to the early 1990s. Importantly, urban poverty too is negatively correlated with per capita income in 1973–4. The value of the coefficient is as high as 0.62 with a negative sign, which is significant at 1 per cent level. The value fluctuates between –0.6 and –0.7 during the period under consideration, as is the case with rural poverty. Surprisingly, for 1993-4, the figure works out as very low at 0.37 (with a negative sign), which is statistically

TABLE 13: SELECT STATISTICAL PARAMETERS CONCERNING POVERTY BASED ON STATE LEVEL DATA

| Year | Coefficient of variation computed from poverty estimates (Modified Expert Group) | | Coefficient of correlation | | |
|---|---|---|---|---|---|
| | | | Of poverty with per capita income | | Between rural and urban poverty |
| | Rural | Urban | Rural | Urban | |
| 1973–4 | 22.18 | 20.40 | -0.714 | -0.620 | 0.408 |
| 1977–8 | 31.70 | 20.25 | -0.639 | -0.715 | 0.449 |
| 1983 | 38.17 | 25.52 | -0.678 | -0.542 | 0.577 |
| 1987–8 | 37.47 | 33.89 | -0.570 | -0.621 | 0.486 |
| 1993–4 | 37.58 | 38.85 | -0.638 | -0.374 | 0.255 |

*Source*: Calculated Using the Select Statistical Tools.

insignificant, even at 10 per cent level. Also, the correlations of urban poverty with other development indicators like per capita consumption, levels of industrial and infrastructural development, etc., also turn out as insignificant during the 1990s (Kundu 2001).

Calorie consumption in per capita terms shows inter-state variation that can be easily explained in terms of selected economic indicators (Tables 14 and 15). The rural figures have strong positive relationship (r = 0.59) with per capita income in 1973–4. A somewhat lower coefficient is noted in case of rural protein consumption (r = 0.44) as well. A similar pattern and interdependencies are noted in case of urban nutritional levels, the two coefficients being 0.52 and 0.36. Two important points, however, emerge as extremely significant. First, the relationship of per capita income with intake of fats is much stronger than that with the other two nutrients. This is understandable as the consumption of calorie and protein in the less developed states do not work out as very low. The average values get pushed up by the high consumption levels of the better-off sections of population and thereby hide high inequality. Also, the richer states do not report high calorie consumption due to diversification of food habits. The higher affordability in richer states, gets reflected in higher intake of fats. The second important trend is that the degree of correlation between income and the consumption of the first two nutrients goes down steadily over the years. The correlation between income and calorie and protein intakes in the year 1993–4 works out as almost zero or negative in both rural and urban areas. This could be because of diversification in the

TABLE 14: CORRELATION MATRIX: NUTRITION AND DEVELOPMENT INDICATORS

| | RKCA L-72 | UKCA L-72 | RKCA L-83 | UKCA L-83 | RKCA L-93 | UKCA L-93 | RPrt 72 | UPrt 72 | RPrt 83 | UPrt 83 | RPrt 93 | UPrt 93 | Rfat 72 | Ufat 72 | Rfat 83 | Ufat 83 | Rfat 93 | Ufat 93 | PR-73 | PU-73 | PR-83 | PU-83 | PR-93 | PU-93 |
|---|---|---|---|---|---|---|---|---|---|---|---|---|---|---|---|---|---|---|---|---|---|---|---|---|
| RKCAL-72 | 1.00 | | | | | | | | | | | | | | | | | | | | | | | |
| UKCAL-72 | 0.87 | 1.00 | | | | | | | | | | | | | | | | | | | | | | |
| RKCAL-83 | 0.94 | 0.84 | 1.00 | | | | | | | | | | | | | | | | | | | | | |
| UKCAL-83 | 0.44 | 0.36 | 0.37 | 1.00 | | | | | | | | | | | | | | | | | | | | |
| RKCAL-93 | 0.83 | 0.78 | 0.84 | 0.60 | 1.00 | | | | | | | | | | | | | | | | | | | |
| UKCAL-93 | 0.35 | 0.57 | 0.40 | 0.56 | 0.65 | 1.00 | | | | | | | | | | | | | | | | | | |
| RPrt-72 | 0.94 | 0.78 | 0.93 | 0.49 | 0.86 | 0.42 | 1.00 | | | | | | | | | | | | | | | | | |
| UPrt-72 | 0.81 | 0.87 | 0.82 | 0.38 | 0.84 | 0.65 | 0.87 | 1.00 | | | | | | | | | | | | | | | | |
| RPrt-83 | 0.90 | 0.75 | 0.95 | 0.37 | 0.81 | 0.36 | 0.97 | 0.85 | 1.00 | | | | | | | | | | | | | | | |
| UPrt-83 | 0.76 | 0.70 | 0.84 | 0.55 | 0.87 | 0.64 | 0.88 | 0.89 | 0.90 | 1.00 | | | | | | | | | | | | | | |
| RPrt-93 | 0.88 | 0.73 | 0.89 | 0.52 | 0.92 | 0.47 | 0.96 | 0.87 | 0.94 | 0.94 | 1.00 | | | | | | | | | | | | | |
| UPrt-93 | 0.71 | 0.68 | 0.76 | 0.53 | 0.87 | 0.71 | 0.84 | 0.90 | 0.85 | 0.97 | 0.91 | 1.00 | | | | | | | | | | | | |
| Rfat-72 | 0.81 | 0.63 | 0.76 | 0.25 | 0.63 | 0.03 | 0.81 | 0.65 | 0.79 | 0.64 | 0.80 | 0.56 | 1.00 | | | | | | | | | | | |
| Ufat-72 | 0.57 | 0.55 | 0.59 | -0.05 | 0.42 | -0.03 | 0.58 | 0.58 | 0.63 | 0.51 | 0.59 | 0.43 | 0.87 | 1.00 | | | | | | | | | | |
| Rfat-83 | 0.71 | 0.53 | 0.65 | 0.13 | 0.51 | -0.11 | 0.67 | 0.53 | 0.69 | 0.54 | 0.70 | 0.45 | 0.97 | 0.87 | 1.00 | | | | | | | | | |
| Ufat-83 | 0.52 | 0.37 | 0.52 | 0.03 | 0.37 | -0.19 | 0.53 | 0.43 | 0.59 | 0.47 | 0.58 | 0.36 | 0.88 | 0.93 | 0.93 | 1.00 | | | | | | | | |
| Rfat-93 | 0.76 | 0.59 | 0.71 | 0.19 | 0.60 | -0.02 | 0.75 | 0.62 | 0.75 | 0.61 | 0.78 | 0.54 | 0.99 | 0.87 | 0.99 | 0.91 | 1.00 | | | | | | | |
| Ufat-93 | 0.58 | 0.46 | 0.58 | 0.02 | 0.40 | -0.11 | 0.61 | 0.54 | 0.66 | 0.53 | 0.63 | 0.45 | 0.91 | 0.97 | 0.92 | 0.97 | 0.92 | 1.00 | | | | | | |
| PR-73 | -0.78 | -0.62 | -0.69 | -0.16 | -0.47 | 0.09 | -0.68 | -0.48 | -0.64 | -0.40 | -0.60 | -0.30 | -0.88 | -0.68 | -0.86 | -0.70 | -0.86 | -0.70 | 1.00 | | | | | |
| PU-73 | -0.44 | -0.51 | -0.31 | 0.05 | -0.26 | -0.09 | -0.27 | -0.38 | -0.21 | -0.09 | -0.18 | -0.08 | -0.29 | -0.27 | -0.25 | -0.19 | -0.28 | -0.21 | 0.41 | 1.00 | | | | |
| PR-83 | -0.61 | -0.43 | -0.59 | 0.06 | -0.33 | 0.30 | -0.51 | -0.29 | -0.52 | -0.27 | -0.47 | -0.12 | -0.81 | -0.69 | -0.84 | -0.75 | -0.82 | -0.70 | 0.92 | 0.31 | 1.00 | | | |
| PU-83 | -0.45 | -0.47 | -0.34 | 0.05 | -0.31 | -0.07 | -0.32 | -0.37 | -0.23 | -0.14 | -0.25 | -0.09 | -0.45 | -0.35 | -0.41 | -0.32 | -0.43 | -0.30 | 0.62 | 0.86 | 0.58 | 1.00 | | |
| PR-93 | -0.36 | -0.23 | -0.31 | 0.15 | -0.16 | 0.50 | -0.21 | -0.03 | -0.21 | 0.02 | -0.22 | 0.15 | -0.65 | -0.60 | -0.71 | -0.67 | -0.68 | -0.60 | 0.72 | 0.22 | 0.86 | 0.40 | 1.00 | |
| PU-93 | -0.36 | -0.37 | -0.21 | 0.12 | -0.27 | -0.11 | -0.24 | -0.35 | -0.17 | -0.14 | -0.24 | -0.17 | -0.39 | -0.29 | -0.42 | -0.27 | -0.42 | -0.26 | 0.51 | 0.70 | 0.45 | 0.88 | 0.26 | 1.00 |
| PCI-73 | 0.58 | 0.52 | 0.52 | -0.02 | 0.36 | -0.19 | 0.42 | 0.36 | 0.45 | 0.26 | 0.42 | 0.16 | 0.73 | 0.76 | 0.79 | 0.80 | 0.76 | 0.75 | -0.71 | -0.62 | -0.72 | -0.59 | -0.72 | -0.46 |

| | | | | | | | | | | | | | | | | | | | | | | | | |
|---|---|---|---|---|---|---|---|---|---|---|---|---|---|---|---|---|---|---|---|---|---|---|---|---|
| PCI-83 | 0.43 | 0.37 | 0.38 | -0.14 | 0.17 | -0.29 | 0.29 | 0.23 | 0.34 | 0.14 | 0.27 | 0.04 | 0.66 | 0.75 | 0.74 | 0.80 | 0.69 | 0.75 | -0.65 | -0.56 | -0.68 | -0.54 | -0.65 | -0.43 |
| PCI-93 | 0.41 | 0.29 | 0.34 | -0.13 | 0.08 | -0.43 | 0.25 | 0.14 | 0.30 | 0.04 | 0.20 | -0.06 | 0.58 | 0.61 | 0.66 | 0.70 | 0.62 | 0.65 | -0.64 | -0.58 | -0.65 | -0.51 | -0.64 | -0.37 |
| FlitR-91 | -0.38 | -0.44 | -0.47 | -0.35 | -0.43 | -0.53 | -0.54 | -0.54 | -0.50 | -0.51 | -0.42 | -0.50 | -0.13 | -0.11 | 0.10 | 0.10 | -0.01 | -0.04 | 0.02 | -0.04 | -0.13 | -0.13 | -0.29 | -0.36 |
| FlitU-91 | -0.46 | -0.49 | -0.56 | -0.35 | -0.54 | -0.52 | -0.60 | -0.56 | -0.58 | -0.56 | -0.52 | -0.57 | -0.22 | -0.16 | -0.01 | 0.04 | -0.12 | -0.10 | 0.09 | -0.14 | -0.05 | -0.20 | -0.17 | -0.39 |
| WPR-RM15+ | -0.01 | 0.10 | 0.13 | -0.11 | 0.01 | 0.02 | 0.06 | 0.07 | 0.11 | 0.05 | 0.00 | 0.01 | -0.04 | 0.19 | -0.15 | -0.02 | -0.10 | 0.08 | 0.20 | 0.20 | 0.14 | 0.40 | -0.04 | 0.64 |
| WPR-UM15+ | 0.53 | 0.32 | 0.42 | 0.01 | 0.29 | -0.43 | 0.40 | 0.14 | 0.35 | 0.06 | 0.34 | -0.03 | 0.68 | 0.59 | 0.68 | 0.65 | 0.68 | 0.61 | -0.71 | -0.37 | -0.76 | -0.40 | -0.85 | -0.21 |
| CasRM | -0.65 | -0.55 | -0.69 | -0.43 | -0.77 | -0.58 | -0.76 | -0.74 | -0.70 | -0.76 | -0.76 | -0.77 | -0.44 | -0.26 | -0.28 | -0.18 | -0.38 | -0.26 | 0.33 | 0.23 | 0.22 | 0.34 | -0.11 | 0.30 |
| CasUM | -0.55 | -0.66 | -0.60 | -0.23 | -0.54 | -0.62 | -0.63 | -0.77 | -0.61 | -0.63 | -0.54 | -0.64 | -0.33 | -0.36 | -0.15 | -0.15 | -0.25 | -0.29 | 0.24 | 0.48 | 0.04 | 0.38 | -0.25 | 0.24 |
| MNF R | -0.44 | -0.48 | -0.56 | -0.32 | -0.32 | -0.46 | -0.52 | -0.51 | -0.55 | -0.55 | -0.41 | -0.48 | -0.20 | -0.09 | -0.08 | 0.00 | -0.12 | -0.09 | 0.29 | 0.04 | 0.16 | 0.12 | -0.25 | -0.01 |
| MNF U | 0.08 | -0.06 | -0.02 | -0.15 | 0.01 | -0.38 | 0.05 | -0.05 | 0.05 | -0.09 | 0.07 | -0.09 | 0.34 | 0.48 | 0.38 | 0.51 | 0.36 | 0.49 | -0.13 | -0.19 | -0.16 | -0.02 | -0.39 | 0.03 |
| UnempR | -0.42 | -0.40 | -0.50 | -0.26 | -0.36 | -0.17 | -0.49 | -0.38 | -0.51 | -0.39 | -0.39 | -0.33 | -0.32 | -0.39 | -0.17 | -0.25 | -0.23 | -0.34 | 0.16 | 0.03 | 0.07 | -0.18 | 0.09 | -0.49 |
| UnempU | -0.63 | -0.47 | -0.68 | -0.27 | -0.49 | -0.02 | -0.69 | -0.45 | -0.69 | -0.49 | -0.61 | -0.39 | -0.70 | -0.64 | -0.57 | -0.58 | -0.62 | -0.64 | 0.59 | 0.03 | 0.53 | 0.06 | 0.46 | -0.22 |

TABLE 15: CORRELATION MATRIX: NUTRITION AND DEVELOPMENT INDICATORS

| | PCI-73 | PCI-83 | PCI-93 | FlitR-91 | FlitU-91 | WPR-RM 15+ | WPR-UM 15+ | CasRM | CasUM | MNF R | MNF U | Unemp R | Unemp U |
|---|---|---|---|---|---|---|---|---|---|---|---|---|---|
| PCI-73 | 1.00 | | | | | | | | | | | | |
| PCI-83 | 0.96 | 1.00 | | | | | | | | | | | |
| PCI-93 | 0.92 | 0.96 | 1.00 | | | | | | | | | | |
| FlitR-91 | 0.24 | 0.31 | 0.34 | 1.00 | | | | | | | | | |
| FlitU-91 | 0.19 | 0.29 | 0.33 | 0.95 | 1.00 | | | | | | | | |
| WPR-RM15+ | -0.10 | -0.16 | -0.20 | -0.65 | -0.66 | 1.00 | | | | | | | |
| WPR-UM15+ | 0.78 | 0.72 | 0.74 | 0.10 | 0.01 | 0.08 | 1.00 | | | | | | |
| CasRM | -0.05 | 0.03 | 0.09 | 0.53 | 0.52 | 0.05 | -0.08 | 1.00 | | | | | |
| CasUM | -0.17 | -0.16 | -0.09 | 0.68 | 0.59 | -0.20 | 0.03 | 0.74 | 1.00 | | | | |
| MNF R | 0.12 | 0.12 | 0.10 | 0.58 | 0.51 | -0.04 | 0.26 | 0.56 | 0.64 | 1.00 | | | |
| MNF U | 0.56 | 0.58 | 0.54 | 0.16 | 0.10 | 0.22 | 0.63 | 0.24 | 0.11 | 0.66 | 1.00 | | |
| UnempR | -0.22 | -0.17 | -0.15 | 0.77 | 0.78 | -0.76 | -0.35 | 0.23 | 0.48 | 0.24 | -0.38 | 1.00 | |
| UnempU | -0.43 | -0.38 | -0.35 | 0.59 | 0.67 | -0.51 | -0.64 | 0.39 | 0.42 | 0.30 | -0.36 | 0.83 | 1.00 |

consumption basket consequent to economic growth. With the level of affordability going up over the years, people have possibly preferred other micronutrients, or increased their consumption of non-food items. In case of consumption of fats, however, the relationships remain high and positive over the years, although there is a decline here as well. The correlation coefficients between rural poverty and all the nutritional intakes are negative and highly significant in 1972–3, as expected. Here again, poverty relates more strongly with consumption of fats than the other two nutrients. Also, the correlations have weakened considerably over the years to become statistically insignificant in 1993–4. Regarding consumption of fats, it has not weakened substantially over the years, similar to what was noted in case of its relation with per capita income.

Average consumption of calorie (urban) as well as protein in per capita terms had strong negative relationship with poverty in the urban areas in early 1970s, although it is less than that of rural areas. This possibly can be attributed to the demonstration effect and exposure to media and publicity, inducing people to spend money on items having low nutritional value. The relationships have become insignificant in the 1990s as was the case in rural areas. The consumption of fats is not linked strongly with urban poverty, possibly due to greater awareness and growing popularity of non-fat items. The correlation coefficient has, however, not changed over the years.

The correlations of employment-related indicators in the 1990s bring out an interesting pattern. The WPR in rural areas does not have any positive relation with calorie intake. This is understandable as the high rural WPR is not an indication of greater income and higher affordability, but of larger distress supply of labour. Urban WPR, however, exhibits strong positive correlation with all the nutrient indicators. Similarly the high percentage of manufacturing workers in rural areas necessarily does not reflect prosperity and higher level of consumption. Urban manufacturing too shows no significant positive correlation except with the intake of fats. These are in conformity with the result of de-linking of poverty with economic development, as suggested above.

The percentage of casual workers is negatively related with all the nutrient indicators in rural and urban areas, and most of the coefficients are significant. The same is the case with the unemployment rate, except in case of calories in urban areas. This can be explained since casualization and unemployment adversely affect the purchasing power of households, bringing down the consumption levels.

The most interesting result is with regard to the correlations of female literacy with income and nutritional indicators in the 1990s. While with income it exhibits a marginally positive relationship (significant only at 5 per cent level), with nutrition these are either negative or insignificant, which is difficult to explain. Its relation with Infant Mortality Rate (IMR) is, however, strongly negative, which suggests that female education has healthy effects on IMR through channels other than calorie or fat intake.

## IMPACT OF NUTRITIONAL LEVELS ON HEALTH-RELATED INDICATORS

The impact of nutritional deficiency on health and related dimensions has been analysed by correlating nutritional intakes with six health-related indicators (pertaining mostly to rural areas) in the 1990s. The total set of indictors included in the analysis are as follows.

1. Average calorie intake (kcal) per day in rural and urban areas, 1993–4.
2. Average protein intake (grams) per day in rural and urban areas, 1993–4.
3. Average intake of fats (grams) per day in rural and urban areas, 1993–4.
4. Percentage of people consuming less than 1,890 calories, 1993–4.
5. Life expectancy at birth.
6. Infant mortality rate, 1997.
7. Percentage of severely 'stunted' children, 1994.
8. Percentage of severely 'wasted' children, 1994.
9. Juvenile sex ratio, 1991.

The percentage of people reporting calorie intake of less than 1890 per day relates negatively and significantly with nutritional intake in rural areas (Table 16). This implies that the states that have a large proportion of calorie deficient people also have a low level of calorie consumption on an average. Understandably, the better-off sections in these states do not report high calorie

TABLE 16: CORRELATION MATRIX FOR NUTRITION AND HEALTH INDICATORS FOR THE NINETIES

| | Rural kcal-93 | Urban kcal-93 | Rural Pro-93 | Urban Pro-93 | Rural Fat-93 | Urban Fat-93 | Percent with <1890 | Life Expedancy 92–6 | IMR-97 | Stunted Children 1994 | Wasted Children 1994 | Juvenile Sex 1991 |
|---|---|---|---|---|---|---|---|---|---|---|---|---|
| Rural kcal-93 | 1.00 | | | | | | | | | | | |
| Urban kcal-93 | 0.69 | 1.00 | | | | | | | | | | |
| Rural Pro-93 | 0.93 | 0.57 | 1.00 | | | | | | | | | |
| Urban Pro-93 | 0.86 | 0.84 | 0.89 | 1.00 | | | | | | | | |
| Rural Fat-93 | 0.64 | 0.21 | 0.80 | 0.58 | 1.00 | | | | | | | |
| Urban Fat-93 | 0.53 | 0.36 | 0.70 | 0.63 | 0.90 | 1.00 | | | | | | |
| Percent with < 1890 kcal | -0.93 | -0.89 | -0.77 | -0.76 | -0.80 | -0.38 | -0.34 | 1.00 | | | | |
| Life Expectancy 92–6 | 0.10 | -0.09 | 0.14 | 0.04 | 0.48 | 0.42 | 0.17 | 1.00 | | | | |
| IMR-97 | 0.30 | 0.34 | 0.24 | 0.30 | -0.14 | -0.10 | -0.45 | -0.86 | 1.00 | | | |
| Stunted Children 1994 | 0.09 | 0.11 | 0.28 | 0.34 | 0.40 | 0.56 | -0.09 | 0.07 | -0.05 | 1.00 | | |
| Wasted Children 1994 | -0.01 | 0.10 | 0.06 | 0.12 | -0.13 | -0.24 | -0.09 | -0.48 | 0.32 | 0.21 | 1.00 | |
| Juvenile Sex Ratio 1991 | -0.65 | -0.09 | -0.78 | -0.51 | -0.80 | -0.56 | 0.38 | -0.25 | -0.05 | -0.21 | -0.09 | 1.00 |

intake but go in for other nutrients, keeping the average calorie consumption low. Surprisingly the infant mortality rate, percentage of severely stunted children, and percentage of severely wasted children do not show any negative correlation with average intake of calories; the coefficients even work out as positive. This in a way questions the significance of calorie, protein and fat consumption in the context of health and quality of life in rural areas.

One important finding is the strong negative correlation of calorie intake with juvenile sex ratio. One would argue that the states with higher nutritional values in the 1990s report fewer females (relative to males) in the 0–6 age group. This can be attributed to the high income and consumption levels of the households in these states, making it possible for them to go for gender determination tests and selectively terminating the pregnancies, giving a low sex ratio at birth. Further, higher nutrition levels seem to have reduced the infant mortality among male children much more than that of females.

## CONCLUSION

The analysis of the linkage between poverty and employment structure in the present paper suggests that an economic environment leading to increase in volume of employment and reduction in unemployment has been helpful in poverty alleviation in the early 1990s. Poverty has been going down systematically and significantly during 1973–93. The development process in the subsequent years has, however, not brought forth many jobs, either of regular or of self-employment variety, which has led to an alarming growth in unemployment and poverty. The importance of the informal labour market in poverty alleviation, therefore, should not be underestimated, at least in the short run. The state must play an important role through a favourable policy package which must include investment in economic infrastructure, particularly in rural areas.

Casualization of workforce and unemployment seem to result in low nutritional intake which may reflect low affordability of households in poor states. This is understandable as casualization enhances poverty both in rural and urban areas. It can be explained in terms of deeper penetration of markets as a result of the economic reforms in the country. This process has unfortunately rendered many of the household-based activities non-viable, particularly those engaging female workers. The dramatic fall in the share of self-employed workers in rural areas must, therefore, be a matter of concern. The other disturbing factor is the volatility of the agricultural sector, which provides employment to a large number of the poor. A fall in its growth rate due to seasonal factors has led to a section of the population being pushed below the poverty line. The State has to play a positive role by helping the small and marginal farmers as also those setting up small-scale units in their survival strategy through a support system. It should also keep a vigil over the developments in the labour market and save the hired workers through implementation of the legislations that already exist with regard to minimum wages and working conditions. The importance of stabilizing agricultural growth through infrastructural investment in the public sector as a step in alleviating poverty on a sustainable basis in rural areas cannot be overemphasized.

The capacity of the government to generate employment directly through anti-poverty programmes in rural or urban areas would remain limited. The past experience suggests that there have been considerable leakages in these programmes. Banks and other financial institutions have shown extreme unwillingness to finance these, as the risk of non-recovery is very high. Also, the assets created through such programmes have not contributed significantly to the development potential or long-term income-generating capacity. Also, the indicators of economic development like work participation rate, percentage of secondary sector workers, etc., do not lead to removal of nutritional deficiency. It is, therefore, recommended that the anti-poverty programmes should primarily be focused on provision of subsidized food grains and other basic amenities to poor and vulnerable sections of the population.

## NOTES

* The assistance of Mr. Bal Paritosh Dash in data analysis and development of ideas is gratefully acknowledged.

1. Scholars had projected the demand for food to grow at a much faster rate than what actually materialized in recent years. The slower growth in cereal demand can partly be attributed to deceleration in population growth in the 1990s. The annual exponential growth rate of 1.93 per cent is much less than what has been incorporated in the

projection models by scholars like Radhakrishna and Ravi, Sarma and Gandhi. The actual growth rate would have been still lower, as experts projected growth rate as low as 1.8 per cent per annum based on the information from the Sample Registration System. The slightly higher growth rate is in no small measure due to the sharp reduction in Infant Mortality Rate in the 1990s, which may partly be attributed to better nutritional levels of both mothers and the children.

2. Assessing poverty trends in India involves serious methodological issues that are being debated with statistical rigour and emotional fervour for the past three decades. The issues get easily intertwined with socio-political considerations as poverty assessment has implications for resource allocation. Even at the macro-level, the methodological issues are extremely challenging.

   One hoped that despite differences among individual researchers, the official estimates of poverty that are to go as policy inputs in planning and resource allocation would be based on the procedure recommended by the Expert Group on Estimation of Proportion and Number of Poor, set up by the Planning Commission (1993), which sought to standardize the methodology and steered clear some of the confusion in the area. This unfortunately has not happened. The Planning Commission itself, through a notification dated 11 March 1997, has introduced a modification in the methodology for constructing the price index for updating the poverty line in urban areas. As a consequence of this modification, the levels of urban poverty in the 1970s, 1980s and 1990s work out as somewhat less than what was obtained earlier following the original (Expert Group) methodology. The trends of poverty as also the pattern across the states, however, remain by and large unaltered. Also, the extensive experiments done by Dubey and Gangopadhaya with alternate poverty lines and methods of price adjustment suggest that differences in the mean levels of poverty notwithstanding, the trend at national level and the pattern across the state level, remain, by and large, unaltered. One would believe that this insensitivity of the poverty pattern to changes in methodological parameters would contribute to their acceptability among researchers and administrators, enhancing at the same time their usability in economic policy.

   A small digression on different data sources and the methodology employed in computing poverty should be in order at this stage. NSSO provides information on consumption expenditure, on yearly as well as five-yearly basis. The sampling design for the quinquennial rounds is prepared in a manner so as to provide reliable estimates at regional (substate) level. These rounds are based on much larger samples, covering over 1,00,000 households. The annual surveys, however, are based on smaller samples, involving 10,000 to 30,000 households only. The estimates based on the latter, therefore, may not be reliable at the state level. Serious doubts have been raised regarding usability of the estimates based on thin sample data, and particularly their comparability with those available from the quinquennial rounds. It is argued that the poverty estimates obtained from these sources, even at the national level, may not be strictly comparable. It is extremely difficult to resolve these problems in any satisfactory manner.

Interestingly, the estimates of poverty based on the full sample data of the 43rd, 50th and 55th Rounds suggest a different trend than that obtained from the annual data for the intervening period. One must also note that the expert group had recommended computation of poverty at national level by aggregating the state level estimates with appropriate weightages. This procedure would be of dubious merit if applied on the thin sample data, as the sample sizes are not adequate for all the states. One would, thus, legitimately ask the question whether the estimates made available for the years 1994, 1995, 1996, 1997 and 1998 from the thin sample are comparable with the regular sample-based estimates of 1993–4 or 1999–2000. Or, have the former served the limited objective and should now be forgotten since the data from the next regular round for the year 1999–2000 have become available. This is exactly what had happened with the annual poverty estimates for the period from 1987–8 and 1993–4. The present paper uses the thin as well as large sample data from NSS in the analysis.

3. This relationship has been ascertained by correlating the poverty levels in a year with per capita SDP for that year.

# 10. Sustainable Livelihood and Economic Access to Food

*Nira Ramachandran*

A sustainable livelihood can be defined as one that comprises the capabilities, assets and activities required for means to live and to cope with and recover from stresses and shocks and maintain or enhance capabilities and assets, both now and in the future, while not undermining the natural resource base (Chambers and Conway 1992).[1]

Poverty in rural areas is largely due to the depletion of assets upon which men and women rely as sources of their livelihoods. In addition to income poverty, rural people are vulnerable to natural disasters such as drought or flooding. A large number of these individuals are landless and rely on seasonal and casual labour as their primary source of livelihood. Working on large farms, these individuals are not provided with adequate wages to meet family needs, reside in poor housing, and are at risk of injury due to unsafe working conditions.

Poverty in urban areas is affected by a combination of factors that produce a wide range of vulnerabilities. Unlike rural people, the urban poor are more immersed in the cash economy and live in unplanned squatter settlements on riverfronts, along railway tracks and on the periphery of urban centres. Their lack of legal status makes them vulnerable, not least because it is compounded by insecure, low-wage employment. With the structural adjustment programmes undertaken since 1991, the urban poor have seen rising food prices, the commercialization of urban land markets, worsening sanitation conditions, unemployment and decline in real wages. In this context, urban men and women are largely dependent on access to the following assets as sources of their livelihoods: income, labour, housing, health, education and social networks (UNDP 1999).

The sustainable livelihoods programme focused on tackling the causes of poverty, hunger, the inequitable distribution of income and low human resource development with the objective of providing everyone with the opportunity to earn a sustainable livelihood. The target groups identified were numerous and included all those who are currently disadvantaged: women, children, and (presumably) senior citizens, the urban unemployed and the urban poor, the rural poor, including the landless, small landholders, pastoralists, artisans, fishing communities, indigenous communities, migrants and refugees. If the livelihood of these people is to be sustainable, it must be secured by economic activities that are sustainable, that do not threaten the integrity of the environmental assets on which they depend.

This has three important implications: first, that individual decisions about the use of environmental goods should take full account of future costs to society; second, that the value of the asset base should be conserved by an appropriate investment strategy, and third, that the distribution of income within the community should meet the needs of the productive and non-productive members alike.

The conditions for the sustainability of the livelihoods of the community are: that there exists an appropriate micro-economic decision environment, an appropriate macro-economic balance between consumption and investment, and an appropriate distribution of income. The important point is that the livelihood of dependent members of society should not be considered in isolation (Perrings 1995).

The concept of sustainable livelihoods is a normative one, and the approach is inherently responsive to people's own interpretations of and priorities for their livelihoods. However, while it starts with people, it does not compromise on the environment. Indeed, one of the potential strengths of the livelihoods approach is that it mainstreams the environment within a holistic framework.

## FOOD INSECURITY: CAUSES AND CONSEQUENCES

The target groups (both urban and rural) identified in the sustainable livelihoods approach are often afflicted by food scarcity, seasonal cycles of hunger, persisting malnutrition, low birth-weight babies, increased vulnerability to disease, high morbidity and mortality rates—all manifestations of food insecurity, either chronic or seasonal.

Food security at country level, results from the interplay of three determining factors: food production, food availability and access to food. Food production, while no longer a matter of acute concern in India, must remain a central pivot of the food security wheel, as notwithstanding current surpluses, the required rate of growth of cereal output according to recent estimates is 3 per cent, as against an actual growth rate of 1.8 per cent recorded during the 1990s. Also, the annual consumption of food grains in the country is around 175 million tons, while international trade in cereals is only about 250 million tons. Thus any large-scale dependence on imports is clearly ruled out. Where availability is concerned, buffer stocks of a size much above the required safety norms ensure stability of supplies. This situation, coupled with the existence of a vast Public Distribution System (PDS) with a well-established network of Fair Price Shops (FPS) and an even more extensive set of private market channels ensures the availability of food throughout the year with a far-flung reach into the remotest of areas.

Hunger in India is not a result of shortage of food, but of lack of entitlement, or in other words, economic access. Existing policies for temporary employment creation fail to take into account the seasonality factor in rural life. Seasonality, coupled with low mean incomes and high seasonal variance in incomes, is one of the primary causes of distress in rural livelihoods. Seasonality will continue to be a major stumbling block in rural development in every LDC where agriculture and rural livelihoods depend on seasonal fluctuations in access to food, employment, income and seasonal changes in status of health/morbidity (Raina 2000). Exacerbating the situation is the impact of recurring shocks in the form of natural calamities.

An overwhelming majority of the food-insecure suffer from transitory food insecurity attributable to the seasonality factor; food security of these households could be secured through measures such as price stabilization, micro-credit, crop insurance and temporary employment creation.

In contrast, those faced with chronic food insecurity suffer from acute poverty. The strategy to overcome this problem includes short-term interventions to raise the purchasing power of the poor through endowments of land and non-land assets, and by generating employment opportunities, as well as long-term growth-mediated interventions to improve food availability and raise incomes by agricultural production programmes, infrastructure, human resource development, etc. (Radhakrishna 2001).

Anti-poverty measures have usually been conceived and implemented from the national level using per capita income or consumption measures and manipulation of sectoral policies as points of departure. Little, if any, attention is paid to the manner in which (or where) people live, the resources (assets) used for pursuing livelihoods, or the human and financial costs associated with the implementation of national programmes through a centralized bureaucracy. On the other hand, participatory development has, on the whole, managed to understand how men and women prioritize needs, exploit resources and offer solutions to their pressing problems. The missing link, however, is examining how macro and sectoral policies affect the livelihood options available to a particular community or individual.

## THE SUSTAINABLE LIVELIHOODS APPROACH TO FOOD SECURITY

Livelihoods are shaped by a multitude of different forces and factors that are themselves constantly shifting. A sustainable livelihoods approach to food security is necessarily, people-centred, and must begin with an investigation of the assets which people have, the objectives that they hope to achieve, and the livelihood strategies that they adopt to achieve them.

Unlike the conventional community needs assessment approach, the sustainable livelihoods approach emphasizes assessing community strengths and assets. This is important in building self-esteem and self-reliance and in breaking the donor-recipient syndrome. The approach is founded on the belief that people require a range of assets to achieve positive livelihood outcomes, no single category of assets on its own being sufficient to yield all the many and varied livelihood outcomes that people seek. This is particularly true for poor people whose access to any given category of assets tends to be very limited. As a result, they have to seek ways of nurturing and combining what assets they do have, in innovative ways to ensure survival.

One of the foundations of the sustainable livelihoods approach is the belief in, and pursuit of, various types of sustainability. This includes, but is not limited to, environmental sustainability. It is not only the existence of different types of natural assets that is important, but also access, quality and how natural assets combine and vary over time.[2]

Human capital can be viewed as an asset or building block in achieving livelihood outcomes and also as an end in itself. Support to the accretion to human capital can be both direct and indirect. In either case, it will only achieve its aims if people themselves are willing and able to invest in their own human capital by attending training courses or schools and accessing preventive medical services. The importance of mobilization and advocacy in this connection cannot be overemphasized.

Social capital has, fortunately, the quality of being in some cases, self-reinforcing. Stocks can be increased rather than depleted by the right type of use. Neglect, on the other hand, can undermine social capital and trust. It can also be actively, though unintentionally, destroyed by wrong interventions that impose new social relations without taking into account the strengths of the old. Most attempts to build social capital focus on strengthening local institutions, either directly through capacity building or leadership training, or indirectly through creating an open democratic environment in which they flourish.[3]

Physical capital comprises the basic infrastructure and producer goods (tools and equipment) needed to support livelihoods. The following components of infrastructure are usually essential for sustainable livelihoods: affordable transport, secure shelter, adequate water supply and sanitation, clean affordable energy, and access to information (communications). Infrastructure is commonly a public good that is used without direct payment. Exceptions include shelter that is often privately owned, and energy supplies that are accessed for a fee related to usage. Lack of a particular type of infrastructure is considered to be a core dimension of poverty. Without adequate access to services such as water and energy, human health deteriorates and long periods of time are spent in non-productive activities like the collection of water and fuel or food.[4]

The opportunity costs associated with poor infrastructure can preclude education, access to health services and income generation. However, development of physical capital must be led by demand from the intended users. Without a perceived need for the service, it is unlikely that the required infrastructure will be used or maintained, making the resource unsustainable in the long run.[5]

Although financial capital tends to be quite versatile, it alone cannot solve all the problems of poverty. People may lack knowledge to put their financial resources to good use or are constrained by inappropriate structures and processes, e.g. underdeveloped markets or a policy environment that hinders micro-enterprise. In the context of credit to access food, the experience of the Rashtriya Mahila Kosh that has extended over Rs. 103 crore in micro-finance through about 800 NGOs all over the country, has led to the conclusion that extending credit to women's Self-Help Groups impacts positively on the food and nutrition status of the family. The single biggest use of micro-credit, as much as 23 per cent, has been seen to be for the purchase of food. Asset creation takes third place, after basic consumption needs are met.

When enhancing food security is the objective, savings can also be held in unconventional forms, e.g. the grain bank scheme being experimented with in Jhabua district of Madhya Pradesh envisages an initial endowment in the form of 50 kg of grain per target household. This can be accessed as a loan by group members to tide them over seasonal food distress periods. Repayment is in the form of equivalent grain, cash or labour. Repayment of the loan makes the household eligible for a further grain loan, thus creating an incentive for repayment as well as sustaining the system. The innovative feature of the scheme is that it seeks to utilize the only asset readily available with impoverished families, i.e. labour (IHD-WFP 2001).

Transforming structures and processes within the livelihoods framework are the institutions, organizations, policies and legislation that shape livelihoods. They operate at all levels from the household to the international arena, and in all spheres from the most private to the most public. They effectively determine access to various types of capital, livelihood strategies, decision making bodies and sources of influence; the terms of exchange between different types of capital and returns (economic or otherwise) to any given livelihood strategy. They can help cushion the impact of external shocks (e.g. policy on drought relief). During the drought of 1987–8, central assistance was extended for the generation of employment for small and marginal farmers as well as for landless agricultural labourers. Of the total drought assistance of Rs. 16,173 million, Rs. 8,421 million was allocated for employment generation in various states. Additional employment for more than 600 million man-days was generated under the National Rural Employment Programme (NREP) and the Rural Landless Employment Guarantee Programme (RLEGP). These programmes provide relief to small and marginal farmers during periods of scarcity and to medium farmers facing drought. The government's response to the currently prevailing situation of drought in eight states of north and central India has been in the form of long-term 'drought proofing' plans for initiating technologies like rainwater harvesting and groundwater recharging in Orissa and Rajasthan, as well as direct support in the form of additional food grains for food for work schemes and the extension of subsidized food grains at lower rates to all families in the affected areas.

Institutions can restrict people's choice of livelihood strategies, e.g. in rigid caste systems. More common are policies that affect the attractiveness of particular livelihood choices through their impact upon expected returns.[6]

Traditional agriculture in the mountains of the Hindu Kush Himalayas focused on mixed cropping, a large variety of crops being grown and consumed. All this changed when the government introduced its Grow More Food campaign and the PDS, which limited the number of crops to three or four which could be sold through the PDS. Government help came only if the farmer grew high-yielding varieties that required intensive cultivation. Mixed cropping decreased, fertility reduced and the farmers became dependent upon chemical fertilizers supplied by the government.

The impact on diet and nutrition have been equally dramatic. Food varieties that contributed to the biological diversity of the region have completely disappeared. The farmer grows only what he can sell or what he gets external support to grow. As a result, households that used to consume over 20 varieties of food items, now consume only five. The food items which have disappeared are those which were environment friendly, resilient, grown to increase soil fertility, or grown at a time when the soil was being rested (Nagpal 1999).

The more choices and flexibility that people have in their livelihood strategies, the greater their ability to withstand or adapt to shocks and stresses. Recent studies have drawn attention to the enormous diversity of livelihood strategies at every level—within geographic areas, across sectors, within households and over time. The pursuit of livelihoods is a dynamic process in which households combine activities to meet their various needs at different times. A common response of the poor to lack of livelihood opportunities locally is 'staddling', whereby different members of the household live and work in different places, temporarily (e.g. seasonal migration) or permanently.

In effect, policies promoting a variety of livelihood options within the constraints set by the resource base would be more effective than job creation in any one specific sector.

## CONCLUSION

Various elements of the sustainable livelihoods approach have been incorporated in government, donor and NGO efforts at ensuring food security to all, as detailed above. However, the lessons drawn from the above experiences indicate that a sharper focus on a few building blocks of the concept that are particularly relevant in the Indian context would yield dividends:

1. Ensuring year-round food security to all across varied geographical regions and in the remotest areas cannot be effectively achieved through a single mechanism, the provision of outside food supplies, however efficient the mechanism. Since traditional support systems in the form of CPR have long provided the back-up for local coping strategies, a renewed focus on CPRs is crucial. The management of these resources could be handed over to a more formalized structure of village communities backed by government support. This would help to regenerate these now defunct resources.
2. As part of the programme to protect and enrich biodiversity, multiple cropping could receive government support at local level. Apart from the positive impact on biodiversity, there could well be a boost in the output of coarse grains providing higher nutritive value in the local diet, as well as ensuring local availability of grain. Linked with the grain bank scheme, this could help to build up the initial capital stock for the grain banks, as well as reduce the inequities created by the Green Revolution.

3. Providing micro-credit to women's groups seems to succeed both in empowering women and in reducing the food insecurity of the family. Coupled with the grain bank scheme in vulnerable areas, the intervention could improve its effectiveness manifold.
4. The introduction of a food guarantee scheme on the lines of the already existing employment and education guarantee schemes, which would ensure a survival level of food grains in cash or kind to all, regardless of their productivity status, could be thought of. Once again, at village level, this could be effectively administered through the grain bank, the government providing additional grain requirements through the existing PDS for those who are physically unable to repay.
5. Support to livelihood creation must take into account the dominance of the seasonality factor in rural areas. The provision of direct food assistance or assured income in areas prone to seasonal food distress must be coordinated with the agricultural calendar, if such schemes are to prove effective.
6. Support to the multifaceted livelihood options already existing in the region, coupled with the introduction of new avenues for diversification within the constraints set by the natural resource base, are called for. These would primarily be based on renewable resources and value addition.

## NOTES

1. The concept of sustainable livelihoods has been refined and legitimized over the last decade through several major international fora. Introduced by the Brundtland Commission (1987), it was initially defined in terms of ownership of and access to resources, basic needs and livelihood security, especially in rural areas. Agenda 21 of the UN Conference on Environment and Development (1992) broadened the concept to include 'sustainable livelihoods for all'. The emphasis was on a programme to combat poverty. The notion arose from the widespread belief that poverty was responsible for environmental degradation, and that once such degradation sets in, a cumulative process is set off which reinforces the trends in both these areas. The reason given for this is that the poor depend to a large extent on natural resources to eke out their livelihood. As there is a higher rate of population growth in poor households, the exploitation of natural

resources also progressively increases. Added to this, the poor also have a high subjective discounting rate, and, therefore, over-exploit natural resources (Vyas 1991).

2. A study of the tribal belt of the southern Aravalis in Rajasthan (Vyas 1995) reveals how the deterioration of the natural resource base in the region has led to a change in the livelihood patterns of the tribal population, accompanied by impoverishment and increasing inequities. With the introduction of modern legislation in the area, the CPR of forests were converted into state property. The rise in economic value of timber and forest products led to large-scale felling of trees, and a major change in the conservationist role of the forest department to a revenue-earning one. The tribal population had to resort to either of two options: to migrate to the nearby plains, or to extend cultivation on fragile lands. Those who resorted to the former found low-paying menial jobs in farms, factories and mines, while the latter group brought progressively larger areas of infertile and marginal lands under the plough with disastrous consequences. This was compounded by the growing dependence on livestock to supplement the meagre income from agriculture. While the numbers of livestock have remained steady, the grazing area has significantly declined, thus overburdening the carrying capacity. Thus, both groups of tribal population have faced a considerable drop in living standards. The privatization of CPR through land redistribution in the villages of West Bengal has led to a denial of gleanings from fields, and the traditional rights to wild fruit, vegetables, greens, herbs and fish from ponds and other water bodies that supplemented the villagers' diets in the lean period. A comparison of food calendars over two time periods revealed a distinct reduction in the number of food items in the diet as well as more prolonged periods of hunger (Mukerjee 2000).
3. With strong local institutions, people can exercise an effective check and control on the functioning of usually inefficient government schemes like the public distribution system, as is evident from the case of Kerala. The existence of a large number of grass-root level organizations provide several fora for consumer complaints by cardholders which are usually taken seriously, as there is always the danger of local organizations pursuing the matter with higher officials. In a related aspact, vast areas of forests in the southern lateritic tracts of West Bengal had become virtually unproductive on account of commercial exploitation, unregulated fuel wood collection by the poor and grazing by village cattle. In 1972, a rehabilitation scheme was introduced focusing on generating sustained productive employment in the forest area, so that people would not have to sell firewood in the market. The project also grew fuel wood so that people could

get it on a token fee, at cost price, and arranged cattle grazing on a rotational basis. It also permitted people to grow paddy on forest lands which was sold to the same people at cost price. Thus, all immediate requirements of the people were taken care of, and with the successful implementation of the project, the government approved the distribution of 25 per cent of the usufruct to the beneficiary families. An erstwhile degraded forest was turned into luxuriant forest with high ecological and commercial value (Saxena 1995). Success stories of this kind are found in all states implementing the Joint Forest Management programme, thus underlining the importance of supporting people's own choices of livelihood options, forming and empowering local organizations, and ensuring their involvement in regenerating the resource base.

4. A participatory study in two remote mountain villages of Pauri Garhwal district of Uttaranchal (Ramachandran 2000), revealed that, on an average, about four hours a day is spent by women on collecting firewood and fodder. As forests are fast depleting, time spent and distances covered in the search for these basic needs have increased.
5. A participatory rural analysis carried out in six villages of a remote mountain block in the Garhwal Himalayas of Uttaranchal analysed the consonance or otherwise in planners' and peoples' priorities for development. The study revealed that certain problems are so dominant that they tend to rank high on the priorities of both outside experts and local people. In the case of Chakrata block, these concerns were health, illiteracy, unemployment and poor road network. Priority areas listed by the local male population, however, were the provision of electricity, drinking water, banking facilities and ration shops that did not find mention on the planners' list. The PRA exercise conducted with women alone brought out distinct gender concerns. The problems prioritized by them were lack of fodder and fuel and the need for toilets. These concerns play a major role in their day-to-day existence, but remain unperceived even by their own menfolk (Ramachandran and Dimri 1999).
6. The transformation of the fishing industry in Kerala from a traditional labour-intensive, caste-based occupation to the modernized/growth-oriented model of today began in the mid-1960s in response to the rising international demand for prawns. Fisheries development soon became synonymous with increasing prawn harvests, and export earnings increased steadily. The earlier caste-bound nature of the fishery sector ceased to be a barrier to entry, and the main investors and beneficiaries of the new development model were non-fishermen. After a boom of one decade, by the mid-1970s, the levels of fish and prawn production began to fall, and by the end of the 1970s, the

state was headed towards an ecological crisis of over-fishing. This implied not only a fall in the fish harvest, but also a very skewed distribution of the benefits and costs in the fish economy. Fish was once considered the poor man's protein in the state, but this is no longer so. The availability and the quality of fish sold in the local market deteriorated, and the retail prices increased faster than the general cost of other food items. The poor consumers, who respond slowly to changes in diet patterns, are the ones most affected by this scarcity of fish (Kurien and Achari 1999).

# 11. Sustainable Livelihood, Gender and Food Security in Rural India

*Saraswati Raju*

As the country moves from protected a *licence-raj* industrial regime to market-led open and competitive growth under the process of globalization, issues relating to social security are coming up and being discussed vehemently. In industrialized countries, there is a consensus that social security, as defined by International Labour Organization (ILO) Convention 102, is a formal protection against a variety of contingencies arising out of old age, sickness, death and disability, unemployment benefits to specific groups and income support. It is understood that essential income and basic welfare is assured through regular participation in work and production. However, it has been argued that in situations where the very right to sustainable livelihood is threatened and/or incomes are low (as is the case with developing countries), social security will have to be go beyond protection against contingencies alone, but also to ensure the basic human development. Within this broadened notion of security, labour security, which has been defined as the 'essence of social and economic development', is of prime importance (Rodgers 1999).[1]

Labour security relates to many dimensions of work, but the most fundamental aspect is about livelihood and its sustainability in the context of at least basic survival, including food security. There is a link between poverty and nature of work. In 1993–4, around 49.4 per cent of the casual workers in rural India were below the poverty line, and although poverty has declined for all classes of workers over the period, the rate of decline was the lowest for casual workers (Dev 1999). Within the wage workers, the plight of women workers is still worse, as the ensuing analysis reveals, but this interconnection between women workers, their waged work and poverty has not been fully examined in the Indian context. Usually, the workforce analysis remains confined to poor households, as if poverty is neutral to gender dynamics operating in the labour market, whereas the data show that in the poor households there are more women, whether the households are poor because there are more women who do not contribute to the economic well-being of the households, or is it that women do contribute to household incomes, but their wages are so low that despite working they are not able to pull the households out from the grip of poverty. Once again, data provide some clues that indicate that in the poor households the sex ratio of workers is higher than the non-poor households, and this sex ratio has become more feminine over time even in those regions that customarily kept women out of the labour market because of prevailing gender ideology of men as the main breadwinners, with women's place being in the household domain, indicating the much-talked-about phenomenon of 'feminization of poverty'.

The preponderance of women in casual wage work and their temporal trends in terms of workdays available has a bearing upon economic access to food. There is considerable evidence that women's employment has a potential to benefit household food intake and nutrition through increasing household income. Indirectly, women's employment may contribute to how the money is spent by increasing their decision-making power.

Drawing data from various NSS reports and qualitative research, this paper discusses the temporal and structural trends in workforce participation rates for various social groups with focus on the gendered nature of casualization of work and poverty and its implication for household food security. The latter part of the paper is based on qualitative information, essentially because of the non-availability of relevant data segregated by sexes. While deriving conclusions, the limitation of the data warrants attention. Subject to availability, the paper has analysed the scenario till 1993–4 and for wages and available workdays till 1987–8. However, data from the 55th NSS round and other recent studies are used to comment upon more contemporary changes.

## WORK FORCE RATES, COMPOSITION AND WAGE STRUCTURE

The 55th round of the NSS pertaining to July 1999–June 2000 on employment and unemployment shows that relative to earlier periods, workforce participation rates have gone down especially

TABLE 1: WORK PARTICIPATION RATES BY USUAL STATUS (PRINCIPAL + SUBSIDIARY)

| Year | Round | Rural | | | Urban | | |
|---|---|---|---|---|---|---|---|
| | | Male | Female | Persons | Male | Female | Persons |
| 1999–2000 | 55th | 53.1 | 29.9 | 41.7 | 51.8 | 13.9 | 33.7 |
| 1993–4 | 50th | 55.3 | 32.8 | 44.4 | 52.0 | 15.4 | 34.7 |
| 1987–8 | 43rd | 53.9 | 32.3 | 43.4 | 50.6 | 15.2 | 33.7 |
| 1977–8 | 32nd | 55.2 | 33.1 | 44.4 | 50.8 | 15.6 | 34.1 |

*Source*: NSS 55th Round.

in rural areas (Table 1). The overall growth rate in female workforce has also been lower in the recent years than the earlier periods, particularly in rural areas, a trend that continues to prevail (Hirway 1999; Rothboeck and Acharya 1999. This downward trend per se is not problematic, as declining workforce participation may be due to decline in child labour or changes in the structure of the working age population.

From our point of view, the more pertinent issue is how this workforce has been appropriated over the period in self employment, regular salaried and/or casual employment. Salaried employment is the most sustained form of livelihood since it offers basic security in terms of regular income and days of work. Self-employment may be in home-based low-paid contractual jobs, but at the other end of the spectrum is the unstable casual labour with irregular and relatively the lowest income with no security. The NSS data show that between 1987–8 and 1993–4, the increase in female workforce participation rate has largely been for casual labour. This is particularly significant for rural female workers who show an increase of 5 per cent from 40.2 in 1987–8 to 45.3 in 1993–4, accompanied by a decline in self- and salaried employment. Rural male casual workers also show a moderate increase from 32.1 to 34.6 per cent in corresponding years. In urban areas, the trend is somewhat similar, but the gender differences are not so stark.

The latest figures for 1999–2000 show a continuing trend of increasing casual labour, albeit at a much slower pace; for rural female workers it has increased from 45.3 per cent in 1993–4 to 46.1 per cent and for males the corresponding figures are 34.6 and 36.6 per cent. As compared to rural workers, in urban areas casual labour has declined for female workers from 28.1 to 23.1 per cent, whereas for male workers the situation remains almost static over the reference period (Table 2).

TABLE 2: PERCENTAGE DISTRIBUTION OF WORKERS BY USUAL PRINCIPAL STATUS

| | | Rural | | | | | |
|---|---|---|---|---|---|---|---|
| Year | Round | Self-employed | | Regular | | Casual | |
| | | Male | Female | Male | Female | Male | Female |
| 1999–2000 | 55th | 54.4 | 50.0 | 9.00 | 3.9 | 36.6 | 46.1 |
| 1993–4 | 50th | 56.9 | 51.3 | 8.50 | 3.4 | 34.6 | 45.3 |
| 1987–8 | 43rd | 57.5 | 55.1 | 10.4 | 4.7 | 32.1 | 40.2 |
| 1983 | 38th | 59.5 | 54.1 | 10.6 | 3.7 | 29.9 | 42.2 |
| 1977–8 | 32nd | 62.2 | 56.3 | 10.9 | 3.7 | 26.9 | 40.4 |

| | | Urban | | | | | |
|---|---|---|---|---|---|---|---|
| Year | Round | Self-employed | | Regular | | Casual | |
| | | Male | Female | Male | Female | Male | Female |
| 1999–2000 | 55th | 41.2 | 38.4 | 41.9 | 38.5 | 16.9 | 23.1 |
| 1993–4 | 50th | 41.1 | 36.4 | 42.7 | 35.5 | 16.2 | 28.1 |
| 1987–8 | 43rd | 41.0 | 38.6 | 44.4 | 34.7 | 14.6 | 26.7 |
| 1983 | 38th | 40.2 | 37.2 | 44.5 | 31.8 | 15.3 | 30.9 |
| 1977–8 | 32nd | 39.9 | 42.2 | 47.2 | 30.8 | 12.9 | 27.0 |

*Source*: Various rounds of NSS.

The process of feminization of casual wage labour is not a feature of the past. According to the recent NCAER report, 'the most interesting result emerge[s] from an analysis of sex ratios of wage earners' and the adverse sex ratios among wage earners are observed in states where the overall female workforce participation rates are lower (Shariff 1999). Along with the process of casualization that has been more marked for female workers until very recently, the increasing gap in wages between male and female workers as well as workdays available have been a cause for concern.

## IMPLICATIONS FOR ACCESS TO FOOD

The Public Distribution System (PDS) of essential commodities is one way of transferring resources and providing for economically marginal sections of society with a minimum level of consumption. This may also work as safety nets in situations of crippled buying capacity of the poor in the face of vulnerable job markets. However, the poors' limited access to PDS in Bihar, Uttar Pradesh and the low offtake by Orissa and Madhya Pradesh, as well as the extent of insignificant income transfer[2] through PDS to the poor, particularly in states under discussion, have been extensively commented upon in the literature. For example, the per capita income transfer in Bihar, Orissa, Rajasthan and Uttar Pradesh has been very small, to the tune of Re. 0.7 to Rs. 1.6 per month as against the poor in Kerala, Karnataka and Andhra Pradesh, although within these states the income transfers were still biased against the poor (Datt 1999). As pointed out by Radhakrishna et al.,

> the efficacy of PDS in distributing food to the poor seems to be bad . . . some of the disquieting features persist [in that there is] virtual exclusion of backward states . . . [and the income transfers had] negligible impact in states with high incidence of poverty. (quoted in Datt 1999; also see Dev 1999)

In such a situation, the instability as reflected in casual wage work combined with its feminization in association with increasingly volatile job markets (particularly in backward states) has serious implications in terms of access to food. As female share of working days vis-à-vis males decline, implying a declining share of her income as well, it can be hypothesized that it would have an adverse effect on the household's economic access to food.

The relationship between a woman's economic productivity and her own family's health status is complex, and it has been argued that working women may not be able to pay much attention to children and other welfare measures because of lack of time. Hard data to substantiate this claim is difficult to come by, but there is a significant body of literature to counter this and to suggest that by and large women's employment has a positive effect on households' access to food as (1) it increases income available for it, and (2) income enhances women's control over how income is used. Documentation shows that on an average, women in agricultural households in Kerala were contributing 98 per cent of their earnings as against 78 per cent by men towards the family's maintenance (Mencher 1988). This is not a feature of south India alone, macro-studies from Punjab, Himachal Pradesh (Sharma 1980), Madhya Pradesh, Uttar Pradesh, Maharashtra and Assam (Dasgupta and Maiti undated), and Andhra Pradesh all report similar patterns (see World Bank 1991 for detailed discussion on these issues).

There is evidence to suggest that wage employment may actually improve a woman's bargaining position within her family (Parthasarathy 1988). Research shows that women's spending priorities differ from those of men and women tend to spend a disproportionately higher share of income on household well-being relative to male counterparts. For example, an early study in Kerala found daily nutritional adequacy in agricultural labour households to be related to females' than to males' employment (Gulati 1978).

## CONCLUSION

The process of casualization among female workers seems to have slowed down considerably in recent years, as the 55th NSS employment data suggest. It may be argued that several governmental and non-governmental safety measures for women have started having effect and slowly making their imprint. However, unless the latest data are fully probed, recent observations remain necessarily conjectural and not conclusive. Moreover, the slowing down of casualization has to be viewed with reference to an overall decline in female work participation rates.

To sum up:

1. It is the vulnerable sections of the society which are trapped in low-skill, low-income, and irregular jobs with least security. This marginalization gets further accentuated in case of female wage workers.
2. The wage gap between sexes has widened both for all classes and Scheduled Castes in case of Andhra Pradesh, Haryana, Madhya Pradesh, Maharashtra, Orissa and Uttar Pradesh. In Rajasthan, the widening of the wage gap is particularly significant for Scheduled Castes. Bihar is an intriguing case, as the wage gap between sexes has narrowed.
3. The widening wage gap is a function of average daily wages and number of workdays available. In all the cases where the wage gap has increased it is because of fewer working days available to women, particularly to those belonging to the Scheduled Castes, as compared to the earlier period. Recent data show a slight reversal of the trend at all-India level, but the share of female workdays continues to be lower.

4. Female workforce participation is significant from the viewpoint of poverty alleviation and food security. However, the nature of work is extremely crucial.
5. The reduced share of workdays of women with a consequent reduction of their income share in the household is likely to impact upon access to food and other welfare means, as their income is more likely to be spent on the well-being of families. Haryana may be the archetype in point. In an otherwise developed context, the state measures very poorly. It also shows the most drastic decline in workdays for women over the reference period.
6. Since it is essentially the socially marginal and poor women who are trapped in the process of casualization, public investment and policy interventions have to intensify to provide them sustainable work opportunities.
7. Several backward states are particularly problematic and require specifically focused attention.

This limited analysis brings out that any policy measure towards hunger-free India needs to address the inter relationships between female work, the sustainability of such work and its impact on intra-household food distribution through women's income (and indirectly their decision-making power).

## NOTES

1. Although outside the scope of this paper, it is important to note that for some groups, in addition to income poverty, social marginality is important, and in case of women, there is additional burden of gendered deprivation.
2. Income transfer to a household through PDS is defined as the difference between the expenditure that the household would have incurred in the absence of PDS, and the actual expenditure under PDS. It is measured by multiplying the quantity purchased from PDS with the difference between open market and PDS price.

ANNEXURE

With a view to examining gap in wages between sexes, the disparity index as developed by Sopher (1980) and subsequently modified by Kundu (1986)[1] is applied to nominal wages for males and females for the years 1974–5 to 1987–8 for rural agricultural and non-agricultural households by social groups. The analysis could not be carried out for 1993–4 because of unavailability of data on workdays. Also, the Scheduled Tribes are not taken into account because of unavailability of comparable data for all states.

Statistically a better tool than the arithmetical difference or gap between the two percentages or the ratios of one to another, the disparity index has an additional property that relates to the question of distributive justice. To compute the disparity index, the maximum wages in individual years are taken as 100, and other values are converted accordingly as a measure of standardization. A disparity value of zero is indicative of no sex differences in wages. Declining disparity values suggest closing gender gaps in wages. Workforce participation, gender ratio disparities in wages, number of days and types of occupation available are given in Tables I to X.

Since wage disparity is a function of average daily wages and workdays available, the increasing gender gap in wages implies declining number of workdays for either male or female workers or both, although the data show that in the majority of cases such a decline is particularly marked in case of female workers, particularly those belonging to Scheduled Castes (Tables III–VIII).[2] It is interesting to note that with the exception of Rajasthan, no other state shows a decline of workdays for male workers during 1974–5 to 1987–8.

For agricultural workers of all classes, the wage gap has widened in case of Andhra Pradesh, Gujarat, Haryana, Karnataka, Madhya Pradesh, Maharashtra, Orissa and Uttar Pradesh. In case of Scheduled Castes, Andhra Pradesh, Haryana, Karnataka, Madhya Pradesh, Maharashtra, Orissa, Rajasthan and Uttar Pradesh show similar trends. It can be seen that the wage gap between sexes for non-agricultural workers in all classes has increased for Andhra Pradesh, Gujarat, Madhya Pradesh, Orissa and Uttar Pradesh, for Scheduled Castes, the increase is observed in Gujarat, Madhya Pradesh, Rajasthan and Uttar Pradesh. Overall also, Madhya Pradesh, Orissa and Rajasthan tend to have fewer numbers of days for both types of wage employment (Shariff 1999).

TABLE I: DISPARITY BETWEEN MEN AND WOMEN'S ANNUAL NOMINAL WAGES FROM AGRICULTURAL WORK

| State | All Classes | | | | Scheduled Castes | | | | Scheduled Tribes | | | |
|---|---|---|---|---|---|---|---|---|---|---|---|---|
| | 1974–5 | 1977–8 | 1983 | 1987–8 | 1974–5 | 1977–8 | 1983 | 1987–8 | 1974–5 | 1977–8 | 1983 | 1987–8 |
| A.P. | 0.34 | 0.30 | 0.23 | 2.79 | 0.35 | 0.31 | 0.22 | 0.43 | 0.26 | 0.22 | 0.27 | 0.26 |
| Bihar | 0.35 | 0.20 | 0.21 | 2.96 | 0.32 | 0.15 | 0.22 | 0.24 | 0.38 | -0.02 | 0.10 | 0.16 |
| Gujarat | 0.29 | 0.17 | 0.26 | 2.77 | 0.30 | 0.12 | 0.21 | 0.28 | 0.39 | 0.25 | 0.21 | 0.38 |
| Haryana | 0.36 | 0.22 | 0.21 | 2.83 | 0.36 | 0.16 | 0.10 | 0.86 | — | — | — | — |
| H.P. | 0.69 | 0.41 | 0.63 | 3.05 | 0.54 | 0.40 | 1.08 | 0.41 | — | — | — | — |
| Kar. | 0.35 | — | 0.12 | 2.93 | 0.39 | — | 0.16 | 0.39 | 0.33 | — | -0.02 | 0.60 |
| Kerala | 0.34 | 0.26 | 0.24 | 2.88 | 0.33 | 0.30 | 0.27 | 0.25 | 0.39 | — | 0.63 | 0.09 |
| M.P. | 0.18 | 0.23 | 0.18 | 2.78 | 0.30 | 0.23 | 0.18 | 0.34 | 0.37 | 0.22 | 0.17 | 0.30 |
| Maha. | 0.39 | 0.36 | 0.33 | 2.87 | 0.36 | 0.28 | 0.29 | 0.63 | 0.50 | 0.37 | 0.27 | 0.34 |
| Orissa | 0.38 | 0.31 | 0.19 | 2.66 | 0.37 | 0.33 | 0.71 | 0.47 | 0.33 | 0.08 | 0.11 | 0.33 |
| Punjab | 0.63 | 0.36 | 0.63 | 3.45 | 0.63 | 0.37 | 0.24 | 0.19 | — | -0.47 | — | — |
| Rajas. | 0.45 | 0.23 | 0.43 | 2.60 | 0.39 | 0.26 | 0.83 | 0.95 | 0.30 | 0.29 | 0.60 | 0.08 |
| T.N. | 0.39 | 0.33 | 0.31 | 2.78 | 0.37 | 0.31 | 0.31 | 0.32 | 0.18 | 0.27 | 0.08 | 0.29 |
| U.P. | 0.42 | 0.32 | 0.31 | 2.63 | 0.40 | 0.30 | 0.33 | 0.60 | 0.10 | 0.12 | — | 0.24 |
| W.B. | 0.33 | 0.15 | 0.09 | 2.93 | 0.43 | 0.29 | 0.14 | 0.31 | 0.16 | 0.06 | 0.09 | 0.11 |

TABLE II: DISPARITY BETWEEN MEN AND WOMEN'S ANNUAL NOMINAL WAGES FROM NON-AGRICULTURAL WORK

| State | All Classes | | | | Scheduled Castes | | | | Scheduled Tribes | | | |
|---|---|---|---|---|---|---|---|---|---|---|---|---|
| | 1974–5 | 1977–8 | 1983 | 1987–8 | 1974–5 | 1977–8 | 1983 | 1987–8 | 1974–5 | 1977–8 | 1983 | 1987–8 |
| A.P. | 0.20 | 0.32 | 0.33 | 0.23 | 0.11 | 0.44 | 0.08 | 0.09 | 0.79 | 0.68 | 0.26 | 0.37 |
| Bihar | 0.46 | 0.30 | 0.37 | 0.37 | 0.53 | 0.24 | 0.41 | 0.49 | 0.21 | — | 0.16 | 0.11 |
| Gujarat | 0.12 | 0.35 | 0.27 | 0.15 | 0.11 | 0.45 | 0.22 | 0.16 | 0.10 | 0.90 | 0.38 | 0.15 |
| Haryana | 0.26 | 0.68 | 0.29 | — | 0.35 | 0.76 | 0.40 | — | — | — | — | — |
| H.P. | 0.27 | 0.11 | 0.31 | — | — | 0.44 | 0.00 | — | — | — | — | — |
| Kar. | 0.26 | — | 0.38 | 0.12 | 0.37 | | 0.36 | 0.06 | 0.47 | — | 0.60 | 0.16 |
| Kerala | 0.44 | 0.50 | 0.58 | 0.26 | 0.24 | 0.31 | 0.67 | 0.16 | 0.41 | — | 0.09 | 0.41 |
| M.P. | 0.41 | 0.27 | 0.24 | 0.46 | 0.40 | 0.21 | 0.33 | 0.64 | 0.43 | — | 0.30 | 0.36 |
| Maha. | 0.44 | 0.56 | 0.40 | 0.33 | 0.31 | 0.46 | 0.06 | 0.13 | 0.39 | 1.22 | 0.34 | 0.48 |
| Orissa | 0.35 | 0.19 | 0.13 | 0.38 | 0.55 | 0.35 | 0.21 | 0.33 | 0.28 | 0.83 | 0.33 | 0.26 |
| Punjab | 0.55 | 0.58 | 0.24 | 0.21 | 0.61 | 0.46 | 0.02 | 0.14 | — | — | — | — |
| Rajas. | 0.44 | 0.38 | 0.15 | 0.37 | 0.39 | 0.16 | 0.10 | 0.66 | 0.61 | 0.42 | 0.08 | 0.30 |
| T.N. | 0.37 | 0.38 | 0.32 | 0.32 | 0.41 | 0.32 | 0.39 | 0.36 | — | — | 0.29 | — |
| U.P. | 0.42 | 0.59 | 0.29 | 0.46 | 0.41 | 0.35 | 0.09 | 0.81 | 0.53 | — | 0.24 | — |
| W.B. | 0.51 | 0.69 | 0.63 | 0.34 | 0.53 | 0.58 | 0.84 | 0.08 | 0.52 | — | 0.11 | 0.43 |

TABLE III: AVERAGE ANNUAL DAYS OF WAGE EMPLOYMENT OF RURAL LABOUR HOUSEHOLDS FOR ALL CLASSES: AGRICULTURAL OCCUPATION

| State | 1974–5 | | 1977–8 | | 1983 | | 1987–8 | |
|---|---|---|---|---|---|---|---|---|
| | Male | Female | Male | Female | Male | Female | Male | Female |
| A.P. | 213 | 147 | 233 | 190 | 230 | 192 | 223 | 147 |
| Bihar | 203 | 122 | 273 | 210 | 265 | 216 | 278 | 206 |
| Gujarat | 232 | 172 | 238 | 198 | 252 | 200 | 263 | 156 |
| Haryana | 228 | 155 | 245 | 204 | 241 | 215 | 260 | 129 |
| H.P. | 287 | 137 | 208 | 148 | 246 | 200 | 279 | 200 |
| Kar. | 229 | 181 | — | — | 239 | 225 | 262 | 171 |
| Kerala | 148 | 112 | 177 | 166 | 199 | 172 | 190 | 174 |
| M.P. | 229 | 144 | 261 | 206 | 260 | 216 | 247 | 165 |
| Mahar. | 244 | 193 | 250 | 198 | 234 | 184 | 247 | 145 |
| Orissa | 189 | 126 | 234 | 166 | 230 | 174 | 220 | 126 |
| Punjab | 245 | 176 | 267 | 255 | 253 | 203 | 253 | 344 |
| Rajas. | 255 | 169 | 202 | 187 | 253 | 210 | 227 | 124 |
| T.N. | 171 | 125 | 202 | 177 | 198 | 169 | 185 | 161 |
| U.P. | 221 | 127 | 223 | 163 | 244 | 190 | 235 | 104 |
| W.B. | 233 | 158 | 254 | 223 | 225 | 206 | 253 | 195 |

TABLE IV: AVERAGE ANNUAL DAYS OF WAGE EMPLOYMENT OF RURAL LABOUR HOUSEHOLDS FOR ALL CLASSES: NON-AGRICULTURAL OCCUPATION

| State | 1974–5 | | 1977–8 | | 1983 | | 1987–8 | |
|---|---|---|---|---|---|---|---|---|
| | Male | Female | Male | Female | Male | Female | Male | Female |
| A.P. | 218 | 235 | 279 | 268 | 258 | 254 | 221 | 214 |
| Bihar | 220 | 145 | 278 | 285 | 283 | 312 | 237 | 147 |
| Gujarat | 266 | 253 | 254 | 266 | 204 | 202 | 242 | 209 |
| Haryana | 239 | 200 | 279 | 190 | 282 | 242 | 150 | — |
| H.P. | 265 | 274 | 245 | 264 | 232 | 213 | 201 | — |
| Kar. | 256 | 250 | — | — | 253 | 257 | 223 | 224 |
| Kerala | 178 | 159 | 223 | 218 | 215 | 209 | 196 | 206 |
| M.P. | 235 | 160 | 270 | 283 | 269 | 264 | 184 | 85 |
| Maha. | 250 | 215 | 291 | 242 | 248 | 236 | 246 | 200 |
| Orissa | 214 | 161 | 252 | 221 | 216 | 244 | 233 | 154 |
| Punjab | 228 | 222 | 277 | 286 | 230 | 269 | 231 | 288 |
| Rajas. | 245 | 187 | 238 | 213 | 247 | 285 | 209 | 119 |
| T.N. | 213 | 200 | 278 | 279 | 244 | 270 | 223 | 209 |
| U.P. | 230 | 186 | 255 | 244 | 254 | 253 | 240 | 133 |
| W.B. | 261 | 213 | 308 | 286 | 261 | 207 | 239 | 260 |

TABLE V: AVERAGE ANNUAL DAYS OF WAGE EMPLOYMENT OF RURAL LABOUR HOUSEHOLDS OF SCHEDULED CASTES: AGRICULTURAL OCCUPATION

| State | 1974–5 | | 1977–8 | | 1983 | | 1987–8 | |
|---|---|---|---|---|---|---|---|---|
| | Male | Female | Male | Female | Male | Female | Male | Female |
| A.P. | 223 | 150 | 251 | 194 | 231 | 194 | 231 | 149 |
| Bihar | 198 | 119 | 273 | 212 | 268 | 201 | 289 | 212 |
| Gujarat | 232 | 176 | 247 | 219 | 264 | 229 | 276 | 179 |
| Haryana | 232 | 154 | 246 | 229 | 246 | 284 | 261 | 71 |
| H.P. | 294 | 180 | 204 | 169 | 275 | 191 | 278 | 174 |
| Kar. | 246 | 183 | — | — | 234 | 214 | 277 | 187 |
| Kerala | 153 | 120 | 171 | 176 | 199 | 174 | 165 | 149 |
| M.P. | 228 | 150 | 258 | 210 | 270 | 232 | 259 | 150 |
| Mahar. | 254 | 212 | 232 | 202 | 229 | 188 | 256 | 119 |
| Orissa | 191 | 129 | 233 | 164 | 231 | 185 | 247 | 119 |
| Punjab | 249 | 176 | 267 | 257 | 256 | 207 | 254 | 340 |
| Rajas. | 270 | 180 | 209 | 196 | 263 | 220 | 237 | 35 |
| T.N. | 154 | 109 | 210 | 179 | 205 | 165 | 201 | 171 |
| U.P. | 224 | 128 | 231 | 161 | 247 | 182 | 231 | 90 |
| W.B. | 243 | 139 | 257 | 198 | 219 | 172 | 251 | 171 |

TABLE VI: AVERAGE ANNUAL DAYS OF WAGE EMPLOYMENT OF RURAL LABOUR HOUSEHOLDS OF SCHEDULED TRIBES: AGRICULTURAL OCCUPATION

| State | 1974–5 | | 1977–8 | | 1983 | | 1987–8 | |
|---|---|---|---|---|---|---|---|---|
| | Male | Female | Male | Female | Male | Female | Male | Female |
| A.P. | 192 | 208 | 291 | 239 | 251 | 279 | 186 | 239 |
| Bihar | 231 | 124 | 289 | 278 | 293 | 302 | 278 | 153 |
| Gujarat | 287 | 279 | 301 | 288 | 211 | 203 | 245 | 218 |
| Haryana | 253 | 198 | 281 | 190 | 287 | 219 | 129 | — |
| H.P. | 268 | — | 247 | 230 | 232 | 167 | 204 | — |
| Kar. | 218 | 187 | — | — | 247 | 210 | 171 | 233 |
| Kerala | 156 | 172 | 193 | 202 | 200 | 188 | 190 | 196 |
| M.P. | 208 | 137 | 286 | 296 | 285 | 239 | 166 | 54 |
| Mahar. | 253 | 242 | 268 | 246 | 236 | 257 | 236 | 266 |
| Orissa | 215 | 132 | 270 | 235 | 199 | 276 | 237 | 164 |
| Punjab | 236 | 214 | 275 | 291 | 207 | 279 | 225 | 275 |
| Rajas | 237 | 203 | 216 | 237 | 228 | 285 | 205 | 76 |
| T.N. | 198 | 156 | 281 | 268 | 232 | 232 | 216 | 179 |
| U.P. | 219 | 183 | 259 | 245 | 229 | 264 | 241 | 93 |
| W.B. | 269 | 237 | 309 | 295 | 247 | 168 | 212 | 356 |

TABLE VII: AVERAGE ANNUAL DAYS OF WAGE EMPLOYMENT OF RURAL LABOUR HOUSEHOLDS OF SCHEDULED CASTES: NON-AGRICULTURAL OCCUPATION

| State | 1974–5 | | 1977–8 | | 1983 | | 1987–8 | |
|---|---|---|---|---|---|---|---|---|
| | Male | Female | Male | Female | Male | Female | Male | Female |
| A.P. | 199 | 157 | 204 | 185 | 241 | 191 | 235 | 190 |
| Bihar | 224 | 148 | 242 | 193 | 257 | 249 | 242 | 207 |
| Gujarat | 249 | 179 | 212 | 150 | 256 | 208 | 268 | 137 |
| Haryana | — | — | — | — | — | — | 288 | — |
| H.P. | — | — | 365 | — | 365 | — | 284 | — |
| Kar. | 239 | 190 | — | — | 241 | 250 | 243 | 113 |
| Kerala | 193 | 145 | 223 | — | 173 | 104 | 196 | 261 |
| M.P. | 242 | 153 | 257 | 205 | 251 | 212 | 233 | 151 |
| Maha. | 258 | 188 | 264 | 204 | 242 | 194 | 259 | 193 |
| Orissa | 198 | 132 | 241 | 162 | 206 | 168 | 215 | 131 |
| Punjab | — | — | 365 | 126 | 243 | 219 | 295 | — |
| Rajas. | 228 | 176 | 196 | 156 | 250 | 149 | 227 | 217 |
| T.N. | 268 | 224 | 200 | 202 | 178 | 199 | 206 | 212 |
| U.P. | 301 | 299 | 241 | 215 | 299 | — | 291 | 243 |
| W.B. | 215 | 194 | 266 | 241 | 246 | 205 | 242 | 212 |

*Source*: *Employment and Unemployment of Rural Labour Households*, 1977–8, 1987–8.

TABLE VIII: AVERAGE ANNUAL DAYS OF WAGE EMPLOYMENT OF RURAL LABOUR HOUSEHOLDS OF SCHEDULED TRIBES: NON-AGRICULTURAL OCCUPATION

| State | 1974–5 | | 1977–8 | | 1983 | | 1987–8 | |
|---|---|---|---|---|---|---|---|---|
| | Male | Female | Male | Female | Male | Female | Male | Female |
| A.P. | 147 | 113 | 265 | 103 | 296 | 214 | 201 | 151 |
| Bihar | 208 | 183 | 281 | 294 | 290 | 309 | 214 | 194 |
| Gujarat | 199 | 190 | 212 | 271 | 195 | 176 | 249 | 152 |
| Haryana | 209 | — | — | — | — | — | 251 | — |
| H.P. | 214 | — | 365 | — | 129 | — | 303 | — |
| Kar. | 295 | 270 | — | — | 187 | 158 | 272 | 236 |
| Kerala | 156 | 198 | 150 | — | 163 | 220 | 231 | 270 |
| M.P. | 230 | 150 | 268 | 244 | 289 | 294 | 139 | 75 |
| Mahar. | 266 | 209 | 262 | 186 | 209 | 246 | 267 | 134 |
| Orissa | 227 | 181 | 235 | 219 | 219 | 244 | 237 | 195 |
| Punjab | 365 | — | — | — | 365 | 365 | — | — |
| Rajas. | 214 | 111 | 210 | 207 | 264 | 329 | 186 | 113 |
| T.N. | — | 365 | 262 | 266 | 183 | 188 | 146 | — |
| U.P. | 365 | 228 | 268 | — | 324 | 104 | 271 | — |
| W.B. | 225 | 172 | 319 | 307 | 299 | 232 | 263 | 175 |

*Source*: *Employment and Unemployment of Rural Labour Households*, 1977–8, 1987–8

It is not accidental that the majority of states having this characteristic feature belong to the proverbial BIMARU (Bihar, Madhya Pradesh, Rajasthan, Uttar Pradesh) state. Bihar is an intriguing case where for both agricultural and non-agricultural work, the gender gap in wages has declined both for all classes as well as Scheduled Castes. This does not indicate an improved situation, as the narrowing gender gap in wages is, in fact, because of relatively more days of work for female workers of all classes, perhaps indicating absence of men due to male migration. In case of Scheduled Castes, the increase in workdays for female workers is slightly more than for their male counterparts. States in which the gender gap in wages has increased for both the agricultural and the non-agricultural workers are Madhya Pradesh, Rajasthan and Uttar Pradesh. Orissa joins the rank in terms of agricultural wages. Punjab, Kerala, Tamil Nadu and West Bengal are characterized by narrowing wage gaps between sexes for agricultural as well as non-agricultural work, both for all classes and Scheduled Castes, and this is essentially due to relatively higher increase in workdays for female workers. This scenario of declining workdays for female workers in backward states needs to be looked at in combination with the disparate wage rate and its growth profile across sectors and between male and female workers within the sectors. As pointed out by Kundu, the growth in average earnings has decelerated substantially (Kundu 1999).

Although the more recent NSS data show a slight reversal of the trend at all-India level whereby days of usual employment seem to be shrinking for men over the period, it is observed that the proportion of person-days of the usually employed utilized for work remain quite low for females compared to males in all the years under scrutiny. During 1999–2000, for rural females it was 68 as against 90 per cent for male workers (Table IX).

A more recent distribution of workdays is provided by the NCAER report; although it cannot be compared with the NSS data, the relative ranking of states in terms of overall availability of work for females does not change too drastically (Shariff 1999).

## POVERTY AND WORK

The hypothesized relationship between female work and poverty is not always straightforward, and in many cases, when poverty has been taken as an independent variable to explain female work

TABLE IX: PER 1000 DISTRIBUTION OF PERSON-DAYS OF USUALLY EMPLOYED (PRINCIPAL AND SUBSIDIARY STATUS) BY THEIR BROAD CURRENT DAILY STATUS FOR VARIOUS SURVEY PERIODS

| Current daily status | Rural | | | | | |
|---|---|---|---|---|---|---|
| | Male | | | Female | | |
| | 1999–2000 | 1993–4 | 1987–8 | 1999–2000 | 1993–4 | 1987–8 |
| (1) | (2) | (3) | (4) | (5) | (6) | (7) |
| Employed | 897 | 909 | 926 | 676 | 663 | 638 |
| Unemployed | 53 | 40 | 27 | 41 | 30 | 26 |
| Not in labour force | 51 | 51 | 47 | 283 | 306 | 336 |
| All | 1,000 | 1,000 | 1,000 | 1,000 | 1,000 | 1,000 |

| Current daily status | Urban | | | | | |
|---|---|---|---|---|---|---|
| | Male | | | Female | | |
| | 1999–2000 | 1993–4 | 1987–8 | 1999–2000 | 1993–4 | 1987–8 |
| | (8) | (9) | (10) | (11) | (12) | (13) |
| Employed | 942 | 949 | 938 | 791 | 766 | 716 |
| Unemployed | 27 | 27 | 37 | 22 | 24 | 37 |
| Not in labour force | 31 | 25 | 25 | 187 | 210 | 247 |
| All | 1,000 | 1,000 | 1,000 | 1,000 | 1,000 | 1,000 |

*Source*: NSS 55th Round Key Results.

participation rates, contrary to nromal expectation, the correlation has been negative. Poverty has declined for all categories of workers over the last decades. Research results show a significant impact of female workforce participation on rural poverty: it accounted for about 10 per cent of inter-state variation. In a classification of states on the basis of female work participation rates and rural poverty, it has been found that out of six states which had a high incidence of poverty in 1993–4 (Madhya Pradesh, Orissa, Assam, Bihar, Uttar Pradesh and West Bengal), except Orissa and Madhya Pradesh, the other four belong to the low-work participation category. Thus, poverty may not always push females to work, but if they work, poverty may decline. Moreover, factors of rural markets are more significant than the forces of economic growth as the 'trickle down effect' of agricultural growth, does not seem to impact reduction in rural poverty (Misra 2000).

It has also been pointed out that the rate of decline in poverty ratios has been the lowest for casual workers vis-à-vis regular workers, clearly indicating a nexus between casualization of labour

TABLE X: EMPLOYMENT STRUCTURE FOR POOR AND NON-POOR[3]

(percentage)

| | Poor | | Non-poor | |
|---|---|---|---|---|
| | 1977–8 | 1987–8 | 1977–8 | 1987–8 |
| Self | | | | |
| Male | 53 | 46 | 68 | 64 |
| Female | 53 | 54 | 69 | 72 |
| Salaried | | | | |
| Male | 10 | 08 | 12 | 14 |
| Female | 05 | 03 | 07 | 05 |
| Casual | | | | |
| Male | 37 | 46 | 19 | 22 |
| Female | 42 | 43 | 43 | 23 |

*Source*: Based on NSS Rounds for States.

and low income with a bias towards female workers as confirmed by poverty line classification of wage labour employment by the NCAER also (Dev 1999; Shariff 1999). A further break-up of casual workers in poor and non-poor segments and their level of casualization reinforces this point (Table X).

## NOTES

1. The disparities are calculated by standardizing the wages as mentioned in the main body of the text and then converting the male and female wages into logits and subtracting the wages for females from wages for males. Since the male wages are more representative of the labour market situations, they are taken first in the disparity group. For details, see Sopher (1980) and Kundu (1986). DIS = log X2/X1 + log (200-X1)/(200-X2).
2. It can be seen that Madhya Pradesh shows increase for male workers and a rather unchanged situation for female workers whereas Haryana and Maharashtra both register decline for females in all classes and Scheduled Castes, while Gujarat and Orissa show a decline for Scheduled Caste females. Rajasthan and Uttar Pradesh have a very marked decline for female workers. Once again, in the less developed states, females, and in developed states, Scheduled Caste females seem to suffer from lack of work the most.
3. This table is derived by dividing the workers by monthly per capita expenditure (MPCE) classes in 'below poverty line' and 'above poverty line' categories. A simple method adopted from Kundu has been used. When the poverty line falls in between the two limits L1 and L2

of consumption classes, the number of observations (X) falling in the range from the lower limit L1 to the poverty line P is estimated by assuming that its proportion to the total oservations (Y) in the category equals the ratio of the range to the total interval of the category. In logarithmic terms: $x/y$ = [log P-log l1]/[log L2-log L1].

# 12. Food Insecurity, Coping Strategy and Livelihood Pattern among Households in Tribal Areas of Orissa

*Kailas Sarap and M. Mahamallik*

Orissa is one of the few states in the country where there is a substantial number of tribes and tribal population. It has more than 11.4 per cent of the total tribal population in the country. As per the 1991 Census, 22.22 per cent of the total population of the state belonged to Scheduled Tribe (ST) categories consisting of 62 communities including 12 primitive groups. About 44.7 per cent of the geographical area of the state has been identified and declared as Scheduled Area under the Fifth Schedule of the Indian Constitution. These communities are mainly found in a continuous belt in the undivided districts of Koraput, Mayurbhanj, Keonjhar, Kalahandi, Bolangir, Phulabani, Sambalpur, Sundargarh and some other pockets of other districts (Table 1). The percentage of ST population varies from 47 to 68 per cent in the Scheduled Area. The most widely-known people are the Khond, Saora, Juanga, Bhuiyan, Ho, Munda and Santhals. The majority of the population is very backward judged on different indicators of development. According to the 1991 Census, only 22.25 per cent of the total tribal population was literate. The female literacy rate is still lower.

The economic growth is negligible, with a high incidence of income poverty and malnutrition. As high as 48.56 per cent of people of the state during 1993–4 were found to be below the poverty line compared to 36 per cent at the all-India level. The state is predominantly rural, with 86.62 per cent people living in villages as against 74.29 per cent at the all-India level. Orissa is characterized by a high Infant Mortality Rate (IMR) and high incidence of malnutrition among children.

TABLE 1: SOCIO-ECONOMIC CHARACTERISTICS OF ST POPULATION IN ORISSA

| District | Scheduled Area | % of ST population to total population | Mandays of employment generated per person | Mandays of employment generated per ST person |
|---|---|---|---|---|
| Gajapati | R. Udayagiri | 67.91 | 4.59 | 3.45 |
| Malkangiri | Whole district | 58.40 | 7.36 | 6.78 |
| Mayurbhanj | Whole district | 57.87 | 3.62 | 3.52 |
| Rayagada | Whole district | 56.04 | 5.91 | 5.52 |
| Sambalpur | Kuchinda tahsil | 55.86 | 3.18 | 2.39 |
| Kalahandi | Th. Rampur block | 55.65 | 2.86 | 3.28 |
| Nawarangpur | Whole district | 55.27 | 5.08 | 1.67 |
| Keonjhar | Keonjhar tahsil | 54.82 | 3.39 | 3.00 |
| Phulbani | Baliguda tahsil | 53.05 | 5.09 | 4.66 |
| Sundargarh | Whole district | 50.74 | 3.74 | 3.34 |
| Koraput | Whole district | 50.56 | 5.14 | 4.87 |
| Balasore | Nilagiri tahsil | 49.85 | 1.78 | 3.81 |
| Kalahandi | Langigarh block | 48.95 | — | — |
| Phulabani | Kandhamal tahsil | 47.80 | — | — |
| Keonjhar | Champua tahsil | 46.58 | — | — |
| Ganjam | Sorada tahsil | 9.01 | 1.31 | 2.18 |
| Orissa | | 22.21 | 0.94 | 1.59 |

*Source*: *Economic Survey of Orissa, 1997-1998.*

The National Health Survey (NHS) also reported both chronic and acute under nutrition in the state. As high as 53 per cent of all children under the age of 4 years were found underweight and 48 per cent were stunted. The mortality rates among the population in general and tribal groups in particular are relatively very high. In tribal belts, the situation is much worse. More than two-thirds (68.90 per cent) of the tribal population living in rural areas was below the poverty line during 1983–4 in comparison to 44.76 per cent for all of rural Orissa. Agricultural labourers constituted 28.68 per cent of the 'main workers' of the Scheduled Tribe population as classified under the Indian Census. It varied from about 30 to 40 per cent in different tribal-dominated districts during 1991 (Table 2). Despite the fact 44.31 per cent of the tribal population comprised 'cultivators', the tribal population in the state is also characterized by landlessness. Poverty and malnutrition are rampant in the state in general and in tribal areas in particular.

TABLE 2: SOCIO-ECONOMIC CHARACTERISTICS OF ST POPULATION IN SCHEDULED AREAS OF ORISSA

| District | % of ST population | % of cultivators to main workers | % of Agli lab to main workers | % of main workers to total population | Employment generation in lakh mandays (ST %) from total | Fertilizer consumption 1996–7 (kg/ha) | Yield rate of rice, 1997–8 (qt./ha) |
|---|---|---|---|---|---|---|---|
| Gajapati | 47.88 | 50.20 | 35.29 | 41.94 | 40.18 | 32.00 | 13.05 |
| Malkangiri | 58.36 | 47.56 | 15.55 | 3739 | 60.29 | 13.50 | 7.25 |
| Mayurbhanj | 57.87 | 48.49 | 31.83 | 37.28 | 59.99 | 20.06 | 13.75 |
| Rayagada | 56.04 | 40.20 | 41.13 | 41.25 | 59.85 | 17.56 | 12.51 |
| Sambalpur | 35.08 | 33.88 | 33.26 | 38.12 | 35.19 | 57.60 | 18.39 |
| Kalahandi | 28.88 | 42.85 | 41.04 | 37.68 | 35.49 | 14.81 | 13.74 |
| Nawarangpur | 55.27 | 52.22 | 35.65 | 38.78 | 55.11 | 25.00 | 11.26 |
| Keonjhar | 44.52 | 47.68 | 24.52 | 32.91 | 45.03 | 13.04 | 13.02 |
| Phulbani | 51.51 | 48.34 | 34.62 | 38.98 | 50.48 | 4.63 | 13.81 |
| Sundargarh | 50.74 | 38.77 | 17.92 | 32.29 | 68.03 | 12.25 | 10.21 |
| Koraput | 50.67 | 48.15 | 31.26 | 41.08 | 57.64 | 8.67 | 11.95 |
| Balasore | 10.57 | 48.58 | 26.78 | 27.09 | 24.86 | 70.80 | 15.17 |
| Kalahandi | — | — | — | — | 35.48 | 14.81 | 13.74 |
| Phulabani | — | — | — | — | 50.48 | 4.63 | 13.81 |
| Keonjhar | — | — | — | — | 45.03 | 13.04 | 13.02 |
| Ganjam | 2.93 | 38.96 | 32.94 | 35.02 | 50.78 | 50.80 | 14.97 |
| Orissa | 22.21 | 44.31 | 28.68 | 32.77 | 37.26 | | |

*Source*: *Economic Survey of Orissa, 1998–1999.*

## AGRICULTURE PRACTICES AND LAND TENURE SYSTEM

Agriculture in Orissa (and the tribal regions in particular) is characterized by underdevelopment with low productivity on account of low use of modern inputs and low percentage of area irrigated. Certain groups of tribals, moreover, practice shifting cultivation. In this type of cultivation, investment is minimal and hence productivity is also very low. The percentage of area irrigated in tribal-dominated districts is much lower than that of other districts. The cropping pattern in these districts is dominated by the cultivation of rice, ragi and other inferior cereals, oilseeds, pulses, etc. These crops cover more than fourth-fifths of the total area cultivated.

Land in the tribal regions can be broadly classified into private land, forest land and unsurveyed (donger or upland) land. Private land is of two categories, namely, land belonging to community and individual holdings. The donger (upland) slopes constitute more than 60 per cent of the land in the tribal districts of southern Orissa. It is considered unfit for cultivation. No private possession rights are given on these lands for reasons of ecological conservation and soil protection. Forest land, on the other hand, is subject to restrictions from the Forest Department of Orissa. A tribal family may have cultivated certain plots of land for generations under the categories of forest/lowland, but his rights to that piece of land are not recognized by the state. Private ownership of land by the tribals is, therefore, very low. Furthermore, whatever ownership of private land they have had in those Scheduled Areas have been eroded over the years due to transfer of land to non-tribals through alienation of land.

There are laws in the state to protect the rights of tribals to their land against land alienation, if land has been transferred to non-tribals. Despite these numerous legislations, large-scale illegal land transfers take place in tribal areas. All these laws have, in fact, become ineffective due to connivance between the lower bureaucracy and the non-tribal people. Since land-ownership amongst tribal households is limited, they have to depend on forests, other common property resources and on wage employment. About three-fourths of the tribal rural population in the state are forest dwellers who reside on the fringes or in the vicinity of forests or within a daily working distance of a forest.

The tribal households thus depend on forests for their food, fuel and medicine. Minor forest products are an important source of income for the tribals, specially during the lean season. The tribals collect minor forest products as and when they want and generally sell it to the authorized leaseholders appointed by the state government. The Tribal Development Cooperative Corporation (TDCC) has been set up with the explicit purpose of facilitating and ensuring fair prices for the products sold by the tribals. The normal practice is to subject the lease to the local businessmen. Nonetheless, some Development of Women and Children in Rural Areas (DWCRA) groups have also been appointed as additional agents in these localities and granted licences for collection and making of finished items (brooms) which are marketed through the Orissa Rural Marketing Apex Society (ORMAS).

The working of TDCC, however, is very unsatisfactory: it has almost become non-functional. It has sublet its work to private businessmen. Monopolistic exploitation takes place in the purchase of minor forest products by the leaseholders. Most minor forest products are sold by the district collector at rates less than 50 per cent of the procurement prices fixed at the district level (Das 1998; Sarap 2000b). It has also been observed that though the sale of these items provides sizeable revenue to the state, the tribal people (including children and old persons) who spend long hours in collecting these items do not realize reasonable prices. In recent years, there has been a decline in access to CPR. Deforestation and state policies to use forest land for industrial purposes including for mining have led to the decline in the access of CPR for the tribals.

### DEVELOPMENT ACTIVITIES IN TRIBAL AREAS

The tribal areas are being developed under the Tribal Sub-Plan (TSP), which was introduced during the Fifth Plan (1974–9). The objectives of TSP are: (1) to improve the socio-economic conditions of the tribal population through strengthening the development of infrastructure, and (2) to protect them against exploitation through administrative and legal support.

Various other development programmes are being implemented through the Integrated Tribal Development Agencies (ITDA), the Modified Area Development Approach (MADA), the Cluster Approach and Dispersed Tribal Development Programme (DTDP). The MADA aims at development of tribals staying outside the

ITDA areas. Since the Seventh Five Year Plan, the Cluster Approach has been adopted for the development of contiguous areas having population of 5,000 where 50 per cent or more of the population are tribals. The DTDP is being implemented by the SC/ST Development Finance Cooperative Corporation for the benefits of tribal families living outside the special project areas like ITDA, MADA, and Clusters and micro-projects.

About 5.67 lakh families in 46 pockets covering parts of 47 blocks of 17 districts are covered under the ITDA and MADA. Besides, a number of anti-poverty programmes including IRDP, TRYSEM, JRY, EAS, IAY, DPAP and MWS are being implemented in the state. As per the guidelines, 50 per cent of the beneficiaries under these schemes are required to be SC/ST families. These programmes are designed to improve the standard of living and quality of life of the poor, including tribals, by providing self- and wage-employment. The bulk of the investment in the tribal sub-plan goes to infrastructure development and the social service sector. The benefits of these programmes have marginal impact on the tribals and other poor due to a variety of reasons, including their implementation and responses of the credit institutions (Drèze 1990). Further, there is widespread default of loans by beneficiaries, so that their ability to borrow later from the formal institutions is reduced. Clearly, despite all the strategies and anti-poverty programmes implemented in tribal areas, the impact of these programmes on reduction of poverty is marginal, and as a result they are vulnerable to food insecurity.

## FOOD CONSUMPTION PATTERN AND ACCESS TO FOOD

The analysis in the following paragraphs is based on the field survey relating to actual access to food, income and food insecurity-coping mechanisms adopted by different groups of households in the study villages. The data have been collected from 3 villages located in Kantabanji tahsil of Bolangir district. One village from each block was intentionally selected taking into account the concentration of SC/ST population/distance from the town as well as hinterland area. Of the 3 villages, 2 are completely tribal. The percentage of ST population varied from 70 to 98 per cent in these villages. In the other village, the percentage of ST population was 37.47 per cent. The SC/ST together constituted 63 per cent of total population in this village.

Field investigations were conducted during the years 1998–9 and 1999–2000. The main source of data relates to the year 1997–8. Collection of data was done through personal interviews on the basis of a suitably designed questionnaire. Besides, the Participatory Research Approach (PRA) method was also adopted to get some special and general information relating to some aspects for households. Secondary information relating to institutions with which the villagers have had transaction was also collected. The data relating to socio-economic and the demographic structure pattern of asset holdings, pattern of consumption of food, expenditure incurred on food and other items, income originating from different sources and borrowing pattern of households were collected from all the households interviewed.

The selected indicators of food security include food consumption, both in terms of physical quantity and expenditure incurred on different food items. Borrowing in cash and kind as well as the extent of loss of collateral in the borrowing are also analysed with a view to understanding the coping mechanisms of the households.

The data relating to food consumption of different items both produced in own/operated land and purchased from the market including from the ration shop (PDS) were collected for a reference period of one month prior to the date of data collection. The data were collected from January to April 1998. The seasonal variation of food consumption of different items has been broadly asked through the recall method. Data relating to consumption of food of different items relate to one month. For non-food items information has been obtained for one year preceding the survey. The expenditure on other food items has been converted into monthly basis.

Production of output of different crops has been collected for the year. It is to be noted that several households belonging to different landholding sizes collected food and non-food items from the CPR at different times. If a household had purchased food grains from a neighbour or shopkeeper, this has been taken into consideration. Similarly, while calculating income, items collected by the members of a household from the CPR have also been taken into account. These items have been converted into value terms (in current market price, both sold and consumed). As the market value of these items (like *achar*, *kendu* leaf, *sal* leaf, *amla*, *kendu*, etc.) is low, the income realized by the households is also low. Besides these, a number of other items mushroom, kardi, and different types of oilseeds are also consumed by tribal households and non-tribal households in the area: all these have not been taken into account while calculating income.

## PATTERN OF FOOD CONSUMPTION

Our enquiries from households in different villages revealed that generally the requirement of rice per adult per day was 500 grams (183 kg p.a.). The requirement of children in the age group of 4 to 14 has been assumed to be half the requirement of an adult member. Besides, they consume other cereals such as mandia, gurji and kudo. Other cereals are consumed as the main course when availability of rice is low/negligible due to rise in price and lack of income. From March to June, the consumption of mandia is, therefore, more in comparison to that of rice. Similarly, during the rainy season in the months of July–August, many households eat *mahua* flower along with *kultha* (a pulse of cheap variety). These items are boiled and utilized for days. Tribal households also consume a variety of spinach collected from the forest during the lean period.

Consumption of different food items in physical quantity has been shown in Tables 3 to 5. Per household consumption of rice was approximately 69 kg per month with a per capita consumption of about 17 kg. Consumption of food grains is thus approximately about 17.50 kg including all other cereals. There is some minor variation of rice consumption between the ST and SC groups and among different size groups. However, in case of Other Caste (OC) groups, consumption of rice was slightly lower that of SC/ST groups. This is due to the consumption of other food items by these groups. There is, however, not much variation in different villages in the case of consumption of rice.

Per household consumption of total food grains including that of pulses is given in the last columns of Tables 3 to 5. There is some marginal increase in the consumption of total food grains as the households move up the size class of landholders. There is slight increase in the amount of consumption of pulses with increase in the status of households, specially among the medium and large farm groups. Further, there is some inter-village variation in the consumption of inferior cereal consumption. It was relatively higher among different size groups of households in Village-3, which is a completely tribal village, followed by Village-1 and Village-2.

TABLE 3: QUANTITY OF DIFFERENT FOOD ITEMS CONSUMED PER HOUSEHOLD PER MONTH IN THE STUDY VILLAGE-1

(in kg)

| Land-holding size (in acre) | Caste | Rice | Inferior cereals | Cereals | Pulses | Total food-grains |
|---|---|---|---|---|---|---|
| 1 | 2 | 3 | 4 | 5(3+4) | 6 | 7(5+6) |
| 00–0.0 | SC | 69.00 (2) | 3.00 | 72.00 | 0.25 | 72.25 |
| | ST | 73.00 (26) | 1.07 | 74.07 | 0.38 | 74.46 |
| | OC | 68.00 (10) | 0.80 | 68.80 | 0.30 | 69.10 |
| Average | | 71.47 (38) | 1.11 | 75.58 | 0.36 | 72.93 |
| 0.01–0.50 | SC | — | — | — | — | 76.63 |
| | ST | 75.00 (4) | 0.87 | 75.87 | 0.75 | — |
| | OC | — | — | — | — | 76.63 |
| | | 75.00 (4) | 0.87 | 75.87 | 0.75 | — |
| 0.51–2.50 | SC | 70.00 (6) | 0.50 | 70.50 | 0.50 | 71.00 |
| | ST | 69.00 (35) | 0.72 | 69.72 | 0.51 | 70.23 |
| | OC | 63.00 (6) | 0.34 | 63.34 | 10.00 | 64.17 |
| Average | | 68.36 (47) | 1.56 | 69.00 | 0.55 | 69.55 |
| 2.51–5.00 | SC | — | — | — | — | — |
| | ST | 65.00 (20) | 1.07 | 66.07 | 0.70 | 66.77 |
| | OC | 61.25 (4) | 0.50 | 61.75 | 1.25 | 63.00 |
| Average | | 64.38 (24) | 0.98 | 65.35 | 0.79 | 66.14 |
| 5.01–10.00 | SC | 69.00 (3) | 1.34 | 70.34 | 0.67 | 71.00 |
| | ST | 70.00 (14) | 1.43 | 71.43 | 1.14 | 72.57 |
| | OC | 62.5 (2) | 0.50 | 63.00 | 0.50 | 63.50 |
| | | 69.05 (19) | 1.32 | 70.37 | 1.00 | 71.37 |
| 10.00–Above | SC | — | — | — | — | — |
| | ST | — | — | — | — | — |
| | OC | 67.00 (3) | 16.67 | 67.17 | 1.34 | 68.50 |
| Average | | 67.00 (3) | 16.67 | 67.17 | 1.34 | 68.50 |
| Overall | SC | 69.55 (11) | 1.18 | 70.73 | 0.50 | 43.95 |
| | ST | 69.63 (99) | 0.98 | 70.62 | 0.62 | 71.23 |
| | OC | 65.11 (25) | 0.54 | 65.70 | 0.72 | 66.42 |
| Average | | 68.79 (135) | 0.93 | 69.72 | 0.63 | 70.34 |

*Source*: Field Survey.
*Note*: Figure in the bracket represents number of households.

The cereal consumption per household in the study villages was relatively higher in comparison with the ICMR norm of 15.48 kg of cereal bundle per month. The high consumption of cereals is partly due to the food habits of the people, availability of cereals and income during the period, and the need for more energy due to the requirement of hard physical labour in harvest and post-harvest work. The general food habit in the area is to eat cereals three to four times per day. Consumption of other food items including pulses is negligible. A majority of households have to derive their energy from cereal only. Households in different villages have reported that the consumption of cereals during the lean months is relatively lower in comparison with the figures given in Tables 3 to 5.

TABLE 4: QUANTITY OF DIFFERENT FOOD ITEMS CONSUMED PER HOUSEHOLD PER MONTH IN THE STUDY VILLAGE-2

(in kg)

| Land-holding size (in acre) | Caste | Rice | Inferior cereals | Cereals | Pulses | Total food-grains |
|---|---|---|---|---|---|---|
| 1 | 2 | 3 | 4 | 5(3+4) | 6 | 7(5+6) |
| 00–0.0 | SC | 70.77 (13) | 1.38 | 72.15 | 0.15 | 72.30 |
| | ST | — | — | — | — | — |
| | OC | 70.23 (3) | 0.67 | 71.00 | 0.33 | 71.33 |
| Average | | 70.68 (16) | 1.25 | 71.94 | 0.19 | 72.13 |
| 0.01–0.50 | SC | 78.00 (4) | 2 | 80 | 0.25 | 80.25 |
| | ST | 81.00 (8) | 1.88 | 82.87 | 0.25 | 83.12 |
| | OC | 71.00 (1) | — | 71.00 | — | 71 |
| Average | | 79.31 (13) | 1.77 | 81.05 | 0.23 | 81.31 |
| 0.51–2.50 | SC | 69.00 (15) | 0.67 | 69.67 | 0.53 | 70.20 |
| | ST | 72.00 (7) | 1.43 | 73.43 | 0.43 | 73.86 |
| | OC | 70.00 (6) | 0.50 | 70.50 | 0.50 | 71 |
| Average | | 69.96 (28) | 0.82 | 70.79 | 0.50 | 71.29 |
| 2.5–5.00 | SC | 68.00 (2) | — | 68.00 | 0.50 | 68.20 |
| | ST | 69.00 (11) | 1 | 70.00 | 0.81 | 70.82 |
| | OC | 63.00 (2) | — | 63.00 | 1.00 | 64.00 |
| | | 68.06 (15) | 0.73 | 68.8 | 0.80 | 69.60 |
| 5.01–10.00 | SC | 61.25 (4) | 0.25 | 61.50 | 1 | 62.5 |
| | ST | 69.00 (1) | 0.50 | 69.50 | 1 | 70.5 |
| | OC | 60.05 (2) | 0.75 | 61.25 | 1.50 | 62.75 |
| Average | | 62.14 (7) | 0.43 | 62.57 | 1.14 | 63.71 |
| 10.00–Above | SC | — | — | — | — | — |
| | ST | — | — | — | — | — |
| | OC | 63.00 (1) | — | 63 | 2 | 65 |
| Average | | 63.00 (1) | — | 63 | 2 | 65 |
| Overall | SC | 69.68 (38) | 0.97 | 70.66 | 0.42 | 71.08 |
| | ST | 73.33 (27) | 1.35 | 74.69 | 0.56 | 75.24 |
| | OC | 67.47 (15) | 0.43 | 67.90 | 0.73 | 68.62 |
| Average | | 70.50 (80) | 1 | 71.50 | 0.53 | 72.03 |

*Source*: Field Survey.

*Note*: Figure in the bracket represents number of households.

TABLE 5: QUANTITY OF DIFFERENT FOOD ITEMS CONSUMED PER HOUSEHOLD PER MONTH IN THE STUDY VILLAGE-3

(in kg)

| Land-holding size (in acre) | Caste | Rice | | Inferior cereals | Cereals | Pulses | Total food grains |
|---|---|---|---|---|---|---|---|
| 1 | 2 | 3 | | 4 | 5(3+4) | 6 | 7(5+6) |
| 00–0.0 | SC | 20.00 | (1) | 2.00 | 22.00 | — | 22.00 |
| | ST | 63.66 | (32) | 1.09 | 64.53 | 0.15 | 64.69 |
| | OC | — | | — | — | — | — |
| Average | | 62.12 | (33) | 1.06 | 63.24 | 0.15 | 63.39 |
| 0.01–0.50 | SC | — | | — | — | — | — |
| | ST | 98.33 | (6) | 1.00 | 99.33 | 0.16 | 99.50 |
| | OC | — | | — | — | — | — |
| Average | | 98.33 | (6) | 1.00 | 99.33 | 0.16 | 99.50 |
| 0.51–2.50 | SC | — | | — | — | — | — |
| | ST | 66.25 | (40) | 2.85 | 69.10 | 0.45 | 69.55 |
| | OC | — | | — | — | — | — |
| Average | | 66.25 | (40) | 2.85 | 69.10 | 0.45 | 69.55 |
| 2.51–5.00 | SC | — | | — | — | — | — |
| | ST | 68.18 | (22) | 0.36 | 68.54 | 0.45 | 69.00 |
| | OC | — | | — | — | — | — |
| Average | | 68.18 | (22) | 0.36 | 68.54 | 0.45 | 69.00 |
| 5.01–10.00 | SC | — | | — | — | — | — |
| | ST | 66.67 | (6) | 0.33 | 67.00 | 0.50 | 67.50 |
| | OC | — | | — | — | — | — |
| Average | | 66.67 | (6) | 0.33 | 67.00 | 0.50 | 67.50 |
| 10.00– | SC | — | | — | — | — | — |
| Above | ST | 71.67 | (3) | — | 71.67 | 2.66 | 74.33 |
| | OC | — | | — | — | — | — |
| Average | | 71.67 | (3) | — | 71.67 | 2.66 | 74.33 |
| Overall | SC | 20.00 | (1) | 2.00 | 22.00 | — | 22.00 |
| | ST | 67.75 | (109) | 1.51 | 69.47 | 0.37 | 69.63 |
| | OC | — | | — | — | — | — |
| Average | | 67.32 | (110) | 1.52 | 68.88 | 0.41 | 69.25 |

*Source*: Field Survey.
*Note*: Figure in the bracket represents number of households.

## EXPENDITURE INCURRED ON FOOD

The expenditure incurred by different groups of households on different food and non-food items such as on health, education and other social expenditure (cloth, social and funeral expenditure) has been collected and calculated for different groups of households. Expenditure incurred per household at current prices for different groups and castes/tribes is given in Tables 6 to 8.

The average mean monthly per household expenditure on food and non-food items for all households varied from Rs. 994 in

TABLE 6: COMPOSITION OF FOOD AND NON-FOOD EXPENDITURE (in Rs.) PER HOUSEHOLD PER MONTH IN THE STUDY VILLAGE-1

| | | | | | | | As % of total non-food expenditure | | |
|---|---|---|---|---|---|---|---|---|---|
| Landholding size (in acre) | Caste | Total food exp. | Total food & non-food exp. | Total food as a % of total exp. | Total non-food exp. as % of total exp. | Total non-food exp. | Health | Education | Other non-food items |
| 00–0.0 | SC | 661 | 684 | 96.63 | 70 | 23 | 91.25 | 9.02 | 0.73 |
| | ST | 723 | 786 | 91.99 | 48 | 63 | 12.22 | 1.01 | 86.77 |
| | OC | 648 | 740 | 87.59 | 39 | 92 | 0.91 | 2.73 | 96.36 |
| Average | | 685 | 753 | 90.92 | 46 | 68 | 9.62 | 1.76 | 88.62 |
| 0.01–0.50 | SC | 767 | — | — | — | — | — | — | — |
| | ST | 767 | 808 | 94.95 | 61 | 41 | 5.11 | 2.55 | 92.34 |
| | OC | — | — | — | — | — | — | — | — |
| Average | | 767 | 808 | 94.95 | 61 | 41 | 5.11 | 2.55 | 92.34 |
| 0.51–2.50 | SC | 849 | 899 | 94.95 | 58 | 50 | 1.39 | 6.35 | 92.26 |
| | ST | 815 | 922 | 88.36 | 38 | 107 | 1.44 | 2.44 | 96.12 |
| | OC | 787 | 857 | 91.82 | 48 | 70 | 0.39 | 5.94 | 93.67 |
| Average | | 816 | 911 | 89.54 | 41 | 95 | 1.34 | 3.03 | 95.63 |
| 2.51–5.00 | SC | — | — | — | — | — | — | — | — |
| | ST | 839 | 986 | 85.13 | 32 | 147 | 3.48 | 3.13 | 93.39 |
| | OC | 868 | 1228 | 70.68 | 16 | 359 | 0.29 | 9.27 | 90.44 |
| Average | | 844 | 1026 | 82.26 | 27 | 182 | 2.43 | 5.15 | 92.42 |
| 5.01–10.00 | SC | 215 | 502 | 42.83 | 22 | 287 | 0.97 | 5.82 | 93.21 |
| | ST | 1108 | 1516 | 73.11 | 18 | 408 | 3.51 | 4.38 | 92.11 |
| | OC | 1137 | 1596 | 71.26 | 17 | 459 | — | 10.82 | 89.18 |
| Average | | 1034 | 1488 | 73.52 | 18 | 394 | 2.78 | 5.34 | 91.88 |
| 10.00– | SC | — | — | — | — | — | — | — | — |
| Above | ST | — | — | — | — | — | — | — | — |
| | OC | 1314 | 1776 | 73.98 | 19 | 462 | 0.91 | 0.84 | 98.25 |
| Average | | 1314 | 1776 | 73.98 | 19 | 462 | 0.91 | 0.84 | 98.25 |
| Overall | SC | 856 | 966 | 88.62 | 39 | 110 | 4.49 | 6.07 | 89.44 |
| | ST | 835 | 978 | 85.37 | 32 | 143 | 3.97 | 3.20 | 92.83 |
| | OC | 863 | 1066 | 80.96 | 26 | 203 | 0.53 | 5.79 | 93.68 |
| Average | | 842 | 994 | 84.73 | 31 | 152 | 3.15 | 4.01 | 92.84 |

*Source*: Field Survey.

*Note*: SC = Scheduled Castes, ST = Scheduled Tribes, OC = Other Castes.

TABLE 7: COMPOSITION OF FOOD AND NON-FOOD EXPENDITURE (in Rs.) PER MONTH PER HOUSEHOLD IN THE STUDY VILLAGE-2

| Landholding size (in acre) | Caste | Total food exp. per HH per month | Total food & non-food exp. per month per HH | Total food as a % of total exp. | Total non-food exp. as % of total exp. | Total non-food exp. per HH per month | As % of total non-food expenditure: Health | Education | Other non-food items |
|---|---|---|---|---|---|---|---|---|---|
| 00–0.0 | SC | 629 | 758 | 82.96 | 28.86 | 129 | 3.42 | 0.60 | 95.96 |
| | ST | — | — | — | — | — | — | — | — |
| | OC | 697 | 700 | 99.61 | 95.52 | 3 | — | 51.02 | 48.98 |
| Average | | 642 | 747 | 85.89 | 33.64 | 105 | 3.40 | 0.56 | 63.54 |
| 0.01–0.50 | SC | 705 | 735 | 95.95 | 66.39 | 30 | 5.60 | 7.00 | 87.39 |
| | ST | 733 | 913 | 80.29 | 25.34 | 180 | 3.47 | 1.45 | 95.08 |
| | OC | 541 | 685 | 79.02 | 23.88 | 144 | — | 5.80 | 94.20 |
| Average | | 710 | 840 | 84.43 | 31.12 | 131 | 3.33 | 2.20 | 94.77 |
| 0.51–2.50 | SC | 710 | 823 | 86.29 | 34.41 | 113 | 5.61 | 9.60 | 84.79 |
| | ST | 738 | 789 | 93.62 | 55.01 | 50 | 4.35 | 56.75 | 38.89 |
| | OC | 739 | 897 | 82.46 | 28.15 | 157 | 1.86 | 7.95 | 90.19 |
| Average | | 723 | 830 | 87.15 | 36.09 | 107 | 4.28 | 14.64 | 81.08 |
| 2.51–5.00 | SC | 845 | 1033 | 81.74 | 27.17 | 189 | — | 13.25 | 86.75 |
| | ST | 776 | 983 | 78.87 | 23.73 | 208 | — | 6.11 | 93.89 |
| | OC | 874 | 1463 | 59.72 | 10.99 | 589 | 2.12 | — | 97.88 |
| Average | | 798 | 1054 | 75.70 | 20.61 | 256 | 0.65 | 4.93 | 94.42 |
| 5.01–10.00 | SC | 857 | 1161 | 73.81 | 19.02 | 304 | — | 6.17 | 93.83 |
| | ST | 1068 | 1464 | 72.96 | 18.36 | 396 | 44.23 | — | 55.77 |
| | OC | 1208 | 2683 | 45.03 | 6.39 | 1475 | — | — | 100.00 |
| Average | | 987 | 1639 | 60.24 | 11.21 | 652 | 3.84 | 1.64 | 94.52 |
| 10.00–Above | SC | — | — | — | — | — | — | — | — |
| | ST | — | — | — | — | — | — | — | — |
| | OC | 1414 | 1843 | 76.74 | 21.56 | 429 | — | — | 100.00 |
| Average | | 1414 | 1843 | 76.74 | 21.56 | 429 | — | — | 100.00 |
| Overall | SC | 704 | 838 | 84.04 | 30.49 | 134 | 3.13 | 6.02 | 90.85 |
| | ST | 764 | 930 | 82.18 | 27.76 | 166 | 5.37 | 8.06 | 86.57 |
| | OC | 843 | 1220 | 69.11 | 15.72 | 377 | 0.75 | 1.55 | 97.70 |
| Average | | 750 | 941 | 79.78 | 24.75 | 190 | 2.91 | 4.96 | 92.13 |

*Source*: Field Survey.

Village-1 to Rs. 859 in Village-3. The expenditure increases slowly with rise in the status of households even among the same caste/tribe. Clearly, there is increase in food and non-food expenditure with increase in the size of landholding groups. There is not much difference in such expenditure between the ST and SC groups of households. However, there is some difference in this expenditure between the ST and OC groups, implying that the ST households incur lower expenditure in comparison with that of OC households.

TABLE 8: COMPOSITION OF FOOD AND NON-FOOD EXPENDITURE (in Rs.) PER MONTH PER HOUSEHOLD IN THE STUDY VILLAGE-3

| Landholding size (in acre) | Caste | Total food exp. per HH per month | Total food & non-food exp. per month per HH | Total food as a % of total exp. | Total non-food exp. as % of total exp. | Total non-food exp. per HH per month | As % of total non-food expenditure: Health | Edu-cation | Other non-food items |
|---|---|---|---|---|---|---|---|---|---|
| 0–0.0 | SC | 155 | 159 | 97.48 | 76.35 | 4 | — | — | 100.00 |
| | ST | 609 | 624 | 97.66 | 77.71 | 15 | 27.32 | 5.72 | 66.96 |
| | OC | — | — | — | — | — | — | — | — |
| Average | | 595 | 610 | 97.66 | 77.69 | 14 | 27.07 | 5.67 | 67.24 |
| 0.01–0.50 | SC | — | — | — | — | — | — | — | — |
| | ST | 603 | 661 | 91.16 | 46.22 | 58 | 52.28 | — | 47.72 |
| | OC | — | — | — | — | — | — | — | — |
| Average | | 603 | 661 | 91.16 | 46.22 | 58 | 52.28 | — | 47.72 |
| 0.51–2.50 | SC | — | — | — | — | — | — | — | — |
| | ST | 726 | 772 | 94.35 | 58.19 | 44 | 10.15 | 7.64 | 82.21 |
| | OC | — | — | — | — | — | — | — | — |
| Average | | 726 | 772 | 94.35 | 58.19 | 44 | 10.15 | 7.64 | 82.21 |
| 2.51–5.00 | SC | — | — | — | — | — | — | — | — |
| | ST | 973 | 1178 | 82.55 | 28.28 | 205 | 3.67 | 2.07 | 96.26 |
| | OC | — | — | — | — | — | — | — | — |
| Average | | 973 | 1178 | 82.55 | 28.28 | 205 | 3.67 | 2.07 | 96.26 |
| 5.01–10.00 | SC | — | — | — | — | — | — | — | — |
| | ST | 1054 | 1325 | 79.57 | 24.51 | 271 | 1.03 | 7.28 | 91.69 |
| | OC | — | — | — | — | — | — | — | — |
| Average | | 1054 | 1325 | 79.57 | 24.51 | 271 | 1.03 | 7.28 | 91.69 |
| 10.00– | SC | — | — | — | — | — | — | — | — |
| Above | ST | 1279 | 1883 | 67.95 | 15.01 | 603 | — | 7.47 | 92.53 |
| | OC | — | — | — | — | — | — | — | — |
| Average | | 1279 | 1883 | 67.95 | 15.01 | 603 | — | 7.47 | 92.53 |
| Overall | SC | 155 | 159 | 97.48 | 76.35 | 4 | — | — | 100.00 |
| | ST | 769 | 865 | 88.85 | 39.89 | 97 | 6.37 | 4.82 | 88.81 |
| | OC | — | — | — | — | — | — | — | — |
| Average | | 763 | 859 | 88.86 | 39.94 | 96 | 6.37 | 4.82 | 88.86 |

*Source*: Field Survey.

A comparison of food and non-food expenditure between caste and tribe and among different size groups reveals the following picture. On the whole, 85 to 89 per cent of total current expenditure has been spent on food items in the tribal villages (V-1 and V-3). It was about 80 per cent in the other village (V-2). The proportion of expenditure spent on food to total expenditure decreases slightly with increase in status of household and caste in all the three villages. A look at coln. 5 of the Tables 4 to 6 shows that the difference between food and non-food expenditure incurred by ST and SC categories, specially among the landless, marginal and small farmer categories is marginal. However, there is some difference among the medium- and large-size categories even among the SC/ST groups.

According to the 53rd round of NSSO (1993–4) as well, food expenditure formed 64.53 per cent of total expenditure in rural Orissa. Similarly, cereals constituted 60.30 per cent of total expenditure incurred by households in rural Orissa. The percentage of expenditure devoted on other food items among all households varied from 15 to 24 per cent of total food expenditure. In the case of tribal households, this expenditure was relatively lower in comparison with the OC and SC groups. Further, it also rises with increase in status of households. On the whole, it is clear that the majority of households belonging to the poor categories (including tribal), devoted more than fourth-fifths of their food expenditure on cereal consumption. This is an implication for supply of adequate nutrition to the households. It appears that in the absence of adequate income, they had to forego other food items.

### PATTERN OF NON-FOOD EXPENDITURE

The amount of expenditure incurred by households on non-food items both in absolute as well as in percentage terms is very low in all the villages as well as among different caste/tribe groups. It varied between Rs. 97 and Rs. 203 for all households. The percentage of non-food expenditure to total expenditure varied between 12 per cent in Village-3 and 20 per cent in Village-1. There is a slight increase in such expenditure with increase in status of households in all three villages.

The composition of non-food expenditure by different groups reveals that the lion's share of it has been spent on other social items and not on health and education. It means that the expenditure on health and education by poor tribal households is minimal, which has implications for human capital formation among the members. It also shows that they are not in a position to satisfy the minimum requirements of expenditure needed for these items.

## COPING MECHANISMS ADOPTED BY HOUSEHOLDS

In this section, the types of coping mechanisms adopted by households is discussed. The main focus is a diversification of income and pattern of borrowing of households. As mentioned in the first section, diversification of income is an important coping mechanism resorted to by households. Similarly, borrowing from a variety of sources is also important in this regard, besides dependence on CPR. In the study area, the extent of reciprocal help among households has declined in recent years due to a variety of reasons, including decline in patent-client relationships. Similarly borrowing at low or nil interest is also negligible. Borrowing on credit is resorted to. But this is also negligible, as we shall see later. First, we shall discuss the income structure and then the pattern and implication of borrowing of households in the study villages. The main focus is to illustrate these two—the income and credit structure—with a view to understanding the nature and structure of coping mechanisms in the area. The composition and sources of income from different sources are given in the groups of households. It is clear that households derived income from a number of sources, including own production, petty business (own business), income from CPR, as well as through wage income. Wage income has been earned both in the village/nearby village as well as through distant migration.

The monthly income per household for different castes/tribes and groups is given in Tables 9 to 11, columns 3 and 4, of which reveal that the income is very low of all households in all the villages. But it is still lower among the landless, marginal- and small-farm cultivation in comparison to that of medium- and large-farm groups. Further, per-household income of ST categories is relatively lower in comparison to that of OC groups in all the villages. There is a positive relationship between the income and status of landholding among the households in all the study

TABLE 9: COMPOSITION OF DIFFERENT FOOD EXPENDITURE INCURRED BY HOUSEHOLDS IN THE STUDY VILLAGE-1

| Size group by land-holdings (in acre) | Caste | Exp. on food items per HH (in Rs.) | Cereal exp. as a % of total food exp. | Inferiror creal exp. as a % of cereal exp. | Pulses as a % of total food exp. | Other food exp. as a % of total food exp. |
|---|---|---|---|---|---|---|
| 00–00 | SC | 661 | 93.57 | 1.28 | 0.76 | 5.67 |
| | ST | 724 | 96.49 | 0.45 | 0.59 | 2.92 |
| | OC | 716 | 89.74 | 0.34 | 0.39 | 9.87 |
| Average | | 718 | 94.58 | 0.46 | 0.55 | 4.87 |
| 0.01–0.50 | SC | — | — | — | — | — |
| | ST | 767 | 90.23 | 0.28 | 1.17 | 8.60 |
| | OC | — | — | — | — | — |
| Average | | 767 | 90.23 | 0.28 | 1.17 | 8.60 |
| 0.51–2.50 | SC | 849 | 75.61 | 0.19 | 0.71 | 23.68 |
| | ST | 815 | 78.64 | 0.30 | 0.75 | 20.61 |
| | OC | 787 | 72.60 | 0.13 | 1.27 | 26.13 |
| Average | | 816 | 77.49 | 0.27 | 0.82 | 21.69 |
| 2.51–5.00 | SC | — | — | — | — | — |
| | ST | 839 | 72.43 | 0.32 | 0.89 | 26.68 |
| | OC | 868 | 60.09 | 0.17 | 1.58 | 38.33 |
| Average | | 844 | 70.32 | 0.29 | 1.02 | 28.66 |
| 5.01–10.00 | SC | 1002 | 65.27 | 0.39 | 0.79 | 3.94 |
| | ST | 1108 | 56.69 | 0.39 | 1.13 | 39.18 |
| | OC | 1137 | 55.13 | 0.13 | 0.62 | 44.25 |
| Average | | 1094 | 60.00 | 0.37 | 1.03 | 38.97 |
| 10.00–Above | SC | — | — | — | — | — |
| | ST | — | — | — | — | — |
| | OC | 1314 | 58.74 | 0.05 | 1.22 | 40.04 |
| Average | | 1314 | 58.74 | 0.05 | 1.22 | 40.04 |
| Overall | SC | 856 | 74.83 | 0.42 | 0.74 | 24.43 |
| | ST | 835 | 78.32 | 0.36 | 0.83 | 20.85 |
| | OC | 863 | 71.89 | 0.19 | 0.95 | 27.16 |
| Average | | 842 | 76.81 | 0.33 | 0.85 | 22.34 |

*Source*: Field Survey.

villages. It is clear that ST households with higher size of land-holding are relatively better as compared to landless and land-poor households.

The composition of income coming from own production among all households varied from 40 to 54 per cent of total income, with some variation among different caste and size groups of households. Further, income from own production increases with rise in status of households. Income from petty business

TABLE 10: COMPOSITION OF DIFFERENT FOOD EXPENDITURE INCURRED BY HOUSEHOLDS IN THE STUDY VILLAGE-2

| Size class by land-holdings (in acre) | Caste | Exp. on food items per HH (in Rs.) | Cereal exp. as a % of total food exp. | Inferior creal exp. as a % of cereal exp. | Pulses as a % of total food exp. | Other food exp. as a % of total food exp. |
|---|---|---|---|---|---|---|
| 00–0.0 | SC | 629 | 95.63 | 0.66 | 0.29 | 4.08 |
| | ST | — | — | — | — | — |
| | OC | 697 | 94.55 | 0.28 | 0.57 | 4.88 |
| Average | | 641 | 95.40 | 0.56 | 0.35 | 4.25 |
| 0.01–0.50 | SC | 705 | 95.28 | 0.85 | 0.43 | 4.29 |
| | ST | 733 | 95.68 | 0.91 | 0.43 | 3.89 |
| | OC | 541 | 93.35 | — | — | 6.65 |
| Average | | 710 | 95.43 | 0.84 | 0.40 | 4.17 |
| 0.51–2.50 | SC | 710 | 89.02 | 0.28 | 0.90 | 10.08 |
| | ST | 738 | 89.97 | 0.58 | 0.69 | 9.34 |
| | OC | 742 | 86.81 | 0.27 | 0.81 | 12.38 |
| Average | | 723 | 88.78 | 0.36 | 0.83 | 10.39 |
| 2.51–5.00 | SC | 845 | 73.42 | — | 0.59 | 25.99 |
| | ST | 780 | 82.34 | 0.41 | 1.05 | 16.61 |
| | OC | 880 | 68.69 | — | 1.15 | 30.16 |
| Average | | 802 | 79.08 | 0.29 | 1.00 | 19.92 |
| 5.01–10.00 | SC | 857 | 40.06 | 0.08 | 1.16 | 58.78 |
| | ST | 1068 | 77.71 | 0.18 | 0.94 | 21.35 |
| | OC | 1208 | 60.39 | 0.28 | 1.24 | 38.37 |
| Average | | 992 | 52.98 | 0.17 | 1.16 | 45.84 |
| 10.00–Above | SC | — | — | — | — | — |
| | ST | — | — | — | — | — |
| | OC | 1414 | 53.46 | — | 1.69 | 44.85 |
| Average | | 1414 | 53.46 | — | 1.69 | 44.85 |
| Overall | SC | 704 | 84.44 | 0.40 | 0.68 | 14.88 |
| | ST | 764 | 87.80 | 0.58 | 0.78 | 11.42 |
| | OC | 843 | 77.09 | 0.19 | 0.96 | 21.95 |
| Average | | 750 | 84.05 | 0.43 | 0.77 | 15.18 |

*Source*: Field Survey.

contributed between 4 and 10 per cent of total income. It is important to note that this source of income is lowest for the ST category, and higher for the SC category of households. It appears that lack of resources may be the factor contributing to doing petty business. Besides, because of illiteracy, they may be unable to do even such business.

After own production, the next important source of income among households is wage income. Such opportunities come from work around and nearby villages as well as from distant migration.

TABLE 11: COMPOSITION OF DIFFERENT FOOD EXPENDITURE INCURRED BY HOUSEHOLDS IN THE STUDY VILLAGE-3

| Landholding size (in acre) | Caste | Exp. on food items per HH (in Rs.) | Cereal exp. as a % of total food exp. | Inferiror creal exp. as a % of cereal exp. | Pulses as a % of total food exp. | Other food exp. as a % of total food exp. |
|---|---|---|---|---|---|---|
| 00–00 | SC | 154 | 51.61 | 6.66 | — | 48.39 |
| | ST | 609 | 94.96 | 0.72 | 0.26 | 4.77 |
| | OC | — | — | — | — | — |
| Average | | 595 | 94.62 | 0.74 | 0.25 | 5.12 |
| 0.01–0.50 | SC | — | — | — | — | — |
| | ST | 603 | 64.29 | 0.65 | 0.34 | 35.37 |
| | OC | — | — | — | — | — |
| Average | | 603 | 64.29 | 0.65 | 0.34 | 35.37 |
| 0.51–2.50 | SC | — | — | — | — | — |
| | ST | 729 | 73.19 | 1.35 | 0.92 | 26.19 |
| | OC | — | — | — | — | — |
| Average | | 729 | 73.19 | 1.35 | 0.62 | 26.19 |
| 2.51–5.00 | SC | — | — | — | — | — |
| | ST | 972 | 70.23 | 0.13 | 0.47 | 29.30 |
| | OC | — | — | — | — | — |
| Average | | 972 | 70.23 | 0.13 | 0.47 | 29.30 |
| 5.01–10.00 | SC | — | — | — | — | — |
| | ST | 1054 | 63.32 | 0.12 | 0.47 | 36.21 |
| | OC | — | — | — | — | — |
| Average | | 1054 | 63.32 | 0.12 | 0.47 | 36.21 |
| 10.00– | SC | — | — | — | — | — |
| Above | ST | 1279 | 56.01 | — | 2.50 | 41.48 |
| | OC | — | — | — | — | — |
| Average | | 1279 | 56.01 | — | 2.50 | 41.48 |
| Overall | SC | 154 | 51.61 | 6.66 | — | — |
| | ST | 769 | 75.54 | 0.74 | 0.56 | 23.90 |
| | OC | — | — | — | — | — |
| Average | | 763 | 75.45 | 0.73 | 0.56 | 23.90 |

*Source*: Field Survey.

It is important to note that share of wage income from outside migration is least for tribal groups. In all villages, by contrast the OC and SC categories of households derived a relatively higher share of their income from this source as compared to tribals. However in the tribal-dominated Village-3, the landless and near-landless derived part of their income from outside migration.

It is important to note that outside migration is a vastly different category, and households have no choice in this. There is connivance between the employers at the other end (e.g. Karim-nagar, Hyderabad), local lenders and instructors who are involved in group migrations to the destination. Individual members of households also migrate, mostly to irrigated areas of Hirakud command area and to Raipur region (Chattisgarh).

The contribution of income from CPR shows the following picture. It is clear that dependence on CPR is more among the landless and land-poor households than that of land-rich households. Further, it is to be noted that this source has been utilized by all the three categories of poor households in all the three villages. In terms of percentage, its share is low. This is due to the fact that the output of CPR has been evaluated at current market prices prevalent at the time of sale of the item (which is much lower than the minimum price fixed by the district committee). Further a part of output consumed by the households has not entered the calculations, as it could not be ascertained correctly. However, this source of income is crucial for the poor groups of all categories, including tribals. Its share is relatively higher among the landless marginal groups of ST: it is a sort of self-insurance mechanism available to them.

Even if the share of income (from CPR) is next in importance to self-production, the income generated from this source is meagre due to very low wage rates (Rs. 20–5 for males and 15–18 for females prevalent during 1997–8) and the low number of days of employment.

Income originating in the service sector (both government and private) is next in importance after wage income. Its share varied between about 9 and 12 per cent (11.62 per cent in V-1, 9.33 per cent in V-2 and 10.77 in V-3). Here also, there is a pattern in all three villages. The share of this income among the OC and SC is much higher in comparison to that of ST people in both V-1 and V-2.

Some income also accrues to households from state intervention. It includes old age pension and income transfer from the PDS, etc. Its contribution varied from 1.26 to 2.17 per cent of total income among all households in these villages (Annexure: Tables X to XII). It is important to note that transfer of income from the state is confined to the poor category, and in view of this the share of income for these groups is slightly higher among all those of the SC/ST and OC categories belonging to the landless, marginal or small-farm groups. The monthly income per household among different groups is not only very low, but there is wide fluctuation during different seasons, which is not reflected in the tables due to aggregation.

The analysis of composition of income shows that the income earned per household is very low in the study villages among all the three categories of households (including the ST group) despite the fact that it has come from diversified sources. There is distress diversification found among the poor households: since the price of output sold and wage rates received by most of these households are low, the diversified sources have not contributed enough income. But given that many of them have no resources of their own or are not in a position to borrow resources from outside they had no choice but to diversify their activities with a view to coping with food insecurity.

## INFORMAL LOAN: ITS SOURCES AND UTILIZATION

Now we discuss the pattern of borrowing (cash and kind) from informal sources by different groups of households in the study villages so as to know the access to borrowing and terms and conditions of borrowing. It is to be noted that access to informal loan borrowing is negligible in the study area and the villages (Sarap 2000a and 2000b). The percentage of households borrowing from formal sources was negligible. In view of the minimal access to formal credit, they had to depend on informal loans.

We broadly point out the nature of borrowing, its utilization and sources of loans by different categories of households. The pattern of cash and kind borrowing is given in Annexure: Tables I to III and IV to VI. The percentage of households borrowing cash varied from 33 per cent in Village-1 to 52 per cent in Village-3. The percentage of borrowing among ST/SC households belonging to landless, marginal and small-farm groups is relatively much higher.

It is to be noted that all categories of households have borrowed both in cash and kind from different sources. The proportion of households borrowing in kind is relatively lower in comparison to borrowing of cash. For instance, the proportion of households borrowing cash varied from 33 per cent to 52 per cent (Annexure: Tables VII-IX). In case of kind, it varied from 28 in Village 1 to 47 per cent in Village-3. The average amount of cash loan varied from Rs. 1,317 to 1,025 per household. In the case of loans in kind, it varied from Rs. 706 to 642 per household. There is not much difference in the overall proportion of households belonging to SC/ST groups. However, it is to be noted that the percentage of households belonging to landless, marginal and small farmers is relatively higher as compared to the other groups, clearly showing their dependence on informal loans. What is more important to note is that a major portion of cash and kind loans has been taken by these households for their bare consumption and to repay old loans. It shows that these households had to borrow to supplement their food needs, especially during the lean seasons. Another fact to note is that a major proportion of such loans has been taken during the lean period, especially during August/September when the possibility of other sources of income is negligible.

Borrowing by households is not a problem if the terms and conditions are reasonable or favourable to them. But the evidence as provided in Annexure: Tables I to III and IV to VI shows that the terms of condition of borrowing are harsh to the majority of the poors borrowers. Many of them have lost collaterals in the process affecting severly their future livelihood. The percentage of borrowers losing collateral is given in Annexure: Tables V to VII. It varied from 46.67 per cent in Village-1 to 30.56 per cent in Village-2. It was 54.39 per cent in Village-3. Of the total number of households losing collateral, the percentage losing land was 28.57 per cent in Village-1, 18.18 per cent in Village-2 and 25.81 per cent in Village-3. Clearly, in such cases these households not only have problems in current borrowing, but also become more vulnerable for future borrowing. As such, their future livelihood is severely affected.

## CONCLUSION AND RECOMMENDATIONS

The analysis relating to the food situation among households in the study villages shows that a majority of tribal and other households are vulnerable to food insecurity. The evidence reveals that even the minimum food security has not been ensured to the majority of the households. Different indicators confirm this situation. They had to spend a lion's share of expenditure on food only. Even among food items, more than three-fourths of the expenditure was allocated to cereals. In such a situation, they are unable to buy other foods that are required to provide them nutrition and other basic needs.

The average income earned per household is very low. In view of this, they had to resort to distress diversification even in order to manage such a low income. Given the fact that the majority of households have no adequate assets (including land) and other regular source of wages or other income, they have to cope with food insecurity through a variety of strategies adopted by them. More than half of the households, in all the villages, had to resort to informal borrowing at very harsh terms and conditions from traders and moneylenders. In such borrowing, about one-fourth of the borrowers lost the collateral, including land, which is the principal source of livelihood to them. In such a situation they are vulnerable to future insecurity of food. Given the widespread poverty, reduced access to CPR and their effectiveness and waning social and community support systems in the region, there is a strong need for state action to protect entitlement and capabilities of households.

The broad strategy, which needs to be focused upon, is:

1. Guarantee of survival and livelihood options;
2. Protection of individual and community rights;
3. Access to control over natural resources;
4. Fulfilment of broader development aspirations of the people in the area.

Clearly, there is need to pursue a two-pronged strategy in order to protect individual households and develop the area so that individuals benefit from it. There is need to provide individual property rights on land (in the name of wife and husband) to the maximum number of tribal households through distribution of land. While doing so, a minimum size of land has to be kept in mind so that the food needs of the household could be produced and their dependence on the market reduced. The evidence on land distribution in Kalahandi, Bolangir and Koraput (KBK) region of Orissa showed that households received very small plots, or land of very inferior quality. In case of the former, it has hardly met 15 to 20 per cent of their food needs. In case of the latter, the production is so low that they are unable to produce even 15 per cent of their food needs. Further, land distribution was not effective due to lack of supply of credit from the financial sector. The majority of the allottees of land had no access to agricultural inputs, credit and output markets. As a result, they could not utilize the plots properly, and in many cases either leased out land or mortgaged it (Sarap 2000).

The rules relating to land alienation in tribal areas should be enforced properly. Connivance of the lower bureaucracy and non-tribals leads to the latter obtaining permission for the sale of tribal land. But land alienation cannot be checked unless the households are provided with alternative sources of income, and credit on reasonable terms.

In view of the above, the state has to implement self-targeting employment-oriented programmes on a wider scale to generate enough income during the lean period. This will not only check distress temporary migration, but also reduce the vulnerability of households to food insecurity. The experience of rural Orissa in terms of implementation of JRY/EAS is minimal, and its impact on income generation is marginal. Evidence from field data in three villages in the district of Kalahandi, western Orissa, showed that the number of days of employment generated through EAS/JRY during the season 1997–8 varied from 8 to 25 days in these villages (Sarap 1999).

There is need for protection and regeneration of CPR, including forests. The tribal community and the state should jointly do the management and maintenance. Unfortunately, degradation of forest and other CPR in the tribal belt of Orissa has increased in recent years due to deforestation/construction of dams in the tribal belt. Further, forest land has been leased for industrial activities (like mining), and recently, forest officials have been given more administrative powers in order to check the use of forest land/produce by users (Das 1998).

The policy of procurement of minor forest products by the state is mostly regressive, in the sense that the rights of the gatherers of minor forest products has been restricted due to procurement of these products by a centralized agency/company. As discussed in the last section, the functioning of these agents is mostly unfavourable to the tribals, as they do not realize fair prices while selling their products. There is an urgent need to change this monopoly procurement policy of state.

Comprehensive land and water development programmes on the principle of the watershed programme should be implemented. These programmes should include soil and water conservation, small-scale irrigation improvement, and animal husbandry activities. These programmes will help the households to generate more and regular income, which will help them to get food throughout the year, and help in sustainable development of the area. The watershed development programmes could fit well within the existing framework of Tribal Sub-Plan and Integrated Tribal Development Area Programme. Currently, tribal development projects emphasize more on administrative activities rather than dealing with the basic issues in development activities leading to food security of tribals.

The present structure of implementing development programmes in the state is highly centralized. It also lacks effective participation of households whose livelihood is affected. People must be given a say in formulating policies implemented by the state and other institutions to protect food security and promote development. Further, there must be some accountability of the implementing agents to the people. Thus, the ideas of participation of stakeholders and accountability of implementing agencies are crucial in maintaining food security.

The state has to create an environment in which local-level participating organizations would grow, spread and acquire capacity for delivering and monitoring a wide range of development services to the tribal people, including implementation schemes for food security. Village panchayats/tribal councils and other local-level participatory organizations should be part of these. The working of Panchayati Raj (PR) institutions in the state and specially in the backward tribal areas, is at a nascent stage, and their functioning is inadequate for the needs of the people. The priority of the PR institutions continues to be for the social sector (school, housing, education, etc.) and infrastructure (rural roads, and construction and renovation of schools, anganwadi centres). Concerted efforts are needed to focus on agricultural activities, including provision of credit through grain banks and so on. The grain bank should store local staples such as bajra, mandia, kudo, guruji, etc., along with national staples (rice and wheat, etc.).

## ANNEXURE

TABLE I: INFORMAL CASH LOAN BORROWED (in Rs.), ITS SOURCES AND UTILIZATION IN THE STUDY VILLAGE-1

| Landholding size (in acre) | Caste | No. of HH* in the group | % of HH borrowed | Avg. amount borrowed per HH | Avg. no. of transaction per HH | As % of total cash loan borrowed | | | | As % of total loan utilized | | |
|---|---|---|---|---|---|---|---|---|---|---|---|---|
| | | | | | | Money Lender | Trader | Friend & Relative | Own landlord | Conscumption | Repayment of old debt | Other purpose |
| 1 | | 2 | 3 | 4 | 5 | 6 | 7 | 8 | 9 | 10 | 11 | 12 |
| 00–0.0 | SC | 2 | — | — | — | — | — | — | — | — | — | — |
| | ST | 26 | 42.31 | 1200 | 1.36 | 50.00 (45.45) | 4.5 (9.09) | — | 45.45 (72.73) | 53.03 (45.45) | 42.27 (45.45) | 4.70 (9.09) |
| | OC | 10 | 50.00 | 702 | 1.40 | 85.47 (60.00) | — | — | 14.53 (40) | 100.00 (100.0) | — | — |
| Average | | 38 | 42.11 | 1044 | 1.38 | 57.45 (50.00) | 3.59 (6.25) | — | 38.96 (62.50) | 62.90 (62.50) | 33.39 (31.25) | 3.71 (6.25) |
| 0.01–0.50 | SC | — | — | — | — | — | — | — | — | — | — | — |
| | ST | 4 | 100 | 1875 | 1.50 | 26.67 (25.00) | 40.00 (50.00) | — | 33.33 (75.00) | 66.67 (75.00) | 26.67 (25.00) | 6.67 (25.00) |
| | OC | — | — | — | — | — | — | — | — | — | — | — |
| Average | | 4 | 100 | 1875 | 1.50 | 26.67 (25.00) | 40.00 (50.00) | — | 33.33 (75.00) | 66.67 (75.00) | 26.67 (25.00) | 6.67 (25.00) |
| 0.51–2.50 | SC | 6 | 66.67 | 2250 | 1.00 | 55.56 (50.00) | 33.33 (100.00) | 11.11 (25.00) | — | — | 88.89 (100.0) | 11.11 (25.00) |
| | ST | 35 | 37.14 | 1400 | 1.38 | 54.95 (45.15) | 32.97 (30.77) | — | 12.08 (23.08) | 28.57 (92.31) | 16.48 (7.69) | 54.95 (7.69) |
| | OC | 6 | 16.67 | 1200 | 1.00 | — | 100 (100.00) | — | — | 100.00 (100.0) | — | — |
| Average | | 47 | 38.30 | 1578 | 1.28 | 52.82 (44.44) | 35.92 (50.00) | 3.52 (5.56) | 7.74 (16.67) | 50.70 (94.44) | 14.08 (11.11) | 35.21 (5.56) |
| 2.51–5.00 | SC | — | — | — | — | — | — | — | — | — | — | — |
| | ST | 20 | 15.00 | 567 | 1.33 | 94.12 (100.0) | — | 5.88 (33.33) | — | 100.00 (100.0) | — | — |

| | | | | | | | | | | | | |
|---|---|---|---|---|---|---|---|---|---|---|---|---|
| | OC | 4 | — | — | — | — | — | — | — | — | — | — |
| Average | | 24 | 12.50 | 567 | 1.33 | 94.12 (100) | — | 5.88 (33.33) | — | 100.0 (100) | — | — |
| 5.01–10.00 | SC | 3 | — | — | — | — | — | — | — | — | — | — |
| | ST | 14 | 14.29 | 1075 | 1.00 | 100 (100) | — | — | — | 100 (100) | — | — |
| | OC | 2 | 50.00 | 1500 | 1.00 | — | — | 100 (100) | — | — | — | — |
| Average | | 19 | 15.79 | 1217 | 1.00 | 58.90 (66.67) | — | 41.10 (33.33) | — | 100 (100) | — | — |
| 10.00– | SC | — | — | — | — | — | — | — | — | — | — | — |
| Above | ST | — | — | — | — | — | — | — | — | — | — | — |
| | OC | 3 | — | — | — | — | — | — | — | — | — | — |
| Average | | — | — | — | — | — | — | — | — | — | — | — |
| Overall | SC | 11 | 36.36 | 2250 | 1.00 | 55.56 (50) | 33.33 (100) | 11.1 (25) | — | 88.89 (100) | 11.11 (25) | |
| | ST | 99 | 33.33 | 1295 | 1.36 | 52.28 (51.52) | 22.46 (21.21) | 0.23 (3.03) | 25.03 (42.42) | 49.24 (78.79) | 24.75 (21.21) | 26.01 (9.09) |
| | OC | 25 | 28.00 | 887 | 1.29 | 48.31 (42.86) | 19.32 (14.29) | 24.15 (14.29) | 8.21 (28.57) | 75.85 (85.71) | — | 24.15 (14.29) |
| Average | | 135 | 32.59 | 1317 | 1.32 | 52.36 (50) | 23.81 (27.27) | 4.49 (6.82) | 19.34 (36.36) | 58.25 (100) | 19.98 (18.18) | 21.77 (15.91) |

*Source*: Field Survey.

*Notes*: Figure in the bracket represents percentage of borrower households.
*HH = Household.

TABLE II: INFORMAL CASH LOAN BORROWED (in Rs.), ITS SOURCES AND UTILIZATION IN THE STUDY VILLAGE-2

| Landholding size (in acre) | Caste | No. of HH* in the group | % of HH borro-wed | Avg. amount borro-wed per HH | Avg. no. of transac-tion per HH | As % of total cash loan borrowed | | | | As % of total loan utilized | | |
|---|---|---|---|---|---|---|---|---|---|---|---|---|
| | | | | | | Money Lender | Trader | Friend & Relative | Own land-lord | Conscumption | Repayment of old debt | Other purpose |
| 1 | | 2 | 3 | 4 | 5 | 6 | 7 | 8 | 9 | 10 | 11 | 12 |
| 00–0.0 | SC | 13 | 53.85 | 260 | 1.71 | 52.75 (42.66) | 28.02 (57.14) | 2.75 (14.29) | 16.48 (28.57) | 67.31 (85.71) | — | 32.69 (14.29) |
| | ST | — | — | — | — | — | — | — | — | — | — | — |
| | OC | 3 | 66.67 | 260 | 2.00 | — | 38.46 (50.00) | 3.85 (50) | 57.69 (50) | 23.08 (50) | 76.92 (50) | — |
| Average | | 16 | 56.25 | 260 | 1.78 | 41.03 (33.33) | 30.34 (55.56) | 2.99 (22.22) | 25.64 (33.33) | 57.48 (77.78) | 17.09 (11.11) | 25.43 (11.11) |
| 0.01–0.50 | SC | 8 | 50.00 | 937 | 2.50 | 51.97 (50) | — | 5.34 (50.00) | 42.69 (50.00) | 57.31 (50.00) | 42.69 (50) | |
| | ST | 4 | 50.00 | 300 | 1.50 | 100 (100) | — | — | — | 100 (100) | | |
| | OC | 1 | 100 | 200 | 1.00 | — | — | 100 (100) | — | — | 100 (100) | |
| Average | | 13 | 53.85 | 468 | 1.71 | 66.40 (71.43) | — | 9.16 (28.57) | 24.44 (14.29) | 69.46 (71.43) | 30.54 (28.57) | — |
| 0.51–2.50 | SC | 15 | 46.67 | 486 | 1.29 | 100 (100.00) | — | — | — | 100 (100) | — | |
| | ST | 7 | 28.57 | 500 | 1.00 | 100 (100.00) | — | — | — | 100 (100) | — | |
| | OC | 6 | 16.67 | 2000 | 3.00 | — | 100 (100) | — | — | 100 (100) | — | |
| Average | | 28 | 35.71 | 640 | 1.40 | 68.75 (90.00) | 31.25 (10) | — | — | 100 (100) | — | — |
| 2.51–5.00 | SC | 2 | 100 | 1098 | 1.00 | 91.32 (50.00) | — | — | 8.68 (50) | 100 (100) | | |
| | ST | 11 | 18.18 | 500 | 1.50 | — | 100 (100) | — | — | 100 (100) | — | — |
| | OC | 2 | — | — | — | — | — | — | — | — | — | — |

| | | | | | | | | | | | | |
|---|---|---|---|---|---|---|---|---|---|---|---|---|
| Average | | 15 | 26.67 | 798 | 1.33 | 62.70 (25.00) | 31.55 (50) | — | 5.95 (25.00) | 100 (100) | — | — |
| 5.01–10.00 | SC | 4 | 25.00 | 1000 | 1.00 | — | — | 100 (100) | — | — | — | 100 (100.00) |
| | ST | 1 | 100 | 2000 | 2.00 | — | 80.00 (100) | — | 20.00 (100) | 80.00 (100) | 20.00 (100) | |
| | OC | 2 | 50.00 | 1500 | 1.00 | 100 (100) | — | — | — | — | — | — |
| Average | | 7 | 42.86 | 1500 | 1.33 | 33.33 (33.33) | 35.56 (33.33) | 22.22 (33.33) | 8.89 (33.33) | 35.56 (33.33) | 31.11 (66.67) | 33.33 (33.33) |
| 10.00– | | | | | | | | | | | | |
| above | SC | — | — | — | — | — | — | — | — | — | — | — |
| | ST | — | — | — | — | — | — | — | — | — | — | — |
| | OC | 1 | — | — | — | — | — | — | — | — | — | — |
| Average | | 1 | — | — | — | — | — | — | — | — | — | — |
| Overall | SC | 38 | 50.00 | 541 | 1.53 | 71.31 (63.16) | 4.96 (21.05) | 11.18 (15.79) | 12.55 (21.05) | 76.71 (84.21) | 17.50 (10.53) | 5.79 (15.79) |
| | ST | 27 | 33.33 | 578 | 1.44 | 42.31 (66.67) | 50.00 (33.33) | — | 7.69 (11.11) | 100 (100.00) | — | — |
| | OC | 15 | 33.33 | 844 | 1.80 | 35.55 (20.00) | 52.13 (40.00) | 5.21 (40.00) | 7.11 (20.00) | 50.24 (40.00) | 23.70 (60.00) | 35.55 (20.00) |
| Average | | 80 | 41.25 | 597 | 1.55 | 56.00 (57.58) | 26.95 (27.27) | 6.95 (15.15) | 10.10 (18.18) | 75.16 (81.82) | 14.21 (15.15) | 10.63 (6.06) |

*Source*: Field Survey.

*Notes*: Figure in the bracket represents percentage of borrower households.
*HH = Household.

TABLE III: INFORMAL CASH LOAN BORROWED (in Rs.), ITS SOURCES AND UTILIZATION IN THE STUDY VILLAGE-3

| Landholding size (in acre) | Caste | No. of HH* in the group | % of HH borro-wed | Avg. amount borro-wed per HH | Avg. no. of transac-tion per HH | As % of total cash loan borrowed | | | | As % of total loan utilized | | |
|---|---|---|---|---|---|---|---|---|---|---|---|---|
| | | | | | | Money Lender | Trader | Friend & Relative | Own land-lord | Conscumption | Repayment of old debt | Other purpose |
| 1 | | 2 | 3 | 4 | 5 | 6 | 7 | 8 | 9 | 10 | 11 | 12 |
| 0.0–0.0 | SC | 1 | — | — | — | — | — | — | — | — | — | — |
| | ST | 32 | 53.13 | 1350 | 1.65 | 88.19 (88.24) | 4.85 (11.76) | — | 0.06 (23.53) | 97.93 (82.35) | 12.85 (23.53) | 39.22 (17.65) |
| | OC | — | — | — | — | — | — | — | — | — | — | — |
| Average | | 33 | 53.13 | 1350 | 1.65 | 88.19 (88.24) | 4.85 (11.76) | — | 0.06 (23.53) | 97.93 (82.35) | 12.85 (23.53) | 39.22 (11.65) |
| 0.01–0.50 | SC | — | — | — | — | — | — | — | — | — | — | — |
| | ST | 6 | 50.00 | 734 | 1.33 | — | — | — | 100 (100) | 100 (100) | — | |
| | OC | — | — | — | — | — | — | — | — | — | — | — |
| Average | | 6 | 50.00 | 734 | 1.33 | — | — | — | 100 (100) | 100 (100) | — | — |
| 0.51–2.50 | SC | — | — | — | — | — | — | — | — | — | — | — |
| | ST | 40 | 37.50 | 979 | 1.07 | 8.45 (20.00) | 4.36 (20) | 0.68 (6.67) | 86.51 (53.33) | 6.81 (40.00) | 86.78 (53.33) | 60.41 (60.67) |
| | OC | — | — | — | — | — | — | — | — | — | — | — |
| Average | | 40 | 37.50 | 979 | 1.07 | 8.45 (20.00) | 4.36 (20) | 0.68 (6.67) | 86.51 (53.33) | 6.81 (40.00) | 86.78 (53.33) | 6.41 (6.67) |
| 2.51–5.00 | SC | — | — | — | — | — | — | — | — | — | — | — |
| | ST | 22 | 81.82 | 800 | 1.11 | 27.80 (40.00) | 69.49 (50) | — | 2.71 (10.00) | 58.30 (50.00) | 27.80 (44.44) | 13.90 (5.56) |
| | OC | — | — | — | — | — | — | — | — | — | — | — |
| Average | | 22 | 81.82 | 800 | 1.11 | 27.80 (40.00) | 69.49 (50) | — | 2.71 (10.00) | 58.30 (50.00) | 27.80 (44.44) | 13.90 (5.56) |

| | | | | | | | | | | | | |
|---|---|---|---|---|---|---|---|---|---|---|---|---|
| 5.01–10.00 | SC | — | — | — | — | — | — | — | — | — | — | — |
| | ST | 6 | 50.00 | 900 | 1.00 | — | 100 (100) | — | — | 100 (100) | — | — |
| | OC | — | — | — | — | — | — | — | — | — | — | — |
| Average | | 6 | 50.00 | 900 | 1.00 | — | 100 (100) | — | — | 100 (100) | — | — |
| 10.00– | SC | — | — | — | — | — | — | — | — | — | — | — |
| above | ST | 3 | 33.33 | 1500 | 1.00 | — | 100 (100) | — | — | 100 (100) | — | — |
| | OC | — | — | — | — | — | — | — | — | — | — | — |
| Average | | 3 | 33.33 | 1500 | 1.00 | — | 100 (100) | — | — | 100 (100) | — | — |
| Overall | SC | 1 | — | — | — | — | — | — | — | — | — | — |
| | ST | 109 | 52.30 | 1025 | 1.26 | 43.62 (45.61) | 27.30 (29.82) | 0.17 (1.75) | 28.91 (29.82) | 45.86 (63.16) | 33.70 (35.09) | 20.44 (8.77) |
| | OC | — | — | — | — | — | — | — | — | — | — | — |
| Average | | 110 | 52.30 | 1025 | 1.26 | 43.62 (45.61) | 27.30 (29.82) | 0.17 (1.75) | 28.91 (29.82) | 45.86 (63.16) | 33.70 (35.09) | 20.44 (8.77) |

*Source*: Field Survey.

*Notes*: Figure in the bracket represents percentage of borrower households.
*HH = Household.

TABLE IV: INFORMAL KIND LOAN BORROWED, SOURCES AND ITS UTILIZATION IN THE STUDY VILLAGE-1

| Land-holding size (in acre) | Caste | Total no. of HH | % of HH borrowed kind loan | Avg. amount borrowed per HH (in Rs.) | As % of total loan borrowed | | | | % utilized for | |
|---|---|---|---|---|---|---|---|---|---|---|
| | | | | | LL* | ML* | Trader | Friend & Relative | Consum-ption | Re-payment |
| 1 | | 2 | 3 | 4 | 5 | 6 | 7 | 8 | 9 | 10 |
| 00–0.0 | SC | 2 | 50.00 | 850 | 100 | — | — | — | 100 | — |
| | ST | 26 | 23.07 | 960 | 13.19 | — | 86.81 | — | 13.19 | 86.81 |
| | OC | 10 | 40 | 240 | 100.00 | — | — | — | 100 | — |
| Average | | 38 | 28.95 | 688 | 33.95 | — | 66.05 | — | 33.95 | 66.05 |
| 0.01–0.50 | SC | — | — | — | — | — | — | — | — | — |
| | ST | 4 | 75.00 | 1280 | 21.87 | 52.08 | 26.05 | — | 78.13 | 21.87 |
| | OC | — | — | — | — | — | — | — | — | — |
| Average | | 4 | 75.00 | 1280 | 21.87 | 52.08 | 26.05 | — | 78.13 | 21.87 |
| 0.51–2.50 | SC | 6 | 50.00 | 575 | 44.35 | — | 55.65 | — | 100 | — |
| | ST | 35 | 37.14 | 394 | 6.25 | 15.63 | 78.13 | — | 100 | — |
| | OC | 6 | 33.34 | 1280 | --- | 78.13 | 21.87 | — | 100 | — |
| Average | | 47 | 38.29 | 522.50 | 11.54 | 29.77 | 58.69 | — | 100 | — |
| 2.51–5.00 | SC | — | — | — | — | — | — | — | — | — |
| | ST | 20 | 20.00 | 800 | 100 | — | — | — | 100 | — |
| | OC | 4 | 25.00 | 960 | — | — | — | 100 | 100 | — |
| Average | | 24 | 20.84 | 832 | 76.93 | — | — | 23.07 | 100 | — |
| 5.01–10.00 | SC | 3 | — | — | — | — | — | — | — | — |
| | ST | 14 | 14.28 | 1280 | — | — | 100 | — | 100 | — |
| | OC | 2 | — | — | — | — | — | — | — | — |
| Average | | 19 | 10.53 | 1280 | — | — | 100 | — | 100 | — |
| 10.00–Above | SC | — | — | — | — | — | — | — | — | — |
| | ST | — | — | — | — | — | — | — | — | — |
| | OC | 3 | — | — | — | — | — | — | — | — |
| Average | | — | — | — | — | — | — | — | — | — |
| Overall | SC | 11 | 36.36 | 643.75 | 62.72 | — | 37.28 | — | 100 | — |
| | ST | 99 | 28.28 | 731.43 | 25.00 | 13.67 | 61.33 | — | 71.48 | 28.52 |
| | OC | 25 | 28.00 | 640 | 21.43 | 44.64 | 12.50 | 21.43 | 100.00 | — |
| Average | | 135 | 28.89 | 706.03 | 27.95 | 17.43 | 51.14 | 3.48 | 78.79 | 21.21 |

*Source*: Field Survey.

*Notes*: Figures in the bracket represents number of households HH.
*LL = Land Lord, ML = Money Lender.

TABLE V: INFORMAL KIND LOAN BORROWED, SOURCES AND ITS UTILIZATION IN THIS STUDY VILLAGE-2

| Land-holding size (in acre) | Caste | Total no. of HH | % of HH borrowed kind loan | Avg. amount borrowed per HH (in Rs.) | As % of total loan borrowed | | | | % utilized for | |
|---|---|---|---|---|---|---|---|---|---|---|
| | | | | | LL* | ML* | Trader | Friend & Relative | Consum-ption | Re-payment |
| 1 | | 2 | 3 | 4 | 5 | 6 | 7 | 8 | 9 | 10 |
| 00–0.0 | SC | 13 | 15.38 | 640 | 100 | — | — | — | 100 | — |
| | ST | — | — | — | — | — | — | — | — | — |
| | OC | 3 | 66.67 | 320 | 100 | — | — | — | 100 | — |
| Average | | 16 | 25.00 | 480 | 100 | — | — | — | 100 | — |
| 0.01–0.50 | SC | 4 | 75.00 | 640 | 100 | — | — | — | 100 | — |
| | ST | 8 | 25.00 | 480 | 100 | — | — | — | 100 | — |
| | OC | 1 | 100 | 640 | 100 | — | — | — | 100 | — |
| Average | | 13 | 46.15 | 587 | 100 | — | — | — | 100 | — |
| 0.51–2.50 | SC | 15 | 26.67 | 506 | — | 20.98 | 79.02 | — | 79.02 | 20.98 |
| | ST | 7 | 42.86 | 533 | — | — | 100 | — | 100 | — |
| | OC | 6 | 66.67 | 346 | — | — | 30.68 | 69.32 | 100 | — |
| Average | | 28 | 39.29 | 455 | — | 8.48 | 72.36 | 19.16 | 91.52 | 8.48 |
| 2.51–5.00 | SC | 2 | 50.00 | 1920 | — | — | 100 | — | 100 | — |
| | ST | 11 | 9.09 | 960 | — | 100 | — | — | 100 | — |
| | OC | 2 | — | — | — | — | — | — | — | — |
| Average | | 15 | 13.33 | 1440 | — | 33.33 | 66.67 | — | 100 | — |
| 5.01–10.00 | SC | 4 | — | — | — | — | — | — | — | — |
| | ST | 1 | 100 | 1385 | 69.32 | — | — | 30.68 | 100 | — |
| | OC | 2 | 100 | 1600 | — | — | 100 | — | 100 | — |
| Average | | 7 | 42.36 | 1146 | 20.94 | — | 69.79 | 9.27 | 100 | — |
| 10.00– | SC | — | — | — | — | — | — | — | — | — |
| Above | ST | — | — | — | — | — | — | — | — | — |
| | OC | 1 | — | — | — | — | — | — | — | — |
| Average | | 1 | — | — | — | — | — | — | — | — |
| Overall | SC | 38 | 26.32 | 715 | 44.79 | 5.95 | 49.26 | — | 94.05 | 5.95 |
| | ST | 27 | 25.93 | 613 | 39.14 | 19.57 | 32.62 | 8.67 | 100 | — |
| | OC | 15 | 60.00 | 512 | 21.83 | — | 61.81 | 16.36 | 100 | — |
| Average | | 80 | 32.50 | 664 | 35.72 | 7.73 | 48.82 | 7.73 | 97.63 | 2.37 |

*Source*: Field Survey.

*Note*: *LL = Land Lord, ML = Money Lender.

TABLE VI: INFORMAL KIND LOAN BORROWED SOURCES AND ITS UTILIZATION IN THIS STUDY VILLAGE-3

| Land-holding size (in acre) | Caste | Total no. of HH | % of HH borrowed kind loan | Avg. amount borrowed per HH (in Rs.) | As % of total loan borrowed | | | | % utilized for | |
|---|---|---|---|---|---|---|---|---|---|---|
| | | | | | LL* | ML* | Trader | Friend & Relative | Consum-ption | Re-payment |
| 1 | | 2 | 3 | 4 | 5 | 6 | 7 | 8 | 9 | 10 |
| 00–0.0 | SC | 1 | 100 | 320 | 100 | — | — | — | 100 | — |
| | ST | 32 | 46.88 | 640 | 91.00 | 3.33 | 5.67 | — | 96.77 | 3.33 |
| | OC | — | — | — | — | — | — | — | — | — |
| Average | | — | 48.48 | 620 | 91.29 | 3.23 | 5.48 | — | 96.77 | 3.23 |
| 0.01–0.50 | SC | — | — | — | | | — | — | — | — |
| | ST | 6 | 66.67 | 640 | 25.00 | — | 75.00 | — | 75.00 | 25.00 |
| | OC | — | — | — | — | — | — | — | — | — |
| Average | | 6 | 66.67 | 640 | 25 | — | 75 | — | 75 | 25 |
| 0.51–2.50 | SC | — | — | — | — | — | — | — | — | — |
| | ST | 40 | 30.00 | 560 | — | — | 76.19 | 23.81 | 100 | — |
| | OC | — | — | — | — | — | — | — | — | — |
| Average | | 40 | 30 | 560 | — | — | — | 76.19 | 23.81 | 100 |
| 2.51–5.00 | SC | — | — | — | | | | | | |
| | ST | 22 | 72.73 | 665 | — | 36.09 | 63.91 | — | 100 | — |
| | OC | — | — | — | — | — | — | — | — | — |
| Average | | — | — | — | — | — | — | — | — | — |
| 5.01–10.00 | SC | — | — | — | — | — | — | — | — | |
| | ST | 6 | 50 | 1067 | — | 50 | — | 50 | 100 | — |
| | OC | — | — | — | — | — | — | — | — | — |
| Average | | 6 | 50 | 1067 | — | 50 | — | 50 | 100 | — |
| 10.00–Above | SC | — | — | — | — | — | — | — | — | — |
| | ST | 3 | 33.34 | 320 | — | — | — | — | 100 | — |
| | OC | — | — | — | — | — | — | — | — | — |
| Average | | 3 | 33.34 | 320 | — | — | — | — | 100 | — |
| Overall | SC | 1 | 33.34 | 320 | 100 | — | — | — | 100 | — |
| | ST | 109 | 46.78 | 648 | 28.36 | 17.43 | 44.50 | 9.69 | 97.09 | 2.91 |
| | OC | — | — | — | — | — | — | — | — | — |
| Average | | 110 | 47.27 | 642 | 29.06 | 17.27 | 44.08 | 9.59 | 97.12 | 2.88 |

*Source*: Field Survey.

*Note*: *LL = Land Lord, ML = Money Lender.

TABLE VII: EXTENT OF LOSS OF COLLATERAL BY THE BORROWERS IN CCLLATERAL BASED LOAN IN STUDY VILLAGE-1

| Land-holding size (in acre) | Caste | Total HH in in the group | Total HH given collateral | % of HH lost collateral | Avg. value of collateral (in Rs.) | As % of the total value of collateral lost: Land (%) | Cycle (%) | Utensils (%) | Ornaments (%) | Others (%) |
|---|---|---|---|---|---|---|---|---|---|---|
| 1 | | 2 | 3 | 4 | 5 | 6 | 7 | 8 | 9 | 10 |
| 00–0.0 | SC | 2 | 1 | 100 | 75 | — | — | 100 (100) | — | — |
| | ST | 26 | 13 | 38.89 | 1584 | 81.15 (28.57) | 6.31 (28.57) | 0.81 (14.29) | 9.02 (14.29) | 2.71 (14.29) |
| | OC | 10 | 6 | 66.67 | 650 | 52.69 (25.00) | 19.23 (25.00) | — | — | 23.08 (50.00) |
| Average | | 38 | 25 | 48 | 1147 | 76.28 (25.00) | 8.72 (25.00) | 1.20 (16.67) | 7.26 (8.33) | 6.54 (25.00) |
| 0.01–0.50 | SC | — | — | — | — | — | — | — | — | — |
| | ST | 4 | 3 | 33.33 | 250 | — | — | 100 (100) | — | — |
| | OC | — | — | — | — | — | — | — | — | — |
| Average | | 4 | 3 | 33.33 | 250 | — | — | 100 (100) | — | — |
| 0.51–2.50 | SC | 6 | 5 | 60 | 933 | 71.43 (33.33) | 10.71 (33.33) | — | 17.86 (33.33) | — |
| | ST | 35 | 2 | 50 | 500 | 100 (100) | — | — | — | — |
| | OC | 6 | — | — | — | — | — | — | — | — |
| Average | | 47 | 7 | 57.14 | 825 | 75.76 (50) | 9.09 (25) | — | 15.15 (25.00) | — |
| 2.51–5.00 | SC | — | — | — | — | — | — | — | — | — |
| | ST | 20 | 6 | 50 | 683 | 68.29 (33.33) | — | 2.44 (33.33) | — | 29.27 (66.67) |
| | OC | 4 | — | — | — | — | — | — | — | — |
| Average | | 24 | 6 | 50 | 683 | 68.29 (33.33) | — | 2.44 (33.33) | — | 29.27 (66.67) |
| 5.01–10.00 | SC | 3 | — | — | — | — | — | — | — | — |
| | ST | 14 | 4 | 25 | 500 | — | 100 (100) | — | — | — |
| | OC | 2 | — | — | — | — | — | — | — | — |

(contd.)

TABLE VII (contd.)

| 1 | | 2 | 3 | 4 | 5 | 6 | 7 | 8 | 9 | 10 |
|---|---|---|---|---|---|---|---|---|---|---|
| Average | | 19 | 4 | 25 | 500 | — | 100 (100) | — | — | — |
| 10.00–above | SC | — | — | — | — | — | — | — | — | — |
| | ST | — | — | — | — | — | — | — | — | — |
| | OC | 3 | — | — | — | — | — | — | — | — |
| Average | | 3 | — | — | — | — | — | — | — | — |
| Overall | SC | 11 | 6 | 66.67 | 719 | 69.57 (25) | 10.43(25) | 2.61 (25) | 77.39 (25) | — |
| | ST | 99 | 33 | 39.39 | 1107 | 75.75 (30.77) | 8.34 (15.38) | 2.71 (23.06) | 6.95 (7.69) | 6.25 (23.08) |
| | OC | 25 | 6 | 66.67 | 650 | 57.69 (25) | 19.23 (25) | — | — | 23.08 (50) |
| Average | | 135 | 45 | 46.67 | 946 | 72.49 (28.57) | 10.07 (19.05) | 2.34 (19.05) | 7.55 (9.59) | 7.55 (23.81) |

*Source*: Field Survey.
*Note*: Figures in the bracket represent percentage of households who lost collateral to total household borrowed.

TABLE VIII: EXTENT OF LOSS OF COLLATERAL BY THE BORROWERS IN COLLATERAL BASED LOAN IN STUDY VILLAGE 2

| Land-holding size (in acre) | Caste | Total HH in in the group | Total HH given collat-eral | % of HH lost collat eral | Avg. value of collat-eral (in Rs.) | As % of the total value of collateral lost: Land (%) | Cycle (%) | Ustensils (%) | Ornaments (%) | Others (%) |
|---|---|---|---|---|---|---|---|---|---|---|
| 1 | | 2 | 3 | 4 | 5 | 6 | 7 | 8 | 9 | 10 |
| 00–0.0 | SC | 13 | 10 | 40 | 319 | — | 47.06 (25.00) | 13.73 (25.00) | — | 39.21 (50.00) |
| | ST | — | — | — | — | — | — | — | — | — |
| | OC | 3 | 1 | — | — | — | — | — | — | — |
| Average | | 16 | 11 | 40 | 319 | — | 47.06 (25.00) | 13.73 (25.00) | — | 39.21 (50.00) |

| | | | | | | | | | | |
|---|---|---|---|---|---|---|---|---|---|---|
| 0.01–0.50 | SC | 8 | 6 | 16.67 | 750 | — | 100 (100) | — | — | — |
| | ST | 4 | 2 | 100 | 450 | — | — | — | 100 (100) | — |
| | OC | 1 | — | — | — | — | — | — | — | — |
| Average | | 13 | 8 | 37.5 | 383 | — | 45.45 (33.33) | — | 54.55 (66.67) | — |
| 0.51–2.50 | SC | 15 | 9 | 11.11 | 1200 | — | — | — | 100 (100) | — |
| | ST | 7 | 2 | 50.00 | 300 | 100 (100) | — | — | — | — |
| | OC | 6 | 1 | — | — | — | — | — | — | — |
| Average | | 28 | 12 | 16.67 | 2100 | 71.43 (50) | — | — | 23.57 (50) | — |
| 2.51–5.00 | SC | 2 | 1 | — | — | — | — | — | — | — |
| | ST | 11 | 3 | 66.67 | 1300 | 61.54 (50) | — | — | 38.46 (50) | — |
| | OC | 2 | — | — | — | — | — | — | — | — |
| Average | | 15 | 4 | 66.67 | 1300 | 61.54 (50) | — | — | 38.46 (50) | — |
| 5.01–10.00 | SC | 4 | 1 | — | — | — | — | — | — | — |
| | ST | 1 | — | — | — | — | — | — | — | — |
| | OC | 2 | — | — | — | — | — | — | — | — |
| Average | | 7 | 1 | — | — | — | — | — | — | — |
| 10.00–above | SC | — | — | — | — | — | — | — | — | — |
| | ST | — | — | — | — | — | — | — | — | — |
| | OC | 1 | — | — | — | — | — | — | — | — |
| Average | | 1 | — | — | — | — | — | — | — | — |
| Overall | SC | 38 | 27 | 22.22 | 538 | — | 41.86 (33.33) | 5.43 (16.67) | 37.21 (16.67) | 15.50 (33.33) |
| | ST | 27 | 7 | 71.43 | 1300 | 70.77 (40) | — | — | 29.23 (60) | — |
| | OC | 15 | 2 | — | — | — | — | — | — | — |
| Average | | 80 | 36 | 30.56 | 884 | 47.30 (18.18) | 13.88 (18.18) | 1.80 (9.09) | 31.88 (36.37) | 5.14 (18.18) |

*Source*: Field Survey.
*Note*: Figures in the bracket represent percentage of households who lost collateral to total household borrowed.

TABLE IX: EXTENT OF LOSS OF COLLATERAL BY THE BORROWERS IN COLLATERAL BASED LOAN IN STUDY VILLAGE-3

| Land-holding size (in acre) | Caste | Total HH in in the group | Total HH given collateral | % of HH lost collateral | Avg. value of collateral (in Rs.) | As % of the total value of collateral lost | | | | |
|---|---|---|---|---|---|---|---|---|---|---|
| | | | | | | Land (%) | Cycle (%) | Utensils (%) | Ornaments (%) | Others (%) |
| 1 | | 2 | 3 | 4 | 5 | 6 | 7 | 8 | 9 | 10 |
| 00–0.0 | SC | 1 | 1 | — | — | — | — | — | — | — |
| | ST | 32 | 18 | 44.14 | 275 | 54.55 (25.00) | 22.73 (12.5) | 22.72 (62.50) | — | — |
| | OC | — | — | — | — | — | — | — | — | — |
| Average | | 33 | 18 | 44.14 | 275 | 54.55 (25.00) | 22.73 (12.5) | 22.72 (62.50) | — | — |
| 0.01–0.50 | SC | — | — | — | — | — | — | — | — | — |
| | ST | 6 | 4 | 50 | 500 | — | 90 (50.00) | 10 (50.00) | — | — |
| | OC | — | — | — | — | — | — | — | — | — |
| Average | | 6 | 4 | 50 | 500 | — | 90 (50.00) | 10 (50.00) | — | — |
| 0.51–2.50 | SC | — | — | — | — | — | — | — | — | — |
| | ST | 40 | 22 | 81.82 | 903 | 61.54 (27.78) | — | 1.54 (22.22) | 36.92 (50) | — |
| | OC | — | — | — | — | — | — | — | — | — |
| Average | | 40 | 22 | 81.82 | 903 | 61.54 (27.78) | — | 1.54 (22.22) | 36.92 (50) | — |
| 2.51–5.00 | SC | — | — | — | — | — | — | — | — | — |
| | ST | 22 | 12 | 16.67 | 1000 | — | — | — | — | 100 (100) |
| | OC | — | — | — | — | — | — | — | — | — |
| Average | | 22 | 12 | 16.67 | 1000 | — | — | — | — | 100 (100) |

| | | | | | | | | | | |
|---|---|---|---|---|---|---|---|---|---|---|
| 5.01–10.00 | SC | — | — | — | — | — | — | — | — | — |
| | ST | 6 | 1 | 100 | 1200 | 100 (100) | — | — | — | — |
| | OC | — | — | — | — | — | — | — | — | — |
| Average | | 6 | 1 | 100 | 1200 | 100 (100) | — | — | — | — |
| 10.00–above | SC | — | — | — | — | — | — | — | — | — |
| | ST | 3 | — | — | — | — | — | — | — | — |
| | OC | — | — | — | — | — | — | — | — | — |
| Average | | 3 | — | — | — | — | — | — | — | — |
| Overall | SC | 1 | — | — | — | — | — | — | — | — |
| | ST | 109 | 57 | 54.39 | 715 | 55.98 (25.81) | 4.29 (6.45) | 3.61 (32.26) | 27.09 (29.03) | 9.03 (6.45) |
| | OC | — | — | — | — | — | — | — | — | — |
| Average | | 110 | 57 | 54.39 | 715 | 55.98 (25.81) | 4.29 (6.45) | 3.61 (32.26) | 27.09 (29.03) | 9.03 (6.45) |

*Source*: Field Survey.

*Note*: Figures in the bracket represent percentage of households who lost collateral to total household borrowed.

TABLE X: COMPOSITION OF INCOME (Y) COMING FROM THE VARIOUS SOURCES IN THE STUDY VILLAGE-1 DURING THE YEAR 1997–8

| Land-holding size (in acre) | Caste | Total no. HH | Monthly Y per HH (in Rs.) | As % of total income | | | | | | | As % of total wage income | |
|---|---|---|---|---|---|---|---|---|---|---|---|---|
| | | | | Own pro-duction | Own buisness | Overall own prod. & business | Y from CPR | Y from state transfer | Y from service sector | wage income | Inside/ Nearby village | Distant migration |
| 1 | | 2 | 3 | 4 | 5 | 6 | 7 | 8 | 9 | 10 | 11 | 12 |
| 00–0.0 | SC | 2 | 953 | — | 2.27 | 2.27 | 3.05 | 5.25 | — | 89.43 | 89.43 | — |
| | ST | 26 | 488 | 0.46 | 11.98 | 12.44 | 7.79 | 6.31 | 7.88 | 65.57 | 65.57 | — |
| | OC | 10 | 512 | — | 8.14 | 8.14 | 5.87 | 3.91 | — | 82.08 | 82.08 | — |
| Average | | 38 | 519 | 0.29 | 10.05 | 10.34 | 6.84 | 5.58 | 5.07 | 72.17 | 72.17 | — |
| 0.01–0.50 | SC | — | — | — | — | — | — | — | — | — | — | — |
| | ST | 4 | 551 | 2.27 | 41.57 | 43.84 | 3.83 | 9.06 | — | 43.27 | 39.61 | 3.66 |
| | OC | — | — | — | — | — | — | — | — | — | — | — |
| Average | | 4 | 551 | 2.27 | 41.57 | 43.84 | 3.83 | 9.06 | — | 43.28 | 39.62 | 3.66 |
| 0.51–2.50 | SC | 6 | 806 | 43.08 | 21.12 | 64.20 | 2.19 | 2.07 | — | 31.54 | 31.02 | 0.52 |
| | ST | 35 | 1147 | 65.41 | — | 65.41 | 0.39 | 1.49 | — | 32.71 | 32.71 | — |
| | OC | 6 | 1674 | 53.75 | — | 53.75 | — | — | 34.84 | 11.41 | 11.41 | — |
| Average | | 47 | 1171 | 61.32 | 1.86 | 63.18 | 0.48 | 1.27 | 6.36 | 28.71 | 28.67 | 0.04 |
| 2.51–5.00 | SC | — | — | — | — | — | — | — | — | | — | — |
| | ST | 20 | 1708 | 76.09 | 0.61 | 76.70 | 0.29 | 0.88 | — | 12.13 | 12.13 | — |
| | OC | 4 | 2069 | 38.67 | — | 38.67 | — | — | 60.43 | 0.90 | 0.90 | — |
| Average | | 24 | 1768 | 68.79 | 0.49 | 69.28 | 0.24 | 0.71 | 11.78 | 17.99 | 17.99 | — |
| 5.01–10.00 | SC | 3 | 2002 | 37.48 | 34.71 | 72.17 | 0.32 | 1.67 | — | 25.82 | 7.77 | 18.05 |
| | ST | 14 | 1834 | 71.57 | — | 71.57 | 0.15 | — | 15.58 | 12.70 | 7.51 | 5.19 |
| | OC | 2 | 1950 | 48.72 | — | 48.72 | — | — | 51.28 | — | — | — |

| | | | | | | | | | | | |
|---|---|---|---|---|---|---|---|---|---|---|---|
| Average | | 19 | 1872 | 63.32 | 5.85 | 69.17 | 0.16 | 0.28 | 16.86 | 13.52 | 6.73 | 6.79 |
| 10.00– | SC | — | — | — | — | — | — | — | — | — | — | — |
| Above | ST | — | — | — | — | — | — | — | — | — | — | — |
| | OC | 3 | 2856 | 28.02 | 31.13 | 59.15 | — | — | 40.85 | — | — | — |
| Average | | 3 | 2856 | 28.02 | 31.13 | 59.15 | — | — | 40.85 | — | — | — |
| Overall | SC | 11 | 1159 | 34.01 | 24.69 | 58.70 | 1.44 | 2.35 | — | 37.51 | 28.82 | 8.69 |
| | ST | 99 | 1160 | 61.58 | 2.31 | 63.89 | 1.19 | 1.65 | 4.35 | 28.92 | 27.69 | 1.23 |
| | OC | 25 | 1436 | 35.93 | 8.58 | 44.51 | 0.84 | 0.56 | 38.99 | 15.09 | 15.09 | — |
| Average | | 135 | 1211 | 53.79 | 5.43 | 59.22 | 1.13 | 1.47 | 11.62 | 26.56 | 25.02 | 1.54 |

*Source*: Field Survey.

TABLE XI: COMPOSITION OF INCOME (Y) COMING FROM THE VARIOUS SOURCES IN THE STUDY VILLAGE-2 DURING THE YEAR 1997-8

| Land-holding size (in acre) | Caste | Total no. of HH | Monthly Y per HH (in Rs.) | Own pro-duction | Own buisness | Overall own prod. & business | Y from CPR | Y from state transfer | Y from service sector | Total wage (in Rs.) | Inside/ Nearby village | Distant migration |
|---|---|---|---|---|---|---|---|---|---|---|---|---|
| 1 | | 2 | 3 | 4 | 5 | 6 (4+5) | 7 | 8 | 9 | 10 | 11 | 12 |
| 00–0.0 | SC | 13 | 903 | — | — | — | 3.19 | 3.41 | — | 93.40 | 92.26 | 1.14 |
| | ST | — | — | — | — | — | — | — | — | — | — | — |
| | OC | 3 | 835 | — | — | — | 3.84 | 4.00 | — | 92.11 | 75.47 | 16.64 |
| Average | | 16 | 890 | — | — | — | 3.32 | 3.51 | — | 93.17 | 89.31 | 3.86 |
| 0.01–0.50 | SC | 4 | 671 | 3.73 | — | 3.73 | 1.77 | 3.73 | — | 90.77 | 80.75 | 10.02 |
| | ST | 8 | 1148 | 0.19 | — | 0.19 | 1.05 | 2.18 | 13.07 | 83.51 | 83.51 | — |
| | OC | 1 | 615 | 5.80 | — | 5.80 | 4.88 | — | — | 89.32 | 67.29 | 22.03 |

(contd.)

TABLE XI (contd.)

| 1 | | 2 | 3 | 4 | 5 | 6 (4+5) | 7 | 8 | 9 | 10 | 11 | 12 |
|---|---|---|---|---|---|---|---|---|---|---|---|---|
| Average | | 13 | 960 | 1.23 | — | 1.23 | 1.39 | 2.41 | 9.62 | 85.35 | 82.12 | 3.23 |
| 0.51–2.50 | SC | 15 | 818 | 36.68 | 13.05 | 49.73 | 3.09 | 0.82 | 8.15 | 38.21 | 38.21 | — |
| | ST | 7 | 1041 | 36.01 | 27.44 | 63.45 | 0.72 | 2.74 | — | 33.09 | 30.01 | 3.08 |
| | OC | 6 | 1257 | 27.85 | 13.35 | 41.20 | 0.49 | — | 37.58 | 20.73 | 20.73 | — |
| Average | | 28 | 968 | 34.04 | 17.01 | 51.05 | 1.73 | 1.11 | 14.15 | 31.96 | 31.13 | 0.83 |
| 2.51–5.00 | SC | 2 | 1910 | 66.52 | — | 66.52 | — | — | 30.54 | 2.94 | 1.64 | 1.30 |
| | ST | 11 | 1627 | 76.82 | 8.15 | 84.97 | 1.16 | 0.56 | — | 13.31 | 13.31 | — |
| | OC | 2 | 2133 | 52.52 | 46.89 | 99.41 | — | — | — | 0.58 | 0.58 | — |
| Average | | 15 | 1732 | 71.32 | 13.31 | 84.63 | 0.81 | 0.38 | 4.48 | 9.51 | 9.51 | 0.19 |
| 5.01–10.00 | SC | 4 | 2000 | 52.52 | 13.03 | 65.55 | — | — | 33.34 | 1.12 | 1.12 | — |
| | ST | 1 | 1268 | 100 | — | 100 | — | — | — | — | — | — |
| | OC | 2 | 1521 | 83.56 | — | 83.56 | — | — | — | 16.44 | — | 16.44 |
| Average | | 7 | 1758 | 65.08 | 8.46 | 72.54 | — | — | 21.67 | 4.79 | 0.73 | 4.06 |
| 10.00 - | SC | — | — | — | — | — | — | — | — | — | — | — |
| Above | ST | 1 | 2929 | 57.32 | 42.68 | 100 | — | — | — | — | — | — |
| | OC | — | — | — | — | — | — | — | — | — | — | — |
| Average | | 1 | 2929 | 57.32 | 42.68 | 100 | — | — | — | — | — | — |
| Overall | SC | 38 | 1013 | 29.45 | 6.86 | 36.31 | 2.08 | 1.56 | 12.55 | 47.50 | 46.33 | 1.17 |
| | ST | 27 | 1320 | 49.55 | 9.71 | 59.26 | 1.01 | 1.41 | 3.36 | 34.96 | 34.33 | 0.63 |
| | OC | 15 | 1393 | 41.14 | 20.37 | 61.51 | 0.79 | 0.48 | 13.56 | 23.66 | 18.62 | 5.04 |
| Average | | 80 | 1188 | 39.56 | 10.89 | 50.45 | 1.40 | 1.26 | 9.33 | 37.56 | 35.74 | 1.82 |

*Source*: Field Survey.

TABLE XII: COMPOSITION OF INCOME (Y) COMING FROM THE VARIOUS SOURCES IN THE STUDY VILLAGE-3, DURING THE YEAR 1997–8

| Land-holding size (in acre) | Caste | Total no. of HH | Monthly Y per HH (in Rs.) | As % of total income | | | | | | | As % of total wage income | |
|---|---|---|---|---|---|---|---|---|---|---|---|---|
| | | | | Own pro-duction | Own buisness | Overall own prod. & business | Y from CPR | Y from state transfer | Y from service sector | Total wage in Rs. | Inside/ Nearby village | Distant migration |
| 1 | | 2 | 3 | 4 | 5 | 6 (4+5) | 7 | 8 | 9 | 10 | 11 | 12 |
| 00–0.0 | SC | 1 | 320 | — | — | — | 6.25 | — | — | 93.75 | 93.75 | — |
| | ST | 32 | 978 | — | 0.05 | 0.05 | 2.31 | 2.88 | — | 94.76 | 93.98 | 0.78 |
| | OC | — | — | — | — | — | — | — | — | — | — | — |
| Average | | 33 | 958 | — | 0.05 | 0.05 | 2.34 | 2.88 | — | 94.75 | 93.98 | 0.77 |
| 0.01–0.50 | SC | — | — | — | — | — | — | — | — | — | — | — |
| | ST | 6 | 445 | 1.56 | — | 1.56 | 5.62 | 7.49 | — | 85.33 | 80.89 | 4.44 |
| | OC | — | — | — | — | — | — | — | — | — | — | — |
| Average | | 6 | 445 | 1.56 | — | 1.56 | 5.62 | 7.49 | — | 85.33 | 80.89 | 4.44 |
| 0.51–2.50 | SC | — | — | — | — | — | — | — | — | — | — | — |
| | ST | 40 | 1020 | 58.94 | — | 58.94 | 0.53 | 2.94 | 8.17 | 29.42 | 29.42 | — |
| | OC | — | — | — | — | — | — | — | — | — | — | — |
| Average | | 40 | 1020 | 58.94 | — | 58.94 | 0.53 | 2.94 | 8.17 | 29.42 | 29.42 | — |
| 2.51–5.00 | SC | — | — | — | — | — | — | — | — | — | — | — |
| | ST | 22 | 954 | 62.89 | 6.95 | 69.84 | 1.03 | 0.96 | 13.50 | 14.67 | 14.67 | — |
| | OC | — | — | — | — | — | — | — | — | — | — | — |
| Average | | 22 | 954 | 62.89 | 6.95 | 69.84 | 1.03 | 0.96 | 13.50 | 14.67 | 14.67 | — |

(contd.)

TABLE XII (contd.)

| 1 | | 2 | 3 | 4 | 5 | 6 (4+5) | 7 | 8 | 9 | 10 | 11 | 12 |
|---|---|---|---|---|---|---|---|---|---|---|---|---|
| 5.01–10.00 | SC | — | — | — | — | — | — | — | — | — | — | — |
| | ST | 6 | 1928 | 46.68 | 19.45 | 66.13 | — | — | 32.42 | 1.45 | 1.45 | — |
| | OC | — | — | — | — | — | — | — | — | — | — | — |
| Average | | 6 | 1928 | 46.68 | 19.45 | 66.13 | — | — | 32.42 | 1.45 | 1.45 | — |
| 10.00– | SC | — | — | — | — | — | — | — | — | — | — | — |
| Above | ST | 3 | 2562 | 58.55 | 8.92 | 67.47 | — | — | 32.53 | — | — | — |
| | OC | — | — | — | — | — | — | — | — | — | — | — |
| Average | | 3 | 2562 | 58.55 | 8.92 | 67.47 | — | — | 32.53 | — | — | — |
| Overall | SC | 1 | 320 | — | — | — | 6.25 | — | — | 93.75 | 93.75 | — |
| | ST | 109 | 1055 | 41.04 | 3.84 | 44.88 | 1.14 | 2.17 | 10.79 | 41.02 | 40.71 | 0.31 |
| | OC | — | — | — | — | — | — | — | — | — | — | — |
| Average | | 110 | 1048 | 40.92 | 3.83 | 44.75 | 1.15 | 2.17 | 10.77 | 41.15 | 40.84 | 0.31 |

*Source*: Field Survey.

SECTION III

# Nutrition, Food Absorption and Utilization

# 13. Approaches to Eliminate Malnutrition

*C. Gopalan*

During the last 50 years, there have been significant changes in India's nutrition scene. The nutrition-related problems which India has been able to overcome during this period is remarkable. However, we still have a long way to go to achieving optimal nutrition status for our people. The nutrition scene is influenced directly or indirectly by several interrelated factors which form part of the developmental process and the fight against under-nutrition and malnutrition is a continuing process.

## THE CHANGING NUTRITION SCENE

Since independence, there has been a remarkable surge in the population: while in the 47 years preceding Independence, the population increase was of the order of over 107 million, in the 47 years following Independence, the increase was of the order of over 580 million. During the colonial era, pestilence and repeated large-scale famines had decimated large sections of the population, and this had resulted in low population growth. Famines have now been practically eliminated and mortality rates have been drastically reduced. But our very success in this respect has resulted in a major nutrition challenge—the 'Population Problem'. Also, since Independence, our land and water resources on which food production programmes depend have been nearly static, we have now to produce a lot more food per unit of land than we did earlier. This is a challenge to agricultural scientists. Population growth has also been associated with progressive ageing of the population and increasing urbanization. While about 15 per cent of our population lived in urban areas prior to Independence, this figure is soon expected to increase to nearly

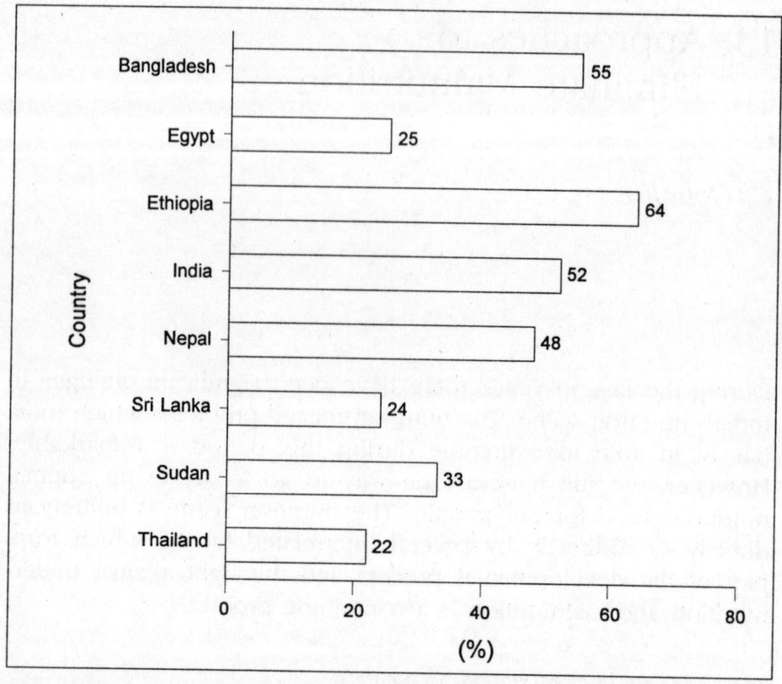


FIG. 1: PREVALENCE OF STUNTING UNDER-5 YEARS OF AGE.
*Source*: UNICEF, *The State of the World's Children*, 1998.

40 per cent. Urbanization involves several changes, in lifestyles, occupation patterns, dietary habits and child rearing practices. All these contribute to the changing nutrition scene. Besides, infant and child mortality have declined significantly. But child-survival does not necessarily mean improved child health and nutrition. Many of the child 'survivors' belong to the poorest sections of the community and they add to the proportion of 'stunted' children; nearly 50 per cent of our under-5 today are stunted (Fig. 1). All this points toward the need for a paradigm shift in our nutrition policy—a shift from emphasis on just child survival to emphasis on child health and child nutrition. Also, a considerable proportion of infants is of low birth weight (less than 2.5 kg)[1,2] which would make them grow and develop at substandard levels.

Thanks to the Green Revolution, food grain production in the country has outstripped population growth, with the result that per capita availability of wheat and rice has increased. This achievement of our agricultural scientists and farmers helped us to stave off famines and acute food shortages. We have had some success with respect to milk production due to pioneering efforts of Dr. Kurien.[3]

Notwithstanding the above achievements, nearly a third of India's population has been estimated to be below the 'poverty line'.[4] Poverty implies not just inadequate access to food, but also deprivation of several basic requisites for healthy life, viz., poor environment, poor educational level skills, and poor access to healthcare. Removal of poverty is the major challenge that has to be addressed in order to achieve adequate nutritional status for our people. Fortunately, available data do show a progressive, though slow reduction in poverty levels.

During the last 50 years, we have had significant success in many areas in the field of nutrition. Apart from completely eliminating large-scale famines, some of the major florid nutrition deficiency diseases, which used to affect millions of the poor in our country[5] have also been totally or nearly eliminated. They are: cardiac, beri-beri and peripheral neuritis, attributable to vitamin B deficiency; cases of pellagra affecting *jowar*-eating population in the Deccan plateau; classical kwashiorkar (of the Cecilly William type), indicator of severe protein calorie malnutrition rampant among children in the southern and eastern parts of the country; and keratomalacia (destruction of the cornea due to malnutrition), and blindness due to vitamin A deficiency. We may, therefore, rightfully claim that the tip of the iceberg of undernutrition has now been done away with in large measure. The elimination of these diseases was brought about not through narrow nutrition intervention programmes involving distribution of synthetic vitamins like vitamin B, nicotinic acid, vitamin A or of food formulations like fish protein concentrates, but through food-based approaches consisting of improved dietary practices and all-round socio-economic development and better healthcare. *As I have often said, we should look to our farms and not to our pharmacies for the solution of our nutrition problems.* The task of bringing about improvement in household diets cannot be evaded, and synthetic vitamins can never be substitute for good, well-balanced diets. Our historical experience serves to confirm this.

## THE PRESENT PICTURE: MAJOR PUBLIC HEALTH PROBLEMS

The major public health problems which we are now witnessing among the poor are: stunting and growth retardation in children; widespread anaemia in all sections of the population and more specially in women in the reproductive age group; iodine deficiency disorders; and, in some pockets of the country, mild forms of vitamin A deficiency. In addition, in recent years there has been an upswing in nutrition-related diseases such as cardiovascular and coronary heart diseases, non-insulin dependent diabetes, hypertension, etc., in affluent sections due to dietary excesses and errors, and faulty lifestyles.

### STUNTING IN CHILDREN

In 50 per cent of children, levels of growth are below international standards. Physical stunting among the poor (Fig. 2) is generally associated with other functional impairments such as impaired mental development and lower level of physical endurance. With

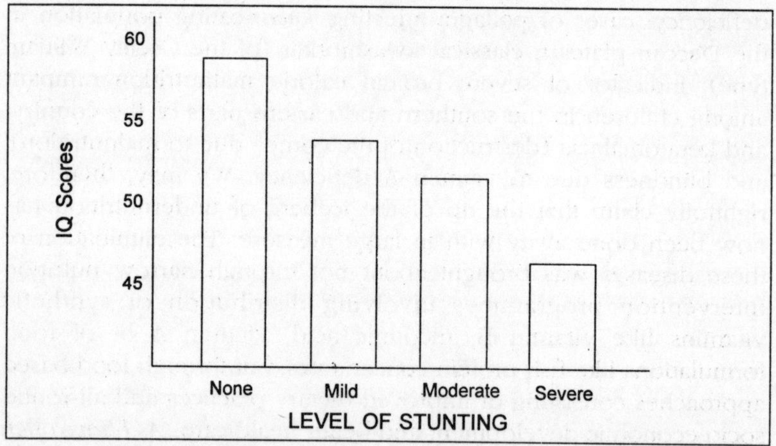


FIG. 2: EFFECT OF PHYSICAL STUNTING.

*Source*: UNICEF. Stunting linked to impaired intellectual development. The State of the World's Children, 1998, Oxford University Press.

*Note*: In a non-verbal intelligence test given to eight-year-olds in the Philippines, scores strongly correlated with children's level of stunting at age 2. Children severely stunted at age 2 had the lowest test scores, while non-stunted children had scores on average 11 points higher.

a proper home environment, not all stunted children need suffer mental impairment. Among the various factors which contribute to stunting, the following require attention: low birth weight due to maternal malnutrition during pregnancy; delayed introduction of complementary feeds; poor quality of diets supplied to children; and frequent episodes of alimentary and respiratory disorders.

The latest NFHS[6] data show that children in whom solid foods were introduced by 6–9 months of infancy showed much less stunting than those who did not receive such food. Educating mothers to introduce solid foods right from the 6 months of infancy will go a long way in preventing stunting.

The quality of the diet and attention to improved feeding practices during crucial periods of growth and development in children is also important. Several studies (Boyd Orr; Aykroyd and Krishnan[7,8]) have found that children who received milk supplement had shown a height gain and also greater alertness than those who had not.

Better healthcare and prompt control of respiratory and alimentary diseases could also contribute to improved growth. The other nutrition-deficiency-related diseases due to iron deficiency (anaemia), iodine deficiency (goitre), etc., are dealt with in detail later in this paper.

## STRATEGIES FOR COMBATING MALNUTRITION

### NEED FOR NUTRITIONAL ORIENTATION OF FOOD PRODUCTION PROGRAMMES

Our food production programmes at present seem to be largely determined by market forces and economic considerations. If we have to solve our nutrition problems, food prodcution policy must have a heavy nutritional orientation. Adequate attention needs to be given to the production of pulses, fruits, vegetables and milk. Among non-vegetarian items, fish and poultry, which are eminently desirable from the nutrition point of view and which make minimum demands on land resources should receive attention. Diversification of food production is thus necessitated more importantly due to nutritional considerations and taking also into account that a large set of our population is vegetarian.

In order to achieve adequacy of food production, we must adopt scientific, safe and ecologically sound agricultural practices. The earlier mistakes, which have led to the present Green Revolution 'fatigue', need first to be corrected. Second, the emerging new technologies in the field of biotechnology that offer promise need to be effectively harnessed and adapted with due considerations for safety and sustainability. Intensive irrigation and heavy use of high-analysis chemical fertilizers should always go hand in hand with periodic soil testing and soil replenishment so that loss of soil micronutrients and soil fertility could be avoided. Irrigation without arrangement for drainage has often contributed to increasing salinity of the soil. The indiscriminate use of pesticides, fungicides and insecticides had upset the biological balance, and tapping of underground water through thousands of tube-wells has led to the rapid exhaustion of this important resource. Exploitative agriculture adopted during Green Revolution should have been based on proper scientific evidence. The Green Revolution has also led to some imbalances because it was solely directed to wheat and rice, to the relative neglect of pulses, millets and vegetables. The per capita availability of pulses, an important source of lysine, riboflavin and folic acid, has now diminished. Millets, which were the main staple of the rural poor, have now been practically displaced by wheat and rice. Pulses and millets are important food items that could have provided much-needed micronutrients. Horticulture has also failed to receive adequate attention, with the result that there have been no great gains with regard to production of vegetables, and nearly a third of vegetables and fruits produced continue to perish. Agro-based industries and village-level technologies for preservation and storage of fruits and vegetables were not adequately encouraged. Post-harvest losses to the tune of about 20 to 30 per cent of horticultural produce can be reduced through provision of adequate infrastructure for post-harvest handling and appropriate technology for on and off farm processing. While we managed to avoid hunger and famine and achieved adequacy with respect to energy requirement, the diets of the poor continue to be unbalanced and deficient in nutrients.

Nutrition security cannot be achieved by reliance on just one staple. Diets exclusively based on rice or wheat will be deficient in a range of micronutrients, apart from being relatively poor in protein quality. Diversification of household diets is necessary, and a national food production policy should aim at the achievement of balanced production and availability of a range of basic essential foods. The achievement of satisfactory levels of milk production in India is, for instance, highly conducive to nutrition security. 'Operation Flood' which has now made India the leading milk producer in the world, is a striking example of what a developing country can achieve through the efficient implementation of a well-thought-out programme. The production of pulses and vegetables and fruits must now, likewise, be augmented. The challenge before agricultural scientists is to ensure balanced, sustainable and ecologically sound agricultural development.

### HARNESSING EMERGING NEW TECHNOLOGY

New genetic technologies offer promise of breeding food crop varieties for resistance, namely tolerance to biotic and abiotic stresses, drought and salinity resistance, and even better nutrient quality. Rice, for example, could be genetically engineered to contain vitamin A. Genetic technology applied to horticulture could result in the production of vegetables and fruits with improved micronutrient content and better acceptability. Large private corporations in the US and Europe are currently making major investments in using these technologies to produce new plant varieties for large-scale commercial agriculture. Much of this action is now occurring in industrial countries under the purview of proprietary science. There is currently widespread concern regarding the safety of some genetically modified foods. A recent statement[9] issued by the Royal Society on genetically modified plants for food use and recent papers on this subject by Swaminathan[10] and Paroda[11] present a balanced and not too euphoric picture.

### UNSUSTAINABILITY OF PHARMACEUTICAL SHORT-CUTS

In recent years, efforts have been made to provide pharmaceutical short-cuts, rather than food-based solutions, to problems of micronutrient deficiencies of populations in developing countries subsisting predominantly on cereal-based diets, even at the public health level. Developing countries are being persuaded to believe that the problems of maternal morbidity and low birth weight can be successfully combated by an arbitrarily chosen concoction of synthetic vitamins. This is an approach that needs to be resisted not only on ground of unsustainability, but also on scientific grounds. Nutrient deficiencies that cannot be solved by foods, especially plant foods, are extremely rare. This is not to argue against selective fortification of foods with appropriate nutrients in order to meet special situations; the issue is examined in detail later in the paper. However, the primary objective in the quest for nutrition security must be to ensure the availability, at the household level, of balanced diets that will meet not only energy needs, but also the requirements of micronutrients and macronutrients.

## THE DISCOVERY OF PHYTONUTRIENTS

During the last two decades, it has been discovered that apart from the conventional nutrients which we had known over the years, foods contain a whole range of bio-active phytochemicals which play an important part in maintenance of health and prevention of disease.[12] A brief list of phytonutrients and their food sources is given in Tables 1 and 2. The discovery of phytochemicals has opened up an entirely new chapter and has given added importance to food-based approaches not only in combating malnutrition, but also in the prevention of diseases including cancer. These new advances provide valuable leads for action to combat malnutrition and to evolve meaningful public

TABLE 1: PHYTONUTRIENTS ASSOCIATED WITH HEALTH PROMOTION

| Phytonutrient class | Food sources |
|---|---|
| Carotenoids | Coloured fruits and vegetables |
| Glucosinolates, isothiocyanates, indoles | Cruciferous vegetables (broccoli), horseradish, mustard and mustard oil |
| Inositol phosphates | Cereals, soyabeans |
| Phenolics, cyclic compounds | Citrus fruits, vegetables |
| Phytoestrogens | Isoflavones: soyabeans, Ligans: flax, rye, vegetables |
| Phytosterols | Vegetable oils, nuts, seeds, cereals, legumes |
| Polyphenols | Fruits, vegetables, tea, red wine, heaflavins and thearubigens in black and oolong tea |
| Protease inhibitors | Soyabeans, other legumes, cereals, vegetables, egg white (duck) |
| Saponins | Soyabeans, other legumes, nuts |
| Sulphides and thiols | Sulphides: allium vegetables (onions), dithiolthiones: cruciferous, vegetables (broccoli) |

*Source*: Beecher, R. Gary, 'Phytonutrients Role in Metabolism: Effects on Resistance to Degenerative Process', *Nutrition Reviews*, 57 (9): S3-S6, 1999.

TABLE 2: AN ILLUSTRATIVE (NOT EXHAUSTIVE) LIST OF COMMONLY AVAILABLE INEXPENSIVE MICRONUTRIENT RICH FOODS

| | |
|---|---|
| Vegetables | Rape leaves, cauliflower greens, amaranth, curry leaves, garden cress, drumstick (leaves), fenugreek leaves, beet greens, spinach, betel leaves, parsley, turnip greens, purslane, mint, carrots, lotus stem, tapioca chips, colocasia, radish, sweet potato, yam, ivy gourd, lettuce, mint, agathi, radish leaves. |
| Condiments and Spices | Poppy, cumin, coriander, oregano, green chillies (fresh/dry), turmeric, ginger, fenugreek, pepper, garlic, mango powder. |
| Nuts & Oilseeds | Coconut (deoiled/dry/milk), groundnut cashew nut, pistachionut, gingelly seeds, garden cress seeds, safflower seeds, mustard seeds, niger seeds. |
| Fruits | Indian gooseberry, watermelon, custard apple, wood apple, tomato, guava, mango, pineapple, orange, papaya, grapes, banana, bael, pomegranate, grapes, gooseberry, apricot. |

*Source*: C. Gopalan, 'Multiple Micronutrient Supplements in Pregnancy', *NFI Bulletin*, 21 (2): 7, 2000.

health approaches towards improving the nutrition status of populations. These advances have made us realize that the nutrition factor plays a far greater role in health and disease, and with this change of perception, nutrition has come to acquire a far more important place in public health than ever before.

## IMPROVING BIOAVAILABILITY OF MICRONUTRIENTS FROM PLANT FOODS

We must strongly propagate ways by which the bioavailability of micronutrients from horticulture plant foods available at the door step can be improved, viz., improved cooking and processing procedures; better preservation techniques that could increase availability throughout the year; home-processing techniques to reduce inhibitors of absorption; simple methods of achieving enzymatic hydrolysis of phytates in cereals and legumes through fermentation and germination; promoting non-enzymatic methods of reducing phytic acid content; invoking home-processing techniques like malting, and use of tomato or lime juice, instead of tamarind as a souring agent in order to facilitate non-haeme iron absorption

There is a wide variety of inexpensive micronutrient rich foods right at the very doorstep of poor village communities (Table 2).

While the nutritive values of some of these are known, there is reason to believe that quite a few plant foods are currently unused and fall in the 'unfamiliar' category and are being currently wasted. The challenge to policy makers and scientists of developing countries is to: increase the production and availability of micronutrient rich foods; enhance their nutritive value using modern tools of biotechnology; prevent their wastage through simple methods of preservation and storage; improve culinary practices to avoid losses of micronutrients during cooking; and develop methods of processing these foods in order to improve their nutritive value, acceptability and shelf life and thereby promote the consumption of these foods.

## SUPPLEMENTATION WITH SYNTHETIC NUTRIENTS

Valid scientific justification and practical need exist for the use of synthetic nutrients in some situations. In these cases, the procedures involved are in consonance with approaches towards overall dietary improvement and national development.

### *Iodine*

Intensive irrigation has apparently led to the leaching out of iodine from the soil. Soil iodine depletion leads to poor content of iodine in foods grown on such soils, and this is reflected in the wide prevalence of neonatal hypothyroidism in endemic areas. Soil testing and soil replenishment which should have gone hand in hand with other aspects of the Green Revolution technology, had apparently been relatively neglected. Furthermore, possibly due to the intensive use of pesticides—again a part of the intensive agriculture technology—it has been found that goitrogens in the environment have increased, thus causing increasing iodine requirements. In view of these conditions, programmes of iodization of common salt with potassium iodate have been successfully undertaken in some countries. Despite recent resistance to this measure from some quarters, this is a programme of proven worth and scientific merit and must continue.[13] The use of iodized oil or of lipiodol injections on the other hand is totally inappropriate, expensive, unsustainable and possibly harmful.[14] Salt iodation, on the other hand, is a perfectly safe and tested procedure and should be the basis of public health programmes designed to control goitre.

*Iron*

Special care should be taken to include higher levels of iron containing food-items in the diets of pregnant women. This is generally not done, the diets in pregnancy in poor populations being no different from the habitual family diets. It is in recognition of this that a national programme of iron/folate supplementation during the last 100 days of pregnancy (200 mg of ferrous sulphate equivalent to 60 mg elemental iron and 500 mg of folate) has been in operation in India though not with much success.

A significant proportion of adolescent girls of poor communities have been found to have low haemoglobin levels.[15] This could mean that many of these girls are anaemic even at the time of conception, and pregnancy only serves to aggravate the anaemia. It is not surprising that iron supplements during the last 100 days of pregnancy, specially given the poor compliance, have not yielded striking results.

The latest data from the survey carried out by NFHS provide some important lessons (Table 3).

Kerala, in the south of India, is a relatively poor state as compared to Haryana, Uttar Pradesh, Bihar in the north and yet the prevalence of anaemia in that state is extremely low. This would highlight the point that micronutrient malnutrition in general can be combated even in poor communities through judicious use of local foods and proper healthcare. Kerala also has the lowest infant and child mortality and birth rates. The Kerala experience would show that importance of nutritional status with respect to micronutrients is likely to be achieved as part of all-round development and not just through narrow vertical programmes.

*Double Fortification of Salt with Iron and Iodine*

Since salt is already being iodized, and since salt is a universal food used by the poor as much as by the rich, there could be a reasonable case for double fortification of common salt with iron and iodine. An added scientific justification for this is the reported finding that iron deficiency could impair the efficacy of iodine supplementation,[16] yet another example of micronutrient interactions. More recently, three techniques for the dual fortification of salt are being investigated at National Institute of Nutrition (Hyderabad): (1) salt fortified with ferrous fumarate plus dextrin

TABLE 3: NFHS II DATA (1998–9)—ANAEMIA AMONG PREGNANT WOMEN

| State | % of preg. women with no anaemia | % of preg. women with mild anaemia | % of preg. women with moderate anaemia | % of preg. women with severe anaemia | % of preg. women with any anaemia |
|---|---|---|---|---|---|
| Andhra Pradesh | 58.2 | 18.8 | 20.6 | 2.4 | 41.8 |
| Assam | 38.1 | 24.5 | 33.4 | 3.9 | 61.9 |
| Bihar | 50.4 | 22 | 25.5 | 2.2 | 49.6 |
| Gujarat | 52.8 | 15.4 | 28 | 3.8 | 47.2 |
| Haryana | 44.4 | 20.7 | 33.1 | 1.7 | 55.6 |
| Himachal Pradesh | 68.2 | 18.3 | 12.9 | 0.7 | 31.8 |
| Kerala | 79.6 | 11.6 | 8.8 | 0 | 20.4 |
| Karnataka | 51.5 | 20.7 | 24.9 | 2.8 | 48.5 |
| Madhya Pradesh | 46 | 22 | 31.1 | 0.9 | 54 |
| Maharashtra | 47.2 | 20.2 | 27.6 | 5.1 | 52.8 |
| Orissa | 39.6 | 26.7 | 33 | 0.7 | 60.4 |
| Punjab | 63 | 20 | 16.4 | 0.6 | 37 |
| Rajasthan | 48.4 | 23.1 | 26.2 | 2.3 | 51.6 |
| Sikkim | 51.6 | 10.8 | 33.2 | 4.5 | 48.4 |
| Tamil Nadu | 42.9 | 25.5 | 27 | 4.6 | 57.1 |
| Uttar Pradesh | 54 | 21.1 | 22.4 | 2.4 | 46 |
| West Bengal | 43 | 30 | 25.6 | 1.4 | 57 |

*Source*: International Institute for Population Sciences. NFHS II, Preliminary Reports, Mumbai, 2000.

encapsulated potassium iodate (developed by the Micronutrient Initiative), (2) fortification with sodium iron Ethylene Diaminete Traacetic Acid (EDTA), and (3) forti-fication with ferrous sulphate, sodium hexa-metaphosphate and potassium iodate. The results of these studies could provide guidance in the search of an iron-iodine salt fortification procedure.

## INTRAFAMILIAL FOOD DISTRIBUTION

The availability of adequate food at the household level does not necessarily imply that the food is distributed to members according to their physiological needs. The worst sufferers in this regard, particularly in households with marginally adequate food supply, are women (especially pregnant women) and children or infants; the male wage earner gets the lion's share. The extra food needed to meet the food and nutritional requirements of women, and, especially children, generally constitutes a small fraction of the total food already available for the household. Faulty intra-familial distribution of food and faulty choice of foods contribute to a considerable part of undernutrition in children and women in poor households. Much of the mild or moderate malnutrition in children of poor communities is directly attributable to poor infant and child feeding practices, due not so much to a lack of food in the household but to faulty child-rearing trends. Significantly, a good part of the high incidence of low-birth-weight deliveries in poor communities is also attributable to lack of awareness of the special nutrient needs of women during pregnancy. This is an area in which nutrition education could make a significant contribution, even in the context of poverty.

## BASIC HEALTH SERVICES, SAFE WATER SUPPLY AND PERSONAL HYGIENE

Improvement of environmental sanitation, provision of safe drinking water and the observance of personal hygiene will make important contributions to nutrition security in poor communities; basic health services have to be accorded high priority in any development programme addressed to poor communities.

Today, most adolescent girls of poor communities enter marriage totally unprepared for the task of motherhood and child-rearing. These girls, more than any other sector of our population, hold the key of the future. Any programme for social development and nutrition security must give proper attention to this group.

A recent report of the NFHS[16] in India has concluded that the prevalence of malnutrition can be reduced by improving educational levels of mothers and that such efforts should be combined with programmes that raise women's awareness of the nutritional requirements of children. An earlier study by Nutrition Foundation of India (NFI)[17] had also recognized that nutrition intervention would be effective when the education of both parents, especially the mothers, was ensured up to middle or high school.

The recent decision by the Government of India to award attractive stipends for schooling to the female children of poor communities is an imaginative step in the right direction; the level of stipends is to be progressively increased with stages of schooling, to discourage school dropouts.

## MOBILIZING AND EMPOWERING THE COMMUNITY

The experience of the past few decades clearly shows that the main focus in programmes designed to bring about nutritional improvement must shift from the provider (the government) to the consumers (the people). The bureaucrats are to act as support group and it is the community that must now take the lead. Once this attitudinal change is accepted, the community can be encouraged and equipped to assume its leadership role. The government's role should be limited to providing such resources as will be needed to facilitate community action. Programmes designed to bring about nutritional improvement involving such community-based activities as home gardening and nutrition education, can be successfully organized and implemented by village-level community organizations using trained local volunteers drawn entirely from the community, generating and using local food resources.

During the twentieth century 'success' was measured in terms of avoiding famines, freedom from hunger, child survival and safe motherhood. In the twenty-first century, our policy makers should set more ambitious targets. Household nutrition security must come to mean a lot more than avoidance of chronic starvation. Foods for families must be adequate, not just meeting the bare energy needs for survival, but providing all the nutrients essential for normal development to enable populations to find full expression of their innate genetic potential.

I acknowledge the help of Ms. Bani Tamber Aeri, Scientist, NFI, in the preparation of this paper.

## NOTES

1. Mahbub ul Haq and Khadija Haq, *Human Development in South Asia*, Karachi: Oxford University Press, 1998.
2. *Human Development Report 1998*, United Nations Development Programme, New Delhi: Oxford University Press, 1998.
3. V. Kurien, 'India's Milk Revolution', *NFI Bulletin*, 21 (1): 1–5, 2000.
4. *Report of Planning Commission*, Government of India, 2001.
5. C. Gopalan, 'The Changing Epidemiology of Malnutrition in a Developing Society—the Effect of Unforeseen Factors', *Current Science* 77 (10): 1257–62, 1999.

6. NFHS, *National Family Health Survey-2, 1998–99*, International Institute for Population Sciences, Mumbai.
7. W.R. Aykroyd and B.G. Krishnan, *Ind. J. Med. Res.*, 24: 1993, 1937.
8. W.R. Aykroyd and B.G. Krishnan, *Lancet*, 11: 153, 1938.
9. Royal Society of London, *A Report on Genetically Modified Plants for Food Use*, 1999.
10. M.S. Swaminathan, *Third Ved Prakash Memorial Lecture* on 'Population and Human Security' at the National Institute of Health and Family Welfare, New Delhi, 1999.
11. R.S. Paroda, 'Genetic modification of foods', *NFI Bulletin*, July 1999.
12. B.S. Narasinga Rao, 'Micronutrient Interactions', Paper Presented at the Indo-US Symposium on Micronutrient Requirements, Hyderabad: NIN, 2000.
13. S. Vir, 'Control of Iodine Deficiency: The National Programme—Current Status', *NFI Bulletin*, 15 (2): 1–4, 1994.
14. K. Kochupillai, 'Prevention and Control of Goitre Demerits of Iodised Oil Injections', *NFI Bulletin*, 12 (4): 1–5, 1991.
15. WHO, 'Nutritional Status of Adolescent Girls and Women of Reproductive Age', Report of Regional Consultations, New Delhi, 1998 (SEA/NUP/14).
16. International Life Science Institute (ILSI), *Project IDEA (Iron Deficiency Elimination Action) Newsletter*, vol. 2, 10 June 2000.
17. C. Gopalan, N. Sharma and H.P.S. Sachdeva, 'Relationship of Current Nutritional Status and Cognitive Functioning in 3-10 Year Olds Living in Slums', New Delhi: NFI, 1998.

# 14. Food Security and Child Rights: Two Priorities

*A.K. Shiva Kumar*

Forty-seven per cent of India's children below the age of 3 years are malnourished—almost twice the rates of malnutrition reported by many countries of Sub-Saharan Africa. In the world today, Bangladesh alone reports a higher rate of child malnutrition than India. Such high levels of malnutrition grossly violate the rights of children to survive and develop into healthy and creative adults. Scientific evidence suggests that compared with the risks facing a well-nourished child, the risk of death from common childhood diseases is doubled for a mildly malnourished child, tripled for a moderately malnourished child, and may be even as high as eight times for a severely malnourished child.[1]

This paper discusses two of the many aspects of food security and child rights that require urgent attention. At a very young age, between 6–18 months, when most infants begin to experience growth faltering, food availability within the household may not be the critical factor causing malnutrition. It is very often inadequate knowledge about feeding practices that are in the best interest of the child. The denial of as little as 200–300 calories in a young child's daily diet is what makes the difference between normal growth and the faltering that starts the descent towards illness and death. Equally critical for preventing malnutrition during early infancy is the quality of care and attention that young infants receive when being fed.

There is a close linkage between child malnutrition and maternal malnutrition. Both child and maternal malnutrition are in turn strongly dependent upon the levels of schooling attained by women. Schooling has to become universal if India is to make a serious dent on the problem of child malnutrition. In this context, food has an especially critical role—serving cooked meals in schools could help achieve universal enrolment, ensure high retention and reduce malnutrition.

## EXPLAINING MALNUTRITION

It has been customary to attribute high levels of child malnutrition to a country's low level of income. However, worldwide at an aggregate level, the correlation of malnutrition with per capita incomes is extremely weak. Income levels are not a good predictor of the levels of malnutrition. Within India too, there is no automatic or obvious linkage between levels of per capita income and malnutrition across the states. States with similar per capita incomes report very different levels of child malnutrition (Table 1).

Again, income poverty is often regarded as a major underlying cause of malnutrition. It is true that at the individual or household level, the absence of purchasing power to establish command

TABLE 1: INCOME LEVELS AND CHILD MALNUTRITION ACROSS INDIAN STATES

| | Per capita net State Domestic Product at current prices Rupees | Weight-for-age percentage of children under 3 years who are moderately and severely malnourished (below 3 SD) |
|---|---|---|
| | 1997–8 | 1998–9 |
| *Low income, high malnutrition* | | |
| *High income, low malnutrition* | | |
| Rajasthan | 9,358 | 50.6 |
| Punjab | 19,500 | 28.7 |
| *Low income, low malnutrition* | | |
| *High income, high malnutrition* | | |
| Manipur | 8,114 | 27.5 |
| Gujarat | 16,251 | 45.1 |
| *Differing incomes, similar malnutrition* | | |
| Orissa | 6,767 | 50.6 |
| Maharashtra | 18,635 | 49.6 |
| *Similar incomes, different levels of malnutrition* | | |
| Kerala | 11,936 | 26.9 |
| Karnataka | 11,693 | 43.9 |

*Sources*: *Economic Survey 1999–2000* and *National Family Health Survey 2.*

over food can lead to starvation and malnutrition. But at an aggregate level, the linkages between income poverty and child malnutrition are not obvious. For instance, as Table 2 reveals, in 1993–4, Tamil Nadu and West Bengal reported similar levels of income poverty (35–6 per cent living below the poverty line), and yet in 1998–9, only 37 per cent of Tamil Nadu's children below 3 years were malnourished as against 49 per cent in West Bengal.

Some people still believe that using international growth

TABLE 2: INCOME POVERTY AND CHILD MALNUTRITION ACROSS INDIAN STATES

| | Percentage of population living below the income poverty line 1993-4 | Weight-for-age percentage of children under 3 years who are moderately and severely malnourished (below 3 SD) 1998-9 |
|---|---|---|
| *Low income poverty, low malnutrition* | | |
| *High income poverty, high malnutrition* | | |
| Goa | 14.9 | 28.6 |
| Bihar | 55.0 | 54.4 |
| *High income poverty, low malnutrition* | | |
| *Low income poverty, high malnutrition* | | |
| Sikkim | 41.4 | 20.6 |
| Andhra Pradesh | 22.2 | 37.7 |
| *Differing income poverty, similar levels of malnutrition* | | |
| Haryana | 25.1 | 34.6 |
| Assam | 40.9 | 36.0 |
| *Similar income poverty, different levels of malnutrition* | | |
| Tamil Nadu | 35.0 | 36.7 |
| West Bengal | 35.7 | 48.7 |

*Sources*: *Economic Survey 1999–2000* and *National Family Health Survey 2.*

standards to assess malnutrition is what explains India's high levels of child malnutrition. It was argued that biologically and genetically, Indian children do not normally grow as fast or as large as children in other countries. This is simply not true. Extensive studies by the Nutrition Foundation of India have established that global standards of height and weight apply to all Indian children as well. And the growth patterns of Indian children who are well-fed and well-looked-after are similar to those of adequately nourished children in other parts of the world, no matter where they are born.

Again, common sense often attributes high levels of malnutrition to the non-availability of food. Nevertheless, there is no predictable relationship between levels of malnutrition and food production within a country. India, for instance, has witnessed an impressive expansion in food production over the years, and it has built up a large buffer stock of food grains. Yet, child malnutrition remains high. The critical element is the way households establish command over food, and how this food is distributed among different members within a household.

In understanding child malnutrition, the focus has to shift from incomes and food availability to an appreciation of how families establish command over food and healthcare, acquire and apply knowledge on child caring and rearing practices, allocate time to look after children, and protect the cleanliness and safety of the environment. Considerable research points out that nutrition and healthy growth are the outcome of three essential factors: accessibility to food within the household, healthcare, and child caring practices. Few would argue over food. It is true that if children do not get food to eat, they will get malnourished. Interventions are needed to address issues of household food and economic security for every member, starting with the child. Similarly, for health, both preventive and curative. It is, however, care which is often the most critical and missing factor that explains the prevalence of child malnutrition despite the availability of food even within the household.

## THE SIGNIFICANCE OF CARE

A major cause for such high rates of child malnutrition is the birth of low-birth-weight babies. Birth weights of less than 2,500 grams are very closely associated with poor growth not just in infancy but throughout childhood. Estimates for India reveal that 20–30 per cent of all babies are born low-birth-weight, suggesting that the child is malnourished in the womb. A major factor adversely affecting the birth of healthy babies is the poor nutritional status of women. Data from the *National Family Health Survey 2* for 1998–9 suggests that more than one-third (36 per cent) of Indian women have a Body Mass Index (BMI) of less than 18.5 kg/m$^2$, indicating a high level of nutritional deficiency. Added

TABLE 3: WOMEN'S AUTONOMY AND CHILD MALNUTRITION IN SIKKIM AND MADHYA PRADESH

| | Sikkim | Madhya Pradesh | India |
|---|---|---|---|
| % of underweight children | 20.6<br>Lowest | 55.1<br>Highest | 47.0 |
| % of women who visit cinema/theatre at least once a week | 19.0 | 7.4 | 10.6 |
| % of women not exposed regularly to any media | 21.5 | 45.2 | 40.3 |
| % of women exposed to family planning messages | 88.0 | 48.9 | 59.9 |
| % of women who do not need permission to visit friends or relatives | 41.6 | 19.5 | 24.4 |
| % of women with access to money | 78.9 | 49.3 | 59.6 |
| Mean age at marriage (years) | 21.9 | 18.9 | 19.7 |

*Sources*: *National Family Health Survey 2, 1998–9*, and *Census of India 2001*.

to this, given the heavy burden of work on most women and the persistent anti-female biases in society, pregnant mothers rarely get adequate attention, care, diet and rest. As a result, the child in the womb is affected, and the birth of a low-birth-weight baby represents an inter-generational transfer of malnutrition.

In general, nutrition of children tends to be better where women enjoy greater freedom and more autonomy. Table 3, for instance, presents comparative data on women's autonomy for Sikkim and Madhya Pradesh, two states reporting the lowest and highest rates of child malnutrition in India. Clearly, women in Sikkim enjoy far greater freedom and autonomy than women in Madhya Pradesh. Women in Sikkim have much more access to money, greater exposure to the media, and more freedom to go out of the house than women in Madhya Pradesh.

The critical relationship between maternal and child nutrition is apparent from an examination of data from Indian states. Table 4 presents selected features of four states reporting the lowest levels, and four states reporting the highest levels of child malnutrition in India. It should not come as a surprise that both sets of states have per capita incomes that are below the national average. And with the exception of Kerala, in both sets of states, income poverty levels are higher than the national average. However, data reveal that the proportion of low-birth-weight babies born in the low malnutrition states is strikingly less than the proportion of such babies born in

TABLE 4: CHILD MALNUTRITION AND RELATED FEATURES ACROSS SELECTED INDIAN STATES

| | Weight-for-age percentage of children under 3 years who are moderately and severely malnourished (below 3 SD) 1998–9 | Percentage of children below 5 years who were weighed at birth and found to be of low birth weight 2000 | Percentage of ever-married women with Body Mass Index (BMI) below 18.5 kg/m$^2$ 1998–9 | Percentage of population living below the income poverty line 1993–4 | Per capita net State Domestic Product at current prices Rs. 1996–7 |
|---|---|---|---|---|---|
| | (1) | (2) | (3) | (4) | (5) |
| *Low malnutrition states* | | | | | |
| 1 Sikkim | 20.6 | 13.1 | 11.2 | 41.4 | 9,472* |
| 2 Nagaland | 24.1 | 7.1 | 18.4 | 37.9 | 11,174 |
| 3 Arunachal Pradesh | 24.3 | 13.6 | 10.7 | 39.4 | 12,032 |
| 4 Kerala | 26.9 | 16.0 | 18.7 | 25.4 | 10,309 |
| *High malnutrition states* | | | | | |
| 1 Uttar Pradesh | 51.7 | 30.3 | 35.8 | 40.9 | 6,713 |
| 2 Bihar | 54.4 | 20.6 | 39.3 | 55.0 | 4,231 |
| 3 Orissa | 54.4 | 26.2 | 48.0 | 48.6 | 5,893 |
| 4 Madhya Pradesh | 55.1 | 24.1 | 38.2 | 42.5 | 7,571 |
| *India* | 47.0 | 21.8 | 35.8 | 36.0 | 12,099 |

*Sources*: *National Family Health Survey 2* for columns (1) and (3), UNICEF MICS 2000 for column (2), Planning Commission (2000) for columns (4) and (5).

*Note*: *Relates to 1995–6.

the high malnutrition states. In fact, the four low malnutrition states rank among the top 5 of the 25 states and 6 union territories in terms of the proportion of low-birth-weight babies born in India. Uttar Pradesh, on the other hand, reports one of the highest proportions of low-birth-weight babies born in India.

The levels of chronic nutritional deficiency among ever-married women are significantly lower in the low child malnutrition states than in the high nutrition states. The four low malnutrition states rank among the top 6 of the 25 states in terms of chronic nutritional deficiency among ever-married women. Orissa, on the other hand, reports the highest levels of chronic nutritional deficiency among ever-married women.

Another factor closely related to child malnutrition is care of the child. Infants have very small stomachs and must be fed frequently. Breast milk provides vital nutrients throughout the first year of life, but breast milk alone is not sufficient. The energy and calories needed for healthy growth can come only from additional food. Beyond 4 to 6 months, infants must be given solid foods to supplement breast milk. Recent data from the *National Family Health Survey 2* suggests that only around a third (33.5 per cent) of children 6–9 months receive solid and mushy foods to supplement breastfeeding. It is, therefore, not surprising that a child typically becomes malnourished between 6 months and 18 months of age, and remains so thereafter. In most cases, nutritional rehabilitation is difficult.

Table 5 shows the strong association that exists between the

TABLE 5: INFANT FEEDING HABITS AND CHILD MALNUTRITION

| | *Weight-for-age* Percentage of children under 3 years who are moderately and severely malnourished (below 3 SD) 1998–9 | | *Infant feeding habits* Percentage of children 6–9 months who receive breast-milk and solid/mushy food | |
|---|---|---|---|---|
| | | Rank out of 25 states | | Rank out of 25 states |
| | (1) | (2) | (3) | (4) |
| *Low malnutrition states* | | | | |
| 1 Sikkim | 20.6 | 1 | 87.3 | 1 |
| 2 Nagaland | 24.1 | 2 | 81.3 | 3 |
| 3 Arunachal Pradesh | 24.3 | 3 | 60.2* | 9 |
| 4 Kerala | 26.9 | 4 | 72.9 | 5 |
| *High malnutrition states* | | | | |
| 5 Uttar Pradesh | 51.7 | 22 | 17.3 | 24 |
| 6 Bihar | 54.4 | 23 | 15.0 | 25 |
| 7 Orissa | 54.4 | 24 | 30.1 | 21 |
| 8 Madhya Pradesh | 55.1 | 25 | 27.3 | 22 |
| *India* | 47.0 | | 33.5 | |

*Source*: *National Family Health Survey 2, 1998–9.*
*Note*: * Based on 25–49 unweighted cases.

introduction of food supplements and child malnutrition. It reveals that a significantly higher proportion of children between 6–9 months receives solid and mushy foods to supplement breast milk in low than in high child malnutrition states. Sikkim, the state reporting the lowest levels of child malnutrition in India, is also the state where the highest proportion of children between 6–9 months (87 per cent) receives solid and mushy foods to supplement breast milk. On the other hand, in the four poor nutrition states, only 15–30 per cent of infants between 6–9 months are given solid and mushy foods.

However, even in regions where infants between 6–9 months are given solid and mushy food to supplement breast milk, proper understanding and caring practices offer the clue to improved child nutrition. Adults and parents do not deliberately deprive infants of solid foods and adequate nutrition. They just do not think about it. Alternatively, they may not know what is in the best interest of the child. Infants at that age do not eat—they need to be fed. In some cases, mothers largely responsible for infant care may not have the luxury of time to feed infants; and so may be forced to leave the babies to the care of elder siblings who simply may not have the patience to handle a child.

## THE NUTRITION-EDUCATION LINKAGE

Reinforcing the critical role of information and knowledge is the strong inverse relationship that exists between levels of women's malnutrition and schooling. Chronic energy deficiency, as Figure 1 reveals, is more than twice as high among illiterate women than it is among those who have completed their high school education.

Similarly, there is a strong inverse relationship between child malnutrition and mother's schooling. Malnutrition among Indian children below 3 years born to illiterate mothers (55 per cent) is more than twice the levels reported among mothers who have completed high school (27 per cent).

Even at the state level, there is a strong correlation between child malnutrition and women's literacy. The higher the level of women's literacy, the lower is the extent of child malnutrition in the state. Regression analysis suggests that close to 42 per cent of the inter-state variation in child malnutrition can be explained by differentials in female literacy rates.[2]

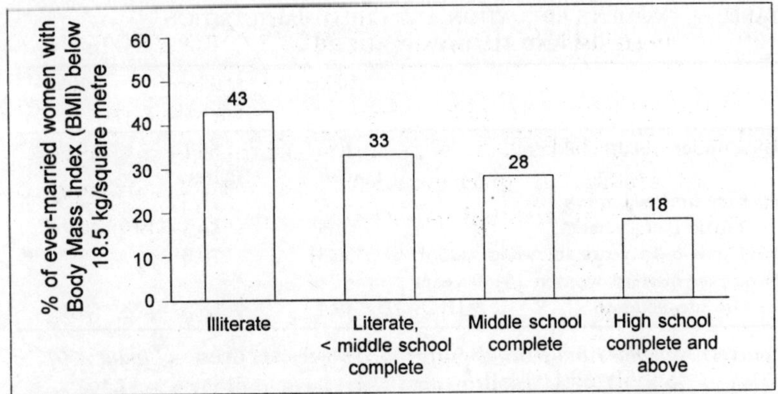


FIG. 1: CHRONIC ENERGY DEFICIENY AND WOMEN'S EDUCATION IN INDIA, 1998-9.

*Source*: *National Family Health Survey 2.*

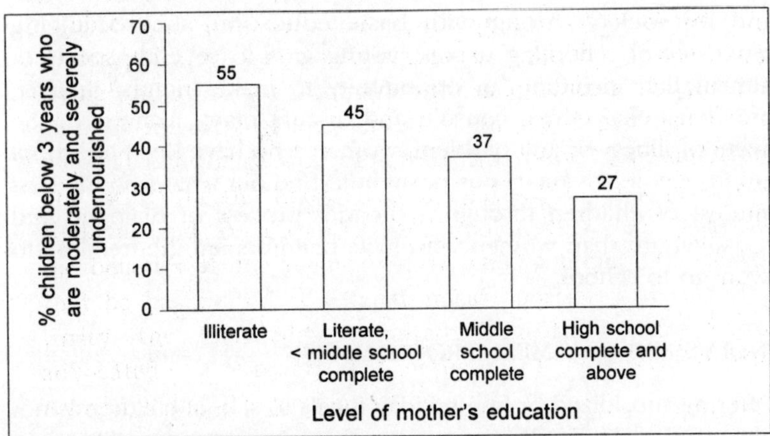


FIG. 2: MOTHER'S EDUCATION AND CHILD MALNUTRITION IN INDIA, 1998-9.

*Source*: *National Family Health Survey 2.*

The importance of literacy and schooling becomes even more evident when we look at the differences between Sikkim and Madhya Pradesh. Close to 83 per cent of girls between 6–17 years attend school in Sikkim. The proportion is only 63 per cent in Madhya Pradesh.

The pathways of influence between women's education and nutritional well-being could be many. Better educated women tend to be better informed, they enjoy better opportunities for employment, they tend to be less superstitious, and they seek out

TABLE 6: WOMEN'S EDUCATION AND CHILD MALNUTRITION IN SIKKIM AND MADHYA PRADESH

| | Sikkim | Madhya Pradesh | India |
|---|---|---|---|
| % of under-weight children | 20.6<br>Lowest | 55.1<br>Highest | 47.0 |
| *Literacy and education* | | | |
| Female literacy rate* | 61.5 | 50.3 | 54.2 |
| % of girls 6–14 years attending school | 88.5 | 70.8 | 73.7 |
| % of ever-married women 15–49 years who are illiterate | 49.4 | 68.5 | 58.2 |

*Sources*: *National Family Health Survey 2, 1998–9* and **Census of India 2001.*

modern healthcare and advice much more readily than less educated women. Educated women also tend to have a greater say in decision making within the household, they enjoy greater self-esteem, and are treated more equally within the household and by society. Along with basic education, the socializing processes of schooling expose young girls to several aspects of human life, including an opportunity to make friends, interact, broaden perspectives, consult, and discuss many matters. In the event of illness or any problem, women who have been to school are in a more advantageous position to find out what is in the best interest of children through a broader process of dialogue and consultations than women who have been denied the freedom to even go to school.

## INDIA'S MID-DAY MEAL PROGRAMMES

Offering subsidized or free midday meals to school-children is not new in India. The Corporation of Madras introduced such a programme in 1925. Kerala introduced a school lunch programme in 1941, Mumbai (Bombay) announced a free midday meal scheme in 1942, and the Corporation of Bangalore in 1946. In 1953, Uttar Pradesh too introduced a similar programme.[3] Providing meals in schools has existed in different forms in Tamil Nadu and Lakshadweep since 1956, in Pondicherry since 1960, in Goa since 1967, in West Bengal since 1977, in Chandigarh since 1980, and in Gujarat since 1984. However, it was only in 1995 that the Mid-Day Meal scheme was introduced uniformly in all states and union territories. Called the National Programme for Nutritional Support to Primary Education (NP-NSPE) and popularly known as the 'Mid-Day Meals

Scheme', the objectives of the programme were 'to give a boost to universalisation of primary education by increasing enrolment, retention and attendance and simultaneously impacting on nutrition of students in primary classes'.

The programme was intended to cover in a phased manner, starting from 1995–6, all government, local body, and government-aided primary schools in all States and Union Territories. Envisaging the serving of hot cooked meals with a calorific value equivalent to 100 g of wheat or rice per student per school day, the central government extended the following assistance.

1. Free-of-cost food grains (wheat and rice) equivalent to 100 g per child per school where cooked or processed hot meal is being served and 3 kg per student per month subject to a minimum attendance of 80 per cent where food grains are being distributed.
2. Reimbursement of costs of transportation through district authorities for movement of food grains from Food Corporation of India (FCI) godowns to the schools at actual costs subject to a maximum of Rs. 50 per quintal. In addition, a Hill Transport Subsidy is provided to the states through the FCI as with the Public Distribution System in the case of hilly areas.
3. The cost of conversion of food grains into hot cooked meals and its distribution to schools is to be met by the states and union territories.

Today, only Gujarat, Kerala, Orissa, Tamil Nadu, Madhya Pradesh (confined to tribal areas) and Pondicherry are serving hot cooked meals. Delhi serves ready-to-eat food. In 1996–7, Haryana and Jammu & Kashmir switched from providing cooked meals to distribution of food grains. All other states and union territories are presently distributing food grains: rice or wheat.

## ASSESSING THE IMPACT OF MDM PROGRAMMES

Even though the programme was initiated nationwide only in 1995, evidence with respect to school feeding programmes in India is extremely encouraging.[4] Most significant are the reported increases in the enrolment of girls, and the benefits that accrue to children belonging to Scheduled Castes, Scheduled Tribes and Other Backward Castes.

According to the *Public Report on Basic Education in India* (*PROBE*) survey in north Indian states, most teachers felt that school meals have boosted school attendance—a view shared by parents as well. Many children reaffirmed the incentive that it offers to them to go to school (they enjoy a free meal) and to be seen as making a useful contribution to their families.

Mid-day meals have had a definite effect on girls' enrolment. In a recent survey, almost all schools (95 per cent) in Tamil Nadu reported that the noon-meal programmes has helped in increasing enrolment and retention of girls. In some other states, the proportion of girls not going to school declined by as much as 50 per cent when the local schools provided meals.

District surveys in Uttar Pradesh point to acceleration in enrolment rates for all children following the announcement of the scheme. School enrolment of children belonging to Scheduled Castes, Scheduled Tribes, and Other Backward Castes in Uttar Pradesh has gone up. In Tamil Nadu, all children eat and share the same meal regardless of who cooks it or who serves the meal. The concerns of caste and class simply seem to have disappeared from the noon meal programmes.

Some qualifying remarks are in order when assessing the impact of school feeding programmes.

First, there are several reasons why millions of Indian children do not go to school, or why they drop out. The Probe Team (1999), for instance, lists many factors that prevent children from going to school. These include high costs, poor quality, unattractive teaching methods, and lack of proper infrastructure in schools. In such a context, offering food alone cannot ensure universal schooling. The report also talks of the 'discouragement effect'—a feeling among parents that teachers are not able to guide children properly, and that even at the end of five years of schooling, children learn very little. At the same time, the reluctance of children to go to school is also another important factor. Typically, children find schools far from exciting, they are often punished and beaten, and worse still, many are humiliated, discriminated against and treated unequally. Of all these factors, high costs do emerge as a significant factor preventing many parents from sending their children to school. Offering meals in school specially for poor families and for all children is surely an incentive for enrolling them in school.

Second, one of the most impressive gains in recent years has been the sharp increase in school enrolment and attendance rates across all states. And more important is the narrowing of gender gaps in school attendance rates. According to the *National Family Health Survey 2*, for instance, in 1998–9, close to 83 per cent of boys and 74 per cent of girls between 6–14 years were attending school. In urban areas, the proportion was as high as 89 per cent for boys and 86 per cent for girls. Some 81 per cent of boys and 70 per cent of girls between 6–14 years were attending school in rural India. The lowest rates of female school attendance were reported by Bihar (54 per cent), Rajasthan (63 per cent), Uttar Pradesh (69 per cent), Madhya Pradesh, and Andhra Pradesh (both 71 per cent). 90 per cent or more of girls between 6–14 years were attending school in Delhi, Himachal Pradesh, Kerala, Punjab, and Mizoram. Many factors including a rising awareness among parents of the importance of education, increased investments in primary schooling, improvements in school and physical infrastructure, rising incomes, increased participation by the community, political decentralization and greater empowerment of women could have contributed to this increase in school attendance over the years. While it is true that serving food helps to increase school enrolment and attendance, how much of the increased enrolment can be attributed to school feeding programmes is a difficult question to answer.

Third, school feeding programmes in India can play only a limited role in pulling children out of work situations and making their parents enrol them in school. The roots of child labour lie to an extent in food insecurity within the household, but very often bonded child labour is more intimately connected to economic insecurity and serious indebtedness. Many children are forced to work to clear the debts of their parents and families. And school feeding programmes may offer only a very small benefit to enable families to get out of a situation of bondage.

Fourth, the nutritional benefits of school feeding programmes are difficult to assess. Much will depend upon both the quantity and quality of food provided to students. Some parents tend to believe that the school meal is a substitute, and not a supplement, for regular food. Consequently, they may be depriving the child of much-needed food at home. In a majority of Indian states where children get food grains instead of a hot cooked meal, it is not at all clear how much of this food is actually consumed by the child. To that extent, assessing the nutritional gains becomes meaningless. Finally, if school meals are provided only on the 186-odd working days of the year, its usefulness as a nutritional intervention is considerably reduced.

Nevertheless, there is increasing evidence to suggest that many benefits of MDM schemes are beginning to accrue, specially to the more disadvantaged children of India. This is indeed a positive sign given the ground reality of how many of the states are implementing the MDM programmes.

## THE GROUND REALITY OF MID-DAY MEAL SCHEMES

The number of children covered under the MDM scheme has gone up from 33.4 million in 1995–6 to 105.1 million in 2000–1. Today, close to 7,92,000 schools are included under the national programme. Yet, following features point to the need for beefing up political and administrative support for the MDM scheme, the effective implementation of which is vital for India's children.

First, almost six years after the announcement of the MDM programme, many states have unfortunately not introduced school meals. They have instead put in place a scheme of 'dry rations' whereby children receive monthly grain rations (3 kg per child) to make up for not providing cooked food. The rations are intended for children with at least 80 per cent attendance, but in practice, most teachers distribute it to all children. The 'dry ration' scheme defeats the very purpose of the school meal programme. It encourages enrolment rather than attendance. In terms of the nutrition and socialization arguments, offering 'dry rations' is utterly useless.

Second, the lack of enthusiasm by the state governments is reflected in the declining proportion of allocated food grains that are lifted by the states. Between 1995–6 and 1999–2000, the proportion of food allocated by the central government lifted by states fell from 75 to 51 per cent (Fig. 3). Many reasons including lack of financial resources, inadequate staffing to implement the midday meal schemes, and logistical difficulties of dealing with the Food Corporation of India are cited for the inability of the states to lift their allocations.

Third, the financial situation of most states is worsening every year. As a result, most of them are cutting back resource allocations for the midday meal programmes.

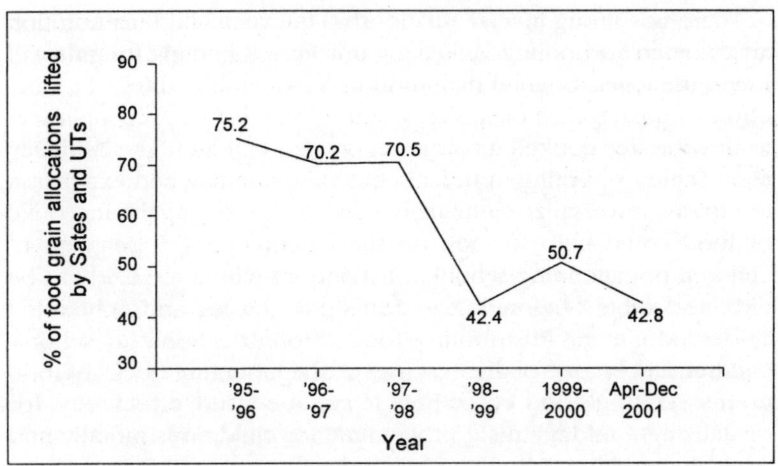


FIG. 3: LIFTING OF FOOD GRAINS ALLOCATED BY THE CENTRAL GOVERNMENT BY STATES.

*Source*: Ministry of Human Resources Development.

## CONCLUDING REMARKS

This paper highlights the importance of care for preventing child malnutrition and argues for making school feeding programmes central to the State's efforts to universalize elementary education—a vital requisite in turn for ending malnutrition in the country.

Tackling child malnutrition requires that careful attention be paid to ensuring proper access to food, health services, a healthy environment and care to all children in the country. In addition to addressing issues of household food and economic security, the most vital intervention has to do with altering feeding and caring practices of children. Behavioural changes call for concerted efforts to improve the knowledge levels of parents and siblings on the nutritional requirement of young children. It is necessary to focus attention on the young child between 0–3 years, and interact intensively with mothers and other child care providers to convince them of the need to introduce supplementary foods at the appropriate time. Given how little infants eat at this stage, it is often not food availability within the household, but lack of knowledge on what to feed, and how to care for the child that makes a difference. Sustained advocacy, supported by health care and food supplements where needed, can bring about dramatic improvements in levels of child nutrition.

There is a strong inverse relationship between child malnutrition and women's schooling. Achieving universal schooling for girls will lower the levels of child malnutrition considerably. Integral to any effort to universalize elementary education must be a commitment to provide free cooked meals in schools for children. The 'Mid-Day Meal Scheme' existing in India needs strengthening and expansion to rapidly universalize elementary education. Offering the incentive of food could help to mop up the remaining 20–5 per cent of children not attending school, a majority of whom are likely to be girls and others belonging to Scheduled Castes and Scheduled Tribes. Moreover, distributing food through schools to school-children can be one of the best uses of the mounting stocks of food grains. Letting food rot when it can be used effectively for revitalizing a midday meal programme for children is morally and ethically revolting. Also, at a time when many parts of the country are reeling under the threat of drought, distributing food through schools may well be the most effective way of protecting the food security of many poor households.

Many possibilities of collaboration exist for implementing a scheme of serving hot cooked meals in schools. Flexibility and innovation need to be combined with effective partnerships and collaborations to meet the different requirements within India. Experience suggests that decentralized management, handing over of funds to local bodies for purchase of requirements, and integrating the serving of food with interventions in health, education, nutrition and water and sanitation yield the best results. Any school feeding programme must also contain an effective information, education and communication component that helps students learn the significance of hygiene, nutrition and other healthy practices.

School feeding programmes, however, need to be well managed and administered. Managers and policy makers need to discuss and agree on *what* problems the school feeding programme will address, *who* the programme will serve, and *which* programme forms are most feasible for implementation, so that effective ways could be devised for achieving universal schooling, addressing the problems of malnutrition and improving food and economic security. Other considerations need to be discussed, specially those relating to targeting and coverage, costs and financing, timing of meals, programme implementation, monitoring and evaluation.[5]

## NOTES

1. See UNICEF (1995).
2. Running a regression yields the following equation: Child malnutrition = 63.9 – 0.43 female literacy 15–49 years; statistic for literacy coefficient = –4.1; $R^2$ = 0.42 and n = 25 states.
3. References have been obtained from the Inaugural Address by Smt. Achala Moulik, Secretary, Elementary Education and Literacy at the workshop on Midday Meal programmes on 15 March 2001.
4. See, for instance, the evidence and discussions in The Probe Team (1999), *Public Report on Basic Education in India*, Oxford University Press, New Delhi; Operations Research Group (1999), 'Evaluation Study to Assess the Efficiency and Effectiveness of the National Programme for Nutritional Support to Primary Education in Ten States of India', Final report submitted to UNICEF, India, New Delhi; Giri Institute of Development Studies, Lucknow (2000), 'National Programme of Nutritional Support to Primary Education (Midday Meals): Comparative Lessons of Experience in Uttar Pradesh and Himachal Pradesh', study sponsored by the Planning Commission; and Nabakrushna Choudhry Centre for Development Studies, Bhubaneswar (2000), 'A Comparative Study of Nutritional Support to Primary Education (Midday Meals Scheme) in Orissa and Tamil Nadu', study sponsored by the Planning Commission.
5. For a useful discussion on these aspects of programme administration, see Joy Miller del Rosso (1999), 'School Feeding Programs: Improving Effectiveness and Increasing the Benefit to Education—A Guide for Program Managers', The Partnership for Child Development, The World Bank: Food and Nutrition Policy: Best Practices/Toolkits at http://wbln0018.worldbank.

# 15. Improving the Effectiveness of ICDS to Fight Malnutrition

*Meera Chatterjee*

The Integrated Child Development Services (ICDS), a centrally sponsored scheme of the Government of India, is over 25 years old. Over the years, the programme has grown to encompass an estimated 25.8 million children and 5.2 million Pregnant or Lactating Women (PLW), and to spend about Rs. 1,560 crore annually (all 1999–2000 figures). 'Encompass' rather than 'cover', because one of the questions surrounding ICDS has always been: How well do its services actually reach its target population? This question has a significant bearing on ICDS' role in fighting malnutrition in the country. The programme originally intended to cover all children and PLW within its project areas, but, over time, its target population has been redefined for different services. For example, supplementary feeding is now provided only for about 40 per cent of the population of 6-month to 6-year-olds and PLW. Nevertheless, the programme's scale and expenditure are large, and its estimated annual per capita cost of approximately Rs. 500 per beneficiary is high by any standards in the country or even the world.[1]

But ICDS is also ambitious in its scope—no other programme in the world attempts to provide maternal and young child health care, nutrition support, health and nutrition education, and early childhood education in an integrated manner, much less through one village-level worker assisted by one 'multi-village' Multi-Purpose Health Worker, under one roof. When ICDS was started in 1975, it was already well-known that supplementary feeding alone did not improve young child nutritional status. Malnutrition was recognized as a complex phenomenon that needed to be addressed by attention to child health in general. It was also believed that mothers' health, nutrition and knowledge were powerful determinants of child health and nutrition, and thereby needed improvement. Further, it was thought that health and nutrition services should be provided in a centre-based mode, which then also offered the opportunity to stimulate the cognitive development of young children. Hence, ICDS developed its integrated package of six services: supplementary nutrition, simple health measures including immunization, health check-ups, and referral (for all children as well as PLW), health and nutrition education for mothers, and pre-school education for 3–6 year-olds. These services are still the core of the programme today.

## NEED FOR AN INTEGRATED CARE

There has been much debate on this integrated model. Is it really possible in the context of the Indian village, tribal area or urban slum to deliver all these services to those at risk of malnutrition, through two briefly-trained workers? How well is this being done? Is it effective? Many of us—policy makers, implementers, practitioners, academicians, or public-spirited citizens—still believe in the approach. Fortunately, international scientific and policy circles also continue to recognize the multiple vulnerabilities of children and women in poor regions, and hence the need for integrated care. The life-cycle and intergenerational approaches to women and child health that are embodied in the 'ICDS Plus' programme have increasingly gained currency. The ICDS can be said to have stood the test of 'scientific time', as well as to be up-to-date in terms of development thought because it is a participatory and equity-oriented programme. It is community-based, targeted at the poorest areas and families, and 'gender friendly' since it aims to at least partially redress the heavier burden of ill health among women and is largely implemented by women workers. Is the high cost of the programme justified by the supposed benefits of this comprehensive approach?

Unfortunately, despite its development soundness, broad scope, high expenditure, vast scale and the political support it has enjoyed (it has survived, virtually unaltered, and expanded through several changes of government at the centre since 1975), ICDS has had insufficient impact on the problem of child malnutrition in the country. With the data from the latest round of the National Family Health Survey (NFHS-2)[2] we can construct the following picture of women and child malnutrition in India.

1. Almost half (47 pre cent) of children under 3 years of age are underweight (i.e. below their expected weight-for-age by more than two standard deviations, 2 SD); 18 per cent are severely underweight (i.e. below their expected weight-for-age by more than 3 SD). Low weight-for-age results from both chronic and acute malnutrition. The proportion of children underweight increases dramatically in the second year of life (59 per cent of 12–23-month-olds are low weight-for-age), and remains high in the third year (58 per cent).
2. Similarly, almost half (46 per cent) of children under 3 are stunted (i.e. below their expected height-for-age by more than 2 SD). Stunting occurs due to chronic undernourishment. Stunting among girl children may result in low adult height and small pelvic size, features that predispose women to high-risk pregnancies as they are associated with obstetric difficulties, premature and/or low-birth-weight infants (see below), and maternal mortality.
3. Sixteen per cent of children under 3 are wasted (i.e. below their expected weight-for-height by more than 2 SD). Wasting is a sign of acute undernourishment.
4. Almost three-quarters (74 per cent) of children aged 6 months to 3 years suffer from anaemia, and over half (51 per cent) have moderate or severe anaemia. In addition to poor diets, anaemia is caused by intestinal parasitism, which can be simply treated. Anaemia in children is associated with lassitude and learning difficulties.
5. More than one-third (36 per cent) of women aged 15–49 years in the country suffer from chronic energy deficiency (measured by Body Mass Index, BMI);[3] the proportion is higher in the states of Bihar (39 per cent), Maharashtra (40 per cent), West Bengal (44 per cent) and Orissa (48 per cent).
6. Over half (52 per cent) of women suffer from anaemia: about one-third of these have a moderate or severe form; although anaemia is higher among illiterate women (56 per cent) and those with a low 'standard of living' (60 per cent) it is still very significant among women with a high standard of living (42 per cent) and those who have completed high school (40 per cent). These are very high levels of adult undernutrition and anaemia, particularly when one considers that a high proportion of poor women in India are manual labourers.

7. Among pregnant women, 28 per cent have moderate or severe anemia, another condition that is associated closely with the birth of underweight babies. Low Birth Weight (LBW) is a disadvantage from which children may not emerge, as the extra nutrition they require for 'catch-up growth' may be unavailable to families whose mothers are undernourished. The LBW infant usually continues on an inadequate growth path in childhood, and is likely to be counted eventually among malnourished adults, completing the 'vicious cycle of malnutrition'.
8. Malnutrition is widespread: more than 20 per cent of children in every state of the country are underweight, and more than half of children in every state except Kerala, Manipur and Nagaland are anaemic. A new configuration of 'BIMARU'—which we might call 'bowrumama'!—emerges from the NFHS-2 data on child malnourishment. The states with the highest prevalence of underweight, stunted and wasted children under 3 are: Bihar, Orissa, West Bengal, Rajasthan, Uttar Pradesh, Madhya Pradesh and Maharashtra. All have malnourishment rates above the national average.
9. Malnutrition is a serious phenomenon in both rural and urban areas: half of rural children and 38 per cent of urban ones are underweight.
10. Improvement in child nutritional status since 1992–3 (NFHS-1) has been small. For example, the percentage of children underweight dropped from 52 to 47 only during the six-year period, and of those severely underweight, from 20 per cent to 18 per cent only. At these rates of change, it would take about 56 years to eliminate moderate and severe malnutrition among Indian children!

The NFHS-2 also gives us information on the reach of some services that aim to address some of the problems listed above. For example:

1. Only 58 per cent of mothers received iron-folate supplements during their last pregnancy (in the three years preceding the survey); the coverage was as low as 24 per cent in Bihar, 32 per cent in UP and 39 per cent in Rajasthan.
2. Only 30 per cent of children between 1 and 3 years of age had received at least one dose of vitamin A: 10 per cent,

14 per cent and 15 per cent in the states of Bihar, UP and Assam respectively. It is of interest that coverage was only 16 per cent in Tamil Nadu, the state that is world-renowned for pioneering work on the epidemiology and treatment of avitaminosis A and its ocular manifestations, for eye treatment facilities in general, and for its Integrated Nutrition Programme (INP)!

3. The potentially greater reach of the health system (public and private combined) is demonstrated by immunization coverage figures: 72 per cent, 63 per cent and 55 per cent of children were vaccinated with Bacillus of Calmette and Guerin (BCG), 3 doses of Polio, and 3 doses of Diphtheria, Pertussis, Tetanus (DPT), respectively. However, only 42 per cent were fully immunized (including measles vaccine).

Health and nutrition education efforts in the country, which include those of ICDS, also appear to have had limited effect. The NFHS-2 reports the following practices which have a direct bearing on the nutritional status of children.

1. Only 16 per cent of children are breastfed within an hour of birth, and only 37 per cent on the first day. Starting breastfeeding immediately after birth is one of the most important messages that health education programmes should give mothers about child nutrition.
2. Two-thirds of mothers discard the first milk before breastfeeding their infants. The colostrum is rich in proteins that protect the newborn from disease and aid growth, and hence this practice must be discouraged by health and nutrition education programmes.
3. Forty-three per cent of mothers do not follow the correct practice of exclusive breastfeeding for at least three months, thus exposing their infants early to infections.
4. Fifty per cent of mothers do not begin appropriate complementary feeding even when their infants are 9 months old. Delayed introduction of solid foods is also associated with the inadequate growth of young children. The combination of inadequate immuno-protection, gastrointestinal infections and late complementary feeding results in the significant increase in malnutrition in the second year of life, that was noted above.

## IMPACT ON NUTRITION

Some might argue that the NFHS data represent the country as a whole[4] and that ICDS could not be expected to change the entire nutrition landscape since it expanded only gradually during the first 10 years of its existence, it does not yet cover the entire country, and, in any case, it does not address the root causes of poverty (such as lack of employment and income) which are also the basic causes of malnutrition. Indeed, we have written at length elsewhere that the achievement of National Nutrition Goals (NNG) by 2010 would require concerted efforts on several fronts including improvement of overall food security at the household level, and development of leadership and institutional capacity to plan and manage nutrition programmes.[5] Nevertheless, we must not derive illusory comfort by pointing elsewhere. A programme that started 25 years ago in the most backward blocks of the country, targeted at the poorest and aiming to change nutrition-related behaviour should have had a significant impact on the country's child nutrition profile. In the absence of robust new data, we are left with earlier evaluations, surveys and micro-studies,[6] the majority of which show that the programme had only a weak impact on nutritional status, even where it was in existence for some time. The main problems affecting ICDS that have a bearing on its ineffectiveness in reducing malnutrition are:

1. Lack of attention to the very young child (0–2-year-olds), particularly to their proper feeding in the home and early treatment of infections. The programme has failed to use growth monitoring as an effective means of counselling mothers. This is due to inadequate training of workers, and also to confusion among programme planners who promoted the tool mainly as a way to target food rations and amass nutrition data.
2. Inadequacy of services to pregnant/lactating women, including early care, effective anaemia prophylaxis, food supplementation, treatment of infections, and health-nutrition education.
3. Insufficiency of food supplementation, while promoting feeding as a 'hand-out' rather than as a means of demonstrating proper feeding practices. Throughout the programme's history, food supplements have failed to cover those who

are most in need of them, and the recommended quantities are inadequate to close the caloric gap of the poorest.

4. Poor training of *anganwadi* and health workers, particularly in nutrition, at programme inception as well as in service, and lack of coordination and supportive supervision over them.
5. Inadequate community involvement in the programme, which has stymied demand as well as supply-side improvements.

Given the persisting high levels of malnutrition and our goal of a hunger-free India, we must ask how these problems can be rectified to improve ICDS' impact on malnutrition. What programme changes must be made, and where should resources be deployed to maximize impact? Some changes may be necessitated by constraints in resources—we must be realistic in forecasting the funds that would be provided for ICDS, the availability of appropriate person-power, and management capabilities to deliver this multifaceted programme. The remainder of this paper is devoted to describing three critical strategies on which I would put my—and the country's—money to improve the effectiveness of ICDS. These are:

1. Enhancing the access of the poor and biologically most vulnerable to the programme, especially to key nutritional inputs;
2. Improving the quality of services, particularly of training in nutrition and coordination with the health services to care for those nutritionally at risk; and
3. Decentralizing the programme to the lowest level capable of performing a particular task, including considerably enhanced community management.

## THE SOLUTIONS

### BUT FIRST, A CAVEAT: IMPROVE QUALITY BEFORE FURTHER EXPANSION

The ICDS extends to about 4,300 blocks and city slums, equivalent to about 76 per cent of the country's 5,652 rural and tribal blocks and urban wards. Targeting to the poorest blocks has been reasonably good, as discussed in a previous paper which elucidated this issue based on an analysis of the blocks covered and a field study.[7] Given this positive situation, and the need for quality improvements and decentralization, the programme should be frozen at its current size. At least the next three years—and possibly five—should be devoted to enhancing effectiveness as described below.[8] The unspent funds sanctioned for expansion during the Ninth Plan and appropriate allocations in the Tenth Plan should be used to improve the programme in existing blocks. Side by side, a review should be carried out to determine whether the 'uncovered' blocks are very disadvantaged or have particularly poor areas that need ICDS services. If so, these should be given priority during future expansion. The review should investigate the socio-economic status of the population and their access to good nutrition, healthcare and pre-school education to determine whether they need ICDS at all, whether needs are confined to specific villages, particular services, and so on. With economic growth and the expansion of education in the country, it is quite possible that these better-off blocks would need only a truncated version of ICDS. Based on the information obtained, appropriate locale-specific strategies should be evolved for covering the needy areas, with implementation beginning three or four years hence.

## ENHANCING ACCESS OF THE POOR TO ICDS: FOCUS ON THE POOR

In the existing project blocks, quality improvement should begin with a rationalization of available resources and enhancements to ensure that services reach those most in need of them. While the study mentioned above showed that block selection has favoured the poor, this was not the case within blocks nor within *anganwadi* catchment areas.[9] A significant proportion of poor (35 per cent) was consistently left out of the programme on account of planning norms or procedures, staff practices, social or physical barriers. Additional poor households were served only sporadically because of other constraints such as mothers' time, lack of awareness, and so on. These excluded families may account for most of the malnutrition that remains unprevented, undetected and/or untreated by ICDS. Thus, rationalization/enhancements in existing blocks would include ensuring the (re)location of *anganwadis* in all poor villages/hamlets, and reorientation of

*Anganwadi* Workers (AWW) to focus on the poorest in their catchment populations when delivering services.

There is strong evidence that among those covered by ICDS (i.e. those with actual access to an *anganwadi*), the poor use the services to a greater extent than do the better-off—they are more dependent on them as they lack suitable alternatives.[10] The poor also use a wider range of *anganwadi* services, while the better-off are more selective.[11] This information suggests that self-targeting and community selection processes are also at work, and could assist purposeful efforts on the part of the programme to focus on the poor. The better-off simply need not be covered by the programme, and the resources saved should be reallocated to the poor.

Improvements in intra-village targeting and effective resource use can be brought about by systematic identification within *anganwadi* areas of families at risk of malnutrition, and systematic follow-up of their young children and pregnant women to ensure that they obtain the services they need. The *anganwadi* worker needs to be given this mandate clearly, and to be supported by supervisory staff as well as by widespread public education on the objectives of ICDS, on who its most important clients are, and so on. Public education must fulfil the dual goals of creating genuine demand among the poor for ICDS services and of ensuring that public pressure is put on service providers to cater to the needy. The 'needy' may be different for different services, in different locations.[12] Enhancing programme efforts to cover the poorest must also take into account the difficulties they face utilizing the services as currently designed or delivered. For example, mothers who leave their homes to work as daily labourers often cannot use the services themselves or for their children because of *anganwadi* timings and/or distances. Hence, targeting the poor requires taking into account local situations and preferences, which may vary by service. In general, there is a major need to target the food available in ICDS to families most at risk of malnutrition, and to the neediest villages and blocks—as mentioned above, quantities available are insufficient to serve everyone.

Within project blocks as a whole, rationalization can be effected and the need for enhancements identified through proper micro-planning. Every block should be encouraged to investigate the nature of its uncovered habitations and make creative recommendations for their coverage, as well as for improved coverage of habitations that already have *anganwadis*, with at least the basic mother-child health and nutrition services focused on the very young (0–2-year-old) child (see below). The block staff should work with the local communities and draw in others as needed to identify how antenatal and post-natal care will be provided to all pregnant women, how infants will be weighed at birth and given special care if LBW, how young children will be fully immunized, and how mothers will be provided counselling for child nutrition care, and food rations where these are necessary and acceptable. Additional *anganwadis* or mini-*anganwadis* should be sanctioned on the basis of this comprehensive plan, and wherever *anganwadis* are not serving an important need, they should be relocated or closed down.

## IMPROVING THE QUALITY OF SERVICES

The crux of improving the impact of ICDS on nutritional status is improving the quality of nutrition-related services. There are many dimensions to quality improvement, of which only the most significant will be discussed here.

### COORDINATE CARE FOR THE BIOLOGICALLY VULNERABLE

The ICDS must be reoriented to focus on the biologically most vulnerable, viz., children from birth to 2 years of age, and pregnant/lactating women.[13] It is widely acknowledged that the programme does not cater to these groups as well as it should, nor even to the extent that it reaches 3–6 year-olds. The very young child and mother form a 'mother-child dyad' that must be approached together, which is best done *within the home*. They need a relatively limited number of services. ICDS can—and must—get better at its outreach function ('home visits') to provide these services on a once-a-week basis. The reach, quality and timeliness of services depend highly on proper coordination between the *anganwadi* worker and health worker [Auxiliary Nurse Midwife (ANM) or Multi-Purpose Worker (MPW)] and Primary Health Centre doctor. The AWW and ANM/MPW already have the 'tools' to focus their joint and separate attention on these vulnerable groups: health check-ups for mothers and 0–2s, immunization, weighing at birth and growth monitoring for counselling mothers, iron folate, vitamin A, simple health treatments such as oral rehydration, and referral when needed. Food supplements too can be provided on home visits when needed, along with proper education and demonstration of infant feeding, which would enhance their effectiveness. All these measures need to be used in a systematic way, covering all those at risk, within clear job protocols designed to ensure timely action.

The NCAER survey suggests that at least the health interventions in ICDS are being provided better today than in the past. Two important areas, however, are extremely weak: education/counselling of mothers in proper nutritional practices in pregnancy and early childhood, and care of growth faltering (or frankly, 'malnourished') children in the home or following referral to a health centre. For example, ANMs know precious little about, and give little priority to, the prevention or treatment of malnutrition, and AWWs who are often capable of being good basic health workers remain mystified about detecting anaemia or vitamin A deficiency. A good referral system would enable a malnourished or sick mother or child to be assisted by the front-line worker to access the necessary health care and complete the course of treatment. (Community-based assistance measures, such as referral funds, are useful in facilitating these processes.) Improvement of these aspects will require considerable training of all the front-line workers and doctors, as well as the provision of appropriate aids.

In effect, the ICDS programme needs to ensure complete coverage of the vulnerable groups with these basic services to improve its contribution to freeing India from hunger. While there may be a need for additional resources for certain items, such as basic medicines and equipment at *anganwadis*, the requirement would not be large compared with current expenditure on health, and better training and coordination between the health and ICDS systems would be a moderate-cost but high-return effort.

### IMPROVE TRAINING IN NUTRITION

There is need to improve training of ICDS workers and managers on a number of fronts. As discussed above, AWWs and ANMs must be able to identify and follow up children and mothers at risk of malnourishment, be technically proficient at delivering the basic health and nutrition services, be well-versed in the contents of health and nutrition education, and be skilled communicators to provide counselling in a convincing manner. They also require better organization skills to carry out their community mobilization, motivation and outreach tasks. They need to be shown how to organize their work efficiently because their job is multifarious and complicated. As most are young women with relatively low levels of literacy, many require confidence building and continuous encouragement. Thus, in addition to training front-line workers, there is also need for better training of supervisors and block level managers (Child Development Project Officers, or CDPOs) to strengthen their role as supporters and instructors of AWWs, and as local-level 'programme designers' and decision makers. Both CDPOs and Supervisors should also perform the role one level below them (i.e. as Supervisors and AWWs, respectively), in order to fully appreciate the tasks they are overseeing.

Further, in order to improve the quality of ICDS for the poor there is a grave need for training to be localized and contextualized, for 'pro-poor' paradigms to form the foundation of training, and for worker skills to be raised to levels that make them confident of taking and implementing the difficult decisions involved in providing services preferentially to the poor. It is also important to break the vicious cycle that causes poor areas to have poor training centres and trainers, who train workers that deliver a poor quality of service, leaving disadvantaged people under-served by the programme. In many areas, training centres have become moribund, calling for their revitalization or for new centres to be established, which has cost implications. Thus, improving training means enhancing financial allocations considerably: to upgrade facilities, improve equipment, purchase more materials, retrain/refresh trainers, improve accommodation for trainees, introduce new methods, and so on.

Over time, training in ICDS has improved in several respects. For example, it has become less didactic and more hands-on and skill-oriented. The introduction of 'sandwich training' has partially addressed the problems of low absorption and AWWs' long absences from families, and the period of work between courses at training centres enables workers to get real experience of running *anganwadis* before returning to learn how to deal with practical situations and problems. In-service training, conducted through various modalities such as mobile teams, monthly cluster- and block-level refreshers and 'cascade' methods, has addressed other problems, particularly the loss of learning and the need to update knowledge and improve skills. In general, however, the

ICDS training system has been unable to meet the challenges of a complex and rapidly expanding programme, of neo- or non-literate workers, of evolving programme-specific knowledge and practices (including training methods), and of more and more difficult working situations. To improve ICDS' impact on malnutrition, specifically, there is need to review the nutrition related contents of the training curricula for appropriateness and consistency of messages, their relevance to and integration with the nutrition services and inputs provided in the programme, and their effectiveness. Though many improvements are being planned under *Udisha*, the nationwide training initiative started in 1999, these have yet to be implemented widely. Ensuring their quality will be a continuous and difficult—but most important—task.

### COMMUNITY PARTICIPATION AND MANAGEMENT

A key need to improve the reach of ICDS, its quality, and overall effectiveness, is strengthening community involvement in management of the programme. To begin with, meaningful community participation could enhance community awareness of the programme and utilization of its services. It would facilitate community assistance when needed, and ensure accountability among workers for service provision. Ultimately, community management would mean that decisions are taken by communities (e.g. on resource allocations) and that the delivery system is fully responsive to their needs and demands.

However, till now, community participation has been one of the weakest elements of ICDS. Communities have generally been involved only in limited ways: providing assistance to the programme by way of a building or land for the *anganwadi*, small quantities of fuel or condiments for the food; helping to select AWWs and/or helping the workers organize household surveys, immunization sessions, and so on. In some areas, village-level committees have been established to assist as well as monitor *anganwadi* activities and oversee the AWW. Effective community participation is still, however, the exception rather than the rule.

Further, inadequate community participation has gone hand in hand with distortions in some of the basic tenets of the programme, compounding its ineffectiveness. For example, the selection of AWWs was intended to be *from* and *by* the communities in which they work, but this was diluted during the programme's rapid expansion, along with other aspects of community mobilization, preparation and involvement. Currently, too many AWWs 'commute' to their villages, are inadequately integrated with their communities and, hence, have difficulty carrying out their community-oriented tasks (such as mobilization and outreach). In effect, they lack accountability to the people they serve and thus deliver poor quality services. To improve ICDS' effectiveness, it is necessary to increase accountability, which in turn calls for better community participation. For example, AWW selection should be carried out by a broad section of the village community, particularly the poor, possibly through gram sabhas where these are representative and functional. Almost all aspects of nutrition-related services in ICDS would benefit from community involvement and management.

However, bringing about community participation in an Indian village or slum community requires great interpersonal efforts to cut through the prevailing social stratification. Ensuring that the poor participate in meaningful ways is even more difficult on account of their low position in the social hierarchy, and because of the great opportunity costs to them of participation. The catalytic agents may be, but are not necessarily only, the workers and supervisors. Gram panchayats (as well as the block- and district level Panchayati Raj institutions, see below) could be instrumental in this, but would need proper orientation. Back-up from public education efforts would be helpful. Community participation, and, ultimately, management of *anganwadis* could also be bolstered by the formation of poor women's groups.

Women's groups are good conduits for nutrition and health information and experience sharing, as well as potential community managers of ICDS. They could be instrumental in ensuring appropriate distribution of ICDS' rations, enhancing village food stocks through management of TPDS outlets and/or community grain banks, and so on. While many basic health and nutritional practices can be improved by increasing awareness within poor households and without additional financial resources, constraints on food availability would need to be eased by increasing household incomes. Experience in India and elsewhere has shown that the quickest route to this is the provision of income-earning opportunities to poor women. Efforts to organize women's groups for thrift and credit and to link them to income-generating schemes are spreading throughout the country. Even when their incomes are increased marginally, the impact on household welfare is apparent. Additional gains include the empowerment that comes with being part of a social support group, with access to information (ranging from health and nutrition to economic and legal information), with newly acquired skills, and with greater exposure to 'the world beyond'. However, as group formation and subsequent activities are difficult to organize and manage, these tasks should not be loaded on ICDS workers. Instead, it is possible to link ICDS' target families to other schemes [e.g. Swaranjayanti Gram Swarozgar Yojana (SGSY), Self-Help Groups (SHG) promoted by NABARD]. The convergence of the the ICDS activities/infrastructure with school feeding programmes (midday meal scheme) could be considered given that there is an overlap in the objectives as well as beneficiaries. Bringing about convergence could be among the most significant developments in ICDS over the next decade.

### DECENTRALIZATION OF MANAGEMENT

In order for the above forms and degree of community orientation, participation and management to take place, it is also necessary for additional ICDS' planning and management functions to be decentralized to the state, district and block levels. The programme is currently highly centralized, with most management functions remaining at the highest level capable of discharging them. Instead, a sound principle of development is to delegate responsibility for tasks to the lowest level capable of carrying them out. Decentralization is desirable in virtually all aspects of ICDS to improve its reach as well as quality. It is as critical in 'soft' areas such as training, to ensure that these cater to local situations and needs, as in the 'harder' aspects of infrastructure provision and food management. Much decision making in ICDS needs to take clients' preferences into account, which calls (in addition to community involvement in planning and resource allocation) for proximity between managers and communities. It should be possible to decide on the allocation of resources (worker time and finances) to different services at the block level, since needs vary from area to area, as described above. For example, food might be provided only at certain times of the year, while at other times the money might go towards the purchase of additional pre-school materials. Decentralization is critical for problem solving (e.g. through development of locale-specific strategies) as well as for the implementation of innovative ideas (e.g. in training).

In addition to improved targeting, which identifies who should (or should not) receive ICDS services, access is also related to service delivery norms that determine spatial distribution of *anganwadi* centres. Over time, norms such as the worker/population ratio have been modified as the programme has entered more sparsely populated areas and it has been recognized that many 'pockets' of poor are still left out. An *anganwadi* can now be opened in a population of 250 only, in contrast with the original figures of 1,000 in rural/urban areas, and 700 in tribal areas. However, another norm—the number of *anganwadis* sanctioned in a block—acts as a constraint and the lower population ratio may not actually be put into practice! This example points to the need for a more decentralized approach to deciding programme norms and strategies. Improving access within some blocks may be a matter of opening a very large number of *anganwadis* for small clusters of habitations, whereas in other areas, properly located and bigger facilities would suffice to cover a large number of clients. The appropriate unit for such decisions is the block, with some rationalization of need and resources taking place at the district level, and ultimate decision making no higher than the state level.

These are only some examples—a full review of the programme would undoubtedly point to other aspects that merit decentralization. Suffice it to say that capacity at the central level is already inadequate to manage the vastly expanded ICDS [leave alone coordination with all the programmes required for implementation of the National Nutrition Policy (NNP)]. The limited capacities even at the state, district and block levels suggest that greater involvement of Panchayati Raj institutions at the latter two levels could be helpful. It goes without saying that gram panchayats have an important role to play in all aspects of *anganwadi* management, particularly to ensure that ICDS serves the poor.

### REALLOCATING RESOURCES

Among the suggested activities to increase access, improve quality, and decentralize management, some require additional resources while others may effect some cost savings, as listed below.

*Where there would be Cost Savings*

1. Freezing expansion (for 3–5 years).
2. Decentralizing training of all cadres (would save in the medium term).
3. Plugging leakages in the food supply system.
4. Reducing or doing away with food supplementation and other services in the non-needy areas.

*Where Additional Resources need to be Allocated*

1. Ensuring coverage of poor areas and families (with food and other services).
2. Ensuring full health coverage of 0–2s and PLW with iron folate, vitamin A supplements, Oral Receipe Solvent (ORS), immunization.
3. Improving the quality of training and expanding training infrastructure in poor areas.
4. Improving and expanding training of MPWs/ANMs and Primary Health Centres (PHC) doctors in referral, nutrition management and rehabilitation, and improvement/provision of facilities at health centres.
5. Orientation of panchayats and women's groups towards community management.
6. Public education.

Many of the other suggestions made above constitute managerial improvements which are, for the most part, no- or low-cost.

## CONCLUSION

It is important to note that a complex and multi-faceted programme such as ICDS, that aims to address several of the causes of malnutrition, requires intensive inputs to be continued and far more effort in order to be effective. The impact achievable would probably not be at low cost. The ICDS should command the resources that it requires to deliver quality services to the poor. Given the budgetary constraints, the possibilities of cost savings should be explored vigorously and only unavoidable additional funding may be provided. India should be willing to invest these resources in its human capital. Investing in the very young child is an important step to making good the country's investment in primary education, as well as a major contribution to population stabilization, which is important for real economic growth in the country.

## NOTES

* The views expressed in this paper are those of the author and should not be ascribed to the World Bank.

1. The per beneficiary cost has been derived by simply dividing the programme's annual expenditure by the officially estimated number of children and women beneficiaries. The actual per capita cost, which might be derived by using actual coverage figures in the denominator, would most likely be higher. Unfortunately, coverage figures are only available for specific services (e.g. feeding, pre-school education), based on *anganwadi* registers and reports. The 1998-9 Concurrent Evaluation of ICDS by the NCAER reports on the coverage of different services based on an *anganwadi* questionnaire and interviews with user households, but did not assess the use of ICDS services by the targeted population as a whole. Also, while it would be useful to cost different services separately, programme expenditure data are not available disaggregated by service.
2. International Institute for Population Sciences, *India: National Family Health Survey (NFHS-2) 1998-99,* IIPS, Mumbai, 2000.
3. The BMI is weight in kilograms divided by the square of height in metres ($kg/m^2$ ). Values less than 18.5 are associated with chronic energy deficiency.
4. Unfortunately, while it may be possible to compare data on nutritional status and services from ICDS blocks and villages with non-ICDS units in NFHS-2, the data are not yet available. And tragically, it will not be possible to assess ICDS' impact on the basis of the NCAER Concurrent Evaluation as it did not measure nutritional status directly, nor (as mentioned earlier) did it collect population-based data on services that would have allowed an independent estimate of their reach.
5. A.R. Measham and Meera Chatterjee, *Wasting Away: The Crisis of Malnutrition in India,* The World Bank, Washington, DC, 1999. We have also argued that all nutrition efforts combined have failed to reduce malnutrition significantly. The new data discussed above are an indictment not only of ICDS but of the Public Distribution System, health services, poverty alleviation programmes, agriculture and food policies, economic growth and 'the market'—all of which must contribute to producing a 'hunger-free India'.
6. For example, National Institute of Public Cooperation and Child Development, *National Evaluation of Integrated Child Development Services,* NIPCCD, New Delhi, 1992; Nutrition Foundation of India,

*The Integrated Child Development Services (ICDS) Scheme*, NFI, New Delhi 1988.

7. Meera Chatterjee, *Does ICDS Alleviate Poverty?* The World Bank, New Delhi, 1997.
8. This plea for consolidation over expansion has been made by many, virtually at every stage since the programme covered only 100 blocks! But the politico-bureaucratic imperative to expand has repeatedly outweighed the advice of hundreds of professionals who have studied the programme and demonstrated need for both technical and managerial improvements.
9. The study found that about 15–25 per cent of block populations (more in rural than tribal areas) did not have an *anganwadi* 'encompassing' them. Of the excluded population, approximately half were in better-off areas, while the other half were in very poor (e.g. highly inaccessible) areas of the block. The more serious problem, however, was the 'under-coverage' within *anganwadi* areas. As much as 25 per cent of the population did not consider themselves covered by *anganwadi* services. This 'intra-village' exclusion was skewed against the poor. Distant hamlets, Scheduled Caste clusters, and dispersed marginal households tended to be left out. By and large—though with significant exceptions—*anganwadis* were located in central, more likely in better-off sections of villages. Further, where the AWW was of high caste or class, the lower castes and poor were often not served.
10. For example, more women from tribal and rural poor households reported that if there were no *anganwadi* health services, they would not seek alternative sources because they lacked time, found alternatives unaffordable, or lacked mobility to access other facilities.
11. For example, mothers interviewed in the field study perceived immunization services to be for both rich and poor, but supplementary nutrition and pre-school education (day care) were for families below the poverty line. Poverty and illiteracy were the major determinants of *anganwadi* use perceived by mothers.
12. For example, in some tribal areas where food availability is relatively good but infrastructure poor, there may be greater need for *anganwadi*-based health care than for nutritional supplements. Conversely, in rural Kerala, where maternity care facilities are widespread, more poor families may need and use good child nutrition services than antenatal care.
13. Again, this is a long-standing recommendation. It has been adopted in the Ninth Plan Strategy for ICDS, and recent guidelines issued by the Department of Women and Child Development, GOI, focus the supplementary feeding in ICDS under the Pradhan Mantri Gramodaya Yojana (PMGY) on this age group. Both are steps in the right direction.

# 16. Improving School Feeding in India

*Ute Meir*

Food insecurity is a multidimensional problem relating to issues such as the amount and quality of food people can grow, their possibility to access food (for example through purchases), the way food is utilized by different members of a family or the particular food vulnerability of specific groups. Education, particularly primary education and education of women and girls, is a key determinant of practically all these dimensions. Better-educated people are better farmers, have better chances for employment or self-employment, and have higher incomes. Educated women tend to have fewer, healthier and better-fed children, and know better how to look after their own health. Education is also central to people's ability to defend their rights and seek out opportunities to improve their condition. Education should, therefore, be a central element of any strategy to improve food security.

## EFFECTS OF HUNGER AND MALNUTRITION ON EDUCATION

There is a mutual influence between education and nutrition. Just as education can help to make people healthier and more food-secure, the health and nutritional problems experienced by school-age children reduce their ability to benefit from educational opportunities. There is a growing body of evidence to show that nutritional and health deficiencies are not limited to children under 6, but that primary-school-age children experience high levels of protein-energy malnutrition, lack certain critical micronutrients, suffer from temporary and chronic hunger, or are infected with parasitic worms.

This affects their education in many ways. In the worst case, children are too hungry and sick to make it to school or are kept out of school to help feed their family, particularly during periods of critical food shortages. Even when children are in school, they may experience short-term hunger as a result of skipping breakfast and having to make long walks from their home. This seriously reduces their concentration span and learning ability. The effects of short-term hunger are worst in, but not limited to, already malnourished children. The lack of micronutrients such as iron, iodine or vitamin A in the children's diet renders them listless and inattentive in class. Protein-energy malnutrition, a widespread condition in school-age children, is another cause of their impaired learning capacity. Children who experience difficulties in learning are also at greater risk of irregular attendance and early dropout. Parasitic infections in children produce malnutrition and other health problems and further reduce their ability to attend school and benefit from the teaching provided to them.

## ROLE OF SCHOOL FEEDING

School feeding programmes can tackle these problems in several ways. If well-designed and properly implemented they can:

1. Alleviate short-term hunger in malnourished or otherwise well-nourished school children;
2. Overcome the lack of specific micronutrients in school-age children;
3. Make it easier for children from poor and food-insecure families to attend and complete school.

This translates into higher enrolment, improved attendance and completion rates and better school performance.

School feeding can operate in two ways: either by feeding children at school, or by distributing dry food rations to students to take home and share with their families. Which option to choose depends on the problems observed and intended results. If there is a need to alleviate hunger in school-age children or improve their diet, then children should eat at school, preferably soon after arriving in the morning so that they will benefit from the energy boost while in class. When food is mostly needed to facilitate enrolment, attendance and retention, it is necessary either to provide a more substantial meal at school (possibly in combination with a morning snack) or to distribute dry food rations. The latter has the additional advantage of improving the food security of the whole family. In each case, the amount and type of food distributed needs to be carefully assessed to suit the problems identified and intended results (nutritional content, incentive value).

School feeding programmes can also have important secondary benefits. For example, they can increase community participation in education, particularly when parents are responsible for running and supervising the feeding programme. This, in turn, is often a key strategy to improve education in general and can have important multiplier effects on community development and the condition of women in the community.

The preparation and distribution of food at school can also provide a setting for many types of practical teaching and learning experiences such as on nutrition, health, hygiene or agriculture.

Lastly, in areas frequently affected by natural calamities, school feeding can be an effective channel for disaster mitigation, not only allowing children to remain in school and maintain their nutritional status even during drought or floods but also bringing more food into their families (in addition to direct distribution of relief food). This requires flexible adjustments in the type and quantities of food distributed.

For greater effects on the health and nutritional status of school-age children, school feeding should be combined with other school health interventions, notably treatment for intestinal parasites (deworming), improvement of sanitary conditions at school (provision of potable water; latrines, preferably separate for boys and girls), or health and nutrition education (outreach to parents will further increase benefits).

To enhance the educational benefits of school feeding, it is important to improve the quality of education provided at school (teacher training, improvements in the curriculum, distribution of textbooks, etc.) and tackle other obstacles to access and retention of children at schools (open more schools closer to children's homes, reduce educational cost to parents, etc.).

## SCHOOL FEEDING IN INDIA: THE CURRENT CONTEXT

School feeding has a long tradition in India; some states (e.g. Tamil Nadu) have had school feeding programmes since as early as the 1920s. They were largely funded by state governments with some external assistance. In 1995, the Government of India launched the centrally-sponsored 'National Programme of Nutritional Support to Primary Education' (NPNSPE) or Mid-Day Meal (MDM) scheme. Its objectives are two-fold:

1. Enhance the nutritional status of children, and
2. Promote universal elementary education by encouraging poorer parents to admit and retain their children in school.

The MDM scheme is part of the Government of India's different food assistance programmes and operates through the Food Corporation of India (FCI). It uses commodities available under the FCI, and distributes them through the network of FCI stores from where they are transported to individual schools/villages.

Under this programme, the central government supports the state governments as follows: 1. provision of food grains (rice or wheat), free of cost, to the implementing state agencies; and 2. reimbursement to district authorities of the cost of food transportation. States pay for additional food items required for cooked meals and salaries of cooks. The scheme offers the states three options: provision of cooked, or pre-cooked, meals at school or distribution of dry food rations. Most states chose dry ration distribution, while some (e.g. Orissa, Gujarat) have opted for provision of cooked meals.

The scheme covered some 13,300 million students in 1998–9 and is proposed to be universalized to all rural blocks and urban slums and disadvantaged sections during the Ninth Five Year Plan. Once universalized, the annual cost of the scheme is estimated to be of the order of Rs. 22.26 billion (US $480.7 million).[1]

Unfortunately, there are numerous problems with the implementation of the programme in different states, as assessed during a recent evaluation.[2] For example, the regularity of provisions is low (only 60 per cent of primary students surveyed had received midday meals during the last 6 months; amongst families receiving dry rations, only 25 per cent reported monthly distribution, and there was mention of frequent delays of 3 months or more). This is partly due to a complicated system of transport between FCI stores and schools and problems with the reimbursement of transport costs to contractors (too late, insufficient amounts). Schools in all states lack adequate food storage and cooking facilities, resulting in loss of food and hygienically unsafe food preparation. Where cooked meals are distributed, there are often delays in contributions from the state government for additional foodstuffs or salaries of cooks, which causes interruption of the programme at school level. There are also complaints about lengthy cooking processes and poor quality of the meals distributed.

Another problem is the lack of community involvement in the programme. While most parents know of the programme, they are unaware of its purpose or their entitlements (for example, for a student to receive a dry ration he/she must have attended school for at least 80 per cent of the month). This lack of awareness, along with the insufficiencies of supplies, breeds hostility between parents and teachers. Teachers also bear the brunt of the workload in implementing the programme, with little support from parents (receipt of food deliveries, supervision of cooks, reporting, purchase of additional food items, sometimes even transport of food from FCI store to school). This not only represents an additional burden on them, but also seriously disrupts the educational process in schools.

The erratic implementation of the programme seriously reduces any effects it may have on the education and well-being of the participating children. Not surprisingly, the evaluation study found a very mixed pattern regarding *educational improvements.* While enrolment seemed to have increased after introduction of the scheme, there were no traceable effects on more regular daily attendance and little change in the generally high rates of dropout. The evaluation did not assess the effects of the scheme on the *nutritional status* of children. However, its current design largely limits any such effects (see under the sub-heading 'Adjust the Design of School Feeding to its Objectives' given below).

On the whole, therefore, the MDM scheme falls far short of its ambitious objectives, and the Government of India as well as state governments reap little benefit for their massive investment in the programme. Yet, school feeding clearly has an important role to play in India. Thirty per cent of primary-school-age children still have no access to school and 40 per cent of those enrolling in school drop out before acquiring even basic skills. The situation is even more serious for girls and children in rural areas and from the poorest families. At the same time, food insecurity, malnutrition and hunger remain widespread. Thirty per cent of the population live on less than 1,700 kcal per day and 49 per cent of the rural population live in poverty;[3] 208 million people are undernourished.[4]

## IMPROVING SCHOOL FEEDING IN INDIA

### ADJUST THE DESIGN OF SCHOOL FEEDING TO ITS OBJECTIVES

India's national MDM scheme pursues two main goals: improving children's nutritional status and their education (enrolment, attendance and retention). However, the current programme design is ill-suited to achieve these objectives.

As mentioned above, where children come to school hungry and there is a need to address their short-term hunger, food needs to be consumed at school and served as early as possible during the school day. Where the main problem is non-enrolment, absenteeism or early dropout, food rations to take home may be the better solution since they provide greater support to parents to enable their children to attend school. Otherwise, a more substantial food ration needs to be distributed at school.

Under the MDM scheme, state governments are free to opt either for on-site feeding or dry rations. Most have chosen the latter, which largely precludes any nutritional benefits for students participating in the scheme. This option is thus not compatible with the first objective of the programme. At the same time, even in those states where food is distributed at school, the meal is usually served only halfway through the school day, after children have been sitting in class hungry for several hours. In fact, the very name of the programme (MDM scheme) attests to this practice. This seriously reduces the effects of the programme on children's learning capacity while they are at school.

The dual objectives of education and nutrition identified for the MDM programme can thus only be adequately achieved through on-site feeding. However, this would require advancing the timing of food distribution, which may have implications for the type of food to be used (see under the sub-heading 'Identify Suitable Rations for On-Site Feeding' given below). If school continues in the afternoon and children cannot return home to eat during lunch time, a combination of mid-morning and mid-day meal or snack may be needed to ensure that children are well-fed and alert throughout the school day. This would also ensure that the total amount of food distributed is substantial enough to enable poor children to attend school. Alternatively, if a snack served early in the day is sufficient to address short-term hunger (for example because of shorter school hours), the incentive role of school feeding could also be enhanced by combining on-site feeding and provision of dry rations. Another case where dry rations may have to be added to on-site feeding could be the particularly disadvantaged and poorest children, including girls, who need an extra boost if they are to attend school.

The actual design of the programme, therefore, needs to be adapted to the local conditions and based on a better analysis of these conditions as well as the problems to be addressed through the programme. Such analysis seems to have been lacking in the current decisions regarding on-site feeding or use of dry rations. To the extent possible, there should be flexibility to use different approaches even within states (e.g. between districts).

At the same time, it must be stated that distribution of food at school, even if served earlier in the day to alleviate temporary hunger, will have limited effects on the overall nutritional status of children unless it is combined with other school health interventions (see under the sub-heading 'Make School Feeding . . . Programme' given below). This needs to be taken into account in the formulation of programme objectives and expected results.

### TARGET SCHOOL FEEDING PROGRAMMES TO WHERE THEY ARE MOST NEEDED

Generally speaking, school feeding is most relevant and should be limited to areas where children are affected in their ability to benefit from educational opportunities as a result of hunger and malnutrition. The aim is to identify and reach families that lack the resources to adequately provide for their school-age children. This not only ensures the effectiveness of school feeding, it is also central to containing its costs.

This has been recognized under the MDM programme with a general focus on 'rural areas, urban slums and other disadvantaged sections'. However, it is unclear to what extent these criteria are adhered to in practice. More importantly, there appears to be scope for further refinement of targeting criteria and more narrow selection of areas and population groups to be covered by the programme. The programme could be targeted at individual districts or even blocks. These should be identified on the basis of indicators reflecting both educational need (low enrolment, attendance and educational performance; high dropout) and high incidence of food insecurity, poverty, malnutrition and ill health amongst school-age children and their families.

At the same time, the government may also want to consider reviewing the current criteria regarding the types of schools to be covered by the programme. Despite the fact that the MDM scheme aims at the promotion of universal elementary education (grades 1 to 7), one of the central development goals of the Government of India since Independence, the programme currently covers only primary schools (grades 1 to 5). This is not only contradictory to its stated objective, it also creates practical problems at school level (many schools include both primary and upper primary sections; assisting only part of the students in a school creates tensions and invites mismanagement of food).

The final decision on programme targeting and coverage (geographical, types of schools) needs to take into account the availability of resources at the level of central and state governments.

### INVOLVE COMMUNITIES/PARENTS IN THE OPERATION OF SCHOOL FEEDING PROGRAMMES

Lack of community participation is one of the main problems that currently affect the functioning of the MDM scheme. Many parents perceive the programme more as an entitlement and responsibility of the government than something for which they might take ownership. There is a need to change this perception and more actively encourage the participation of parents.

Insufficient awareness and participation of parents not only creates tensions over the distribution of food within the community as well as between teachers and parents, it also negatively affects the educational process at schools if teachers and students (particularly girls) are left to manage the feeding programme. Moreover, greater community participation could save costs for the government (in states with on-site school feeding, state governments pay for 2 cooks per school as well as fuel wood and additional food items).

The programme should thus become a joint responsibility of government and communities. Village Education Committees or similar bodies should jointly manage the programme with the teacher/headmaster; the participation of women would be of particular importance.[5] This could include the following: verification of food deliveries and follow up in case of delays; regular control of food store room; spot checks on food preparation and distribution; ensure adherence to entitlement criteria such as the need for minimum attendance; provision of additional food items, fuel wood and water where necessary; or, possibly, prepare and distribute food on a voluntary basis. Parents could also be made responsible for ensuring that schools have the necessary infrastructure for school feeding. This should include at least a good store room for food (safe, close to the school) and a cooking shed.

Parents should be fully informed and consulted about their contribution and a clear system developed for distribution of responsibilities between all concerned. Training should be provided as necessary, e.g. to strengthen the functioning of parents groups. The inclusion of a school in the programme could be made dependent on the signing of an agreement between parents, school staff and programme authorities to ensure that all have understood and accepted their tasks.

### IDENTIFY SUITABLE RATIONS FOR ON-SITE FEEDING

As mentioned above, the type of school meal that is currently provided under the MDM scheme is not suitable to adequately address the problem of short-term hunger in school children. For example, in Orissa the daily ration per student consists of rice (115 g), pulses/*dal* (15 g) and vegetable oil (1 g), plus vegetables purchased from the cash contribution of the state government (allocation of 10 paisa/student/day). While this type of meal corresponds to local eating habits and may be sufficient in terms of daily nutritional requirements of students it takes too long to cook to be served as early in the day as would be necessary. Longer cooking times also result in higher consumption of fuel wood and thus higher costs. Moreover, the problems in food deliveries often result in only part of the three commodities being available at a school, and hence incomplete rations being served.

There is thus a need to review the ration to be used under the programme. A suitable ration could be identified on the basis of the following considerations.

1. Identify the necessary number of meals/snacks to be provided per day, depending on timing and duration of school hours (short-term hunger); this should always include a meal/snack to be provided as early as possible after children arrive at school.

2. Identify the necessary nutritional value of the ration in terms of the percentage of children's daily nutritional requirements to be covered (these will depend on the age of students to be reached); in general, a school snack or meal should provide from one-third to half of the recommended daily allowance for energy and protein for the age group targeted by the programme.
3. Identify the necessary incentive value of the ration and whether it should be achieved through on-site feeding only or in combination with provision of dry rations;[6] this can be assessed by comparing the nutritional and financial value of the ration to average household incomes/food consumption amongst the children's families or to the (estimated) value of the child's labour (the ration should at least partly compensate families for the loss of children's labour when they attend school); since there is no fixed rule in this area this needs to be decided on the basis of discussions with parents.
4. Use ready-to-eat food or food which requires little preparation time to reduce time spent on cooking and fuel wood consumption; blended foods such as the Indiamix used by WFP under the ICDS may be particularly relevant. This would also eliminate the need to handle several commodities at the same time and reduce costs to state governments for additional food items.
5. Ensure that food is appealing and acceptable to children and can be prepared in a hygienically safe manner.
6. Use commodities which are easy to transport and store and have a sufficient shelf life.
7. Ensure that rations are of minimum cost to the government.

Care has to be taken to keep the criteria flexible and easily implementable. As a general rule, however, any ration to be used for school feeding must be based on the commodities available under the FCI.

### IMPROVE FOOD LOGISTICS AND MANAGEMENT

School feeding can only be effective if food is available at schools regularly, in sufficient quantities and of satisfactory quality. However, this is a major bottleneck of the programme at present. Typically, private contractors, who are later reimbursed for the cost of transport, lift food from FCI stores to schools. However, these reimbursements are often late and insufficient to meet the real costs of transport in often-difficult terrain. As a result, many companies refuse to deliver or do so only when funds are available. There is thus a need to review the current system of food transportation and delivery to schools to identify an arrangement that is feasible, reliable and cost-effective. For example, food godowns could be made available closer to schools and parents requested to ensure the last leg of transport up to the school.

### IMPROVE MONITORING AND EVALUATION OF SCHOOL FEEDING

The evaluation of the MDM programme[7] revealed the lack of sufficient and reliable data to adequately assess its outcomes, either in educational or nutritional terms. As a result, the government lacks vital information to assess the effectiveness of the programme, the degree to which intended results are achieved, and the actual benefits accruing as a result of the investments made. A monitoring and evaluation system should be developed for the programme which not only allows tracking the flow of commodities and programme implementation but also programme results as per stated objectives (changes in enrolment, attendance, retention, academic performance, broken down by gender; possible changes in children's nutritional status if relevant interventions are added to school feeding). Baseline data should be collected to track changes resulting from school feeding. In order to simplify reporting requirements, the system should build as much as possible on data already collected, for example as part of the annual school census. Whenever possible, collection of additional data on wider programme effects should be considered (e.g. on household food security of targeted families, general functioning of schools and involvement of parents, status of women and girls in the community).

### MAKE SCHOOL FEEDING PART OF A LARGER SCHOOL HEALTH PROGRAMME

As mentioned above, the current design of the MDM programme largely precludes any nutritional benefits for participating children, which is one of the stated objectives of the programme. Adjustments are necessary to ensure better alleviation of the short-term hunger in school-children. However, distributing food at school will have little effects on their overall nutritional status if they suffer from 'hidden hunger' (lack of essential micronutrients and vitamins) or are unable to adequately absorb the food due to intestinal parasites.

School feeding should thus be combined with other school health interventions to increase its nutritional and health benefits and bring it more in line with the stated programme objectives. These should include, at the minimum, micronutrient supplementation and control of parasitic worms. For example, the food distributed at school could be fortified with micronutrients lacking from the children's regular diet. Deworming of students can be carried out at limited cost and effort (drugs are relatively inexpensive and easy to deliver; no previous testing for infection is required). Adding other school health interventions such as nutrition and health education or improvements in sanitary conditions at school will enhance programme benefits even further, not only for the children concerned but also their families.

## TASKS AHEAD

Putting the above recommendations into practice will require action on many fronts. The following should be particularly considered.

1. While the current MDM scheme is faced with many problems, there are also many positive experiences with school feeding in India. For example, some states (Tamil Nadu, Kerala) have operated successful school feeding programmes for many decades, and in Gujarat the MDM programme has been improved by adding biannual treatments against intestinal parasites and providing vitamin A and iron to school-children. These experiences should be analysed with a view to drawing lessons that would facilitate their mainstreaming.
2. The World Food Programme has almost 40 years of experience in operating school feeding programmes all over the developing world. The government should draw on this experience in order to build models for improved school feeding in India. This should form part of the larger partnership between the Government of India and WFP in working towards greater food security in India.

3. The government should also consider linking with an initiative launched by several other UN agencies at the recent 'World Education Forum' (WEF) (Dakar, Senegal, April 2000). The initiative is known as 'FRESH' (Focusing Resources on Effective School Health) and currently supported by UNESCO, UNICEF, WHO and the World Bank. It is built on the recognition of the important links between education, health and nutrition, and aims to promote a package of school health services to be provided at every school, including school feeding.

## NOTES

1. At an exchange rate of US $1 = Rs. 46.31 (UN exchange rate for April 2001).
2. Operations Research Group, 'Evaluation Study to Assess the Efficiency and Effectiveness of the National Programme for Nutritional Support to Primary Education in Ten States of India: Final Report', UNICEF, New Delhi, July 1999.
3. World Food Programme, 'Enabling Food Aid for Development: A Policy Review of the India Country Programme', WFP, New Delhi, 1999.
4. *The State of Food Insecurity in the World*, FAO, Rome, 2000.
5. For example, under the ICDS programme in Orissa 'Food Committees' have been set up which are composed exclusively of women and with rotating membership. This could be replicated also at primary schools.
6. The commodities currently used for dry ration distribution (wheat/rice) seem appropriate since they form part of the staple foods in the country and are thus attractive to families. However, the per-student allocation (3 kg per month) may have to be reviewed on the basis of the above considerations.
7. Operations Research Group, op. cit., n. 2 above.

# 17. Care for Development: Contributions toward a Hunger Free India

*Patrice L. Engle and A. Dustagheer*

The most recent census data suggest that great strides forward are possible with concerted effort; literacy has increased dramatically in some areas of the country. Yet in the area of nutrition and health, indicators still lag; the change in the percentage of underweight children under 3 has been from 51 per cent to 47 per cent, less than 1 percentage point a year. The Infant Mortality Rate (IMR) has changed little. Girls face greater threats: the chances of a girl child surviving to the age of 6 is less than it was 10 years ago (933 girls to 1,000 boys in the year 2000, compared to 945 girls to 1,000 boys in 1991). Only 37 per cent of India's children aged 3–6 are attending any kind of a pre-school programme. Are the conditions of their rearing providing children the opportunities they need for realizing their right to survival and development guaranteed under the Convention for the Rights of the Child, ratified by India in 1992?

Although India has achieved food sufficiency, its children are still suffering high levels of child malnutrition, low birth weight, and nutritional deficiencies such as vitamin A deficiency and anaemia. A report from the Planning Commission indicated that there is almost no relation between per capita intake and percentage of children who are malnourished (Fig. 1). Many investigations within apparently homogeneous towns and villages have shown that there is considerable variation between families, and even between children within families, in the chances of being malnourished. Improving income levels and per capita food production is not enough to prevent malnutrition. While food is important, food availability is insufficient to explain children's nutritional status.

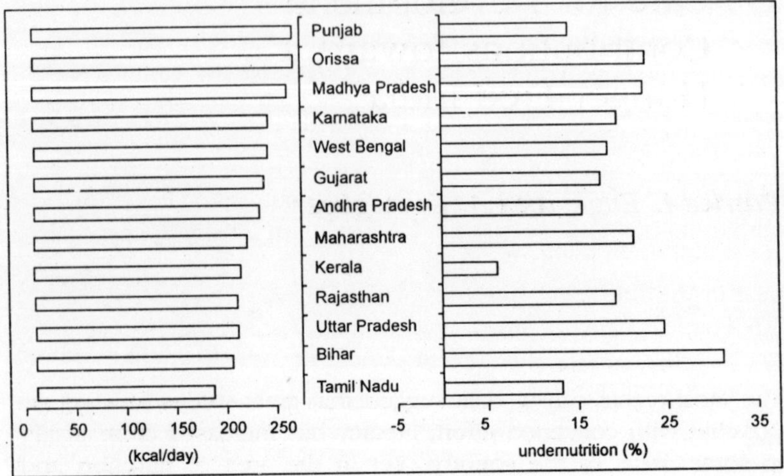


FIG. 1: AVERAGE ENERGY INTAKE AND UNDER-NUTRITION, IN CHILDREN BELOW 3 YEARS.

Household food security is generally considered to be a function of four factors: food availability, access to food at the household level, vulnerability of the household to shocks such as natural disasters or drought, and food utilization (a combination of factors such as absorption of nutrients, intra-household distribution of food, and caring practices that affect food intake). These factors have a particularly large impact on the most vulnerable, young children and children who are of lower status in the family (girls, especially later-born girls). The average calorie deficit that a child from birth to 12 months suffers, which results in malnutrition, is of the order of 100 to 200 kcal per day, approximately 20 per cent of the child's daily needs. However, this amount of food is only 2 per cent of the total food intake of the average family. Therefore, one must conclude that factors in addition to food itself have a role to play in the child's malnutrition.

The productivity of a population depends not only on health and nutrition, but also on cognitive ability. Experience suggests that early interventions in child learning have long-term effects on adult productivity. A series of studies in India has indicated that children who attended ICDS pre-school were more likely to profit from schooling (Vazir study).

The lead editorial from *Indian Pediatrics* (17 February 2001) suggests that countries that have shown dramatic improvements in their human development indicators, such as Sri Lanka or Thailand, have invested in the human resources—health, nutritional status, and child development—of its youngest citizens (Bhutta 2001). Women's equality has to be a key component of this investment strategy. Governments have to understand the importance of investing in human resources, the long-term pay-off of these interventions, and the importance of malnutrition not only for health, but also for children's development. An intelligent response is to invest in children, especially in their earliest years, and to invest in the future parents of those children.

This paper proposes that child nutrition, women and adolescent girls' nutrition, and child development are inextricably linked. Numerous studies show that optimal child development requires good nutrition; the effects can be over half a standard deviation on cognitive tests, or 8–10 points. Well-nourished and healthy children are more able to profit from schooling opportunities. They are more likely to stay in school, and learn more when they are in school. What is less often recognized is that even in their earliest years, the well-nourished are more cheerful and energetic, they are able to solicit attention from busy caregivers. More attention and interaction further enhances their cognitive and socio-emotional abilities. More interaction also increases the chances that the child will receive better feeding and care. Thus, from the earliest months of a child's life, a positive upward cycle can begin linking survival, growth and development.

The purpose of this paper is to evaluate the evidence that interventions to improve early childcare for survival, growth and development, particularly in the first three years of life, will have an impact on the child's eventual development and productivity. More specifically, the paper will:

1. Define early childcare and resources for care;
2. Examine evidence that care practices are associated with nutrient intake and growth;
3. Outline the mechanisms through which early childcare, particularly psychosocial care, influences growth and development; and evaluate the evidence that interventions to improve care practices can have an impact on growth and development; and
4. Recommend strategies for improving children's care for survival, growth and development.

## CONCEPTUAL MODEL AND DEFINITION OF CARE PRACTICES

Childhood malnutrition is a major public health problem throughout the developing world and is one of the principal underlying causes of infant and child mortality (Murray and Lopez 1997a, 1997b). Typically, growth faltering begins at around 6 months, as infants progress from a diet based on breast milk alone to one that includes additional flavours and textures coinciding with newly emerging developmental skills (Birch and Fisher 1995; WHO 1998). The provision of safe and adequate amounts of local foods appropriate for infants just learning to eat is complex because of linkages among behavioural, cultural and nutritional factors (Pelto 1999). Interdisciplinary formative research is required to identify appropriate and effective interventions to improve complementary feeding, infant growth and development in various country settings (Dickin et al. 1997; Caulfield et al. 1999).

The central importance of cultural and behavioural factors in children's nutrient intake, growth and development, particularly during the first 18 months of life, has been recognized only recently (WHO 1999). Research has shown that even chronically malnourished infants in developing countries often do not eat all of the food that is available to them (Garcia et al. 1990; Brown et al. 1988; Caulfield et al. 1999). The UNICEF conceptual framework (UNICEF 1997) suggests that care and feeding, in addition to food security, health care services and a healthy environment, are critical for children's survival, growth and development (Engle, Bentley and Pelto 2000). Even when poverty causes food insecurity, enhanced caregiving can optimize the use of existing resources to promote good health and nutrition in women and children. In fact, it is under these circumstances that improving care behaviour is most important. The UNICEF framework, which recognizes that environmental, socio-cultural and individual factors interact to influence child health, is essentially an ecological model (McElroy and Townsend 1979; Pelto 1999). Many factors influence nutrition other than food intake, and care practices play a major role in influencing these other factors that affect good nutrition. Providing food is not enough.

Ghosh (1997) has argued that the high rates of malnutrition in India are not primarily caused by poverty; rather, the behaviour of delayed initiation of breastfeeding, early introduction of water and liquids, and delay in complementary feeding results in a period of 'perpetual hunger for the child'. This occurs 'because the child was dependent on someone else to feed him/her and this person did not have the knowledge and awareness (or time) regarding how much food this child needed and how often'.

## DEFINING CARE

In 1990, UNICEF proposed a conceptual framework that suggested that not only were food security and health care services necessary for child survival, but care for girls and women and children was equally important (UNICEF 1990). It was argued that food, health, and care are all necessary, but none alone is sufficient for healthy growth and development. All three elements must be adequate in order for children to have the opportunity to be well-nourished. Even when poverty causes food insecurity and limited health care, enhanced caregiving can optimize the use of existing resources to promote good health and nutrition in women and children. In fact, it is under these circumstances that care is most important. Breastfeeding is an example of a practice that provides food, health and care simultaneously.

The term 'care' refers to the way caregivers feed children, care for illnesses, provide hygienic environments, prepare food, and provide a responsive and stimulating environment for the child. Such behaviour plays a significant role in the child's growth and development. These daily actions of caregivers translate food in the household, sanitary facilities, and health care services into good nutrition for children. Food on the shelf will not help a young child to grow; it must be prepared and given to the child. An immunization campaign will have no effect if no one takes the child to the ANM. A new latrine is ineffective if the child continues to defecate in the household space. In order to provide all children their right to optimal growth and development, families must be supported in providing the best care possible (Engle et al. 1997).

Six kinds of care practices have been defined (Engle et al. 1997). First, care for girls and women represents a pattern of behaviour on the part of the family, including making sure that they receive adequate prenatal care and safe birthing, and have equal access to education. Second, food preparation takes enormous amounts of caregiver time and effort. Adequate stoves prevent women's exposure to indoor air pollution. Third, hygiene practices have long been recognized as critical for child nutrition. Fourth, home health practices include diagnosing illness in the home, use of preventive health care, and protection from pests and accidents. Fifth, good psychosocial care, including warmth, verbal interaction, and encouragement of learning causes improved cognitive development of children, and is related to complementary feeding styles. Feeding, including both breastfeeding and complementary feeding, is the sixth care practice.

In order for caregivers to carry out these practices, they must have resources for care. Resources for the provision of care may be human, economic, or organizational, ranging from the beliefs, knowledge and health of the caregivers, and their control of money, time, and decisions, to the degree of community support such as sharing of workloads and supervision of children. At the national level, resources for care are influenced by expenditure priorities, poverty levels, landlessness and other limitations on the distribution of available resources. Political, cultural, social and economic structures constitute basic determinants of the use of resources in support of families and caregivers for children. Economic conditions, governmental policies and the ecological environment can have influences on care practices and resources for care (Engle, Lhotska and Armstrong 1997).

For example, mothers are often told to increase the frequency of feeding, but they have too much work to have the time for giving an additional feed. Instead of being helped, they may find themselves blamed for providing inadequate care. We must avoid this situation by being aware of the resources required, and helping the caregivers to increase their resources. Focusing on care practices without a concern for resources may lead to the unfortunate result of 'blaming the mother' for inadequate care, rather than recognizing a lack of resources. *The notion that a child is the combined responsibility of both parents needs to be reinforced continually and at all levels.*

To define 'resources for care' adequately, one must assess who is providing the care, where young children are cared for, who provides the economic support, and *who makes the decisions.* Telling a mother to breastfeed six times a day will not be effective if her mother-in-law requires her to be working in the fields all day long: the mother-in-law also needs to be convinced.

Health care and ICDS programmes will be more effective if caregivers are recognized and supported for their positive practices as well as being guided to adopt improved practices. Providing support to empower the caregiver should be recognized as an important vehicle for behaviour change, and as a strategy to increase resources for care.

These care practices and resources for care are not only important for children's good nutritional status, but also for their growth and development. In fact, they have now been recognized as the building blocks of Early Childhood Care for Survival, Growth and Development (ECC for SGD), UNICEF's integrated approach to young children.

Caring practices and resources vary tremendously by culture, yet there is some evidence that variations among families within one culture may be greater than those between cultures (Engle, Menon and Haddad 1997). Children's basic needs for food, health care, protection, shelter and love are the same in all cultures. Differences may be seen in how each culture and each family attempts to meet these needs. Traditional knowledge may be valuable, but widespread changes in families due to urbanization, women's increased economic roles, expansion of primary education, and population increase may require changes and adaptations in care practices, for which families may be ill prepared. These changes may undermine positive traditional practices.

## DESCRIPTION OF SAMPLE CARE PRACTICES

### *Home Health Care*

Good home health practices help prevent illnesses, and through good treatment reduce the negative impact that illnesses have on children's growth and development. Studies in a variety of countries show that 70 to 80 per cent of health care treatment is performed at home by women, particularly by mothers (World Bank 1994).

*Home management of illness* includes the prevention of illness, its diagnosis and subsequent home treatment. Caregivers recognize and diagnose diarrhoea and provide home remedies, including oral rehydration solution. Because diarrhoea and other illnesses often result in anorexia, caregivers must use their skills to increase feeding during illness and convalescence. Continued or increased breastfeeding during illness helps compensate for lowered intake of other foods.

*Utilization of health services*, including growth monitoring and immunization, takes time and effort. When children cannot be adequately treated at home, curative health services must be availed as soon as the child seems to need help. Sometimes, the caregiver cannot take the child to the health care services because she does not have enough decision-making power to be able to decide alone, and must wait for other family members to return home. Initiatives such as the Integrated Management of Childhood Illnesses will improve the effectiveness of first-line medical care if sought early enough. After visiting a health care centre, following medical recommendations also takes time and resources. Health services can support caregivers by providing community-based services, keeping waiting times at clinics short, informing caregivers fully and accurately, and treating them with respect.

*Home-based protection* includes control of pests (e.g. insects, rats), and avoiding accidents (burns, falls, poisoning). Malaria has a major impact on nutrition of children, and prevention of mosquito bites through use of bednets is thus important care behaviour. When a child's caregiver is also a child, protection from dangerous situations and prevention of accidents may be lacking. Children also need protection from common forms of abuse, such as severe physical punishment or other physical harm, which can occur both within and outside the family. Abuse can affect children's psychosocial and mental development, as well as their growth.

## CARE FOR GIRLS AND WOMEN

One of the most neglected areas of work is finding ways to encourage families to support care for girls and women. During pregnancy and lactation, the family should support the women in obtaining extra and higher-quality foods, reducing workloads, attending antenatal clinics and obtaining safe birthing, and receiving adequate postpartum rest. There is evidence that factors such as workload have a significant effect on birthweight (Launer et al. 1990).

Family support is also important for reproductive health, including helping the adolescent girl delay her age at first birth, and supporting women in their use of family planning. A third area concerns physical health, including provision of a fair share of the family food, and protection of girls and women from abuse. Fourth, mental health, stress, and self-confidence are domains which families can support or undermine depending on their attitudes and behaviour. Fifth, women need support in having adequate autonomy in decision making when needed, and access to the family's income and assets. Support in sharing the workload is also a domain of care for girls and women. Finally, the family's ability to assure girls' equal access to school and women's access to continuing education is extremely important both for the current and for the subsequent generation.

#### BREASTFEEDING

Current UNICEF recommendations are to initiate breastfeeding in the first hour after birth, to breastfeed exclusively for about the first 6 months (no water), and to continue breastfeeding until the child is at least 2 years of age. Only 51 per cent of children were reported to be exclusively breastfeeding from 0–3 months, and the percentages have changed little in the NFHS-2 study (55 per cent). The percentage of children exclusively breastfeeding from 4–6 months has dropped from 26 per cent to 24 per cent according to the NFHS studies.

Although India is a country very supportive of breastfeeding, exclusive breastfeeding is quite uncommon, as mothers begin to supplement with top milks and water early in the child's first months. Some studies have shown rates of 18 per cent or less (Phillips 2000) when a more stringent definition is used than the NFHS-2. When the definition of exclusive breastfeeding explicitly excluded children receiving water, the rate fell to about 25 per cent as well, except in the coolest states (e.g. Himachal Pradesh). (MICS II data from UNICEF, summarized by Parikh 2001.)

Resources for breastfeeding, such as education, beliefs, and time, have a significant effect on this care practice. Although most traditional beliefs support breastfeeding in India, some undermine good breastfeeding regimes. For example, there is a strong belief that colostrum is highly undesirable and prelacteal feeds of sweetened water, goat's milk, or diluted cow's milk are commonly given in the first two-to-three days postpartum (Reissland and Burghart 1988).

Perceptions about the child's state of health have also been reported to influence decisions about breastfeeding, particularly duration of breastfeeding. Adair and Popkin (1996) have reported that a mother's perception that her infant was small increased the likelihood of her not breastfeeding, even when she had the intent to do so before the birth of the infant, and perceiving that the infant was doing well increased the likelihood that breastfeeding would continue (Adair, Popkin and Guilkey 1993).

Women are increasing their work for income around the globe, and often this work is not recognized because it is contrary to prevailing norms about men's and women's roles. It is commonly believed that the most significant factor associated with declines in breastfeeding is women's work for income. Although studies generally do find that work contributes to less breastfeeding, there are many mothers who can continue to breastfeed despite working outside the home, and work is not the most significant factor reported. Aggarwal et al. (1998) reported that perceived breast-milk insufficiency, often based on the crying of the infant, was the most commonly cited reason, rather than needing to work or lack of childcare for supplementing breast milk among low-income urban women in Delhi. They began topfeeds before 4 months of age (non-human milks, usually highly diluted and prepared without proper hygienic conditions).

### COMPLEMENTARY FEEDING

UNICEF recommends initiating complementary feeding around 6 months of age, providing high-quality and nutrient-dense foods, and feeding five times a day from 6 months onwards, while continuing breastfeeding until 24 months.

Indian data in general show very delayed introduction of complementary foods; according to the 1992–3 National Family Health Survey data (NFHS 1992–3), only 31 per cent of children 6–9 months were receiving foods other than breastmilk, although they were receiving water and other liquids. The data from 1998–9 have improved little; 33 per cent of children are reported to receive foods other than breast milk from 6–9 months. A recent study in Pune, Maharashtra, suggested that these rates vary by location, with urban mothers introducing complementary food earliest (Philips et al. 2000),[1] followed by peri-urban and rural mothers. Children from the urban slum were also most likely to be stunted.

Beliefs can influence this timing. Although there are many reasons for this delay, including income level and education, one study of poor families in five states reported that mothers delayed because they perceived that the child was not interested. Mothers and grandmothers reported that one should wait until the child shows hunger before giving any kinds of foods (Chirmulay and Bhagwat 1997). Thus, how one defines and perceives a child's hunger can play a major role.

The caregivers' behaviour during feeding of complementary foods contributes significantly to the adequacy of children's nutrient intake, and, therefore, to their nutritional status. Clearly, dietary quality and quantity are important for nutrient intake, but they do not account for all of the variance. Practices related to how food is provided to children and fed to them are also important (e.g. Bentley et al. 1991; Shanker et al. 1998; Dettwyler, 1989; Gittelsohn et al. 1998). Feeding complementary foods requires much from the caregiver in addition to food selection and preparation (Engle et al. 1997). For example, caregivers must feed a child several times a day, and must decide when and under what circumstances to feed. They may encourage intake with praise, or may use demands or threats. They may feed children with spoon or fingers, or expect children to feed themselves. Caregivers often must decide how to deal with children who are uninterested in food or refuse it.

Good complementary feeding behaviour has three components: (1) adapting the feeding method to the child's psychomotor abilities (e.g. spoon handling); (2) feeding responsively, including feeding when the child is hungry, encouraging a child to eat, recognizing possible low appetite, balancing child versus caregiver control of eating, and using an affectionate or warm style of relating to the child during feeding; and (3) creating a satisfactory feeding situation by reducing distractions, developing a consistent feeding schedule, and supervising and protecting children during eating.

## PSYCHOSOCIAL CARE

Care practices that influence both growth and development of children are the kinds of social, emotional, and cognitive interactions between caregivers and children (Engle, Lhotska and Armstrong 1997; Engle and Riccuiti 1995).

*Responsiveness to developmental milestones and cues* affects children's growth and development. This includes the extent to which caregivers are aware of their children's signals and needs, interpret them accurately, and respond to them promptly, appropriately and consistently (Engle and Riccuiti 1995). Responsiveness can be illustrated by the caregiver's behaviour when a child cries or fusses. If the caregiver does not have time to respond, or misinterprets the reason for the crying, the caregiver may miss an opportunity to feed the child when the child is hungry. Responsiveness is also important for developing language. Even before they can talk, children understand simple adult speech, and can learn the give-and-take of conversation. Caregivers who talk to their children in simple language, and respond to children's verbal play, will help their children learn language earlier.

*The attention, affection and involvement* that caregivers show to children influence their growth and development. The most important factor in a child's healthy development is to have at least one strong relationship (attachment) with a caring adult who values the well-being of the child. Lack of a consistent caregiver can create additional risks for children. The child needs frequent positive interaction. To the extent possible, valuable traditional practices should be identified and sustained. Examples are infant massage in India, postpartum rest of mother and child in many Muslim countries, and responsiveness to child's desires in Bali. These customs may be undermined by an encroachment of Western values and urbanization.

*Encouragement of autonomy, exploration and learning* by caregivers can improve children's intellectual development and nutritional status. Young children are born with the ability to learn, but they need the encouragement and freedom to be able to develop that ability. Caregivers need to provide safe conditions for play, encourage exploration and provide learning opportunities in addition to good nutrition. Feeding may provide an opportunity for autonomy, as children learn to feed themselves at a young age. Enhanced opportunities for exploration and autonomy have been shown to affect growth (Super et al. 1990).

Hygiene and sanitation and food preparation, processing and storage are both groups of behaviour that have significant impacts on children's survival, growth and development.

## CAN INTERVENTIONS TO IMPROVE CARE PRACTICES AFFECT GROWTH?

International infant feeding guidelines promote (1) exclusive breastfeeding through 6 months of age; (2) the gradual introduction of soft and semi-solid puréed or mashed foods, followed by finely chopped foods; and (3) a transition to a family diet of appropriate quantity and quality to support adequate growth and cognitive development (WHO 1998, 1999). In actual practice, there is tremendous variation in the timing, type, and amounts of complementary foods that are offered to infants, which are related to cultural beliefs and norms (Piwoz et al. 1994; Bentley et al. 1997, 1999c; Engle et al. 1996; Zeitlin 1996).

Breastfeeding is a care practice that has been shown to be positively affected by interventions. Several recent studies have illustrated that breastfeeding counselling and promotion interventions can increase the initiation and duration of breastfeeding (e.g. Morrow et al. 1999). The effects may be due to related behavioural changes. In Ghana, mothers who stopped and burped children in the midst of a feed had children who ingested significantly more breastmilk than those who were not provided this opportunity. Zeitlin in Bangladesh reported that mothers who allowed children to terminate a breastfeed had significantly better patterns of growth than those who did not (Zeitlin et al. 1998).

Complementary feeding behaviours can also be changed. In Lima, Peru, a community-based communications project was developed to promote exclusive breastfeeding during the first 6 months of life and improved complementary feeding practices (Creed-Kanashiro 1994). Formative research was conducted to develop the messages and the intervention strategies. A significant increase in the prevalence of exclusive breastfeeding to around 6 months was found (from 32.7 per cent to 43.1 per cent of the population), primarily due to the reduction in the use of water and infusions, and a delay in the introduction of first foods, typically early in this population. Mothers were able to increase their preparation of thick foods (purées) and reduce giving very watery foods (soups) in line with the messages. The percentage of children 6–12 months age receiving 2 servings per day of energy-dense foods increased from 15 per cent to 28 per cent, thus increasing the energy density of intake. Complementary food demonstrations and horizontal or face-to-face communication within the community were found to be important communication methods.

In Uttar Pradesh, a formative research study by Linkages project of AED identified behavioural practices in breastfeeding and complementary feeding that could reduce intake of complementary foods. The mothers in the study all valued breastfeeding on demand. However, breastfeeding initiation was delayed in almost all cases (more than 50 per cent did not begin for 48 hours), pre-lacteal foods were usually given, exclusive breastfeeding only continued through the second month, and feeds were generally short, without emptying one breast. Hahjeboy et al. (1998) performed household trials to improve breastfeeding. Results showed that the most effective messages about breastfeeding were telling the woman to give longer breastfeeds, to empty each breast when the benefits of doing so were explained, to stop giving 'top milk' or animal milks. Mothers reported that the amount of breast-milk that they had available had increased when they followed these recommendations.

The researchers identified three problem behaviours in complementary feeding: late introduction of complementary foods, using food as a 'distracter' rather than as an element of the diet, and the belief that children less than 12 months cannot digest adult food. From 6–9 months children received only 114 calories a day, resulting in a deficit of 167 kcal per day. From 9–11 months, the children's diet was short by over 200 kcal per day. In the household trials, several messages regarding complementary feeding were found to be effective: giving higher density food, and giving family food. Mothers were willing to give higher density food, and reported that babies were happier, more active, and allowed the mother more time for her work. Mothers were also willing to give family food to the child, as opposed to special food, because it did not take additional time.

Interventions to improve infant feeding practices have demonstrated that behaviour change can lead to improvements in growth. Recently, Caulfield et al. (2000) reviewed 16 studies from 14 developing countries that promoted improved complementary feeding practices through simple, action-oriented messages. The results of these studies suggest that even in resource-poor settings, caregivers were willing to prepare and feed new recipes and foods. The range of positive impacts was of the order of +0.24 to +0.87

Structure Deviation (SD) for either weight-for-age or height-for-age.

A community-based study recently published in the *Lancet* promoted exclusive breastfeeding among Bangladeshi mothers and showed significant delay in the introduction of complementary foods and improvements in infant weight gain (Hyder et al. 2000). In Bangalore, a recent study showed that a home-visiting intervention that provided only counselling, without food, resulted in a significant improvement in growth velocity of girls from 6 to 10 months of age (Ganapathy et al. 2001). There is strong evidence then, that interventions to improve care practices can have significant effects on child nutrition and growth in developing countries.

### CHANGING FEEDING PRACTICES: FEEDING STYLES AND CULTURAL VARIABILITY

Complementary feeding behaviour is not easy to change, and cannot rely on mass media alone, as can other interventions (e.g. purchase of iodized salt). Programmes that have successfully modified complementary feeding practices have found that formative research to clarify messages, face-to-face communication, and the strategies of behaviour change are necessary (AED 1995, 1996; Manoff Group 1991; Creed de Kanishiro et al. 1991).

It is not surprising that interventions based on good communication strategies have been able to demonstrate changes in feeding practices. Not just food availability and quality, but also behaviour of child and caregiver restrict food intake. Research has shown that chronically malnourished infants in developing countries often do not eat all of the food that is available to them (Garcia et al. 1990; Caulfield et al. 1999). Poor appetite related to repeated infections and non-responsive feeding styles have been hypothesized to be explanatory factors (Dettwyler 1989; Engle and Riccuiti 1995; Bentley et al. 1991a, 1996, 1997).

Feeding behaviour often appears in patterns that represent an overall 'style' of feeding. Three caregiver feeding styles have been conceptualized by Birch and Fisher (1995) and further developed by Bentley et al. (1999a): controlling, laissez-faire, and responsive. In a highly controlling style of feeding, the caregiver has the intention to control when and how much the child eats, either through dietary restriction or overfeeding/control. Under these circumstances, some children may be unable to self-regulate their energy intake (Birch and Fisher 1995).

At the opposite end of the continuum, caregivers may provide little physical help or encouragement to eat, and this style of feeding may be based on cultural beliefs that a 'child knows' when and how much he should eat, or that children should develop independent feeding styles at an early age. This feeding style, described as 'laissez-faire', does not imply neglect or withholding of food, but rather describes low levels of caregiver-child interaction during feeding episodes. The amount of food that children consume may depend as much on the caregivers' active encouragement of eating as the amount offered (Gittelsohn et al. 1998; Bentley et al. 1991; Engle and Zeitlin 1996). Caregivers may not understand or respond to their infant's cues of appetite or satiety, and this may be particularly maladaptive when children have low appetites and reject food (Dettwyler 1989; Bentley et al. 1997). Parental beliefs or 'ethnotheories' provide the cultural rationale for these feeding styles (Harkness and Super 1994, 1996). These include the view that parents should not insist on a child eating more, because the child's stomach 'knows its own limits' (Dettwyler 1989; Engle et al. 1996). Eating may also be regarded as moral training, in that a child must learn not to demand food, but rather learn to eat according to parents' schedules. There is also a general belief that children will develop naturally, and that specific parental intervention (e.g. interactive feeding) is not needed unless the child is refusing food, or is ill (Bentley et al. 1991a; Engle et al. 1996).

Responsive feeding refers to the level and kind of interaction between caregiver and child that leads to a positive feeding experience, adequate dietary intake, and enhanced developmental opportunities. Some specific items of behaviour that encompass responsive feeding are the active provision of physical help, verbal encouragement, role-playing of food behaviour, offering more spoonfuls or helpings, persistence, positive strategies to improve dietary intake, monitoring of child cues of appetite and satiation, and increased maternal-infant interaction in general. A responsive caregiver perceives her child's cues, interprets them accurately, and responds in a contingent manner (Ainsworth et al. 1978). This is the essential component of feeding and care that is outlined in the UNICEF conceptual framework.

### HYGIENE PRACTICES

Improved hygiene and sanitation practices will also impact children's nutrition, and should be a key part of the ICDS programme. Recent research in five districts (data from UNICEF Water Section 2000) suggested that less than 50 per cent of parents understood that children's feces are sources of infection. A national survey (MICS II) showed that across the country, less than 10 per cent disposed of children's faeces in a toilet or latrine. Episodes of diarrhoea are well-known contributors to poor nutritional status, but efforts to improve these practices are often not included in health and nutrition programmes.

### IMPROVING RESOURCES FOR CARE

Many evaluations of the nutritional status of Indian children emphasize the need for childcare or day care for the young children of working mothers (e.g. Chirmulay and Bhagwat 1997; Udipi and Merchant 1995). Despite large government programmes to support food distribution, these day care needs are not met. Although one might think that children raised in a joint family would have a better chance for good nutritional status, data do not always support that perspective (Chirmulay and Bhagwat 1997). An extensive review of studies relating childcare time to children's nutritional status found that most studies did not find a simple association between increased time of the mother in childcare and improved nutritional status (Engle, Menon and Haddad 1998). More important factors appeared to be the woman's rate of pay, her control of her income, the flexibility of her work situation and the adequacy of alternate childcare (resources for care).

The hypothesis that increasing men's involvement in the care of their children will improve care practices remains to be tested adequately in India, although it seems to be reasonable. Family or intra-household dynamics clearly result in different care provided by gender and as a function of other characteristics, such as birth order (see review of benefits of increased father involvement in childcare by father in Engle and Breaux (1998).

In addition to poverty and social marginalization, the status of women may be an underlying variable explaining the Asian Enigma; children are better nourished in most African countries than in South Asia, even though incomes are similar (Ramalingaswamy, Jonsson, and Rodhe 1996). The authors suggest that the low status of women affects not only her care practices, but also her access to resources for care: autonomy in decision making, control over time and resources, access to resources, health and nutritional well-being. In many families the key decision maker is not the mother but the parents-in-law, and targeting the mother for behaviour change may be ineffective. Other family members must also be involved in behaviour change. Improving family care for women and girls needs to be a key intervention.

## IMPROVED PSYCHOSOCIAL CARE PRACTICES AND GROWTH AND DEVELOPMENT?

Evidence over the past 20 years clearly illustrates that early interventions to improve psychosocial care can have a significant impact on a child's cognitive and affective development, both through highly controlled experiments and in broad programme initiatives such as home visiting of high-risk families (Ramey and Ramey 1998; see WHO 1999 for a review). Factors that determine the size of the impact include earlier initiation of the intervention, more intense programmes, working directly with children in addition to improving parenting skills, and resources of parents, and factors related to the child, such as the perception that their child needs increased care, e.g. with low birth weight or premature infants) (Pelto, Dickin and Engle 1999).

Increasingly powerful evidence suggests that there is a link between nutrient intake and child development (Pollitt 1993; Pollitt et al. 1995) and that care practices can enhance both of these (Pelto et al. 1999). Several recent publications have outlined these positions (Engle et al. 1997; Engle, Menon and Haddad 1999), and the recent WHO/UNICEF/UC Davis/ORSTOM report on complementary feeding includes a discussion of care practices in feeding (Brown et al. 1998).

Three different models for the interactions of nutritional status and child development can be postulated. First, improved nutritional status can have a direct effect on a child's development through biological mechanisms of brain growth and function. Second, improved nutritional status of a child can have an indirect effect on both growth and development by changing child behaviour, which in turn will influence the caring environment, resulting in more responsive care. Third, improved care practices may have parallel effects on both growth and development.

### DIRECT EFFECTS

The effects of micronutrients such as iodine on brain development have been recognized for many years. Hetzel's groundbreaking work showed that even relatively minor levels of iodine deficiency can have negative effects on cognitive function (e.g. Hetzel et al. 1987). Interventions to improve iron intake have been shown in some trials to improve cognitive function, although not all studies have supported these findings (Pollitt 1993). In 1995, a review of studies designed to improve children's nutritional status concluded that there is a clear impact of improvements in overall nutritional status on children's cognitive development (Gorman 1995).

### INDIRECT EFFECTS

Evidence is also accumulating for indirect effects. In 1993, Pollitt et al. proposed that the effects of the nutritional intervention from the INCAP study in Guatemala were in part mediated by different care practices. As children became better nourished they were more active, and more demanding of attention. Research suggests that for children in poor homes, frequency of feeding is often related to child demand and interest in food. A malnourished child is less likely to express interest in food, and, therefore, less likely to receive it (e.g. Garcia et al. 1990). Parents may need help in recognizing the need for food intake among children who are passive and less demanding, particularly if they do not believe that children need food.

### PARALLEL EFFECTS

Third, parallel effects of improved parenting and parent availability may be seen for both nutrition and development. A key variable that has been identified is parental responsiveness to a child's changing abilities and to the child's messages or cues. These are often hard to understand before language is well developed, and attentive caregivers will note and interpret these attempts at communication.

Controlled trials show that improving parental responsiveness can have significant effects on young children's psychomotor development (Poley-Strobel and Beckman 1987). Riksen-Walraven (1978) assigned 100 Dutch mothers of 9-month-olds to four groups. In other studies, sensitivity or responsivity has been shown to be associated with children's learning and cognitive development (Murray and Hornbacker 1997). Responsiveness is not a single construct but a 'domain consisting of a complex of related constructs and variables' (Martin 1989: 7). Increasing responsivity during feeding would also influence responsiveness to the child more generally, which would have positive effects on the child's psychomotor development. Black et al. (1998) found a significant correlation between parents who were active feeders and those who were active participants in children's play. Interventions have been shown to affect both growth and development (see studies by Grantham-McGregor 1991; and Pelto Dickin and Engle 1999).

## EFFECTIVENESS OF INTERVENTIONS ON CARE

Overall, criteria for an effective intervention include the quality of the intervention, the appropriateness of the intervention for the conditions in the environment, and the interaction between environment and the child. For example, providing information about feeding frequency will not be helpful if the caregivers have no option but to leave the child alone all day in the house in order to earn the family food. Often there is an interaction between the intervention and the characteristics of the child; in some cases they can be effective for some kinds of children and families, whereas not for others.

The paper clearly argues that improving care practices can have a significant impact on nutrient intake, and, therefore, on growth and development. Second, it suggests that improving psychosocial care will affect both growth and development. It is important, therefore, to define the conditions under which improving care practices are likely to have the expected impact.

The characteristics of a child will influence outcomes for that child. Anorexic children require more persistent feeding than children with strong appetites do, and a difficult or irritable child will probably evoke different and perhaps less patient caregiving than a sunny, easy-to-manage child. In addition to temperament (easy or difficult), the child's health and nutritional status (well or poorly nourished, anaemic or iron-replete) affects how responsive a child is, and can have impacts on caregiving behaviour. Lozoff (1998) argues that one of the major effects of anaemia is increased fearfulness and reactivity in young children, which may reduce the child's ability to solicit care.

Some children, such as low-birth-weight infants, should have an immediate claim on resources, but they may be less able to demand attention. A review of 80 studies of low-birth-weight infants, mostly in developing countries, showed that LBW children generally have poorer levels of development than normal-birth-weight children (Aylward et al. 1989). Grantham-McGregor et al. (1999) summarized the literature regarding effects in children's growth and development of being Small for Gestational Age (SGA): SGA children are born at term, but are low-weight, suggesting that they were malnourished in utero. The literature suggests that whereas not all SGA children are lower in cognitive ability in the first two years, there are likely to be negative effects in middle childhood. These effects are less evident later in life. The negative effects of SGA are particularly marked when combined with an impoverished home environment.

Other child characteristics represent risks for children due to parental perceptions or cultural values. Haddad (1999) documents the significant negative effects on children of being born female. In many South Asian countries, girls are less preferred, less likely to receive healthcare, and have higher mortality rates. These effects operate through differential care practices and allocations of resources within the household.

## CONCLUSION

The most common intervention is to change behaviour related to care, or support positive existing behaviour. Other successful interventions are to have improved resources for care, such as setting up community childcare facilities, improving community response to needs for child referral, or strengthening women's capacity to make decisions affecting community decisions.

Doing a good communication package relies on careful formative research and testing of messages for their use. Research currently underway in Bangalore (Belaku 2001) suggests that factors associated with increased growth velocity are to change food consistency (more like a purée than a soup), offer more bites even if the caregiver suspects that the child will refuse (increase persistence and offering of new food), and increase feeding frequency. These are all care practices. However, the first two are rarely included in communication strategies to improve nutritional status, which tend to focus on food rather than feeding behaviour. Communication tools may introduce milestones of development, but rarely do they include information about what parents can do to improve care for development. Careful formative research will permit the construction of effective messages that will result in behaviour change. In successful behaviour-change projects, messages often incorporated the concept that food and nutrition are related to children's development. Parents are more likely to be motivated by the belief that they are improving a child's chances of doing well in school than by the belief that the child will grow bigger.

The elements of a successful behaviour-change intervention include, but are not limited to:

1. Formative research initially to define and refine key messages—can be done as a community process.
2. Development of simple, clear and consistent messages.
3. Messages tested for acceptability and use.
4. Identification of channels of communication, key actors and enablers.
5. Use of interpersonal communication and negotiation strategies.
6. Multiple sources of messages, from mass media to interpersonal communication.
7. All influential parties express the same messages.
8. Messages are linked to existing behavioural practices.
9. Actions expected are both feasible and important for the long-term goal.
10. Community is involved and supportive of change.
11. Motivation of individuals to change behaviour is assessed and strengthened.

What actions are recommended? Table 1 contains simple recommendations for care behaviour that could be recommended at each age level to be made to caregivers. They are part of a larger list of key actions based on IMCI standards. Other behaviour

TABLE 1: SELECTED EXAMPLES OF PSYCHOSOCIAL CARE FROM TWENTY KEY ACTIONS FOR FAMILIES AND COMMUNITIES TO IMPROVE CHILDREN'S SURVIVAL, GROWTH AND DEVELOPMENT: EARLY CHILDHOOD CARE PRACTICES*

| Action | Supported by |
|---|---|
| 4. Promote child's mental and social development by being responsive to the child's needs for care, and stimulating the child through talking, playing, and other age-appropriate physical and affective interactions. | AWW |
| *From birth onwards* | |
| Smile at your child, look into her eyes. | |
| Show your child that you love him or her. | |
| Give your child opportunities to see, feel, hear, and move. | |
| *From 4–6 months* | |
| Have large, colourful things for your child to see and reach for. | |
| Talk to your child and get a conversation going (sounds or gestures). | |
| *From 6–12 months* | |
| Give your child clean, safe items to handle, and things to make sounds. | |
| Respond to your child's sounds. | |
| *From 12 to 24 months* | |
| Give your child things to stack up, to put into containers and take out. | |
| Play games like 'bye', and encourage your child to name things. | |
| *From 24 to 36 months* | |
| Help your child count and compare things; make simple toys for her. | |
| Encourage your child to talk and answer your child's questions. Teach your child stories, songs, and games. | |
| 9. Look for child's slow development or low activity levels, bring them to the attention of service providers (AWW, ANM, and Supervisor), and provide additional encouragement for learning. | AWW, referral |
| 11. Ensure that men actively participate in early childcare for boys and girls, including teaching, verbal interaction, playing and communication, and physical care. | AWW, referral |
| 17. Ensure a nurturing environment without yelling and physical abuse to prevent child abuse/neglect, and take appropriate action when it has occurred. | Community pressure, AWW education |

(contd.)

TABLE 1 (contd.)

| Action | Supported by |
|---|---|
| 18. Support girls and women in the following ways:<br>*Young girls*: Equal access with boys to breastfeeding, other food, health care, and psychosocial care.<br>*School age*: Completion of primary education, equal access to school for boys and girls.<br>*Adolescents*: Get and take IFA tablets weekly for 52 weeks per year, help delay age at marriage and first birth.<br>*Women*: Support for participation outside home, dignity and respect in home. | Community pressure |
| 20. Strengthen the family's ability to provide care through information, training, and policies such as maternity leave legislation. | Government, civil society |

*Note*: IMCI standards.

for change include more responsive (less passive) feeding, using more and different strategies for dealing with children's food refusal, and increasing feeding frequency. Other care practices that might be amenable to change are too-early-expectations for self-feeding, and lack of attention to children's excessive food refusal. Psychosocial care can be improved by focusing parents' attention and awareness of developmental changes in children, and increasing their awareness of the importance of the first few years of life. Interventions to improve resources for care, such as education of caregivers, decreased workload, and community supports such as childcare centres are likely to improve children's nutrition. The existing government interventions through programmes such as ICDS and other related schemes could be reoriented to incorporate these changes.

## NOTE

1. The areas studied were representative of rural, urban and peri-urban locations: 400 mothers, each with a 6–24-month-old-child were interviewed for the study. The mean age of introduction of complementary foods was 7.6 ± 2.3 months for the whole sample. Only 13.2 per cent were getting complementary foods regularly by the sixth month. There was a significant difference in the time of introduction ($F = 8.5$, $p < 01$) and regular introduction ($F = 5.7$, $p < .01$) between

the three areas of study. The villages had the highest rate of late introduction with 47.9 per cent introducing after the 9th month, while the urban locations had the lowest rates of late introduction. The nutritional status also showed a statistically significant difference between the three locations (WAZ, $F = 24$, $p < .01$) (WHZ, $F = 6.67$, $p < .01$) (HAZ, $F = 37.3$, $p < .01$). The children of urban mothers, who were introducing complementary foods earlier, showed a higher rate of stunting compared to the others. One-way Analysis of Vairance (ANOVA) and ANCOVA analysis controlling for a number of social and economic variables indicated that there was no significant differences in nutritional status based on the timing of complementary feeding. Maternal time use and quality of the diet were the two variables associated with the nutritional status of the child.

SECTION IV

# Globalization and Food Insecurity

# 18. Food Security and Globalization

*Biplab Dasgupta*

Until recently, for about four decades, the concept of food security for a country like India was taken as quite simple and straightforward: it implied a goal of self-sufficiency to be fulfilled mainly by way of increased food production. Ever since India's Independence, achievement of 'food self-sufficiency' has been taken as a major goal of the Indian economy and of its five-year plans. Later, the term 'food security' came in currency, though for all practical purposes these two terms were taken as interchangeable; no one ever thought that food security could be achieved substantially excepting by way of increased food production. Internally, food security implied the maintenance of domestic food supply, both in order to provide protection against natural calamities such as drought, flood, or earthquake and also to meet domestic consumption needs during normal years. Internationally, this raised the very important issue of achieving self-sufficiency in food production, and correspondingly, minimizing reliance on food imports.

Some of the largest countries in Asia, such as India, Pakistan or Bangladesh, historically relied on food imports to bridge the gap between domestic demand and domestic supply. In all these countries, the underlying logic behind the drive towards self-sufficiency was that a country, particularly an agricultural one, should at least produce enough food for its citizens or should reduce import to the minimum, food supply being too important an item to be left to the mercy of the foreigners. Food was considered to be the 'basic' of all 'basic needs', even more important than shelter, job, health, drinking water supply or education.

There were other related issues, like the operation of Engel's law, that the expenditure on food as a proportion of total expenditure was likely to decline with progress, and that, over time, there was likely to be a shift in food consumption towards a more diversified and better-quality menu. Concern was expressed that the intra-family distribution of food was biased again women. There were debates on balanced diet, whether rice and wheat seeds should be so developed that a protein element was built into them, or that the menu itself, taking the cereals, vegetables, and pulses together, should provide such balance.

The importance of providing food to the non-food producers and distress-sellers by way of a Public Distribution System (PDS) was debated, as also the issue of an optimal food reserve that took care of the needs of the PDS and emergencies, while keeping the cost of storage at its lowest. It was also asked whether everything should be left to the market and the PDS should wither away in course of time, or whether PDS should be narrowly targeted for the poorest. Some asked whether such targeting was administratively feasible.

Agriculture being a way of life for more than two-thirds of the population, most of whom mainly produced for their own consumption, concern for food security was linked with that for agricultural development. Should the government bear responsibility for building rural infrastructure, for power, irrigation, fertilizer and what not, or should this task be left to the market, the latter charging the consumers the full cost of such development plus normal profit? The population policy also featured in the debate, in order not to let the growth of demand for food go out of control. At the end, the issue of 'poverty' and 'entitlement' came to the fore, with the recognition that the distributional issues could not be overlooked. Towering above all these was the issue of meeting the minimum calorie needs of everyone, which was taken as a major goal by most poor-country governments. The fact that per capita food availability per day, measured in grams, had declined since 1991, despite 13 successive good monsoons (a freak), worried planners. It also forced them to take account of the alarming possibility that, some time in the future, there could be a succession of droughts, like what happened in the first half of the 1960s. What action should be taken now to avert a further, drastic, fall in food availability in those future years?

## FOOD SECURITY BY WAY OF TRADE

In recent years, under the impact of 'structural adjustment' sponsored by the World Bank and the slogan of 'globalization' that has been vigorously championed by the recently established

World Trade Organization, it is being said that such quest for domestic self-sufficiency in food production is no longer necessary. It is being argued that, in today's integrated world, it is possible to bridge the gap between domestic demand and supply by way of food import. This is described, in sophisticated international jargon, as food security 'by way of trade'.

What this implies is that a country should produce only those commodities that it is good in producing at low and competitive prices. Whatever it earns by exporting a large part of the production of goods in which it has a comparative advantage, should be used to import goods that it does not (or should not) produce. The assumption underlying this view is that global integration is by now complete, the global trade is perfect and fully competitive, hence self-reliance is no longer necessary in this modern integrated world of free-flowing trade. If the country concerned does not enjoy comparative advantage in food production, then, according to this view, the option of securing it from the food-surplus countries should be the preferred one, rather than putting in more energy, time, and money in an enterprise in which it is not so good, comparatively speaking.

We should also recognize the economic philosophy underlying such a view. One of the main exponents of this view is Ann Krueger, who sees this policy of 'food security via trade' as an integral part of a much wider policy towards economy in general and agriculture in particular. She takes the view that in many of the agricultural policies in the less-developed countries a strong bias in favour of urban-industrial consumers is implicit. Food prices are controlled and not allowed to go beyond an upper limit, as it would affect the powerful urban consuming interests (Krueger 1992; Krueger 1974; Krueger et al. 1991).

Domestic production of agricultural inputs involves, according to this view, either subsidizing the domestic industrialist or allowing the prices of domestic production to be higher than international ones. In order to protect the high-cost domestic industries, the cheaper foreign sources are barred from entering the market by way of quantitative import restrictions or by subjecting them to high import duties. Both of these make agricultural inputs costlier than these would be had there been no control over imports and had the domestic industry not been protected. In other words, the policy of import substitution, and the accompanying controls and high tariffs, as also control over agricultural prices, work for the benefit of the urban-industrial interests, and against the agriculturist. It also involves a policy of discrimination in favour of non-tradables (things that cannot be exported, and in which the country concerned enjoys no comparative advantage), and against tradables, e.g. much of agriculture. Removal of controls of all types would, therefore, reduce the cost of agricultural production, and make those agricultural products, not necessarily food items, cheaper and competitive in the international market.

Therefore, this policy approach—against any idea of self-sufficiency, and for following a country's 'comparative advantage' in deciding on production and exports—involves a much wider scenario about the government's attitude towards subsidies, prices, controls on price, production, import, and so on, than simply the issue of self-sufficiency in food grain production. Underlying this policy approach is also a particular kind of political economy, that has come to be known as the 'New Political Economy', which proclaims itself to be pro-agriculturist, and which even calls for the beneficiaries—the agriculturists—to be rallied politically behind reform (Dasgupta 1998; Dasgupta 1997).

This new policy has much older roots. For a long time, the United States had been advocating that the poor countries should dispense with food self-sufficiency. John Block, US Agriculture Secretary, said at the outset of the Uruguay Round in 1986, that '. . . the idea that developing countries should feed themselves is an anachronism from a bygone era. They could better ensure their food security by relying on US agricultural products, which are available, in most cases, at lower cost.' This was one of the first occasions that the 'food security by way of trade' argument was mooted, and the context makes it clear that one of the motives was to find a market for the US agricultural surplus (Watkins 1992). The less-developed countries account for half of world food imports, and provide a large, actual as also potential, market for the US food exporters. There is a conflict of interest among the poor countries (between food importers and the self-sufficient and exporting ones) that keeps them divided in international forums, to the advantage of the rich ones. The food importing countries have a vested interest in cheap food prices, no matter where the food comes from (Hopkins 1993).

Such a view, arguing that food self-sufficiency was not necessary, and that food security can be obtained by way of trade, involves a number of important assumptions, including the following:

1. That global trade is so integrated that it is possible for any country to buy anything from any market, at a price ruling in that market.
2. That every country in the world makes production decisions on the basis of its 'comparative advantage', and imports the other required commodities from the integrated world market.
3. That non-economic factors, such as the needs for diplomacy or war do not influence the production and export-import decisions of a country.
4. That both the rich and the poor countries adhere to such rules of global trade.

Let us examine these assumptions in turn.

## FEW OPTIONS FOR FOOD IMPORT

The view that anybody can buy anything from the world market is, at best, naive and unreal. At its worst, it has been concocted in order to serve neo-colonial interests. In one recent instance, in the early 1990s, India's request for wheat was turned down by the US on the ground that the year before India had permitted the supply of one boatload of rice to its archenemy, Cuba (Mukherjee 1994).

Besides, the number of countries holding food surplus in the present-day world is alarmingly small, and most of those are rich, Western countries. The United States (US), Canada, Western Europe, Australia and Argentina are among the wheat surplus countries, while the number of rice surplus countries is even smaller, Thailand and Vietnam being notable among them. Besides, food consumers like Russia and China are so large that they can mop up the entire global surplus production of a year when they are suffering from natural calamities. India too is so big and its demand is so large, that its sizeable entry into the world food market is capable of effectively raising global food prices, to India's further disadvantage (Atkin 1995). Thus, the option for the purchase of food in the world market is not as wide as the protagonists of food security via trade would make us believe.

## FOOD DIPLOMACY

Taking the history of the past five decades into account, food had always been an important ingredient of the foreign policy of the United States [Webb and Krasner 1989; Frankel et al. 1979). Food was used as a weapon to force Pakistan and several other countries facing severe drought in the early 1950s to join military alliances led by the US. In the 1960s, countries depending on US wheat imports under the PL 480 agreement had to orient their economic and external policies in tune with US diplomatic, defence and economic needs. India, dependent as it was on PL 480 in the 1960s, had to carry out a devaluation of currency in 1966 that no one in India wanted. What was more humiliating was that India, a recognized leader of the non-aligned movement in the world, was forced to maintain its silence on the Vietnam war that was raging at that time. This pathetic subservience was brought about by two successive droughts and forced the government to rely for 10–15 per cent of the country's food needs on US bounty (Lateef 1994).

Nor should one forget the anxieties that the government and the people of the time had to undergo, as the country's survival was dependent on the next shipment of wheat from the US. In terms of economic policy changes induced by wheat imports, in addition to the forced devaluation, the Second Five-Year Plan had to be drastically pruned, and the planning exercise itself was made to lose its significance. Indian foreign policy changed and the Indian Government began speaking out again, taking a strong stand during the Bangladesh war in 1971, only after the country had achieved self-sufficiency in food, thanks to the new Green Revolution technology.

That was also the time when the Paddock brothers, having carefully examined the demand and supply conditions for world food, found that these two were grossly out of balance with one another, and within a few years, by 1975, the food surplus countries (particularly the USA, the sole food surplus country by then) would have to make the cruel but inevitable choice as to which countries were to be 'saved' and which countries 'could not be saved'. They concluded that, if such a decision had to be taken, it would be wiser to save a large number of small countries than a small number of large countries. It goes without saying that in the list they drew up, India was placed by them in the second, 'cannot be saved' category.

Of course, with the Green Revolution, the international food scenario changed radically, and in India itself production tripled in three decades from the mid-1960s, but the potential danger of a large country with many hungry mouths in a world with few food surplus countries, cannot be underplayed. Today, with similar crop varieties being cultivated in a large part of the globe, worldwide epidemics in a particular year sharply bringing down food cannot be ruled out, and in such a contingency, India would be one of the worst sufferers, more so if it relies heavily on foreign sources for its food.

As one commentator once observed, taking this historical experience into account: 'to stave off hunger and deprivation, attention to rural development was critical' (Lateef 1994). What he meant was that the basic task of producing food for meeting domestic needs cannot be ignored. Only scholars blissfully unaware of this historical perspective would urge 'removing controls and distortions associated with the "food security" complex', as if the fear associated with the issue of food security is a figment of the imagination and not embedded in the reality of the 1960s (Pursell and Gulati 1995; Dasgupta 1977). In addition, such PL 480 type food aid had several other negative consequences for all the aid recipient countries, e.g. these imports kept domestic agricultural prices as also the incentive for domestic production low (Kim 1995).

## JAPAN: FOOD SELF-SUFFICIENCY IN PRODUCTION

While the rich countries render to the poor countries the profound advice that they should not seek food self-sufficiency, as history shows, when it comes to the needs of their own economies and societies, they have always treated food security as one of the key national priorities. In 1988, the Japanese Diet passed a resolution confirming self-sufficiency in rice as a political objective. Its rice imports amounted to only 50,000 tons at that time, compared with the domestic demand of around 10 million tons a year, thanks to their quantitative restrictions over rice imports. The Japanese had always been reluctant to replace such quantitative restrictions by tariff, as tariffication alone would not dispel the Japanese fear of dependence on others for food. 'The government maintained that to the Japanese public such a radical change of policy appears highly dangerous due to the vulnerability of the Japanese rice market to climatic changes and other factors liable to cause wide fluctuations in supplies and prices on the world market.'

Further, 'there is the issue of food security. Any cut in domestic producer prices would reduce the area under rice cultivation', while such land is not suitable for non-rice cultivation (Hemmi 1994). Japan's present level of tariffication for rice is perhaps the highest in the world. It sees a protectionist policy as legitimate in national interest (Hopkins 1993).

If Japan, one of the richest countries in the world, with a per capita income that is one hundred times more than that of India and which can buy anything from anywhere in the world at any price, continues to provide more than 1,000 per cent cover to its domestic rice production on the ground that rice supply is too important to be left to the foreigners, then what ground could there be to abandon this target of food self-sufficiency in India now? (Hoekman and Cremoux 1993).

Historically speaking, one of the reasons why Japan carried out extensive land reforms in both Korea and Taiwan, their colonies for the early part of the twentieth century until the end of the Second World War, was to ensure a steady supply of rice for the Japanese consumers. The beneficiaries of land reforms, small farmers in both countries, were more open to training in modern technologies of rice production than the landlords they replaced, and helped Japan to maintain a good supply of the rice varieties of its choice within the territory it controlled (Nafziger 1995; Amsden 1988; Brautigam 1995). Japan's Food Agency has the monopoly to import and sell to domestic consumers at regulated prices (Atkin 1993).

## THE EU AND US: SELF-SUFFICIENCY

Similarly, both the US and Europe have, as the core of their agricultural policy, the objective of self-sufficiency in food. The Common Agricultural Policy (CAP) of the European Common Market was evolved on the assumption that the European economy would remain dependent on food imports for a long time to come. In their urge to reduce imports, domestic production was highly subsidized and imports of wheat were taxed fully to take away their competitive edge. However, in their overzealous drive to boost domestic production by way of subsidies, Europe, a food deficit region even in 1970, achieved self-sufficiency in 1980, and became transformed into a food exporting region—in cereals, beef, sugar, and dairy products—in 1986 (Moyer and Josling 1990). It is instructive to take note of four types of support mechanisms that were introduced in Europe in the late 1950s.

1. Minimum product prices were guaranteed through variable levies for cereals, sugar, milk, beef, pork, a number of fruits and vegetables and table wine.
2. For poultry, eggs, various types of fruits and vegetables, flowers and wines it was agreed not to intervene in the domestic markets, and to limit support to external protection.
3. For durum wheat, olive oil, cotton, tobacco, oilseeds, and sheep, support was primarily given by way of producer subsidies (called 'deficiency payments'). This enabled the food industry (bread from durum wheat, margerine from oilseeds) and the producers of animal feed (from oilseeds) to benefit from lower input prices.
4. A flat rate of 'producer subsidy' was given on the basis of area harvested or on production quantity for durum wheat, cottonseed, flaxseed, hops and silkworms (Folmer et al. 1995).

Thus, what was originally a concern for food security has taken Europe beyond self-sufficiency. Europe has been transformed into a major exporter of wheat, milk, and other primary products, mainly by way of heavy subsidy. In the US also the same concern for food self-sufficiency was so successful that, thanks to a colossal subsidy, it became the number one exporter of wheat in the world. The subsidy became so high, exceeding $40 billion a year, that even a very rich country like the US found it hard to continue subsidy on this scale. It proposed in the mid-1980s to subsidize farmers, 'not to plant and produce', in order to economize on storage and subsidization costs (Moyer and Josling 1990).

The Food Security Act of 1985 of the US has restricted the scope for the entry of food products of the poor countries. A whole battery of non-tariff measures has been deployed by the rich-country governments to keep the poor-country food exports out of their own markets.

Tapioca from Thailand was subjected to 'Voluntary Export Restraint' (VER), by no definition a 'voluntary' trade restriction, in Europe. Thailand canned food exports were subjected to chemical tests in the US, while frozen sea food and maize faced quantitative restrictions from Japan (Leeahtam 1991). Of 236 VERs the world over in the mid-1990s, 60 covered food and agricultural products (Low 1995).

The Western countries, generally speaking, have made far greater use of the 'safeguard' provisions in the General Agreement on Tariffs and Trade (GATT) agreements to their advantage than their poor counterparts, including those relating to food products. In 1993, out of 18 safeguard actions taken by European Economic Community (EEC), 13 were on processed foodstuff, and in case of the US, one such action was against imported preserved mushroom (Schott 1994).

In both the US and Europe, the farmers' lobby is recognized as politically powerful. 'In the US there is one bureaucrat for every five farmers and the budget of the US Department of Agriculture exceeds the net income of all farmers. In the European Community, two-thirds of the Community's budget goes to support farmers (Atkin 1993).

One scholar echoed the official European sentiment on this issue as follows:

> . . . even if the EU (European Union) does not intend to be major food exporter, it should not rely on the world market to satisfy its food needs under every emergency (like war, droughts, nuclear and other catastrophe in any part of the world) . . . The EU should preserve at least its capacity to produce food, even when it chooses temporarily to allocate its arable land to other uses. Unless specific restrictions are imposed, it will hardly be possible to ever reconvert agricultural land back to food production once it has had a non-agricultural use. 'Asphalt is the land's last crop', as they say. Therefore, the safeguarding of the productive capacity of land should become a major preoccupation of European agricultural policy in the future. (Folmer et al. 1995)

An authentic advocacy for food security, by the rich countries themselves that bears no resemblance to the globalization rhetoric they deploy for the poor-country listeners. For the rich countries, the old fashioned definition of food security would apply, globalization or no globalization. For the poor countries, it is food security 'by way of trade'.

## ADVANTAGE OF US/EUROPE IN FOOD PRODUCTION?

This issue also raises the question: what is comparative advantage? In case of wheat, neither of the two leading players in the international arena, the US and Europe, enjoys comparative advantage in its production, but can still manage to make their costly production cheap in the world market by way of enormous subsidies, around $40–50 billion each, every year. In case of United Kingdom (UK), subsidies to farmers that were equal to the difference between the 'desired' and the average market price were in vogue even prior to its accession in the EEC, in order to maintain a low food price for the consumer. In the US, floor price for wheat is determined by the 'loan rate' fixed by the Department of Agriculture, at which the farmer can secure a loan from the government against his crop. He can take back the crop if the market price is high. Otherwise, the stock accumulates in the hands of the government, and the latter sells or uses it as food aid or for subsidizing exports (Atkin 1993).

Though Article 39 of the Treaty of Rome signed in 1957 by the six original members of the European Community incorporates an agricultural policy in general terms, CAP was formalized in 1962. The main basis of CAP is a 'target' or desired price that provides satisfactory return on agricultural investment by domestic farmers. The CAP also refers to a 'threshold price' below which an import is not permitted, irrespective of the world market price. The European Commission (EC) charges a 'variable levy' that is equal to the difference between the 'world market price' and the 'threshold price'. The 'intervention price' is the price at which the member governments buy agricultural produce. Domestic prices fluctuate between 'threshold price' and 'intervention price'. For export surpluses that arise because the domestic market cannot absorb all that is produced and are sold to the interventioning authorities, a subsidy is given to bridge the difference between European and world market prices (Atkin 1993; 1995). If these subsidies are withdrawn, not a single grain of wheat from these sources would be sold anywhere in the world. Taking the rich Organization for Economic Cooperation and Development (OECD) countries together, in the early-1990s their aggregate subsidy for agricultural products amounted to $240 billion, which was equal to one-third of the income of their agricultural producers (Watkins 1992).

## ENVIRONMENTAL NEEDS FOR FOOD PRODUCTION

The Brundtland Commission on World Environment also recognized the highly protectionist nature of rich-country agriculture, and that such protection was many times what was given to their agriculturists by poor-country governments (Brundtland 1987). The commission also pointed to the gross abuse of environment by the rich-country agricultural subsidy. It pointed out that every year 10,000 people died and 4,00,000 suffered from pesticide poisoning in the less-developed countries, soil erosion had become widespread, while the interests of the small producer were being neglected (Brundtland 1987). The commission urged government intervention to protect forests, as private business, guided by the lust for profit, was prone to ignore ecological considerations (Brundtland 1987). The commission advocated land reform and an equitable distribution of resources for protecting the environment (Brundtland 1987).

The commission also took the view that food security was essential, and to achieve this, 'Most developing countries need more effective incentive systems to encourage production, especially of food crops.' Further, such concern for food security should be buttressed by land reforms, as also by policies to protect the vulnerable, biodiversity and tropical forests (Brundtland 1987).

Excessive commercialization is also making agricultural production less stable, vulnerable to vagaries of international prices and subject to environmental degradation. Over the past two decades, under structural adjustment the area under forest has been drastically reduced in countries like Thailand, the Philippines and Malaysia, the annual rates of depletion during 1990–5 being alarming: 2.6 per cent, 3.5 per cent, and 2.4 per cent, respectively (World Bank 1998–9).

The spread of shrimp farming has exposed the traditional mangrove-covered coastline in many countries to serious ecological risk. Shrimp farming is causing irreversible changes in land use. As saline water is intruding into paddy fields, such land cannot be restored to paddy cultivation even after the shrimp bonanza ends. Shrimp cultivators are becoming increasingly vulnerable to oscillations in world prices, emergence of new and cheaper supply sources, periodic epidemics, bans imposed by major consuming countries on health grounds, and other ills that were unknown to them when they began this commercial venture. A large volume of non-target, that is non-shrimp, fish is being destroyed every day as the commercial agriculturist is focusing on one particular item (Skladany and Harris 1994; Barraclough and Finger-Stich 1996; Shiva et al. 1997).

Such issues are particularly relevant for Asia, as this continent boasts of some of the most sensitive biospheres in the world. Countries like Indonesia or Malaysia, as also to a greater and lesser extent almost all the other countries in South and South-East Asia including India, contain enormous biodiversity in terms of both flora and fauna. In this area one finds the largest number of biological species that need to be carefully preserved. Such biodiversity is coming under severe threat because of deforestation and commercialization of agriculture. It is also increasingly coming under the serious threat of 'bio-piracy' by Western MNCs (Dasgupta 1998).

No less important is the fact that, over time, more and more land is being devoted to non-agricultural urban-industrial uses. In the early days of Indian planning, it was thought that some increase in food production would come about by way of extension of cultivation. Even now, a large part of India's geographical land area is cultivable, in proportion, more than any other country in the world except Bangladesh and Ukraine. China, three times bigger than India, possesses less cultivable land than India. This shows how lucky we are. By the late 1950s, it dawned on our planners that such extension was no longer feasible: further increase in food production should come by way of increased land productivity. There is no doubt that a massive increase in production has come about by way of land productivity over the past three decades, particularly through new agrarian technologies and inputs, but we are now facing a real danger of shrinking agricultural land, with the growing use of land for urban-industrial purposes. Yet, the fact remains that, despite recent increases, our land productivity is still low, comparing it with the figures for China and other comparable countries, and there is room for increasing land productivity by more intensive application of modern inputs.

## AGRICULTURE AND INDUSTRY: COMPARATIVE ADVANTAGE

The view in favour of 'food security by way of trade', as we have seen above, also postulates a hostile relationship between the urban-industrial interests on the one hand, and the agricultural-rural interests on the other. It suggests that, going by their comparative advantages, the poor countries should specialize in agriculture, and within agriculture, in non-food items, if food production is not in line with their comparative advantage. Normally, they should not venture into industries, but if they do, such activity should remain confined to light industries like textiles. One rough approximation of what is and what is not in tune with the comparative advantage of a country can be made in terms of the ratio of domestic prices to international ones. If the domestic price is higher than the landed price of a commodity imported from outside, then the country concerned does not enjoy comparative advantage in that item, and it should not be produced.

We have already noted that this simplistic measure does not take into account the fact many of the internally traded commodities contain in their prices a large subsidy element. And if such subsidies were removed, the landed prices of the internationally traded commodities would, in fact, be much higher than the domestic prices. World trade is far from fair and competitive, and world prices are not determined by the autonomous interaction of the forces of demand and supply. The so-called 'world prices' do not reflect comparative advantages, and should not form the basis for domestic production decisions. Neither the US nor Europe enjoy a comparative advantage in wheat production and exports, but still they manage to control and dominate world trade in wheat because of the enormous subsidies their governments give.

Further, because the rich countries dominate world trade in practically everything, they are the ones who fix the rules of international trade. As long as the US was happy to give heavy subsidies to its agriculture, agriculture was not made a part of the GATT trade negotiations. When subsidies reached a level that even a rich country like the US was unable to sustain, it began advocating a reduction in the level of subsidies, and the item became a matter for GATT negotiations in its eighth (that is the last) round of negotiations.

Again, when it came to subsidy reduction, it prescribed a percentage-wise reduction that, given the very high level of US subsidy, maintained subsidy at a very high absolute level despite the 36 per cent reduction in value and 21 per cent reduction in volume, over a period of six years (between 1995 to 2000). They did not agree to the complete elimination of subsidy or a reduction of subsidy in absolute terms, or on the basis of per head of agricultural population, that could whittle down their level of subsidies to poor-country levels. Further, they arbitrarily decided to classify subsidies into good ones that were not production- or trade-distorting, and the baddies that distorted production and trade. It goes without saying that they classified their own massive subsidies as 'good' ones, after some changes in definition and some tinkering with the method of giving subsidies, while continuing to classify the small, poor country subsidies as the 'bad' ones.

The very idea that the poor countries should only develop their agriculture, and should refrain from participating in heavy and chemical industries can be challenged on the basis of the history of industrialization. As it can be seen from the statistics provided by the World Development Report for 1998–9, the contribution of agriculture to GDP becomes less as the country becomes more industrialized, while, at the same time, its agriculture becomes more productive and efficient in its utilization of land resources and rural labour power. In case of Japan, the share of agriculture in GDP is only 2 per cent, followed by 6 per cent in case of South Korea, 11 per cent in Thailand, 13 per cent in Malaysia, 16 per cent in Indonesia, 20 per cent in China, 26 per cent in Pakistan, 27 per cent in India, and 30 per cent in Bangladesh. This is more or less the order in which they appear in terms of GDP per capita and other major indicators. In other words, the ultimate solution to the land problem lies outside agriculture, while a productive agriculture, by producing a large enough surplus, enables people to move off the land for urban-industrial occupations.

The logic of the view that the poor countries should only engage themselves in agriculture and small industries can be challenged on other grounds too. The industries of Japan, South Korea, Taiwan, Singapore and Hong Kong could grow because they rejected this profound advice (Amsden 1988; Wade 1990). Going by the history of industrialization world over, the transition from 'less developed' to 'developed' status comes along with a move to grow out of food and textiles and venturing into a wide array of industries, both for meeting domestic needs and for exports.

The relationship between agriculture and industry is, in contrast with the view of the global trinity that it is antagonistic, essentially a symbiotic one. Agriculture alone cannot solve all the major problems that arise in the countryside. The development of industry and towns is a logical outcome of agricultural prosperity. Indeed, generation and mobilization of agricultural surplus and its productive use in industry has been the key to industrialization in every country that is developed today. The growth of towns and industries, on the other hand, has created opportunities for migration in search of employment in the urban areas. By projecting the relationship as being hostile, and by playing the agriculturist against the urban population, the global trinity and the protagonists of the New Political Economy are attempting to divide the people and to divert attention away from exploitation of the poor countries by the rich-country MNCs.

This so-called 'pro-agriculture' policy has not led to the development of either agriculture or industry anywhere in the poor world, since structural adjustment was introduced two decades ago in 1980. Whatever the agriculturist has gained in terms of cheaper inputs and higher food and other agricultural prices has been negated by the withdrawal of subsidies—for food, fertilizer and inputs—and under-investment in agriculture (Mukherjee 1994; Dasgupta 1997a). The decline in the rate of growth in Indian agriculture in recent years has been largely because of this policy of withdrawal of subsidy to fertilizer and the reduction in expenditure on agricultural infrastructure. In 1991 itself, at the very beginning of the reform process, fertilizer subsidies were cut, mainly on fiscal grounds, that led to a rise of 40 per cent in the issue price of fertilizer. At the same time, some of the low-analysis fertilizers—(ammonium sulphate, calcium chloride and sulphate of potash) were decontrolled. After three weeks, the average price of fertilizer was reduced by 10 per cent and small and marginal farmers were exempted from high prices: by then, the cultivation season was tapering off, and the dual pricing created administrative problems. The rate of growth of fertilizer consumption declined (Dasgupta 1997b; Mukherjee 1994).

Domestic agricultural producers have also suffered from the liberalization of agricultural imports. With the complete removal of quantitative restrictions in April 2001, their production has remained unsold and/or the prices of their products have registered sharp falls. Though the official analysis finds no evidence of a torrent of imports, the adverse impact of this policy might be felt after a time lag. It might also be that the official statistics have failed to capture the intensity of the problem. Already, the domestic small industries are up in arms against cheaper and qualitatively better 'Chinese exports', and their sharp reaction from all over the country shows that such imports are hurting them. Once the door is opened, how can one control who would be coming and who would not? Despite much hype, agricultural exports have failed to take off, and have remained fixed at around one-fifth of the total value of exports. So much for the New Political Economy of the World Bank.

## THE FATE OF PDS

Even where the agriculturist has gained from higher agricultural prices, there have been other, poor and non-poor, households that have suffered because of higher food prices. The distress-selling poor agricultural producer, who sells cheap during harvesting only to buy at a high price several months later, is one such segment of population. Among others, one can mention the agricultural labourer, artisan, urban poor and industrial worker.

One way by which the agriculturist could be given higher prices for his toil, while not hurting the food-purchasing sections, was by putting in place a comprehensive public distribution system that covered the basic needs such as those for food, kerosene oil, sugar, salt, etc., at reasonable prices. The current trend is not only not to build and develop such a system, but wherever these exist, to dismantle those. While the World Bank and its two ideological partners would like to dispense with the public distribution system, they know that such a decision cannot be easily implemented because of political opposition. They are, therefore, asking for a 'targeted' public distribution system that would only supply the very poor. But targeting that involves the identification of the poor is often, as the experience of the FAO with several countries indicates, more costly in terms of administrative and other expenses than the saving in expenses it manages to achieve (Knudsen and Nash 1991; Islam 1991; Development Committee 1993).

In fact, a kind of targeting is implicit in the way the PDS works. Given the quality of food supplied by the PDS, only the most desperate would be willing to take advantage of it. The offtake usually goes down when people feel that they are better-off, and goes up in years of crisis. Such targeting always goes on, without incurring a heavy administrative expenditure to identify the poor. I am not suggesting that bad-quality food should be reserved for the poor, nor that high-quality basmati should be supplied via the PDS system. As the figures suggest, in normal times, only a part of the identified poor population rush for PDS supply.

## COMMERCIALIZATION AND EXPORT OF AGRICULTURE AND ITS CONSEQUENCE ON TERMS OF TRADE

The view of the global trinity—Fund, Bank and World Trade Organization (WTO)—that food security is not necessary has its counterpart in the drive towards commercialization. As we have already noted, according to the global trinity, the comparative advantage of the poor countries lies in agriculture, in its production and exports. Had this advice been given to a country or two, this had the possibility of succeeding for those. But the global trinity was quite generous in rendering such advice, and gave it to any country that was willing to listen. As a consequence, this has led to an excess of production of agricultural products at the world level, and a corresponding sharp drop in their international prices.

The global terms of trade between agriculture and industry have been moving consistently against agriculture over the past few decades, and this trend is likely to persist, according to the World Bank itself, at least until the end of the first decade of this century. The index of real commodity prices fell by half between 1980 and 1993. According to Lewis T. Preston, President of the World Bank in the mid-1990s, the fall of $100 billion, in non-oil commodity prices between 1980 and 1993 was more than double the net aid flows to developing countries in 1993 (Development Committee 1994). More alarming, from the point of view of the subject matter of this article, the share of food in world trade has declined from 21.4 per cent in 1962 to 9.5 per cent in 1992, and of non-food agriculture from 10.2 per cent to 2.1 per cent (ECLAC 1994).

In this situation, further emphasis on agricultural production for exports can only increase the glut of agricultural commodities at the world level, leading to a situation where the poor countries of the world would continue producing more and more to earn less and less. During the 1980s, the volume of world agricultural exports increased by 2.3 per cent, while their value increased by only 1.4 per cent a year, confirming what has been stated above (ECLAC 1994). This movement of terms of trade would undoubtedly help the importing rich countries, but would at the same time ruin the poor-country economies in general and agriculture in particular.

Further, this excessive commercialization has led to a shift in land use away from subsistence crops, particularly those that comprise the diet of the poor household, e.g. wheat replacing inferior cereals like sorghum or millet. At the same time, it is making the poor countries more dependent on the food-surplus rich countries/regions, such as the US, Canada, or western Europe for their subsistence. The inequality is likely to grow further if the export-orientation of agriculture gives rise to further concentration of land in the hands of the richer farmers and even MNCs (Mukherjee 1994).

Third, it has brought the MNCs into the countryside as producers or as suppliers of inputs. This is a new phenomenon in the context of Asian agriculture. In India, even under British colonial rule (leaving aside their early incursions into indigo and poppy cultivation in the countryside soon after their conquest, and their involvement with tea and coffee plantation latter in sparsely-populated areas), the British refrained from active participation in crop production. In Africa, the British farmers were active in Kenya, Rhodesia, and South Africa, the French colonies in Morocco, Algeria and Tunisia, and the Italians in Libya, but nothing like this happened in Asia under colonial rule. But what did not happen during foreign rule is now happening in these countries under their own, independent governments.

## GROWING MNC PARTICIPATION IN AGRICULTURE

As a corollary of the policy of globalization, MNCs are increasingly participating in Asian agriculture, both as producers and exporters of agricultural outputs and as suppliers of agricultural inputs. In many cases, their production is displacing indigenous agricultural production, e.g. Coca Cola replacing coconut water. Sometimes they operate their own plantations and work with their own agricultural labourers, but sometimes they enter into contracts with the existing agriculturists. The contracts entered into by companies like Monsanto with a large number of small farmers, are by their very nature one-sided and unequal.

The farmer is expected to produce in accordance with detailed specifications laid down by the company, use inputs supplied only by the company and deliver the entire output only to the company. He is told what to produce and by what combination of inputs. Both the prices of inputs used by the farmers and the prices of the products delivered by the farmers to the company are unilaterally determined by the company. Once having entered this dependency relationship, the farmer can seldom extricate himself from the company and recover his independence. While this relationship is producing millions of dollars for the MNCs, the poor farmer is remaining as poor as he had been at the beginning of the agreement.

In many cases, the objective of the multinational company is not so much agricultural production, but the sale of input packages, in this case to farmers who have not entered into supply contracts with them. Monsanto, one of the leading multinational agribusiness farms, specialized in weed-killing chemicals during the days of the Vietnam war in the 1960s; their weedicides were deployed to destroy the rich foliage of Vietnam to remove the natural cover to the movement of the nationalist/communist guerrilla forces. Though later they moved into seed production too, they specialized in producing those seeds that were compatible with the weedicides that Monsanto produced. In this way, a package of inputs, corresponding well with the seeds of a multinational company, is being delivered, thus making the agriculturist completely dependent on the latter company, even when he is not under any contract with it. Once entering into this dependency relationship, the farmer would hardly be able to extricate himself from the company, and the dependence would be perpetuated.

The obsessive urge for profits has led the MNC seed-breeding companies to develop what has come to be known as 'terminator seed'. Here, the objective is to force the farmer out of the habit of multiplying seeds initially procured from the MNC, and to make him buy seed from the company every time he goes for cultivation. While agriculture is identified, in popular perception, with reproduction and regeneration, this technology makes the seed sterile after single use, so that the agriculturist is forced to go back to the seed manufacturing firm again and again.[1]

## CONCLUSIONS

This paper shows that the concept of food security has undergone a radical change in recent years. While for four decades since Independence this implied an emphasis on self-sufficiency in domestic food production, over the past one decade or so the emphasis has been shifted to what has come to be described as 'food security by way of trade'. As our paper shows, this shift is unwarranted and motivated. Global trade is not so integrated that one can buy as much of what one needs from the world market, very few countries of the world having a surplus in food production, and such supply is not available without political costs. Even a rich country like Japan is averse to 'food security by way of trade', and is doing everything possible to achieve domestic food self-sufficiency at an enormous cost, food being so important and basic according to their thinking.

Our paper shows that all the rich, industrialized countries strove to reach the target of self-sufficiency in domestic food production, and while achieving this target, they did so well that they were transformed into leading global food exporters. But the competitiveness of their exports does not lie in their comparative advantage, but in the colossal subsidies they give to their agricultural producers. While, with the formation of WTO they had to scale down their subsidies, this was done on a percentage basis, and not on per head basis or by way of an absolute limit to subsidies. This more or less helped them to retain their comparative price advantage over poor, agricultural, countries. Further, definitions of subsidies were formulated in a manner that categorized the massive rich-country subsidies as not being production- or trade-distorting, while much smaller subsidies of the poor countries were castigated for trade or production distortion.

The New Political Economy of the global trinity—World Bank, International Monetary Fund (IMF) and WTO—provides theoretical justification for structural adjustment, stabilization and globalization, and projects such a policy to be pro-agricultural and opposed to urban-industrial interests. The fact is that the countries that follow their prescription seldom do better in agriculture than those who do not. 'Under-developing' Sub-Saharan Africa, a region which followed the prescriptions of the global trinity almost line by line, presents a sad and horrifying contrast with East Asia (not the southern tier of Thailand, Malaysia, Indonesia and the Philippines), where the State intervened, directed saving and investment, gave generous subsidies to activities that they wanted to promote, made the public sector an instrument of development in banking, steel, automobiles, chemicals and other heavy industries, and in every possible way did everything 'wrong' according to the theology emanating from the World Bank, in the course of their development (Amsden; Wade).

One of the most worrying features of the food industry in the developed countries of today is that gradually agriculture is being delinked from the food industry, and is becoming smaller in comparison with the latter. Agriculture is now one of several options as inputs available with the food industry, along with bio-mass, hydrocarbons and chemicals, and more and more food items are being produced and consumed that are not grown in the fields or on the trees, like hamburgers, Pepsi and sweeteners. While this tendency is not as pronounced in India as in the rich countries, it is noticeable that advertising is making a tremendous impression on people's tastes and preferences, at the cost of domestic production. The impact of this change is going to be comparatively more severe in the poor countries where agriculture is a way of life. Even many small rural industries, on which the livelihood of millions depends, is based on food and fruit processing by using simple technologies (Goodman 1991; Fried-man; Barrat-Brown and Tiffen 1994).

## NOTE

1. However, the Protection of Plant Varieties and Farmers Rights Bill, 2001, currently before the Select Committee of the Parliament provides for farmers' rights to save, use, sow, and save the seeds. Terminator seeds will also not be permitted in the Indian situation.

# 19. WTO and Food Security: Issues in the Context of Small Farmer Economies like India

*D. Narasimha Reddy*

As is well known, the WTO was established after a highly controversial Uruguay Round of negotiations of GATT spread over eight years. One of the contentious issues relates to the provisions and implementation of the Agreement on Agriculture (AOA). One of the central issues of cause for concern under AOA is 'food security'. Interestingly, the concern for food security is shared both among a group of developed countries which would like to preserve the multi-functionality of agriculture and among developing countries, which aim at a reasonable self-reliance in food production and economic accessibility.

The World Food Summit of 1996, building on the earlier internationally-agreed definition of food security, states: 'Food security exists when all people, at all times, have physical and economic access to sufficient, safe and nutritious food to meet their dietary needs and food preferences for an active and healthy life.' The emphasis is not only on the physical availability of food but also on the economic accessibility, meaning ability to buy food, which is linked to remunerative employment, which in turn, in many developing countries, is associated with access to land and employment opportunities in agriculture and related activities. Until transition to a higher stage of development, the link between physical access through domestic production and economic access through employment in agriculture can only be ignored at the cost of jeopardizing food security.

In contrast, the WTO approach to agriculture and food security is trade-linked. It considers that aiming at food self-sufficiency or agriculture-linked employment and income security as inefficient.

The trade-induced agricultural development and food security are based on well-known endowments-related production strategy. It advocates boost to food production in countries where it can be produced at lowest cost, including the many developing countries whose agriculture is affected by subsidy practices abroad. It is argued that such a global specialization in food production would lead to improved efficiency, reduced costs and lower prices. Lower food prices will make food more affordable, it is argued, particularly for the poor. The AOA is, therefore, aimed at limiting, if not removing, all production- and market-distorting interventions like subsidies, protective measures such as quantitative restrictions and high tariffs. It considers all non-market or non-trade-related arguments as impediments to global welfare. These premises of WTO have been extensively contested. The second part of this paper analyses the provisions of the AOA and the related Sanitary and Phytosanitary Standards (SPS), Technical Barriers to Trade (TBT) and Trade-Related aspects of Intellectual Property Rights (TRIPS) and the effects of their implementation during the last five years. The third part of the paper discusses the 'trade-plus' issues, including multi-functionality of agriculture and their relevance to food security. The last part argues for a negotiating strategy with an emphasis on more room for trade-plus issues in the AOA and related agreements with a view to ensuring food security for the small farmer-based economies through a 'food security box' or 'development box'.

## WTO PROVISIONS, IMPLEMENTATION AND FOOD SECURITY

This section discusses the provisions and implementation of AOA and related agreements like the SPS, TBT, the Ministerial Decision concerning least developed and Net Food Importing Developing Countries (NFIDCs), and agriculture-related part of the TRIPS and their implications for food security. Let us first examine the provisions and implementation of AOA.

The AOA has three components: (1) *market access*, which aims at freeing imports from quantitative restrictions and introduction of tariffs with specified upper bounds; (2) *domestic support*, which aims at reducing domestic subsidies to farmers, and (3) *export subsidy*, which is intended to reduce government subsidies to agricultural exports. In the case of market access and export subsidy, instead of fixing any absolute limits, a differential reduction on existing levels is proposed. Domestic support differentiates different support for agriculture and also fixes a differential limit on what is felicitously defined as 'subsidies'. Apparently, the provisions relating to all these measures give an impression that less-developed countries are given more concessions, while the developed countries are subjected to more discipline. In reality, it is quite the contrary. True, in some provisions, the transition period for the developed countries is shorter and the new provisions would come into effect from AD 2000, while the less-developed countries are given time up to 2004. But there ends the discretion. The AOA equates farming systems of the industrialized countries with those of the subsistence systems like those of India, which is grossly iniquitous. To this theme, we shall return in the third section. Presently, we shall analyse the provisions under each one of the three measures under the agreement with a view to unravelling the underlying inequity.

### MARKET ACCESS

The objective of 'Market Access' is to promote relatively free imports. The agreement under Market Access has two measures, 'tariffication', and reduction of tariffs by a certain percentage. Removal of all kinds of quantitative restrictions like import quotas, minimum import prices, discretionary licensing, state trading, total ban of certain imports and switching towards tariffs in the place of these measures, is called 'tariffication'. This means that, after AD 2000, the developed countries cannot ban any imports of agricultural commodities, except for reasons of sanitary and phytosanitary conditions. And the less-developed countries too will have no such right to ban agricultural imports after 2004. Some countries like India, which do not have balance of payments problems, are forced to comply with it much earlier. The only way left to regulate imports is through tariffs, which, in any case, have to be reduced. The sly here lies arriving at tariff equivalents of non-tariff measures. Most of the less-developed countries have left their schedules blank or ended up with very low tariff equivalents.

Regarding the reduction of tariffs, the AOA stipulates that the developed countries should reduce their tariffs by 36 per cent by 2000, whereas the less-developed countries should reduce the tariffs by 24 per cent by 2004. Apparently, it looks as if the less-developed countries are permitted to retain higher tariffs since the reduction requirement is only 24 per cent compared to 36 per cent of the developed countries. The developed countries, which have been protecting their agricultural products for a long time, have retained very high tariffs and even after 36 per cent reduction, the tariffs will be very high. Some of these typically high tariffs are (Das 1998):

| | | |
|---|---|---|
| US | : | sugar (244.4), peanuts (173.8), milk (82.6) |
| EU | : | beef (213.0), wheat (167.7), sheep meat (144) |
| Japan | : | wheat products (388.1), wheat (352.7), barley products (361) |
| Canada | : | butter (360), cheese (289), eggs (236.3) |

In contrast to these prohibitive tariffs of the developed countries, most of the less-developed countries, which do not have much experience in protecting their agricultural commodities, field very low tariffs. Though many developing countries have adopted bound tariffs ranging from 100 to 150 per cent, the applied tariffs are much lower, ranging from 10 to 40 per cent. An FAO study of 14 developing countries shows that none of them could use the full range of bound tariffs because of the following reasons: (1) their commitment to international financial organizations; (2) fear of ruining trade relationships with big exporters, and development aid givers; and (3) the necessity to maintain low consumer prices (FAO 1999). Not many developing countries could make use of Tariff-Rate Quotas (TRQ), which is a way of retaining a protective measure by charging two levels of tariff rates for the same product.[1] But the tariffs retained by the rich countries, as shown by the example of the US, EU and Japan for some of the commodities, are very high.

The net result is that even after meeting the reduction requirement, developed countries will end up with high tariffs and less-developed countries with low tariffs. Even after five years of implementation of the AOA, the agricultural tariffs of the developed countries remain six times higher than industrial tariffs, and there is little impact of AOA on promoting developing countries' access to agricultural trade (FAO 1999). 'Market Access' thus ends up as access of the rich countries to the markets of the poor countries and *not* vice versa.

DOMESTIC SUPPORT

'Domestic Support', or what is termed 'Aggregate Measure of Support' (AMS), is calculated in terms of product and input subsidies provided by the government to the agricultural sector as a proportion of the total value of agricultural output. It is argued that the provision of product-specific subsidies like support prices and non-product-specific input subsidies like fertilizer, credit, power and irrigation subsidies will distort the real resource costs below the market levels and offer undue advantage to the countries with high domestic production and input subsidies. It is pointed out that the existence of such subsidies would amount to distortion of markets, causing inefficient allocation of resources and loss of welfare. The AOA provisions under 'domestic support' are supposed to correct market distortions by minimizing the domestic production subsidies and shifting production to locales with comparative advantage.

Under the AOA, a certain *de minimis* level is fixed on the agricultural production and investment subsidies. For the developed countries, the *de minimis* level is fixed at 5 per cent of the value of total agricultural production. For the developing countries, the *de minimis* subsidy is fixed at 10 per cent. And the subsidies have to be reduced to these levels by the respective implementation periods, i.e. 2000 for developed countries and 2004 for developing countries. A differential limit on the subsidies for developed and developing countries is fixed apparently to show that developed countries are subjected to more discipline since their 'subsidies' are limited to 5 per cent, while developing countries will have the limit at 10 per cent of the value of the total agricultural output. But in reality, as in the case of 'market access', under 'domestic support' provisions too, there is a sly.

The definition of 'subsidies' under the AOA is distorted and it differentiates between production-promoting subsidies and certain other expenditures on farms or payments made to farmers by the government, which are designated as 'Green Box' measures. These Green Box measures include, inter alia: general services to agriculture such as research and extension, and pest and disease control; public stocking for food security purposes; structural adjustment programmes; environmental programmes; crop and income insurance schemes; and certain direct payments and income supports that are not linked to agricultural production.

These Green Box payments are exempt from the calculation of subsidies under the AOA. A spurious argument is advanced in justification. The Green Box subsidies are not meant to promote production, and, therefore, do not distort trade. These payments are called 'production-neutral', and exempted from being counted as subsidies. But the facts speak a different story, and, indeed, substantial increase in agricultural production in the EU is attributed to Green Box payments, which have often been used as the basic investment by farmers.

The artificial distinction drawn between price support and input subsidies on the one hand and the Green Box subsidies on the other, and excluding the latter from subsidy cuts, is again an unfair discrimination against the developing countries like India. It is well-known that 'set-aside' payments made directly to farmers to withdraw from production constitute not only huge amounts in the USA and EU, but also act as the source of new investment by farmers. Since the 1980s, 'set-aside' payments to farmers account for a growing proportion of subsidies provided under the European Union's Common Agricultural Policy (CAP). The argument that 'set-asides' do not promote production lacks credibility. According to certain estimates, the direct payments made under 'set-asides' generated enough new investment by farmers, which resulted in an increase in the cereal production in EU by 30 million tons during the mid-1990s compared to the mid-1980s (Watkins 1999). Since 1992, due to EU reforms through CAP, there has been a growing shift from price support to direct 'set-aside' payments. By 1996, about 25 per cent of subsidies going to farmers in the industrialized countries are in the form of direct payments. Exempting these direct payments from the subsidies at one stroke reduced the level of EU subsidy cuts by over $3 billion in the case of wheat alone (Watkins 1999).

Table 1 shows the magnitude of Green Box subsidies paid by the developed countries. Of the total expenditure on Green Box, the developed countries account for 85 to 88 per cent during 1995 and 1996. If we exclude Brazil, South Korea and Thailand, all the developing countries put together accounted for only about 9 per cent of the global Green Box payments in 1995, but it had slipped further to just 4 per cent in 1996. 'These subsidies are huge—the US and EU spent over $15.7 billion in 1995 subsidizing wheat and maize production alone—and far outstrip the financial support available to farmers in the South. As a result, trade in cereals is

TABLE 1: TOTAL EXPENDITURE ON 'GREEN BOX' MEASURES

| Sl. No. | WTO Members | 1995 | | 1996 | |
|---|---|---|---|---|---|
| | | Amount (US$ billion) | Percentage Share in Total | Amount (US$ billion) | Percentage Share in Total |
| 1. | Total by all WTO Members | 129.44 | 100.00 | 126.74 | 100.00 |
| 2. | Developed Countries | 110.17 | 85.10 | 110.96 | 87.60 |
| | USA | 46.04 | 35.57 | 51.82 | 40.88 |
| | EC | 24.11 | 18.63 | 28.38 | 22.39 |
| | Japan | 32.86 | 25.39 | 25.02 | 19.74 |
| 3. | Developing Countries | 19.27 | 14.91 | 15.78 | 12.50 |
| | Brazil | 4.88 | 3.77 | 2.60 | 2.05 |
| | South Korea | 5.17 | 4.00 | 6.44 | 5.08 |
| | Thailand | 1.35 | 1.05 | 1.62 | 1.28 |

*Source*: FAO (1999), Paper 4, Table 3, pp. 141–2.

massively distorted in favour of Northern producers, which can dump their surpluses on the South at heavily subsidized prices. The average subsidy, for example, to a US farmer producing wheat for export is around 25 times the total average per capita income in the 42 countries classified by the World Bank as 'low-income', and more than three times the average per capita income of the middle-income countries of South-East Asia and Latin America. Even these figures, however, underestimate the level of distortion in international food trade, since the producers of staple foods, who have to compete in local markets against US exports, usually have incomes far below the national average. On the Philippines island of Mindanao, for instance, over half a million corn farmers, who earn less than $100 a year, 'compete' against the corn imported from the US, which has been produced with a subsidy amounting to one hundred times their income, even without taking into account subsidies for transport and marketing infrastructure (Watkins 1999).

This situation would continue substantially even after the implementation of the AOA stipulation to bring down the agricultural subsidies to less than 5 per cent of the total value of agricultural production in developed countries because of the exclusion of the Green Box subsidies from the purview of WTO subsidy cuts. In contrast, most, if not all, agricultural subsidies in developing countries are 'production' or 'input' subsidies, which have to be reduced under AOA.

Countries, which exceed the *de minimis* AMS are supposed to enter 'Amber Box', which necessitates their undertaking measures to reduce the AMS to *de minimis* level. In contrast, out of 100 developing countries, only 12 reported AMS above the *de minimis.* The remaining 88 countries cannot exceed the limit in future. Most of the developed countries, which exceeded their AMS limit of 5 per cent, got away with a reduction programme of 20 per cent of their AMS. There is no commitment as to when the AMS would be brought down to the *de minimis.* The invention of the Green Box has come very handy. The US, by shifting from market price supports to direct payments, shifted from Amber Box to Green Box and put itself in a strong negotiating position for the future. The European Union and others have shifted towards policies in the 'Blue Box' (direct set-aside payments) and Green Box. The result of these games that developed countries have been playing is that WTO, which is supposed to create a framework for reduction of subsidies, has actually contributed to huge increases in subsidies, Green, Blue, Amber or call it what you will. In 1996, the OECD's total support to agriculture had increased to $335 billion, of which $251 billion are producer support payments. The developing countries remain without access to these highly protected agricultural markets of the developed countries.

A further discrimination against the interests of the farming community in countries like India is that under Article 13, the production and input subsidies extended mostly by developing countries (Article 6, Annexure 1) are subject to countermeasures and countervailing duties, whereas the Green Box subsidies enjoyed by the developed country farmers (Article 6, Annexure 2) are exempt from these countermeasures and actions (Das 1999a). It is clear that the stipulations of Domestic Support under the AOA are heavily loaded against the farmers of the developing countries, and cleverly camouflaged in the pursuit of finding markets for the farm products of the developed countries.

## EXPORT SUBSIDIES

The commitment on export subsidy is on two themes, reduction in the total budgetary outlays on export subsidies, and reduction in the total quantity of exports covered by the subsidy. These reductions are on product-specific basis (Khor 1999). The developed countries should reduce the value of their expenditure on export subsidies by 36 per cent and reduce the quantity covered under export subsidies by 21 per cent. For the developing countries, lower percentage reduction and longer implementation are provided. For the least developed countries, there is no restriction, and longer implementation is provided. The subsidies given on transport, processing and packaging of agricultural exports of both developed and developing countries are also exempt from reduction requirements (Das 1998). But the facts on agricultural exports show that while developed countries subsidize their exports heavily, there are hardly any subsidies provided by the developing countries for agricultural exports. Therefore, even after meeting the reduction requirements, the developed countries will still be left with substantial subsidization of their agricultural exports.

Export subsidies are singled out as the most trade-distorting practice. In developing countries with strong agricultural export potential, the export subsidies of the developed countries severely limit the ability of commodity producers to compete on the international market. With the pressure on export subsidies, there is a shift in the OECD towards export credits to circumvent the cuts on export subsidies. According to OECD estimates, the US is the largest user of export credits, which accounted for $12.8 billion between 1995 and 1998. Though the US accounts for the majority of distortions in world markets caused by officially-supported export credits, Australia ($6.8 billion), EU ($4.3 billion) and Canada ($3.6 billion) are also major users of export credit. It is reported that Greg Frazier, former top agricultural negotiator for the US, observed: 'There is little disagreement that USDA's export credit programmes are one of the most significant, if not the single-most instrumental, tool the US is employing both to maintain market access in a number of critical markets and to open new ones. There is just as little disagreement that additional disciplines on export credits, those of the US as well as other countries, would contribute to greater liberalization.'

## TRADE RELATED ASPECTS OF INTELLECTUAL PROPERTY RIGHTS

That part of the TRIPS Agreement which deals with patents or effective sui generis legislation on property rights to plant and animal varieties as well as to Genetically Modified Organisms

(GMOs) is also relevant in the context of food security. Developing countries face two kinds of disadvantages. First, these countries lack the scientific capability to innovate and patent new materials and are not even in a position to fully catalogue the natural resources of bio-materials they currently possess. Second, there is growing concentration of transnational corporations in biotech industries, notably in the seed sector. This concentration enables these industries to exact monopoly rents from farmers worldwide. Dependence on MNCs for such critical inputs as seeds are feared to bring in a chain of developments which would undermine the very survival of small farmer economy.

## SANITARY AND PHYTOSANITARY STANDARDS (SPS) AND TECHNICAL BARRIERS TO TRADE (TBT)

The WTO agreement on SPS poses a challenge to developing countries in terms of raising the quality to internationally recognized levels. The challenge becomes a serious impediment to food trade by developing countries, if developed countries, on risk assessment grounds, adopt higher standards than correctly recognized by international bodies. This does happen frequently. During 1996–7, the US Food and Drug Administration detected 11,166 contraventions of imports, of which 44 per cent were not on any technical grounds, but just on filth and microbiological contamination (FAO 1999). The SPS and TBT, in the absence of transparency, may pose an additional constraint on the developing countries' access to markets.

The Agreement on Agriculture and the related agreements have so far been a failure in implementing market access for developing countries. It raises serious doubts about free-trade-based food security. On the contrary, developing countries, as a whole, experienced increased food imports, loss of domestic markets due to import competition and loss of public-sector institutional capacity. The FAO case studies of 14 developing countries show increased productivity and competitiveness, but at a very heavy cost of increasing marginalization of small producers and added unemployment and poverty (FAO 1999). The net losers have been the small farmers, and this has increased the risk of local food security. The WTO has hardly conceived any social safety nets to face the trade-induced distress.

## SPECIFICITIES OF SMALL-FARMER ECONOMIES AND MARKET-PLUS APPROACH

### NON-COMMERCIAL FARMING

One of the major problems with the AOA lies in the basic premises of the agreement that agriculture, across the countries, is similar. But in reality, the agricultural situation differs vastly between countries. Equating the land-abundant and capital-cheap farming system of North America with land-scarce and capital-expensive systems like India is unjust (Marglin 1996). Treating dissimilar situations similarly is bound to harm the interests of the disadvantaged. For a vast majority of farming communities in developing countries, agriculture is still not entirely a commercial venture. Agriculture continues to be subsistence cultivation and a way of life. Many farmers take to agriculture not as a commercial venture, but as a family activity passed down over generations. The proportion of small-marginal farmers with less than five acres of operational holding is very high and it is growing. For instance, in India, small-marginal farmers constitute more than two-thirds of the operational holdings and in some states, it is as high as 90 per cent of the holdings. If these farmers are exposed to international competition from the high-tech farming of the developed countries like the US, the livelihoods of these households are likely to be threatened on a colossal scale.

In the industrialized countries, agribusiness is less and less 'agri' and more and more business. A substantial value of food and fibre is made up of inputs produced off the farm than in the field, which has raised questions of sustainability (Marglin 1996). Pushing farming systems of the Third World in that direction would cause untold suffering to the poor farmers.

> . . . most developing countries are struck with one simple fact: most of their population is in agriculture, not because that is where they want to be but because the development process has failed. That is in stark contrast to the developed countries, where subsidies have to be given to keep people in agriculture and money is thrown away to that end. How to bring a semblance of economies of scale to millions of poor people and help them increase their production in a way, which does not destroy incentives or create inefficiencies? That is the old development question, and for most people in developing countries, that is where the problem lies. (Abhijit Sen in FAO 1999)

## AGRO-CLIMATIC SPECIFICITY

Further, farming in the majority of the less-developed countries is not only increasingly small-farm based, but is also conditioned by the regional agro-climatic variations. Most of the crops become region-specific. For instance, rubber and copra are specific to Kerala, and so are many spices. Oilseeds are more or less specific to dry and rainfed areas. Rice goes with heavy rainfall areas, besides the irrigated areas. In these regions, there is no room for flexibility in the cropping pattern. If edible oil is imported freely because of its price being less in the international market, there is no choice for the dry-land farmers to switch to other crops. The economies of some of these regions, which have emerged as oilseed monocrop areas, would be put to serious turmoil. Agro-climatic specificity of most of the crops and consequent absence of choice or flexibility in crops are likely to cause destitution to many farming communities if they are exposed to 'free trade', even if there is really some such trade.

## TRANSITORY STAGE AND PROTECTION

A large proportion of the small-marginal farmers in developing countries like India are on the verge of transition to high-productivity crops. They are being slowly drawn into cultivation of high-yielding varieties and hybrid varieties because of improvement in their levels of literacy and education, exposure to the gains reaped by the better-off farmers who have taken to new varieties and their own urge to live better. They are just at the threshold of entering into high-productivity agriculture. But such a transition needs heavy investments in irrigation, infrastructure like roads, storage facilities, better marketing facilities and assured price, besides access to credit facilities at reasonable interest, subsidized inputs like fertilizers, pesticides, better seeds with quality assurance and fair price for the produce. Extension facilities and better cultural and agronomic practices also become essential when the small farmers are entering new crops, which depend relatively less on their traditional knowledge. Every one of these external sources poses a high risk to the capacities of the small-marginal farmers. The recent incidents of a large number of suicides of small-marginal farmers in Andhra Pradesh, Karnataka, Punjab and Assam are instances where farmers were forced to bear on their own risks of high interest on credit, poor-quality pesticides, absence of any extension, lack of remunerative prices for the commodities and poor marketing facilities and the failure of groundwater-based irrigation on which heavy investments were made by the small-marginal farmers themselves. The compounding of all these risks on the small-marginal farmers was too big a burden for them to bear. As a consequence, some of them were forced to the extreme step of committing suicide. The history of small-marginal farmers successfully graduating to high-productivity crops has been exclusively the history of East Asia, and it is more relevant to countries like India. The East Asian experience like that of Japan, South Korea and Taiwan shows that small-marginal farmers could experience transition to high-productivity agriculture essentially because of heavy state support in the form of rural infrastructure, credit facilities, extension, marketing and appropriate price policy—all of which involved substantial subsidies to the agriculture sector. Instead of extending state support at this critical stage, if small-marginal farmers in countries like India are exposed to the so-called 'free trade' under AOA of the WTO, there will be widespread distress.

## FOOD SECURITY AND MULTI-FUNCTIONALITY OF AGRICULTURE

To augment food supplies, the World Food Summit of 1996 suggested a Plan of Action involving seven commitments. Of these seven commitments, two are very critical for 'food security' in the context of non-trade concerns. The 'Objectives and Actions' of Commitment Three is a complex agenda involving 'a statement on human-centred, gender-sensitive, participatory, resource- conserving, small-scale, local knowledge-using, bottom-up agricultural and rural development into which food security is woven as an integral part' (FAO 1999). This is contrasted with an efficiency-seeking, large-scale, technology- and profit-driven, top-down development where food security may well improve, but not necessarily equitably so, either spatially or socially. The latter is often associated with the WTO liberalized regime of trade, which needs to change in response to the conditions of less-developed countries, which often conform to the statement under Commitment Three mentioned above. Commitment Two of the summit further broadens the scope, to focus, additionally, on economic access to food and hence the need for 'secure and gainful employment' as well as 'equitable and equal access to productive resources such as land, water and credit'. Underlying this concern is the need to focus attention on 'vulnerable and disadvantaged individuals, households and groups', including women. This brings into focus that imported food is accessible to groups which are different compared to domestically produced food, which has place for self-provisioning groups. Often, the proceeds of traded food products may not percolate to vulnerable groups, including women (FAO 1999).

There are a number of scholars who have emphasized the link between 'food security' of less-developed countries and domestic food production, which challenges the premises of AOA (Raghavan 1999; Das 1999c; Griffin 1999). As discussed above, the AOA is based on the theoretical premise of comparative advantage, which suggests that a country must import agricultural products from those countries which produce cheaply. Das points out that under the agreement, developing countries can buy food at market prices and supply it at lower prices, but that is not real food security. Real food security is not only providing food needed to satisfy domestic consumption, but also augmenting purchasing power of the vulnerable to enable them to buy food. This involves improving small-farmer domestic food production. It is like national security (B.L. Das in FAO 1999). Less-developed countries may run into serious problems of lack of food security because of the following reasons (Das 1999c).

1. The chronic shortage of foreign exchange may result in difficulties and uncertainties from depending on food imports.
2. Privatization of agriculture trade may result in uncertainties and frequent high increases in the prices of food, which may jeopardize food consumption of the poorer sections.
3. Further, even if foreign exchange is available, imports may not be readily available at times of need for various reasons. Less-developed countries with substantial concentration of population can ill afford such uncertainties.
4. Dependence on imports for staple food may reduce the foreign policy options of a country, at least on critical occasions, thus constraining its sovereignty.

Above all, a large proportion of small-marginal farmers in countries like India are net buyers of food. The rise in food prices, instead of bringing more income, would mean additional burden on small-marginal farmers. The domestic incomes of the poor in developing countries cannot be raised as easily as the escalation of domestic prices of food to match the global prices.

## MULTI-FUNCTIONALITY

In recent years, there is growing emphasis on the positive externalities of agriculture and these are referred to as 'multiple functions of agriculture'. Failure of markets in promoting these functions merits policy interventions such as subsidies or other means of agricultural support to ensure their continued 'production'. These multi-functions are defined as genuine externalities and not simply extensions of agriculture's primary economic function of producing food, fibre, etc. By this definition, the following is a short list of these functions (FAO 1999).

- Food security, including nutritional and food safety aspects, sometimes termed 'strategic' functions.
- Environmental: protection of natural resources, including natural habitats and biodiversity and so contributing to the sustainability of food production systems; disaster prevention (floods and landslides); protecting rural landscapes.
- Social and Cultural: linked to employment and income generation in rural areas and hence sustaining the viability of rural communities and maintaining rural society.

What is interesting is that a large number of developed countries, including the EU, Switzerland, Norway, Japan and countries like South Korea have been emphasizing the need to protect their agriculture on the basis of its multi-functionality. For instance, it is revealing to note the contents of Norway's food security policy, which has four components: first, the need to protect arable land from degradation and alternative use; second, to maintain food self-sufficiency from domestic production; third, to maintain a 'fairly sizeable', well-trained and experienced farming population; and fourth, to maintain decentralized food production structures as being less vulnerable in times of crisis. Norway is one of the richest countries with hardly 7 million population. Policy makers in Japan and South Korea consider protection to rice agriculture as 'psychic' investment, which preserves the culture, nature and country and are not predisposed to explore the 'risky' path of dismantling protection to agriculture (Burmeister 2000). They are not even favourable to the proposal of the APEC Food System (AFS), which suggests a region-wise strategy but insists on country-specific food security (Gilbert et al. 2000).

If such is the fervour of these developed countries to protect their agriculture for reasons of multi-functionality or market-plus considerations, countries like India, with the majority of the population depending on agriculture and with most of these farming communities highly vulnerable to any external vagaries of the market, need to be treated with considerable exception from the provisions of the AOA.

## STRATEGY FOR REVIEW OF AOA

### FREE-MARKET MYTH

The AOA is built on the widespread propaganda that 'free trade' in agriculture is more beneficial to predominantly agricultural countries like India. It is argued even in India that global agricultural prices are higher than domestic prices, and if trade in agricultural commodities is liberalized, then Indian farmers would export and get higher returns on agriculture, which in turn would lead to increased investment and growth in agriculture. But the premise that there could be 'free trade' in agricultural commodities is a tenuous one. As Watkins points out, in the real world, agricultural production and trade is determined not so much by comparative advantage as by comparative access to subsidies. Industrialized countries, as is well-known, dole out much more in subsidies than the developing countries. And a substantial proportion of trade in agricultural commodities is dominated by a handful of developed countries. Watkins points to the case of cereals.

> These are the largest internationally traded foodstuffs, generating around \$20 billion annually. Between them, the United States and the European Union account for over half of all exports of wheat and wheat flour, while the US alone accounts for over three-quarters of maize exports. Because producers in the US and EU dominate world cereal markets, the prices at which they export effectively dictate world cereal prices—and hence the prices against which producers in importing countries have to compete. The subsidies paid to the US and European producers, therefore, play a key role in determining the price at which cereals are traded, not just in the North but worldwide. (Watkins 1999)

Contrary to the benefits accruing under free trade, even the liberalization mooted under the Structural Adjustment Programme (SAP) has caused considerable damage to the interests of small-marginal farmers. According to a report (1995) of the United Nations Research Institute for Social Development (UNRISD), the SAPs had adverse impact on small farmers.

Poor farmers in developing countries undergoing adjustment programmes have had no cushion of social security. In region after region, governments have eliminated subsidies, and as a result, small farmers have lost access to essential inputs and services, and many have suffered a steep fall in income or have had to leave farming altogether. Farmers producing food for local markets have also been suddenly subjected to the cold wind of international competition—and may find it impossible to compete with technologically advanced farmers in Europe or North America, who can sell cheaply in part because they have benefited from massive subsidies. Expanding international markets may have created vast opportunities for some wealthier farmers but the impact on the livelihood of the rural poor in developing countries has been harsh (Quoted in Khor 1999).

Based on a case study of the impact of lowering agricultural tariffs in the Philippines, Watkins (1999) concludes: 'Silently, relentlessly, and away from the glare of the world's media, "free trade" is displacing communities and destroying their livelihoods with all the ruthless efficiency of a civil war.'

Again, in a case study of the effects of the WTO agreement on agriculture in the Philippines, an Oxfam report estimated that average household incomes of maize farmers will be reduced by as much as 30 per cent over the six years, as cheap imports from the US will drive down prices in the local markets. 'The report estimates that in the absence of trade restrictions, US maize could be marketed at less than half the price of maize grown on the Philippine island of Mindanao and that the livelihoods of up to half a million Philippine maize farmers (out of the total of 1.2 million) are under immediate threat' (Khor 1999).

## FOOD SECURITY: GLOBAL AND NATIONAL SCENARIO

During the period 1960 to 1994–6, globally, food availability for human consumption increased by 19 per cent to 2,720 kcal/day. The increase for the developing countries was higher by 32 per cent.

But food availability still remains highly uneven, with 2,150 kcal/day for Sub-Saharan Africa to 3,570 kcal/day for North America. In the 1990s, there was a slowdown in the growth of world agricultural production. World cereal output stagnated and fluctuated widely in the first half of the decade, though the decline was largely in the developed countries. Globally, the per capita availability of cereals fell from 342 kg in the mid-1980s to 311 kg in 1993–5 and rose again marginally to 323 kg in 1996–8 (FAO 1999). The major problem continues to be chronic undernourishment in developing countries. Table 2 shows the magnitude of the problem. Raising food production along with the physical and economic access to food is the major challenge of food security.

Studies on the prospects of supply and demand for cereals in the next two decades suggest a serious deficit. Bhalla et al. (2000) estimate that cereal deficit for India may range between 36 and 64 million tons by 2020. Pradumn Kumar's (2000) projections show an annual growth rate of 1.6 per cent in the supply and 2 per cent in the demand for cereals in the next 20 years. By 2020, there will be a cereal shortage of 39 million tons. The growth of food production is constrained by the lack of favourable factors of the

TABLE 2: NUMBER AND PERCENTAGE OF UNDERNOURISHMENT IN THE DEVELOPING COUNTRIES (ANNUAL AVERAGE)

| Region | Number of undernourished (millions) | |
|---|---|---|
| | 1990–2 | 1994–6 |
| Sub-Saharan Africa | 196<br>(40) | 210<br>(39) |
| Near East and North Africa | 34<br>(11) | 42<br>(12) |
| East and South-East Asia | 289<br>(17) | 258<br>(15) |
| South Asia | 237<br>(21) | 254<br>(21) |
| Latin America and Caribbean | 64<br>(15) | 63<br>(13) |
| All Developing Countries | 822<br>(20) | 828<br>(19) |

*Source*: FAO, 1999, p. 94.

*Note*: Figures in parenthesis show the percentage of undernourished population.

past growth, fast declining factor productivity in major cropping systems and rapidly shrinking resource base. Added to this, the research and education intensity measured by investment in terms of percentage to agricultural GDP, which showed much improvement up to the 1980s, has been stagnating at 0.49 per cent in the 1990s. Similarly, extension intensity, which is about 0.4 per cent for developing countries and 0.9 per cent for developed countries, is one of the lowest for India at 0.15 per cent and has been stagnating at that in the 1990s (Kumar 2000).

With decline in the rate of growth of global food production, with declining global terms of trade for agriculture during the past few decades and with the share of food in world trade declining from 21.4 per cent in 1962 to 9.5 per cent in 1992 and non-food agriculture from 10.2 per cent to 2.1 per cent, it would be highly untenable to hope for an external trade-based solution for India's food security (Dasgupta 2000). Past experience shows negative welfare effects of external trade-based food management (Chandra 2000). 'Producing additional food with limited and degraded natural resources and to provide economic access to food at the household level for ensuring food security for all will be the major challenge for the country' (Kumar 2000).

## TOWARDS A 'FOOD SECURITY BOX' OR 'DEVELOPMENT BOX'

The experience of the last five years with the WTO has made possible a consensus among many developing countries towards a two-pronged approach. One is to insist on limiting production- and trade-distorting measures of developed countries and thereby ensure market access to developing countries. The other is adding more flexibility to the existing provisions in the areas of interest to developing countries (FAO 1999). The suggestions of more flexibility for developing countries include recalculation of the AMS; revision of country schedules; raising *de minimis* levels for non-product-specific AMS; giving due credit for negative product-specific AMS; and assisting least developed countries under the Marrakesh Decision without placing the burden of proof on these countries. For developing countries, more important in this regard are: enhancing the capacity to produce, safeguarding domestic market stability, building institutional capacity and ensuring food security. All these are interrelated and could be combined under a special provision like a 'food security box' or 'development box'. Access to the food security box may be provided to developing countries satisfying appropriate developmental indicators like the percentage share of population depending on agriculture, the percentage share of agriculture in the national product, rate of undernourishment of the population, the productivity growth rate, population growth rate and the extent of dependence on imported food.

The 'food security box' would permit developing countries to tailor their domestic programmes in order to meet goals related to a broad range of issues, including rural-urban income disparities, rural development, structural adjustment, the environment, and of course, food security. Any support measures included in the proposed 'food security box' would be exempt from reduction commitments. These may include support mechanisms to either cushion the effect of trade reforms or provide compensation to small producers. Such mechanisms could include targeted programmes to increase productivity and competitiveness as well as stimulate rural economic diversification. This could also facilitate considerable improvement in social safety nets for the small producers and vulnerable workers.

## NOTE

1. The TRQ facility was available as a part of the tariffication package, but since many developing countries had prohibitively high levels of tariffs, no provision was required for minimum access in their case.

# 20. Implications of WTO on Food Security

*V.K. Mehta*

Food is the most important product, as it is indispensable for the maintenance of human life and health. According to an estimate made by the FAO, about 790 million people in developing countries and 34 million in developed countries and in countries with economies in transition, currently suffer from undernourishment.[1] Over three-fourths of undernourished people live in Asia, the Pacific and Sub-Saharan Africa, and the malnutrition in those countries coexists with affluence in other parts of the world. Although the undernourished population all over the world is expected to decrease over the next decade, FAO predicts that the target set at the 1996 World Food Summit to halve the number of people suffering from hunger and malnutrition by 2015 might get delayed by 15 years, i.e. until 2030. This has heightened the concerns on the need for ensuring global food security on an urgent and sustainable basis by undertaking suitable policy measures at national and international levels. In this context, the Plan of Action adopted at the 1996 World Food Summit calls for international cooperation for securing sustainable food security which exists 'when all people, at all times, have physical and economic access to sufficient, safe and nutritious food to meet their dietary needs and food preferences for an active and healthy life'. From the foregoing definition, it is clear that the elements of food security are: (1) *Availability of Food*—to meet demands of the growing world population and changing dietary habits; (2) *Accessibility to Food*—physical and economic access, the latter is especially serious in developing countries; (3) *Stability of Food Supply*—at reasonable prices, given the price inelasticity of supply and demand for major agricultural commodities; and (4) *Food Safety/Quality and Preference*—assurance that food is safe and in good quality to satisfy the dietary needs and preference of consumers.

The World Trade Organization (WTO), which came into existence in 1995, is a rule-based organization and places several obligations on the member countries to bring their policies in conformity with the commitments under different agreements.[2] The legal interpretation of the WTO agreements is undertaken through an integrated dispute settlement mechanism that provides an assured access to the panel process, time limits for each stage, provision for appeals and semi-automatic adoption of panel and appellate body reports. The Dispute Settlement Body (DSB) is empowered to authorize suspension of an equivalent amount of trade benefits by the complaining party against the party in default, making the dispute resolution very prompt and effective. Given the bound nature of commitments under WTO, several existing WTO agreements put limits on the range of policy options available to member countries to pursue their domestic policy goals including food security concerns. The present paper provides an overview of the relevant provisions of WTO agreements that have implications for food security, specially for developing countries. There are concerns that unless appropriate changes are made in the existing agreements by providing flexibility to developing countries for furthering food security (which is of paramount importance to them), and also simultaneously restraining the developed world from distorting agricultural trade, the interests of the developing countries would be seriously jeopardized in the WTO regime, with severe social and economic consequences. As a part of the built-in agenda on agriculture and discussions in several WTO committees, the issues relevant to food security are being deliberated upon and negotiating proposals have been made by several member countries. The paper provides an assessment of the effects of these developments, and offers suggestions on the strategies that may be pursued by India to get a favourable outcome in future WTO negotiations so that appropriate WTO-compliant policies could be put in place to eradicate hunger and malnutrition and achieve food security as early as possible.

## WTO AGREEMENTS AND FOOD SECURITY

### AGREEMENT ON AGRICULTURE

At the start of the Uruguay Round, the world agricultural trading system was characterized by severe restrictions and distortions in the form of quantitative import restrictions, variable import levies, minimum import prices, discretionary licensing, voluntary export restraints and other protective measures in virtually every country of the world. One of the major achievements of the Uruguay Round Agreement on Agriculture (AOA) was to establish new rules and new types of binding, quantitative commitments to reduce trade-distorting measures in three main areas: market access, domestic support and export competition. As stated in the preamble, the long-term objective of the AOA is 'to establish a fair and market-oriented agricultural trading system, through the binding commitments on progressive reduction in agricultural support and protection sustained over an agreed period of time and through the establishment of strengthened and more operationally effective GATT rules and disciplines'. It was agreed that in implementing their commitments on market access, developed-country members would take fully into account the particular needs and conditions of developing-country members by providing for greater improvement of opportunities and terms of access for agricultural products of particular interest to developing-country members, including the fullest liberalization of trade in tropical agricultural products. The preamble also mentions that agricultural reforms should have due regard to non-trade concerns, including *food security,* and the need to protect the environment and also take into account the possible negative effects of the implementation of the reform programme on least-developed and net food-importing developing countries. Article 20 of the AOA, which lays down the principles on which future negotiations should be conducted, recognizes the 'long-term objective of substantial progressive reductions in support and protection . . .', and also lays down that further negotiations shall take into account, inter alia, experience gained from implementing the existing agreement, non-trade concerns and special and differential treatment.

The AOA consists of two parts. One part is a set of general commitments which spell out the new GATT rules. The second part is a series of country schedules that contain the commitments of the country in three main areas: market access, domestic support and export competition. The product coverage of the AOA as defined in Annex 1 to the agreement comprises a total of 280 Harmonized System (HS) 4-digit headings of HS Chapters 1 to 24 (excluding fish and fish products), plus several other items like sorbitol, essential oils, finishing agents, hides and skins, raw silk, wool, cotton, flax and hemp. India has suggested rationalization of product coverage by bringing primary agricultural commodities such as rubber, jute, coir, abaca and sisal, etc., under the ambit of the AOA.

*Market Access*

In respect of market access in agriculture, the following issues are important: (1) tariffs; (2) tariff quotas; (3) special safeguard provisions; and (4) tariff peaks and escalation.

*Tariffs*

The AOA required that defined Non-Tariff Barriers (NTBs)[3] be converted into their tariff equivalents or eliminated (exception to this requirement was allowed to a few countries, specifically Japan and Korea in case of rice, in lieu of enhanced minimum access import levels, and for developing countries in commodities that are staples in traditional diet). Non-Trade Measures (NTMs) were to be converted to ad valorem equivalents based on the price gap in the base period 1986–8 between the administered price (i.e. domestic price under NTMs) and the c.i.f. import price of the product concerned. Such exercises for arriving at tariff equivalents have often resulted in prohibitively high tariff rates, thus providing an even higher level of protection than under NTMs. The initial tariff bindings in many cases are far higher than the actual tariff equivalents in 1986–8. The EU, for example, has set them on average at about 60 per cent above the actual tariff equivalents of the CAP in recent years, while the US has set theirs about 45 per cent above recent rates.[4] Developing countries were given the option to submit new base and bound tariffs for previously unbound tariff items, with the additional proviso to remove all agriculture-specific non-tariff measures.

The bound tariffs were to be reduced by 36 per cent on average over six years (i.e. by 1 January 2000) by developed countries and 24 per cent over 10 years (i.e. by 1 January 2005) by developing countries (subject to the condition that reduction for each tariff line would be at least 15 per cent). The fact that tariff reductions were aggregated introduced a bias in favour of lowering the higher tariff rates on sensitive products by the minimum level of around 15 per cent, and by effecting larger cuts on low tariffs, thereby leading to the maintenance of high tariffs on some products like sugar, rice or dairy products by making substantial reductions on less sensitive tariff lines in which there is little trade.[5] The average tariffs in OECD countries in 1995 were 214 per cent for wheat, 197 per cent for barley, and 154 per cent for maize.[6]

### TARIFF RATE QUOTAS

As part of the tariffication package, the AOA introduced two provisions for tariff quotas to ensure that in 1995, current and minimum market access opportunities combined represented at least 3 per cent of the base-period consumption and were progressively expanded to reach 5 per cent of that consumption in the year 2000 (developed countries) or 2004 (developing countries), respectively. First, to maintain 'current access opportunities' in products previously subject to non-tariff measures, imports were required to be maintained through explicit quotas at levels prevailing in the 1986–8 base period. Second, in products where current access had been less than 5 per cent of the domestic consumption, the agreement required an (additional) minimum access opportunity on a Most Favoured Nation (MFN) basis. No provision was made for minimum access for products where previous tariffs had been at prohibitively higher levels. A two-tier tariff structure was introduced: a 'lower' tariff rate (a maximum of 32 per cent of the bound tariff rates) for the in-quota imports, and a higher 'bound rate' for the rest of the imports. Tariff quotas under the 'minimum' access commitment were in principle treated as global quotas to be allocated to supplier countries on an MFN basis. However, countries were allowed to incorporate their preferential trade arrangements into the market access opportunities available through the tariff quota system. This has resulted in some portion of the 'minimum' access tariff quotas being earmarked for specific supplier countries under bilateral, regional or interregional preferential trade agreements. Thirty-seven members have tariff quota commitments shown in their schedules, with a total of 1,371 individual tariff quota commitments. These quotas are concentrated in 12 product categories, with fruits and vegetables accounting for the largest number (355 tariff quotas), followed by meat products (247), cereals (217), dairy products (181), oilseeds products (124) and sugar (51). The major users of tariff quotas were Norway (232 tariff quotas), Poland (109), Iceland

(90), EU (87), Bulgaria (73), Hungary (70), Colombia (67), Korea (67), Venezuela (61), and US (54). It is estimated that about 28 per cent of the overall global trade is governed by such Tariff Rate Quotas (TRQ). The existence of disparate types of the TRQ administration methods among TRQ-providing countries, or even among products within a country, and conditions attached to certain TRQ imports have allegedly presented difficulties in obtaining access to markets under TRQs. Traders in developing countries reported a lack of information about export opportunities under market access measures.[7]

*Special Agricultural Safeguards*

The provision on special safeguards applies only to products that were subject to tariffication and was incorporated in the AOA to address concerns that tariffication would bring about massive increase of imports and decrease in prices of domestic goods. The Special Agricultural Safeguards allow an importing country to impose additional duties up to specified limits in case of a precisely defined surge of import quantity, or cases of imports at prices below a precisely defined reference level (only one, either quantity-triggered or price-triggered safeguard can be invoked at a time). The quantity-triggered safeguard can be invoked if imports surge in relation to the base imports to a level of over 105 per cent (and existing imports are over 30 per cent of domestic consumption averaged during the previous three years), 110 per cent (the existing imports are over 10 per cent but less than 30 per cent) and 125 per cent (the existing imports are less than 10 per cent). The price-triggered safeguard can be invoked if the import price in local currency falls below a trigger price based upon the 1986–8 average import price. The additional duty that can be levied is variable and is a function of how far the import price falls below the trigger price.

Thirty-eight countries have reserved that right, on a varying number of products. For all relevant members combined, these reservations imply a potential for imposing special safeguards on 6,072 tariff lines spread across 12 broad categories. Of these, the major product categories for potential application of safeguard measures include: animal and animal products (1,327 tariff lines), cereals (1,087), fruits and vegetables (809), dairy products (715), oilseeds (706), beverages (329), sugar (291), coffee, tea, etc. (277), and other agricultural products (371). The actual use of the safeguard mechanism has, however, been quite limited.

It has been proposed that developing countries and least-developed countries should also have the right of recourse to the special safeguard provisions. As seasonal and perishable agricultural products have difficulty in inventory adjustments and although consumption itself remains stable, prices are elastic, these products are more susceptible to a sharp fall in prices, resulting from an increase in imports, thus having a huge impact on producers over a short period of time. The proposed new safeguard mechanism should be possible to be applied automatically and effectively, based on simple and basic conditions.

### *Tariff Peaks and Escalation*

The agricultural sector remains one of the sectors that are most affected by tariff peaks and tariff escalation problems. A joint United Nations Conference on Trade and Development (UNCTAD)/WTO study[8] shows that more than half of the peak tariffs of developed countries are found in the agricultural (including food industry) and fishery sectors. One-fifth of the peak tariffs of the US, a quarter of those of the EU, about 30 per cent of those of Japan and about one-seventh of those of Canada exceed 30 per cent. The study further reports that the most important areas with the highest tariff rates include the major agricultural staple foods, cereals, meat, sugar, milk, butter and cheese as well as tobacco products and cotton. In the EU, for instance, the out-of-quota tariff for bananas is 180 per cent; in Japan these tariffs range between 460 and 600 per cent for dried beans, peas and lentils, about 1,000 per cent on rice and in the US, groundnuts in shell attract a tariff of 164 per cent.

Tariff escalation[9] persists in the post-Uruguay Round tariff environment, especially in a number of products that are of importance to developing countries, including coffee, cocoa, oilseeds, vegetables, and fruits and nuts. Escalation appears to be less significant in meat and dairy products (OECD, *The Uruguay Round Agreement on Agriculture and Processed Agricultural Products*, 1997). This provides extra protection for processing industries in the importing country, and is particularly perverse for developing countries since it virtually 'taxes' efforts to diversify production and to move into higher stages of processing.[10]

## INDIA'S MARKET ACCESS COMMITMENTS

As India was maintaining Quantitative Restrictions (QRs) due to balance of payments reasons (which is a GATT-consistent measure), it did not have to undertake any commitments in regard to market access. The only commitment India has undertaken is to bind its primary agricultural products at 100 per cent; processed foods at 150 per cent and edible oils at 300 per cent. For some agricultural products like skimmed milk powder, maize, rice, wheat, millets, etc., which had been bound at zero or at low bound rates, negotiations under Article XXVIII of GATT were successfully completed in December 1999, and the bound rates have been raised substantially.[11] The present rates applied are lower than the bound rates in case of several agricultural commodities, implying that rates can be raised up to bound levels if the need arises in future for protection of agriculture. For 2000–1, the average basic duty rate for all agricultural tariff lines is 34.9 per cent as against the negotiated bound rate of 114.9 per cent. Against 686 agricultural commodities for which India stood committed for tariff reduction, 2000–1 levels of its MFN tariff rates are lower than those of Uruguay Round final bound rates for as many as 676 commodities;[12] in fact, in respect of more than 85 per cent of the commodities, the difference was 50 per cent and more. Consequent to the WTO ruling that the QRs maintained by India on balance of payments considerations are not justified, these have been dismantled in two phases, with the latest Exim Policy for 2001–2 removing import restrictions on the final batch of 715 goods, including a large number of agricultural products. In addition to tariff protection announced in the Union Budget, the Exim Policy has instituted some WTO-compliant restrictions so that highly subsidized food grains and other food products do not enter indiscriminately and pose a threat to domestic small farmers in the post-QR regime. For instance, major and sensitive agricultural products such as wheat, rice, maize, other coarse cereals, copra and coconut oil can only be imported by nominated state trading enterprises.[13] All imported edible/food products are required to comply with the provisions of the Prevention of Food Adulteration Act, 1954, and Rules, 1955, in the same way as domestically manufactured and sold food products. The import of primary products of plant and animal origin has been subjected to a permit system for assessing their bio-security implications as also sanitary and phytosanitary standards. Several facilitation measures have been announced to boost farm incomes from exports. The Market Access Initiative, a leaf out of the US book, will make available government funds for market research and development. Export/trading houses would be entitled to status and facilities at par even if export of agri-produce by them is just a third of the threshold set for exporters of other goods. Agri-export zones are to be created with the help of willing States, so that the best of the domestic food produce is able to find its due markets overseas. But facilitation alone may not be adequate: the state governments and their agri-horticulture departments and research institutions must take on their supportive roles more purposefully so that domestic produce meets global quality standards on a sustained, consistent basis.

## DOMESTIC SUPPORT

Under this provision, member countries are required to undertake reduction commitments on the Aggregate Measurement of Support (AMS).[14] The total AMS is to be reduced by 20 per cent over the six-year-period in developed countries and by 13 per cent over a ten-year-period in developing countries. The following support measures are allowed to be specifically excluded from AMS calculations: measures having minimal impact on trade, provided that support is provided through a publicly funded programme and does not have the effect of price support to producers (so-called 'Green Box'); production limiting programmes (so-called 'Blue Box' measures); governmental assistance to encourage agricultural and rural development provided by developing countries in the form of investment subsidies to agriculture, and agricultural input subsidies to low-income or resource-poor farmers Special and Differential (S&D) treatment-related support), and *de minimis* support up to 5 per cent of the value of production of individual product for product specific support, or the value of total agricultural production in case of non-product-specific support (10 per cent for developing countries). Green Box (Annex 2) subsidies are 'non-actionable' and are completely immune from countermeasures and countervailing duty under the Due Restraint Clause in Article 13. In fact, of all the types of supports where protection is accorded—Blue Box; *de minimis*; special and differential treatment supports; and export subsidies—it is only Annex 2 subsidies that are completely protected.[15]

India does not provide any product-specific support other than market price support. During the reference period (1986–8), India had market price support programmes for 22 products, out of which 19 are included in our list of commitments filed under GATT. The products are rice, wheat, *bajra*, *jowar*, maize, barley, gram, groundnut, rapeseed, *toria*, cotton, soyabean (yellow), soyabean (black), *urad*, *moong*, *tur*, tobacco, jute, and sugar cane. Three relatively minor crops, viz., *ragi*, safflower, and sunflower seed are not included in the list, as due to inadequacy of data it has not been possible to calculate the relevant product-specific support. The total product-specific AMS was (-) Rs. 24,442 crore during the base period. The negative figure arises from the fact that during the base period, except for tobacco and sugar cane, international prices of all products were higher than domestic prices, and the product-specific AMS is to be calculated by subtracting the domestic price from the international price and then multiplying the resultant figure by the quantity of production.

Non-product-specific subsidy is calculated by taking into account subsidies given for fertilizers, water, seeds, credit and electricity. During the reference period, the total non-product-specific AMS was Rs. 4,581 crore. The calculations for the marketing year 1995–6 show the product-specific AMS figure as (-) 38.47 per cent and non-product-specific AMS as 7.52 per cent of the total value of production. The present rules do not permit setting off of the negative product-specific support against the positive non-product-specific AMS support, thus disadvantaging countries like India. Even though our aggregate AMS at 7.52 per cent is still below the *de minimis* level of 10 per cent, the scope for extending additional non-product-specific general support for protection of small farmers' livelihoods, food security, agricultural development and productivity is quite limited, particularly as the present structure of the Green Box is tailored in line with the provisions widely used by the developed world. In 1996, developing countries provided only 12.5 per cent of all Green Box supports, with developed countries providing the other 87.5 per cent. The majority of developing countries do not even provide 0.5 per cent of total Green Box supports. The budgetary constraints make it further difficult for developing countries to utilize even some of the existing exempted provisions, like support for general services.

The list of programmes exempted from reduction commitments under the Green Box covers: (1) general services including research, training, inspection, extension and advisory services, pest control, marketing and promotion services, capital costs of infrastructural services; (2) public stockholding for food security purposes, public distribution system for urban and rural poor in developing countries; (3) decoupled income support; (4) income insurance and safety net programmes; (5) crop insurance; (6) structural adjustment assistance through producer retirement, resource retirement and investment aids; and (7) payments under environmental and regional assistance programmes.

It is imperative that the Green Box should have provisions for the general development of agriculture including its diversification in developing countries, which in turn would help them to take care of their rural employment and food security. For instance, input subsidies given by developing countries for crops wherein productivity levels are below the world average should be covered under the Green Box. Sufficient flexibility should be allowed to developing countries to administer such policies.

The Public Distribution System, which forms an integral part of the food security programme in the country, is covered under 'public stockholding for food security purposes' and domestic aid clause. It has, however, been provided that the volume and accumulation of public stocks should correspond to predetermined targets related solely to food security, and the process of stock accumulation and disposal should be financially transparent and conducted in accordance with officially published objective criteria identified in the national legislation. In this context, it is felt that the adoption of the recent recommendation of the Expenditure Reforms Commission (ERC) to limit the operational requirement for PDS at 7 million tons (assuming a 4-monthly stock rollover norm and annual PDS requirement of 21 million tons) and food security related buffer of 10 million tons (6 million tons of rice and 4 million tons of wheat) could seriously hamper the flexibility of operation and maintenance of the PDS and food security, as the extra buffer stocks beyond the target would count as 'producer subsidy' under WTO stipulations, and would come under reduction commitment.

## EXPORT COMPETITION

As a part of the special treatment to agriculture, the AOA subjects the listed subsidies provided by members to reduction commitment only while many of these types of export subsidies in the industrial sector are prohibited. The export subsidies subject to reduction commitments include: (1) direct subsidies, in cash or kind, contingent on export performance to a firm, industry, producers/association of producers, marketing board, etc., by the government or its agencies; (2) export at prices lower than domestic prices of non-commercial stocks of agricultural products by the government or its agencies; (3) payment on the export of agricultural products financed by government action including levy; (4) subsidies on agricultural products contingent on their incorporation in exported products; (5) subsidies to reduce the cost of marketing exports of agricultural products (widely available export promotion and advisory services are allowable) including the handling, upgrading and processing costs; and (6) subsidizing the internal transport of exports.

Only those countries which had notified the use of export subsidies in their original schedules could continue to use them, albeit in a restrained manner, while other countries are not permitted to introduce them thereafter (Article 3.3 of the AOA). A majority of the developing-country members are deprived of their right to provide export subsidies, which are otherwise permitted under Article 27, read with Annex VII of the Subsidies and Countervailing Measures (SCM) Agreement. According to the so-called 'Peace Clause', until 31 December 2003, export subsidies for products covered by the AOA in conformity with the budgetary outlay reduction commitments specified in the respective national schedules and for products listed in the respective national schedules are exempt from challenges under the subsidies agreement. Thereafter, these will become 'prohibited subsidies' in accordance with the provisions in SCM.

Developed countries were required to reduce the budget outlay on export subsidies by 36 per cent and the volume of subsidized exports of each commodity by 21 per cent in six years (between 1995 and 2000). The corresponding reduction commitments by developing countries are only two-thirds, e.g. 24 per cent budget outlay and 14 per cent of volume over an extended period of 10 years (between 1995 and 2004). Developing countries also are exempt from commitments on subsidies to reduce the cost of marketing exports and internal freight subsidies for the implementation period.

Developed countries are the major users of, and account for most of the export subsidies reduction commitments. For instance, subsidies provided by six industrial countries in 1995 accounted for more than 75 per cent of the global value of the export subsidies subject to reduction commitments. The share of all developing countries combined, on the other hand, accounted for just over 20 per cent. The principal commodities, which have high incidence of export subsidies, include wheat, coarse grains, oilseeds, vegetable oil, sugar, dairy products and fruits and vegetables, which also happen to be products of export interest to many developing countries. The effects of export subsidies are frequently associated with the depression of international prices, the lowering of the non-subsidized farmer income, the displacement of competitive exports, the use of environmentally unsustainable methods of production, and, last, the perpetuation of rural poverty in developing countries reliant on agricultural exports and/or having inherent comparative advantage. Export subsidies do not favour medium- or long-term 'food security' even in net food-importing countries, as subsidized imports may reduce their potential to develop agricultural production.

Article 10.2 of AOA stipulates that WTO members should '. . . work towards the development of internationally agreed disciplines to govern the provision of export credits, export credit guarantees or insurance programmes . . .' and to abide by those disciplines once they are established. Despite some work conducted on this subject in OECD, no agreed outcome has yet been reached in the WTO before the end of the Uruguay Round implementation. This has led to circumvention of export subsidy reduction commitments, and has neutralized to a great extent the effects of export subsidy reduction commitments under the agreement.

The current rules and disciplines concerning exports, including export prohibitions and restrictions and export subsidies, remain less strict than the rules and disciplines on imports. For instance, a member instituting the export prohibition or restriction shall give due consideration to the effect on an importing member's food security and shall consult, upon request, with any other member having a substantial interest as an importer (Article 12). Export prohibitions and restrictions, which an exporting country may take temporarily, can severely affect the food security of an importing country, even if it can be considered a necessary measure for the exporting country in view of ensuring its own food security.

## FOOD AID

The concept of food aid, a prominent form of external assistance, is by nature and intention specifically designed to enhance food security. Despite the explicit provision in Article 10.4 to prevent the circumvention of export subsidy commitments by food aid transactions, in certain cases the main objective of food donations seems to be to help reduce price-depressing surplus stocks in the donor countries, as well as promoting market development to displace normal commercial transactions and local production. The Preamble of the Food Aid Convention, 1999, enjoins that the capacity of the international community to respond to food emergency situations and to improve food security should be enhanced through the assurance of supplies of food aid irrespective of world food price and supply fluctuations, and the ultimate objective of food aid should be the elimination of the need of food aid itself, and that the effectiveness of food aid as a tool in support of food security in developing countries should be improved simultaneously, avoiding negative impacts on the enhancement of their domestic production. The global food aid deliveries to LDCs and NFIDCs have declined in recent years, from 17.4 million tons in 1993 to 8.0 million tons in 1998.[16]

## AGRICULTURAL TRADE AND FOOD SECURITY

The main features of the world agricultural trade are as follows. (1) The amount of major agricultural commodities traded in the international market is small as compared with total amount domestically produced. For example, the amount of wheat traded is around 18.5 per cent of the world's production, and in the case of rice the ratio is about 4.5 per cent.[17] Consequently, fluctuation in yields in major exporting and/or large consuming countries easily affects world prices. (2) A limited number of exporting countries dominate international markets. According to the Food and Agriculture Organization Statistical Databases (FAOSTAT) data, the share in major grains exports by the top three largest country/areas in 1998 in quantity terms was: wheat (60.7 per cent), rice (60.5 per cent), barley (71.1 per cent), maize (89.4 per cent), and soyabeans (89.7 per cent). The concentration of suppliers makes fluctuations in world market prices greater in cases of abnormal weather conditions in those countries. (3) A small number of large-scale multinational 'grain majors' and export state trading enterprises ('single desk sellers') dominate the world market situation in major agricultural commodities, causing further concerns on the ability of the importing countries to secure a stable food supply in terms of price and quantity. (4) Hedge funds controlling more than US $200 billion can unduly interfere with markets. (5) Measures by exporting countries such as embargoes and/or export restrictions threaten the food security of importing countries. In addition, developing countries have limited foreign exchange reserves to import foodstuffs.

In recognition of these realities, the FAO Plan of Action in 1996 suggests that 'increased production, including traditional crops and their products, in efficient combination with food imports, reserves, and international trade can strengthen food security and address regional disparities'.

The agricultural sector contributes to the GDP and provides productive employment opportunities and income for the bulk of the population, specially the rural population. The sector plays a crucial role in eradicating poverty through a structure and pattern of production that allow small farmers and landless agricultural workers to share in benefits of agricultural growth. The sector also contributes to the achievement of food security for the rural people, because generation of rural income determines the capacity of the rural population to access sufficient and appropriate food. The sector plays an important role in improving the balance of payments through increased foreign exchange earnings and saving, as well as reduced dependence of the economy on foreign sources. Against this background, it is important to adopt policies aimed at preserving the viability of rural employment and development in order to protect the livelihood of farmers and their families from adverse affects of trade liberalization in agriculture.

## SANITARY AND PHYTOSANITARY (SPS) AGREEMENT

Many developing countries' exporters are encountering additional difficulties in the SPS and TBT areas. Trade harassment through arbitrary use of such measures tends to be growing. Developed-country members should not be allowed to use SPS measures for protectionist purposes by prescribing overly stringent trade-restrictive SPS measures for denying market access to developing countries. Simultaneously, quarantine and inspection measures should be improved and strengthened to meet genuine consumer concerns on food safety. Appropriate international rules should also be established under the auspices of the Food Standards Committee of Alimentarious Commission for Harmonization of Food Standards (CODEX) with regard to the labelling of Genetically Modified Organisms (GMO).

## TRADE RELATED INTELLECTUAL PROPERTY RIGHTS

### PROTECTION OF PLANT VARIETIES

The TRIPS Agreement obligates members to provide for protection of plant varieties, either by patent or by an effective sui generis system such as the plant breeder's rights established in the International Union for the Protection of New Varieties of Plants (UPOV) convention. As the extension of patent protection to plant varieties is likely to prove more onerous, India has decided to provide a UPOV type system to protect the exclusive rights of plant breeders with adequate safeguards for the farming community. The preamble to the Protection of Plant Varieties and Farmers Rights Bill, 2001, states that . . .

> . . . whereas for accelerated agricultural development in the country it is necessary to protect plant breeders' rights to stimulate investment for research and development, both in the public and private sectors for the development of new plant varieties.
>
> . . . and whereas, such protection will facilitate the growth of the seed industry in the country which will ensure the availability of high quality seeds and planting materials to the farmers. . . .

The Bill includes a separate chapter on farmers' rights conferring: (1) the farmer with the right to registration and other protection similar to that provided to the breeder of a variety; (2) the farmer engaged in the conservation of genetic resources will be entitled for recognition and reward from the National Gene Fund; (3) the right to save, use, sow, exchange, share or sell his farm produce, including seeds of a variety protected under the Act (he would not be entitled to sell branded seeds varieties protected under the Act); (4) protection of innocent infringement (wherein the farmer is not aware of the infringement); (5) the farmer can seek compensation if the propagating material which he procured does not match the claimed performance; (6) a governmental or NGO, or a group of persons can take up the cause of infringement of the rights of a local community and fight for redressal or adequate compensation; (7) a breeder applying for registration of any variety should mandatorily disclose, in the application, information regarding the use of genetic material conserved by any tribal or rural families in the breeding or development of the variety.

The free exchange of germ-plasm (seeds) has been vital in meeting food needs by increasing the food productivity of farmers. New laws allowing breeders to claim exclusive rights over seeds may benefit research, but would also restrict sharing of new varieties of the grain, thus posing a threat to food security. The developments in modern biotechnologies based on recombinant DNA techniques, monoclonal antibodies, new cell and tissue technologies has given a fillip to the privatization of agricultural research, and has fostered a trend towards increased reliance on IPR with far-reaching implications on agriculture. There is a need to reorient and enhance public funding for agriculture R&D to deal with emerging challenges.

## GENETICALLY MODIFIED FOODS

As a result of technology development in GMO, production of GMO and food using such technology has substantially increased. The potential of present-day agriculture to meet future demands is under strain. The area of available arable land is decreasing with urban development, and productivity growth is levelling off (partly due to the diminishing potential of 'traditional' breeding technologies). But GM technologies, if developed under appropriate conditions, offer the potential of providing solutions. A number of issues have, however, emerged concerning production, exports/imports, labelling and the protection of intellectual rights for GMO.

Indian farmers encounter serious disease problems of blast in rice, rust in wheat, leaf rust in coffee, viruses in tomatoes and chillies and leaf-spot in groundnuts, besides pests such as shoot borers in brinjal and bollworm in cotton. Conventional plant breeding or use of chemicals have little ammunition to deal with these in an expedient and efficient manner. Cotton farmers alone spend a staggering Rs. 1,600 crore annually on pesticides to combat the American bollworm menace, with diminishing results. These problems can be significantly minimized by using genetically-reprogrammed seeds designed to resist disease attacks, while economizing on costly and harmful pesticide sprays. Further, biotechnology can also help address the dilemma posed by the presence of hazardous substances in several Indian foods—neurotoxin in kesar dal, cyanide in tapioca, aflatoxins in groundnuts and anti-metabolites in chick-pea, horse gram and sweet potato.

It is estimated that more than 18 per cent of children in India suffer from some level of Vitamin A deficiency. About 25 per cent of the population suffers from significant illnesses, including impairment, inability to absorb proteins and nutrients and reduced immune functions because of Vitamin A deficiency. Golden rice—the genetically engineered rice fortified with Vitamin A—has been targeted for enrichment with Vitamin A to improve the health and nutritional security of the vulnerable sections of the population.

The gene revolution is potentially more scale-neutral and small-farmer-friendly than the Green revolution, as its potency revolves entirely around genetically-reprogrammed seeds and there is less dependence on the conventional package of inputs, specially pesticides and other costly chemicals. However, there are concerns that large multinational biotech corporations, which are spear-heading the genetically engineered seeds, will try to dominate Indian agriculture. Corporate control would increase over seed and agrochemical markets at the expense of the poor farmers. Potential opportunities are likely to bypass small farmers due to lack of investment in research on relevant crops. Special exemptions on intellectual property rights protection for crops widely used by farmers and government agencies of developing countries, and more general policies of sharing GM technologies, have been proposed as part of a number of private/public ventures.

Biotechnological applications in agriculture and food can help Indian farmers tackle global competition, provided the related technological and social issues are properly addressed. There is also a related issue of impairment of traditional comparative advantage of countries in several agricultural products vis-à-vis Genetically Modified Foods (GMF) on cost terms. The Indian Government has decided to continue the work on transgenic plants for improving productivity, nutritional and environmental security with stringent bio-safety regulations. Before releasing any GMF, bio-safety assessment including safety of food to human and animal health is mandatory under the Indian Environment (Protection) Act. Genetically modified crops of cotton, tobacco, tomato, potato, brinjal, cauliflower, cabbage and mustard have been permitted to undergo field trials in Indian environmental conditions. Studies on food safety of transgenic crops conducted in India have indicated that these crops were safe from environmental and health hazards.

## GEOGRAPHICAL INDICATIONS

The TRIPS Agreement establishes protection of the indications which identify a good as originating in a country, or a region or locality where a given quality, reputation or other characteristic of the good is essentially attributed to its geographical origin. Under Article 23.1, additional protection has been conferred for geographical indications for wines and spirits, including the establishment of a multilateral system of notification and registration. Products other than wine and spirits can also be considered for additional protection. To claim protection as a geographical indication for a good, legal protection is required in the law of the country of origin. India has already enacted the Geographical Indications of Goods (Registration and Protection) Act, 1999. Proposals have been made to expand the existing protection level for wines and spirits to, among others, agricultural and foodstuffs originating in developing countries. The additional protection for agricultural and foodstuffs at international level could go a long way in ensuring higher income for farmers and improve food security.

## CONCLUDING OBSERVATIONS

Food security in developing countries depends in part on agricultural development and in part on raising income and eradication of poverty. The FAO, in its paper on 'Issues at stake relating to Agricultural Development, Trade and Food Security', has concluded: '. . . significant progress in promoting economic growth, reducing poverty and enhancing food security cannot be achieved in most of these countries without developing more fully the potential capacity of the agriculture sector and its contribution to overall economic development.' Food security can only be secured through an appropriate combination of WTO-consistent measures, such as domestic supports, border measures, stronger disciplines for export restriction/prohibition measures and an adequate level of food aid for NFIDCs, taking into account the specific situations in various countries. Appropriate flexibility should be reflected in future negotiations and agreements in the area of market access, domestic support and export competition. Tariff levels of processed agricultural products should be determined, fully considering the sound development of agro-industries, in particular those involved in processing staple foods which play a significant role in the stable supply of good-quality food and fosters enhanced food security. The trade-related risks and concerns on food security are much more serious in developing countries than in developed ones because, in developing countries, the Engel index is higher and consumers spend a larger portion of their income on food.

It must be ensured that the WTO policy reform is consistent with other relevant multilateral commitments such as the Convention on Biological Diversity and commitments relating to the right to food, such as the International Covenant on Economic, Social and Cultural Rights which emphasizes the importance of adequate food supply, alongside the continuous improvement of living conditions, and the World Food Summit which highlights the multifunctional role of agriculture and the concerns surrounding issues such as rural development and outmigration, high- and low-potential areas and food security.

The agricultural negotiations should be conducted by bearing in mind the importance of global food security, which includes assistance to developing countries suffering from problems such as starvation and malnutrition, and also by maintaining close coordination with other organizations, such as the FAO. An idea of a possible framework for international food stockholding should be examined, which should complement existing bilateral and multilateral food aid schemes, and which will enable loan of food in case of temporary shortage.

## NOTES

1. See FAO, *The State of Food Insecurity in the World*, Rome: FAO, 2000.
2. The WTO agreement incorporates some 29 individual texts covering subjects ranging from agriculture to textiles and clothing, services, rules of origin, and intellectual property rights. In addition, ministerial declarations, decisions and undertakings spell out further obligations and commitments for WTO members. Under the 'single undertaking

approach', membership in WTO entails accepting all the multilateral agreements without exception.

3. The NTBs that are specifically covered include quantitative import restrictions, variable import levies, minimum import prices, discretionary import licensing, non-tariff measures maintained through state trading enterprises and voluntary export restraints. Quantitative restrictions on agricultural products are, however, allowable on balance of payments considerations and those permitted under other non-agriculture-specific provisions of various WTO agreements.
4. M.D. Ingco, 1996, 'Tariffication in the Uruguay Round: How Much Liberalization?', *The World Economy,* 19(4): July.
5. Australian Bureau of Agricultural and Natural Resource Economics (ABARE), 2000, 'The Impact of Agricultural Trade Liberalisation on Developing Countries'.
6. FAO, 1996, 'Policy Options for Developing Countries to Support Food Security in the Post Uruguay Round Period'. Panos Konandreas and Jim Greenfield, Rome.
7. FAO, 1999, 'Agriculture, Trade and Food Security: Issues and Options in the forthcoming WTO Negotiations from the Perspective of Developing Countries', FAO Symposium, 23–4 September 1999, Geneva.
8. UNCTAD/WTO Joint Study (TD/B/COM.1/14/Rev.1, 1999), 'The Post-Uruguay Round Tariff Environment for Developing Country Exports: Tariff Peaks and Tariff Escalation'.
9. Tariff escalation occurs when tariffs are increased as the level of processing in a production stage is increased. Tariff escalation prevents development of value-added activities in developing countries, and also leads to more pollution due to higher-weight transport.
10. WTO, Tariff Escalation, WT/CTE/W/25, Document Prepared by the Secretariat.
11. As per the agreement, India has reduced its tariffs on almonds to be imported from the US from Rs. 55 per kg to Rs. 35 per kg. and duties on imports of fresh fruits and juices, such as apples, oranges, plums and pears from 60–70 per cent to an average of 40 per cent. These concessions amount to around $40 million annually. In return, the bound duties on milk powder and corn (maize) has been increased (from zero per cent) to 15 per cent for in-quota imports, and to a higher duty of 60 per cent for out-of-quota imports.
12. A. Dhar and S. Chaturvedi, *WTO Agreements and Agricultural Sector: Implications for India*, Research and Information System for Non-Aligned and other Developing Countries, October 1999.
13. Import State Trading Enterprises (STE) are perceived to play an important role in mitigating the impacts of a fluctuating international agricultural market, stabilizing domestic prices and in ensuring

adequate supplies for food security purposes. Article XVII of GATT sets out certain rules for state trading agencies, including non-discriminatory treatment, operation in conformity with commercial practices, notification requirements on their operations and limit on price mark-ups on domestic sales only up to relevant tariff bindings. However, these disciplines are quite weak, and efforts are on in the WTO to develop new and effective rules to deal with the perceived market power of STE.

14. The AMS means the annual level of support, expressed in monetary terms, separately for each basic agricultural product or total non-product-specific support provided in general to agricultural producers. Total AMS is the sum of all domestic support provided in favour of agricultural producers, calculated as a sum of aggregated support for all basic agricultural products and all aggregated non-product-specific support.
15. Blue Box and export subsidies can be challenged if there is proof of injury or threat to another member. Investment subsidies and input subsidies exempt from domestic support reduction commitments for developing countries have been equated with the Blue Box payments, in the sense that no countervailing duties could be imposed unless a determination or injury of threat thereof is made in accordance with anti-dumping agreements and the SCM agreement. In contrast to that, Green Box subsidies are fully exempt, being non-actionable.
16. Monitored by WFP. See a background paper by the Secretariat of the WTO Committee on Agriculture, G/AG/NG/S4, pp. 3–6, for details.
17. Including trade of wheat flour, milled rice, etc. Based on the data of 1989–98 of FAOSTAT.

SECTION V

# Policy Response to Food Security

# 21. Public Distribution System: Safety Net for the Poor?

*S.S. Meenakshisundaram*

A Public Distribution System (PDS) through Fair Price Shops (FPS) providing food grains at affordable prices has been the key element of the food security system in India. The national agenda for governance of the present government while specifically promising to ensure food security for all and create a hunger-free India by 2007, proposes to 'reform and improve the PDS so as to serve the poorest of the poor in rural and urban areas'. While the PDS and its efficiency and effectiveness have been largely criticised by some, the role of the PDS as a lifeline in times of crisis has also been highlighted by others. With the advent of the new economic policy and the consequential structural adjustment, the role of the PDS has become even more crucial. While the government cites the system as a safety net for the poor in view of the backlash of a market economy in an era of globalization, other opinions tend towards leaving incomes and quality of life to market forces in the hopes of positive spill over effects of liberalization. In this context, this paper seeks to review the functioning of the PDS, in times of both surplus and scarcity, as a safety net for the poor.

The PDS in India has a long history. Rationing was first introduced in India in 1939 in Bombay (Mumbai). In 1943, the first Food grain Policy Committee recommended continuation of rationing due to the fall of Burma (Myanmar), which was a major supplier of rice to India and the great Bengal famine in the preceding year. Immediately after Independence, rationing was abolished, only to be reintroduced in 1950 as food shortages led to high prices. The rationing system thus introduced due to scarcity of food evolved into a PDS in the mid-1960s. The PDS, over the years, became an important instrument of governments policy of ensuring availability of food grains to the public at affordable prices, regulating the open market prices of essential commodities and enhancing food security at the household level.

Under the PDS, the central government has assumed responsibility for procurement and supply of essential commodities, namely wheat, rice, sugar, imported edible oil and kerosene to the states for distribution. These commodities are made available at fixed Central Issue Prices (CIPs) which are determined by the central government and generally involve subsidies borne by the central government. Some states also distribute additional items of mass consumption through the PDS outlets, namely, the fair price shops (FPS). The implementation of PDS is the joint responsibility of the central and the state governments. The Centre is responsible for procurement, storage and transportation of the commodities upto the central godowns and making them available to the states. The responsibility for distribution to the consumers through the FPS and administration of the PDS rests with the state governments. Statewise population, number of households, number of ration cards and number of FPS are given in Annexure: Table I.

## TARGETTED PUBLIC DISTRIBUTION

With a network of around 4,51,000 FPS distributing commodities worth over 150 billion rupees to about 180 million households, India's PDS is perhaps the largest distributing network of its type in the world. The system is designed to help both the producers and consumers of food grains by linking procurement to support prices and ensuring their distribution along with other essential commodities at affordable prices throughout the country. This huge network can play a meaningful role, provided the system is able to translate the macro-level self-sufficiency into a micro-level availability of food grains for the poor household. Unfortunately the PDS has experienced several implementation problems. It was criticised for its failure to serve the people Below Poverty Line (BPL), its urban bias, negligible coverage in the states with the highest concentration of rural poor and lack of transparent and accountable arrangements for delivery. Realizing this, the Government of India streamlined the PDS into a Targeted Public Distribution System (TPDS) so as to raise the cost-effectiveness in reaching the poor.

The TPDS offers two separate distribution channels, one aimed at BPL households, and the other at Above Poverty Line (APL) households. Under the channel for BPL households, the central government transfers wheat and rice at about half the CIP set for the PDS to the state governments. To start with, the monthly ration under the TPDS was kept at 10 kg per poor household. However, keeping in view the general consensus on increasing the allocation of food grains to BPL families, the Government of India later increased the allocation to 20 kg per family with effect from 1 April 2000.

At present, a quantity of about 15.65 million tons per annum has been earmarked for benefiting around 65 million BPL families. The end retail price is fixed by the States/UTs after taking into account margins for wholesalers/retailers, transportation charges, levies, local taxes, etc. Under TPDS, the states are required to issue food grains at a margin of not more than 50 paise per kg over and above the CIP for BPL families. For APL families, the states can fix the margin keeping in view the actual expenses incurred.

From December 2000 the allocation of food grains for BPL families is being made on the basis of population projections of the Registrar General (of India) as on 1 March 2000, instead of the previous base of projected population of 1995. The identification of the poor is done by the states as per statewise poverty estimates of the Planning Commission based on the methodology enunciated by an expert group on 'estimation of proportion and number of poor' chaired by late Prof. Lakdawala. The states also design and implement appropriate targeting mechanisms to reach the poor. The thrust is to include only the really poor and vulnerable sections of the society such as landless agricultural labourers, marginal farmers, rural artisans/craftsmen, urban slum dwellers, urban workers in the informal sectors, etc. The state governments, after identifying the poor, issue special cards and deliver food grains to the intended beneficiaries through the FPS. The central government monitors the performance of the states and the TPDS can even be discontinued if the states do not target and deliver adequately.

Under the second channel, which deals with APL households, the central government transfers wheat and rice at CIP, which is usually fixed closer to the market rates. Access through the APL channel is universal. This channel will be gradually phased out, leaving just the BPL households to be catered by the TPDS, although there are agruments in favour of its continuation for the

APL population in chronically food-deficit areas such as the hilly regions and states like Kerela. Allocation of food grains to the states is based on the average offtake of rice and wheat over the last 10 years under PDS. The quantum of food grains in excess of the requirement of BPL families is provided to the states as 'transitory allocation', for which a quantum of 10.3 million metric tons (mt) of food grains is earmarked annually. This transitory allocation is intended for the continuation of the present benefit of subsidized food grains to the APL population, as any sudden withdrawal of PDS from them may not be possible.

The Government of India has issued a model citizens' charter in November 1997 for adoption by the state governments. It contains essential information, viz., entitlement of BPL families, fair average quality of food grains, information regarding FPS, procedure of issue of ration cards, inspection and checking, right to information, vigilance and public participation. In the guidelines issued in June 1999 for the involvement of the Panchayati Raj Institutions (PRIs) in the implementation of the TPDS, it is mentioned that the Gram Panchayat/Gram Sabha should be encouraged to form vigilance committees at the FPS level. The main functions of the vigilance committees are to ensure smooth functioning of the PDS and redressal of problems related with it.

## PDS IN INDIA: AN EVALUATION

Having described briefly the salient features of the PDS, let us now attempt an analysis of its utility. We shall examine how effective the PDS is in meeting the needs of the hungry poor for whose benefit it was designed and implemented, and what has been the impact on household income as well as food security. The PDS has been functioning for almost five decades now. Its greatest achievement lies in preventing famines in India. It has no doubt played a great role by making available rice and wheat at fixed prices to consumers all through the country. This distribution network also supplied grains for the food for work type programmes taken up from time to time to fight droughts and also the normal rural employment programmes. However, all is not well with the PDS. The annual food subsidy involved in maintaining the system is huge (Table 1). One of the major problems involved in the operation of the PDS is the issue of containing the food subsidy at reasonable levels. It is also said that the PDS is not cost-

TABLE 1: FOOD SUBSIDY OF THE CENTRAL GOVERNMENT

(Rs. in crore)

| Year | Amount | As % of total govt. expenditure |
|---|---|---|
| 1990–1 | 2,450 | 2.33 |
| 1991–2 | 2,850 | 2.53 |
| 1992–3 | 2,785 | 2.27 |
| 1993–4 | 5,537 | 3.90 |
| 1994–5 | 4,509 | 2.80 |
| 1995–6 | 4,960 | 2.78 |
| 1996–7 | 5,166 | 2.46 |
| 1997–8 | 7,500 | 3.23 |
| 1998–9 | 8,700 | 3.11 |
| 1999–2000 | 9,200 | 3.03 |
| 2000–1 | 8,100 | 2.39 |

*Source*: Government of India, Planning Commission, *Mid-Term Appraisal of Ninth Five Year Plan (1997–2002)*, October 2000, New Delhi.

effective, its operations are costly and the ratio between procurement and transportation is high, pointing to wasteful movements sometimes. The storage losses are also reported to be high (Nawani 1994).

Another valid criticism of the PDS is its marginal impact as far as income transfer to poor households is concerned. In a study based on the National Sample Survey (42nd round), it has been observed that

> the value of the subsidy is very little even for those households who make all their purchases of cereals from rationshops. For the bottom 20 per cent of the rural population, the subsidy is no more than Rs. 2.08 per capita per 30 days. With the average family size of six, the subsidy per family is almost Rs. 12.50 per month. In other words, it is useful to note here, one person day of additional employment per family per month would provide the same income support as provided by the cereals distributed under PDS. (Parikh 1994)

The coverage and popularity of the PDS appears dependent upon the demand and the political, administrative and infrastructural facilities available at the level of the states. Only 33 per cent of the rural households in India have reported use of the PDS on a regular basis (*India Human Development Report 1999*). It is likely that this proportion may fall further for short periods of time such as during the harvesting season. An increase, however, depends upon the vibrancy of the programme and regularity of PDS supplies. Available data indicate that the programme is working fairly efficiently in all the four southern states, two western states, and Himachal Pradesh, and at modest levels in Madhya Pradesh. The proportion of households using PDS is 82 per cent in Tamil Nadu, 78 per cent in Kerala, 70 per cent in Karnataka, and 66 per cent in Andhra Pradesh. On the other hand, only about 5 per cent of rural households have reported PDS utilization in Uttar Pradesh, Bihar, Orissa and Punjab. With the exception of Punjab, the other three states have a very high level of undernutrition both among children and adult populations. Low PDS utilization in Punjab and Haryana is primarily a consequence of lack of demand, since these are agriculturally prosperous states with substantial marketable surpluses. The distribution network is very weak in the states of Uttar Pradesh, Bihar, Orissa, and West Bengal. The proportion of users is very low and the proportion of requirement met by the PDS is also low in all the poorly performing PDS states (Parikh 1994).

The main weakness pointed out in the PDS has been its inability to reach the poor effectively. The advent of the TPDS may to some extent remedy the situation. Earlier evidence from the village studies on TPDS undertaken for the World Bank suggests that targeting measures taken under TPDS may have at least significantly increased the amount of PDS food grains reaching the poor: BPL lists have been developed in the majority of study villages and the new ration cards actually distributed in over half of them. Many of the study respondents felt that most of the poor—particularly the very poor—were included in the lists, although researchers also heard numerous reports of inappropriate inclusion and exclusion. Nevertheless, TPDS suffers from some of the same implementation problems as the PDS. For example, the poor said they were discouraged from using PDS by irregular hours of store operation, lack of information about when rations would be available, insults from shopkeepers and high transport costs relative to expected savings. The poor in one state complained that by the time they learnt of a delivery, most of the grains had already been distributed to the wealthier households living near the shop.

Another criticism against the PDS is that the states making the greatest use of the PDS are not necessarily the poorest. Some of the poorest states, namely, Bihar, Uttar Pradesh and Madhya

Pradesh chose to draw a much lower share of PDS subsidies than what they are entitled to, and also far less than their share of poverty. Targeting within the state is likewise weak. One of the studies on the PDS estimates that only about 40 per cent of the total quantity of wheat and nearly 47 per cent of the total quantity of rice supplied through the PDS is consumed by the poorest 40 per cent of people in India (Ahluwalia 1993). This would be the expected pattern if the PDS were not at all targeted at the poor, but distributed its rations randomly. Moreover, the high administrative costs again raise questions about the cost-effectiveness of the PDS. In general, it is reported that it costs the government between Rs. 2 and 7 (with the highest value reported for the PDS) to provide Re. one to the poor (World Bank 1997). The impact of the PDS as a check on open market food grain prices and as a safety net for the weaker sections of the society is also minimal in most of the states, particularly where the per capita distribution is low and social and economic inequalities are more pronounced. With wide variations in the employment situation, consumption levels, percentage of the population below the poverty line, etc., between the states, it would be difficult to ensure equitable allocation of food grains to different states under the PDS.

As regards the criticism of urban bias and pro-rich nature of the PDS, a study has shown that 'in case of all commodities except coal, more than 50 per cent of the total quantity purchased under PDS is in the rural areas. . . . PDS is rural biased at all India level for rice, coarse cereals, sugar and cloth. These items constitute more than 60 per cent of the total PDS purchases. Hence it appears that PDS is not urban biased but pro-rural' (Mahendra Dev and Suryanarayana Rao 1991). As regards its being pro-rich, the same study shows that 'more or less all the population (income) groups depend uniformly to the same extent on the PDS with respect to all commodities in rural areas, even though there were slight variations'. Thus, even though the PDS appears to be even-handed for all income groups, this very finding points out its failure in achieving its basic goal of helping the poor.

One other drawback that invites abuse and diversion of grains from the poor to the non-poor under the current TPDS is the expectation that the retail dealer will supply the same variety of grains at half-price to the poor (theoretically those with red colour ration cards) and at the regular price to the non-poor. Given past experience with similar arrangements for kerosene and cooking oil (Radhakrishna and Subbarao 1997), it is unrealistic to expect anything but a high level of fraud. Although the central government plans to enforce strict monitoring, such control is likely to be difficult and administratively costly.

In view of several complaints made regarding diversion of PDS commodities into the open market, a study was conducted by the Tata Economic Consultancy Services (1998) to know how much of PDS supplies were diverted from the system. At the national level, it was found, there was a diversion of 36 per cent of wheat supplies, 31 per cent of rice and 23 per cent sugar. Statistically, at 90 per cent confidence level, the actual diversion of wheat would fall in the range of 32–40 per cent, rice in 27–35 per cent and sugar 20–6 per cent. Table II in Annexure shows the extent of diversion in various states and Union Territories. The table shows that the diversion is more in northern, eastern and north-eastern regions; it is comparatively less in southern and western regions. As high as 64 per cent diversion of rice is estimated in Bihar and Assam. In the case of wheat, the diversion is an estimated 100 per cent in Nagaland and 69 per cent in Punjab.

It is significant to note that the diversion is estimated less in the case of sugar as compared to rice and wheat. The PDS is better organized in towns where sugar is consumed while its infrastructure is weak in rural areas, specially in poorer northern, eastern and north-eastern states.

A study of the delivery system for PDS in Bihar reported that dealership and even membership of vigilance committees there are seen as positions where money can be made. The procedure to appoint them is highly politicized, and mostly clients of MLAs are appointed. Sub-district infrastructure to handle food grains is poor; Ranchi had only 11 godowns for 20 blocks. The Civil Supplies Corporation has no working capital to buy from the Food Corporation of India (FCI), vans are in poor condition or have no money for petrol, the staff do not receive salaries for months. On the whole, only government staff, agents and retailers seem to benefit from the scheme (Jharwal 1999).

Problems of lack of infrastructure and shortage of funds with government agencies are not unique to Bihar. Most states suffer such handicaps, except for a few in the west and the south. Some states, do not have regular paid staff to manage the PDS, and often have to depend upon the services of the wholesalers in their region. The centre may have to ensure adequate infrastructural capacities in districts and at block levels to plug leakage of scarce resources, which reportedly help only contractors and corrupt government staff and keep the poor and the needy away. One study claimed that each fair price dealer has to 'maintain' on an average nine government functionaries. It is significant that the allocation to poorer states like UP, Bihar and Assam got more than doubled after the switchover to TPDS, but the offtake by the states was poor, and by actual BPL beneficiaries, even poorer. The scheme has not made any impact on nutrition levels in those states.

A detailed study on TPDS carried out among 2,250 households across 120 villages in 25 districts in 4 economic regions of Uttar Pradesh (UP) showed that savings through TPDS in UP accounts for only 1.3 per cent and 1.1 per cent of the cereal budget of households in the two lowest units (Srivastava 2000). The scheme is seen to hardly help the poor. This, it was stated, is because the Government of UP does not lift its quota due to bad administrative arrangements, and a substantial portion of whatever is lifted is often sold in the black market. Pricing provides a hefty incentive for an estimated 41 per cent of leakage. Imperfect targeting has led to exclusion of eligible households. The basis for selecting beneficiaries lacks transparency and is too complicated for local officials to administer. There is a lack of political commitment to the TPDS, it was stated, as well as administrative cynicism, while the PDS shopkeeper does not have adequate incentive. Multiplicity of agencies, poor coordination and low administrative accountability have combined to cripple the delivery machinery. Greater local supervision and a clear enunciation of entitlements could perhaps help in reducing the extent of leakage.

A few other problems associated with the scheme are the inability of the poor to buy 20 kg food grains at a time as they are not permitted to buy the same in instalments, the low quality of food grains, lack of transparency, and inadequate accountability of officials to the community they are expected to serve.

## CONCLUSION AND RECOMMENDATIONS

To summarize, an assessment of the current PDS indicates that there are a number of problems: only partial success in targetting the poor: often complex administration, high administrative costs;

poor accountability and beneficiary participation. Though the latest TPDS appears to be well-targeted, it cannot be said that under this system, food distribution would be regular, adequate and timely. It may also not succeed in meeting the needs of the targeted poor to a significant extent leading to any notable impact on household income and food security. This programme which involves huge subsidy may not be cost-effective. Finally, there have been no efforts to integrate the ongoing poverty alleviation programmes relating to self-employment, wage employment or area development with the PDS.

The PDS no doubt offers great potential for providing extra food to poor households, if only it can successfully reach them. The main weakness in the PDS, i.e. not reaching the poor effectively, stems from the universality of its coverage. Every household, irrespective of its income, can have an entitlement card and draw food grains against it under the PDS. This, in turn, leads to low scales per household and 'first-come first-served' system of delivery. These two combine to allow leakages and diversion on the one hand, and a 'no commitment syndrome' on the part of the poor households on the other. If the PDS could be targetted at the poor, a larger proportion of the household's requirement could be met by enhancing the scale, and it would also be able to generate a commitment on the part of the cardholders to the system. Beneficiaries could then be organized and educated. They would then monitor the supplies and sales themselves to ensure that supplies reach the FPS in proper quantity and quality and are sold to genuine beneficiaries. The entitled households would also then demand their quota from the FPS. Targeting of PDS to the really needy is, therefore, a sine qua non for an effective PDS. The advent of the TPDS in 1997 to some extent may remedy the situation. The ultimate solution will, however, lie in eliminating the non-poor entirely from the TPDS and restricting its coverage to the targeted poor only.

Second, for the TPDS to have any impact on nutrition allocation to poor households must be increased. An intake of 10 kg per household provides an additional 100 calories per person per day, which is inadequate for the poorest households. If the TPDS is to bring caloric levels for the poorest 30 per cent from the current average of about 1,500 calories per person per day to even a modest average of 1,900 calories, allocation of an additional 30 kg of cereals per households is necessary, presuming that the very poor households would maximize their expenditure on food when it is highly subsidized. Provision of additional grains during the months when they are most needed, such as the pre-harvest and rainy seasons, will definitely help preventing vulnerable children and pregnant women from declining in nutritional status during these periods.

Although rice, wheat, sugar, edible oil, pulses and kerosene are sold through PDS outlets, four of these items, namely, rice, wheat, sugar and kerosene account for 86 per cent of the total PDS sales. The share of pulses, the main source of protein for the poor, is less than 0.2 per cent. Sugar, rice and kerosene are relatively more important items sold through the PDS in the rural sector, while rice, sugar, kerosene, wheat and edible oils in the urban sector. Thus, there is some basis for the general impression that the composition of PDS commodities is weighted in favour of items supposed to be consumed largely by the relatively richer sections of the society (Suryanarayana 1995). It is, therefore, necessary to identify the PDS commodities which confer higher income benefits on the poor through extensive consumer surveys, and to gradually shift those which are used by the non-poor to the open market. To help the effective transfer of income to the poor, the gap between the issue prices of essential commodities and the market prices can be maintained in such a manner so as to attract the poor to buy PDS commodities.

There is also a general feeling to choose only those foods most consumed by the poor, such as coarse grains and unrefined sugar as transfer instruments for the poor under the PDS. The introduction of coarse grains, which are purchased only by the lower income groups, could no doubt help in better targeting, but there are several restricting factors. First, coarse grains are grown by small farmers for their own consumption and are difficult to collect in sufficient quantities. Second, the production is totally from rainfed lands and may collapse in a drought year. Third, the prices of coarse grains are sometimes higher even than those of wheat and rice, and last, the short shelf life of coarse cereals would not permit their procurement, stocking and distribution through the FCI. The only alternative would be to organize grain banks at the village itself (preferably through the PRIs), making use of the local facilities available for stocking and the local FPS for distribution. Such a system can also help the distribution of food grains at the work spots wherever the food for work programmes are in operation.

Even if the public distribution of grains is restricted only to the targetted poor, the problem of identifying the genuine poor will have to be addressed. This requires strategies which, without ignoring political economy considerations, can minimize, if not eliminate, the accrual of benefits to the non-poor. A possible solution could be to identify the poor through the Gram Sabhas (village councils) which have now become an integral part of India's Panchayati Raj system of local governance. By transferring the task of identification from the bureaucracy to PRIs, the selection process will become transparent and the access of non-poor to TPDS can be drastically reduced. The plan to issue new cards for households below the poverty line has to be implemented through the PRIs, which can also be given the responsibility to supervise the distribution of cereals through the FPS within their jurisdiction.

To ensure that the really vulnerable sections living in the rural areas are covered under TPDS, the criteria for distribution of cards must include: (1) all households participating in the ongoing poverty alleviation programmes; (2) single mothers with children, or widows without support; (3) all non-income tax paying households; (4) small and marginal farmers; and (5) all landless agricultural labourers and petty artisans who can be identified in the open Gram Sabha meetings. The running of the grain banks, wherever established, through local purchase of coarse grains, can also be entrusted to the village panchayats. This will ensure market friendly procurement, local storage and timely utilization. Discussions on procurement, stocking and distribution policies at the Village Panchayat/Gram Sabha levels will greatly enhance participation of the beneficiaries in food security measures, besides ensuring transparency.

Even after taking all necessary steps to exclude the non-poor under TPDS, there can still be a possibility of its being usurped in time by those who do not require subsidized food. To prevent this, a few more safety mechanisms have to be designed. For instance, the contracts for FPSs can be given to community groups, particularly womens groups and cooperatives, as against individuals. These shops will have to be located in areas where the poor and the vulnerable live. Participation by the beneficiary groups must be insisted upon both in the location of fair price shops and also in their actual running. The performance of the

FPS must also be put down as a subject for discussion during the annual meetings of the Gram Sabha.

As the organization of the PDS is carried out through FPS, the economic viability of these shops is relevant to the efficient functioning of the system as well as curbing malpractices such as diversion of commodities to the open market. Particularly in rural areas, the poor return on investments made by FPS owners does not make the business attractive. It may, therefore, be necessary to encourage FPS owners to have their own private business in addition to the distribution of commodities under PDS. Further, if the distribution of PDS is organized on a weekly basis as in Kerala, the invested capital would be continuously utilized and only smaller amounts of cash would be required for working capital at any time. From the purchasers' point of view also, a weekly system of allotment would be much more beneficial as many of the poor families cannot afford to purchase their whole entitlement in the few days when the stocks are available.

Finally, greater emphasis on consumer awareness rather than official vigilance committees may be more effective in streamlining the PDS. People can exercise an effective check and control on the functioning of the PDS as is evident from the example of Kerala. The existence of a large number of grass-root-level organizations will also provide adequate fora for consumer complaints and their timely redressal.

While well targeted coverage under the PDS can definitely ensure reasonable food security, it can only provide temporary relief. For the purpose of providing enduring food security to the poor, it would be necessary to emphasize strategies which reduce poverty and enhance their purchasing power. The need for rapid economic growth with larger employment generation, therefore, assumes crucial importance. Moreover, since hunger debilitates people physically and psychologically, they get trapped in a vicious cycle of hunger—low productivity—poverty—hunger. The links between hunger, labour productivity and employment make a strong case for 'food for work' type of programmes to assist the hungry and the poor to achieve food security, as that is the only way to make them productive and self-reliant.

Since it may be difficult to cover all villages under the food for work programmes, this purpose can be achieved to some extent by linking the ongoing State sponsored wage employment programmes with distribution of food grains as a part of wages at the work spots. Implementing the TPDS through food for work projects and employment generation programmes appears to be a better alternative, because in such programmes the poor derive a double benefit. First, the error of inclusion of non-poor is minimized since non-poor generally do not undertake employment under these programmes. Second, besides transferring purchasing power to the hands of the poor through employment generation programmes, additional income transfer can also take place through PDS supplies to the participants. The state government or the PRIs can distribute food stamps/vouchers to the workers employed under these programmes, which can be utilized to purchase food grains from the local FPS. Since the responsibility to execute the employment generation programmes is now vested in the PRIs, it would not be difficult for the PRIs to link these programmes with the local FPS for distribution of a portion of the wages in the form of grains. To check deviations from the intended purpose by the PRIs/FPS and also at the work spots, it would be useful if NGOs with a proven record of helping the poor are involved in supervising the entire procedure.

While taking up employment programmes, it may be desirable to allot a proportion of food grains exclusively for women. This will ensure that more women participate in these programmes and that they are not excluded because of physical or traditional gender segregation of work activities. All workers, rather than only one member of the family, must be made eligible for rations when they work in such projects. This will ensure that women who work alongside their male family members get equal opportunity to receive food directly. This will also result in the children of the family getting some food. If the food for work activities can generate around 100 work-days per person per year, that will provide reasonable food security to the participating families.

When all these considerations are combined with the evidence available from the various evaluation/research studies, the highest gains to the poor from the PDS are likely to come from: (1) subsidizing only rice, wheat and kerosene (for environmental considerations) under the TPDS; (2) phasing out completely the second and untargetted channel of the PDS; (3) progressively shifting more public spending from food subsidies to public works programmes; (4) linking payment of wages under poverty alleviation programmes with the PDS; (5) encouraging the distribution of food grains through the PRIs, which will also be responsible for targeting the poor; (6) organizing grain banks at the local level which can procure even coarse grains if necessary and distribute them to the poor through the FPSs organized at the panchayat level which will reduce costs of buffer-stocking and transportation; and (7) involving non-government organizations which can organize community groups and cooperatives that can take over the targeting and distribution of food grains wherever panchayats do not have a strong presence.

In a country where there is mass poverty, where food consumption is low and where expenditure on food accounts for the bulk of total family expenditure, we need to expand and strengthen, and not undermine and disband the PDS. Its utility as a safety net for the poor is beyond doubt. Unfortunately, the implementation of PDS has been rather poor. There are large differences in the coverage and functioning of PDS across the states. This is not surprising, given the differences in the class character and politics of different state governments. Even though key parameters of food distribution may be determined by the central government, the state governments do have a final say on policy, including quantity, prices and coverage of the PDS and are responsible for its implementation. The diverse experience among states shows that strong political support is essential to establish and maintain an effective PDS. It also points to differences in the quality of governance and the level of government commitment to the effective provision of public goods and services such as through the PDS. Given that the PDS could not succeed in several parts of the country, the task ahead is to restructure it so as to make it an effective safety net for the poor, and here again, good governance seems to hold the key to success.

## ANNEXURE

TABLE I: STATEWISE NO. OF HOUSEHOLDS, BPL HOUSEHOLDS, FPS AND NO. OF RATION CARDS

| State/UT | Population 1998 (in lakh) | No. of house holds 1998 (in lakh) | No. of BPL House Holds (in lakh) | Fair Price Shops | | | Ration cards (in lakh) | | | No. of cards per FPS | Reported as on |
|---|---|---|---|---|---|---|---|---|---|---|---|
| | | | | Rural | Urban | Total | BPL | APL | Total | | |
| Andhra Pradesh | 741.71 | 155.50 | 38.39 | 32,813 | 7,040 | 39,853 | 113.02 | 51.53 | 164.55 | 413 | Oct. 1998 |
| Arunachal Pradesh | 11.28 | 2.29 | 0.94 | 842 | 103 | 945 | 0.78 | 2.22 | 3.00 | 317 | June 1998 |
| Assam | 256.46 | 43.99 | 17.97 | 27,466 | 3,753 | 31,219 | 19.06 | 22.68 | 41.74 | 134 | Aug. 1998 |
| Bihar | 969.55 | 157.39 | 86.50 | 47,293 | 10,242 | 57,535 | 84.26 | 88.74 | 173.00 | 301 | Nov. 1997 |
| Goa | 15.13 | 3.03 | 0.45 | 429 | 161 | 590 | 0.07 | 2.87 | 2.94 | 498 | Oct. 1998 |
| Gujarat | 470.98 | 85.48 | 20.69 | 10,358 | 3,766 | 14,124 | 33.62 | 67.59 | 101.21 | 717 | June 1998 |
| Haryana | 193.43 | 30.70 | 7.69 | 5,052 | 2,615 | 7,667 | 5.62 | 28.51 | 34.13 | 445 | Oct. 1998 |
| Himachal Pradesh | 64.23 | 12.03 | 4.93 | 3,418 | 240 | 3,658 | 2.84 | 8.96 | 11.80 | 323 | May 1998 |
| Jammu & Kashmir | 95.35 | 18.10 | 6.17 | 2,237 | 689 | 2,926 | 3.36 | 10.12 | 13.48 | 461 | Sep. 1997 |
| Karnataka | 509.83 | 92.36 | 30.63 | 14,540 | 5,353 | 19,893 | 59.50 | 43.57 | 103.07 | 518 | Oct. 1998 |
| Kerala | 317.8 | 60.19 | 15.31 | 12,279 | 1,982 | 14,261 | 20.61 | 40.04 | 60.65 | 425 | Sep. 1998 |
| Madhya Pradesh | 774.00 | 137.00 | 58.25 | 20,489 | 3,652 | 34,141 | 42.36 | 91.45 | 133.81 | 554 | Sep. 1998 |

| | | | | | | | | | | | |
|---|---|---|---|---|---|---|---|---|---|---|---|
| Meghalaya | 23.05 | 4.25 | 1.74 | 3,257 | 572 | 3,829 | 0.97 | 0.98 | 1.95 | 51 | Mar. 1997 |
| Mizoram | 9.01 | 1.58 | 0.65 | 874 | 193 | 1,067 | NA | 1.64 | 1.64 | 154 | Feb. 1997 |
| Nagaland | 15.91 | 2.86 | 1.17 | 138 | 213 | 351 | 0.96 | 1.05 | 2.01 | 573 | Nov. 1997 |
| Orissa | 353.04 | 66.86 | 32.47 | 20,980 | 3,620 | 24,600 | 42.21 | 38.80 | 81.01 | 329 | Aug. 1998 |
| Punjab | 231.01 | 39.02 | 4.53 | 8,680 | 3,072 | 11,752 | 4.88 | 45.54 | 50.42 | 429 | May 1998 |
| Rajasthan | 520.05 | 86.10 | 23.60 | 14,041 | 4,551 | 18,592 | 31.16 | 76.58 | 97.74 | 526 | Sep. 1998 |
| Sikkim | 5.29 | 1.00 | 0.41 | 519 | 359 | 878 | NA | NA | 0.66 | 75 | Oct. 1997 |
| Tamil Nadu | 608.81 | 136.81 | 47.92 | 18,426 | 7,228 | 25,654 | 55.00 | 89.12 | 144.12 | 562 | Oct. 1998 |
| Tripura | 35.82 | 6.84 | 2.79 | 1,185 | 174 | 1,359 | 2.31 | 4.48 | 6.79 | 500 | May 1998 |
| Uttar Pradesh | 1640.41 | 263.73 | 107.73 | 64,393 | 12,326 | 76,719 | 95.48 | 159.96 | 255.44 | 333 | July 1998 |
| West Bengal | 772.50 | 142.00 | 50.64 | 15,628 | 4,790 | 20,418 | 47.07 | 106.41 | 153.48 | 752 | Apr. 1998 |
| A&N Islands | 3.65 | 0.08 | 0.03 | 286 | 118 | 404 | 0.12 | 0.73 | 0.85 | 210 | Aug. 1998 |
| Chandigarh | 8.40 | 1.92 | 0.22 | 46 | 201 | 247 | 0.01 | 1.96 | 1.97 | 798 | Sep. 1998 |
| D&N Haveli | 1.80 | 0.03 | 0.02 | 76 | NA | 76 | 0.17 | 0.32 | 0.49 | 403 | Oct. 1998 |
| Daman & Diu | 1.32 | 0.02 | 0.000 | 7 | 6 | 13 | 0.02 | 0.25 | 0.27 | 2,077 | Feb. 1998 |
| Delhi | 130.40 | 25.98 | 3.82 | 428 | 2,739 | 3,167 | NA | NA | 30.51 | 963 | Dec. 1996 |
| Lakshdweep | 0.67 | 0.11 | 0.03 | 21 | 14 | 35 | NA | 0.12 | 0.12 | 343 | Oct. 1998 |
| Pondicherry | 10.52 | 2.12 | 0.79 | 153 | 208 | 361 | 0.89 | 1.62 | 2.51 | 695 | Sep. 1998 |
| Total | 9709.32 | 1757.16 | 632.21 | 360,496 | 90,512 | 451,008 | 715.18 | 1,121.66 | 1,868.01 | 414 | |

*Source*: Government of India, Department of Food and Civil Supplies, *Annual Report 1998–1999*, New Delhi.

TABLE II: STATE AND NATIONAL LEVEL DIVERSION OF PDS COMMODITIES

| Name of State/UT | Estimated diversion (%) | | |
|---|---|---|---|
| | Wheat | Rice | Sugar |
| Northern Region | | | |
| 1. Delhi | 53 | 53 | 25 |
| 2. Haryana | 53 | 44 | 28 |
| 3. Himachal Pradesh | 47 | 18 | 8 |
| 4. Jammu & Kashmir | 28 | 29 | 28 |
| 5. Punjab | 69 | 40 | 6 |
| 6. Uttar Pradesh | 46 | 49 | 36 |
| Western Regon | | | |
| 1. Goa | 23 | 28 | 6 |
| 2. Gujarat | 23 | 21 | 18 |
| 3. Maharashtra | 26 | 30 | 22 |
| 4. Madhya Pradesh | 20 | 24 | 32 |
| 5. Rajasthan | 31 | 36 | 17 |
| Southern Region | | | |
| 1. Andhra Pradesh | 15 | 19 | 16 |
| 2. Karnataka | 30 | 18 | 19 |
| 3. Kerala | 28 | 23 | 25 |
| 4. Tamil Nadu | 24 | 33 | 28 |
| Eastern Region | | | |
| 1. Bihar | 44 | 64 | 47 |
| 2. Orissa | 39 | 54 | 28 |
| 3. Sikkim | 52 | 21 | 41 |
| 4. West Bengal | 40 | 34 | 24 |
| North Eastern Region | | | |
| 1. Arunachal Pradesh | 47 | 56 | 23 |
| 2. Assam | 61 | 64 | 52 |
| 3. Manipur | 48 | 19 | 37 |
| 4. Meghalaya | 62 | 54 | 39 |
| 5. Mizoram | 63 | 54 | 41 |
| 6. Nagaland | 100 | 46 | 24 |
| 7. Tripura | 27 | 33 | 13 |
| Union Territories | | | |
| 1. Chandigarh | 24 | 12 | 35 |
| 2. Dadra & Nagar Haveli | 18 | 7 | 26 |
| 3. Daman & Diu | 40 | 38 | 13 |
| 4. Pondicherry | 40 | 20 | 39 |
| National Level | 36 | 31 | 23 |

*Source*: Total Economic Consultancy Services (TECS), 'Study to Ascertain the Extent of Diversion of PDS Commodities' (a study undertaken on behalf of the Ministry of Food and Consumer Affairs, Government of India), New Delhi, February 1998.

# 22. Targeted Food Distribution in Karnataka and Bihar

*Jos Mooij*

The origins of the Indian food Public Distribution System (PDS) can be traced back to the Second World War and the Bengal Famine in 1943, when the colonial government felt the need to develop a food policy for the country. Over the years, the system expanded enormously in area covered, quantity of food grains handled and costs involved (Mooij 1998). There have been several important watersheds in the course of the history of the PDS, such as marked, for instance, by the establishment of the Food Corporation of India (FCI) and the Agricultural Prices Commission (now Commission on Agricultural Costs and Prices) in 1964–5. This meant a watershed in India's rice and wheat price regime, as the objective of food policy changed fundamentally. 'While earlier the thrust of policy was towards preventing agricultural prices from rising, [now] the emphasis was on establishing price levels which would act as an incentive to domestic production' (Mundle 1981). A more recent watershed took place in the 1990s, when the government started to pursue an economic reform process. The PDS became part of a safety net, but at the same time an attempt was made to prune the system and reduce the subsidy. In 1997, the so far largely universal PDS was converted into a Targeted PDS (TPDS), meant to benefit especially the poor. According to the TPDS, Below Poverty Line (BPL) families are entitled to 10 kg of food grains per month at a subsidized rate, while Above Poverty Line (APL) families are entitled to a variable quantity for a higher price, and, initially it was said, only for the transition period. Because there was always a huge mismatch between state-wise poverty levels and food grain allocation to the various states, the introduction of the TPDS implied not only a redistribution of food grains between rich and poor, but also a reallocation of food grains between the various states in India (Table 1).

TABLE 1: REALLOCATION OF FOOD GRAINS AS A RESULT OF TPDS IN SELECTED STATES

(in 000 tons)

| State | | Before Targeting | | After Targeting | |
|---|---|---|---|---|---|
| | Percentage of people below the poverty line[a] | Allotment of food grains in 1995–6[b] | Allotment for BPL families[c] | Additional allotment for APL families[c] | Total BPL and APL |
| Andhra Pradesh | 22 | 2,812 | 392 | 2,005 | 2,397 |
| Bihar | 55 | 1,087 | 1,031 | — | 1,031 |
| Gujarat | 24 | 1,244 | 239 | 562 | 801 |
| Haryana | 25 | 263 | 88 | 9 | 97 |
| Karnataka | 33 | 1,803 | 345 | 555 | 900 |
| Kerala | 25 | 2,385 | 184 | 1,592 | 1,776 |
| Madhya Pradesh | 43 | 1,164 | 640 | — | 640 |
| Maharashtra | 37 | 1,958 | 725 | 764 | 1,489 |
| Orissa | 49 | 1,210 | 382 | 45 | 427 |
| Punjab | 12 | 172 | 52 | — | 52 |
| Rajasthan | 27 | 1,506 | 260 | 402 | 662 |
| Tamil Nadu | 35 | 1,900 | 549 | 461 | 1,010 |
| Uttar Pradesh | 41 | 1,735 | 1,146 | — | 1,146 |
| West Bengal | 36 | 1,955 | 559 | 895 | 1,454 |
| INDIA | 36 | 25,564 | 7,038 | 9,448 | 16,486 |

*Sources*: [a]Government of India, 1997, Appendix IV.
[b]Based on Radhakrishna et al., 1997, Table 3.6.
[c]Government of India, 1997, Appendix II.

The main reason for the introduction of the TPDS was the increasing subsidy burden. Till the end of the 1960s, food subsidy was negligible, but since then it has increased steadily. By the mid-1990s, the subsidy was more than Rs. 50,000 million, and this was considered by many as too much. In this context, the appeal of targeting is understandable. Targeting, it seems, can solve two problems at the same time: it is a way to reduce the costs of state intervention, while at the same time it enhances the effectiveness of PDS.[1]

So far, to my knowledge, there are no comprehensive studies of the effects of the TPDS on food intake and food security of the poor. There are, however, enough reasons to conclude that targeting has not fulfilled its promises. The food subsidy has continued to rise. The food subsidy for the year 2000–1 may have reached the all-time high of Rs. 11,500–12,000 crore [although only Rs. 8,100 crore was budgeted: editorial *Economic and Political Weekly* (*EPW*) 2001]. At the same time, the offtake of the PDS has declined seriously (Table 2). In almost all states, there has been a decline in per capita offtake between 1991 and 1995. In some states, there was an increase again between 1995 and 1998. It is likely that this is related to the introduction of the Targeted PDS in 1997, which meant lower PDS prices for BPL families, and, therefore, more and cheaper food grains for states with high levels of poverty. Indeed, what we observe in the 1995–8 period is a substantial increase in offtake in the poor states: Bihar, Madhya Pradesh, Maharashtra, Orissa and Uttar Pradesh. After 1998, the overall offtake came down again. It is estimated 'that the offtake of wheat and rice taken together from the PDS during 2000–1 would see a 30 per cent decline over the previous year when again it has witnessed a decline of over 45 per cent over the preceding year' (editorial, *EPW* 2001). In short, less and less people (can) make use and/or have access to the subsidized food grains. The latter is, probably, immediately related to the persistent rise in PDS prices in the 1990s, especially for the APL families, but detailed studies of what exactly happens 'on the ground' are not available.

TABLE 2: ANNUAL PER CAPITA FOOD GRAIN OFFTAKE UNDER PDS IN SELECTED STATES

| State | Annual per capita food grain offtake (kg) | | | | | % change | |
|---|---|---|---|---|---|---|---|
| | 1973–89 | 1981 | 1991 | 1995 | 1998 | 1981–91 | 1991–8 |
| Andhra Pradesh | 13.79 | 11.00 | 35.90 | 33.91 | 28.58 | 222.34 | -20.39 |
| Bihar | 9.46 | 8.00 | 6.83 | 2.29 | 9.48 | -14.67 | 38.89 |
| Gujarat | 16.72 | 12.00 | 27.28 | 14.10 | 13.80 | 127.35 | -49.42 |
| Haryana | 10.71 | 7.00 | 10.49 | 3.32 | 5.30 | 49.85 | -49.48 |
| Karnataka | 19.48 | 18.00 | 22.84 | 23.47 | 23.38 | 26.91 | 2.37 |
| Kerala | 51.39 | 46.00 | 70.37 | 53.32 | 66.65 | 53.02 | -5.31 |
| Madhya Pradesh | 8.81 | 10.00 | 9.24 | 4.63 | 8.02 | -7.56 | -13.29 |
| Maharashtra | 25.81 | 25.00 | 24.57 | 10.70 | 19.10 | -1.73 | -22.27 |
| Orissa | 12.84 | 11.00 | 16.86 | 15.35 | 27.99 | 53.24 | 66.07 |
| Punjab | 13.62 | 12.00 | 4.56 | 0.14 | 0.46 | -61.99 | -89.98 |
| Rajasthan | 11.56 | 6.00 | 20.19 | 10.23 | 9.32 | 236.57 | -53.86 |
| Tamil Nadu | 24.38 | 24.00 | 20.75 | 29.51 | 24.91 | -13.55 | 20.04 |
| Uttar Pradesh | 7.77 | 8.00 | 7.37 | 2.89 | 8.68 | -7.92 | 17.78 |
| West Bengal | 36.30 | 38.00 | 23.41 | 17.74 | 16.37 | -38.39 | -30.09 |

*Source*: Swaminathan, 2000, Table 4.4.

## PDS IN KARNATAKA AND BIHAR

The rest of this paper discusses some experiences with the PDS in two Indian states: Karnataka in south India and Bihar in the north.[2] Karnataka is a more or less average state with regard to poverty. It is estimated by the Planning Commission that about 33 per cent of the people in Karnataka live below the poverty line. The World Food Programme (WFP) regards it as a state with low levels of food insecurity (Daly and Bhattacharya 2001). Bihar, on the other hand, is the only state, according to the WFP, where the level of food insecurity is extreme. It is estimated that 55 per cent of the population lives below the poverty line.[3] The PDS was reasonably well organized in Karnataka (Mooij 1999b). Since the mid-1980s, there is a special scheme (Green Card Scheme) for the rural poor. Bihar, on the other hand, used to make very bad use of the PDS in the past.[4] It is clear that the PDS performance is very different in these two states.

## THE DELIVERY SYSTEM: PDS WHOLESALE

In most states, there are state civil supplies corporations which lift food grains from the FCI, and there are private persons, licenced by the state governments, who retail the commodities. In many states, both activities are financially problematic, and sometimes the TPDS has only intensified the problems. In both Karnataka and Bihar, PDS wholesale is the main activity of the state food and civil supplies corporations. These corporations are usually overstaffed, with often 1,500–2,000 employees or more. In Bihar, there is a fundamental problem with the basic infrastructure. As Jharwal (1999) states

> For example, in Gumla district of Bihar, the nearest godown at Padra was 12 kms away while the farthest at Kurdegin was 220 kms away from the FCI depot at Ranchi. In the whole district of Gumla, there were only 8 godowns for 18 blocks. In the district of these godowns, six were reported to be not very safe for storage. . . . Even in Ranchi district, there were only 11 godowns for 20 blocks. In the district of Lohardagga, there were 3 godowns for 5 blocks out of which 2 were at the district headquarters. In the district of Chaibasa (Singhbhum), . . . there were only two FCI depots . . . , and one of the State Food & Civil Supplies Corporation (SFC) godown was as much as 90 kms away from the FCI depot.

Apart from lack of warehouses, moreover the corporation is in extremely poor financial shape. There is no working capital to purchase the PDS commodities from the FCI; it is the PDS dealers who have to advance the money every month. The mobile vans meant to bring the food grains from the godowns to the shops are all in need of repair, or there is no driver and no money for fuel. There are districts in which the depot managers and other corporation staff members have not received their salary for 12–18 months or longer. Given this fact, it is not surprising that some of them try to get some payment in kind, if they do not get it in cash. And indeed, malpractices such as illegal sales of the commodities and misappropriation of money occur regularly.[5]

The introduction of the TPDS has eased the financial problems to a certain extent. After 1997, lifting has gone up considerably. The higher turnover means that there is more income (through the wholesale margins fixed for the commodities). It will, however, take a very long time, if ever, before the financial problems of the Bihar Food and Civil Supplies Corporation are over.

In Karnataka, the situation is different: PDS wholesale is done by the Karnataka Food and Civil Supplies Corporation and by cooperatives. When the allotment is reduced, as happened with the introduction of TPDS, the actual offtake is also likely to come down, and when the commission is not adjusted, the wholesalers land in trouble. This was the case in 1997 when the Government of India decided to halve the allotment to Karnataka. Fortunately, this decision was soon withdrawn, but it is hard to imagine that the ongoing decreasing offtake would not be a problem for the Karnataka Food and Civil Supplies Corporation (but this should be substantiated by more fieldwork).

## THE DELIVERY SYSTEM: PDS RETAIL

Generally, PDS retail is hardly viable. In Bihar, after the introduction of the TPDS, the situation improved somewhat. The more food grains, the higher the (official) income, but even then the income remains low. Let me take the example of Ranchi district in South Bihar (now Jharkand). The monthly allotment to this district briefly after the introduction of targeting was: 1,853 tons wheat for BPL families, 1,237 tons rice for BPL families, 629 tons wheat for APL families, 419 tons rice for APL families,[6] 1,218 tons sugar and 1,836 kilolitres of kerosene. There are 1,624 PDS dealers in Ranchi district. The commission for the PDS dealers is 3.15 per cent for food grains, Re. 0.09 per litre for kerosene and Rs. 5.85 per 100 kg of sugar. Altogether, this means an average monthly income for each PDS dealer of Rs. 479.57.[7] This is based on full offtake of the commodities. When only 50 per cent is available or lifted by the PDS dealers, the income is proportionately less. There are some additional earnings from the sale of the gunny bags, but there are also expenses. The PDS dealers themselves have to pay for the transportation of the commodities from the warehouses to their premises. This involves a bullock cart and some payment for the coolies who load and unload the cart. All this means that, when the whole business is run according to the official rules, the earnings are not more than Rs. 500–600 per month. This is comparable to what a landless labourer earns on average, and much lower than the salary of the lowest office staff (attendant or sweeper).[8]

In addition to the official expenses, there are many unofficial expenses. To illustrate, I will quote from an interview with one of the PDS dealers at the outskirts of the capital of Ranchi district.[9]

Each month I get 10 bags of sugar, which I have to collect from the FCI warehouse. First, I have to obtain a release certificate. This costs me Rs. 10. Then I have to go to the bank for a demand draft, which costs me Rs. 15. Then I go back to the FCI. The coolie who carries the bags demands Rs. 10 per bag. I have to pay Rs. 10 to the person who counts the bags and certifies the release order. Then I have to get a gatepass, Rs. 7. Transportation charge is about Rs. 10 per bag, and the coolie for unloading demands Rs. 5 per bag. This is for sugar. In the case of rice and wheat there are similar costs involved, with the exception that these have to be weighed in the godown, which means Rs. 5 per bag for the person who fills the bags. In addition to all this, there are other expenses. I have to pay Rs. 250 per month to the Supply Officer and Rs. 150 to the Marketing Officer. Twice a year, during festival season, they demand double the amount.

It is obvious that, despite these expenses, it is pretty lucrative to be a FPS dealer. People are willing to pay large amounts of money to get a licence to become such a dealer. The same person explained me how he manages.

According to official policy, each shop should have at least 300 cards attached to it. Of these 300 cards, 50 per cent is genuine, and the rest is held by me. [He showed me some of the bogus cards held by him. He also showed me a pile of application forms which he could use to apply for (bogus) cards.] These forms are sold by the Supply Officer to us for about Rs. 40–50 each. So, I can lift a much larger quantity of all the commodities and sell it in the free market. The only thing I take to my shop is 50 per cent of the kerosene, and some of the BPL food grains, and that only rarely. I estimate that my net earnings are around Rs. 10,000 per month.[10]

Both the official income through sale of the PDS commodities to cardholders as well as the unofficial income through diversion of the commodities is likely to have risen in Bihar as a result of the TPDS. There is more interest among the cardholders to purchase the commodities (i.e. the BPL commodities), and the increased difference in price between the PDS price and the open market price makes blackmarketeering more profitable. As Table 2 shows, the offtake of food grains has increased more than fourfold between 1995 and 1998 in Bihar. By legal or illegal means, the viability of the ration shops will have improved.

In Karnataka, the situation is different. Initially, the new policy resulted in a reduction of the amount of food grains distributed to each cardholder. Previously, in Bangalore, the capital, cardholders were entitled to a maximum of 21 kg of food grains (depending on family size). This was reduced to 10 kg for BPL families and 5 kg for APL families. So cardholders experienced a severe reduction of food grain distribution, and PDS dealers experienced an equivalent loss of income. Already, in 1991–2, I found that the financial situation of many ration dealers was precarious. Their net income at that time was about Rs. 550–600 monthly,[11] but they had to make large investments relative to their small earnings. In Karnataka, the dealers have to collect the allotted quantities of food grains and sugar once per month only.[12] This means they have to dispose of a relatively large amount of money: the value of one month's stock, which came to approximately Rs. 15,000 in 1991–2. Many of them survived by selling a part of the food grains and sugar in the free market.

The reduction of PDS food grains only increased the financial problems of the fair price shop dealers. The monthly allotment to their shops was cut, initially by 50 per cent. This reduced the monthly cash requirement, but the income also came down because the commission remained unchanged.[13]

In short, the viability of PDS retail and wholesale can easily be undermined when the offtake comes down. Immediately after the introduction of the TPDS, the effect was only temporary, because the Government of India restored allotment to the old level before any serious damage was done to the delivery system. It is, however, likely that the present overall decreasing interest in APL food grains has a negative impact on the viability of both retail and wholesale, and will harm the delivery system. This will also affect BPL food distribution. Honest PDS dealers see their income decreasing and may no longer regard the business as profitable. Others will try to compensate by selling part of the BPL commodities on the black market. The lesson here is that before cuts in allotment are made, the viability of the delivery system is something to look at very seriously.

## WHO BENEFITS? EXPERIENCES IN A FEW LOCALITIES

There are a few studies on leakages and losses before the introduction of the TPDS. Ahluwalia (1993) found that in the whole of India, 31 per cent of the rice and 36 per cent of wheat was lost.[14] In Bihar, these percentages were 74 and 83 respectively. This would mean that only 17 per cent of the wheat was lifted in Bihar from the FCI reached the cardholders. In Karnataka, the percentages were 31 for rice and 44 for wheat. In another study, done by Tata Economic Consultancy Services (quoted in Asthana 2000), it was found that 31 per cent of the rice in the whole of India and 36 per cent of the wheat was diverted to the open market in the 1980s. According to this study, in Bihar these percentages were 64 and 44 respectively, and in Karnataka 18 and 30.

These high leakage percentages in Bihar correspond with my own findings. As is clear from the quotations above, some PDS dealers themselves confirmed that they possessed bogus cards and that they diverted part of the commodities to the open market. Also in Karnataka, in the early 1990s, I found evidence of diversion to the open market, but not to the same extent.

Card distribution to the consumers is poor in Bihar, so there are many poor people who should have a card, but who have never received one. In our fieldwork in south Bihar (now Jharkand), we found many people complaining about the fact that they had never received a card, or that the food grains never arrived or that the dealer made false entries in their cards. On the other hand, we also found villages in which most people were satisfied.

The main problem (also see Table 3) is that PDS commodities arrive late and irregularly, if at all. The villagers are poorly informed, and certainly not in advance. This means that the poorest among them may not have sufficient cash readily available when the food grains arrive in the shop. The PDS dealer will only transport as much as he expects to sell within one or two days. In short, there is a problem of physical access, in the sense that the commodities may come with irregular intervals or not at all. There is also a problem of economic access, in the sense that the poorest people do not have cash ready at the moment the stocks arrive. Yet, on the positive side, all villagers we interviewed knew about the PDS and knew what a 'red card' (a card meant for the BPL

TABLE 3: PDS IN SOUTH BIHAR (JHARKAND): EXPERIENCES IN 15 VILLAGES

| | | |
|---|---|---|
| Palamu District Chandwa Block | Village 1 | Almost everybody satisfied. PDS shop run by a cooperative. |
| | Village 2 | Reasonable supply, but rice not available for last few months; sometimes people have no money when shop is open. |
| | Village 3 | Many poor households without red cards; erratic supply and false entries in the cards. |
| | Village 4 | Many poor households without red cards; erratic supply and false entries in the cards; food grains finished within 1–2 days. |
| | Village 5 | Erratic supply, except to local Vigilance Committee members; villagers not informed about stock arrival. |
| Ranchi District Silli Block | Village 1 | Poor distribution of red cards; those with red cards purchase the commodities, but often do not have money when food grains have arrived; influential people close to the PDS dealer have no problem in lifting. |
| | Village 2 | Random distribution of red cards. Those with cards were satisfied, although supply was irregular. |
| | Village 3 | Reasonable distribution; some complaints about late arrival of stocks, and stocks finished within 3 days. |
| | Village 4 | No major complaints. Many people do not take sugar. |
| | Village 5 | Many people without red cards. Some people with red cards had problems in arranging the money when stock had arrived. |

(contd.)

TABLE 3 (contd.)

| | | |
|---|---|---|
| Ranchi District Kanke Block | Village 1 | Village with two shops, one doing well, the other much less: irregular supply of food grains; late arrival; and food grains finished within a day. |
| | Village 2 | Many deserving people without cards, false entries in the cards; irregular supply of food grains; sugar and kerosene somewhat better. |
| | Village 3 | Preferential treatment to people close to the PDS dealer; rice and wheat often not available. |
| | Village 4 | Many people without red cards; small quantities of rice and wheat in the shop, and poor people sometimes not able to purchase on the day the stocks are available. |
| | Village 5 | Irregular supplies; false entries in the cards; if the food grains arrive at all, they are sold out in no time. |

*Source*: Fieldwork done by Alok Deo Singh, 1999. The table summarizes the main findings in 15 villages on the basis of 10 interviews in each village with randomly selected villagers and occasional group interviews. The villages are spread over the blocks: some close to the block capital, others more remote.

population) was. This, I have been told, was very different 15–20 years ago.

Since 1997, as per Government of India guidelines, vigilance committees have been introduced at various levels: district, subdivisional, panchayat or ward, and shop level. Membership of the first three types of vigilance committees is almost completely politicized, and it is mainly local level politicians who are appointed. At the shop level, the members are usually selected by the PDS dealers themselves, and are often not aware of the tasks they have to do.

During the fieldwork, we tried to find out whether there are examples of positive experiences, for instance villagers who organized themselves to fight for a better PDS system. We came across one interesting example in Bhojpur district, not far from Patna, where villagers had started to protest against malpractices. This was then taken up by the local Communist Party of India (Marxist Leninist) [CPI(ML)] and together they had forced the officials to suspend the PDS dealer. But, while these kind of cases abound in a state like Kerala, where on the whole PDS works much better, in Bihar they are rare.

The situation in Karnataka is better compared to Bihar. The main fieldwork took place around Bangalore and in Bijapur, north Karnataka (Table 4). Most cardholders in Bijapur (a fairly remote area in Karnataka) were reasonably satisfied. Surprisingly, not many cardholders complained about the quality of the rice, but some of the PDS dealers did. One of the reasons may be that the villagers in this region of Karnataka are less accustomed to eating rice. Most of them purchased the rice, but in their overall consumption pattern, this rice is unimportant. Many people mentioned that they would rather receive jowar or more wheat (rather than 8 kg of rice and 2 kg of wheat per BPL card/family). Some of the saffron cardholders (APL) did not purchase all the food grains. Most people purchased sugar.

Generally, the shops are open only during one or two days a

TABLE 4: PDS IN NORTH KARNATAKA: EXPERIENCES IN 10 VILLAGES

| | | |
|---|---|---|
| Bijapur District<br>Bijapur Taluka | Village 1 | Almost everybody satisfied. Prices a little bit above prescribed prices. APL families pay Re. 1 more for a kg of sugar. Villagers prefer jowar, rather than rice (of which the BPL families can get 8 kg). Shop only open during 1 or 2 days per month. |
| | Village 2 | Most people had no major complaints. Some price variation: APL households seem to pay slightly more for kerosene. Shop opens only once per month. Rice and wheat prices a little higher than what is fixed by the government. Some complaints about rice quality, and people prefer wheat and *jowar* to rice. |
| | Village 3 | Good distribution. Some big or self-sufficient farmers have a green (BPL) card, but not all buy from the PDS. Preference for jowar. Shop opens only once per month. Some complaints about rice quality. APL cardholders do not take all food grains. |
| | Village 4 | Many people have no complaints, but some who considered themselves poor complained that they did not have a BPL card, and said that some rich people do have BPL cards. Preference for *jowar* and other coarse grains. |
| | Village 5 | No major complaints. APL families do not purchase wheat. Overpricing of all the commodities. Some complaints about rice quality. Shop opens maximally 3 days in a month. |

(contd.)

TABLE 4 (contd.)

| | | |
|---|---|---|
| Bijapur District<br>Indi Taluka | Village 1 | Two PDS shops in this village. One is run by a youth organization and functions well. There are some complaints about the other shop (does not distribute kerosene well). Many people paid Rs. 50 (APL) or Rs. 100 (BPL) for their card. |
| | Village 2 | People satisfied. Cardholders can buy more from the PDS shop if they pay somewhat higher prices. So APL cardholders do not take all the food grains. Shop only opens for 1-2 days. |
| | Village 3 | Distribution reasonably good. Some people who consider themselves poor do not have a BPL card. Problems with kerosene distribution. |
| | Village 4 | Most people buy from the PDS, but they prefer *jowar* to rice. |
| | Village 5 | Many people had paid Rs. 50 for their cards. Preference for wheat and *jowar* over rice. Some APL cardholders do not purchase the food grains. Shop only opens for 1–2 days. |

*Source*: Fieldwork done by A.S. Shrinidhi and J.H. Paramesha in 1999. The table summarizes the main findings in 10 villages on the basis of 10 interviews in each village with randomly selected villagers and occasional group interviews. The villages are spread over the talukas: some close to the taluka capital, others more remote.

month. The villagers are informed through a drum-beating man who makes a round through the village. There were no complaints about irregularity in the supply. In Bijapur taluka, we found systematic evidence of overpricing of the commodities. This issue was not investigated in Indi taluka, but it might be that some overpricing takes place there as well. Vigilance committees were sometimes established, according to the PDS dealers, but the cardholders were never aware of them.

In short, these small surveys suggest that cardholders in Bijapur in Karnataka benefit to a larger extent than those in south Bihar (now Jharkhand). Also in Karnataka, PDS dealers find their ways to increase their income somewhat, mainly through selling at a slightly higher price. However, we did not find any evidence for the large-scale diversion of food grains that seems to take place in Bihar. These findings, though based on evidence in a few localities only, correspond with the findings of larger-scale studies undertaken before the introduction of the TPDS.

The fact that many of the would-be cardholders in Bihar do not receive the food grains (every month) does not mean that nobody in Bihar benefits from the PDS. There are large groups of beneficiaries, including the PDS dealers, many officials involved in 'inspection' and 'monitoring', local politicians who can appoint people to the vigilance committees, the food minister and others. I analysed the system in Bihar (Mooij 2000) in much more detail and concluded that many people participate or benefit from the diversion of food grains. Although there is also dissatisfaction with the way the system works, there are also vested interests and the whole 'malfunctioning system' functions actually very well when one looks at it from the perspective of an overall predatory state. This is the subject I will attend to in the next section.

## EMBEDDEDNESS OF TPDS IN STRUCTURES OF STATE AND SOCIETY

The political economy of the two states of Karnataka and Bihar is, of course, very different. With regard to Karnataka, there are two important characteristics. First, the fact that Karnataka's social and political history has not witnessed many extreme situations and/or periods. According to Manor (1989), Karnataka 'has long possessed what must, in the Indian context, be seen as a comparatively cohesive society'. Processes of economic development have been steady and moderate, and have not led to marginalization and social exclusion of large numbers of people. The extreme forms of rural inequality and exploitation that exist in many other parts of India did not and do not exist in Karnataka, partly because landownership is less unequal—many agricultural labourers still have a minimal landholding—and partly because there is no ritual component to the structure of rural dominance (Manor 1989) The two dominant rural caste groups, the Lingayats and the Vokkaligas, are both peasant-cultivator jatis, belonging to the Sudra caste.

A second important characteristic of Karnataka is its somewhat benign form of populism. This started with the regime of Devraj Urs in the 1970s. During his rule, several welfare measures were introduced: land reform, a small farmers programme, minimum wage legislation, caste reservations, etc. Although the redistributive effects of these measures may have been limited, as Kohli (1987) argues,[15] the ideological effects were substantive. According to Srinivas and Panini (1984), Urs 'established the norm that the task of any elected government was to work for the betterment of the living conditions of the poor who constituted the majority'.

This norm continued to exist. In the 1980s, a minimum needs programme was introduced, including provision of drinking water, clothing, health facilities, rural roads, etc. Food distribution was also taken much more seriously than before. In 1985, the Green Card scheme was introduced, which entitled poor rural households to 10 kg of subsidized food grains. Of course, it was not only a changing norm which led to the introduction of this scheme. There were also acute political compulsions: the first non-Congress (and minority) government in Karnataka faced the possibility of losing a mid-term election, and it then decided to follow the Andhra Pradesh example of distributing cheap food. Nevertheless, it is clear that since the 1980s, politicians in Karnataka are trying to appeal to voters by promising, formulating or implementing populist programmes (including food distribution). As a result, these programmes (not only the fact that they exist in name, but to a certain extent also their performance) have become important for both the intended beneficiaries as well as for the political leaders. The political survival of the latter partly depends on them.

The structures of state and society in Bihar are very different. First of all, while Karnataka is characterized by a moderate but steady and cohesive type of development, Bihar is characterized by economic underdevelopment and stagnation, combined with extreme inequalities. In the 1990s, Bihar's growth rate has been between 1 and 1.2 per cent per year, while the national average for the whole of India was around 6 per cent. Both industrial and agricultural development are poor, and there is a retrogression in the employment structure, to the extent that even the absolute number of people employed in the secondary sector declined (Sharma 1995).

As a result, an increasing number of people depend on agriculture for their livelihood. The agricultural performance is, however, unfortunately also not very good. One of the main reasons is the prevailing agrarian structure, which is often characterized as semi-feudal because of the prevalence of 'pre-capitalist' economic relationships such as sharecropping, usury and bonded labour.

In this situation of an increasing population depending on a stagnating agriculture, conflicts are bound to arise. The total cake is not growing, but those who dominate the social structure continue to try to increase their share by intensifying surplus appropriation. This is not possible without force, debt bondage, reference to a rigid caste hierarchy and other semi-feudal mechanisms (Kohli 1991; Sharma and Kumar 1997). At the same time, people have become increasingly vocal and do not accept the extreme exploitation. This has led to very violent rural conflicts.

This underdevelopment and economic stagnation also explains in part why the state itself has become the prize over which rival caste groups are fighting (Frankel 1989). In the absence of economic development and growth of the private sector, the state is the main provider of jobs and other resources. This makes it understandable that there is still a considerable interest in getting a licence to run a PDS shop. Even though, strictly speaking, the business is unviable, it is better than nothing since it gives access to food, relations and local influence.

A second contrast with Karnataka is related to the political structure. For a long time, Bihar's political landscape was dominated by the 'twice-born' castes, but their dominance was successfully challenged in the 1990s. In caste terms, it is the upper *jatis* among the backward castes who have become the new ruling castes: the Yadavs, the Kurmis and the Koiris. Among them, the Yadavs dominate, both in number and in terms of political representation. In class terms, it is the kulaks who have taken over. As far as there has been some agricultural development, it was this class of farmer which benefited, and it has been successful in cornering most of the loans and other benefits from the government.

The political leaders of this OBC-dominated regime are certainly populist, in the sense that they aim to appeal to large parts of the population with slogans and issues such as social justice and self-respect. Many of their more tangible promises—for instance, a promise made in the 1996 elections to provide free saris and dhotis to the poor—remain, however, unfulfilled, and more ambitious issues, such as welfare programmes or food distribution, have never been part of the political agenda. In the political context of Bihar, the promise and effective delivery of such services and programmes, is not (yet) crucial. What matters more is that politicians are strong and powerful. Muscle power is especially important in Bihari politics. This criminalization of politics has a lot to do with the distinct political culture in the state, as Prasad (1997) argues.

The majority of the voters are illiterate and unsophisticated, but at the same time socially and politically alert. They do not hold the authority of the government in high esteem. In a state where the administrative machinery has been rendered by and large dysfunctional, the voters are inclined to elect someone who can act tough and 'get things done' by the administration. The search, therefore, is not for the one who can conceive good legislation or initiate an informed debate in the house, but for the ones who can arm-twist the right person at the right place and have things delivered. This partially explains how and why undesirable elements get nominated by all political parties across the board and why elections in Bihar have been increasingly rough, violent and corrupt (Prasad 1997).

So, in two important respects, the Karnataka and Bihar context in which food policy is implemented differs a lot. First, with regard to the type of development. Karnataka has experienced steady growth, which has never caused a major social disruption. There are definite social inequalities, but as compared to elsewhere in India, they are less blatant and extreme. Bihar, on the other hand, is characterized by underdevelopment and economic stagnation. There is not much development in agriculture, and also not outside agriculture. In the absence of development of the private sector, the state remains the main provider of (relatively secure) jobs, positions and other resources. There are extreme social inequalities and suppression of the lower classes/castes takes a very violent form.

Second, with regard to the political regime. Since the 1970s, Karnataka has had political leaders who have tried to secure votes by formulating and implementing various kinds of welfare schemes. The idea that governments are there to serve the people (including the poor) has taken root, at least to some extent. True, there is also corruption and misappropriation, but the intended beneficiaries continue to have some positive expectations, and, since they are also voters, these have to be fulfilled to some extent. This means that both political leaders as well as the potential beneficiaries have a common interest in (a somewhat) effective implementation of welfare programmes, etc. In Bihar, welfare issues do not play an important role in political agendas. The general public does not expect much from the government, and tends to vote for tough musclemen.

This is a very short and schematic description of some of the main differences of the contexts in Bihar and Karnataka in which food distribution is implemented. Of course, it is too schematic and perhaps too much of a caricature. Bihar is more diverse than I could acknowledge here, and it is also important to keep in mind that Karnataka is not the extreme positive counterpoint. Never-theless, the comparison does point at some important factors explaining the differences in food policy implementation in these two states. Knowing and understanding the structures of state and society, one can understand, indeed, that among other things, first, there are different expectations among the potential beneficiaries in these two states. In Karnataka, the general public/voters/cardholders expect some performance in service delivery, while in Bihar many people have become so cynical that they do not expect much from the government. They are also less inclined to reward effective service delivery in the elections, as other things matter more.

Second, the attitude of the PDS dealers differs. In a context of overall development, one can expect PDS dealers to drop out if they find the business no longer profitable (as compared to alternative employment or activities). In the absence of alternative employment or income-earning activities, people will remain eager to do the job and get as much earning as possible (through legal or illegal means).

Third, redistributive programmes including the PDS are interpreted in different ways. The PDS can be seen as an attempt to support the poor, but it can also be seen as a major resource base: these is/are money, food, positions, licences, jobs, discretionary power, etc., all to be distributed to those who are from the same caste, have been loyal in the past, have to be rewarded for past actions, etc.

Fourth, a different importance is given to redistributive policies. In a situation where the poor (used to) belong to some extent to the same social groups as the ruling groups, one can expect more willingness to share than in a situation in which there always have been large social cleavages between the rich and the poor.

## CONCLUSION AND RECOMMENDATION

What one could, perhaps, conclude is that the necessary conditions for a proper implementation (i.e. an implementation that benefits the officially targeted beneficiaries) are much better fulfilled in a state like Karnataka than in a state like Bihar. Or, put more generally proper implementation of the PDS is much easier in some states than in other states. In the design of the PDS, some particular contextual structures are assumed or taken for granted, probably not explicitly but implicitly, without even realizing it. These structures do not exist in each and every state. These have to do, among other things, with the contextual structures of state and society, which may enable or put constraints on the implementation process. In some states, the contextual structures are such that a proper implementation is possible, while in other states it is much less likely that implementation can take place as intended.

So, an important conclusion is that there are 'conditions for implementation' of a policy like the PDS. On the basis of the Karnataka–Bihar comparison, one could hypothesize that these conditions include: (1) the absence of extreme social inequalities; (2) the existence of some economic growth and development; (3) the presence of a benign form of populism (i.e. politicians woo voters by promising and delivering welfare programmes, and political leaders themselves have an interest in proper implementation, to some extent); and (4) the expectation among the beneficiaries that the government is there for them and has to deliver. This list may not be exhaustive (and, of course, there is an important question of whether all these conditions are equally essential).

If (some of) these conditions are crucial, indeed, the immediate question that follows is, of course: what should be done in a context in which these conditions are not fulfilled? Can anything be done at all, or is it justified to become cynical and believe that nothing can be done at all? This latter interpretation is widespread in Bihar, indeed, where many IAS officers and others have become rather cynical and/or feel that they are wasting their time and talents in office (but no alternatives are available to them). In my view, however, this interpretation is too negative.

At the most general level, the answer is that proposals for reform and improved performance should take the structures of state and society into account, and are doomed to fail when they do not, i.e. when they assume a political-economic vacuum in which policies are implemented. This seems fairly obvious, almost a trueism, but the point is often overlooked. Often, policy making does not differentiate between different contexts of implementation. The Government of India has developed an all-India public distribution system, with all-India guidelines, and it wants these to be implemented in all the states. Some individual state governments have made their own adjustments to some extent, and some states have complemented the GOI policies and subsidies with state-wise programmes. On the whole, however, policy thinking about the PDS happens in terms of grand schemes and big overall solutions. The particular contexts of the various states (let alone the specificities at a sub-state level) are rarely taken into account. The only variable that is considered is the level of poverty, but this has no implication for the design of the programme as such, but only affects the allotted quantities of food grains.

But apart from general knowledge about the contextual structures of state and society, locally specific knowledge about the various stakeholders, their activities, interests and strategies is also necessary. On the basis of my fieldwork in Bihar, I concluded that there are opportunities for change and reform (Mooij 2000). There are some people from all normally-benefiting stakeholder groups (PDS dealers, officials, local politicians, MLAs) who are dissatisfied and who could be brought together. Potential beneficiaries may also be willing to fight for a better PDS,[16] and there are journalists and other people who take the cause of the poor. All these people could be brought together in a kind of 'multi-stakeholder platform towards a better PDS'. Some money would be required to solve some of the practical problems. A small pilot project in one or two blocks will not threaten the vested interests in a serious way. In due course, of course, this has to change. When the project is successful and people in other parts of the state start demanding something similar, there could be a real income loss. The success will then depend on the strength of the people's demand for a clean PDS.

The initiation and monitoring of such a project is not easy, and this brings me to the third requirement: willingness to act politically. What is needed is a rather unconventional approach in the field of policy making: political manoeuvring, lobbying and strategic alliance building, rather than the formulation of new all-India policy directives from the state capital or from Delhi, more squads or guidelines. Improving food distribution policy has to be a political process in which the (few) well-wishing stakeholders come together to act strategically and in which a lot will depend on the pressure exercised by the would-be beneficiaries.

## NOTES

This paper is one of the outcomes of a larger research project on 'Social Policies and Legislation in India'. From Independence to Structural Adjustment, financed by the Indo-Dutch Programme for Alternatives in Development (IDPAD). I would like to thank Mr Alok Deo Singh, Mr A.S. Shrinidhi and Mr J.H. Paramesha for their research assistance.

1. See Mooij (1999a) for more discussion about the appeal and assumptions of targeting.
2. Fieldwork took place between 1997 and 2000, when the state of Bihar was not yet divided into the new Bihar and Jharkand.
3. These poverty estimates come from the 'Expert Group on Estimation of Proportion and Number of Poor' constituted by the Planning Commission under the Chairmanship of late Prof. Lakdawalla. The percentages calculated by the Expert Group refer to 1993–4. These figures of the Planning Commission are very high. According to the Market Information Survey of Households of the NCAER, 14 per cent of the Karnataka population lived below the poverty line in 1997–8, and 29 per cent of the Bihar population. The all-India figure according to this survey is 17 per cent (Lal et al., 2001: Tables 2B and 3).
4. Of course, actual supplies are always less than the allotment, but the difference in Bihar is more marked than in the rest of India. For India as a whole, 56 per cent of the allotted quantity was lifted in 1995–6 (25.6 million tons allotted, 14.3 million tons lifted), while Bihar lifted only 23 per cent. Generally, 1995–6 was a very bad year in this respect. In 1993–4, 67 per cent of the allotted food grain was lifted in the whole of India and 50 per cent in Bihar. (Based on Radhakrishna et al., 1997: Table 3.6.)
5. Statement based on newspaper reports and interviews with officials of the Bihar State Food and Civil Supplies Corporation and some other officials.
6. According to the official guidelines of the Government of India, there should be no distribution of food grains to APL families in Bihar, but in reality there is some.
7. On average, each PDS dealer can sell 1,141 kg BPL wheat, 761 kg BPL rice, 387 kg APL wheat, 258 kg APL rice, 750 kg sugar and 1,131 litres kerosene. BPL wheat costs Rs. 3 per kg, BPL rice costs Rs. 4 per kg, APL wheat costs Rs. 5.12 per kg and APL rice costs Rs. 8.38 per kg.
8. It is important, however, that being a fair price shop dealer is normally not a full-time job. Sometimes the dealers do not need more than a few days per month to finish the job. However, their urgency to get rid of the commodities as quickly as possible (and therefore not lift more from the warehouse than they can sell in a short time span) adds to access problems of the consumers/cardholders.

9. This story was confirmed by other PDS dealers. In Patna, the capital of Bihar, the fixed monthly payments to the Rationing Inspector seem even higher than in Ranchi.
10. This picture is confirmed by other PDS traders as well as by official figures. In 1995 there were 32 million ration cards in Bihar, while there are only 15.6 million households. This means more than 50 per cent of the cards are bogus cards. In the whole of India, this was 14 per cent (based on Government of India, 1996, Appendix II).
11. In 1991–2, 7,73,700 tons food grains were distributed through 17,364 fair price shops. This means each fair price shop sold 44,558 kg of food grains on average. That is just over 3,700 kg per month. The profit margin for the retailer was Rs. 10 per 100 kg. This means that by selling PDS food grains, the fair price shop dealers could earn an average monthly income of Rs. 370. The profit margin on sugar was Rs. 3.50 per 100 kg. On average, there was 800 kg sugar per month per fair price shop in 1991–2. Kerosene was sold through other outlets. The price of used gunny-bags was Rs. 7. This means that the total monthly gross income of a fair price shop owner came to Rs. 750. The expenditure (rent, labour, travel expenses to and from the warehouses, small tips and bribes, electricity and stationery) came to Rs. 200 on average.
12. There is no official rule prescribing that all monthly allotted commodities should be collected at once. However, due to late arrival of stocks, subsidized transport of the commodities once a month and bureaucratic obstinacy, many fair price shop owners are forced to collect and pay for the whole monthly allotment at one time.
13. This problem was acknowledged by the Government of Karnataka, and in order to meet the problems of the dealers the government started to allow the PDS dealers to trade in other non-controlled commodities as well. Previously, this was forbidden, because this non-PDS business was thought to interfere with the PDS. This relaxation of the rules, however, only solved the problem of a small number of PDS dealers: those with skills, necessary capital and contacts to build up another business.
14. Ahluwalia calculates leakages as a residual by subtracting the total quantities of wheat and rice that were actually bought from the PDS between July 1986 and June 1987 (NSS 1989) from the quantities that the Government of India supplied to the system in this period. This estimate seems rather crude.
15. But not everybody would agree with this, as Kohli himself acknowledges. Manor (1978), for instance, writes that Urs' land reform law is 'unusually practicable'.
16. Although many people in Bihar are caught up in extremely exploitative relations and depend for their immediate survival on

landlords and moneylenders, they are willing to involve themselves in various struggles. So far, there struggles have hardly centred around the PDS (or any anti-poverty programme for that matter), but there is no reason why they could not be, provided there is a possibility to change things for the better.

# 23. Public Distribution System in Rural Uttar Pradesh

*Ravi S. Srivastava*

With average food grain production of about 35.9 million tons and per capita production of 247 kg per year, the third-highest among major states, UP is considered to be a food grain surplus state.[1] There are, however, large variations between different regions in the state. Food grain production per hectare is highest in the agriculturally developed western region. During 1993–6, food grain production per hectare in the western region was 22.96 quintal (1 quintal equals 100 kg)—nearly twice the level of the Bundelkhand region (11.22 quintals) and 30 per cent higher than the yield levels in the eastern region (17.88 quintals per hectare). However, in per capita terms, food grain production (both cereals and pulses separately) in the agriculturally poor Bundelkhand region was nearly 19 per cent higher than the state average in 1992–3.

The growth of food grain production in the state has, however, decelerated sharply during the current decade. During the triennium ending 1980–90, food grain production in the state grew at an impressive rate of 4.92 per cent per annum. More remarkably, the eastern region of the state, considered a laggard, grew at a faster rate of 5.81 per cent per annum. But during the 1990s, the growth of food grain production, though still higher than the rate of growth of population, declined to 2.6 per cent per annum.

Despite the relatively high levels of food grain production, income poverty in the state is, however, still high. Estimates given by Haque, Lanjouw and Ravallion (1998) and discussed in World Bank (1998) show that the state was the fourth-poorest in terms of the Head-Count Ratio (HCR) and the Poverty Gap Index, as well as the fifth-poorest in terms of the Squared Poverty Gap Index. Compared to other states, the state's rank in rural poverty is lower compared to the incidence of urban poverty. Poverty incidence is the highest in the southern region of the state (Bundelkhand), and the lowest in the hill and western regions. According to estimates prepared by Dubey and Gangopadhyay (1998), the head-count poverty ratio was 23.69 per cent in the hills and 28.44 per cent in the western region. The central and eastern regions had HCRs of 49.1 per cent and 47.74 per cent, while the HCR in the Bundelkhand region was as high as 65.98 per cent. Among the NSS regions, the Bundelkhand region is among those with very high and stubborn levels of poverty (Srinivasan and Drèze 1997; Dubey and Gangopadhyay 1999).

Per capita consumption of cereals has been declining in UP in tandem with the trends in both rural and urban India since the early 1970s According to the NSSO, the average per capita cereal consumption in rural Uttar Pradesh was 13.9 kg during 1993–4, higher than the national average of 13.4 kg for rural India. In urban UP, average cereal consumption was estimated at 11.06 kg again slightly higher than the national average of 10.63 kg. Per capita cereal consumption in the rural areas was, however, only 10.83 kg for the lowest consumer expenditure class, increasing to 17.33 kg for the highest expenditure class. In urban UP, while the cereal consumption in the lowest class is only 9.73 kg, per capita consumption does not show a rising trend thereafter. Food hunger, measured by households reporting not being able to get two square meals a day, was reported by 3.4 per cent households in 1993–4 (NSS 1996) for the entire state, and by 6.2 per cent households in the Survey of Living Conditions (SLC) survey carried out in eastern UP and Bundelkhand in 1997–8. The share of food in total consumption expenditure in rural UP was estimated at 61.5 per cent, while in urban areas, this was 55.9 per cent.

The per capita per diem intake of calories is estimated at 2,153 kcals in rural UP and 2,114 kcals in urban UP, with cereals contributing 68.68 per cent and 59.37 per cent of the calorie intake in the rural and urban areas respectively. This average is well below the 2,400 kcal benchmark used in poverty measurement, and compares to all-India levels of calorie intake of 2,153 kcals and 2,071 kcals in the rural and urban areas respectively. Nearly 31 per cent of rural households have a per capita calorie intake, which is less than 90 per cent of the NSS norm of 2,700 kcals (NSS 1996).

Several recent surveys provide estimates of malnutrition in the state. These find malnutrition among children in UP as being higher than the national average. Using the weight for age criteria, the National Family Health Survey (NFHS) for 1992–3 estimates malnutrition (< 3 SD) among children 0–4 years at 13.8 per cent for females and 19.3 per cent for males (Gopalan 1995). Using various criteria (height for age, weight for height and body mass) the NCAER Human Development Survey reports a higher prevalence of malnutrition among children in the age groups 0–4 and 5–12 compared to the national level (Shariff 1999). The health status of females is generally poor in the state and mortality rates are higher leading to extremely low sex ratios in the state (Drèze and Gazdar 1997).

In general, therefore, despite higher per capita food grain availability in UP, cereal and food grain consumption and calorie intake are still quite low among the poorer classes. In terms of income poverty, UP is among the poorest states in the country. Nutritional deficiency among children is higher compared to the national status, and there is a strong selective gender bias against women. There is, thus an urgent need for public policy to address issues relating to the food and nutrition security of the poor, especially poor women and children. In this paper, however, we focus on one dimension of policy, namely the PDS and its role in addressing food security concerns in UP.

## THE PDS: OVERALL TRENDS IN UTTAR PRADESH

There has been a long and intense debate on the role and efficacy of the Public Distribution System in India, including its efficacy vis-à-vis other anti-poverty programmes such as the Employment Guarantee Scheme (EGS) (Suryanarayana 1995a; Dev 1996; Parikh 1994; Radhakrishna and Subbarao 1997). The continuation of the PDS is demanded not only on grounds of fiscal transfer to poor households, but also because it is argued that subsidized food grain may reverse the declining trend of cereal consumption, change the consumption basket of the poor and raise their calorific intake. The poor, it has been argued are not nutrition-conscious (Suryanarayana 1995). This debate has become more intense since the government's fiscal concern has led it to reign in the food subsidy through redesign of the system, first by introducing a form of geographical targeting in 1993–4 through the Revamped Public Distribution System (RPDS) and then replacing this with a means-tested Targeted Public Distribution System (TPDS). Along with reducing the burgeoning subsidy bill, the 'targeting' of the PDS is also expected to provide better coverage to poor households. This is sought to be achieved in two ways. First, by bifurcating state-level allocations from the central pool and relating the heavily subsidized BPL allocations to the proportion of poor households (along with historical levels of offtake). This has improved the share of BPL allocation to poor states. Second, within each state, the distribution of BPL rations was to be restricted to poor households identified through means-cum-occupation criteria. Initially, the targeted poor households were entitled to a monthly ration of 10 kg of cereals, which has since been increased to 20 kg. In the changes introduced in 2000, (1) the issue price of rice and wheat has been increased, while simultaneously increasing the entitlement of eligible poor households to 20 kg. of cereals; (2) subsidies on cereal purchases to Above Poverty Line (APL) households has been completely removed; (3) sugar has been removed from the list of subsidized commodities; (4) there has been a hefty rise in the price of kerosene distributed through the PDS.[2]

One of the main objectives of this paper is to examine whether, in the light of recent changes, access of the poor households to subsidized cereals appears to have improved significantly, both through improved absorption in poor states/regions and through the targeting of poor households. In doing so, the paper focuses on some of the constraints on the demand side and offers suggestions regarding restructuring of the PDS.

Historically, the PDS has played a much smaller role in Uttar Pradesh compared to states such as Kerala, Tamil Nadu or West Bengal. Between 1986–7 and 1995–6, the state lifted only 4.5 per cent of the national PDS offtake of rice and wheat. Household surveys confirm the marginal role of the PDS in the supply of food grains in the state, particularly in the rural areas. The 42nd round of the NSS estimated that only 2.1 per cent of the rural population in the state purchased cereals from the PDS, while this percentage was as high as 88 per cent in Kerala, 60 per cent in Andhra and 62 per cent in Karnataka (Parikh 1994). The per capita purchase from PDS was only 0.21 kg in the rural areas (1.33 per cent of total cereal consumption) and 0.32 kg in the urban areas (2.72 per cent of cereal consumption). Cereal purchases for the two poorest classes in the rural areas were only 0.11 kg, and 0.13 kg, or only 0.95 and 0.97 per cent of their cereal consumption (Radhakrishna and Subbarao 1997).

For 1993–4, the NCAER Human Development Survey (Shariff 1999) estimated that 5.2 per cent of rural households in the state had used the PDS (compared to 33.2 per cent nationally) to purchase 33.4 kg of cereals per household. Cereals purchased through the PDS met 24.5 per cent of the cereal requirement and 15.2 per cent of the total food grain requirement of these reporting households. Other surveys in approximately the same period found an even more limited role of the PDS in the supply of cereals to rural households. In a sample survey of villages in eastern UP, Srivastava (1996) found that during 1995–6, except in RPDS villages, there was no supply of cereals through the PDS shops. This was also accounted for by closing of the gap between the issue price of PDS cereals and the open market price of wheat and rice. The PDS shops, in the villages studied, were also expected to stock and distribute cereals to labourers employed in public employment programmes, but there was no evidence that this had been done.

However, in 1997/98, soon after the inception of the TPDS, N. Srivastava (1997) and Khare (1997) found that, despite confusion surrounding the identification of beneficiary households, several poor households had purchased cereals from the PDS for the first time at the subsidized prices.

TABLE 1: ALLOCATION AND OFFTAKE OF CEREALS, UTTAR PRADESH AND MAJOR STATES

| UP | 1993–4 | 1994–5 | 1995–6 | 1996–7 | 1997–8 | 1998–9 | 1999–2000 | 2000–1 |
|---|---|---|---|---|---|---|---|---|
| Total offtake ('000 mt) | 465.00 | 394.60 | 419.00 | 713.60 | 519.16 | 925.01 | 925.01 | 479.98 |
| % offtake/allocation | 43.41 | 35.90 | 38.12 | 67.04 | 58.78 | 73.13 | 62.53 | 32.54 |
| % BPL offtake/allocation | | | | | 61.48 | 87.27 | 70.63 | 38.63 |
| 16 States | | | | | | | | |
| % All/APL offtake/allocation | 71.80 | 60.78 | 64.09 | 72.62 | 79.38 | 84.31 | 81.17 | 53.43 |
| % BPL offtake/allocation | | | | | 77.81 | 84.26 | 96.16 | 80.94 |
| % UP/16 states | | | | | | | | |
| Total allocation | 4.90 | 4.64 | 4.20 | 3.92 | 4.91 | 5.59 | 6.02 | 6.35 |
| Total offtake | 2.96 | 2.74 | 2.50 | 3.62 | 3.64 | 4.85 | 4.64 | 3.87 |
| BPL allocation | | | | | 10.18 | 9.77 | 9.62 | 10.48 |
| BPL offtake | | | | | 8.05 | 10.11 | 7.07 | 5.00 |

An analysis of the PDS state-level data shows that the overall offtake from the PDS changed only marginally as a result of the introduction of the TPDS. Compared to a total cereal offtake of 6,61,000 mt during 1986–7 to 1995–6, and 7,13,000 mt in 1996–7, the total offtake was 5,19,000 mt during 1997–8, rising to 9,25,000 mt during 1998–9 and 1999–2000. However, available estimates for 2000–1 show a decline in offtake.

As a percentage of total offtake, too, UP's share shows a small increase (by about 1 per cent), from 3.6 per cent in 1996–7 and 1997–8 to 4.8 per cent and 4.6 per cent respectively during 1998–9 and 1999–2000, and a fall to 3.8 per cent during 2000–1 (Table 1). However, UP's share in food grains lifted under the BPL allocation has been higher—around 8 per cent in 1997–8, 10.1 per cent in 1998–9, 7.1 per cent in 1999–2000 and 5 per cent in 2000–1.

Figure 1 shows the average offtake per BPL household during 1997–2001. The figure for UP (54 kg per BPL household) per year is less than one-fourth the figure for states such as Kerala, Orissa, Tamil Nadu and Assam.

Separate figures for the urban-rural distribution of the TPDS are not known, but as discussed earlier, some part of the small increase in cereal offtake appears to have been absorbed in the rural areas of the state.

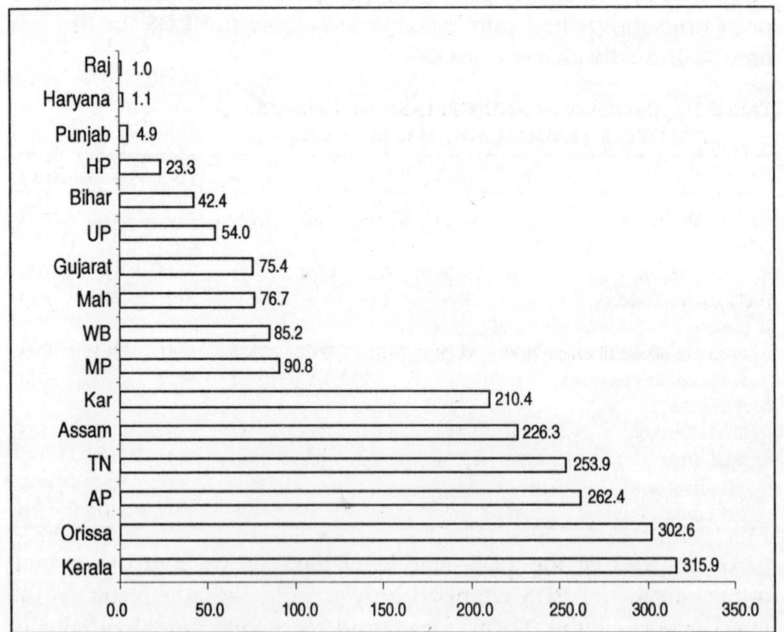


FIG. 1: AVERAGE OFFTAKE PER BPL HOUSEHOLD (kg per year).

## REACHING THE RURAL POOR THROUGH TPDS: SOME EVIDENCE

Although the macro-evidence analysed above shows that there has not been any significant change in cereal offtake in UP since the launch of the TPDS, it would be useful to examine whether the offtake is now better directed towards the poor households in need of food and nutrition security. This section examines some of the available evidence on (1) identification of eligible households; (2) purchase of cereals by rural households; and (3) leakage from the amounts intended for purchase by households.

### IDENTIFYING ELIGIBLE BENEFICIARIES IN THE TPDS

After experimenting with geographical targeting through the RPDS, the Indian government moved over to a TPDS in 1997, which has been implemented in UP since June 1997.

At inception, the TPDS promised 10 kg of cereal per month to all urban and rural poor households (i.e. those below the poverty line or BPL) at specially subsidized prices. State allocations for BPL households have been made on the basis of the estimated number of poor households in 1993–4. Transitory allocations have also been made for APL households based on the difference between average lifting of grains in the last 10 years and the BPL allocation. Under the scheme, UP's APL allocation has been nil due to poor lifting in the ten years preceding 1997.

The identification of poor households which will benefit under the TPDS is crucial to the new system. Under the new guidelines, the states were required to formulate and implement foolproof arrangements for the identification of the poor households. The TPDS guidelines initially provided guidelines for the identification of poor households 'belonging to the really poor and vulnerable sections of society such as landless agricultural labourers, marginal farmers, rural artisans/craftsmen . . . etc. (GOI 1998). The total number of poor so identified across villages and districts was expected to be equal to or less than the proportion of the poor (33 per cent in the case of UP) estimated by the government as the basis of the BPL allocation.

The Gram Sabhas in UP were initially involved in the identification of the BPL households, but the list of households prepared by the Gram Sabhas was screened and whetted by the functionaries of the rural development department, who were also concurrently involved in a separate survey to update the list of poor households eligible for assistance under poverty alleviation programmes. The BPL Census conducted by the Ministry of Rural Development (GOI), which finally became the basis of identification of BPL households, consists of a preliminary enquiry based on easily identifiable criteria such as ownership of high-value domestic and farm assets and land. Households are further screened on the basis of their income. In the preparation of the BPL list, the state government ordered three different income iterations (at Rs. 20,000, Rs. 11,000 and Rs. 9,000) and only in the last instance, the number of households identified fell below the number estimated by the central government (41 per cent in rural UP) as the basis of the BPL allocation (Kriesel and Zaidi 1999).

Given the lack of transparency which this procedure ultimately involved (the final identification had little relation to the initial proposals made by the Gram Sabhas), the complicated procedure of means testing and the influences which could work on the local bureaucracy to make these lists, it is worthwhile asking how well 'targeted' the rural poor in the TPDS in UP are.

Fig. 2 gives the characteristics of respondent households in the BPL list, on the basis of a sample survey of households in 60 villages in eastern and southern UP (hereafter called the Survey of Living Conditions or SLC study).[3]

It is quite clear from this list that households with characteristics correlated with poverty (caste status, landlessness, dependence on wage labour) were much more likely to be on the BPL list. Thus, 56 per cent of SC households, 50 per cent of landless households and 49 per cent of labour households found a representation on the BPL list in UP. Means testing is a more difficult exercise, but even here poorer households were (almost four times) more likely to be on the BPL list compared to other less poor households.

That the poor had a greater chance of being represented on the BPL list than the non-poor is quite heartening. But the magnitude of inclusion and exclusion errors have to be closely examined before reaching an overall verdict. On the first issue, Kriesel and Zaidi (1999) have carefully compared the characteristics of BPL households with those screening characteristics which have been used in the survey to exclude households. These characteristics include ownership of more than 2 ha land, *pukka* houses and specified domestic and farm assets. On the basis of these criteria, they find

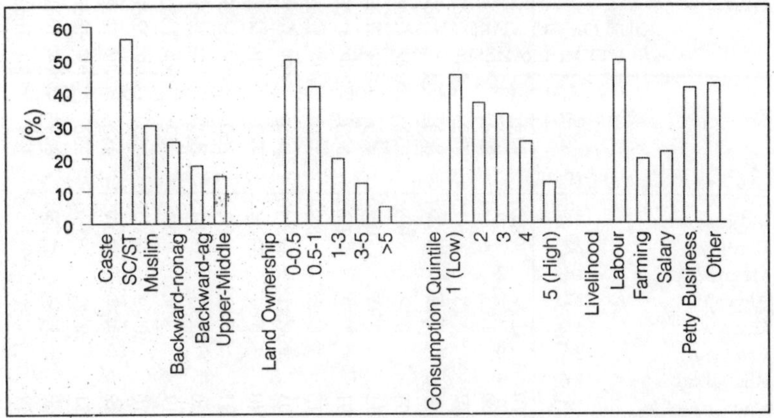


FIG. 2: PERCENTAGE OF HOUSEHOLDS IN THE BPL LIST (GROUP-WISE).

that (1) 2.2 per cent BPL households had more than, 2 acres of land; (2) 14.4 per cent had *pukka* houses; (3) 9.1 per cent had ineligible domestic assets; (4) 3.2 per cent had ineligible farming assets. Kriesel and Zaidi do point out that confirming to these characteristics did not rule out other inclusion errors, since 70 to 87 per cent of rural households, in any case, fulfilled these criteria. Further, their conclusions confirm that *at least* 15 per cent of BPL households—if these characteristics of ineligibility strictly overlapped—were clearly ineligible: a figure which compares with the clear inclusion of about 20 per cent of ineligible households in other anti-poverty programmes such as the IRDP (see Lieten and Srivastava 1999).

Using the data on per capita consumption level of households as a proxy for means testing above, they find that 46.7 per cent of the BPL households were not in the lowest two quintiles (i.e. an error of inclusion), whereas nearly three-fifths of poor households (in the lowest two quintiles) were not in the list of BPL households (i.e. an error of exclusion). If one notes, however, that: (1) estimates of income poverty in this region are considerably higher than 40 per cent; (2) that the exercise of identification began with an estimated income poverty line of Rs. 20,000 per household which was reduced to Rs. 9,000 per household; (3) nutrition poverty in UP is higher than income poverty, a significant proportion of poor households requiring food security are not covered in the TPDS in UP. On the whole, therefore, means testing has not provided a reliable way of targeting poor households for the TPDS, leading to fairly costly inclusion and (costlier) exclusion errors.

TABLE 2: WEALTH-RANKING STATUS OF HOUSEHOLD AND ISSUE OF BPL CARD IN SAMPLE VILLAGES/DISTRICTS OF UTTAR PRADESH, 1999–2000

| | Ranked as poor/ very poor | BPL cards issued | Ranked as avg. | BPL cards issued | Ranking as rich | No. of BPL cards issued | Total | No. of BPL cards |
|---|---|---|---|---|---|---|---|---|
| Pithoragarh | 21 | 17 | 24 | 11 | 15 | 1 | 60 | 29 |
| Bareilly | 22 | 7 | 22 | 4 | 16 | 1 | 60 | 12 |
| Meerut/Bagpat | 14 | 2 | 21 | 0 | 25 | 0 | 60 | 2 |
| Aligarh | 27 | 6 | 14 | 0 | 19 | 1 | 60 | 7 |
| Unnao | 33 | 17 | 17 | 6 | 10 | 2 | 60 | 25 |
| Fatehpur | 25 | 10 | 22 | 3 | 13 | 0 | 60 | 13 |
| Allahabad | 14 | 0 | 8 | 0 | 8 | 0 | 30 | 0 |
| Kaushambi | 18 | 8 | 8 | 1 | 4 | 0 | 30 | 9 |
| Jaunpur | 20 | 11 | 29 | 15 | 11 | 0 | 60 | 26 |
| Kushi Nagar | 20 | 8 | 3 | 2 | 7 | 3 | 30 | 13 |
| Deoria | 14 | NA | 5 | NA | 11 | NA | 30 | NA |
| Hamirpur | 11 | 7 | 10 | 0 | 9 | 2 | 30 | 9 |
| Mahoba | 12 | 1 | 12 | 0 | 6 | 0 | 30 | 1 |
| Total | 251 | 94 | 195 | 42 | 154 | 10 | 600 | 146 |
| Percentage | | 37.5 | | 21.5 | | 6.5 | | 24.3 |

*Source*: Planning Commission Project on Decentralization and Anti-Poverty Programmes in Uttar Pradesh (ongoing).

Another recent survey in 20 villages spread over 10 districts of UP has compared the probability of inclusion and exclusion of poor households in the BPL list on the basis of wealth ranking and stratification of sample households done by a group of poor villagers themselves. Again, although the poor have a greater probability of being in the list of BPL cardholders, the majority of those considered poor by the villagers are not in the BPL lists, confirming that the risks of exclusion are very high under the procedures being adopted for identifying eligible households.

## BENEFITS FROM THE TPDS: DISTRIBUTIONAL IMPLICATIONS

Based on the SLCC survey, Table 3 provides commodity-wise figures of percentage of rural households purchasing from the PDS during the last 30 days. The overall purchases of cereals from the PDS are restricted to only 12.9 per cent households. This compares with 46.7 per cent households purchasing sugar from the PDS,

TABLE 3: PERCENTAGE OF HOUSEHOLDS BUYING EACH PDS ITEM IN THE LAST 30 DAYS

| Classification | Rice | Wheat | Sugar | Kerosene |
|---|---|---|---|---|
| Caste Group | | | | |
| Upper-middle | 6.24 | 5.46 | 54.37 | 86.51 |
| Backward agri. | 6.24 | 6.01 | 46.94 | 91.48 |
| Backward non-agri. | 12.03 | 12.32 | 39.4 | 84.75 |
| SC/ST | 25.88 | 26.20 | 46.72 | 86.69 |
| Muslim | 8.16 | 8.16 | 47.59 | 94.12 |
| Land ownership gp (acres) | | | | |
| 0–0.5 | 24.64 | 24.66 | 40.05 | 88.39 |
| 0.5–1 | 15.41 | 14.60 | 43.38 | 92.02 |
| 1–3 | 6.26 | 6.01 | 45.25 | 88.72 |
| 3–5 | 4.60 | 5.28 | 53.66 | 85.37 |
| > 5 | 1.93 | 2.15 | 63.26 | 85.86 |
| Per capita consumption quintile | | | | |
| 1 (Low) | 19.23 | 18.59 | 32.00 | 91.00 |
| 2 | 14.15 | 15.72 | 37.04 | 89.62 |
| 3 | 14.56 | 13.66 | 48.28 | 86.15 |
| 4 | 10.27 | 9.83 | 53.10 | 85.62 |
| 5 (High) | 6.94 | 7.18 | 60.63 | 88.46 |
| Main source of livelihood | | | | |
| Farming | 7.29 | 6.74 | 51.04 | 89.76 |
| Labour | 24.29 | 26.60 | 40.74 | 85.62 |
| Salary | 10.56 | 7.73 | 43.73 | 89.02 |
| Business | 18.37 | 18.91 | 44.45 | 89.10 |
| Other | 12.03 | 9.35 | 33.41 | 78.34 |
| Total | 12.89 | 12.84 | 46.66 | 88.25 |

and 88.25 per cent households purchasing kerosene from the PDS.

What is disappointing is that as compared to 29.9 per cent beneficiaries identified for the TPDS, only 12.9 per cent (43.1 per cent of those considered eligible) made purchases of wheat and rice from the TPDS. Even in the two lowest quintiles, only about 17 per cent households (compared to 40 per cent considered eligible) had made cereal purchases. As noted earlier, the incidence of poverty in the survey regions is estimated at 50.1 per cent. Thus, even if all beneficiaries were correctly identified (no exclusion errors), only a quarter of the estimated poor income households in the region had been able to use the TPDS for making purchases from the TPDS.

Although targeting is leading to high exclusion errors, it does appear to have increased the relative probability of inclusion of the poorer groups compared to the non-poor. The probability of poor households purchasing wheat or rice from the TPDS is significantly higher than for non-poor households. For instance, 19 per cent of households in the poorest quintile purchased wheat, compared to 6.94 per cent in the highest quintile. This is reversed in the case of sugar, which is untargeted, and where a higher proportion of non-poor households make purchases. For instance, while only 32 per cent of households in the poorest quintile made purchases of sugar, 60.6 per cent of households in the upper-most quintile made sugar purchases from the PDS.

Table 4 summarizes the information on the percentage of PDS commodities received by different groups. The results here strengthen the conclusion reached above: 51 per cent of PDS wheat and rice have been purchased by 40 per cent households in the bottom two consumption quintiles. But these households purchased only 28.5 per cent of the PDS sugar. However, their share in the PDS kerosene (39.5 per cent) is nearly equal to their numerical weight. On the other hand, the richest 20 per cent households (in terms of per capita consumption) purchased about 13 per cent cereals, 24 per cent kerosene and 31 per cent sugar.

Analysis of prices paid for PDS cereals shows that these were, on average, 42 paise per kg higher than those designated by the UP government (Rs. 3 for wheat and Rs. 4 for ordinary rice). Table 5 brings together the information on PDS quantities purchased per household (both participant as well as non-participant). In the case of rice, average purchases from the PDS were 0.5 kg per household in the bottom 3 quintiles, declining to 0.4 kg in the 4th quintile and 0.2 kg in the highest quintile. For wheat, average purchases were 1.1 kg in the bottom two quintiles, declining to 0.5 kg in the highest quintile. The total benefit due to cereal purchases from the PDS amounts to only Rs. 3.57 per month for the poorest 40 per cent households. This progressively declines, and in the highest quintile, the net benefit derived per household is only Rs. 1.65. Had all households in the poorest two quintiles secured 10 kg of cereals from the PDS at the issue price determined by the central government, their net benefits would have been an estimated Rs. 31 per household. Compared to these figures, the actual benefit derived by poor households is indeed very low—only 11.5 per cent of the intended benefit. As a percentage of the total benefit derived by rural households from PDS

TABLE 4: PERCENTAGE OF PDS COMMODITY OBTAINED BY EACH QUINTILE GROUP

| Classification | Rice | Wheat | Sugar | Kerosene |
|---|---|---|---|---|
| Per capita consumption quintile | | | | |
| 1 (Low) | 31.58 | 30.65 | 14.51 | 21.82 |
| 2 | 19.40 | 21.65 | 14.03 | 17.95 |
| 3 | 21.87 | 20.60 | 20.03 | 18.90 |
| 4 | 14.33 | 13.78 | 20.47 | 17.45 |
| 5 (High) | 12.83 | 13.33 | 30.95 | 23.88 |
| Land ownership gp (acres) | | | | |
| 0–0.5 | 64.41 | 64.73 | 28.92 | 33.75 |
| 0.5–1 | 15.82 | 15.05 | 12.31 | 13.80 |
| 1–3 | 13.28 | 12.80 | 26.52 | 27.50 |
| 3–5 | 4.55 | 5.24 | 14.65 | 12.33 |
| > 5 | 1.94 | 2.17 | 17.60 | 12.63 |
| Caste group | | | | |
| Upper-Middle | 7.84 | 6.89 | 18.75 | 15.75 |
| Backward agri. | 14.54 | 14.07 | 30.03 | 30.90 |
| Backward non-agri. | 19.14 | 19.67 | 17.19 | 19.53 |
| SC/ST | 53.87 | 54.75 | 26.68 | 26.14 |
| Muslim | 4.60 | 4.61 | 7.36 | 7.68 |
| Main source of livelihood | | | | |
| Farming | 30.37 | 28.16 | 58.70 | 54.58 |
| Labour | 43.96 | 48.32 | 20.36 | 22.63 |
| Salary | 7.24 | 5.32 | 8.28 | 8.91 |
| Business | 15.07 | 15.58 | 10.08 | 10.68 |
| Other | 3.36 | 2.62 | 2.58 | 3.19 |
| Total | 100.00 | 100.00 | 100.00 | 100.00 |

cereal purchases, the 40 per cent households in the poorest two quintiles secure 51 per cent benefit.

In the case of sugar purchases, the picture is quite different, and the net benefit per household is progressively higher among richer households. While the net benefit to the poorest 20 per cent households is only Re. 0.96 per household, for the richest 20 per cent, the benefit is much higher—Rs. 2.72 per household.

Overall benefits per household are the highest for kerosene purchases through the PDS. In the case of kerosene, as we noted earlier, a higher percentage among the poorest households take recourse to the PDS. However, the per household quantity purchased is higher for the better-off groups. As a result, the net benefit from PDS kerosene purchases is the lowest for the poorest quintile (Rs. 8.61) and the highest for the richest quintile (Rs. 12.8).

Since the distribution of benefits from sugar and kerosene is

TABLE 5: PDS PURCHASES AND ESTIMATED NET BENEFIT

(Rs. per household)

| | Consumption quintile | | | | | Total |
|---|---|---|---|---|---|---|
| | 1 | 2 | 3 | 4 | 5 | |
| Rice qty | 0.5 | 0.5 | 0.5 | 0.4 | 0.2 | 0.4 |
| Price paid | 4.4 | 4.3 | 4.6 | 4.4 | 4.2 | 4.4 |
| Market price | 6.7 | 6.7 | 6.7 | 6.7 | 6.7 | 6.7 |
| Benefit per HH (Rs.) | 1.15 | 1.2 | 1.05 | 0.92 | 0.5 | 0.92 |
| Wheat qty | 1.1 | 1.1 | 1 | 0.7 | 0.5 | 0.9 |
| Price paid | 3.4 | 3.4 | 3.6 | 3.5 | 3.3 | 3.5 |
| Market price | 5.6 | 5.6 | 5.6 | 5.6 | 5.6 | 5.6 |
| Benefit per HH (Rs.) | 2.42 | 2.42 | 2 | 1.47 | 1.15 | 1.89 |
| Sub-total | 3.57 | 3.57 | 3.05 | 2.39 | 1.65 | 2.81 |
| % to total benefit | 25.58 | 25.58 | 21.14 | 15.54 | 12.16 | 100 |
| Sugar qty | 0.6 | 0.8 | 0.9 | 1.1 | 1.7 | 1 |
| Price paid | 12.4 | 12.3 | 12.5 | 12.5 | 12.4 | 12.4 |
| Market price | 14 | 14 | 14 | 14 | 14 | 14 |
| Benefit per HH (Rs.) | 0.96 | 1.36 | 1.35 | 1.65 | 2.72 | 1.6 |
| Kerosene | 2.1 | 2.2 | 2.3 | 2.4 | 3.2 | 2.5 |
| Price paid | 3.9 | 3.9 | 3.9 | 3.9 | 4 | 3.9 |
| Market price | 8 | 8 | 8 | 8 | 8 | 8 |
| Benefit per HH (Rs.) | 8.61 | 9.02 | 9.43 | 9.84 | 12.8 | 10.25 |
| Total benefit | 13.14 | 14 | 13.83 | 13.88 | 17.17 | 14.66 |
| % to total benefit | 18.24 | 19.44 | 19.20 | 19.27 | 23.84 | 100 |

regressive, the distribution of total per household benefits is also regressive, slowly increasing from Rs. 13.14 per household for the poorest 20 per cent households to Rs. 17.17 per household among the richest 20 per cent households. As far as the distribution of total benefits is concerned, the poorest 40 per cent households managed to secure only 37.7 per cent of the total benefit of the PDS, while households in the highest quintile secured 23.8 per cent of total benefits accruing from the TPDS. The overall significance of the TPDS to the consumption of cereals by rural households in UP is given in Table 6. First, the quantities of cereals purchased through the PDS are only 3.8 and 3.6 per cent of cereals purchased and consumed by the two poorest quintiles respectively. Since higher quintiles purchase smaller quantities of cereals, the share of the PDS in their cereal purchases is nearly the same in the highest quintile.

TABLE 6: QUANTITATIVE AND VALUE SIGNIFICANCE OF PDS PURCHASES OF WHEAT AND RICE

| | Consumption quintile | | | | | Total |
|---|---|---|---|---|---|---|
| | 1 | 2 | 3 | 4 | 5 | |
| % PDS qty to purchased cereal | 3.8 | 3.6 | 3.8 | 3.1 | 3.6 | 3.6 |
| % PDS qty to total cereal consumed | 2.1 | 1.7 | 1.5 | 1.0 | 0.7 | 1.4 |
| % saving to total purchase | 2.6 | 3.5 | 2.6 | 2.4 | 3.2 | 2.8 |
| % saving to total value consumed | 1.3 | 1.1 | 0.8 | 0.5 | 0.4 | 0.8 |

The net saving through the TPDS (as a percentage of value of cereals purchased) is also only 2.6 per cent in the lowest quintile and 3.5 per cent in the 2nd quintile. As a percentage of the total value of cereals consumed, savings through TPDS accounts for only 1.3 per cent and 1.1 per cent of the cereal budget of households in the two lowest quintiles. Overall, the contribution of the PDS to savings in the cereal and food budget of poor households in UP appears to be very small.

## CONSTRAINTS ON THE SUPPLY SIDE AND LEAKAGE FROM THE TPDS

Both operative constraints (on the demand as well as supply side) as well as under-identification of poor households (exclusion) have significantly reduced the efficacy of the TPDS in rural UP—to the extent that a smaller percentage of poor households—whether identified on the basis of caste, landholding, per capita consumption or livelihood source buy cereals from the PDS relative to making purchases of kerosene or even sugar—commodities which were untargeted in the PDS. As shown in Table 6, among households in the lowest quintile, about 19 per cent had purchased rice or wheat, but 32 per cent had purchased sugar and 91 per cent had purchased kerosene from the PDS in the last 30 days.

Supply-side constraints have been analysed in a number of studies (Sharma 1996; Kriesel and Zaidi 1999; Mazumdar forthcoming). First, the PDS shopkeepers operate under excessively small margins and have to cater to the illegal demands of influential persons. Both these factors increase the inducement to siphon grain off to the black market. The dual pricing provides another hefty incentive for leakage. This is compounded by a lack of political commitment to the PDS in the state, administrative cynicism and the lack of adequate incentives to the PDS shopkeeper. Multiplicity of agencies with poor coordination has led to lower administrative accountability of the delivery machinery (Kriesel and Zaidi 1999).

Leakage occurs at all points in the distribution chain, from the FCI and block godowns, right down to the retail shop. Two independent estimates of the leakage from the PDS estimate it at approximately 40 per cent of the state's offtake. Based on the estimates of grain purchased by rural households in Eastern UP and Bundelkhand regions, and the urban-rural distribution, Kriesel and Zaidi (1999) find that as much as 41 per cent of the grain intended for supply through the TPDS may have ended somewhere else. Another nationwide study by Tata Consultancy Services estimates the leakage from the PDS system at even higher levels: 46 per cent for wheat, 49 per cent for rice and 36 per cent for sugar. For each of these commodities, this was substantially higher than the national estimates (36 per cent, 31 per cent and 23 per cent respectively) (Planning Commission 2000).

Although the system envisages the setting up of local vigilance committees, these do not function effectively, although the move towards bringing the shopkeeper under the control of Panchayats has, on the whole, had positive impact. There is little transparency in the system: lists of quantities received and distributed are rarely displayed, and households have no method of verifying the information orally provided by the shopkeeper. Greater local supervision, transparency and a clear enunciation of entitlements could reduce the leakage at the shop level, but clearly other steps are needed to strengthen the system.

## CONSTRAINTS ON THE DEMAND FOR PDS CEREALS

In most of the studies on the PDS, emphasis has been laid on the supply side factors, while the role of demand has been relatively neglected. Obviously, these are not independent factors, but the nature of demand for PDS food grain has a very significant bearing on the PDS system. A striking feature in UP is the lack of political commitment and support for the PDS. This is in contrast to the extent and nature of political support for the PDS in states such as Kerala, Tamil Nadu or Andhra Pradesh. Why is this the case? An argument analysed in this paper is that, given the pattern of production and consumption of food grain in UP, there is very

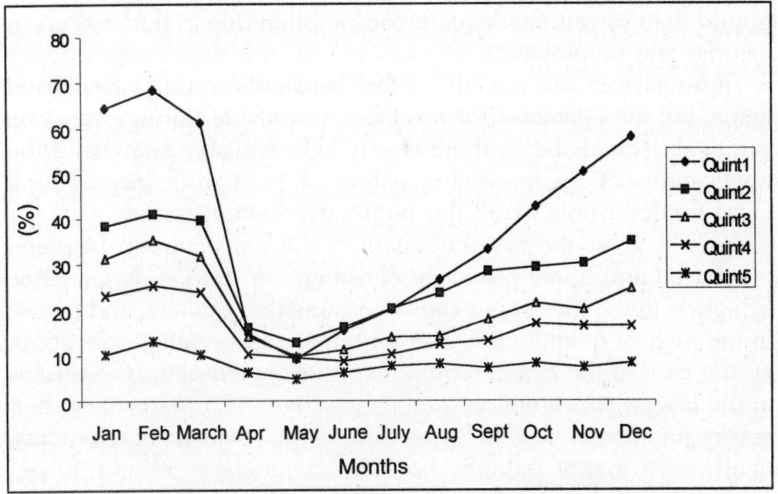


FIG. 3: PERCENTAGE OF HOUSEHOLDS PURCHASING WHEAT MONTHWISE IN EACH PER CAPITA CONSUMPTION QUINTILE.

While this weakens their support for the PDS, the demand for PDS cereals is also eroded by sharp seasonality in the purchase of cereals by rural households, a fluctuating but smaller price wedge between PDS and market prices when production is good, and shortage of cash in the hands of the poor.

The pattern of cereal and food grain consumption, calorific intake and nutritional deficiency in UP was discussed in the first section. This section focuses on certain specific features of cereal consumption among rural households in the state, focusing on seasonality and market dependence. It is commonly understood that there are considerable differences between urban and rural consumers, inasmuch as the former access food grains and other food items principally through the market, whereas the latter also take recourse to self-produced items for consumption, reducing their dependence on the market. There are also differences between groups of rural households in their dependence on the market for meeting their food requirements. Poor households depend on the market to a larger extent (Parikh 1994).

Seasonality is also another important factor. The access of rural households to self-produced food items is expected to vary seasonally, hence, also their dependence on purchased food items. In the case of poor households, seasonal fluctuations may compound their overall inadequate consumption due to fluctuations in income and employment.

These factors do not affect the demand for purchased food items, but also demand for food items available through the PDS yet, as discussed above, there is very little available analysis of the implications of the prevailing nature of food insecurity in rural areas for food policy and the public distribution system.

Table 7 gives the distribution of cereal consumption between purchased and home-produced consumption. Market dependence is highest in the lowest per capita consumption quintile, and lowest in the highest quintile. But even in the lowest quintile, only about 48 per cent of the cereal requirements are purchased. Households in the lowest consumption quintile purchase 53.5 per cent of their rice requirements and 46.8 per cent of their wheat requirements. In the next lowest quintile, households purchase 34 and 30 per cent respectively of their rice and wheat requirements. But in the highest quintile, households buy less than 15 per cent of their cereal requirements, including 18.8 per cent of rice requirements and 11.9 per cent of wheat requirements.

There are also very significant seasonal variations in the con-

TABLE 7: PER CAPITA MONTHLY CONSUMPTION OF RICE, WHEAT AND OTHER CEREALS, PURCHASED AND HOME PRODUCED (in kg)

| | Consumption quintile | | | | | | | | | | | |
|---|---|---|---|---|---|---|---|---|---|---|---|---|
| Item | 1(Low) | | 2 | | 3 | | 4 | | 5(High) | | Total | |
| Purchased qty | | | | | | | | | | | | |
| Rice | 2.3 | 53.5 | 1.7 | 34.0 | 1.9 | 37.3 | 1.6 | 27.1 | 1.3 | 18.8 | 1.8 | 32.7 |
| Wheat | 2.9 | 46.8 | 2.3 | 30.3 | 2.4 | 27.3 | 1.8 | 19.8 | 1.2 | 11.9 | 2.1 | 25.0 |
| Rice + Wheat | 5.2 | 49.5 | 4.0 | 31.7 | 4.3 | 30.9 | 3.4 | 22.7 | 2.5 | 14.7 | 3.9 | 28.1 |
| Other cereals | 0.4 | 36.4 | 0.2 | 20.0 | 0.3 | 23.1 | 0.3 | 18.8 | 0.2 | 14.3 | 0.3 | 23.1 |
| Total cereal | 5.6 | 48.3 | 4.2 | 30.9 | 4.6 | 30.3 | 3.7 | 22.3 | 2.7 | 14.7 | 4.2 | 27.6 |
| Home produced | | | | | | | | | | | | |
| Rice | 2.0 | 46.5 | 3.2 | 64.0 | 3.2 | 62.7 | 4.3 | 72.9 | 5.6 | 81.2 | 3.7 | 67.3 |
| Wheat | 3.3 | 53.2 | 5.3 | 69.7 | 6.4 | 72.7 | 7.2 | 79.1 | 8.9 | 88.1 | 6.3 | 75.0 |
| Rice + Wheat | 5.3 | 50.5 | 8.5 | 67.5 | 9.6 | 69.1 | 11.5 | 76.7 | 14.5 | 85.3 | 10.0 | 71.9 |
| Other cereals | 0.8 | 72.7 | 0.7 | 70.0 | 1.1 | 84.6 | 1.3 | 81.3 | 1.3 | 92.9 | 1.0 | 76.9 |
| Total cereal | 6.1 | 52.6 | 9.2 | 67.6 | 10.7 | 70.4 | 12.8 | 77.1 | 15.8 | 85.9 | 11.0 | 72.4 |
| Total consumption | | | | | | | | | | | | |
| Rice | 4.3 | 100 | 5.0 | 100 | 5.1 | 100 | 5.9 | 100 | 6.9 | 100 | 5.5 | 100 |
| Wheat | 6.2 | 100 | 7.6 | 100 | 8.8 | 100 | 9.1 | 100 | 10.1 | 100 | 8.4 | 100 |
| Rice + Wheat | 10.5 | 100 | 12.6 | 100 | 13.9 | 100 | 15.0 | 100 | 17.0 | 100 | 13.9 | 100 |
| Other cereals | 1.1 | 100 | 1.0 | 100 | 1.3 | 100 | 1.6 | 100 | 1.4 | 100 | 1.3 | 100 |
| Total cereal | 11.6 | 100 | 13.6 | 100 | 15.2 | 100 | 16.6 | 100 | 18.4 | 100 | 15.2 | 100 |

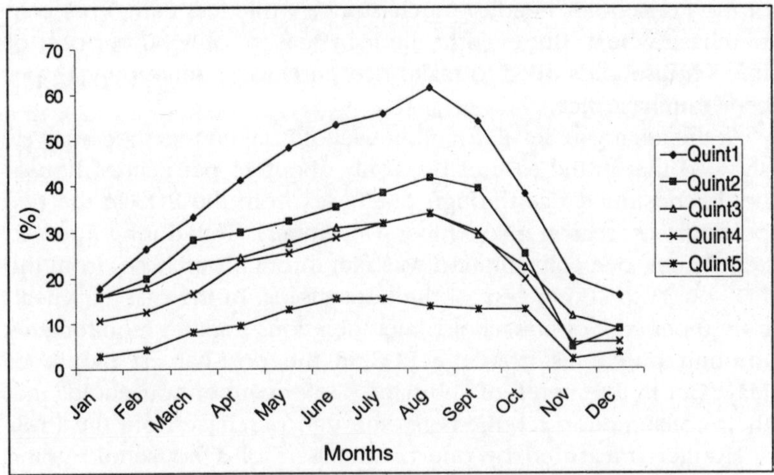


FIG. 4: PERCENTAGE OF HOUSEHOLDS PURCHASING RICE MONTHWISE IN EACH PER CAPITA CONSUMPTION QUINTILE.

sumption and purchase of cereals. Qualitative surveys carried out by this author in 1996, as well as the SLCC survey in 1997–8, showed that the seasonal pattern of cereal consumption in east UP-Bundelkhand was itself determined by the seasonal availability of cereals (mainly rice and wheat in eastern UP and rice, wheat and coarse cereals in Bundelkhand). Thus consumption of any cereal, whether met through home production or purchases, tends to decline for most groups of rural households in the lean season for that cereal.

As far as the purchase of cereals in any given month is concerned, considerations of availability from all sources, the pattern of consumption, and the economic status of the household determines the percentage of households purchasing the cereal. Figs. 3 and 4 show the percentage of households in each consumption quintile purchasing wheat and rice respectively in different months of the year.

The greater market dependence of the poorer groups stands out in this analysis, but at the same time, their dependence on purchases is also highly seasonal. In the post-harvest period, only 16 per cent of the poorest households purchase rice while only 9 per cent purchase wheat. But in the lean season, as many as 61 per cent purchase rice, and 68 per cent purchase wheat. In the highest quintile, in the post-harvest seasons, only about 2 per cent of the households need to purchase rice while less than 5 per cent of the households need to purchase rice while less than 5 per cent purchase wheat. But even in the lean season, only 30 per cent of these households need to make rice purchases, while only 13 per cent purchase rice.

At the aggregate level, for all households taken together, analysis showed that in the case of rice, only about 11 per cent of households consumed rice through purchases from the PDS in the rice post-harvest season (November–December). But during June to September, rice consumption was met through purchases from the PDS by 35 to 40 per cent of the households. In the case of wheat, only 6 per cent of households met their consumption requirements through purchases from the PDS in the post-harvest month of May. But in the month of February, 33 per cent of households met their consumption requirements through purchase from the PDS.

Hunger (measured by one or members of a household going without 2 square meals for some time during the year) is also seasonally distributed. More than 6.2 per cent of the sample households in the SLC reported going without two square meals for some time during the year. The households also reported the periods (months) in which they do not eat two square meals. An analysis of these monthly data on 'hungry' households shows sharp peaks in the lean season (see Fig. 5). For instance, in April–May, in the wheat-harvesting season, only 2.8 per cent such households report going without two square meals. This percentage increases to 37 in August–September. Another peak of hunger occurs in January, when 33 per cent of such households report going without two square meals.

Wages-in-kind are an important source of consumption in UP. In the case of households reporting 'labour' as their principal means of livelihood, access to home-production, and wages-in-kind, are significant sources of consumption in certain seasons. Together, home production and wages-in-kind account for the consumption needs of almost 80 per cent of labour households in the rice postharvest season, and 84 per cent households in the wheat post-harvest season. In the case of rice, 73 per cent households depend on purchases in the lean season. In the case of wheat, market dependence increases to 68 per cent in the lean season.

For households depending upon purchases, the behaviour of prices of cereals in the local rural markets determines the source of purchase. Local prices are often lower than what they are in urban centres, and this is specially the case in glut years. Thus, the

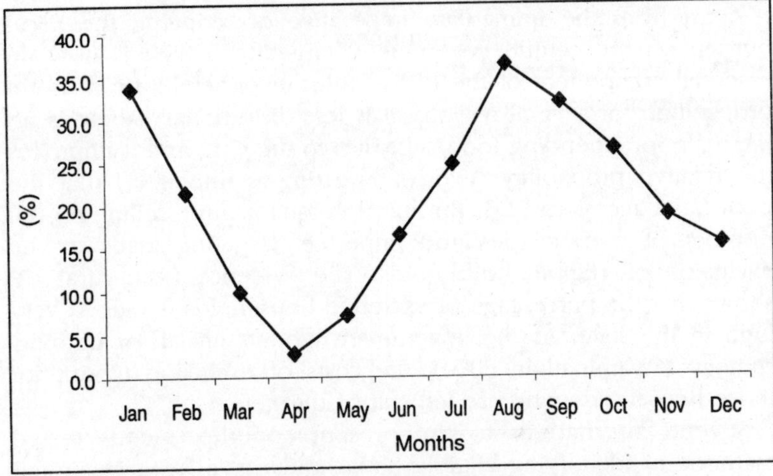


FIG. 5: PERCENTAGE OF 'HUNGRY' HOUSEHOLDS GOING WITHOUT TWO SQUARE MEALS IN ANY GIVEN MONTH.

rural areas of the state. In fact, with the increase in the Central Issue Price (CIP) of rice and wheat in 2000–1 for the TPDS, local prices are reported to be lower than the TPDS prices.

Added to this are the other issues often mentioned: lack of knowledge among the poor regarding availability of PDS cereals, lack of sufficient cash to purchase the quota, and the time taken to effect the purchases.

Thus, the current nature of rural transactions and production activity in the rural areas in UP provides access to cereals in kind to poor households, reducing their overall market dependence to almost half. Food deficits as well as market dependence are both highly seasonal in the rural areas. Demand for PDS cereals is constrained both by cash requirement and a smaller price difference than would be the case in urban areas. A well-designed PDS would need to take care of these factors in order to maximize impact and have a high demand among the rural poor.

## CONCLUSION

The recent results in UP bring out some of the dilemmas confronting PDS policy and suggest that the system may need significant changes to effectively meet the challenge of providing food security to the rural poor.

Apart from the immediate imperative of reducing the fiscal burden on the central government, targeting, which is now an essential component of the PDS, could, in principle, be a useful proposition for several reasons: it is less distortionary, there is no rationale for extending food subsidies to the rich, and it improves the relative probability (even if targeting is imperfect) that the poor have access to PDS. But the tight quantitative ceiling on the number of beneficiaries and imperfect targeting leads to the exclusion of eligible households. The evidence from rural UP shows that the percentage of excluded households is indeed very high in the state. As the government mounts an 'all or nothing' strategy (Swaminathan 2000), the costs of exclusion mount for those households who are left out of the net.

Several alternatives to the present complex means tested methods of identifying eligible households have been suggested in the past. These include simple indicator based targeting which could vary regionally, linking PDS to other programmes and food stamps, and so on. Each of these have some advantages but apart from indicator-based targeting, run the risk of reducing the coverage of the PDS even further. One possibility is to try out these alternatives on an experimental basis, by including households covered in the Social Assistance, Employment and other similar programmes, involving self-selection of poor households, and to link this with the new *Antyodaya* scheme which is intended to cover the poorest households.

The above scheme should be used in conjunction with a more broad-based PDS scheme, which can use some other self-selecting criteria (such as the distribution of low-quality rice) to keep diversions low. In the context of the scenario in rural UP where even the rural poor have sizeable access to cereals in the peak season, any scheme must focus on flexibility and removal of shortages in the lean seasons. Food stamps and/or grain passbooks issued to the poor could meet their needs more flexibly, with less distortion and leakage, and could be tried out.

At present, the dual pricing provides a hefty incentive for leakage. This is compounded by a lack of political commitment to the PDS in the state, administrative cynicism and the lack of adequate incentives to the PDS shopkeeper. Multiplicity of agencies with poor coordination has led to lower administrative accountability of the delivery machinery. There is an urgent need to improve local supervision through the Panchayati Raj Institutions (PRI), introduce transparency, and create clear PDS entitlements.

## NOTES

1. Assuming a nutritional requirement for adults at 15 kg food grain per month and for a child at half that level, GOI (1998) estimates the average annual per capita requirement at 146.45 kg or approximately 150 kg per year. Accordingly, states with cereal production above that level are categorized as 'surplus' states.
2. The issue price of common rice increased from Rs. 244 in 1990 to Rs. 537 per quintal in 1994. In June 1997, after the introduction of the TPDS, the issue price became Rs. 650 for APL families and Rs. 350 for BPL families. The former was revised to Rs. 700 in December 1997 and Rs. 900 with effect from January 1999. In the case of wheat, the issue price increased from Rs. 204 in 1990 to Rs. 402 in 1994. In June 1997, the issue price was fixed at Rs. 250 for BPL families and Rs. 450 for APL families. The latter was raised to Rs. 650 in January 1999. Since 2000, the issue prices of wheat and rice are Rs. 4.20 per kg and Rs. 5.85 per kg. Kerosene prices have been raised by Rs. 2.50 per litre.
3. The Survey of Living Conditions was carried out in a representative sample of 120 villages in north/central Bihar and eastern/southern UP during 1997–8. For the purposes of this paper, data on food consumption and food security from the UP sample villages have been analysed.

# 24. Food Security and Public Distribution System in Rajasthan

*Pradeep Bhargava*

Survival in a fragile ecosystem characterized by dryland areas and uncertain rainfalls is the major struggle for the poor in Rajasthan. It is to the credit of the people that they have developed and sustained some of their survival strategies in harsh and uncertain environmental conditions. In recent years, however, their survival strategies have come under severe strain due to external interventions and demographic factors wherein the sustainability of the ecosystem has been driven to the margin (Bhargava 1995).

Survival for a very large majority (around 70 per cent of the population) is based on agriculture and animal husbandry, which contributes around one-third to the State Domestic Product (SDP). In the severe drought year of 2000–1 it is expected to contribute only 28 per cent to the SDP. Adverse climatic conditions characterized by erratic rainfall and frequent visitations of droughts have resulted in wide fluctuations in agricultural output and the number of livestock. In several years, the agricultural output has fallen short of the output in the previous year.

High population pressure offsets the positive impact of growth. Population increase in the state is one of the highest in the country. In 1991, the decennial growth rate of population was 28.44 per cent, which has very marginally come down to 28.33 per cent in 2001.

The gross cropped area in the state has increased from 14 million hectares in 1958–9 to 21 million hectares in 1998–9 (achieving a peak of 22 million hectares in 1997–8), but there are wide fluctuations from year to year due to erratic rainfall. The coefficient of variation in area sown of food grains alone was 8 per cent in the last three decades (1971–2001) (Table 1). The fluctuations are far more for kharif crops and more so in the arid dryland regions

TABLE 1: COEFFICIENT OF VARIATION IN AREA SOWN AND PRODUCTION OF FOOD GRAINS AND OILSEEDS

(Various years)

| | 1970s | 1980s | 1990s | 1971–2000 |
|---|---|---|---|---|
| *Food grains* | | | | |
| Area | 4.9 | 10.0 | 8.6 | 7.9 |
| Production | 19.2 | 21.7 | 20.2 | 28.6 |
| *Oilseeds* | | | | |
| Area | 11.8 | 26.5 | 12.9 | — |
| Production | 23.0 | 47.5 | 16.9 | — |

*Source*: Government of Rajasthan, Department of Economics and Statistics.

of the state. The net cropped area has stabilized around 17 million hectares. The gross irrigated area in 1998–9 was 7 million hectares, which is around one-third of the gross cropped area. Out of this, two-thirds is irrigated by wells and tube-wells, the recharge of which is directly dependent on rainfall. The remaining 28 per cent is irrigated by canals, and 5 per cent by other sources including tanks. In a fragile ecosystem, both the increase in area under cultivation and under irrigation has been a cause of much concern and forms a part of the debate on sustainability of food security being achieved by increased irrigation.

## CHANGING CROPPING PATTERN

The gross cropped area in the state increased from 16.9 million hectares in TE 1974–5 to 20.9 million hectares in TE 1997–8. Until the 1970s, the cropping pattern was heavily biased towards food grains. In the 1980s, a major shift in the cropping pattern was witnessed in favour of oilseeds. While the average area under food grains has remained around 12.7 million hectares, the area under oilseeds increased from 1.2 million hectares to 4.0 million hectares (Table 2). The share of food grains in gross cropped area declined from 75 per cent in the TE 1975–6 to 61 per cent in TE 1997–8. Within food grains, the relative decline is more pronounced in small millets, minor cereals and pulses. Land vacated by cereals has been occupied by soyabean in the *kharif*, and to an extent rapeseed and mustard in the *rabi*. The share of oilseeds in the gross cropped area increased from 8 per cent in TE 1975–6 to 19 per cent in TE 1997–8. This shift is also important from an environmental perspective, as

TABLE 2: DISTRIBUTION OF AREA UNDER *KHARIF* AND *RABI* MAJOR CROPS (VARIOUS YEARS)

(million ha)

| | TE 1975–6 | TE 1997–8 | 1999–2000 | 2000–1 |
|---|---|---|---|---|
| *Kharif* | | | | |
| Cereals | 6.4 (38) | 6.2 (30) | 5.6 (29) | 5.6 |
| Pulses | 2.2 (13) | 2.1 (10) | 1.4 (8) | 2.0 |
| Oilseeds | 0.7 (4) | 1.1 (5) | 1.1 (5) | 1.3 |
| *Rabi* | | | | |
| Cereals | 2.3 (14) | 2.7 (13) | 2.8 (14) | 2.1 |
| Pulses | 1.7 (10) | 1.8 (9) | 1.0 (5) | 0.9 |
| Oilseeds | 0.6 (4) | 3.0 (14) | 2.6 (13) | 1.6 |
| *Total (Kharif and Rabi)* | | | | |
| Cereals | 8.7 (52) | 8.9 (43) | 8.4 (43) | 7.7 |
| Pulses | 3.9 (23) | 3.9 (19) | 2.4 (13) | 2.9 |
| Oilseeds | 1.3 (8) | 4.1 (19) | 3.7 (18) | 2.9 |

*Source*: Government of Rajasthan, Department of Economics and Statistics.
*Note*: Figures in parentheses are percentages of the gross cropped area. For the year 2001–1 the figures are estimated. Gross cropped area for the year is not available.

oilseeds require almost one-sixth the irrigation of wheat, which has been vacated for oilseeds. However, expansion of rapeseed and mustard has also been on marginal lands which have come under cultivation and also irrigation using water saving devices. The sustainability of such a shift in the cropping pattern, therefore, requires a more careful analysis.

Yet another impact on the cropping pattern is of the prices received by the farmers for their produce vis-à-vis the expenditure incurred. The barter terms of trade have deteriorated in Rajasthan, particularly in the 1990s (Acharya 2000). The prices received by farmers for rapeseed and mustard, wheat and gram either decreased or increased only marginally. In 1994–5 they were considerably lower than in the previous year. In 1994–5, the government liberalized imports of edible oils and pulses and reduced the custom duty on these commodities to abysmally low levels. The prices received by farmers did not compensate for the increase in input prices, resulting in the deterioration of the barter terms of trade. Even increase in productivity could not compensate for the same. The impact on production of oilseeds is beginning to be felt, although it is too early to predict a decline based on the production figures of a drought year.

## PRODUCTION OF FOOD GRAINS AND THEIR COMPOSITION

The gross food grains production in the state grew at the annual rate of 2.1 per cent during the period 1971–2001, accelerating mainly in the 1990s (Tables 3 and 4). Between the TE 1975–6 and TE 1997–8, the average annual cereal production doubled from

TABLE 3: GROWTH RATE OF PRODUCTION OF FOOD GRAINS AND OILSEEDS

(Various years)

| | 1970s | 1980s | 1990s | 1971–2000 |
|---|---|---|---|---|
| Food grains | -1.87 | 0.83 | 3.3 | 2.1 |
| Oilseeds | -2.52 | 16.12 | 2.9 | 9.5 |

*Source*: Based on CMIE Data.

TABLE 4: GROWTH RATES OF SOME IMPORTANT CROPS BETWEEN TE 1972–3 AND TE 1994–5

| Crop | Rajasthan | | | India | | |
|---|---|---|---|---|---|---|
| | Area | Production | Yield | Area | Production | Yield |
| *Jowar* | -1.9 | -1.7 | 0.2 | -1.5 | 1.2 | 2.7 |
| *Bajra* | -0.1 | 1.3 | 1.3 | -0.9 | 0.5 | 1.4 |
| Maize | 0.8 | 0.7 | -0.1 | 0.2 | 2.0 | 1.8 |
| Small millets | -4.6 | -6.8 | -1.8 | -3.8 | -3.0 | 0.8 |
| Wheat | 1.9 | 4.5 | 2.6 | 1.5 | 4.2 | 2.7 |
| Barley | -3.4 | -2.4 | 1.0 | -4.7 | -2.6 | 2.2 |
| Gram | -0.3 | 0.1 | 0.3 | -0.7 | -0.1 | 0.6 |
| *Arhar* | -1.2 | -1.6 | -0.3 | 1.4 | 1.3 | -0.1 |
| Total food grains | 0.1 | 1.8 | 1.8 | 0.0 | 2.5 | 2.5 |
| *Kharif* food grains | -0.3 | 0.8 | 1.1 | -0.2 | 2.1 | 2.3 |
| *Rabi* food grains | 0.5 | 2.6 | 2.0 | 0.5 | 3.4 | 2.9 |
| Groundnut | -2.6 | 2.3 | 2.7 | 0.5 | 1.5 | 1.1 |
| Rapeseed, mustard | 9.9 | 12.1 | 1.8 | 2.7 | 5.2 | 2.4 |

*Source*: CMIE, July 1996, cited in Vyas, 1996.

TABLE 5: DISTRIBUTION OF PRODUCTION UNDER *KHARIF* AND *RABI* CROPS (VARIOUS YEARS)

(lakh tons)

| | TE 1975–6 | TE 1997–8 | 1999–2000 | 2000–1 |
|---|---|---|---|---|
| *Kharif* | | | | |
| Cereals | 23 | 34 | 27 | 22 |
| Pulses | 4 | 5 | 1 | 3 |
| Oilseeds | 2 | 9 | 9 | 9 |
| *Rabi* | | | | |
| Cereals | 28 | 68 | 71 | 58 |
| Pulses | 6 | 14 | 8 | 7 |
| Oilseeds | 2 | 24 | 25 | 16 |
| *Total (Kharif and Rabi)* | | | | |
| Cereals | 51 | 102 | 98 | 80 |
| Pulses | 10 | 19 | 9 | 10 |
| Oilseeds | 4 | 33 | 34 | 25 |

*Source*: Government of Rajasthan, Department of Economics and Statistics.
*Note*: Figures for 2000-1 are provisional.

51 lakh tons to 102 lakh tons (Table 5). In TE 1997–8, this production averages 231 kg per capita per annum, amounting to a 2,195 daily calorie equivalent. However, this is only part of the story. The hidden truth lies in the composition of output and its distribution between *kharif* and *rabi*.

Vyas (1996) has shown concern over decline in area and production of *bajra* and small millets (Table 4), the coarse grains for the arid region, which are also more nutritive than wheat. Similarly, the area under pulses shows a declining trend. Wheat and oilseeds have shown an increasing trend in area, production and yield.

In the TE 1997–8, 12.8 million hectares were under food grains. Two-thirds of this area was under *kharif*, very largely rainfed, and contributed only 38 per cent of the total output as against one-third of the area being under rabi but contributing 62 per cent of the food grain output. While Rajasthan's agriculture is correctly defined as 'rain-fed', the contribution of *rabi* cereals was double the *kharif* cereals in the TE 1997–8. In the two severe drought years of 1999–2000 and the following year, the rabi output is estimated to be 2.8 times the *kharif*. In such years, the drawal of groundwater is far in excess of the recharge. Large investments are made by farmers to deepen their wells, increasing their costs, which in the final analysis may turn out to be both economically and environmentally unviable.

To sum up, three aspects of composition of area and output in the state need to be emphasized:

1. Both area and output are characterized by wild year-to-year fluctuations. This puts livelihoods of small and marginal farmers, particularly those 45 per cent without irrigation under strain. These, along with agricultural labourers, need food security at all times.
2. The shift to cash crops, namely oilseeds, which provided substantial cash flows even to the small farmer, is threatened by deterioration in the barter terms of trade.
3. The increasing biotic pressure on the fragile ecosystems, absence of adequate investments and appropriate management to augment and conserve land and water resources, population growth, macroeconomic policies that provide inducement to overexploit the natural resource are factors that contribute to explain the environmental factors that will influence the food security of the state in the long run.

## DROUGHTS IN RAJASTHAN AND FOOD INSECURITY CONCERNS

Droughts visit Rajasthan frequently. In the last 45 years (1956 to 2001), one or the other area in the state has been affected by drought (Annexure: Table I). Drought conditions are declared by the government based on information collected on 'damage caused to crops'. Droughts are a result of wide annual fluctuations in rainfall and the failure to meet the demand for water in a particular region.

While the level and growth of food production in the state is satisfactory, the sustainability of the same is questionable. Besides, the fluctuation in production of food grains, specially those in the kharif season affect those households the most which are entirely dependent on rainfed agriculture. Almost 45 per cent landholdings of size less than 2 hectares do not have irrigation facilities. Moreover, there are households which need food security at practically all times, given their livelihood patterns.

Table 6 is based on a survey of 4 sample chronically drought-prone districts with 160 cultivator households selected at random

TABLE 6: PERCENTAGE DISTRIBUTION OF HOUSEHOLDS BY MONTHS OF FOOD GRAIN REQUIREMENTS THAT ARE MET BY OWN PRODUCTION

| | 12 months or more | | 0–3 months | |
|---|---|---|---|---|
| | NY* | DY** | NY* | DY** |
| Overall | 45 | 7 | 27 | 88 |
| Ajmer | 49 | 8 | 20 | 83 |
| Jaisalmer | 22 | 5 | 51 | 86 |
| Pali | 59 | 11 | 6 | 79 |
| Udaipur | 25 | 1 | 19 | 89 |

*Source*: Survey Data.
*Note*: *NY = Normal Year (1996-7); **DY = Drought Year (1999-2000).

in each district. (We shall refer to this as Survey 1.) It shows how in a drought year only 7 per cent households are able to grow the requirements for household consumption for the entire year compared to 45 per cent in a normal year. Moreover, 27 per cent households in the 4 districts produce food grains that last them less than 3 months and they, of course, are more vulnerable in a drought year. It is for these households that food security needs to be ensured throughout the year. In most of these households, at least one member migrates seasonally for wage labour.

## ENSURING FOOD SECURITY AND PUBLIC DISTIBUTION SYSTEM

Ensuring food security at the household level can be done in two ways. The first is through the Public Distribution System (PDS) and the other is through ensuring entitlements of poor households through wage programmes or programmes such as Food for Work.

The *Economic Review* of the Government of Rajasthan describes the PDS as 'an essential element of the government's safety net to the poor'. The Food and Civil Supplies Department of the state is managing the PDS. There are 19,346 authorized Fair Price Shops (FPS) in the state. Out of these, 14,710 are operational in rural areas and the remaining in the urban areas. The cooperative sector manages 5,188 shops and the remaining are in the private sector. The FPS get their quota of rationed commodities from wholesalers appointed by the state government, who in turn collect the allocated quota of these commodities from the FCI godowns (or a depot of an oil company). A 'Doorstep Delivery System' is in place wherein wholesalers collect commodities from the FCI after making payment, and in turn supply the commodities to FPS on credit. The transportation cost is borne by the government.

Sagar (2000) finds that this system does not function strictly in this order. According to his study on the PDS in Rajasthan, the wholesalers first collects money from FPS owners and delivers the commodity 15 or 30 days later. A number of leakages are reported including underweighing, collection of unloading charges and in some cases transportation costs as well. The main findings of the study of sample households in four districts include the following:

- Households covered by Poverty Alleviation Programmes (PAP) purchased 58 to 170 per cent more wheat from FPS than the non-PAP households did. In one RPDS village, the PAP households took their entire entitlement of wheat.
- The main beneficiaries of the PDS wheat purchases are the poor marginal and small farmers and agricultural labourers.
- The share of PDS wheat in cereal consumption of households declined with the increase in Monthly Per Capita Expenditure Classes (MPCE) in 2 districts out of the 4 covered by the study. In the other 2 districts, this relationship was found to be neutral.
- Sagar also finds that the FPS provide support to the scanty market infrastructure particularly in underdeveloped villages. The importance of PDS operations in the state is high due to the fact that it provides access to food by reinforcing the tenuous market infrastructure in large parts of the state.

## SOME FINDINGS OF A RECENT SURVEY OF FPS

A survey of the PDS in 18 blocks of 12 districts of the state was undertaken in January 2001. The reference period was October–December 2000. The main findings are summarized below:

- In one-sixth of the FPS, no wheat had been distributed during the reference months. Only one-third of the villages had regular distribution (i.e. every month for these three months).
- In FPS where wheat reached, all BPL households drew their full quota of 20 kg per month. Thus, low offtake of PDS

wheat cannot be attributed to the failure of households to draw their rations. Instead, low offtake seems to be due to inadequate coverage and irregular distribution.

- It is sometimes claimed that offtake is low because many households do not have cash to buy their monthly quota. The survey found that such households are a small minority.

## PDS SUPPLIES AS PERCENTAGE OF TOTAL CONSUMPTION

The households in Survey 1 mentioned above consumed an appreciable proportion of wheat from FPS as a percentage of total food grain consumption. This was higher in drought years than in normal years (Table 7). Also, the dependence of the BPL is also found to be higher, which corroborates the Sagar (2000) findings. In the most vulnerable areas like Udaipur, the dependence on FPS is far more than in other districts. In districts like Jaisalmer in the arid region, the preference is for *bajra*, which incidentally does not form part of the PDS.

In spite of its limitations, the PDS has helped maintain the average annual consumption of food grain as is evident from Table 8. In the 1987 drought survey of the same villages, the per annum consumption was reported to be 160 kg per capita in normal years and 167 kg in drought years (Acharya 1989).

The performance of the PDS in Rajasthan when compared to other main wheat consuming states in terms of offtake as percentage of allocation by the central government is the lowest though it has improved through the years (Table 9).

The overall offtake by FPS is 61 per cent of their allotted quota in 2000–1. There are significant district-wise variations, as can be seen in Table 10.

TABLE 7: OFFTAKE FROM FPS AS PER CENT OF TOTAL CONSUMPTION

| Year | Ajmer | Jaisalmer | Pali | Udaipur | Total |
|---|---|---|---|---|---|
| *BPL* | | | | | |
| DY | 11 | 23 | 18 | 43 | 24 |
| NY | 8 | 22 | 9 | 34 | 19 |
| *APL* | | | | | |
| DR | 15 | 21 | 13 | 41 | 17 |
| NR | 8 | 20 | 5 | 31 | 12 |

*Source*: Survey Data.

TABLE 8: AVERAGE CONSUMPTION OF GRAIN BY HOUSEHOLDS IN DROUGHT AND NORMAL YEARS

(in kg.)

| | |
|---|---|
| *BPL* | |
| DY | 1,019 |
| NY | 1,051 |
| *APL* | |
| DY | 1,063 |
| NY | 1,091 |

*Source*: Survey Data, 1999.

TABLE 9: OFFTAKE OF WHEAT: SELECT STATES FOR BPL HOUSEHOLDS

(in per cent)

| State | 1997–8 | 1998–9 | 1999-2000 |
|---|---|---|---|
| Bihar | 93 | 93 | 103 |
| Gujarat | 110 | 110 | 99 |
| Madhya Pradesh | 62 | 62 | 76 |
| Maharashtra | 83 | 83 | 87 |
| Rajasthan | 55 | 55 | 73 |
| Uttar Pradesh | 96 | 96 | 97 |
| West Bengal | 92 | 92 | 96 |

*Source*: Government of India, *Foodgrains: Monthly Bulletin*, November 2000.

## WHY SOME FPS DO NOT OBTAIN THEIR ALLOTMENT

In the current year, only BPL households are availing their quota of 20 kg from FPS. The prices fixed for APL households is the 'economic cost' which is more than the market price, hence their offtake is negligible. The doorstep delivery is made possible by the wholesaler only if the FPS allocation is 100 quintals (100 kg) or more. If less than this, they are paid a transport allowance of Rs. 6 per quintal. In one such FPS, the monthly quota is 44 quintals. The actual transport cost to transfer this is Rs. 500, while the FPS receives only Rs. 284. Besides, loading and unloading costs of Re. 1 each are to be borne by the FPS owner. The FPS also has to pay in advance to the wholesaler. In such circumstances, the distribution line is weak. Unless such weak links like credit facilities are corrected and doorstep delivery ensured, the offtake will continue to lag.

TABLE 10: DISTRIBUTION OF DISTRICTS BY OFFTAKE OF FOOD GRAINS AS PER CENT OF ALLOTMENT FOR BPL HOUSEHOLDS

| Per cent | Districts |
|---|---|
| Up to 20 | Jhalawar, Kota, Tonk |
| 20–40 | Alwar, Baran, Bundi, Dausa, Sawaimadhopur |
| 40–60 | Ganganagar, Jaipur, Karauli |
| 60–80 | Banswara, Barmer, Dholpur, Jalore, Jhunjhunu |
| 80–100 | Bikaner, Churu, Dungarpur, Jaisalmer, Jodhpur, Nagaur, Pali, Rajsamand, Sikar, Sirohi, Udaipur |
| Overall | 61 per cent |

*Source*: Government of India, *Foodgrains: Monthly Bulletin*, November 2000.

Providing entitlements can ensure access to food. In a severe drought year such as the present one, there is dire need to ensure access to food. Reports of deaths due to combined effect of dwindling livelihoods, declining health, decline in food intake, surviving merely on corn gruel have been reported in a section of the press (Mishra 2001). This year, the people's own strategy to migrate to Gujarat for work has failed due to the earthquake. There have been demonstrations outside the FCI godowns for release of food grains.

The state government's financial position is weak. It has opened works according to the allocations made in the Calamity Relief Fund. However, the work days fall far short of the demand for relief works. According to Survey 1 of the 1987 and 1999 drought situations, the demand for work was fulfilled far more in the former year (Table 11). Table 12 shows that 77 per cent men and 68 per cent women who were available for work did not get employment in relief works in the year 1999–2000. This situation of large-scale unemployment is likely to be more in the current year.

## PERCEPTION OF CIVIL SOCIETY ORGANIZATIONS

Leading civil society organizations which are playing an advocacy role for the last one year or more, have two major demands for ensuring food security. The first demand is to increase the quota of food grains to 10 kg per unit per month in the household as was the case in the 1987 drought, and the distinction between the BPL and APL be removed till the next crop is harvested. The second demand is to raise the employment ceiling to 20 lakh

TABLE 11: A COMPARISON OF 1987 AND 1999 RELIEF WORKS

| Individual's employment in relief works | 1987 | 1999 |
|---|---|---|
| Did not need employment | 16.3 | 10.0 |
| Partially employed | 78.7 | 39.3 |
| Full employment as per need | 1.6 | 5.8 |
| Did not get employment but available for work | 2.8 | 44.9 |

*Source*: Survey Data.

TABLE 12: EMPLOYMENT IN RELIEF WORKS: 16 VILLAGES IN 4 DISTRICTS (1999–2000)

| | |
|---|---|
| *Male* | |
| Percentage of those available for work employed in relief works (143/612) | 23.3 |
| Mean number of days employed | 12 |
| Mean wages paid (Rs.) | 36.47 |
| *Female* | |
| Percentage of those available for work employed in relief works (167/528) | 31.6 |
| Mean number of days employed | 17 |
| Mean wages paid (Rs.) | 33.15 |

*Source*: Survey Data.

person days of employment per day for 4 months to help people mitigate drought (though even this will fall short of employment to all who demand work. (According to the 1991 Census, there were 1.4 million agricultural labourers and 8.18 million cultivators.) A part of this, payment may be made through the Food for Work Programme at the rate of 10 kg wheat as part of wages and Rs. 14 per day be paid in cash. The total wage would then be Rs. 60 per person per day, valuing wheat at the rate of Rs. 4.60 per kg. This employment programme would require 2.4 lakh tons of wheat, which is only 5 per cent of the total food grain stock with the FCI.

## CONCLUSION

Recurrent droughts in the state are enough justification for continuance of the food security initiatives through the PDS. At an aggregate level, the state has achieved self-sufficiency in food production in a normal year. But these normal years are very few and far between. The same cannot be said of food security at the household level for more than half the population of the rural areas, which survives on its own meagre production and incomes from casual farm and non-farm employment. Even the 'self-sufficiency' achieved by mining scarce water resources may not be viable both from the economic and environmental perspectives. The PDS in the state is functioning, but needs a further push to ensure door step delivery and probably short term credit facilities to the FPS. The BPL households presently buy their full quota of 20 kg of wheat whenever it is made available at the FPS. The perceived reluctance of the BPL of not buying their full quota is a false perception. The demands raised by civil-society organizations to increase the quota to 10 kg per unit and this be made applicable for all households in the severe drought conditions alongwith the demand to release 2.4 lakh tons for Food for Work is justified. The justification lies in the fact that the shortfall in food grain production in 2000–1 is projected to be 18 lakh tons less than in 1999–2000, and 22 lakh tons less than in TE 1997–8.

## ANNEXURE

TABLE I: DROUGHT SITUATION IN RAJASTHAN (*SAMVAT* 2013–56)

| Year | *Samvat* | No. of districts affected | No. of villages affected | Affected population in crore |
|---|---|---|---|---|
| 1 | 2 | 3 | 4 | 5 |
| 1956–7 | 2013 | 7 | 1,353 | 00.92 |
| 1957–8 | 2014 | 14 | 6,581 | 22.72 |
| 1958–9 | 2015 | 6 | 1,309 | 10.77 |
| 1959–60 | 2016 | — | — | — |
| 1960–1 | 2017 | 18 | 4,634 | 20.91 |
| 1961–2 | 2018 | 5 | 379 | 04.07 |
| 1962–3 | 2019 | 10 | 1,248 | — |
| 1963–4 | 2020 | 18 | 6,367 | 47.25 |
| 1964–5 | 2021 | 15 | 3,156 | 12.85 |
| 1965–6 | 2022 | 24 | 11,452 | 55.00 |
| 1966–7 | 2023 | 24 | 10,079 | 45.25 |
| 1967–8 | 2024 | 12 | 2,383 | 15.24 |
| 1968–9 | 2025 | 26 | 22,915 | 131.63 |
| 1969–70 | 2026 | 23 | 11,977 | 71.12 |
| 1970–1 | 2027 | 7 | 480 | 03.02 |
| 1971–2 | 2028 | 13 | 6,139 | 30.60 |
| 1972–3 | 2029 | 26 | 18,722 | 136.88 |
| 1973–4 | 2030 | — | — | — |
| 1974–5 | 2031 | 25 | 19,873 | — |
| 1975–6 | 2032 | — | — | — |
| 1976–7 | 2033 | — | — | — |
| 1977–8 | 2034 | 19 | 12,253 | 92.45 |
| 1978–9 | 2035 | 26 | 5,609 | 33.20 |
| 1979–80 | 2036 | 26 | 31,095 | 240.00 |
| 1980–1 | 2037 | 26 | 21,395 | 167.79 |
| 1981–2 | 2038 | 26 | 23,246 | 200.12 |
| 1982–3 | 2039 | 26 | 22,606 | 171.62 |
| 1983–4 | 2040 | 3 | 282 | — |
| 1984–5 | 2041 | 21 | 10,276 | 92.02 |
| 1985–6 | 2042 | 26 | 26,859 | 219.80 |
| 1986–7 | 2043 | 27 | 31,936 | 252.70 |
| 1987–8 | 2044 | 27 | 36,252 | 317.37 |
| 1988–9 | 2045 | 17 | 4,497 | 43.45 |
| 1989–90 | 2046 | 25 | 14,024 | 120.67 |
| 1990–1 | 2047 | — | — | — |

(contd.)

TABLE I (contd.)

| 1 | 2 | 3 | 4 | 5 |
|---|---|---|---|---|
| 1991–2 | 2048 | 30 | 30,041 | 289.00 |
| 1992–3 | 2049 | 12 | 4,376 | 34.66 |
| 1993–4 | 2050 | 25 | 22,586 | 246.81 |
| 1994–5 | 2051 | — | — | — |
| 1995–6 | 2052 | 29 | 25,478 | 273.82 |
| 1996–7 | 2053 | 21 | 5,905 | 55.29 |
| 1997–8 | 2054 | 24 | 4,633 | 14.91 |
| 1998–9 | 2055 | 20 | 20,069 | 215.07 |
| 1999–2000 | 2056 | 26 | 23,406 | 261.79 |
| 2000–1 | 2057 | 31 | 30,583 | 330.41 |

*Source*: Government of Rajasthan, Department of Agriculture.

# 25. Role of Food in Sustainable Development: The Case of Jhabua in Madhya Pradesh

*Wasim Akhtar*

Jhabua is a predominantly tribal district located in the western part of Madhya Pradesh. It is surrounded by Panchamahal and Baroda districts of Gujarat, Banswara district of Rajasthan and Dhar and Ratlam districts of Madhya Pradesh. The river Narmada forms the southern boundary of the district. The terrain is hilly, undulating, typically known as 'Jhabua hills topography'. In this Jhabua hill topography, the difference between the highest and the lowest points varies between 20 and 50 metres. But this difference goes on increasing as we move towards south of Jhabua. In Alirajpur division which is in the south of Jhabua the areas is almost entirely hilly and intersected by narrow valleys and low Vindhyan ranges covered with jungles. But most part of Jhabua (except Katthiwada) is without any forest cover because of low fertility of land and soil erosion. The area suffers from poor and skeletal soils with shallow to very shallow depth and erratic rainfall and high temperature. The area comes under Agroclimatic zone no. 12 namely, 'Jhabua hills' covering an area of 0.68 million ha (1.5 per cent of geographical area of MP). The district has three distinct subzones namely Petlawad (Malwa), Jhabua (low rainfall) and Katthiwada (high rainfall) zones.

The normal level rainfall of the district is recorded as 828.00 mm p.a., but there has been decline in the recorded rainfall from 1,260 mm in 1997–8 to 588 mm in 1999–2000 and just 366 mm in 2000–1. The main *kharif* crops grown in the district are maize, *urad*, soyabeen, cotton, while wheat and gram are the major *rabi* crops. The productivity of agricultural crops in the district is less than both state and national averages. The low productivity is attributable to irregular rains and long dry spells; paucity of short-duration varieties of maize, paddy and soyabeen crops; unbalanced use of fertilizers, etc.

Jhabua is a sparsely-populated area with a total population of 13.96 lakh according to 1991 census. The total area is 6,793 sq km. There are about 1,313 inhabited villages. About 85 per cent of the population is tribal, while 3 per cent of the population belongs to the Scheduled Castes; 47 per cent of the people live below the poverty line. The literacy rate according to the 1991 census is 19.1 per cent, with female literacy of only 4 per cent. Jhabua is thus an overwhelmingly tribal and poor district.

## WATERSHED DEVELOPMENT MISSION

The Rajiv Gandhi Mission on Watershed Development started in October 1994 was the first attempt at sustainable livelihood development. Presently, 249 micro-watersheds have been taken up under EAS, DPAP, IWDP and IJRY schemes. A total of 1,47,066 ha has been taken up under integrated watershed development with an estimated project cost of Rs. 5,277 lakh. In order to effectively launch the project, 12 governmental and 8 NGO Project Implementing Agencies (PIA) were carefully selected. Using RRA/PRA techniques and thematic maps by remote sensing, action plans were prepared by the PIAs for every micro-watershed. At the district level, a Watershed Advisory Committee has been formed which monitors the programme and tries to resolve observed shortcomings every fortnight. The Collector, PIAs, relevant district-level departments and people's representatives are part of this committee. There are Watershed Development Teams for each PIA, consisting of block-level officials of various departments. The PIAs are linked with Watershed Development Committees of local villagers, which consist of Self-Help Groups and User Groups in watershed villages. Watershed Development Committees and Watershed Associations were formed and registered with District Rural Development Agency (DRDA), Jhabua. Presently, 2,181 Women SHGs (*Baira-ni-kuldis*) are doing thrift activities in the watershed villages.

Confidence building and people's participation are ensured through numerous meetings and RRA/PRA techniques before taking up preparation of the Action Plan. User Groups and Self-Help Groups initiate people's involvement in watershed activities, and use their knowledge and wisdom in the preparation of the

Action Plan. Members of User Groups, Self-Help Groups and representatives from Gram Panchayats are included in Watershed Development Committees (WDC). A chairman is elected and secretaries selected for each WDC. An extensive land literacy campaign was launched to find out various geographical, geomorphological and geohydrological problems and situations. House-to-house contacts and PRA/RRA activities were used to identify social, economical, ecological and geohydrological needs, problems and perceptions of the villagers.

The President, Zila Panchayat is the patron of the Watershed Advisory Committee at the district level. District, Janpad and Gram Panchayats' representatives are involved in watershed development activities at all levels. The help of the people's representatives is taken in PRA exercises and preparation of Action Plans also. Every Watershed Development Committee necessarily includes three to four Gram Panchayat members.

## ACTIVITIES UNDERTAKEN

### *Soil and Water Conservation*

A very thoughtful and targeted approach to achieve effective, efficient and site-specific soil and water conservation was adopted. Ridge-to-valley treatment was strictly followed. Contour trenches, staggered pits, gully control measures, drainage line treatment along with fodder development and plantation of suitable species were taken up in recharge zones. Contour bunds, earthen embankments, nalla bunds, sub-surface dykes, percolation tanks and other water conservation and harvesting structures were taken up in transition and discharge zones. Agronomic measures like intercropping, intensive cropping, etc., along with pasture development and silvi-pastural activities were taken up on transition and discharge zone. Intensive soil and water conservation treatment work has been completed on 33,430.50 ha.

### *Regeneration of Degraded Forests*

Assisting and ensuring natural regeneration from dormant seeds, coppices and gap planting has been taken up in 2,900 ha of degraded forest areas. Informal groups or village forest committees under Joint Forest Management (JFM) have been protecting these areas for the last two to three years. Approximately 27.12 lakh plants are found to be regenerating in watershed areas through social fencing by WDC. *Tectona grandis* (teak), *Butea monosperma* (*palash*), etc., are major coppicing species. Some teak plants today are 3–4 m high.

### *Community-assisted Water Harvesting Tanks*

A total of 350 community-assisted water harvesting tanks have been constructed. Sites for all these tanks were selected by the villagers themselves. Without any outside support, the villagers have successfully constructed these tanks with local knowledge and wisdom, and contributed 50 per cent of the total costs.

## WFP-ASSISTED TANK PROJECT

A major portion of the land in the district (85 per cent) is hilly and undulating. This kind of topography provides immense possibilities for constructing small tanks and stop dams. Small and medium tanks have proved to be the most effective and appropriate in the limited amount of irrigation (15 per cent) that is being carried out in the district at present. Studies and survey have revealed that approximately Rs. 10 lakh will be sufficient to construct an irrigation tank having a catchment area of nearly 0.2 sq km. The length and height of such a tank are nearly 150 m and 8–10 m respectively, with storage capacity of 3 million cu ft of water, sufficient for protective irrigation of about 35–40 ha. Normally 70 per cent of the total cost of a tank is incurred on labour while the remaining 30 per cent is on material. A total of 83 tanks have been constructed under this project and have helped bringing additional land under irrigation and improving the economic conditions of the population engaged in agriculture. It is estimated that net production from irrigated land would go up to as high as seven times as compared to unirrigated land. Besides this, horticulture, agro-forestry, fisheries and sericulture activities could be undertaken.

## PROJECT IMPLEMENTATON

The cash component was met by the rural development schemes of EAS, ITDP and DPAP; the food grain was contributed by the WFP (2,600 mt wheat). The implementing agencies for the works are Water Resources, Rural Engineering Services, Agriculture and Project Implementing Agencies for Watershed Mission, etc. The labourers are distributed wheat up to 2.5 kg a day at Rs. 4 a kg, only at the work site. People's participation is assigned to the extent of 10 per cent for the purpose of creation of '*gramkosh*'. In watershed areas, people's participation can be achieved up to 30 per cent of the wages. Community Lift Irrigation Schemes are proposed to be set up from *Nistar*-cum-irrigation tanks to increase irrigation facilities. Cases of Self-Help Groups for finance of Lift Irrigation Schemes are proposed to be prepared under the recently-launched Swaranjayanti Gram Swarojgar Yojana (SGSY) scheme.

## FOOD FOR WORK ASSISTANCE BY GOVERNMENT OF INDIA

Going by the success of the food for work project of tanks under WFP, the district administration and the state policies became more inclined towards such ventures. Fortunately, the Government of India also worked on similar lines and provided 10,000 tons of food grains for assistance to combat drought under food for work programmes in the current year to complement existing works under other schemes up to 5 kg of wheat per manday.

A positive feature in the utilization of the food grains has been its association with water conservation, development and recharge works wherein it was supported by a massive and popular public movement and contribution under the state-run *Pani Roko Abhiyan.*

## *PANI ROKO ABHIYAN* WITH FOOD GRAINS OF GOI AND WFP

Water harvesting works are being taken up in the district as a popular movement in order to combat existing drought conditions and also to increase water holding capacity of the district to minimize similar natural crises in the future. The items of works undertaken include micro-tanks; stop dam; dug well construction deepening/desiltation; dugout ponds; dug well and tube well recharge; roof water harvesting; and field bunding. The focus is on people and their contribution towards such efforts, voiced, led and implemented through panchayats under the existing schemes of the government and all other sources of the district, including GOI's food grain, WFP's and UNICEF's contribution.

TABLE 1: FOOD FOR WORK ASSISTANCE UNDER VARIOUS FOOD FOR WORK PROGRAMMES

| Name of project | Food grain received (in mt) | | Remarks |
|---|---|---|---|
| | Wheat | Pulses | |
| Central Assistance for Scarcity Works | 10,000 | 0 | Converged with ongoing Rural Development (RD) schemes, UNICEF assistance and panchayat works for water conservation. |
| WFP–assisted Micro-Dam Project | 2,600 | 0 | Matched with 80 % cash from RD schemes such as EAS, ITDP, DPAP. |
| WFP–assisted Intensive Intervention Project | 1,512 | 296 | Converged with state funds under food security mission. |
| Total | 14,112 | 296 | |

## UNICEF-ASSISTED TANK PROJECT

A project similar to that of WFP's has been taken up under the assistance received by the district through UNICEF to combat drought. The grain component is provided with the grain assistance of GOI 32 micro-tanks are under construction with 25 per cent of labour being provided by local people on their own, free of wage.

The total cost of a tank will consist of a public contribution of 25 per cent and the remaining cost will have cash/food grain components. However, in some works the limit imposed by the revenue department may increase from Rs. 3 lakh per structure to make it more feasible from the livelihood angle. The cash component will be met from the amount provided by UNICEF, and the food grain (4,600 mt wheat plus 80 mt rice) made available free by the central government under Scarcity Works. The implementing agencies assigned for the works are Water Resources, Rural Engineering Services, Agriculture and Project

Implementing Agencies for Watershed Mission, etc. Partial payment of the labour would be done in the form of food grains. The labourers will be distributed 5 kg of wheat or 4 kg rice per day. This distribution of grain will be made only at the work site. The cost of food grains works out to a total of Rs. 23.25 per day for wheat, or Rs. 24 for rice as opted for by the labourer.

People's participation is assigned to an extent of 25 per cent for this purpose, The labourers would be motivated to work without wages. In watershed areas, people's participation can be achieved up to 30 per cent of the wages. Community Lift Irrigation Schemes are proposed to be set up from *Nistar*-cum-irrigation tanks to increase irrigation facilities. Cases of Self-Help Groups for finance of Lift Irrigation Schemes are proposed to be prepared under the SGSY scheme.

## INTENSIVE INTERVENTION PROJECT (IIP) OF WFP: JHABUA PILOT

The IIP was envisaged in the year 2000–1 to augment the livelihood of families living below the poverty line in the 129 most backward, interior and food-insecure villages of the district. Low human development indicators such as low literacy rates (especially of women), low enrolment in schools (especially of girls), high migration, low fertility of soil and low productivity in agriculture due to lack of irrigation facilities have characterized these villages located in the three most southern blocks of the district. The idea was to assist in the uplift of these low indicators by focusing on the various aspects of food insecurity.

### OBJECTIVE OF IIP

1. Improved literacy of the adult population, specifically women.
2. Improved attendance and education of girls in the primary schools.
3. Pre-positioning of commodities to strengthen coping mechanisms for the vulnerable population during periods of sudden shortfall due to disasters.
4. Creation of individual and community assets through food for work activities to enable sustainable livelihood security.
5. Group feeding for vulnerable women and children to prevent malnutrition.

6. Organize and train women groups (especially women from landless families) in income generation activities.
7. To improve the quality of Indiamix at the Meghnagar plant and make it financially feasible. (This WFP–assisted project provides nourishing food to the ICDS centres in Meghnagar block of the district.)
8. To provide sustainable means of agriculture and allied livelihood to identified families living below the poverty line.
9. Integrated efforts for improved implements, seeds, fertilizers, etc.
10. To popularize the drip irrigation method for backyard horticultural practices.
11. To improve irrigation facilities by constructing water conservation structures under various schemes.
12. To motivate the families for improved hygienic practices through flush/dry latrines, smokeless *chulhas*, biogas, nadep, etc.
13. Popularizing alternative energy sources in place of conventional ones.
14. Access to health services/activities like immunization, blindness eradication, leprosy, and family planning programmes for all identified families.

### ACTIVITIES UNDER THE JHABUA PILOT

After several rounds of discussions with the WFP and with the local population, several activities were identified to be undertaken in an integrated manner with an added focus on women and children. The successful implementation of the following identified activities is expected to generate tangible results in the form of individual and/or community assets: (1) improvement in literacy of the population (specifically girls and women); (2) minor watersheds including field bunding and dug wells; (3) grain banks to address sudden shortfall of food; and (4) supplementary nutrition for children 6 months to 6 years old with special focus on those 6 months to 3 years old, and pregnant and lactating women. Besides these specific IIP. activities, the Food Security Mission funded by the state government also has provisions to undertake other activities in same villages. These include: grain bank, improved agriculture implements, bucket drip irrigation sets, nadep pits, toilet construction, biogas construction, water harvesting structures, and solar cooker distribution.

## FOOD FOR LITERACY: INCENTIVE FOR WOMEN IN ADULT EDUCATION

Jhabua district is already pursuing the implementation of an adult education programme. The programme, marked *Parna Barna* (reading, developing) is a village-based programme. A local educated person in the village has the responsibility of teaching the village population. Three comprehensive modules have been developed on the lines of Improved Pace and Contents of Learning (IPCL). The programme is supported by the Rajiv Gandhi Education Mission. On a cursory monitoring of the programme, it was found that while in some places the response is good, there are problems in getting the tribals to attend classes. Specifically, the participation of women was lesser, even in areas where the programme was deemed successful. Various reasons have been attributed for this including the work at home and time spent in fetching water and firewood, taking care of the children, etc., As the proposed villages are food insecure, it was suggested that food would be provided as incentive to the adolescent girls and women in the age group 15–50 to attend these classes. Incentive in the form of food would also be given to the teacher to conduct the classes as there is no other compensation provided to them right now.

The three comprehensive modules enable people to learn the alphabet from words and then move to reading (Hindi) and arithmetic. Issues on health, nutrition, environment, agriculture, plantation, and economic issues such as banking and savings are also covered. The first module contains nine chapters, the second seven and the third nine. After the completion of a few chapters there is an examination and after all the three modules are taught, an examination is conducted and certificates are issued. The teaching, as said above, is conducted by a local educated person, who is currently given Rs. 100 for every person who has attained literacy. It has been suggested that provision of food as an incentive would help to improve attendance and consequently increase the literacy.

### *Implementation*

1. Illiterate women from the identified BPL families attending the *Parna Barna* literacy campaign were selected.
2. These were 5,000 women from 129 villages, who were given 10 kg of food grain on passing each of the three primers.

3. The teachers of *Parna Barna* classes were also given 20 kg of food grain for all the three primers on similar norms.

The case of Udaigarh block shown in Table 2 brings out the importance of intensive intervention to tackle the problem of illiteracy. The villages covered under IIP in the block have been more successful in increasing literacy among women as compared to those in the non-IIP project areas.

*Primary School Feeding (Improved Education for Girls)*

Mid-day meals are being provided in the schools. Even with this provision, it was found that the attendance of the girls was low. The rural literacy rate for rural women (in all blocks) was in single digits. The reduced attendance of the girl child is attributed to traditional reasons, such as looking after the siblings, house work, etc. It was proposed to pilot food incentives for the girls in the primary schools and measure the impact on attendance and literacy. For attracting girl students of the identified BPL families to primary education, 10 kg of food grains is being given, if attendance is above 80 per cent. This is in addition to the existing MDM.

Under this scheme, 5,000 girl students of 129 identified villages (39 girls from each village) have been selected and are being given 10 kg ration per month. The scheme has tended to influence the attendance of girls in schools. The increase recorded in various

TABLE 2: UDAIGARH BLOCK

| IIP Project | | | | Non-IIP Project | | | |
|---|---|---|---|---|---|---|---|
| Name of village | No. of enrolled women | No. of successful women | % | Name of village | No. of enrolled women | No. of successful women | % |
| Thandla | 46 | 43 | 93 | Talawad | 46 | 31 | 67 |
| Umeri | 9 | 5 | 56 | Amabi | 13 | 6 | 46 |
| Pangola | 18 | 17 | 94 | Bawadi Khurd | 17 | 9 | 53 |
| Terka | 20 | 18 | 90 | Kundalwasa | 27 | 13 | 48 |
| Jhiri Chotti | 14 | 14 | 100 | Kandala Raw | 16 | 9 | 56 |
| Jhiri Badi | 27 | 22 | 81 | Pipliya | 25 | 17 | 68 |
| Jamli Badi | 64 | 50 | 78 | Dhamanada | 54 | 21 | 39 |
| Jamli Chotti | 37 | 29 | 78 | Bayada | 39 | 27 | 69 |
| Total | 235 | 198 | 84 | Total | 237 | 133 | 56 |

villages of Udaigar block in the district varies from 14 per cent in Umeri, to 57 per cent in Jamil Chotti, 57 per cent in Pangola, 64 per cent in Thandla, 66 per cent each in Jhiri Chotti and Badi and 77 per cent in Terka and Jamli Badi.

### *Vulnerable Group Feeding: Supplementary Nutrition for Women and Children*

The malnutrition situation in the selected blocks is severe. Even the availability of the basic cereals is below the actual needs of the communities. In many of these villages, there are no vegetables, fruits and milk. Meat, poultry products and fish are also scarce and expensive and people basically survive on maize and lentils. One of the problems in Jhabua is scattered hamlets consisting of 20–30 households and therefore the incapability of the ICDS to reach this population. To cover these hamlets with vulnerable group feeding, it was proposed to ask the *anganwadi* workers to have weekly ration distribution at these hamlets. Growth monitoring and vaccinations is to be provided at the hamlets on a regular basis on one of the distribution days. Convergence with the health department is ensured.

A novel beginning was made of distributing rations to children below 6 years of age and lactating mothers in villages where ICDS services are not available. This has led to a 6 per cent increase in beneficiaries and 7.5 mt ration has been distributed through 120 outlets.

### *Individual and Community Asset Creation: Food for Work Activities*

An important component of the pilot is creation of assets to enable improvement in livelihood security of poor families, specifically women. The topography of Jhabua is a serious constraint to agriculture. With consecutive years of drought and no major watershed schemes, agricultural production has been stagnant. The local population has realized that the answer to the water problem lies in water harvesting through conservation. The district administration, through people's organizations (panchayats) has been working hard to create water harvesting structures: 79 minor tanks have been sanctioned in the district through WFP's assistance. Additionally, field bunds in 129 villages and 645 new dug-wells and 645 deepening of old wells are proposed under this pilot. The construction of these assets is funded through 50 per cent contribution from WFP (thorough food assistance) and 50 per cent contribution from the beneficiary through labour and materials. Food assistance is in the form of 3 kg of wheat and 300 g of pulses for every manday of work. For a 6 m diameter and 10 m deep dug well excavation, the beneficiary will get 1,500 kg wheat and 150 kg pulse in 3 stages. For deepening of 2 m depth, the beneficiary gets 300 kg of wheat and 30 g of pulses.

Drainage line treatment and field bundings on private fields in villages is also being taken up. The valuation of work is done by a committee led by the Chairman of the Food Security Committee along with members like the Gram Prabhari, Sarpanch, POFSM and a representative from the district administration. The field bunding and dug wells are expected to increase the *kharif* crop production by 25 per cent as a result of increased coverage. The *rabi* crop yield, which is currently very low, is expected to increase by at least 50 per cent as a result of the water and moisture. Additionally, availability of vegetables and fruits would increase, thereby resulting in additional nutrition, income and better food security. The dug wells will be a constant source of water supply to the entire village.

Water conservation is very important for plant growth in dry climates and difficult terrain. Anything that helps to get more water into the soil or keeps it there by reducing evaporation provides more water for plant growth. Improved plant growth in turn helps reduce wind erosion as well as water erosion.

### *Linkage with Agroforestry and Horticulture*

The district has a World Bank-assisted nursery of social forestry which specializes in cloning of fast-growing and good-quality agroforestry plants such as eucalyptus, *amla*, bamboo and others. A special project report and action plan has been prepared with a combination of these plants with fast-growing papaya and vegetables such as tomato. The returns on this irrigated agroforestry-horticulture project is up to Rs. 5,000 pm averaged over 4 years per ha. The clonal eucalyptus and bamboo are extremely fast-growing with the former reaching a height of up to 7 m in one year, which makes it advantageous for agroforestry. Moreover, the activity will ensure some drought-proofing because such a project gives returns even in dry years. The beneficiaries of the assets created under IIP are being linked through credit facilities in schemes such as SGSY to take up these activities. Already, about 75 farmers have been identified and are now being linked.

### *Grain Banks*

Grain banks help prepositioning of commodities at required places and lead to an enhanced coping mechanism in times of disasters. There are 368 grain banks that are running in the district, including 129 in these selected villages. In the current pilot, the grain banks are being strengthened with WFP's help. The returns are in the form of commodities. However, if there are no borrowings in a particular year, the grains are consumed by the member families (mandatorily) at the end of the year and returned in kind the following year (without interest). The district administration provides the necessary infrastructure in terms of storage and weighing equipment in each of these villages.

## TRIBAL WOMEN COMMUNITY ENTREPRENEURSHIP: MEGHNAGAR INDIAMIX PLANT

With assistance from WFP, funds generated from the forestry project and from the district administration, a 1.5 mt/day capacity Indiamix plant has been set up in Meghnagar, Jhabua. This plant is run by a cooperative comprising tribal women. The plant became operational in November 1998 and has since been running with few problems. The plant is run by a women's cooperative, the Amrut Mahila Udyog having 75 women who are members of self-help groups formed under the watershed programme. The Indiamix prepared is marketed directly to ICDS centres of Meghnagar block. The plant is running in profit of up to Rs. 3 lakh per year, being divided equally among the equity members.

## CONCLUSION

Jhabua district has been a pioneer in focusing on sustainable development and on human development index through successful initiatives in the sectors of development like lift irrigation schemes, joint forest management and participatory watershed development. These programmes have enriched the poverty-stricken people by altering their socio-economic status. The area of *rabi* crop during the last decade has tripled from about 40,000 ha to more than a lakh and a quarter. The district, from being a net importer, is today self-sufficient in food and fodder production. Over 5,000 self-help groups today are functioning in the remote villages of the district, engaging a cumulative thrift of about Rs. 120 million. Socio-economic growth has also given a fillip to educational and health programmes. The District Primary Education Programme and Total Literacy Campaigns have also made a mark. Jhabua is also a successful model for the implementation of Panchayati Raj and Gram Swaraj in the Scheduled Areas: 612 village bodies (panchayats) and 12 block level Janpad Panchayats under the supervision of the District Panchayat deliver rural development schemes in the remotest villages. Reservation for women has also seen the fairer sex making important local decisions and implementing them. The experience of Jhabua has important lessons for other similar areas in the country.

# 26. Strengthening India's Food Assistance Programmes

*Wolfgang Herbinger*

Despite strong economic growth (approximately 6 per cent per annum in the 1990s) and the achievement of self-sufficiency in cereals at the national level, India is still home to 208 million undernourished people.[1] India alone accounts for a quarter of the chronically food-insecure people in the world. The worst affected are infants, girl children and women, those belonging to the Scheduled Tribes (ST) and Scheduled Castes (SC), landless, marginal and small farmers, agricultural labourers and those whose coping mechanisms are seriously affected by recurring disasters. The presence of chronic hunger means that mothers are more likely to give birth to underweight babies (low birth weight rate of 33 per cent) and children are more susceptible to disease and death (infant mortality rate of 69/1,000, under-5 malnutrition rate of 47 per cent). School age children may not go to school or have a reduced ability to concentrate (primary school net enrolment of 64 per cent for girls and 78 per cent for boys, primary education dropout rate of 40 per cent); and adults may lack the energy for a productive working life (adult chronic energy deficiency of 48.5 per cent).

Since food insecurity is a multidimensional problem that affects different people in different ways, simply focusing on national food supplies is not enough to solve the problem. Food security is not just about growing more food; it is about who can buy that and where the food is available; it is also about who eats what kind of food and when. It encompasses the status of women and girls' education, public health issues like water supply and sanitation, and levels of protection against loss of lives and assets as a result of recurrent disasters.

Although India already has a unique set of national food assistance programmes that seek to tackle food insecurity, there are constraints in their reach to the identified sections and areas. Moreover, these programmes could be strengthened if they were based on a more thorough analysis of food insecurity and its four principal dimensions: food availability, food access, food utilization, and vulnerability to recurrent shocks.

## FOOD AVAILABILITY

At first sight, food availability seems less of a problem in India. Food grain production has grown steadily over the past decades. However, the high growth rate of 3.5 per cent of the 1980s could not be sustained in the 1990s. With 1.8 per cent annual growth, food production was only marginally higher than the population growth rate of 1.7 per cent. Today, India's macro availability dimension of food security is premised on self-sufficiency in wheat and rice, and on net imports of pulses and vegetable oil. However, the current policy of aiming at self-sufficiency in cereal production has its downsides. Government-held food stocks are large, and carrying costs represent a considerable budgetary burden. Twice over the past 10 years, stocks overshot buffer stock norms, first in 1995 by more than 10 million tons, and in 2000 by about 20 million tons of rice and wheat. Many analysts trace the excess stocks to a price regime that, on the one hand, offers floor prices to producers that are too high, and, on the other hand, does not provide enough subsidies for the country's Targeted Public Distribution System (TPDS) to charge affordable prices and improve outreach to the poor.

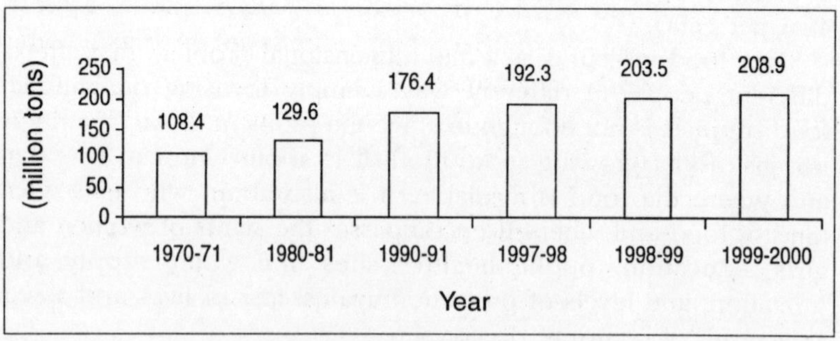


FIG. 1: FOOD GRAIN PRODUCTION IN INDIA.
*Source* : GOI, Ministry of Finance, *Economic Survey, 2001-2001.*

National-level gains in cereal production are not easily translated into adequate food availability for all. Even today's average 2,470 calories per capita available for daily consumption are not sufficient to ensure adequate nutrition for all, taking into account inequalities in income distribution within the country and inequity within households. Moreover, considering the likely demand for food grains in the future, current national-level food surpluses could change back into a cereal import gap.[2]

Food availability is by no means the same in all parts of the country. Food grain production is concentrated in only a few of India's 28 states. Around 70 per cent of the area under crops remains dependent on good rains. Infrastructure constraints, market imperfections and government regulations affect free movement of food across state borders, leading to variation across the states in levels of food intake independently of variations in levels of incomes and prices.[3]

In low potential areas, to keep up food production, fallow cycles are shortened, leading to loss of soil fertility, poor harvests, expansion of the cultivated area on to more and more marginal lands, and an increased dependence on forests for an alternate livelihood. As a result, neighbourhood populations particularly in tribal areas, often rely for subsistence on the forest areas as a source of agricultural land, though it is not sustainable. This development reflects the increasing marginalization of small-scale agriculture. Currently, 31 per cent of rural households fall into the category of near landless families, more than twice as many as three decades ago.

Apart from policies to promote domestic food grain production to maintain self-sufficiency in cereal production, India's basic food security system consists of government-guaranteed minimum farm support prices, public distribution of subsidized food and maintenance of buffer stocks. While this system has resulted in surplus production at the national level, adequate food availability in all deficit and remote regions remains a goal.

## FOOD ACCESS

Even where food is available in the local market, it does not mean that all people have adequate access to it. Food access is determined by people's purchasing power in relation to the price of food. With around one-third of the population below the (calorie based) poverty line, there are hundreds of millions who by definition are not able to procure their minimum food requirements.

Realizing this, the government seeks to integrate production with food distribution systems and link these with employment and income generation programmes. India has probably the most sizeable food assistance programmes in the developing world.[4] All of them aim at improving access to food, and all programmes, except the TPDS, which simply offers a monthly transfer of 20 kg of subsidized cereals to below poverty line families, also aim at improving the longer-term food security of their participants.

Employment and income generation programmes are increasingly being linked to the creation of rural assets such as irrigation and drainage channels, wells and tanks, check dams, bunds and roads. The government also aims at making more use of food payments in employment programmes. However, targetting of the poor and local-level participation in programme delivery remain serious challenges. Poverty reduction has been sluggish in the 1990s, particularly in rural areas. The ST and SC are distinctly poorer than the general population. And importantly, poverty reduction has varied greatly between states.

The Mid-Day Meal Scheme (National Programme for Nutritional Support to Primary Education) seeks to ensure school access and retention for all primary school-age children and improve their nutritional status. The programme provides a daily meal or a monthly take-home ration during the school year and is entirely funded by the Indian government. There is, however, widespread agreement that 'on-site feeding' and not the provision of 'dry rations' would yield the greatest benefits. Moreover, to obtain maximum educational results, the feeding programme should rather be in the form of a mid-morning breakfast than a mid-day meal.

## FOOD UTILIZATION

Most food-insecure people not only have poor access to food, but also suffer from poor food utilization. Utilization of food has three aspects: nutrition practices, intra-household distribution, and physiological absorption. Inadequate food utilization contributes—perhaps more than any other dimension of food insecurity—to the high prevalence of child malnutrition and micronutrient deficiencies among expectant and nursing mothers. Among young children in India (very similar for boys and girls), 47 per cent are underweight, 45 per cent are stunted and 16 per cent are wasted (weight-for-height). Micronutrient deficiencies like anemia affect 88 per cent of pregnant women in India. Also, vitamin A and iodine deficiency are widespread.

India's malnutrition is clearly linked to inappropriate caring and feeding practices, including lack of micronutrient intake. Poor food utilization tends to be correlated with the low level of female literacy and women's status. Not even every second adult woman in India is literate (43 per cent for women compared to 67 for men). Literacy is lowest among tribal women in rural areas (16 per cent).

Gender inequality at birth perpetuates a vicious cycle. Girls are either not 'permitted to be born' or are born with a disadvantage. 18 per cent more girls than boys die before their fifth birthday. In the most vulnerable states of India, 57 per cent girls are married before the age of 18. Undernourished girls who are married early give birth to low birth weight babies, thus perpetuating the problems of malnutrition. Gender discrimination leads to high rates of malnutrition, morbidity and mortality. The poor social status of women may best be expressed in the sex ratio that has hardly improved over the past years (927 women/1,000 men). Persistently low levels of education and ill health, exacerbated by social and structural barriers, severely reduce women's opportunities for escaping poverty.

Poor physiological absorption of food is closely related to access to safe water, sanitation and health facilities. While 81 per cent of the population has access to 'improved water sources', only 16 per cent have access to sanitation.

India's National Nutrition Policy and Action Plan aims at: reducing the incidence of moderate and severe malnutrition and chronic undernutrition among pre-school children by half; reducing the incidence of low birth weight to less than 10 per cent; eliminating blindness due to vitamin A deficiency; and reducing iron deficiency anaemia among pregnant women to 25 per cent. High priority is also accorded to improving reproductive health care services.[5]

Programmes such as the Integrated Child Development Services (ICDS) are central to this effort. The ICDS seeks to provide supplementary food rations, pre-school education and nutrition/health messages and health services. The target groups are children under

6 years and pregnant and nursing women. State governments, Cooperative for Assistance and Relief Everywhere (CARE) and WFP provide the food resources for the programme. It is planned to universalize the ICDS programme to cover the entire country. However, evaluation studies have identified that more attention needs to be given to reaching under-3-year-old children and improving complementary feeding practices if the programme is to make a more significant impact on the nutritional status of young children.

Management of micronutrient deficiencies is another strategy in addressing the food utilization problem. Programmes for the control and elimination of micronutrient malnutrition include popularization of low cost nutritious foods, fortification of food and micronutrient supplementation. Programmes for prevention of Iodine Deficiency Disorders (IDD), anaemia and blindness due to vitamin A deficiency have been initiated by the Department of Health and Family Welfare. The current approaches include provision of oral iron folate prophylactic therapy to all pregnant women and provision of massive doses of vitamin A to children between 1 and 5 years. However, the outreach of the micronutritient supplementation programmes has been reported to be insufficient, ranging in the case of iron-folic acid from as low as 20 per cent in Bihar to 75 per cent in Andhra Pradesh.

## VULNERABILITY TO DISASTERS

Many poor people are very vulnerable to food shocks as a result of a variety of disasters including floods, droughts, cyclones and earthquakes. In the decade of 1988–97, disasters affected an average of 40 million people every year.[6] These disasters can play havoc on household livelihood systems and turn transitory food insecurity into chronic situations of poverty and undernutrition. The severity of natural disasters and the devastating effects are steadily increasing interdependent with environmental degradation. 19 per cent of India's total area, with 12 per cent of its population, is considered drought-prone. Rajasthan, Madhya Pradesh and Gujarat are the most drought prone states while Bihar, Uttar Pradesh, Assam and West Bengal suffer from periodic floods.

The extent of transitory food insecurity can be gauged from the peak annual number of Indians affected by disasters (since 1980): drought, 300 million (1987); floods, 130 million (1993); earthquakes,

20 million (1988); cyclone, 15 million (1999); and landslides, 2.5 million (1986).

Although not emphasized in the five-year plan and not conceptually linked to food insecurity, the Government of India has a long history of mitigating natural disasters and there are several programmes in place. Planned expenditure on these programmes amounts to US$174 million in 2000–1. Major schemes include: the Integrated Wasteland Development Programme, Drought Prone Areas Programme, Desert Development Programme and Flood Management Schemes.

In areas prone to floods, droughts, cyclones and earthquakes, the government routinely prepares contingency plans on a district basis. Responsibility for these plans lies with district administrators who coordinate disaster mitigation and disaster response activities. Disaster contingency plans are updated on an annual basis. However, appropriate integration of development programmes and prevention and preparedness measures in areas prone to recurrent disasters has only most recently become a concern of the government.[7]

So on the one hand, India has made significant progress in food grain production and great strides in reducing food insecurity through a myriad of programmes over the past few decades. On the other hand, far too little headway has been made in reducing the number of undernourished people—in line with the commitment of heads of states at the 1996 World Food Summit to halve the number of hungry people by 2015. Government policies and programmes had limited impact in addressing food insecurity as defined by its four dimensions. There is general agreement among policy makers and agencies working in the area that the effectiveness of food assistance programmes needs improvement. There is a continuing need for food assistance, and the government is in the process of finalizing its approach on this subject. This will enable India to better target the investments needed towards its most food-insecure people.

## MAKING FOOD ASSISTANCE PROGRAMMES MORE EFFECTIVE

Broadly speaking, the current food assistance programmes fail due to weaknesses with respect to a few key issues. Greater attention to these will go a long way in improving the impact of food-based interventions. These are as follows:

## DECENTRALIZED MANAGEMENT

Greater decentralization and participation in planning, implementation and monitoring of food assistance programmes is the single most important factor in improving their effectiveness. While food assistance programmes are well thought out at the central level, where they fail is in the local execution. An informed strategy of decentralized management through clear understanding of the respective roles and limitations of local entities such as panchayat institutions, user groups, NGOs and local administration will be the key to the success of any food assistance programme.

## SYNERGY

The Government of India runs various food assistance programmes. Convergence of these programmes, which address different dimensions of food insecurity at the household level, can maximize the benefits through tapping synergies. This would result in a much larger and better-quality impact on food insecurity than a single programme working by itself. While TPDS can ensure food availability in remote areas and FFW improve food access through creating opportunities for employment, ICDS assists in improving health and nutrition status of mothers and children. Additionally, greater complementarity of food and non-food resources can be expected to ensure food security for the maximum number of households.

## BETTER TARGETING

Targeted food is a fast track to the poor. It requires understanding food insecurity at both national and local levels; responding with appropriate activities to reach the right people at the right times; developing clear programme objectives as well as sound activity design and monitoring. Insufficient targeting by many of the government food assistance programmes has made them fail in significantly reducing food insecurity. Reaching the right people depends on identifying who they are, where they live, and when and why they are food insecure. WFP's Vulnerability Analysis and Mapping (VAM) was put in place to help improve effectiveness of programmes by accurately identifying food-insecure areas and hungry populations, and targeting them for food assistance.

## WOMEN AS KEY AGENTS OF CHANGE

Hunger and poverty affect women disproportionately. Thus, strengthening opportunities and options for women is the key to the solution of the problems of hunger and poverty. An explicit focus on women as key agents of change is essential to any worthwhile strategy of food assistance. While empowerment is an end in itself, it also improves household food security and nutritional status of future generations. Women's educational level, nutritional status and their control over food resources and assets are interlinked determinants of household food security. Educated women tend to follow better childcare and nutrition practices, use health services more frequently, have a higher share in family and community decision making, and are more likely to send girls to school. In addition, women's own nutritional status largely determines the physical and mental potential of the next generation.

## IMPROVED DISASTER RESPONSIVENESS

Tens of millions of Indians are affected by recurrent disasters every year: they are victims of transitory food insecurity. Food assistance is most essential and immediately required where it mitigates disaster-induced food shortages. Vulnerability to recurrent disasters should be a prominent indicator in any food security analysis and choice of target areas. Responding to the food needs of disaster-affected people helps to preserve their assets, and is thus an integral component of any development strategy for these groups. Disaster responsiveness as part of development food assistance interventions involves knowing when to respond (early warning, trigger points) and how to respond (what food rations, which procedures, how to coordinate).

## GREATER ATTENTION TO DEVELOPMENT OUTCOMES

Today, the key challenge is to enable undernourished and vulnerable people to become food-secure in a sustainable way. For the food assistance programmes to reach beyond providing temporary support, they must also try to enable development. Food aid should work as an enabler, a pre-investment, which can free people to take up development opportunities, to increase human capital or acquire assets. Food should be used to give poor people scope for their ingenuity and efforts, leveraging their access to the benefits of development.

## WFP'S NEW COUNTRY STRATEGY IN INDIA

WFP is currently testing these directions to improve effectiveness of food aid interventions in three Intensive Intervention Projects (IIP) pilot districts. The interventions in Koraput (Orissa), Jhabua (Madhya Pradesh) and Banswara (Rajasthan) represent a first step towards a new country strategy that aims at *promoting immediate and longer-term food security in the most food-insecure districts in the least developed states of India* by playing *a catalytic role in strengthening ongoing food assistance programmes and leveraging policies and resources for the hungry poor.*

Development assistance from international and bilateral donors does not amount to more than 1.5 per cent of India's annual development budget. The WFP's food aid to India amounts to 80,000 mt per annum against a national food grain production of more than 200 million mt. Given this, the agencies such as WFP should ensure that expenditure made by them has a positive demonstrative effect through facilitating of learning from best practices, new ideas and policy advocacy so that the development expenditure made by national authorities is well spent. *Multilateral food aid should*, therefore, *be seen in terms of its contribution towards providing a critical momentum and direction rather than a critical mass in the fight against hunger and poverty.*

For WFP, this means concentrating on the development of innovative models that better reach the most vulnerable groups and enable them to participate in the development process. New approaches will be tried and monitored and the results integrated into wider programming. Two conditions need to be fulfilled if successful strategies are to be replicated by the government and aid partners:

### PARTNERSHIP IN ANALYSIS, DESIGN AND IMPLEMENTATION

Identification of hotspots of food insecurity and of priority groups for food assistance as well as design of innovative food interventions will require partnership between the government and aid agencies. Thus, consistency with national strategies and objectives, and support from national authorities are prerequisites to effectiveness of any WFP endeavour. Using food aid to bring poor households to development opportunities means working in partnerships. The WFP's assistance should be viewed as a support for the efforts of a government committed to tackling hunger.

### DEMONSTRATING RESULTS

Novel institutional models of enabling food interventions will only have a chance of being replicated if their effectiveness is demonstrated. For WFP this means: first, introduction of the concept of Results-Based Management in all food interventions, not only to improve management effectiveness, but also to enable measurement of progress against set objectives; and second, systematic dissemination of lessons learned from design and implementation and advocacy of results to inform national food assistance interventions and policies.

Areas for WFP interventions will be selected on the basis of their concentration of food insecure people, i.e. food aid will be targeted at those people for whom food consumption is a problem. Selection criteria will include: under-5 malnutrition, level of food production, Dietary Energy Supply (DES), poverty, gender bias (e.g. literacy gaps), micronutrient deficiency (e.g. anaemia rates), frequency and magnitude of recurrent shocks (e.g. natural disasters), and, importantly, capacity to implement and monitor food assistance interventions. Local-level assessments of people's food security needs will determine the activities and direction of the future country programmes.

The WFP's VAM exercise shows that there are several categories of food-insecure people who live in a given geographical area. While it would be inappropriate to simply add up these often overlapping categories, it becomes apparent that food insecurity has multiple dimensions that requires a multi-pronged response. Based on the VAM exercise and the vulnerability profile, WFP's future strategy will focus on the following three strategic areas for food intervention.

### SUPPLEMENTARY FEEDING

For Improving the nutritional status of children and women, the ICDS scheme has proved to be a unique tool to reach women and children suffering from malnutrition. The WFP will continue to provide nutritious supplementary food rations to vulnerable women and children. It will also strongly promote the regular provision of complementary inputs (such as training and the delivery of health and nutrition services) that are required to bring behavioural changes. Special attention will be given to reaching children below 3 years and children and mothers in far-off hamlets. The WFP will continue to tackle the issue of micronutrient deficiencies by promoting the use of fortified food and by supporting sustainable initiatives to enhance the local production of enriched food. Community participation and strengthened partnerships with concerned government departments, UN agencies and NGOs will be key programmatic features. Partnerships created with NGOs in the past have resulted in significant improvements in the quality of ICDS services.

### FOOD FOR EDUCATION

For investing in human capital with special emphasis on girls in order to support children's enrolment and retention in schools, WFP will use a variety of food-based approaches. A mid-morning snack initiative will aim at providing a model for the improvement of the existing national Mid-Day Meal Scheme. Combined with the provision of appropriate micronutrient fortified food (for example Indiamix) and school health activities (such as deworming), the mid-morning snack should result in improved learning ability among children (both girls and boys). A take-home ration scheme (exclusively for girls) will enable food-insecure families for which girls' labour is an essential household coping strategy to send their girls to school. The WFP would also consider providing technical support to strengthen government capacity to plan and implement school feeding activities. The future Country Programme will also provide food support to non-formal education for women. This component would normally be linked with income-generating projects promoted by NGOs and government departments.

### FOOD FOR WORK

For improving food security through creation and preservation of assets, WFP will assist the poor and vulnerable households to gain access to food through food for work. The activities undertaken will provide employment for 90 to 120 days, specially during the time when households require food incomes the most, thus saving them from the stress of unemployment and migration. All activities will be identified and executed after a thorough community needs assessment. It is expected that the assets created with people's participation will assist in strengthening their livelihoods and enhancing their ability to cope with recurrent shocks and crises. The WFP recognizes that the creation of assets alone will not ensure longer-term food security, and hence will place greater importance on strengthening people's ability to maintain and preserve the assets created.

Activities that will be considered under food for work interventions include: irrigation structures to increase food production; water harvesting and grain banks to decrease the impact of droughts; and, eco-restoration to stabilize yields and mitigate floods and droughts. To ensure that women equally benefit from WFP-supported activities, special emphasis will be on changing unequal power relations. Several steps, of which WFP can only take initial ones, are required to achieve this longer-term goal. This will involve: ensuring equal access to food for work employment and control over assets created; promoting greater participation in management and decision making (at least one-third of community group members must be female); and special training and support in attaining functional literacy.

A primary objective of WFP interventions will be to build capacity for communities and households to effectively respond to environmental and natural disasters. The WFP's development assistance in these areas will focus on activities that reduce the vulnerability of poor families, enhance the preparedness to cope with disasters, and support speedy recovery measures after a disaster has struck. The WFP will use district disaster contingency plans as the entry point for its emergency preparedness and response arrangements. This will be the basis for pre-designed plans for scaling up of food for work and vulnerable group feeding activities. Additionally, women group-run grain banks will be encouraged and strengthened to be able to help people through crises.

## CONCLUSION

Although international food aid is small in quantity, there is a role for food aid agencies to play in improving food security by adding to the quality of national programmes. India has a large domestic food grain production and also numerous food assistance programmes. But the national food assistance programmes often do not reach the vulnerable sections of the population, and are not very effective in the most food-insecure areas. In such a scenario, multilateral food aid can play a catalysing role as it has more freedom to adapt its programmes over time than the government. Hence, an important task of food aid would be in piloting new food assistance approaches that are feasible for the national government to scale up. Results from piloting will help develop models of enabling food aid interventions, which will further serve as the basis for advocating for the hungry poor and strengthening the ongoing and new programmes. By demonstrating successful food assistance models, WFP aims to leverage policies and resources for the hungry poor.

## NOTES

* This paper draws heavily on the WFP Country Strategy Outline for India (WFP/EB/May 2001) and a draft paper prepared by Ms Archna Kaushal and Shalini Kala, WFP Consultants.

1. FAO, 2000, *The State of Food Insecurity in the World*, Rome.
2. International Food Policy Research Institute, 1999, *Prospects for India's Cereal Supply and Demand to 2020*, Washington, DC.
3. N. Krishnaji, T.N. Krishnan, 2000, *Public Support for Food Security: Strategies for Human Development in India*, vol. 1, New Delhi.
4. See Annexure.
5. Department of Women and Child Development, 1995, *National Plan of Action on Nutrition*, New Delhi.
6. Centre for Research on the Epidemiology of Disasters database, 2000.
7. Keynote address of K.C. Pant at IGNOU, 'National Workshop on Livelihood Options for Disasters Risk Reduction', New Delhi, 23–4 March 2001.

ANNEXURE 1: MAJOR FOOD ASSISTANCE PROGRAMMES IN INDIA*

| Name of programme | Cost per year (in million US$) | Food per year (1000 tons) by commodity | Target population | Targeted per year | Funding agency |
|---|---|---|---|---|---|
| Trageted Public Distribution System (TPDS) | 900 | 6,000 rice and wheat | People below poverty line | 60 million households | Ministry of Food |
| Integrated Child Development Services (ICDS) | 176 | 550 cereals (GOI), 54 blended food (WFP) 141 blended food and oil (CARE) 1,797 cereals | Pregnant and lactating mothers, children 6–60 months | 23.5 million people | Ministry of Human Resource Development, CARE, WFP |
| Mid-Day Meal Scheme | 246 | | Primary school-age children | 97.5 million students | Ministry of Human Resource Development |
| Forestry activities in tribal areas | N/A | 30 wheat and pulses | Vulnerable and tribal castes | 1.2 million people | WFP/ Ministry of Agriculture |
| Jawahar Rozgar Yojana (village asset creation scheme) and Employment Assurance Scheme | 1,232 | N/A | Unemployed below poverty line in rural areas | 326 million workdays | Ministry of Rural Development |

*Note*: * World Food Programme, 2001a, 'Enabling Development: Food Assistance in South Asia', New Delhi.

APPENDIX

# Ten Point Agenda for Action during the Tenth Five Year Plan Period (2002–2007)

## Adopted at the Closing Session of the Consultation on 26 April 2001

The participants in this consultation on 'Towards a Hunger Free India' convened jointly by the Planning Commission of the Government of India, the M.S. Swaminathan Research Foundation of India, and the United Nations World Food Programme, firmly believe that hunger is the worst form of human deprivation and that there is now no technological, social or economic justification for its widespread persistence. Targeting our resources at the most under-privileged is hence an absolute imperative. We will be able to partly judge the success of the Consultation's long term achievement in the light of two key dates: the number of Indians who remain undernourished in 2007, which is the 60th anniversary of India's Independence and also the final year of the 10th Five Year Plan; and 2015, the target date set by the Rome World Food Summit for reducing the number of children, women and men going to bed hungry by 50 per cent. Both the Government of India and the respective ministries and organizations we represent, hereby pledge ourselves to work towards a significant reduction in the number of hungry in India by these dates.

We, would like to reaffirm the definition of food security accepted by the Heads of States who attended the World Food Summit in Rome in 1996: 'food security exists when all people, at all times, have physical and economic access to sufficient, safe and nutritious food to meet their dietary needs and food preferences for an active and healthy life'. In the light of this

*The Planning Commission was not party to this Agenda since that required the approval of the full Planning Commission/National Development Council.

definition, we would like to reiterate the right of everyone to have access to safe and nutritious food, clean drinking water, primary health care and education.

The question of hunger needs to be viewed in a framework of food insecurity which covers the following dimensions; (a) Availability of food, which is a function of home production and net imports, (b) Access to food, which is a function of purchasing power, sustainable livelihoods and employment opportunities, (c) Absorption and Utilization of food, which is a function of access to clean drinking water, environmental hygiene and primary health care and nutrition practices, (d) Vulnerability, which covers external factors affecting food security, viz., natural and human-made disasters, and (e) Sustainability, which involves attention to the conservation and enhancement of natural resources like land, water, forests and biodiversity.

After a detailed debate and analysis of the above dimensions of hunger and food insecurity, we affirm that the real challenge is not only one of achieving self-sufficiency in the production of food grains, but also of reducing disparities in regional food availability and making use of production potentials in an environmentally sustainable manner. Creating employment opportunities and promoting sustainable livelihoods are critical for ensuring that the poorest gain access to food. Better health care facilities, access to safe drinking water and sufficient micronutrient intake will ensure that food is properly absorbed. Ending gender discrimination, and in particular, increasing female literacy are crucial for improving childcare and nutrition practices. In areas prone to disaster, development must be safeguarded through investments in disaster mitigation.

Our strong belief is that to have an effective programme, we need to first understand the region and culture specific problems at the grass roots level of a village, a community and individuals within a household. We call upon policy planners and administrators to develop a set of policies and programmes and to achieve convergence and synergy among existing programmes, so as to ensure sustainable food security at the national level and the elimination of household level poverty-induced chronic hunger by the year 2007.

We have identified the following ten action points, which could be initiated at various levels as integrated components of a 'Freedom from Hunger Movement'.

## 1. IDENTIFICATION OF THE VULNERABLE INDIVIDUALS

The first step is to identify families and individuals suffering from endemic hunger and malnutrition. This is best done by the Gram Sabha. Usually, such families/individuals tend to have limited or no access to productive assets like land, cattle, fishponds and education. They often live by daily unskilled wage work. The methodology of the *Food Insecurity Atlas of Rural India* is a tool that can help in identifying the hotspots of hunger.

## 2. INFORMATION EMPOWERMENT

Families/individuals identified as vulnerable to endemic hunger can be given Household Entitlement Cards which give information on all government projects (both Central and State Government) relating to poverty and hunger elimination, to which they are entitled. The various government projects should be dis-aggregated by gender, age, class and caste and precise information provided on methods of accessing the benefits to which people are entitled. Land ownership records should be periodically updated and made available to all concerned. Such steps will enable all eligible persons to derive benefit from their entitlements, for which provisions exist in the budget of the Central and State Governments. Also the Panchayats/local bodies should be empowered legally, administratively and financially to assume the responsibilities assigned to them under Schedule 11 of Constitution Amendment 73.

## 3. ELIMINATING PROTEIN CALORIE MALNUTRITION AND ENERGY DEPRIVATION

Existing projects like the targeted Public Distribution System and nutrition programmes (e.g. Integrated Child Development Services, Mid-Day Meals and *Antyodaya Anna Yojana*) will have to be mobilized to ensure that they reach those who have so far been bypassed by such schemes. The PDS should include the distribution of nutritious cereals like *jowar*, *bajra*, *ragi* and millets because they have a low-cost and high caloric/protein/micronutrient advantage. Knowledge on childcare and health care practices as well as support services should be targeted to pregnant and nursing mothers, so as to ensure effective protein-calorie nutrition of young children. ICDS should encourage increased involvement of women in the management of feeding programmes. Greater attention is needed to appropriate supplementary nutrition for children in the 0–2 age group, the most critical period in terms of brain and body growth, and also the most neglected in ICDS, and the group with the highest established levels of malnutrition. This will ensure better health and nutrition of both the infants and mothers. Reaching the un-reached and giving operational content to Gandhiji's concept of *Antyodaya* are major challenges.

Food assistance agencies should accord priority to cost-efficiency and programme-effectiveness. The large surplus food reserves available with Government provide unique and uncommon opportunities for establishing a national grid of Community Grain Banks. Such Banks administrated by local self-help groups could become the vehicle for administering food for work, *Antyodaya Anna Yojana*, targeted public distribution system and all such schemes designed to assist the vulnerable sections of the population.

## 4. ELIMINATING HIDDEN HUNGER GAUSED BY MICRONUTRIENT DEFICIENCIES

A multi-pronged strategy consisting of direct interventions like the fortification of food, the administration of oral doses of vitamin A, iron and iodine fortified salt, as well as the promotion of the cultivation of vegetables and trees like *amla* in the small areas surrounding huts/homes (home garden), can be introduced in every village. 'India-mix', which is fortified with essential vitamins and distributed through ICDS centres in selected States, should be extended to all States and Union Territories. The highest priority should go to the elimination of hidden hunger as soon as possible since this is an easily achievable task. The programmes can be designed on a campaign mode as in the case of vaccination for important diseases.

## 5. SAFE DRINKING WATER AND ENVIRONMENTAL HYGIENE

Environmental hygiene can be improved through cooperation among local communities. Every village and town should have a plan for the treatment and recycling of solid and liquid wastes.

Waste recycling could also become a remunerative enterprise and self-help groups can be trained to take up such environment enhancing enterprises. Clean drinking water is necessary to ensure the efficient biological absorption and digestion of food in the body. In addition, the consumption of boiled water should be encouraged and facilitated. This one step could help in reducing infant and child mortality rates significantly.

## 6. ENHANCING PURCHASING POWER THROUGH SUSTAINABLE LIVELIHOODS

There is need for synergy among the farm and non-farm employment programmes in different agro-climatic zones. Efforts should include the corporate and business sectors in contract farming and buy-back arrangements of the farm products. This will increase employment opportunities in the rural areas. Productivity enhancement and market development need priority attention. Livestock and agro-forestry are important to livelihood security in semi-arid and arid areas. Appropriate infrastructure for perishable commodities including livestock and poultry products as well as fruits, vegetables and flowers should be developed as soon as possible. The Rural Infrastructure Development Fund needs to be harnessed for this purpose. Every individual should be able to earn his/her daily bread through economically and ecologically viable means of self-employment. To this end, the organisation of an innovative National Programme for Sustainable Livelihood Security with provisions for both skilled and unskilled work and for value-added on-farm and non-farm employment should be considered for inclusion in the Tenth Five Year Plan. Assistance under such a programme can take the form of food, cash and infrastructure.

## 7. SPECIAL ATTENTION TO WOMEN AND CHILDREN

While all the above programmes should accord equal attention to men, women and children, special steps are essential to attend to the needs of pregnant and nursing mothers and pre-school children. There are several national and State schemes intended to help adolescent girls, pregnant and nursing women. They can be listed in the Household Entitlement Cards, to ensure that the coverage of such projects includes the excluded. Education, social mobilization and regulation are essential for overall empowerment of women including prevention of female foeticide and infanticide. The highest priority in Panchayat (elected local bodies) level monitoring should go to both the incidence of Low Birth Weight (LBW) children and the male-female sex ratio. The serious consequences of LBW in relation to brain development and subsequent health should become widely known. Sex ratio is an important indicator of the status of women in the society. Women's role as nutritional caretakers as well as their work outside the house have to be equally acknowledged. Their educational level, nutritional status and control over food resources and assets are all determinants of household food security. Thus strengthening opportunities and options for women and making them key players is the first step to alleviate hunger.

## 8. STRENGTHENING FOOD BASED SAFETY NETS

There is an immediate need to strengthen food-based safety nets in a manner that food assistance plays an important role in ensuring minimum nutritional intake for the most undernourished people. ICDS and the Mid-Day Meal Programme are very relevant examples. The focus of food assistance should shift from merely appeasing hunger in the short term towards enabling development of human faculties. Programmes such as FFW (Food for Work) should use food consumption to encourage investment and leave behind a lasting asset which will continue to help the community, household or individual into the future. With respect to natural resource management and disaster mitigation, FFW can be used to promote sustainable livelihoods for the food insecure.

This requires action by concerned Ministries, Government and Non-Government Organizations, in a variety of sectors, integrated under a coherent policy framework for food assistance. Action with respect to geographic and gender targeting as well as to age and social status together with refocusing on specific nutritional gaps, will lead to greater and more speedy impact. Drawing from the best experience available, there is an urgent need to develop more effective mechanisms for the delivery of food assistance programmes.

## 9. LINKING DISASTER MITIGATION WITH DEVELOPMENT

Both at the national and global level there is an immediate need to link disaster mitigation with development. Without disaster preparedness, development itself is at risk. Increased attention is needed to find ways of mitigating the effects of natural disasters so that a single calamity does not push some people over the edge. An example of a mitigation activity is local level grain and water banks, which provide assistance at both the community and household level. Food assistance is a powerful tool in tackling hunger at times of natural disasters: the challenge is to ensure that distributions are in accord with the demands of development, while at the same time safe-guarding the most vulnerable sections of society.

Where appropriate, additional food assistance should be targeted to disaster-prone areas that are home to many food insecure people. It should strengthen the ability of these households to cope better with short term shocks. Food assistance should combine with other investments under the umbrella of a broad food security strategy.

## 10. GREATER MARKET ACCESS TO FARM PRODUCTS

Industrialized countries must provide greater market access to the farm products of developing countries. If trade and not aid is to become the pathway for poverty reduction, trade should become not only free but also fair. At the same time, greater attention and investment will be needed to strengthen our efforts in the areas of ecotechnology, post-harvest technology, sanitary and phytosanitary measures and adherence to FAO *Codex Alimentarius* standards. Emphasis on food quality and safety is vital not only for attracting and retaining global markets, but even more importantly to protect the health of the poor. In addition, restrictions on farmers selling their products anywhere in the country should be removed. If foreign farmers could enjoy the privilege of removal of quantitative restrictions on exports to India, Indian farmers should enjoy the same privilege not only abroad but also within the country.

In conclusion, we are of this firm view that given an appropriate blend of political will and action, professional skill and people's participation, India can make substantial progress in realizing Mahatma Gandhi's vision of a hunger free nation by 15 August 2007. There could be no better way of commemorating the 60th anniversary of India's Independence.

# Glossary

*Achar*: Pickle

*Amla*: Gooseberry

*Anganwadis*: Community Based Pre-school in India

*Antyodaya Anna Yojana*: Food Scheme for Upliftment of the Poorest

*Bajra*: Millet

*Dal*: Pulses

Dalit : The Downtrodden of the Lower Caste

*Gud*: Jaggery

*Jati*: Caste

*Kaal Baisakhi*: Thunder Squalls

*Kendu Leaf*: Beedi Leaf

*Kharif*: Cropping Season (October-March)

*Kultha*: A Pulse Variety

*Licence Raj*: Permit System

*Mahua*: Variant of Country Liquor

*Mamlatdar*: Deputy Collector

*Nistar*: Irrigation Tank

*Pani Roko Abhiyan*: Water Harvesting Movement

*Panjrapol* : An Institution Dedicated to the Preservation of Animal Life

*Parna Barna*: Reading, Developing

*Pukka*: Concrete Structure

*Rabi*: Cropping Season (April-September)

*Sal* Leaf : Leaf of Teak Tree

*Samvat*: Hindu Calendar

*Talati*: Lower Level Revenue Official

*Udisha*: National ICDS Training

# Bibliography


Acharya, S.S., 1999, 'Food Security and New International Trade Agreement Perspectives from India', Paper for ICSSR-MSH Joint Seminar under India-France Cultural Exchange Programme, Paris.

———, 2000, 'Socio-Economic Impact of 1987 Drought in Rajasthan', Udaipur: Department of Agricultural Economics, Rajasthan Agricultural University.

———, 2000, 'Terms of Trade for Agricultural Sector in India at the State Level', Jaipur: Institute of Development Studies, Mimeo.

Adair, L.S. and B.M. Popkin, 1996, 'Low Birth Weight Reduces Likelihood of Breast-feeding among Filipino Infants', *Journal of Nutrition*, 126 (January): 103–11.

Adair, L.S., B.M. Popkin and D.K. Guilkey, 1993, 'The Duration of Breastfeeding: How is it Affected by Sociodemographic, Health Sector, and Food Industry Factors?', *Demography*, 30 (1): 63–80.

Aggarwal, A., S. Arora and A.K. Patwari, 1998, 'Breastfeeding among Urban of Low Socio-economic Status: Factors Influencing Introduction of Supplemental Feeds before Four Months of Age', *Indian Pediatrics*, 35: 269–73.

Agragamee, 1991, 'Baseline Socio-economic Study and Preparation of Action Plan of Rehabilitation and Re-settlement for Upper Indravati Project, Koraput', Kasipur, Koraput, Orissa.

Ahluwalia, D., 1993, 'Public Distribution of Food in India: Coverage, Targeting and Leakages', *Food Policy*, vol. 18, no. 1 (February): 33–54.

Ahluwalia, Montek, 1978, 'Rural Poverty in India', in Ahluwalia et al., *India: Occasional Papers*, World Bank Staff Paper No. 279.

Aldington, T.J., 1999, 'Food Security and the WTO Trade Negotiations: Key Issues Raised by the World Food Summit', in FAO, 1999.

Alyward, G.P., S.I. Pfeiffer, A. Wright and S.J. Verhulst, 1989, 'Outcome Studies of Low Birth Weight Infants Published in the Last Decade: A Meta-analysis', *Journal of Pediatrics*, 115: 515–20.

Amsden, Alice, 1988, 'Taiwan's Economic History: A Case of Etatisme and a Challenge to Dependency Theory', in Robert H. Bates, ed., *Toward a Political Economy of Development—A Rational Choice Perspective*, Berkeley: University of California Press, Ch. 4, pp. 141–75.

———, 1989, *Asia's Next Giant—South Korea and Late Industrialization*, New York and Oxford: OUP.

Asthana, M.D., 2000, 'Rationale for Recent Changes in Foodgrains Distribution under the Targeted Public Distribution System', Paper Presented at a Seminar on 'Food Security in India: The Emerging Challenges in the Context of Economic Liberalization', held at the Centre for Economic and Social Studies (CESS), Hyderabad, 25–7 March.

Atkin, Michael, 1993, *Snouts in the Trough: European Farmers, the Common Agricultural Policy and the Public Purse*, Cambridge: Woodhead Publishing.

———, 1995, *The International Grain Trade*, 2nd edn., Cambridge: Woodhead Publishing.

Australian Bureau of Agricultural and Natural Resource Economics (ABARE), 2000, 'The Impact of Agricultural Trade Liberalisation on Developing Countries'.

Aykroyd, W.R. and B.G. Krishan, 1937, *Ind. J. Med. Res.*, 24: 1993, 1937, ———, 1938, *Lancet*, 11: 153.

Banerjee, N., 1992, 'Poverty, Work and Gender in Urban India', Occasional Paper No. 133, Calcutta: Centre for Studies in Social Sciences.

Barraclough, Solon and Andrea Finger-Stitch, 1966, *Some Ecological and Social Implications of Commercial Shrimp Farming in Asia*, Geneva: United Nations Research Institute for Social Development.

Barratt Brown, Michael and Pauline Tiffen, 1994, *Short Changed: Africa and World Trade*, London and Boulder, Pluto Press, with Transnational Institute.

Baumwell, L., C.S. Tamis-LeMonda and M.H. Bornstein, 1997, 'Maternal Verbal Sensitivity and Child Language Comprehension', *Infant Behavior and Development*, 20 (2): 247–58.

Bentley, M.B., P.E. Engle, L. Caulfield, H. Creed and M. Penny, 1999, 'Caregiver Style of Infant Feeding as a Determinant of Dietary Intake: The Need for Promotion of "interactive feeding"', *Federation of American Societies for Experimental Biology (FASEB) Journal.*

Bentley, M.E., M.M. Black and E. Hurtado, 1995, 'Child-feeding and Appetite: What can Programmes Do?', *Food and Nutrition Bulletin*, 16 (4): 340–9.

Bentley, M.E., R.Y. Stallings, M. Fukumoto and J.A. Elder, 1991, 'Maternal Feeding Behaviour and Child Acceptance of Food During Diarrhoea, Convalescence, and Health in the Central Sierra of Peru', *American Journal of Public Health*, 81: 43–7.

Bhalla, G.S. and Peter Hazell, 1998, 'Foodgrains Demand in India to 2020: A Preliminary Exercise', *Economic and Political Weekly* (*EPW*), 32 (52), December.

Bhalla, G.S. and G. Singh, 2001, *Indian Agriculture—Four Decades of Development*, New Delhi: Sage.

Bhalla, G.S., Peter Hazell and John Kerr, 2000, 'Prospects for India's Cereal

Supply and Demand 2020', National Seminar on 'Food Security in India: The Emerging Challenges in the Context of Economic Liberalization', Hyderabad: CESS.

Bhargava, Pradeep, 1995, 'Rajasthan', Jaipur: Institute of Development Studies, Mimeo.

Bhatt, Ela, 2001, 'Reconstructing Gujarat', *The Hindu*, 10 February.

Bhutta, Z.A., 2001, Editorial: 'Beyond the Millennium: What Can be Done to Improve Child Health in South Asia?', *Indian Pediatrics*, 38, 17 February.

Binswanger, H.S.R. Khandker and M. Rosenzweig, 1993, 'How Infrastructure and Financial Insituations Affect Agricultural Output and Investment in India', *Journal of Development Economics*, 41 (2): 337–66.

Birch, L.L. and J.A. Fisher, 1995, 'Appetite and Eating Behavior in Children', *Pediatric Clinician of North America*, 42 (4): 931–53.

Birch, L.L., 1998, 'Psychological Influences on the Childhood Diet', *Journal of Nutrition*, 128 (2 suppl): 407S–10S.

Birthal, P.S., 2000, 'Technological Change in India's Livestock Sector and its Impact', in the Eighth Annual Conference, on 'Livestock in Different Farming Systems' held at TNVASU, Chennai, on 28–9 December, Chennai: Agricultural Economics Research Association (India).

Birthal, P.S., Anjani Kumar, A. Ravishankar and U.K. Pandey, 1999, 'Sources of Growth in India's Livestock Sector', Policy Paper 9, New Delhi: NCAP.

Black, M.M., J.J. Hutchinson, J. Dubowitz, R.H. Starr and J. Berenson-Howard, 1996, 'The Roots of Competence: Mother-Child Interaction among Low Income Urban African-American Families', *Journal of Applied Developmental Psychology*, 17: 367–91.

Brautigam, Deborah, 1995, 'The State as Agent: Industrial Development in Taiwan, 1952–72', in Howard Stein, ed., *Asian Industrialisation and Africa—Studies in Policy Alternatives to Structural Adjustment*, St Martins Press, Ch. 5, pp. 145–81.

Brown, K.H., K.L. Dickin, M.E. Bentley, G.A. Oni, V.T. Obassaju, S.A. Esrey, S. Mebrahtu, I. Alade and R.Y. Stallings, 1988, in D. Alnwick, S. Moses, and O.G. Schmidt, eds., *Improving Young Child Feeding in Eastern and Southern Africa Household-level Food Technology*, Proceedings of a workshop held in Nairobi, Kenya, 12 October 1987, Ottawa, Canada: IDRC.

Brundtland, Gro Harlem, 1993, *Population, Environment and Development*, New York: UNFPA.

Burmeister, Larry L., 2000, 'Dismantling Statist East Asian Agriculture? Global Pressures and Responses', *World Development*, vol. 28, no. 3.

Caulfield, L.E., S.L. Huffman and E.G. Piwoz, 1999, 'Interventions to Improve the Complementary Food Intakes of 6–12 Month Old Infants in Developing Countries: Impact on Growth, Prevalence of Malnutrition and Potential Contribution to Child Survival, *Food and Nutrition Bulletin*, 20: 183–200.

Census of India, 2001, *Provisional Population Totals*, Paper 1 of 2001 Series 1, Registrar General and Census Commissioner, India.

Centre for Environment Education, 2001, 'An Attempt Toward Rehabilitation', *Astha*, vol. 1, March.

Centre for Monitoring Indian Economy, 2001, *Monthly Review of the Gujarat Economy*, Regional Monitoring Service, March.

Centre for Research on the Epidemiology of Disasters (CRED) Database, 2000.

CEPT, 2001, 'Rehabilitation of Earthquake Affected Villages in Kachchh: Some Ideas', Prepared by CEPT Students, Ahmedabad.

Chambers, R. and G. Conway, 1992, 'Sustainable Rural Development: Practical Concepts for the 21st Century', IDS Discussion Paper No. 296, Sussex: Institute of Development Studies.

CHETNA, 2001, 'Rebuilding Lives of Women and Children in Earthquake Affected Areas—CHETNA's Plans and Efforts'.

Chirmulay, D., I.P. Bhagwat, 1997, 'Factors Influencing Nutritional Status of Preschool Children from Selected Areas in Five States of India', Pune: BAIF Development Research Foundation, India, Report No. IHPP/1.

Chopra, Kodekodi and Murty, 1990, 'Participatory Development: People and Common Property Resources: Studies in Economic Development and Planning', New Delhi: Institute of Economic Growth, Mimeo.

Commission on the Nutrition Challenge of the 21st Century, 2000, 'Ending Malnutrition by 2020: An Agenda for Change in the Millennium', Final Report Submitted to the ACC/SCN Sub-Committee on Nutrition.

Confederation of Indian Industries, 2001, 'The Earth Shrugged: Now You Shouldn't—Rehabilitation and Reconstruction of Quake-hit Gujarat'.

Corbett, J.E.M., 1988, 'Famine and Household Coping Strategies', *World Development*, vol. 16, no. 9: 1099–1113.

Daly, Gerald and Deepayan Bhattacharya, 2001, 'Food Insecurity and Child Work in Rural India: Space Dimensions', Paper Presented at the IHD-WFP Consultative Workshop on Food Insecurity and Child Work, 15–17 March.

Das, Bhagirath Lal, 1998, *The WTO Agreements: Deficiencies, Imbalances and Required Changes*, Penang: Third World Network.

———, 1999a, 'The AOA: An Imbalanced and Inequitable Agreement', *Third World Resurgence*, nos. 100/101.

———, 1999b, 'Proposed Specific Changes Needed in WTO Agriculture Agreement', *Third World Resurgence*, nos. 100/101.

———, 1999c, 'The "Big Bang" in Agriculture', *Third World Resurgence*, nos. 100/101.

Dasgupta, Biplab, 1997, 'The New Political Economy: A Critical Analysis', in *EPW*, 32 (4), January.

———, 1997a, 'Indian Agriculture in the Global Context and Under Structural Adjustment', in G.K. Chaddha and Aloke N. Sharma, eds., *Growth, Employment and Poverty in Rural India: Change and Continuity*, New Delhi: Allied Publishers.

———, 1998, *Structural Adjustment, Global Trade and the New Political Economy of Development*, London and New Delhi: Zed and Sage-Vistaar.

———, 2000, 'Food Security for India: Some Major Issues', National Seminar on 'Food Security in India', Hyderabad: CESS.

Dasgupta, S. and A. Maiti, n.d., 'The Rural Energy Crisis, Poverty and Women's Roles in Five Indian Villages', Geneva: ILO.

Dastagiri, M.B., 2000, 'Demand for Livestock Products towards 2020', in the Eighth Annual Conference on 'Livestock in Different Farming Systems' held at TNVASU, Chennai, on 28–9 December, Chennai: Agricultural Economics Research Association (India).

Datt, R., 1999, 'Food Security in India', in *Social Security in India*, Seminar Papers, New Delhi: Institute for Human Development, 15–17 April.

Das, Vidya, 1996, 'Minor Forest Produce and Rights of Tribals', *EPW*, 31 (50), December.

———, 1998, 'Human Rights Inhuman Wrong, Plight of Tribals in Orissa', *EPW*, vol. 33, no. 11, 14–20 March.

Department for International Development, 1999, *Sustainable Livelihood Guidance Sheets.*

Desai, Rajendra and Rupal Desai, 2001, 'Disaster Rehabilitation—The Basic Tenets', Ahmedabad: National Centre for People's Action in Disaster Preparedness.

Dettwyler, K.A., 1989, 'Interaction of Anorexia and Cultural Beliefs in Infant Malnutrition in Mali', *American Journal of Human Biology*, 1: 683–95.

Dev, S. Mahendra, 1996, 'Food Security: PDS versus EGS', *EPW*, 31 (27), July.

———, 1999, 'An Overview of Social Security in India', *The Indian Journal of Labour Economics*, 42 (3): 361–92.

Dev, S. Mahendra and M.H. Suryanarayana, 1991, 'Is PDS Urban Biased and Pro-Rich: An Evaluation', *EPW*, 26 (41), October.

Dhar, A. and S. Chaturvedi, 1999, *WTO Agreements and Agricultural Sector: Implications for India*, Research and Information System for Non-Aligned and other Developing Countries, October.

Dickin, K., M. Griffiths and E. Piwoz, 1997, *Designing by Dialogue: Program Planners' Guide to Consultative Research for Improving Young Child Feeding*, Washington, DC: Academy for Educational Development.

Drèze, Jean and Amartya Sen, 1989, *Hunger and Public Action*, New York: OUP.

Drèze, Jean and Amartya Sen, eds., 1997, *Indian Development: Selected Regional Perspectives*, New Delhi: OUP.

Drèze, Jean and Harris Gazdar, 1997, 'Uttar Pradesh: The Burden of Inertia', in Jean Drèze and Amartya Sen, eds., *Hunger and Public Action*, New York: OUP.

Dutta, Rupnayan, 2001, 'Cyclone Risk Management: Social Issues and Community Capacity Building—A Case for Sagar Island', Ahmedabad: School of Planning, CEPT.

Dvorak, K., 1992, 'On-farm Experiments as a Diagnostic Method: Constraints to Nitrogen Fertilizer use on Sorghum in Semi-arid Tropical India', *Experimental Agriculture*, 28 (2) (April): 155–64.

Dyson, Tim and Amresh Hanchate, 2000, 'India's Demographic and Food Prospects', *EPW*, 35 (45), November.

EARRS, 2001, Documentation Prepared on the Earthquake, February–April.

ECLAC (United Nations Economic Commssion for Latin America and Caribbean), 1994, *Policies to Improve Linkages with the Global Economy*, Santiago, Chile.

Economic and Political Weekly, 2001, 'Food for the Poor: Rs. 30 per kilo', editorial comment in *EPW*, vol. 36, nos. 5/6: 428.

Economic Survey of Orissa, 1993–4, 1996–7, 1998–9, *District Statistical Handbook: Bolangir District*.

Engle, P.L. and C. Breaux, 1998, 'Fathers' Responsibility for Children: A Cross-cultural Perspective', *Social Policy Report of the Society for Research in Child Development*, vol. 12, no. 1: 1–23.

Engle, P.L. and H. Riccuiti, 1995, 'Psychosocial Aspects of Care and Nutrition', *Food and Nutrition Bulletin Supplement*, 26, 4: 356–77.

Engle, P.L., M. Bentley and G. Pelto, 2000, 'The Role of Care in Nutrition Programs: Current Research and a Research Agenda', *Proceedings of the British Nutrition Society*, 59: 25–35.

Engle, P.L., P. Menon and L. Haddad, 1997, *Care and Nutrition: Concepts and Measurement*, Washington, DC: IFPRI.

———, 1999, 'Care and Nutrition: Concepts and Measurement', *World Development*, 27, 8: 1309–38.

Engle, P.L., G. Pelto and M. Bentley, 2000, 'Care for Nutrition and Development', *Journal of Indian Medical Association*, 9: 530–5.

Engle, P.L., K. Gorman, R. Martorell and E. Pollitt, 1993, 'Food Supplementation and Infant and Preschool Psychological Development', *Food and Nutrition Bulletin* 14 (3): 201–20.

Engle, P.L., M. Zeitlin, Y. Medrano and L.H. Garcia, 1996, 'Growth Consequences of Low Income Nicaraguan Mothers' Theories about Feeding One Year Olds', in C. Super, S. Harkness, eds., *Parental Cultural Belief Systems*, New York: Guilford Press, pp. 428–46.

Evenson, R.E. and M. Rosegrant, 1995, 'Developing Productivity (non-price yield and area) Projections for Commodity Market Modeling', Washington, DC: International Food Policy Research Institute, Mimeo.

Fan, S. and P. Hazell, 1999, 'Are Returns to Public Investment Lower in Less-favored Rural Areas? An Empirical Analysis of India', EPTD Discussion Paper No. 43, Washington, DC: International Food Policy Research Institute.

Fan, S., P. Hazell and S. Thorat, 1998, 'Government Spending, Growth and Poverty: An Analysis of Inter Linkages in Rural India', EPTD Discussion Paper No. 33, Washington, DC: International Food Policy Research Institute.

Food and Agriculture Organisation, United Nations (FAO), 1996, *World Food Summit.*

———, 1996, 'Policy Options for Developing Countries to Support Food Security in the Post Uruguay Round Period', Panos Konandreas and Jim Greenfield, Rome.

———, 1999, 'Agriculture, Trade and Food Security: Issues and Options in the Forthcoming WTO Negotiations from the Perspective of Developing Countries', FAO Symposium, 23–4 September 1999, Geneva. (fao.org.)

———, 1999, *The State of Agriculture.*

———, 2000, *The State of Food Insecurity in the World*, Rome.

Focus on the Poor (Guidelines for the Implementation of the Targeted Public Distribution System), Ministry of Civil Supplies, Consumer Affairs and Public Distribution, 1997.

Folmer, C., M.A. Keyzer, M.D. Merbis, H.J.J. Stolwijk and P.J.J. Veenendaal, 1995, *The Common Agricultural Policy Beyond the Maastricht Reform*, North Holland, Amsterdam.

Frankel, Francine R., 1989, 'Caste, Land and Dominance in Bihar: Breakdown of the Brahminical Order', in Francine R. Frankel and M.S.A Rao, eds., *Dominance and State Power in Modern India: Decline of a Social Order*, vol. 1, New Delhi: OUP, pp. 46–132.

Frankel, Richard M., Don F. Hadwiger and William P. Browne, eds., 1979, *The Role of US Agriculture in Foreign Policy,* New York: Praeger.

Friedman, Harriet, 1991, 'Changes in the International Division of Labor: Agri-food Complexes and Export Agriculture', in William H. Friedland, Laerence Busch, Frederick H. Buttel and Alan P. Rudy, eds., *Towards a New Political Economy of Agriculture*, Boulder: Westview, Ch. 3, pp. 65–93.

———, 1995, 'Food Politics: New Dangers, New Possibilities', in Philip McMichael, ed., *Food and Agrarian Orders in the World Economy,* London: Praeger, pp. 15–33.

Galler, J.R., F.C. Ramsey, R.H. Harrison, R. Brooks and S. Weiskopf-Bock, 1998, 'Infant Feeding Practices in Barbados Predict Later Growth', *Journal of Nutrition*, 128: 1328–35.

Ganapathy, S. et al., 2001, 'Findings from the Belaku Trust Longitudinal Study', Paper Presented at IUNS Conference, August 2001.

Gandhi, V., G. Desai, S.K. Raheja and Prem Narain, 1994, 'Fertilizer Response—Function: Environment and Future Growth of Fertilizer use on Wheat and Rice in India', in G. Desai and A. Vaidyanathan, eds., *Strategic Issues in Future Growth of Fertilizer Use in India*, New Delhi: Macmillan India.

Garcia, S., L. Kaiser and K. Dewey, 1990, 'Self-regulation of Food Intake among Rural Mexican Preschool Children', *European Journal of Clinical Nutrition*, 44: 371–80.

George, P.S., 1996, 'Public Distribution System, Food Subsidy and Production Incentives', *EPW*, 31 (38), September.

Ghosh, A.K., 1999, 'Current Issues of Employment Policy in India', *EPW*, 34 (36), September.

Ghosh, S., 1997, 'Integrated Child Development Services Programme—Need for Reappraisal', *Indian Pediatrics*, 34: 911–18.

Gilbert, J. et al., 2000, 'The APEC Food System: Implications for Agricultural and Rural Development Policy', *Developing Economies*, vol. XXXVIII, no. 3.

Giri Institute of Development Studies, Lucknow, 2000, 'National Programme of Nutritional Support to Primary Education (Midday Meals): Comparative Lessons of Experience in Uttar Pradesh and Himachal Pradesh', Sponsord by Planning Commission.

Gittelsohn, J., A.V. Shankar, K.P. West, F. Faruque, T. Gnywali and E.K. Pradhan, 1998, 'Child Feeding and Care Behaviors are Associated with Xerophthalmia in Rural Nepalese Households', *Social Science and Medicine*, 47: 477–86.

Goodman, David, 1991, 'Some Recent Tendencies in the Industrial Reorganization of the Agri-Food System', in William H. Friedland, Laerence Busch, Frederick H. Buttel and Alan P. Rudy, eds., *Towards a New Political Economy of Agriculture*, Boulder: Westview, Ch. 2, pp. 37–64.

Gopalan, C., 1995, 'Towards Food and Nutrition Security', *EPW*, 30 (52), December.

———, 1999, 'The Changing Epidemiology of Malnutrition in a Developing Society—the Effect of Unforeseen Factors', *Current Science*, 77 (10): 1257-62.

Gopalan, C., N. Sharma and H.P.S. Sachdeva, 1998, 'Relationship of Current Nutritional Status and Cognitive Functioning in 3-10 Year Olds Living in Slums', New Delhi: NFI.

Gorman, K.S., 1995, 'Malnutrition and Cognitive Development: Evidence from Experimental/Quasi-experimental Studies among the Mild-to-moderately Malnourished', *Journal of Nutrition*, 125 (8S): 2239S–44S.

Government of Gujarat, Directorate of Information, 2001, 'Nature's Fury—Devastating Earthquake—Human Approach Towards Earthquake Victims'.

———, 2001, 'Package of Rehabilitation and Reconstruction for Earthquake Victims in Gujarat'.

Government of India, 2001, *Economic Survey (2000–2001)*, New Delhi.

———, Department of Food and Public Distribution, 2001, *Interim Report of the High Level Committee on Long-Term Grain Policy*, New Delhi, May 2001.

———, Department of Women and Child Development, 1995, *National Plan of Action on Nutrition*, New Delhi.

———, Ministry of Agriculture, *Area Production and Yield of Principal Crops in India*, Various Issues.

———, Ministry of Finance, 2000, *Economic Survey*, New Delhi.

———, Ministry of Food and Consumer Affairs, *Annual Report, 1997-8 and 1998–9.*

———, Ministry of Consumer Affairs, Food and Public Distribution, *Annual Report 2000–2001*, New Delhi.

———, Ministry of Rural Areas and Employment, 1995, *Guidelines for Watershed Development*, New Delhi.

———, Ministry of Rural Development, 1994, *Report of the Technical Committee on Drought-prone Areas Programme and Desert Development Programme,* New Delhi.

———, National Centre of Disaster Management, 1998, 'Natural Disasters in India, Some Recent Case Studies', New Delhi.

———, National Sample Survey Organisation, 1988, 'A Note on the Third Quinquennial Survey on Employment and Unemployment', *Sarvekshana*, 11 (4), Issue 35.

———, National Sample Survey Organisation, 1990, 'Employment: Past Trends and Prospects for 1990s', Working Paper, New Delhi.

———, National Sample Survey Organisation, Department of Statistics, 1990, *Key Results of Employment and Unemployment Survey*, All India (Part I), New Delhi.

———, National Sample Survey Organisation, 1992, *Eighth Five-Year Plan*, vol. II, New Delhi.

———, National Sample Survey Organisation, 1994, *Report on Level and Pattern of Consumer Expenditure*, 50th Round, July 1993 to June 1994, New Delhi.

———, National Sample Survey Organisation, Department of Statistics, 1996, *Key Results on Employment and Unemployment*, 50th Round, New Delhi.

———, National Sample Survey Organisation, Department of Statistics, 1996a, *Level and Pattern of Consumer Expenditure*, Fifth Quinquennial Survey, 50th Round, 1993–4, Report No. 402.

———, National Sample Survey Organisation, Department of Statistics, 1996b, *Nutritional Intake in India*, Fifth Quinquennial Survey, 50th Round, October 1993–4.

———, National Sample Survey Organisation, Department of Statistics, 1998, *Household Consumer Expenditure and Employment Situation in India*, 54th Round (January–June 1998), New Delhi.

———, Planning Commission, 1988, *Report of the Study Groups in Landholding Systems in Tribal Areas*, New Delhi.

———, Planning Commission, 2000, *Population and Human Development Part-I, II and III*, Publications of the Planning Commission (Health, Nutrition and Family Welfare Division), New Delhi.

———, Planning Commission, 2000, *Ninth Five Year Plan (1997–2002)*, New Delhi.

———, Planning Commission, 2000, *Mid Term Appraisal of Ninth Five Year Plan (1997-2002)*, New Delhi, October.

Grantham-McGregor, S.M., C.A. Powell, S.P. Walker, J.H. Himes, 1991, 'Nutritional Supplementation, Psychosocial Stimulation and Mental Development of Stunted Children: The Jamaican Study', *Lancet*, 338: 1–5.

Griffin, David, 1999, 'Agricultural Globalization: A Threat to Food Security', *Third World Resurgence*, nos. 100/101.

Gujarat State Disaster Management Authority, 2001, 'Earthquake Rehabilitation Policy—Draft', Gandhinagar: Government of Gujarat.

———, *Gujarat Earthquake Rehabilitation: Rebuilding Lives—Village Partnership Procedure Manual*, Gandhinagar: Government of Gujarat.

Gulati, A. and C.H.H. Rao, 1994, 'Indian Agriculture: Emerging Perspectives and Policy Issues', *EPW*, 31, December, A158–A169.

Gulati, L., 1978, 'Profile of a Female Agricultural Labourer', *EPW*, 13 (12).

Guldan, G.S. et al., 1993, 'Maternal Education and Child Feeding Practices in Rural Bangladesh', *Social Science and Medicine*, 36: 925–35.

Gurjar, R.K., ed., 1994, *Drought Planning in India*, Jaipur: Printwell.

Hahjeboy, N. and N. Keith, 1998, 'Formative Research on Breastfeeding and Complementary Feeding in Uttar Pradesh', Washington, DC: AED, Linkages.

Haller, A., 1999, 'National Food Surpluses and Food Aid in India', New Delhi: World Food Programme, Regional Office for South Asia, Mimeo.

Haq, Mahbub ul and Khadija Haq, 1998, *Human Development in South Asia*, Karanchi: OUP.

Hauser, Walter, 1997, 'General Elections 1996 in Bihar: Politics, Administrative Atrophy and Anarchy', *EPW*, 32 (41).

Hemmi, Kenzo, 1994, 'The Japanese Perspective', in K.A. Ingersent, A.J. Rayner and R.C. Hine, eds., *Agriculture in the Uruguay Round*, New York: St Martin's Press, pp. 140–56.

Herbinger, W., B. Crawshaw and John Shaw, 1999, 'Beneficiary Participation in a Context: Practical Experiences from a Food-aided Project in Ethiopia', in Joseph Mullen, ed., *Rural Poverty, Empowerment and Sustainable Livelihoods*, Ashgate: Aldershot Hants.

Hetzel, B.S., J.T. Dunn, J.B. Stanbury, eds., 1987, *The Prevention and Control of Iodine Deficiency Disorders*, Oxford: Elsevier.

Hirway, Indira, 1999, 'Social Security for Women Workers: Some Issues', in *Social Security in India*, Seminar Papers, New Delhi: Institute for Human Development, 15–17 April.

———, 2000, 'Water Crisis in Gujarat: Turning Adversity into Opportunity', Paper Presented to the Chief Minister, Government of Gujarat.

———, 2001, 'After the Earthquake: Towards Rehabilitation and Reconstruction—Some Suggestions', Paper Prepared for Discussion at the Meeting of NGO Networks, Ahmedabad, Ahmedabad: Centre for Development Alternatives, February 2001.

Hirway, Indira and Unni, 1990, *Employment and Occupational Diversification of Women in India,* ARTEP Working Paper, New Delhi: ILO.

Hobbs, P. and M. Morris, 1996, *Meeting South Asia's Future Food Requirements from Rice-Wheat Cropping Systems: Priority Issues Facing Researchers in the post-Green Revolution Era*, Natural Resources Group Paper 96–101, Mexico City: International Maize and Wheat Improvement Center.

Hoekman, Bernard M. and Patricia Cremoux, 1993, 'Perspectives for Multilateral Reductions in Agricultural Support Policies', in Robert M. Stern, ed., *The Multilateral Trading System: Analysis and Options for Change*, New York: Harvester-Wheatsheaf, Ch. 11, pp. 277–307.

Hopkins, Raymond F., 1993, 'Developing Countries in the Uruguay Round: Bargaining under Uncertainty and Inequality', in William P. Avery, ed., *World Agriculture and the GATT*, Boulder and London: Lynne Rienner Publishers, Ch. 7, pp. 143–63.

Howes, S. and S. Jha, 1992, 'Urban Bias of the Public Distribution System', *EPW,* 9 May.

ICRISAT and FAO, 1996, *The World Sorghum and Millet Economies: Facts, Trends and Outlook*, A joint study by the Basic Food Stuffs Service, Rome and Hyderabad: FAO Commodities and Trade Division, and the International Crops Research Institute for the Semi-Arid Tropics.

Ingaco, M.D., 1996, 'Tariffication in the Uruguay Round: How Much Liberalization?', *The World Economy*, 19 (4), July.

International Food Policy Research Institute (IFPRI), 1998, *Overcoming Child Malnutrition in Developing Countries: Past Performance, Future Possibilities*, Washington, DC.

———, 1999, *Prospects for India's Cereal Supply and Demand to 2020*, Washington, DC.

Institute for Human Development and World Food Programme of the

United Nations, 2001, *Workshop on Food Insecurity and Child Work in Rural India: Synthesis of Technical Papers and Conclusions*, New Delhi.

International Institute for Population Sciences (IIPS) and ORC Macro, 2000, *National Family Health Survey (NFHS-2), 1998-99*, Mumbai.

Islam, Nurul, 1991, 'Comments', in Vinod Thomas, Ajay Chibber, Mansoor Dailami, Jaime De Melo, eds., *Restructuring Economies in Distress Policy Reform and the World Bank*, World Bank, OUP, Ch. 7.

Janpath Citizen's Initiative, 2001, 'Janpath Citizen's Initiative: Earthquake Relief Action Plan'.

Janvikas, 2001, 'Gujarat Earthquake: Strategy Building for Rehabilitation and Reconstruction: A Preliminary Appraisal'.

Jha, Shikha and P.V. Srinivasan, 2000, 'On Improving the Effectiveness of PDS in Achieving Food Security', Paper Presented in National Seminar on Food Security in India: The Emerging Challenges in the Context of Economic Liberalisation, at Centre for Economic and Social Studies, Hyderabad, 25–7 March.

Jharwal, S.M., 1999, *Public Distribution system in India: Ressessed*, New Delhi: Manak Publication.

Jodha, N.S., 1986, 'Common Property Resources and Rural Poor in Dry Regions of India', *EPW*, 21 (27), July.

Jones, Stephen, 1998, 'Liberalised Food Marketing in Developing Countries: Key Policy Problems', Oxford: Oxford Policy Management.

Joshi, P.K, 1997, 'Farmer's Investments and Government Intervention in Salt-affected and Water Logged Soils', in J.M. Kerr, D.K. Marothia, K. Singh, C. Ramaswamy and W.R. Bantley, eds., *Natural Resource Economics: Concepts and Applications to India*, New Delhi: Oxford and IBH.

Joshi, Y.G., 1999, *Perception of Drought and the Adoption of Control Strategy in the Jhabua Region of Madhya Pradesh*, Ujjain: Madhya Pradesh Institute of Social Science Research.

Karuppaiyan, E., 2000, 'Alienation of Tribal Land in Tamil Nadu: Panel Data Analysis', *EPW*, 35 (37), September.

Share, Sandip, 1997, 'Qualitative Assessment of Poverty in Tarkullah Village of Gorakhpur', Report Prepared for the World Bank Study on Qualitative Assessment of Poverty in some of India's Poor Regions, Mimeo.

Khor, Martin, 1999, 'Macroeconomic Policies that Affect the South's Agriculture', *Third World Resurgence*, nos. 100/101.

Kim, Si Joong, 1995, 'Korean Direct Investment in China: Perspectives of Korean Investors', in Sumner J. la Croix, Michael Plummer and Keun Lee, eds., *Emerging Patterns of East Asian Investment in China: From Korea, Taiwan and Hong Kong*, New York and London: Eastgate, M.E. Sharpe, Armonk, Ch. 12.

Knudsen, Odin and John Nash, 1991, 'Agricultural Policy', in Vinod Thomas, Ajay Chibber, Mansoor Dailami, Jaime De Melo, eds., *Restructuring Economies in Distress Policy Reform and the World Bank*, World Bank, OUP, Ch. 7.

Kohli, Atul, 1987, *The State and Poverty in India: The Politics of Reform*, Cambridge: Cambridge University Press.

———, 1991, *Democracy and Discontent: India's Growing Crisis of Governability*, Cambridge: Cambridge University Press.

Kochupillai, K., 1991, 'Prevention and Control of Goitre Demerits of Iodised Oil Injections', *NFI Bulletin*, 12 (4): 1-5.

Kotchabhakdi, N.J., P. Winichagoon, S. Smitasiri, S. Dhanamitta and A. Valyasevi, 1987, 'The Integration of Psychosocial Components of Early Childhood Development in a Nutrition Education Programme of Northeast Thailand', *Asian Pacific Journal of Public Health*.

Kriesel, S. and S. Zaidi, 1999, 'The Targeted Public Distribution System in India: An Evaluation', Washington, DC: World Bank, Mimeo.

Krishna Rao, Y.V, 2000, 'WTO Pressure and Issues for Millennium Round: Impact on Indian Agriculture', *New Challenges Facing Indian Agriculture*, New Delhi: AIKS and ILO.

Krishnaji, N., T.N. Krishnan, 2000, *Public Support for Food Security: Strategies for Human Development in India*, vol. 1, New Delhi.

Krueger, Anne O., 1974, 'The Political Economy of the Rent-seeking Society', *American Economic Review*, 64 (3), June.

———, 1992, *The Political Economy of Agricultural Pricing Policy*, vol. 5: *A Synthesis of the Political Economy in Developing Countries*, A World Bank Comparative Study, Washington.

Krueger, Anne O., Maurice Schiff and Alberto Valdes, eds., 1991, *The Political Economy of Agricultural Pricing Policy*, vol. 2: *Asia*, A World Bank Comparative Study, Baltimore: John Hopkins University Press.

Kumar, P., 1998, 'Food Demand and Supply Projections for India', Agricultural Economics Policy Paper 98-101, New Delhi: Indian Agricultural Research Institute.

Kumar, Pradumn, 2000, 'Productivity and Supply of Cereals in India', National Seminar on Food Security in India: The Emerging Challenges in the Context of Economic Liberalization, Hyderabad: CESS.

Kundu, A., 1986, 'Inequality in Educational Development: Issues in Measurement, Changing Structure and its Socio-economic Correlates with Special Reference to India', in M. Raza, ed., *Educational Planning: A Long Term Perspectives*, New Delhi: NCERT.

———, 1994, *Employment Growth, Changing Workforce Structure and Poverty Employment Linkages in Urban Areas*, New Delhi: International Labour Organisation.

———, 1997a, 'Trends and Structure of Employment in the Nineties—Implications for Urban Growth', *EPW*, 32 (24), June.

———, 1997b, 'Trends and Pattern of Female Employment in India: A Case of Organised Informalisation', *The Indian Journal of Labour Economics*, 40 (3).

———, 1999, 'Urban Informal Sector in India: Macro Trends and Policy Perspectives', Discussion Paper No. 25, New Delhi: ILO.

———, 2001, 'Poverty Trends and Employment Structure in India: Implications for a Development Strategy', Paper Presented at the NGO-Academics Seminar on Poverty Alleviation, Ahmedabad: CFDA.

Kurien, J. and T.R. Thakappan Achari, 1999, 'Overfishing along Kerala Coast: Causes and Consequences', *EPW*, 1–8 September.

Kurien, V., 2000, India's Milk Revolution', *NFI Bulletin*, 21 (1): 1-5.

Kutch Nav Nirman Abhiyan, 2001, 'An Introduction of Abhiyan and the Earthquake Relief and Rehabilitation Initiative'.

———, 2001, 'Rapid Assessment of Earthquake Affected Areas in Gujarat—Interim Report', Government of Gujarat, 12 February 2001.

———, 2001, 'Rebuilding Lives—Not Just Houses: A Brief Note on Concept and Setting up of Sub-Centres for Post-Earthquake Relief and Rehabilitation'.

———, 2001, 'Recommendations for Shelter Policy—Draft, Post Earthquake Reconstruction in Kutch, Gujarat'.

Lal, Deepak, Rakesh Mohan and I. Natarajan, 2001, 'Economic Reforms and Poverty Alleviation: A Tale of Two Surveys', *EPW*, 36 (12), September.

Lateef, K. Sarwar, 1994, *The Evolving Role of the World Bank, the First Half-centurty: An Overview*, Washington, DC: World Bank.

Launer, L.J., J. Villar, E. Kestler, M. de Onis, 1990, 'The Effect of Maternal Work on Fetal Growth and Duration of Pregnancy: A Prospective Study', *British Journal of Obstetrics and Gynecology*, 97 (1): 62–70.

Leeahtam, Pisit, 1991, *From Crisis to Double Digit Growth—Thailand's Economic Adjustment in the 1980s*, Bangkok: Doya Publishing House.

Levinger, Beryl, 1986, 'School Feeding Programs in Developing Countries: An Analysis of Actual and Potential', AID Evaluation Special Study No. 30 (Document Order No. PN-AAL-060), U.S. Agency for International Development (1986) at http://www.edc.org/INT/CapDev/sfp.txt.

Lieten, G.K. and Ravi Srivastava, 1999, *Unequal Partners: Power Relations, Devolution and Development in Uttar Pradesh*, New Delhi: Sage.

Low, Patrick, 1995, *Trading Free—The GATT and the US Trade Policy, Twentieth Century Fund*, New York.

Lozoff, B., 'Explanatory Mechanisms for Poorer Development in Iron-deficient Anaemic Infants', in *Nutrition, Health, and Child Development: Research Advances and Policy Recommendations*, Pan American Health Organisation, Tropical Metabolism Research Unit of the University of the West Indies, and the World Bank, Scientific Publication 566, 1998: 162–78.

Majumdar, Bhasker, 2001, 'Public Distribution System of Essential Commodities as a Social Safety Net: A Study of the District of Allahabad, Uttar Pradesh', Draft Report, Submitted to the Planning Commission, Government of India.

Manor, James, 1978, 'Where Congress Survived: Five States in the Indian General Election of 1977', *Asian Survey*, vol. 18, no. 8, pp. 785–803.

———, 1989, 'Karnataka: Caste, Class, Dominance and Politics in a Cohesive Society', in Francine Frankel and M.S.A. Rao, eds., *Dominance and State Power in Modern India: Decline of a Social Order*, vol. 1, New Delhi: OUP, pp. 322–61.

Marglin, Frederique Affel and S.A. Marglin, eds., 1996, *Decolonizing Knowledge from Development to Dialogue*, Oxford: Clarendon.

Marglin, S.A., 1996, 'Farmers, Seedmen, and Scientists: Systems of Agriculture and Systems of Knowledge', in F.A. Marglin and S.A. Marglin, eds., *Decolonizing Knowledge from Development to Dialogue*, Oxford: Clarendon.

Mathur, Kuldeep and Niraja Jayal, 1993, *Drought, Policy and Politics: The Need for a Long Term Perspective*, New Delhi: Sage.

Mavlankar, Dilip, 2001, 'Issues in Disaster Management', Note for Discussion at the Meeting of the Advisory Committee on 23 March 2001.

Maxwell, S. and T.R. Frankenberger, 'Household Food Security: Concept, Indicators, Measurements—A Technical Review', UNICEF and IFAD.

McElroy, A., and P. Townsend, 1979, *Medical Anthropology in Ecological Perspective*, North Scituate, MA: Duxbury Press.

Measham, Anthony R. and Meera Chatterjee, 1999, *Wasting Away: The Crisis of Malnutrition in India*, Washington, DC: World Bank.

Mencher, J., 1988, 'Women's Work and Poverty: Women's Contribution to Household Maintenance in two Regions of South Asia', in J. Bruce and D. Dwyer, eds., *A Home Divided: Women and Income Control in the Third World*, California: Stanford University Press.

Milla, 1991, cited in K. Brown, K. Dewey and L. Allen, 1996, 'State of the Art Paper in Complementary Feeding', Paper Prepared for the UNICEF/WHO Consultation, 27 November–1 December 1995, France: Montpelier.

Miller del Rosso, Joy, 1999, 'School Feeding Programs: Improving Effectiveness and Increasing the Benefit to Education—A Guide for Program Managers', The Partnership for Child Development, The World Bank: Food and Nutrition Policy: Best Practices/Toolkits at http://wbln0018.worldbank.

Miller del Rosso, Joy, Marek and Tonia Marek, 1996, *Class Action: Improving School Performance in the Developing World through Better Health and Nutrition*, Washington: World Bank.

Mishra, Neelabh, 2001, 'Post-Mortem of Hunger', *Hindustan Times*, 4 April.

Misra, V.N., 2000, 'Role of Female Labour Force Participation in Rural Poverty and Non-farm Employment: Indian Experience', *The Indian Journal of Labour Economics*, 43 (2): 221–46.

Mohapatra, L.K., 1994, *Tribal Development in India: Myth and Reality*, New Delhi: Vikas.

Mooij, Jos, 1998, 'Food Policy and Politics: The Political Economy of the Public Distribution System in India', *Journal of Peasant Studies*, vol. 25, no. 2: 77–101.

———, 1999a, 'Real Targeting: The Case of Food Distribution in India', *Food Policy*, vol. 24, no. 1: 49–69.

———, 1999b, *Food Policy and the Indian State: The Public Distribution System in South India*, New Delhi: OUP.

———, 2000, 'Food and Power: The Political Economy of the Public Distribution System in Bihar', IDPAD Occasional Papers and Reprints 2000–1, New Delhi and The Hague: Indo-Dutch Programme for Alternatives in Development.

Morrow, A.L., M. Lourdes Guerro, J. Sjults, J.J. Calva, C. Lutter, J. Bravo, G. Ruiz-Palacios, R.C. Morrow and F.D. Butterfoss, 1999, 'Efficacy of Home-based Peer Counselling to Promote Exclusive Breastfeeding: A Randomized Controlled Trial', *Lancet*, 353: 1226–31.

Moyer, H. Wayne and Timothy Josling, 1990, *Agricultural Policy Reform: Politics and Process in the EC and the USA*, New York: Harvester Wheatsheaf.

Mukharjee, Amitava, 1994, *Structural Adjustment Programme and Food Security*, Aldershot: Avebury.

———, 2000, 'Perspectives of Rural Women on Food Security from Tribal Villages in West Bengal, 1993–9', Paper Presented in the National Seminar on 'Food Security in India: The Emerging Challenges in the Context of Economic Liberalization', Hyderabad: CESS, 25–7 March.

Mundle, Sudipto, 1981, *Surplus Flows and Growth Imbalances: The Intersectoral Flow of Real Resources in India, 1951-71*, Bombay: Allied Publishers.

Murray, A.D. and A.V. Hornbaker, 1997, 'A Maternal Directive and Facilitative Interaction Styles: Associations with Language and Cognitive Development of Low Risk and High Risk Toddlers', *Development and Psychopathology*,.9: 507–16.

Murray, C.J., and A.D. Lopez, eds., 1997a, *Global Burden of Disease: A Comprehensive Assessment of Mortality and Disability from Diseases, Injuries, and Risk Factors in 1990 and Projected to 2000*, Cambridge, Massachusetts: Harvard University Press.

Murray, C.J., and A.D. Lopez, 1997b, 'Mortality by Cause for Eight Regions of the World: Global Burden of Disease Study', *Lancet*, 349: 1269–76.

Nafziger, E. Wayne, 1995, 'Japan's Industrial Development, 1868–1939: Lessons for Sub-Saharan Africa', in Howard Stein, *Asian Indus-*

*trialisation and Africa—Studies in Policy Alternatives to Structural Adjustment*, New York: St. Martins Press, pp. 53–85.

Nabakrushna Choudhry Centre for Development Studies, Bhubaneswar, 2000, 'A Comparative Study of Nutritional Support to Primary Education (Midday Meals Scheme) in Orissa and Tamil Nadu', Sponsord by the Planning Commission.

Nagpal, S., 1999, 'Food Security in the Hindukush Himalayas', *EPW*, 24 (36), September.

Narasinga Rao, B.S., 2000, 'Micronutrient Interactions', Paper Presented at the Indo-US Symposium on Micronutrient Requirements, Hyderabad: MIN.

Narasimha Reddy, D., 1998, 'Intellectual Property Rights (IPRs): Protection of Farmers' Rights in a Changing Scenario', International Seminar on Biotechnologies for Dryland Agriculture: Prospects and Constraints, 16–18 July, Hyderabad: IPE.

———, 1998a, 'The New World Trade Order and Certain Concerns about the Indian Agrarian Prospect', in R.P. Singh, ed., *Implications of GATT/WTO on Agriculture and Rural Development*, Hyderabad: NIRD.

———, 2000, 'World Trade Organization, Agreement on Agriculture and Small Farmer Economies', in Y.V. Krishna Rao, ed., *New Challenges Facing Indian Agriculture*, New Delhi: AIKS and ILO.

Nawani, N.P., 1994, 'Indian Experience on Households Food and Security', Paper Prepared for Regional Expert Consultation, Bangkok: FAO-UN.

Oldeman, L.R., ed., 1988, *Global Assessment of Soil Degradation (GLASOD): Guidelines for General Assessment of Status of Human-induced Soil Degradation*, Wageningen, The Netherlands: International Soil Reference and Information Centre.

Operation Research Group, 1999, 'Evaluation Study to Assess the Efficiency and Effectiveness of the National Programme for Nutritional Support to Primary Education in Ten States of India', Final report submitted to UNICEF, India, New Delhi.

Paddock, William and Paul Paddock, 1967, *Famine–1975*, Boston: Little, Brown.

Pant, K.C., 2001, Keynote Address at IGNOU 'National Workshop on Livelihood Options for Disaster Risk Reduction', 23–4 March, New Delhi.

Parikh, G., 2000, *Breastfeeding Patterns,* Report for UNICEF, New Delhi.

Parikh, K.S., 1994, 'Who Gets How Much from PDS: How Effectively Does it Reach the Poor?' *Sarvekshana*, vol. XVII, no. 3, January–March.

Paroda, R.S., 1999, 'Genetic modification of foods', *NFI Bulletin*, July.

Parthasarathy, G., 1988, 'Public Policy and Trends in Women and Development', Paper Presented at Workshop on 'Women in Agriculture', Trivandrum: Centre for Development Studies, 15-17 February.

Patel, Anil, 2001, 'Emerging Health Scenario in Kutch, Arch-Vahini Camp, Bhuj'.

Pelto, G., K.L. Dickin and P.L. Engle, 1999, *A Critical Link: Interventions to Promote Growth and Development*, Geneva, Switzerland: Department of Child and Adolescent Health and Development, World Health Organization.

Pelto, G.H., H. Tuomainen, 1996, 'Evaluating Social and Psychological Responses to Vitamin A Interventions', in C. Garza, J.D. Haas, J.P. Habicht, D.L. Pelletier, eds., *Beyond Nutritional Recommendations: Implementing Science for Bealthier Populations*, Ithaca, New York: Cornell University Division of Nutritional Sciences, pp. 145–62.

Pender, J. and J. Kerr, 1996, 'Determinants of Farmers' Indigenous Soil and Water Conservation Investments in India's Semi-arid Tropics', EPTD Discussion Paper No. 17, Washington, DC: International Food Policy Research Institute.

Perrings, C., 1995, 'Sustainable Livelihoods and Environmental Soundness', in I. Ahmed and J.A. Doeleman, *Beyond Rio: The Environmental Crisis and Sustainable Livelihoods in the Third World*, ILO Study Series, ILO.

Philips, N., Deepti Chirmulay, F. James Levinson, Patrice Engle, 2001, 'Comparison of Rural and Urban Children in Pune, Maharashtra', Submitted for Publication.

Pingali, P., M. Hossain and R. Gerpacio, 1997, *Asian Rice Bowls: The Returning Crisis?*

Piwoz, E.G., R.E. Black, G. Lopez de Romaña, H.C. de Kanashira and K.H. Brown, 1994, 'The Relationship between Infants' Preceding Appetite, Illness, and Growth Performance and Mothers' Subsequent Feeding Practice Decisions', *Social Science and Medicine*, 39 (6): 851–60.

Poley-Strobel, B.A., C.A. Beckman, 1987, 'The Effects of a Teaching-Modeling Intervention on Early Mother-Infant Reciprocity', *Infant Behavior and Development*, 10 (4): 467–76.

Pollitt, E., 1993, 'Iron Deficiency and Cognitive Function', *Annual Reviews of Nutrition*, 13: 521–37.

Pollitt, E., K.S. Gorman, P.L. Engle, J.A. Rivera and R. Martorell, 1995, 'Nutrition in Early Life and Fulfillment of Intellectual Potential', *Journal of Nutrition*, 125 (4S): 1111S–18S.

Pollitt, Ernesto, 1990, *Malnutrition and Infection in the Classroom*, Paris: UNESCO.

Prasad, Binoy S., 1997, 'General Elections, 1996: Major Role of Caste and Social Factions in Bihar', *EPW*, 32 (47).

PROBE Report, 1999, *Public Report on Basic Education in India*, New Delhi: OUP.

Pursell, Gary and Ashok Gulati, 1995, 'Liberalizing Indian Agriculture: An

Agenda for Reform', in Robert Cassen and Vijay Joshi, eds., *India—The Future of Economic Reform*, Bombay: OUP, pp. 261–311.

Radhakrishna, R., 1997, 'Food, Nutrition and PDS: Emerging Issues', Mimeo.

———, 2001, 'Food Security: Emerging Concerns', in M. Dev et al., eds., *Social and Economic Security in India*, New Delhi: Institute for Human Development.

Radhakrishna, R. and K.V. Naraina, 1993, 'Nutritional Programmes in India: Review and Assessment', Hyderabad: CESS.

Radhakrishna, R. and K. Subbarao, 1997, 'India's Public Distribution System: A National and International Perspective', World Bank Discussion Paper No. 380, Washington DC: World Bank.

Raghavan, C., 1999, 'India Calls for a "Market Plus" Approach to Agriculture', *Third World Resurgence*, nos. 100/101.

Raina, R.S., 2000, 'Countering Seasonal Rural Problems: Integrated Participatory Information System', *EPW*, 9 September.

Ramachandran, N., 2000, *Review and Field Testing of Guidelines for Formulating and Implementing National Plans of Action for Nutrition*, Prepared for the Nutrition Planning, Assessment and Evaluation Service, Food and Nutrition Division, Rome: FAO.

Ramachandran, N. and A.K. Dimri, 1999, 'Participating in the Planning Process—A Must for Sustainable Development', *Social Change*, vol. 26, no. 1.

Ramesh Chandra, 2000, 'Trade Liberalization, Agricultural Prices and Net Social Welfare: A Study of Selected Crops', National Seminar on 'Food Security in India . . .', Hyderabad: CESS.

Rao, C.H.H. and R. Radhakrishna, 1997, 'National Food Security: A Policy Perspective for India, Paper Presented at the XXII Conference of International Association for Agricultural Economists, Sacramento, CA, August.

Rao, D.L. Prasad, 1999, 'Explanation in Tribal Areas: With Special Reference to Land Alienation', in Behera and Pfeffer, eds., *Contemporary Society: Tribal Development Issue*, New Delhi: Concept Publishing.

Reissland, N. and R. Burghart, 1988, 'The Quality of a Mother's Milk and the Health of her Child: Beliefs and Practices of the Women of Mithila', *Social Science and Medicine*, 27 (5): 461–9.

Repetto, R., 1994, *The 'Second India' Revisited: Population, Poverty and Environmental Stress over Two Decades*, Washington, DC: World Resources Institute.

Robert Houser, I.P. Bhagwat, 2000, 'Comparison of Early Child Feeding Practices between Rural, Urban and Periurban Locations in Maharashtra, India', Paper Submitted for Publication.

Rodgers, G., 1999, 'Poverty, Exclusion and Insecurity: Issues and Policy

Frameworks', *The Indian Journal of Labour Economics*, 42 (3): 327–40.

Rosegrant, M.R., M. Agcaoili and N. Perez, 1995, 'Global Food Projections to 2020: Implications for Investment', Food, Agriculture and the Environment Discussion Paper 5, Washington, DC: International Food Policy Research Institute.

Ross, Jay and Susan Horton, 1998, *Economic Consequences of Iron Deficiency*, Ottawa: Micronutrient Initiative.

Rothboeck, S. and S. Acharya, 1999, 'Gender-based Segregation in the Indian Labour Market', *The Indian Journal of Labour Economics*, 42 (4): 581–96.

Roy Burman, B.K., 'Critical Issues Relating to Tribal Development During the Eighth Plan', in Pfeffer and Behera, eds., *Contemporary Society: Tribal Development Issue*, New Delhi: Concept Publishing.

Royal Society of London, 1999, *A Report on Genetically Modified Plants for Food Use.*

Sagar, Vidya, 1995, 'Public Intervention for Poverty Alleviation in Harsh Agro-Climatic Environment: Case of Rajasthan', *EPW*, 30 (41-2), October.

———, 2000, 'PDS and Food Security: Rajasthan', in N. Krishnaji and T.N. Krishnan, eds., *Public Support for Food Security: The Public Distribution System in India*, New Delhi: Sage.

Sankat Nivaran Society (Gujarat), 2001, 'Report of Activities, Sarvodaya Ashram, Amirgadh'.

Sarap, K., 1998, 'On the Operation of the Land Market, in Backward Agriculture: Evidence from a Village in Orissa, Eastern India', *The Journal of Peasant Studies*, vol. 25, no. 2, January: 102–30.

———, 2000a, 'Flow of Production and Investment Credit through Cooperatives and LAMPS in Orissa: Study from Kalahandi and Sambalpur', Report Prepared for the Orissa State Cooperative.

———, 2000b, 'Agrarian Structure, Land Reforms Measures and Livelihood Pattern in KBK Region, Orissa', Unpublished Project Report of Department of Economics, Sambalpur University, Prepared for the State Bank of India, Mumbai.

Sarma, J.S. and V. Gandhi, 1990, *Production and Consumption of Food Grain in India: Implications of Accelerated Economic Growth and Poverty Alleviation*, Research Report 81, Washington, DC: International Food Policy Research Institute.

Saxena, N.C., 1995, *Forests, People and Profit: New Equations for Sustainability*, Dehradun: Natraj Publishers.

———, 2000, 'Remarks Made at the Joint Session of the Executive Boards of UNDP/UNFPA/UNICEF/WFP', New York.

Scherr, S.J. and P. Hazell, 1994, 'Sustainable Agricultural Development Strategies in Fragile Lands', EPTD Discussion Paper No. 1, Washington, DC: International Food Policy Research Institute.

Schott, Jeffrey J., 1994 (assisted by Johanna W. Burman), *The Uruguay Round*, Washington, DC: Institute for International Economics.

Sehgal, J. and I.P. Abrol, 1994, *Soil Degradation in India: Status and Impact*, New Delhi: Oxford and IBH.

Sen, Amartya, 1981, *Poverty and Famines: An Essay on Entitlement and Deprivation*, Oxford: Clarendon Press.

Shah, Amita, 1998, 'Watershed Development: Integration is Far Behind', in C.V.J. Verma, A.R.G. Rao and T.N. Murthy, eds., *Watershed Management and Conservation*, Proceedings of an International Conference, New Delhi: Central Board of Irrigation and Power.

———, (forthcoming), *Who Benefits from Watershed Development? Evidence from Gujarat*, IIED Gatekeeper Series, London.

Shah, Anil, 2001, 'Limits to Patience', *Naya Marg*, 1 March.

Shah, Kirti, 2001, 'Earthquake Rehabilitation: A 24-Point Strategy for Shelter and Settlements Development', Ahmedabad Study Action Group.

Shah, Mihir et al., 1998, *India's Drylands: Tribal Societies and Development through Environmental Regeneration*, New Delhi: OUP.

Shankar, A.V., J. Gittelsohn, K.P. West, R. Stallings, T. Gnywali and F. Faruque, 1998, 'Eating from a Shared Plate Affects Food Consumption in Vitamin A Deficient Nepali Children', *Journal of Nutrition*, 128: 1127–33.

Shariff, A., 1999, *India: Human Development Report: A Profile of Indian States in the 1990s*, New Delhi: OUP.

Sharma, Alakh N., 1995, 'Political Economy of Poverty in Bihar', *EPW*, 30 (41/42).

Sharma, Alakh N. and Ajay Kumar, 1998, 'Peasant Mobilisation in Bihar: Implications for Rural Labour Markets', in R. Radhakrishna and Alakh N. Sharma, eds., *Empowering Rural Labour in India: Market, State and Mobilisation*, New Delhi: Institute for Human Development, pp. 395–414.

Sharma, U., 1980, *Women, Work and Poverty in North West India*, London: Tavistock Publications.

Shiva, Vandana and Gurpreet Karir, 1997, *Towards Sustainable Aquaculture: Chenmmeenkettu*, New Delhi: Research Foundation for Science, Technology and Ecology.

Singh, P. and A.B. Majumdar, 1992, 'Current Status of Feed and Fodder Management of Livestock: Agricultural Situation in India', August.

Singh, R.P. and M.L. Morris, 1997, 'Adoption, Management, and Impact of Bybrid Maize seen in India', Economic Working Paper 97–106, Mexico City: International Maize and Wheat Improvement Center.

Skladany, Mike and Craig K. Harris, 1994, 'On Global Pond: International Development and Commodity Chains in the Shrimp Industry', in Philip McMichael, ed., *Food and Agrarian Orders in the World Economy*, London: Praeger.

Sopher, D., 1980, 'Sex Disparity in Indian Literacy', in D. Sopher, ed., *An Exploration in India: Geographical Perspective in Society and Culture*, New York: Cornell University Press.

Srinivas, M.N. and M.N. Panini, 1984, 'Politics and Society in Karnataka', *EPW*, 19 (2), January.

Nisha Srivastava, 1997, 'Qualitative Assessment of Poverty in Chitauri Village of Allahabad', Report Prepared for the World Bank Study on Qualitative Assessment of Poverty in some of India's Poor Regions, Mimio.

Srivastava, Ravi, 1996, 'Agricultural Reforms and the Rural Poor in Eastern Uttar Pradesh', *Background Paper, India: Country Economic Memorandum 1996*, Washington, D.C: World Bank.

———, 2000, *Food Security and the Targeted Public Distribution System in Uttar Pradesh*, Hyderabad: National Institute of Rural Development.

———, 2001, 'Inequality and Education Security', in M. Dev. et al., eds., *Social and Economic Security in India*, New Delhi: Institute for Human Development.

———, (ongoing), 'Decentralisation and Anti-Poverty Programmes in Uttar Pradesh', Ongoing Research Project Sponsored by the Planning Commission.

Subbarao, K., 1989, 'Improving Nutrition in India: Policies and Programs and their Impact', World Bank Discussion Paper No. 49, Washington, DC: World Bank.

Sub-Committee on Nutrition, 2000, *Nutrition Throughout the Life Cycle: Fourth Report on the World Nutrition Situation*, Geneva: United Nations.

Suryanarayana, M.H., 1995, 'PDS Reform and Scope for Commodity-Based Targeting', *EPW*, 30 (13), April.

———, 1995, 'Some Experiments with Food Stamps', *EPW*, 30 (52), December.

———, 1995, 'Growth, Poverty and Levels of Living; Hypotheses, Methods and Policy', *Journal of Indian School of Political Economy*, 7; 2, April–June.

———, 2001, 'The Budget and the Food Economy', *The Hindu*, 20 March.

Swaminathan, M.S., 1999, *Third Ved Prakash Memorial Lecture* on 'Population and Human Security' at the National Institute of Health and Family Welfare, New Delhi.

Swaminathan, Madhura, 2000, *Weakening Welfare, The Public Distribution of Food in India*, New Delhi: LeftWord.

Swaminathan, Madhura and V.K. Ramachandran, 1999, 'New Data on Calorie Intakes', *Frontline*, 12 March: 109–11.

Thamarajakshi, R., 1997, 'Economic Reforms and State Intervention in Foodgrain Market', *EPW*, 26 July.

———, 1999, 'Food Production in the New Millennium', *Economic Times*, 24 July.

The Partnership for Child Development, 1999, *School Feeding Programs: Improving Effectiveness and Increasing the Benefit to Education—A Guide for Program Managers*, June.

The Probe Team, 1999, *Public Report on Basic Education in India*, New Delhi: Oxford University Press.

Tyagi, D.S., 1990, *Managing India's Food Economy: Problems and Alternatives*, New Delhi: Sage.

UNCTAD/WTO Joint Study (TD/B/COM. 1/14 Rev. 1, 1999), 'The Post-Uruguay Round Tariff Environment for Developing Country Exports: Tariff Peaks and Tariff Escalation'.

UNICEF, 1990, 'Strategy for Improved Nutrition of Children and Women in Developing Countries', *UNICEF Policy Review 1990–1* (E/ICEF/1990/L.6), New York.

———, 1995, 'The Progress of Indian States', New Delhi: UNICEF India.

———, 1997, *The Care Initiative Assessment, Analysis, and Action to Improve Care for Nutrition*, New York: UNICEF Nutrition Section.

———, 1999, *Annual Report: The States of the World's Children*, 1999, New York: OUP.

———, 2001, 'Multiple Indicator Cluster Survey 2000—MICS 2000', New Delhi: UNICEF India Country Office.

United Nations, 1992, *Report of the United Nations' Conference on Environment and Development*, Rio de Janerio, 3–14 June, vol. 1, New York.

———, 1999, *World Survey on the Role of Women in Development*, New York.

United Nations Development Programme, 1998, *Human Development Report 1998*, New Delhi: OUP.

———, 1999, Sustainable Livelihoods Documents: *Rural and Urban Poverty: Similarities and Differences.*

Verma, R.K. (n.d.), *Dimensions of Mid-Term Lok Sabha Elections in Bihar.*

Vyas, V.S., 1995, 'Agrarian Structure and Sustainable Livelihoods of Tribal People in Indian Forestry', in I. Ahmed and J.A. Doeleman, *Beyond Rio: The Environmental Crisis and Sustainable Livelihoods in the Third World*, ILO Study Series, ILO.

———, 1996, 'Agriculture in the Ninth Plan of Rajasthan: Background, Issues and Approaches', Working Paper No. 73, Jaipur: Institute of Development Studies.

———, 2000, Presidential Address, Third Annual Conference of Asian Society of Agricultural Economics, held at Institute for Development Studies, Jaipur, 18–20 October.

———, 2000, 'Ensuring Food Security: The State, Market and Civil Society', *EPW*, 35 (50), December.

Vir, S., 1994, 'Control of Iodine Deficiency: The National Programme—Current Status', *NFI Bulletin*, 15 (2): 1-4.

Wade, Robert, 1990, *Governing the Market: Economic Theory and the Role of the Government in East Asian Industrializaiion*, Princeton.

Watkins, Kevin, 1992, *Fixing the Rules: North-South Issues in International Trade and GATT Uruguay Round*, London: Catholic Institute for International Relations.

———, 1999, 'Free Trade and Farm Fallacies: From the Uruguay Round to the World Food Summit', *Third World Resurgence*, nos. 100/101.

Webb, M.C and S.D. Krasner, 1989, 'Hegemonic Stability Theory: An Empirical Assessment', in *Review of International Studies*, vol. 15, pp. 183–98.

Webb, Patrik, 1998, 'Strategic Implications of the Food Policy for WFP Strategy in India', Mimeo.

Webb, Steven B. and Karim Shariff, 1992, 'Designing and Implementing Adjustment Programs', in Vittorio Fischer, Corbo Stanley and Steven B. Webb, eds., *Adjustment Lending Revisited—Policies to Restore Growth, A World Bank Symposium*, Washington, DC: World Bank, pp. 69–98.

WFP, UNESCO, WHO, 1999, *School Feeding Handbook*, Rome: WFP.

World Bank, 1991, *Gender and Poverty in India*, Washington, DC.

World Bank, Development Committee, 1993, 47th Meeting, September 1993, Washington, DC.

———, 1994, 48th Meeting, April 1994, Washington, DC.

———, 1993, 'India: Public Expenditure Review', Sector Report IV: Social Sectors. C: Nutrition. South Asia Country Department (India). Population and Human Resources Operations Division.

———, 1996, *India Livestock Sector Review: Enhancing Growth and Development*, Washington, DC: World Bank.

———, 1998, *Reducing Poverty in India: Options for More Effective Public Services*, Report No. 17881-IN, Poverty Reduction and Economic Management Unit, South Asia Region, Washington, DC.

———, 1998, *India: Water Resources Management Sector Review, Report on Irrigation*, Washington, DC: South Asia Rural Development Unit.

———, 1999, 'Towards Rural Development and Poverty Reduction', Paper Presented at the NCAER-IEG-World Bank Conference on 'Reforms in the Agricultural Sector for Growth, Efficiency, Equity, and Sustainability', 15–16 April, New Delhi, India.

———, 1999, *World Development Report, 1998–1999*, Washington.

World Bank and Asian Development Bank, 2001, 'Gujarat Earthquake Recovery Program: Assessment Report to the Governments of Gujarat and India'.

World Commission on Environment and Development, 1987, *Our Common Future*, New York: OUP.

World Food Programme (WFP), 2001a, *Enabling Development: Food Assistance in South Asia*, Regional Office for South Asia, New Delhi: OUP.

———, 2001b, *Country Strategy Outline for India*, Rome.

World Health Organization, 1998, 'Complementary Feeding of Young Children in Developing Countries: A Review of Current Scientific Knowledge', WHO/NUT/98.1, Geneva: World Health Organization.

———, 1998, 'Nutritional Status of Adoloscent Girls and Women of Reproductive Age', Report of Regional Consultations, New Delhi (SEA/NUP/14).

———, 1999, *A Critical Link Interventions for Physical Growth and Psychological Development: A Review*, Department of Child and Adolescent Health and Development.

WTO, Tariff Escalation, WT/CTE/W/25, Document Prepared by the Secretariat.

Zeiltin, M., 1996, 'My Child is My Crown: Yoruba Parental Theories and Practices in Early Childhood', in S. Harkness and C. Super, eds., *Parents' Cultural Belief Systems*, New York: Guilford Press, pp. 407–27.

———, 1996a, *Child Care and Nutrition: The Findings from Positive Deviance Research*, Ithaca, New York: Cornell International Nutrition Monograph Series No. 27.

# Index